GLOBAL  STUDIES

THE MIDDLE EAST

STAFF

GLOBAL STUDIES

THE MIDDLE EAST

William Spencer

The Dushkin Publishing Group, Inc., Sluice Dock, Guilford, Connecticut 06437

The Middle East

OTHER BOOKS IN THE GLOBAL STUDIES SERIES

- Latin America
- China
- Africa
- The Soviet Union and Eastern Europe
  India and South Asia
  Western Europe
  Japan and the Pacific Rim
  Southeast Asia

- Available Now

First Edition

Manufactured by George Banta Company, Menasha, Wisconsin 54952

ISBN: 0-87967-610-8

The Middle East

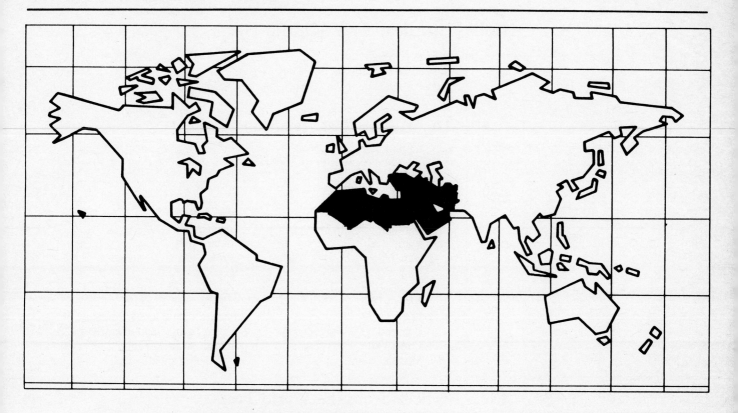

AUTHOR AND EDITOR

Dr. William Spencer

The author and editor for *Global Studies: The Middle East* was formerly Professor of Middle East/North African History at the Florida State University and in recent years has been Visiting Professor at Rollins College, Jacksonville University, and the University of Florida. During a thirty-year career specializing in Middle Eastern affairs, he has published and lectured extensively and has held various US government and international organization and foundation assignments. His special area of interest is Islamic North Africa. As a curriculum consultant for school systems, colleges, and universities, Dr. Spencer has developed workshops and short courses designed to help US educators develop a better understanding of this region.

CONSULTANT

Elizabeth Spencer

Elizabeth Spencer is an artist and teacher who has travelled with her husband to the Middle East on many research trips. She is responsible for much of the material in this book on home and family life, architecture, and housing, aside from her contributions as grammarian and amanuensis extraordinary.

SERIES CONSULTANT

H. Thomas Collins
Washington, DC

Contents

Global Studies: The Middle East

Page 11

Page 23

Page 42

Introduction viii
United States Statistics and Map x
Global Map xii
Middle East Map 2

4 | **The Middle East: Islam in Ferment**

15 | **The Middle East: Theater of Conflict**

26 | **Country Reports**

Algeria 26
Bahrain 32
Egypt 35
Iran 44
Iraq 52
Israel 57
Jordan 67
Kuwait 72
Lebanon 75
Libya 80
Morocco 86
Oman 92

Qatar 96
Saudi Arabia 99
Sudan 104
Syria 108
Tunisia 113
Turkey 117
United Arab Emirates 122
People's Democratic Republic
  of Yemen (South Yemen) 125
Yemen Arab Republic
  (North Yemen) 128

132 | **Articles from the World Press**

Annotated Table of Contents for Articles 132
Topic Guide 134
Articles:

Middle Eastern Region

1. **Mideast Turning Point,** *World Press Review,* October 1985, p. 136.
2. **The Teflon Palestinian,** *The Economist,* December 21, 1985, p. 139.
3. **Bedouins, Poets and Pirates of the Dunes,** Bruton Bernstein, *Science Digest,* January 1983, p. 141.
4. **Arab Linguists Toil to Keep Language from Being Written Off,** David Lamb, *New Haven Register,* September 1, 1985, p. 142.
5. **Cradle of Civilization May Also Be Birthplace of Haute Cuisine,** Erik Eckholm, *Gainesville Sun,* October 12, 1985, p. 144.
6. **Expats' Future in the Gulf,** Zafar Samadani, *Pakistan & Gulf Economist,* June 29 - July 5, 1985, p. 145.
7. **The Gulf Countries Making Headway,** Zafar Samadani, *Pakistan & Gulf Economist,* August 10-16, 1985, p. 146.

Algeria

8. **Crop Production Under Wraps,** David Bradshaw, Special Report—Algeria, *South,* December 1985, p. 147.
9. **Finding Strength in National Culture,** Kamel Belkacem, Special Report—Algeria, *South,* December 1985, p. 148.

Bahrain

10. **Diversification of Economy,** IMF Survey, *Pakistan & Gulf Economist,* August 17-23, 1985, p. 149.

Egypt

11. **Mubarak Walks a Shaky Tightrope,** Stanley Reed, *The Nation,* December 28, 1985/January 4, 1986, p. 151.
12. **Egypt's National Film Archive,** Khaled Osman, *The Unesco Courier,* August 1984, p. 155.
13. **Letter from Alexandria,** Geoffrey Bower, *Middle East International,* August 9, 1985, p. 156.

Iran

14. **War and Hardship in a Stern Land,** *Time,* August 26, 1985, p. 157.
15. **In Iran, the Stamp of Islam Is Everywhere,** *The Christian Science Monitor,* August 6, 1985, p. 158.

Page 70

Page 88

Iraq

16. **Iraqis Insulated from Economic, but Not Human, Costs in Gulf War,** Mary Curtius, *The Christian Science Monitor,* November 21, 1985, p. 161.
17. **Iraq Grapples with Sandy Solar Collectors,** Richard Wilson, *The Christian Science Monitor,* March 21, 1983, p. 162.

Israel

18. **Israel at a Crossroads,** Xan Smiley, *World Press Review,* September 1985, p. 163.
19. **Israel Is Threatened by an Enemy Within: Its Economy,** Lawrence Meyer, *The Washington Post National Weekly Edition,* January 6, 1986, p. 166.
20. **Student Life in Jerusalem,** Hannah Brown, *Congress Monthly,* April 1985, p. 168.

Jordan

21. **West Bank: Core of Middle East Conflict,** Ned Temko, *The Christian Science Monitor,* October 21, 1985, p. 170.
22. **Letter from Amman,** Paul Harper, *Middle East International,* December 20, 1985, p. 173.

Kuwait

23. **Kuwait Living on Its Nerves,** K. Celine, *Merip Reports,* February 1985, p. 174.

Libya

24. **Revolution in Recession,** Jon Bearman, *South,* October 1985, p. 176.
25. **A Rare Glimpse of Colonel Qaddafi,** Judith Miller, *The New York Times,* January 11, 1986, p. 178.

Lebanon

26. **Life in Lebanon: In the Camps,** *Middle East International,* December 6, 1985, p. 180.
27. **Who Won Lebanon?** *The Economist,* May 25, 1985, p. 181.

Morocco

28. **Libya and Morocco—Marriage of Necessity,** George Henderson, *Middle East International,* October 11, 1985, p. 183.

Oman

29. **Oman Gives Super Party: It's Come a Long Way,** John Kifner, *The New York Times,* November 19, 1985, p. 185.

Saudi Arabia

30. **Cheers for the Saudi Camel Race,** George Joseph Tanber, *The Christian Science Monitor,* March 21, 1983, p. 186.
31. **After OPEC,** S. Fred Singer, *The New Republic,* October 21, 1985, p. 187.

Sudan

32. **Sudan's Hidden Tragedy,** Robert Watkins, *Africa Report,* November-December 1985, p. 190.

Syria

33. **Syria: Key Arab Factor in Mideast Equation,** Mary Curtius, *The Christian Science Monitor,* December 30, 1985, p. 193.

Turkey

34. **In Turkey, a Gain for Rights,** Jeri Laber and Alice H. Henkin, *The New York Times,* December 24, 1985, p. 194.
35. **The Magician Who Lost His Touch,** Ergin Yildizoglu, *South,* May 1985, p. 196.

United Arab Emirates

36. **Rapid Progress in Education,** Fatima Jamal, *Pakistan & Gulf Economist,* July 13-19, 1985, p. 198.

People's Democratic Republic of Yemen (South Yemen)

37. **Like Clockwork,** *The Economist,* January 18, 1986, p. 200.

Yemen Arab Republic (North Yemen)

38. **North Yemen Has Many Reasons for Playing Down Oil Potential,** Ian Steele, *The Christian Science Monitor,* November 12, 1985, p. 200.

Credits 202
Glossary of Terms and Abbreviations 203
Sources for Statistical Summaries 205
Bibliography 206
Index 209

Introduction

THE GLOBAL AGE

As we approach the end of the twentieth century, it is clear that the future we face will be considerably more international in nature than ever believed possible in the past. Each day of our lives, print and broadcast journalists make us aware that our world is becoming increasingly smaller and substantially more interdependent.

The energy crisis, world food shortages, nuclear proliferation, and the regional conflicts in Central America, the Middle East, and other areas that threaten to involve us all make it clear that the distinctions between domestic and foreign problems are all too often artificial—that many seemingly domestic problems no longer stop at national boundaries. As Rene Dubos, the 1969 Pulitzer Prize recipient stated: ". . . [I]t becomes obvious that each (of us) has two countries, (our) own and planet earth." As global interdependence has become a reality, it has become vital for the citizens of this world to develop literacy in global matters.

THE GLOBAL STUDIES SERIES

It is the aim of this Global Studies series to help readers acquire a basic knowledge and understanding of the regions and countries in the world. Each volume provides a foundation of information—geographic, cultural, economic, political, historical, artistic, and religious—which will allow readers to better understand the current and future problems within these countries and regions and to comprehend how events there might affect their own well-being. In short, these volumes attempt to provide the background information necessary to respond to the realities of our Global Age.

Author and Editor

Each of the volumes in the Global Studies series has been crafted under the careful direction of an author/editor—an expert in the area under study. The author/editors teach and conduct research and have travelled extensively through the countries about which they are writing.

In this Middle East volume, the author/editor has written the regional essays and the country reports. In addition, he has been instrumental in the selection of the world press articles which relate to each of the regional sections.

Contents and Features

The Global Studies volumes are organized to provide concise information and current world press articles on the regions and countries within those areas under study.

Regional Essays

For *Global Studies: The Middle East,* the author/editor has written two narrative essays focusing on the religious, cultural, sociopolitical, and economic differences and similarities of the countries and peoples in the region. The purpose of the regional essays is to provide readers with an effective sense of the diversity of the area as well as an understanding of its common cultural and historical backgrounds. Accom-

(United Nations photo/Yutaka Nagata)

The Global Age is making all countries and all people more interdependent.

panying the regional essays is a two-page map showing the political boundaries of each of the countries within the region.

Country Reports

Concise reports are written for each of the countries within the region under study. These reports are the heart of each Global Studies volume. *Global Studies: The Middle East* contains twenty-one country reports.

The country reports are comprised of five standard elements. Each report contains a small, nondetailed map visually positioning the country amongst its neighboring states; a detailed summary of statistical information; a current essay providing important historical, geographical, political, cultural, and economic information; a historical timeline offering a convenient visual survey of a few key historical events; and four graphic indicators, with summary statements about the country in terms of development, freedom, health/welfare, and achievements, at the end of each report.

A Note on the Statistical Summaries

The statistical information provided for each country has been drawn from a wide range of sources. The eight most frequently referenced are listed on Page 205. Every effort has been made to provide the most current and accurate information available. However, occasionally the information cited by these sources differs to some extent; and, all too often, the most current information available for some countries is dated. Aside from these discrepancies, the statistical summary of each country is generally quite complete and reasonably current. Care should be taken, however, in using these statistics (or, for that matter, any published statistics) in making hard comparisons among countries. We have also included comparable statistics on the United States, which follow on the next two pages.

World Press Articles

Within each Global Studies volume are reprinted a large number of articles carefully selected by our editorial staff and the author/editor from a broad range of international periodicals and newspapers. The articles have been chosen for currency, interest, and their differing perspectives on the subject countries and regions. There are a total of thirty-eight articles in *Global Studies: The Middle East.*

The articles section is preceded by a *Topic Guide* as well as an *Annotated Table of Contents.* The Annotated Table of Contents offers a brief summary of each article, while the Topic Guide indicates the main theme(s) of each article. Thus, readers desiring to focus on articles dealing with a particular theme, say, religion, may refer to the Topic Guide to find those articles.

Spelling

In many instances articles from foreign sources may use forms of spelling that are different from our own. Many Third World publications reflect the European usage. In order to retain the flavor of the articles and to make the point that our system is not the only one, spellings have not been altered to conform with our system.

Glossary, Bibliography, Index

At the back of each Global Studies volume, readers will find a *Glossary of Terms and Abbreviations,* which provides a quick reference to the specialized vocabulary of the area under study and to the standard abbreviations (OPEC, PLO, etc.) used throughout the volume.

Following the Glossary is a *Bibliography,* which is organized into general works, national histories, literature in translation, current events publications, and periodicals which provide regular coverage on the Middle East.

The *Index* at the end of the volume is an accurate reference to the contents of the volume. Readers seeking specific information and citations should consult this standard index.

Currency and Usefulness

This first edition of *Global Studies: The Middle East,* like other Global Studies volumes, is intended to provide the most current and useful information available necessary to understand the events that are shaping the cultures of the region today.

We plan to issue this volume on a regular basis. The statistics will be updated, regional essays rewritten, country reports revised, and articles completely replaced as new and current information becomes available. In order to accomplish this task we will turn to our author/editor, our advisory boards and—hopefully—to you, the users of this volume. Your comments are more than welcome. If you have an idea that you think will make the volume more useful, an article or bit of information that will make it more current, or a general comment on its organization, content, or features that you would like to share with us, please send it in for serious consideration for the next edition.

(United Nations photo/John Isaac)
Understanding the problems and lifestyles of other countries will help make us literate in global matters.

United States of America

Comparing statistics on the various countries in this volume should not be done without recognizing that the figures are within the timeframe of our publishing date and may not accurately reflect today's conditions. Nevertheless, comparisons can and will be made, so to enable you to put the statistics of different countries into perspective, we have included comparable statistics on the United States. These statistics are drawn from the same sources that were consulted for developing the statistical information in each country report.

The United States is unique. It has some of the most fertile land in the world, which, coupled with a high level of technology, allows the production of an abundance of food products—an abundance that makes possible the export of enormous quantities of basic food stuffs to many other parts of the world. The use of this technology also permits the manufacture of goods and services that exceed what is possible in a majority of the rest of the world. In the United States are some of the most important urban centers in the world focusing on trade, investment, and commerce as well as art, music, and theater.

GEOGRAPHY

Area in Square Kilometers (Miles):
9,372,614 (3,540,939)
Capital (Population): Washington,
DC (638,432) (1980)
Climate: temperate

PEOPLE

Population
Total: 236,413,000 (1984)
Annual Growth Rate: 0.9%
Rural/Urban Population Ratio:
26.3/73.7
Ethnic Makeup of Population: 80%
white; 11% black; 6.2% Spanish
origin; 1.6% Asian and Pacific
Islander; 0.7% American Indian,
Eskimo, and Aleut

Health
Life Expectancy at Birth: 70.4 (male),
78 (female) (1982)
Infant Death Rate (Ratio): 11.2/1,000
Average Caloric Intake: 138% of FAO
minimum
Physicians Available (Ratio): 1/520

Religion(s)
31% Protestant; 21% Roman
Catholic; 2.5% Jewish; 45.5% other

Education
Adult Literacy Rate: 99.5%

COMMUNICATION

Telephones: 182,558,000
Newspapers: 1,679 dailies; approximately 60,000,000 circulation

TRANSPORTATION

Highways—Kilometers (Miles):
6,208,552 (3,866,296); 5,466,612
(3,398,810) paved (1982)
Railroads—Kilometers (Miles):
270,312 (167,974) (1981)
Commercial Airports: 15,132 (1981)

GOVERNMENT

Type: federal republic
Independence Date: July 4, 1776
Head of State: President Ronald
Wilson Reagan
Political Parties: Democratic Party;
Republican Party; others of minor
political significance
Suffrage: universal at 18

MILITARY

Number of Armed Forces: 2,178,300
(1984)
*Military Expenditures (% of Central
Government Expenditures):* 29.1%
(1983)
Current Hostilities: none

ECONOMY

Currency ($ US Equivalent): —
Per Capita Income/GNP:
$12,530/$3,363.3 billion (1983)
Inflation Rate: 4%
Natural Resources: metallic and
nonmetallic minerals; petroleum;
arable land
Agriculture: food grains; feed crops;
oilbearing crops; cattle; dairy
products
Industry: diversified in both capital-
and consumer-goods industries

FOREIGN TRADE

Exports: $334.2 billion (1983)
Imports: $366.4 billion (1983)

U.S.

CANADA

NORTH AMERICA

UNITED STATES

MEXICO

CARIBBEAN

CENTRAL AMERICA

SOUTH AMERICA

EUROPE

N

W   E

S

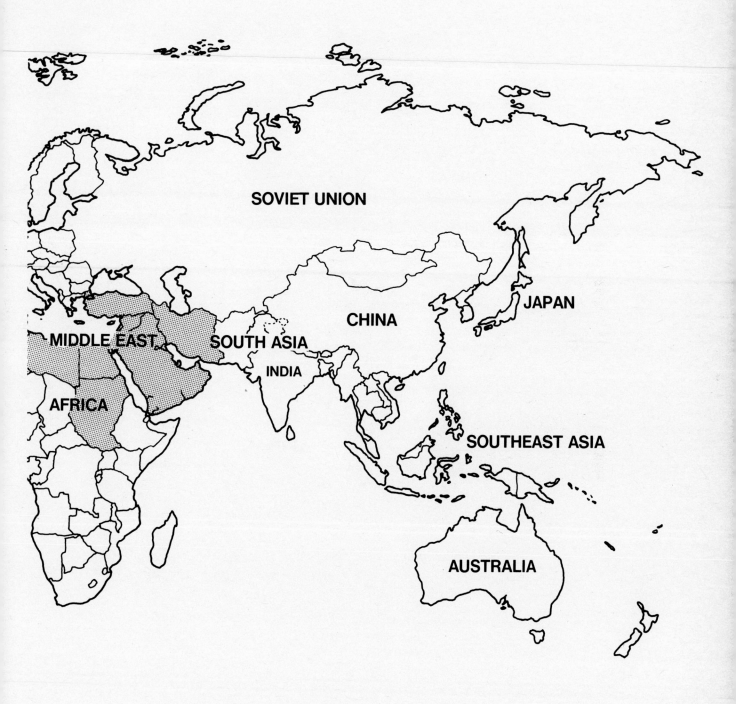

SOVIET UNION

JAPAN

CHINA

MIDDLE EAST

SOUTH ASIA

INDIA

AFRICA

SOUTHEAST ASIA

AUSTRALIA

This map of the world highlights the Middle East countries that are discussed in this volume. All of the following essays are written from a cultural perspective in order to give the readers a sense of what life is like in these countries. The essays are designed to present the most current and useful information available today. Other books in the Global Studies series cover different global areas and examine the current state of affairs of the countries within those regions.

The Middle East

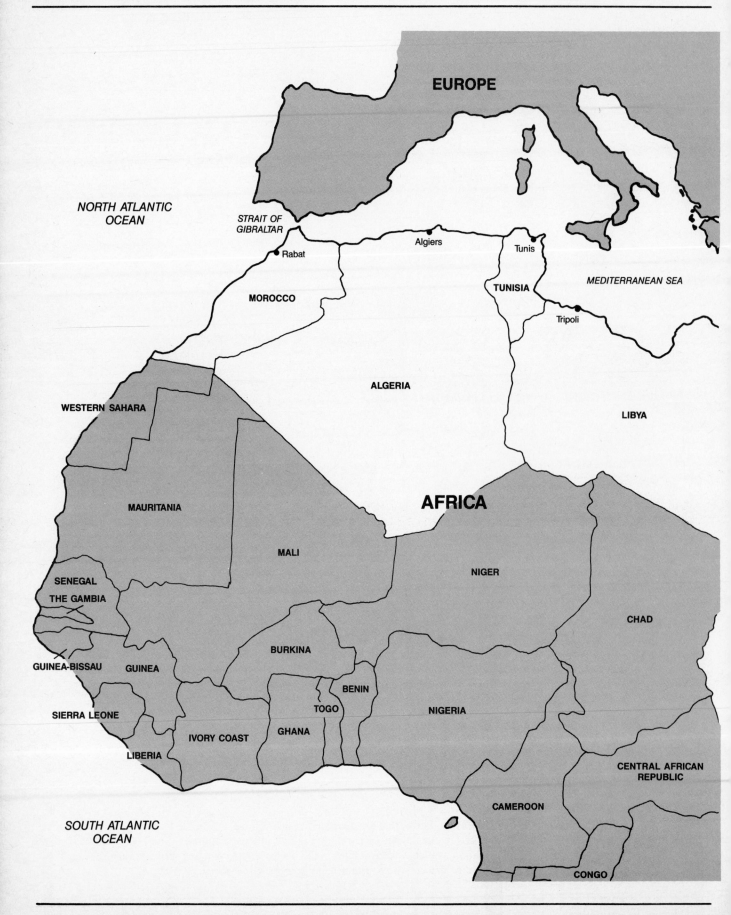

EUROPE

NORTH ATLANTIC
OCEAN

STRAIT OF
GIBRALTAR

Rabat

MOROCCO

Algiers

Tunis

TUNISIA

Tripoli

MEDITERRANEAN SEA

ALGERIA

LIBYA

WESTERN SAHARA

MAURITANIA

AFRICA

MALI

NIGER

CHAD

SENEGAL

THE GAMBIA

BURKINA

GUINEA-BISSAU   GUINEA

BENIN

TOGO

SIERRA LEONE

NIGERIA

IVORY COAST   GHANA

LIBERIA

CENTRAL AFRICAN
REPUBLIC

CAMEROON

SOUTH ATLANTIC
OCEAN

CONGO

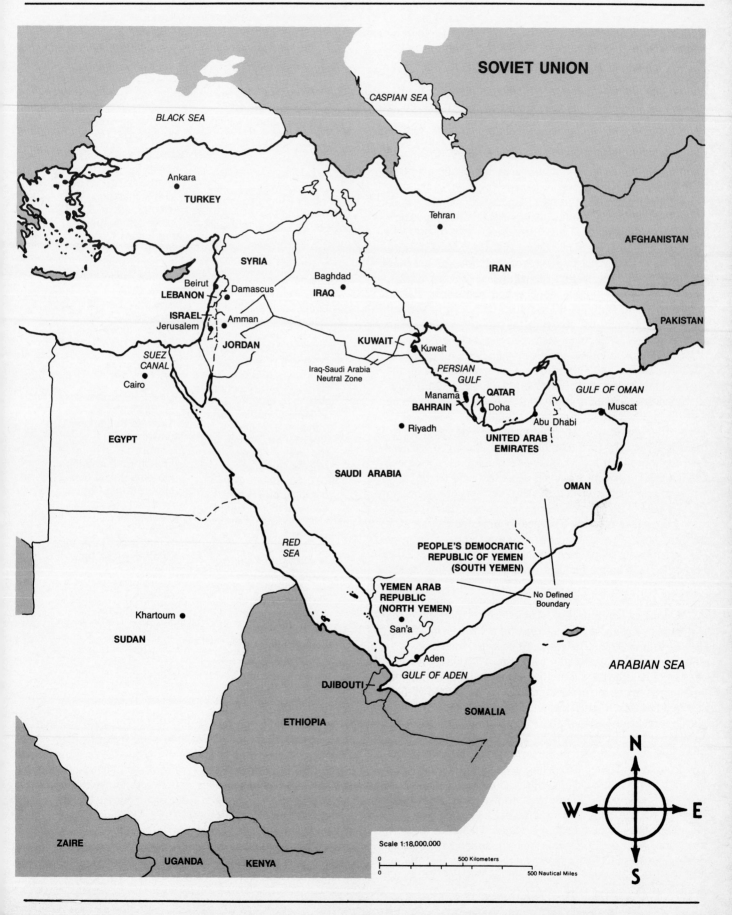

SOVIET UNION

CASPIAN SEA

BLACK SEA

Ankara

TURKEY

Tehran

AFGHANISTAN

SYRIA

IRAN

Baghdad

Beirut

LEBANON   Damascus

BAGHDAD

IRAQ

PAKISTAN

ISRAEL

Jerusalem   Amman

JORDAN

KUWAIT

Kuwait

SUEZ
CANAL

Iraq-Saudi Arabia
Neutral Zone

PERSIAN
GULF

GULF OF OMAN

Cairo

Manama   QATAR

BAHRAIN   Doha

Abu Dhabi   Muscat

EGYPT

Riyadh

UNITED ARAB
EMIRATES

SAUDI ARABIA

OMAN

RED
SEA

PEOPLE'S DEMOCRATIC
REPUBLIC OF YEMEN
(SOUTH YEMEN)

No Defined
Boundary

Khartoum

YEMEN ARAB
REPUBLIC
(NORTH YEMEN)

SUDAN

San'a

ARABIAN SEA

Aden

DJIBOUTI

GULF OF ADEN

SOMALIA

ETHIOPIA

N

ZAIRE

W   E

UGANDA   KENYA

Scale 1:18,000,000

500 Kilometers

0

0   500 Nautical Miles

S

3

The Middle East: Islam in Ferment

Until quite recently the world of Islam, centered in the Middle East, was a remote grey area to most Americans. To those who passed through the area en route to the invasions of occupied Europe in World War II, it was a hot, dusty place, peopled by swarthy men dressed in what appeared to be bed sheets, who sat in fly-blown cafes at the outskirts of military bases drinking endless glasses of hot sweet tea and speaking an incomprehensible language. This image changed little in the intervening years except for the addition of the little state of Israel, whose Jewish peoples made the desert bloom and more than stood their ground militarily against the children of those men in bed sheets.

Seen against the strong image of Israel, that country's Middle Eastern neighbors seemed unimportant. Americans knew little of their history, or of their struggle to attain dignity and stability in the new world of independent states. Many Americans shared only a vague awareness of a religious group called Muslims (mistakenly called Mohammedans), who inhabited the Middle East in large numbers and practiced a religion known as Islam. But in political terms, the Muslims seemed powerless, disorganized, always on the brink of conflict. With the exception of Israel, often seen as an extension of the United States, the maturity that Americans had come to expect of governments like their own was not to be found among the quarrelsome leaders of these new Middle Eastern states. Thus the thunderous impact of Islam on the United States has come with little advance warning or preparation.

The first shock was the 1979 occupation of the US Embassy in Teheran by Iranian militants, with American hostages held for more than a year before their release. In October 1983, a truck carrying what was described later as the most powerful non-nuclear device ever exploded was driven by two men into the United States Marine barracks in Beirut, Lebanon, killing 241 marines assigned to Lebanon as part of a multinational peacekeeping force. Subsequently, a mysterious organization calling itself Islamic Jihad carried out a series of murders and kidnappings of Americans, including Benjamin Weir, a Presbyterian missionary with thirty years' experience in Lebanon. Weir was subsequently released.

The most telling impact of Islamic ferment to date was the hijacking by Lebanese Shia terrorists of a TWA jet in Athens, Greece in June 1985. The plane, filled with American vacationers, was taken eventually to Beirut. Thirty-nine Americans were held hostage there for seventeen days, in support of demands by the terrorists to release seven hundred of their coreligionists taken into Israel and jailed after the 1985 Israeli withdrawal from Lebanon.

This sequence of shocks, particularly the hijacking because of its vast press coverage in the form of "crisis journalism," has brought the United States face to face with what appears to be a new phenomenon of confrontation in the Middle East between Muslims and Westerners. To give the phenomenon a name, we call it "Islam in ferment."

United States involvement in Lebanon intensified the confrontation. After the 1983 truck bombing, an anonymous caller warned press and US Embassy representatives that the attack would be followed by others, until the "enemies of Islam"

ATTACKS CLAIMED BY ISLAMIC JIHAD

APRIL 18, 1983 Truck bombing of the US Embassy in Beirut, killing 63 people.

OCT. 23, 1983 Suicide bombings of US and French military headquarters in Beirut, killing 241 Americans and 58 French.

DEC. 12, 1983 At least six bombings in Kuwait, including one at US Embassy.

DEC. 21, 1983 Explosion at French military command post in Beirut, killing 18.

JAN. 18, 1984 Shooting death of Malcolm Kerr, president of American University of Beirut.

FEB. 8, 1984 Shooting deaths in Paris of former Iranian martial law administrator, Gen. Gholam Ali Oveissi, and his brother Gholam Hosein Oveissi.

SEPT. 20, 1984 Car bombing of US Embassy annex in Beirut, killing at least 8 people.

SEPT. and OCT. 1984 Shootings of two Saudi Arabians on Spain's Costa del Sol.

MAY 25, 1985 Suicide car bomb attempt against the Emir of Kuwait.

JUNE 14, 1985 Probably behind hijacking of TWA flight between Athens and Rome.

KIDNAPPINGS: Islamic Jihad has also claimed responsibility for numerous kidnappings of Westerners in Lebanon since March 1984.

Americans:
William Buckley, embassy official.
Jeremy Levin, reporter (now free).
The Rev. Benjamin Weir (now free).
Peter Kilburn, librarian.
The Rev. Lawrence Jenco.
Terry Anderson, reporter.
David Jacobsen, hospital official.
Thomas Sutherland, professor.

French:
French Embassy employees Marcel Fontaine, Marcel Carton, and Danielle Perez (later freed).

British:
Brian Levick (now free).
Geoffrey Nash (now free).
Alec Collett.

Robin Wright, in *The Christian Science Monitor,* June 17, 1985.

had been driven from sacred Islamic soil. The difficult process of negotiation to free the TWA hostages demonstrated not only the number and variety of militant Lebanese Muslim groups, but also the virulent anti-American feelings (which were also transferred to a broader plane due to American involvement in Lebanon) of most of them. Previously unfamiliar organizational names such as Amal, Hizbullah, al-Dawa, and the omnipresent Islamic Jihad became household words in the United States even though most Americans did not know what they stood for.

Responsibility for the TWA hijacking in 1985 was claimed by the Islamic Jihad. This terrorist was one of the Shia gunmen who held the flight crew hostage in Beirut, Lebanon.

What has caused this ferment? What does it consist of, and why is it directed so violently against the United States? Is it a new phenomenon, or is it a natural progression for Islam, arising out of the circumstances in which Muslims find themselves in the late twentieth century? What are the elements in the Islamic ferment? We address these questions in this report.

THE CONCEPT OF JIHAD

Jihad is one of the most important elements in the Islamic ferment. Three events serve to illustrate jihad which may be defined as "struggle," "striving" (of the individual to realize God's will), or "holy war." In November 1979 a group of zealous Muslims seized the Great Mosque in Mecca, Islam's holiest shrine, barricaded themselves inside, and said they would remain until the government of Saudi Arabia halted its progressive movement away from observance of basic Islamic law and principles. Members of Jamaat al-Jihad ("Society of the Struggle") assassinated Egyptian President Anwar al-Sadat in 1981, justifying their actions on the grounds that under Sadat's leadership, Egypt was no longer a true Islamic state. And in Syria in the 1980s, members of the Muslim Brotherhood, a group dedicated to regional Islamic unity, assassinated a number of government leaders belonging to the minority Alawite (Shia) community which rules that country. These three militant events have not occurred in isolation. They are part of the struggle of Muslim peoples to come

to terms with the modern world, and to define an appropriate role for Islam in that world.

The difficulty for fundamentalist Muslims in defining such a role stems from the fact that their religion operates under very specific divine rules of conduct. These rules were laid down fourteen centuries ago by Muhammad the Messenger, who received them as revelations from God. The sum total of these revelations is the Koran, the Holy Book of Islam. Because Muslims believe that the Koran is the literal Word of God, they also believe that it is not subject to change but only to interpretation within a narrow range.

The conflict over interpretation of jihad has had a great deal to do with the ferment visible in Islam today. For example, members of Islamic Jihad believe that their interpretation of a *holy war* against the enemies of Islam is the correct one. The "holy war" definition of jihad is the one most familiar to non-Muslims. Muslims have always believed that God intended them to struggle to establish Islam as a universal religion, although conversion of other monotheists (Jews and Christians) would not be required as long as these communities recognized the superiority of Islam. The military interpretation of jihad has led to the division of the world into the Dar al-Islam ("House of Islam") and the Dar al-Harb ("House of Dissidence"), the area yet to be brought into the House of Islam.[1]

Members of al-Dawa, on the other hand, interpret jihad as a *struggle* to overthrow the Islamic government of Iraq, because they deem it unjust and believe that it does not follow correct Islamic principles or apply strict Islamic law to the state. The Muslim Brotherhood, an Arab organization, believes that the current leaders of all Islamic Arab states should be overthrown and replaced by a new Arab caliph, reviving the ancient Islamic theocratic state of Muhammad's successors.

A third definition of jihad, the *striving* of the individual for justice, is perhaps the most controversial. Islam teaches that if rulers, appointed or elected over some Islamic territory, become unjust, their subjects should bear the injustices with fortitude since God will, in due course, reward their patience. Some Muslims interpret this injunction to mean that they should strive to help the leaders to see the error of their ways by whatever action is necessary. Centuries ago a secret society, the Hashishin ("Assassins," so called because they were reportedly users of hashish) carried out many assassinations of prominent officials and rulers, claiming that God had inspired them to rid Islamic society of tyrants. Since Islam emphasizes the direct relationship of man to God, and therefore man's responsibility to do right in the eyes of God and to struggle to help other believers follow the same right path, it becomes most dangerous when individuals feel that they do not need to subject themselves to the collective will, but rather to impose their own concept of justice on others.

In our own day, jihad is associated with the struggle of Shia Muslims for social, political, and economic rights within Islamic states. Inspired by the example of Iran, they seek to establish a true Islamic government in the House of Islam.

One of the Five Pillars of Islam, or five basic duties of Muslims, is to go on a pilgrimage to Mecca in Saudi Arabia once in their lifetime. Once there they circle seven times around the Black Box (the Ka'ba, pictured above), kiss the Black Stone, drink from the well of Zam Zam, and perform other sacred rites.

But in order to establish such a government, alien influences (particularly those of the "infidel" West) must be weeded out, all Islamic territory must be recovered, and unjust leaders must be removed to make way for those best qualified to lead the community.

ISLAMIC ORIGINS

Despite the fact that Islam has coexisted with Christianity for fourteen centuries, the long history of conflict between these two religions makes mutual understanding difficult. F.E. Peters notes that "holy war against the Franks did not spring immediately to the mind of every Muslim . . . until the Franks made it clear by their behavior and propaganda (in the Crusades) that they were engaged in a holy war over Jerusalem.[2] The most negative view of Islam by Westerners is largely the result of the Crusades, highly colored by gener-

ations of Sunday-school textbooks. However, Islam developed among a particular people, the Arabs, was built on earlier foundations of Christianity and Judaism, and was primarily concerned with the transmission of the spiritual message of God to mankind as a corrective measure. It is an article of faith among Arab nationalists and Muslim Arab scholars that the Arabs were chosen as a people to receive God's revelations because they were cousins of the Jews through Abraham and therefore were included in the Judeo-Christian tradition. But they did not have scriptures of their own.

Islam was founded in the seventh century AD by Muhammad, a merchant in the small town of Mecca in southwestern Arabia. Muslims believe that Muhammad's religious teachings came from revelations which he received orally from God via the Angel Gabriel. After Muhammad's death, these revelations were put into book form in the *Koran* ("Recitation"), the Holy Book of Islam.

During Muhammad's lifetime, the various revelations he received were used to guide his followers along the "Way" of conduct (*Sharia*, in Arabic) acceptable to God. The Arabs followed traditional religions in Muhammad's time, worshipping many gods. Muhammad taught belief in one God—Allah—and in the Word of God sent down to him as Messenger. For this reason, Muhammad is considered the prophet of Islam.

The total of Muhammad's teachings and revelations make up a formal religious system called *Islam* (literally "submission," to God). Those who submit are called *Muslims*. The Islamic religious system developed by Muhammad is essentially a simple one. It has five basic duties or requirements, usually called the *Five Pillars* because they are the foundations of the House of Islam. They are:

1. The confession of faith: "I testify that there is no God but God, and Muhammad is the Messenger of God."
2. Prayer, required five times daily, facing in the direction of Mecca, the holy city.
3. Fasting during the daylight hours in the month of Ramadan, the month of Muhammad's first revelations.
4. Alms giving, a tax or gift of not less than two-and-one-half percent, to the community for the help of the poor.
5. Pilgrimage, required at least once in one's lifetime, to the House of God in Mecca.

It is apparent from the above description that Islam has many points in common with Judaism and Christianity. All three are monotheistic religions, having a fundamental belief in one God. Muslims believe that Muhammad was the "seal of the Prophets," the last messenger and recipient of revelations. But they believe that God revealed Himself to other prophets before Muhammad, starting with Abraham, Moses, and the Old Testament prophets, down through history to Jesus. Muslims part company with Christians over the divinity of Jesus, the resurrection, and the Trinity. They stay close to Judaism on matters of dietary restrictions and the interpretation of divine law by a body of religious scholars.

In addition to the revelations in the Koran, Muhammad based his leadership on his own wisdom and understanding

THE KORAN: THE HOLY BOOK OF ISLAM

Muslims believe that the Koran is the literal Word of God, and that Muhammad was chosen to receive God's Word through the Angel Gabriel as a *rasul* (messenger). But the Koran does not cancel out the Bible and Torah, which preceded it. The Koran is viewed, rather, as providing a corrective set of revelations for these previous revelations from God, which Muslims believe have been distorted or not followed correctly. To carry out God's Word, as set down in the Koran, requires a constant effort to create the ideal Islamic society, one "that is imbued with Islamic ideals and reflects as perfectly as possible the presence of God in His creation."*

The Koran was revealed to Muhammad over the twenty-two-year period of his ministry (AD 610-632). The revelations were of varying lengths, and were originally meant to be committed to memory and recited on various occasions, in particular the daily prayers. The first authoritative text was compiled in the time of the third caliph, Uthman. Uthman's text was divided into 114 *suras* (chapters), with the longest at the beginning and the shortest at the end. (The actual order of the revelations was probably the reverse, since the longer ones came mostly during Muhammad's period in Medina, when he was trying to establish guidelines for the community.)**

Many of the revelations provide specific guides to conduct or social relationships:

When ye have performed the act of worship, remember Allah sitting, standing and reclining . . . Worship at fixed times hath been enjoined on the believers. . . .

(IV, 103)

Establish worship at the going down of the sun until the dark of night, and at dawn. Lo! The recital of the Koran at dawn is ever witnessed.

(XVII, 78-79)

Make contracts with your slaves and spend of your own wealth that God has given you upon them. . . .

(XXIV, 33)

If you fear that you will be dishonest in regard to these orphan girls, then you may marry from among them one, two, three or four. But if you fear you will not be able to do justice among them, marry only one.

(IV, 3)

Much of the content of the Koran is related to the ethical and moral. It is an Arab Koran, given to Arabs "in clear Arabic tongue" (*sura* XLI, 44) and characterized by a quality of style and language that is essentially untranslatable. Muslim children, regardless of where they live, learn it in Arabic, and only then may read it in their own language (but always accompanied by the original Arabic.) Recitals of selections from the Koran are a feature of births, marriages, funerals, festivals, and other special events, and are extraordinarily effective whether the listener understands Arabic or not.***

*Peter Awn, "Faith and Practice," in Marjorie Kelly, ed., *Islam: The Religious and Political Life of a World Community* (New York: Praeger, 1984), pp. 2-7.
**On this topic see Fazlur Rahman, *Major Themes of the Qur'an* (Chicago: Bibliotheca Islamica, 1980), *passim*.
***"The old preacher sat with his waxen hands in his lap and uttered the first Surah, full of the soft warm coloring of a familiar understanding . . . His listeners followed the notation of the verses with care and rapture, gradually seeking their way together . . . like a school of fish following a leader, out into the deep sea." Lawrence Durrell, *Mountolive* (London: Faber and Faber, 1958), p. 265.

---

of human behavior. Muhammad's own life is considered by Muslims as a model to follow. His decisions, called *hadith* ("sayings" or "traditions"), supplement the Koran as a guide to the correct conduct or mode of behavior of Muslims. This code is called the *Sunna*, translated literally as "Beaten Path."

ISLAMIC DIVISIONS: SUNNI AND SHIA

The great majority (ninety percent) of Muslims are called *Sunni Muslims*. They follow the Sunna, practice the rituals of the religion, and accept the progression of Islamic history from Muhammad through a line of successors called *caliphs* (in Arabic, *Khalifa*—"agent," "successor," or "deputy") acting on his behalf down to the present division into sovereign Islamic states. But a significant minority (ten percent), while accepting the bases of Islam, reject its historical and political development. They are called *Shia Muslims* (commonly, but incorrectly, Shiites). The split between these two groups dates back to the aftermath of Muhammad's death in AD 632.

Muhammad left no instructions as to a successor (caliph). Since he had said that there would be no more revelations after him, a majority of his followers favored the election of a caliph who would hold the community together and carry on his work. But a minority felt that Muhammad had intended to name his closest male blood relative, Ali, as his successor. Supporters of Ali declared that the succession to Muhammad was a divine right inherited by his direct descendants. Hence they are known as Shia ("Partisans") of Ali.

The first three caliphs were elected by the majority. Under their leadership, Arab armies carried the Prophet's green banner deep into Asia and as far as the Atlantic coast of Morocco. But these successes merely intensified the political divisions between Sunni and Shia. The conquest and conversion of new non-Arab peoples to Islam compounded the problems. Peoples who already had definite sociopolitical and cultural patterns of their own, such as the Egyptians and Iranians, resented being given an inferior status to the Arabs, since theoretically all Muslims are equal. These peoples worked to undermine the authority of the Arab caliphs.

Ali was eventually elected as the fourth caliph, but by this time the divisions were so deep that his election was disputed, and he was murdered by a rival. One of his sons, Hasan, was poisoned. The other son, Husayn, was ambushed and killed by the armies of his father's rival. This rival not only assumed the title of caliph, but also established a hereditary dynasty and moved the capital of Islam from sacred Mecca to the city of Damascus, Syria. When, later, another revolution overthrew the Damascus caliphs and the new rulers moved the capital to Baghdad, the Shia Muslims were subjected to periodic persecution because they opposed the established order. Shia rebellions were put down with bloody massacres by the ruling Sunnis. Forced to go underground, the Shia Muslims began to practice *taqiya* ("concealment"). Outwardly they bowed to the authority of Sunni rulers, but secretly they continued to believe in the divine right of Ali's descendants to rule the Islamic world.

Most Shia Muslims recognize a line of twelve direct descendants of Muhammad, through Ali and Husayn, as their *Imams*, or spiritual leaders. When the twelfth Imam died, a number of Shia religious leaders declared that he was not dead but hidden (alive, present in this world, but invisible) and would return at the end of time to pronounce the Day of Judgment. Until the hidden Imam returned, the religious leaders would provide leadership and interpretation of God's will and make decisions on behalf of the Shia community. This doctrine gave the Shia religious leaders more authority over Shia Muslims than Sunni religious leaders have over Sunni Muslims. This helps to explain the tremendous power and prestige that the Ayatollah Khomeini, a Shia, holds in Iran.

With one exception, Shia Muslims remained a minority in Islamic lands and did not acquire political power. The exception was Iran. In the early 1500s Shaykh Safi, the leader of a religious brotherhood in northern Iran, preached a jihad against the Ottoman Turks, accusing them of unjust practices and discrimination against the non-Turkish subjects of their empire. His successor, as head of the brotherhood, claimed to be descended from Ali, which entitled him to act on behalf of the Hidden Imam. In order to obtain further sanction for his wars with the Ottomans, the successor reached an agreement with Shia religious leaders, whereby they would recognize him as ruler of Iran in return for a commitment to establish Shia Islam as the majority there.

Since that time, Shia Islam has been the strongest bond unifying the Iranian people, regardless of ethnic, linguistic, or social differences. The relationship between the shahs of Iran and the clergy has undergone many vicissitudes, from coexistence, to persecution, to a grudging acceptance, since the Safavid period began. But it was not until Shah Mohammed Reza Pahlavi began to tamper with the bonds linking the Iranian people with their religious leaders, through his programs of social modernization, particularly in the areas of emancipation and literacy, that the relationship became a totally adversary one.

SHIA MUSLIMS AND MARTYRDOM

The murder of Husayn made him a martyr for Shia Muslims. They have identified themselves with him ever since, in terms of their heroic struggle against continual persecution. Shia Muslims observe the anniversary of Husayn's death annually, with ritual dramas reenacting his tragic last days and death. The tombs of Ali and Husayn at Najaf and Karbala (Iraq) are second only to Mecca as holy shrines for Shia Muslims. This sense of martyrdom among Shia Muslims is reinforced by their low socioeconomic status in most Islamic countries outside Iran. Their martyr complex and belief in their leaders makes Shia Muslims more willing to give their lives for their cause of social justice and defense of Islam than their Sunni brethren. The Iranian children who walk through minefields in Iraq ahead of advancing Iranian troops are following an ancient tradition of sacrifice built into the Shia credo.

THE FIRST CALIPHS OF ISLAM AND THE SUNNI-SHIA SPLIT

Roman numerals number Muhammad's successors (caliphs). Single line indicates kinship ties; double line signifies spiritual succession of caliphate.

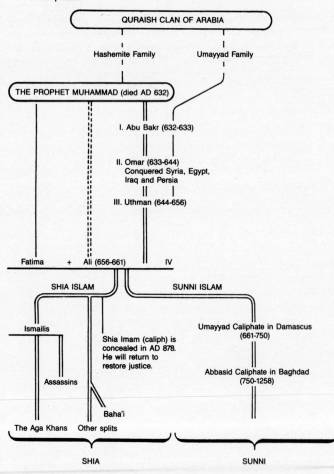

The Sunni Muslims and Shia Muslims split over the question of who should succeed Ali as caliph.

Henry Bucher, Jr., *The Third World: Middle East*, The Third World Series (Guilford, CT: The Dushkin Publishing Group, Inc., 1984), p. 44.

ISLAM AND EUROPE: CHANGING ROLES

In November 1979 the Islamic world marked the start of fourteen centuries since the founding of the religion. The early centuries were marked by many brilliant achievements. An extensive network of trade routes linked the cities of the Islamic world. It was a high-fashion world in which the rich wore silks from Damascus ("damask"), slept on fine sheets from Mosul ("muslin"), sat on couches of morocco leather, carried swords and daggers of toledo steel. Islamic merchants developed many institutions and practices used in modern economic systems, such as banks, letters of credit, checks and receipts, accounting, and bookkeeping. Islamic agriculture, based on sophisticated irrigation systems developed for the arid Middle East, introduced to the Western world the cultivation of citrus fruits, vegetables such as eggplant and radishes, coffee, cotton, and sugar.

Islamic medical technology reached a level of excellence in diagnosis and treatment unequalled in Europe until the nineteenth century. Muslim mathematics gave us our Arabic numerals and the concept of zero. Muslim navigators made possible Columbus's voyages through their knowledge of seamanship and inventions such as the sextant and the compass. Their libraries were the most extensive in existence at that time.

The level of achievements of Islamic civilization during these centuries (roughly AD 750-1200) was far superior to that of Europe. The first Europeans to come in direct contact with Islamic society were Crusader knights who invaded the Middle East in order to recapture Jerusalem from its Muslim rulers. The Crusaders marveled at what they saw, even though they were the sworn enemies of Islam. Those who returned to Europe brought with them new ideas and products from the Islamic world, as well as many English words derived from Arabic, including sofa, algebra, crimson, and admiral.

The hostility between Muslims and Christians, generated by the Crusades, was intensified by the rise of the Ottoman Turks, one of the many newly converted Islamic peoples, to power in the Islamic world. By the 1400s they had established

THE ISLAMIC CALENDAR

The Islamic calendar is a lunar calendar. It has 354 days in all, divided into 7 months of 30 days, 4 months of 29 days and 1 month of 28 days. The first year of the calendar, AH 1 (*Anno Hegira,* the year of Muhammad's "emigration" to Medina to escape persecution in Mecca), corresponds to AD 622.

Another difference between our calendar and the Islamic one is that the Islamic months rotate with the moon, coming at different times in the year from year to year. It takes an Islamic month thirty-three years to make the complete circuit of the seasons. The fasting month of Ramadan moves with the season and is most difficult for Muslims when it takes place in high summer.

a powerful Islamic military state. In 1453 the Ottomans captured Constantinople, capital of the East Roman (Byzantine) Empire, and then controlled most of Eastern Europe.

Large numbers of Christians became converts to Islam during the centuries of Ottoman domination. Today there are large Muslim minorities in Yugoslavia, Bulgaria, Rumania, and Greece. Albania is the only country in Europe with a Muslim majority (seventy percent) in the population.

The Ottoman state not only ruled Eastern Europe for nearly four centuries, but also dominated such emerging European nations as Russia, Austria, France, and England. These nations were struggling to limit the powers of absolute monarchs, develop effective military technology, and build a system of representative government. The Ottomans and the various Islamic peoples they governed did not think that any of these things were necessary. The Ottoman sultan was also the caliph of Islam. He was convinced that God had given him the right to rule and to know what was best for the people. Ottoman military success against Europe seemed to prove that God had given the Islamic world a stronger army, superior military technology, and a more effective way of life. The Ottomans were so sure of the superiority of Islam over anything that could be devised in the Christian West that they allowed Christian and Jewish communities under their control to practice their beliefs and rituals freely under their own leaders, in return for payment of a special tax and admission of their inferior military and political status in exchange for Ottoman protection.

Gradually these roles were reversed. The first reversal came with the defeats of Ottoman armies by various European powers. The Ottoman sultans were forced to sign treaties with rulers they deemed inferior. Worse yet, they lost territories with each defeat. In the early nineteenth century France and then the United Kingdom seized control of Egypt, while in Eastern Europe the Greeks, Rumanians, Serbs, and other subject peoples won their independence with European support. The defeat in Egypt was particularly shocking to Ottoman leaders, because Egypt had been part of the Islamic heartland for a thousand years.

An even greater shock came with the discovery by Muslims that the despised Europeans had developed a relatively advanced technology. Upper-class Muslim visitors to European lands in the late nineteenth century were astonished by this technology. Electric lights, railroads, broad boulevards sweeping through cities, telegraph lines, factories, and a long list of labor-saving inventions were all new to the Muslims. Most Islamic peoples were still living much as their ancestors had lived for centuries. When this apparent superiority in technology was added to European military dominance, it seemed to thoughtful Muslims that something had gone wrong.

The question was, what had gone wrong? How had it happened that the Islamic world had fallen behind Europe? Some Muslims believed that all one could do was to await the inevitable; God Himself had decided that it was time to bring the world to an end, and, therefore, the decline of Islam was a logical consequence. Other Muslims believed that the problem had developed because they had not been true to their religion or observed correctly the obligations of the faith. A third group of Muslims were convinced that Islam itself had to be "changed, modified, adapted or reformed to suit modern conditions . . . so as to overcome Western domination."[3]

The contrast between the second and third approaches to Islamic reform has been important in forming the Middle Eastern states of today. Two states, Saudi Arabia and, more recently, Iran, developed out of a movement to reestablish the Islamic community of Muhammad in its original form, basing their campaign on calls for strict adherence to the Koran and the Sunna. The other Middle Eastern states developed on an ad hoc basis through Western tutelage and gradual acceptance of Western methods and technology.

ISLAMIC FUNDAMENTALISM

The fundamentalism which appears to pervade the Islamic world today has its roots in earlier, nineteenth-century movements that sought to revitalize Islam through internal reform, thus enabling Islamic societies to resist foreign control. Some of these movements sought peaceful change; others were more militant. The most prominent of the militant groups was the Wahhabi movement, which laid the basis for the Saudi Arabian state, a pure Islamic state in form, law, and practice. Another was the Sanusiyah, founded by a prominent scholar who sought to unite the nomadic and seminomadic peoples of Libya into a brotherhood. This movement was also based on strict interpretation and application of the Koran. A third movement, Mahdism, developed in the Sudan; its purpose was not only to purify Sudanese Islam but also to drive out the British who had invaded the Sudan from Egypt.

Fundamentalism is a somewhat incomplete term to apply to the twentieth-century successors to these nineteenth-century Islamic movements, because it suggests to Westerners a religious view which is antimodernist, literal in interpretation, and with a strong emphasis on traditional ethics. Some fundamentalists would reestablish Islamic society peacefully through internal change, but others would revolutionize Islam in the manner of Marxist or other European revolutionary movements. Shia Muslim factions such as the Hizbullah view the revolutionary struggle as one aimed at expelling foreign influences first and achieving social justice second. This revolutionary movement, centered around Khomeini in Iran, is committed to the rule of the religious leaders, while Libya's Muammar al-Qadhafi would eliminate the influence of the religious leaders entirely, substituting rule by "people's committees." The only common ground for these movements and groups is their fundamental opposition to the onslaught of materialistic Western culture. Their desire is to reassert a distinct Islamic identity for the societies they claim to represent.

The great danger to Islam is that, rather than being a true revival of the religion, these movements have disfigured its nature. Some of them would modernize Islam by grafting onto the religion negative and spiritually devastating ideas borrowed from the West. In the name of religious fervor, they

close the door to the kind of open dialogue that could produce general agreement or understanding of what form Islam should take. A common concern among Muslims is how to achieve *Islamic modernization,* meaning a future wherein political and social development and economic progress appropriate for the realities of the twentieth century are firmly rooted in Islamic history and values.

Islamic modernizers and fundamentalists alike view Islam as a divinely ordained alternative to capitalism and communism. Where they differ is that many leaders and professional persons throughout the Islamic world are Western educated; they seek to superimpose Western principles and values on Islamic society. The struggle of fundamentalists to reestablish *Islamic* law as the law of the land, prohibit banks from charging interest, emphasize propriety of dress and decorum for women, and reform the curriculum in universities for greater Islamic emphasis, sets the two groups at odds, although their long-term goals are essentially the same.

On the political level, the difference between modernizers and fundamentalists is illustrated by comparing and contrasting the policies of Iran and Libya. The Islamic Republic of Iran challenges existing Islamic regimes on the basis that they are un-Islamic, since they have followed the path of Western secularism with its man-made laws, separation of church and

A common concern among Muslims is how to achieve Islamic modernization, wherein social development considers the realities of the twentieth century. This dichotomy is illustrated by these Egyptian women in traditional dress waiting for a bus, a modern convenience.

state, and "godless" technology. The Libyan regime of Muammar al-Qadhafi also challenges these regimes, on grounds that all Western institutions of government eventually become corrupt and hostile to the interests of the people.

Both Qadhafi and Khomeini share the conviction that Islam, when properly interpreted, provides a blueprint for a just society. Where they part company is over the question of participation by religious leaders in building this just society. Qadhafi believes that every thinking Muslim is capable of *ijtihad* ("correct interpretation of Islamic principles") and can contribute to Islamic state building. To Khomeini, however, no Islamic state can be either just or representative unless it is governed by religious leaders, since they alone have the training and knowledge to interpret these principles. And within this hierarchy of knowledge only one person, the Grand Ayatollah, possesses the necessary wisdom and insight for final interpretation, and is, therefore, the only legitimate ruler of the Islamic community.

ISLAMIC SOCIETY IN TRANSITION

I have come, I know not where,
  but I have come.
And I have seen a road before me,
  and have taken it.[4]

Most Muslims inhabit a world still dominated by Islamic law, custom, spirituality, and belief, despite the waves of violence, puritanical reaction, revolution, idealogical conflict, and power struggles among leaders that have threatened it. Islam is not only the bond which unites diverse peoples over a vast territory; it also brings equilibrium to counterbalance the visible disruptions that increasingly affect Islamic life.

Islam is a complete system providing spiritual, social, moral, and, to a considerable extent, political rules and guidelines for its followers. To become a Muslim is to enter into that system. But there are vast cultural differences among the world's estimated 836 million Muslims. Other than religion, an Indonesian Muslim has little in common with an American Muslim.[5] The only time these differences disappear is during the annual Great Pilgrimage (*Hajj*) to Mecca. At that time all Muslims, rich and poor, famous and unknown, become merely pilgrims, indistinguishable from one another in their seamless white *ihrams* as they circle seven times around the Ka'ba, kiss the Black Stone, drink from the well of Zam Zam, and perform the other rites associated with the return to the sacred center of their faith.[6]

In the Islamic lands of the Middle East, however, Islam provides a cultural uniformity that transcends ethnic, linguistic, or other differences between social groups. This Middle Eastern Islamic cultural order has many components, both real and intangible. The former include architecture, dress, arts and crafts, food, and living accommodations. In addition to these physical aspects of the culture, a wide range of social activities has evolved, built on religious foundations. The traditional social rituals of childbirth, marriage, adulthood, and death, the festival celebrations, are duplicated with minor variations across the region. The intangible compon-

ents of the system are harder to define, and they are perhaps more Middle Eastern than purely Islamic. Yet there is a common pattern of behavior. Most Middle Easterners practice bargaining in both business and personal relationships, emphasize the family as the responsible social unit above political parties and even nations, and follow a formal code of etiquette governing all aspects of behavior.

ARCHITECTURE: CONCRETE EXPRESSION OF RELIGIOUS FAITH

Islamic architecture is centered on the *mosque*, the house of worship. The first mosque was a simple structure of palm branches laid over a frame of tree trunks to provide shade from the desert sun for worshippers. As time passed, Muslim architects built more magnificent structures, dedicating their work to the glory of God, much as Medieval Christian artisans did with the great cathedrals of Europe. The mosque today remains the dominant architectural feature of every Islamic village and town. The presence of at least one mosque in every city neighborhood or district provides Islamic cities with a distinctive skyline of domes and minarets.

The mosque at Khan El Khalili, Egypt.

Until recently all Islamic cities were also marked by a distinct spatial order, and many still are. The order began with an encircling series of massive walls and gates, closed at night to frustrate invasion or criminal actions. There was a separate, often fortified quarter marking the presence of the central government, the market (*suq*) with its tiny artisans' shops and sacks of spices, residential quarters, and religious institutions. Residential suburbs and subdivisions similar to those of many American cities have developed only in recent years. Traditionally, one was either in the city or out of it, one was either a city dweller or a rural peasant.

HOUSING AND FAMILY LIFE

Within the residential quarters of Islamic cities there existed, and in large measure still exists, a kinship arrangement very different from that of the typical American subdivision. The households of each quarter claim either a kinship relation or close personal ties to one another. Everyone knows everyone else, and most households are related. In one residential quarter of the town of Boujad, Morocco, the great majority of households claim descent from a common ancestor, the founder of the group from which they descended patrilineally. Other households regard themselves as being under the protection of that group.

The resulting close cooperation establishes what anthropologists call the notion of "closeness" (*qaraba*), which defines the social organization of the quarter. Closeness is essential to the proper functioning of society. Christine Eickelman describes the *hayyan* (family cluster) in inner Oman as an essential support network for village women. The hayyan consists of those women (some of them relatives, others not related) whom each woman regards as her confidantes, and to whom she will confide matters which she may not reveal even to her own husband or immediate family. Visits among hayyan members are made on a daily basis, aside from the support provided in stressful situations such as birth, marriage, or death. Hayyan members also provide mutual protection and even share housework and child care.[7]

MUSLIM HOUSING: FORM FOLLOWS FUNCTION

Muslim families in the Middle East live in many different kinds of houses. A common feature is the suitability of the traditional Islamic residence to the surrounding environment. Nomads in the desert live in woven goat-hair tents, easily dismantled when ready to break camp. In Syria and Turkey one finds the cone-shaped beehive house, built of mud brick, which can be put up easily by unskilled labor and costs little in the way of materials. The high dome of the beehive collects the hot, dry air and releases it through narrow openings, while the dome shape sheds rainfall before the mud brick can absorb moisture and crumble. The construction provides natural air conditioning; interior temperatures remain in the 75° F - 85° F range, while the outside temperatures may reach 140° F. The beehive house illustrates Frank Lloyd Wright's dictum that "form follows function."

Further illustrations of ingenious designs to suit the harsh climate are the cave houses in southern Tunisia. Caves have been hollowed out from a central shaft below the desert floor. (The movie *Star Wars* was filmed here.) Most residences on the Persian/Arab Gulf, where strong winds blow, have open-sided towers above the rooftops to catch any wind and funnel it into the rooms below. Many city residences are built with tiny windows, and are joined together and covered by deep overhangs to provide shade for passers-by.

In San'a in the Yemen Arab Republic, houses are several stories high, gaily decorated and painted with slatted overhangs for women to look out of without being seen. Some farmers in northern Tunisia utilize hay to construct their houses. These hay houses are sometimes elaborate and contain windows and wooden doors.

Mud brick, cut and sun dried, has been the Middle East's common building material for eight thousand years. Today, with the increased use of reinforced concrete, steel, and other prefabricated building materials, and air condition-

This cave house in the Matmata Mountains suits the harsh climate of southern Tunisia.

ing, Middle Eastern cities have begun to take on the look of cities everywhere. Not only have most Middle Eastern cities lost their distinctive look, but widespread use of cement instead of the traditional and easily available building materials has had more dire consequences. To raise the cash to buy cement for housing in rural areas, someone must leave the village, thus disrupting family life.

Communities in the Middle East emphasize the private over the public life of residents. It is not possible for someone walking along a town or city residential street to know much about the economic or social circumstances of those who live there. Homes have blank, windowless walls which face the street; entry is usually through a massive studded door set in the wall, a brass hand serving as a knocker. Inside one may find, in a wealthier home, low-ceilinged rooms furnished with rich carpets, banquettes, and ottomans in lieu of chairs and sofas (though this is disappearing), and in the center an open courtyard with flowers, fruit trees, and a plashing fountain.

FAMILY CELEBRATIONS

Throughout the Middle East, the family is still the most important social unit, so much so that when rulers like King Hussein of Jordan and Hassan II of Morocco describe their relationship with their subjects they do so in terms of "my family" or "my children." Economic dislocations, the gap between illiterate parents and educated children, and new social legislation have all affected the family. But the extended family is still where the individual places his or her trust, loyalty, and obedience.

Islamic and Jewish families provide a network of support relationships and activities for members. These activities are

PASSOVER SEDER

Religious holidays the world over are associated with food traditions. This is especially true of the Jewish celebration of Passover.

A thin, crisp cracker called *matzo* is one of the main ingredients of the Passover feast, or *Seder,* meaning "order." It is the first food eaten at the Seder, and is also served with bitter herbs as a symbolic sandwich later in the meal.

A traditional plate is filled with special foods that serve as symbols of the long history of the Jewish people. Some of these foods are bitter herbs as reminders of the bitter years spent in captivity in Egypt, a shankbone symbolic of religious sacrifice, and a roasted egg for mourning. A mixture of fruit and nuts called *haroset* represents the mortar used by Jewish slaves while building the pyramids in Egypt. Parsley symbolizes the slaves' springtime release.

During the holiday, Jewish families gather in their homes to celebrate the Seder feast, sharing the story of Exodus, singing hymns, praying, and enjoying foods that make up this beautiful "service within a meal."

Throughout the week many families use a separate set of dishes, cutlery, and cooking utensils, and everyone enjoys this opportunity to set a fine table. In modern homes the Seder menu, although festive, may be lighter, with fewer courses.

During the eight days of Passover, celebrants will eat no products made from regular flour and no foods with leavening agents. Before the festival, houses are thoroughly cleaned to remove any trace of leavening; traditionally, a feather is used to remove any last suspected traces.

nearly always connected with religion. The main Islamic festivals celebrate historic events in the development of Islam, just as those among Jews are keyed to the experiences of the Jewish people. Thus, Jewish children building a hut of certain kinds of branches to celebrate Succoth, or gathering with their parents to observe the elaborate ritual of a Passover Seder, are commemorating events in Jewish history and helping to keep their memory alive.

The same is true of Muslim households. The entire month of Ramadan, for example, is set aside as a period of fasting to commemorate God's first revelations to Muhammad. Fasting Muslims go without any nourishment—not even a drop of water may pass their lips—during the daylight hours, until a white thread cannot be distinguished from a black one after sunset. Then a cannon booms to mark the end of the fast, and families gather for the evening meal, followed by sweets for the children and visits to friends and neighbors. Shops and cafes remain open all night, mosques are crowded with worshippers, and a *hafiz* ("reciter") reads from the Koran on street corners until by the twenty-seventh of the month the entire Koran has been read. When the month ends and the cannon booms for the last time, Muslims celebrate *Id al-Fitr,* the "Breaking of the Fast." This festival may last for several days. Its main feature is the ritual slaughter and serving of a sheep at each family's ceremonial banquet.

A CUISINE SUITED TO THE ENVIRONMENT

Middle Eastern cooking largely transcends political, linguistic, religious, and other differences. It is a highly varied cuisine which makes much use of natural, unrefined foods. The pungent smells of lamb roasting over charcoal, stuffed eggplant and roasted sweet peppers, tiny cups of thick coffee and hot, sweet tea are common across national boundaries. The basics of Middle Eastern cooking originated in ancient Persia (modern Iran) and have been continually refined, with subtle differences developing from country to country.

Beef is relatively scarce in the region due to the aridity and lack of pasture, although this is changing with the introduction of Texas cattle and other breeds suited to the arid climate. There is abundant lamb and chicken, and people eat a great variety of seafood. Because of the lack of cattle, more olive oil is used in cooking than butter, and goat and sheep cheeses are more common than cheese made from cows' milk. Yogurt is a staple dessert, but it is also used in soups and sauces. Potatoes are seldom used, but rice pilaf made with chicken broth, onions, and currants is popular. There is an almost limitless variety of herbs and spices.

Little milk is drunk, due to the lack of dairy cows and pasteurization. Fresh orange juice and guava juice are common, along with other fruit juices. Desserts are usually fruit, and sometimes cheese. Middle Easterners are also fond of rich, sweet pastries such as baklava and cakes, which are reserved for holidays and special occasions.

Coffee was discovered growing wild in the mountains of Yemen hundreds of years ago, and was brought to Europe by Ottoman Turkish soldiers during the siege of Vienna, Austria. Coffee is usually drunk strong and heavily sugared in tiny cups. Mint tea is also very popular in the Middle East, particularly in Morocco, where it is heavily laced with sugar and is drunk from small glasses. The elaborate tea-making ceremony is an important part of a formal meal.

Middle Easterners are very conscious of their need to make use of every part of the things they grow. The date palm is a good illustration of this ecologically sound practice. The leaves of the date palm provide rope, baskets, mats and rugs, cleaning pads, and shelter for people and animals. People eat the dates, and camels feed on the pits. The trunk of the palm is used for roof beams, rafters, and window frames.

As is true elsewhere in the world, in the Middle East the traditional distinctive culinary arts and specialties are giving way to a homogenized "international" cuisine, just as shoes or plastic sandals now adorn Middle Eastern feet. Labor-saving devices such as microwave ovens and refrigerators simplify the task of meal preparation in Middle Eastern homes, and McDonalds and Kentucky Fried Chicken houses have introduced a fast-food wedge into Middle Eastern life. But a strong undercurrent of traditionalism pervades Islamic society in the region. This undercurrent has been strengthened by the relative success of Khomeini's revolution in Iran and the appeal of this revolution to Muslims as a third force independent of both the United States and the Soviet Union. Traditions die hard anyway, and the more isolated Muslims become by their own choice from Western thought, behavior, and practice, the more likely it is that all elements in their social system that reflect preferences and values, including food, will remain appropriate to the system.

CHALLENGES TO THE MUSLIM FAMILY

The Muslim family in the Middle East today is subject to many of the same strains and stresses as those which affect families everywhere. These stresses and strains have somewhat greater impact on Muslim families because of their suddenness. The Middle East did not have the lengthy period of conditioning and preparation which Europe and the United States had due to the Industrial Revolution. The story is told that when some Turkish villagers saw their first automobile, early in the 1940s, they could not believe that it ran on its own power. Where is the donkey that will pull it? they wondered. Similarly, King Ibn Saud, former ruler of Saudi Arabia, was faced with angry opposition by the religious leaders of the kingdom when he wished to install a radio network to link the far-flung cities and towns of his realm. He satisfied the religious leaders by having the Koran read over a radio hookup between Mecca and Riyadh, his capital, pointing out to them that if the machine could carry the Word of God, then God must have approved its use.

One of the challenges which puts strains on the family in the Middle East is secular education, which separates illiterate parents from their children who have acquired university degrees and have moved into computers and microchip technology. From Jordan alone, sixty thousand students are studying abroad, and one out of every three Jordanians is a student. Family solidarity and unity are also threatened by overseas labor emigration. Several million Middle Eastern Muslim men work in European or other Middle Eastern countries, leaving their families at home. The family is challenged by new mores and values, often imported (or observed on TV) from Western countries. And family unity is threatened perhaps most particularly by changing male-female relationships. At the University of Jordan, for example, half of the twelve-thousand-member student body is female. Traditional Islamic society is a male-dominated one; *Sura* 4:34 of the Koran is often cited as placing men in charge of women "since God has endowed them with the necessary qualities and made them breadwinners."

After a long period of development of women's rights and status as contributors to the economy, beginning with the reforms of Mustafa Kemal Ataturk in Turkey, these rights seemed to enter a period of reversal after the 1979 Revolution in Iran. The emphasis set by that revolution in modesty of costume and decorum for women, prohibition on public dating, removal of women from the labor force and their return to housework and child bearing has spread to other countries. This is an important element in the "ferment of Islam" that was discussed earlier in political terms. Thus we see that women in emancipated Egypt, in freewheeling Lebanon, and in other determinedly secular states, increasingly identify with their Iranian sisters in modesty of dress and behavior.

But the wheel is unlikely to come full circle, nor is the Muslim family likely to become fully fragmented. A law passed recently by the Egyptian parliament annulling divorce rights for women was revoked under pressure not only from feminist groups but also from intellectuals, professionals, civil servants, and a considerable number of landowners. Egypt's parliament is predominantly male, but it heeds the voice of domestic politics, the squeaky wheel getting the benefit of the grease.

FOOTNOTES

1. Peter Awn, "Faith and Practice," in Marjorie Kelly, ed., *Islam: The Religious and Political Life of a World Community* (New York: Praeger, 1984), p. 26.

2. F.E. Peters, "The Early Muslim Empires," in Kelly, *op. cit.*, p. 86.

3. Seyyed Hossein Nasr, "Islam in the West Today, an Overview," in C.K. Pulapilly, ed., *Islam in the Contemporary World* (Notre Dame, IN: Cross Roads Books, 1980), p. 7.

4. Eliya Abu Madi, quoted in Michael Asher, *In Search of the Forty Days' Road* (London: Longman, 1984), p. 132.

5. There are between 1.5 million and 3 million Muslims in the United States and Canada. Most are immigrants, but the number of converts from the black and white communities, particularly in the US, is growing rapidly. See Yvonne Y. Haddad, "Muslims in the United States," in Kelly, *op. cit.*, pp. 258-272.

6. The American Muslim leader Malcolm X has a moving description of the pilgrimage in which he participated, in his autobiography, *The Autobiography of Malcolm X* with Alex Haley (New York: Ballantine Books, 1973).

7. Christine Eickelman, *Women and Community in Oman* (New York: New York University Press, 1984), pp. 80-111.

The Middle East: Theater of Conflict

The Middle East, a region approximately equal in size to the continental United States and slightly larger in population, extends from the Atlantic coast of Morocco, in North Africa, to the mountains of Afghanistan, where the Indian subcontinent begins. The Middle East is thus intercontinental rather than continental, with the diversity of topography, climate, and physical and social environments characteristic of the two continents, Africa and Asia, which define its territory. Geography and location have dictated a significant role in world affairs for the Middle East throughout recorded history; mankind's earliest cities, governments, organized societies, and state conflicts were probably located there. In the twentieth century this traditional role has been confirmed by the exploitation of mineral resources vital to the global economy, and by the rivalries of nations which regard the Middle East as strategically important to their national interests.

The Middle East of the 1980s is very different, however, from its predecessor of the 1880s or, for that matter, the 1780s. One important difference is political. When the United States became independent of England there were three more or less "sovereign" Middle Eastern nation-states and empires: the Sherifian Sultanate of Morocco; the Ottoman Turkish Empire; and Iran, reunited by force under the new Qajar dynasty, which would last another century and a half. These states were still in place a century later, but European influence and control over their rulers had effectively robbed them of most of their independence. Since then—a process accelerated since World War II—the Middle East map has been redrawn many times. The result of the redrawing process is the contemporary Middle East, twenty-one independent states with diverse political systems overlaying a pastiche of ethnic groups, languages, customs, and traditions.

The diversity of these twenty-one states is compensated for, in part, through the cohesion provided by various unifying factors. One of these factors is geography. The predominance of deserts, with areas suitable for agriculture compressed into small spaces where water was available in dependable flow, produced the "oasis-village" type of social organization and agricultural life. Beyond the oases evolved a second type of social organization suited to desert life, called "nomadism." A third type of social organization, villages within the numerous mountain ranges of the region, developed. This type of social organization was similar to that of the oases but was adapted more to defense. Peoples living in the region mirrored one of these three lifestyles, with the Middle Eastern city developing as an urban refinement of the same traditions.

The broad set of values, traditions, historical experiences,

Mankind's earliest governments, cities, and organized societies were probably located in what today is known as the Middle East. This ancient Roman town of Timgad, Algeria testifies to man's continued attempts to live in the arid expanses of this part of the world.

kinship structures, and so on, usually defined as "culture," is a second cohesive factor for the Middle East's peoples. Islam, for example, is either the official state religion or the leading religion in all but one (Israel) of the twenty-one states. The Arabic language, due to its identification with Islam, is a bond even for those peoples who use another spoken and/or written language (e.g., Turkish, Hebrew, or Farsi), and in any case the social usages of Islam are common throughout the region.

A third unifying factor, while it is intangible and difficult to define, is the cohesion provided by a common historical experience. Without exception, the twenty-one states of the Middle East are the products of twentieth-century international politics and the clash of interests of outside powers. Clashing national interests and external involvement in regional affairs have set the tone for the internal and regional conflicts of Middle Eastern states. Thus, the intercommunal violence in modern Lebanon has its roots in foreign (French and British) support for various communal groups in the 1860s, setting the groups against one another under the guise of protecting them from the Ottoman government and its misrule. But Lebanon is only one narrow example of a broad historical process. Throughout Middle Eastern history, invaders and counterinvaders have rolled across the region, advancing, conquering, and being conquered, while below the surface of conflict other peoples crisscrossed the land in peace, building homes, establishing cities, forming the bedrock of settlement and social development.

THE LAND ISLAND

Until recently the Middle East was compartmentalized. Its peoples had little awareness of one another and even less of the outside world. Months of arduous travel were needed for a directive from the caliph in Baghdad, the chief personage of the theocratic Islamic state, to reach his viceroy in far-off Morocco. Communications within the region were relatively poor, so that often residents of one village would know nothing of what was going on in other nearby villages—that is, if they were at peace and not feuding. Travel for caravans between cities was uncertain and often dangerous; the Tuareg of the Western Sahara Desert, a nomadic society, made a good living by charging tolls and providing mounted escorts for merchants crossing the desert.

Consequently, the combination of vast distances, poor communications, and geographical isolation brought about the early development of subregions within the larger Middle East. As early as the tenth century AD, three such subregions had been defined: North Africa; the Arab lands traditionally known to Europeans as the Near East; and the highland plateaus of Turkey and Iran. In the twentieth century these three areas were further separated from one another by foreign political control—the French in North Africa, the French and British jointly in the Arab lands, with Turkey and Iran nominally independent but subject to pressures from various outside powers. Alan Taylor's phrase "the Arab balance of power," referring to the "patterns of equilibrium, disloca-

tion and readjustment that unfolded among the Arab states . . ." applies equally well to the interaction of peoples and nations within the subregions.[1]

Many years ago Alfred Theyer Mahan, an American naval historian, defined the Middle East as a central part of the "land island" or heartland whose possession would enable some powerful nation to dominate the world. Mahan's definition stemmed from his view of naval power as an element in geopolitics; he saw the US, as a growing naval power, and Russia, expanding across Asia, as the competitors for world domination in the twentieth century.

Mahan was not original in his geopolitical assessment. In the nineteenth century the United Kingdom and Russia, the two superpowers of the period, were engaged in a "Great Game" of imperial expansion in Asia—the British *from* India, and the Russians moving southward from Moscow across the steppes *toward* India.[2] Each power worked assiduously to expand its territory or sphere of interest at the expense of the other. The powers' perceived national interests were thousands of miles from London and Moscow, in the mountains of Tibet, the Caucasus, or along the Amu Darya (Oxus) River that today separates Afghanistan and Iran from Soviet Central Asia. The Great Game is still being played in different locations, but under similar rules by the United States and the Soviet Union. Thus US President Ronald Reagan insisted in 1983-1984 that American marines were in Lebanon to defend vital US interests, while insisting as well that they were there also on a peacekeeping mission. He warned Iran and Iraq that any attempt to close the Strait of Hormuz to oil-tanker traffic would be regarded as a threat to the free world's access to Middle East oil, and therefore to American national interests. The Soviet Union has from time to time made equally strong pronouncements.[3]

SUBREGIONAL CONFLICTS

Currently each Middle Eastern subregion is the theater of a major conflict which has developed its own internal rhythm and thrust of events. In order of their intensity of conflict and impact on regional stability, the conflicts are the Iran-Iraq War, the on-going Arab-Israeli conflict, and the conflict in the Western Sahara between Morocco and the Saharan nationalist movement Polisario (Popular Front for the Liberation of Saquia al-Hamra and Rio de Oro), which is fighting to establish an independent state. A fourth conflict between Soviet occupation forces in Afghanistan and Afghan *mujahideen* ("fighters for the faith") is peripheral to the Middle East. But as it has become an important factor in the geopolitical relations of superpowers and regional powers in the Persian/Arab Gulf, it is discussed in this report.

The fact that each subregion is the theater of an active conflict has caused great concern, not only among US policymakers but also among the general public, that any one of these conflicts might spread and involve other nations in a wider war, possibly proving or at least demonstrating the effectiveness of the "domino theory" often invoked as a guide to modern international relations.

The domino theory holds that tensions or unresolved disputes between two nations will inevitably widen as neighboring nations are drawn inevitably into the dispute, even without taking sides. The uninvolved nations will then become involved, as the particular dispute becomes buried in the rivalries of competing national interests. At some point a specific incident ignites a general war, as nation after nation falls like a set of dominos into the widening conflict. The classic example of the theory is World War I.

While none of the four Middle Eastern conflicts has yet proven the workability of the domino theory, their lengths and increasing levels of intensity suggest that they are becoming less and less susceptible to rational negotiation assisted by outside mediators. Thus far these conflicts have not affected global commerce, nor motivated terrorism on an international scale, nor threatened the survival of any of the nations involved. But there are very real limits to involvement or effective management, even by the superpowers. US President Reagan recognized these limits implicitly by withdrawing American marines from Lebanon; and when Egypt's then President Anwar al-Sadat ordered the withdrawal of all Soviet military advisers from his country some years ago, home they went.

A final point about these conflicts is that they are all direct results of European intervention in the Middle East. For much of its history the Middle East was a region without defined borders, other than the intangible limits fixed for Muslims by their religion. Even the Ottoman Empire, the major power in the region for over five centuries, did not mark off its territories into provinces with precise boundaries until well into the 1800s. But the European powers brought a different set of rules into the area. They laid down fixed borders sanctified by treaties, played ruler against ruler, divided and conquered. It is this European ascendancy, building on old animosities while creating new ones, that laid the groundwork for today's conflicts.

THE IRAN-IRAQ WAR: BATTLE OF ISLAMIC BROTHERS

The current Iran-Iraq War broke out in September 1980, when Iraqi forces invaded Iran and occupied large portions of Khuzestan Province. As is the case with most Middle Eastern conflicts, the causes of the war are complex.

One factor is the ancient animosity between Iranians and Arabs, which dates back to the seventh century AD when invading Arab armies overran the once powerful Sassanid Empire of Iran, defeating the Iranian army at the famous battle of Qadisiyya in 637. The Iranians were converted to Islam with relative ease, yet they looked down on the Arabs as uncivilized nomads who needed to be taught the arts of government and refined social behavior. The Arabs, in turn, despised the Iranians for what they considered their effeminateness—their love of gardens and flowers, their appreciation of wine and fine banquets. These attitudes never entirely disappeared.[4] After the recent invasion the controlled Iraqi press praised

ARABS AND IRANIANS: SOME DIFFERENCES

Arabs and Iranians (or Persians) are nearly all Muslims, but they have very different ethnic origins and linguistic and geographical backgrounds, as well as a different history.

The Arabs originated in the Arabian Peninsula and began to migrate to other parts of the Middle East after the rise of Islam. The Iranians were originally nomadic tribespeople from Central Asia who migrated into the Iranian plateau three thousand years ago and became sedentary farmers and herders. A gifted people, they organized what is usually called the world's first true empire around 600 BC, under Cyrus the Great and his successors. Despite a checkered history since then, they retain a lofty sense of their contributions to civilization beginning with this period.

The Arabs, in contrast, gained their sense of unity and leadership through Islam. Today the Arabs form the majority of the population in North Africa, the Near Eastern Arab states, and the Sudan, and are an important minority in Iran. Except for Iraq and the Persian Gulf states, where there are significant Iranian communities, Iranians have remained in their country of origin.

it as Saddam Hussain's Qadisiyya, reminding its readers of the earlier Arab success.

Iraq also accused Iran of persecuting the predominantly Arab population (in ethnic origin) of Khuzestan, charging the Khomeini government with cancellation of the shah's policy of internal autonomy for the province.

Iraq also resented the efforts by Iranian agents to incite rebellion among its own Shia Muslim population. Iraqi governments have been dominated by the Sunni Muslim population since independence, although fifty-five percent of the population is Shia. The regime of Saddam Hussain, like its predecessors, is paranoid about opposition in general but Shia opposition in particular.[5]

The personal hatred existing between Iraq's Hussain and Iran's Ayatollah Khomeini is another strong contributing factor to the war. These two leaders have totally opposing views about politics and economics. Hussain is committed to development under secular socialism, Khomeini to a clergy-dominated republic in pure Islamic form. Khomeini lived in Iraq for fifteen years (1963-1978) after his expulsion from Iran, and then was summarily expelled on the grounds that he had become a danger to the Iraqi state. As long as the two leaders are in power, their animosity clearly stands in the way of any mediation by outside powers.

Although today it is Islamic brothers who battle one another in the Hawizeh marshes and in the skies over Baghdad and Teheran, the major cause of the war is a territorial dispute which goes far back in history, but which has been aggravated by European intervention in the Middle East. The dispute concerns the Shatt al-Arab, the 127-mile waterway from the junction of the Tigris and Euphrates Rivers south to the Persian/Arab Gulf. The waterway was a bone of contention between the Ottoman and Iranian Empires for centuries, due to its importance as a trade outlet to the Gulf. It came entirely under Ottoman control in the nineteenth century. But with the collapse of the Ottoman Empire in World War I, the new kingdom of Iraq set up by the United Kingdom came in conflict with a revitalized Iran over navigation and ownership rights. Iran demanded ownership of half of the Shatt al-Arab under international law, which would mean to mid-channel at the deepest point. Iraq claimed the entire waterway across to the Iranian side. Conflict intensified as both countries built up their oil exports in the 1960s and 1970s. In 1969 Iranian Shah Reza Pahlavi threatened to occupy Iran's side of the waterway with gunboats, and began a program of military support to Kurdish (Sunni Muslims) rebels fighting the Iraqi government.

Iran was much wealthier and militarily stronger than Iraq at that time, and Iraq could do little about Iranian support for the Kurds. But the Iraqis did have the Shatt al-Arab as a bargaining chip, in that their rights were embodied in several treaties. In 1975, after lengthy negotiations, Houari Boumedienne, the president of Algeria, interrupted an oil ministers' conference in Algiers to announce that "our fraternal countries Iran and Iraq have reached agreement on their differences."[6] Iraq agreed to recognize Iranian ownership of the Shatt from bank to mid-channel, and Iran agreed to stop supporting Kurdish rebels in Iraq.

The advantage to Iraq of bringing an end to the Kurdish rebellion was offset by the humiliation felt by Iraqi leaders because they had bartered away a part of the sacred Arab territory. Hussain considered the agreement a personal humiliation because he had been the chief negotiator. When he became president, he said that he had negotiated it under duress and that Iraq would one day be strong enough to revoke it.[7]

The fall of Shah Rezi Pahlavi and the internal upheaval in Iran after the 1979 Revolution seemed to Hussain to be an excellent opportunity to reverse Iraq's humiliation. In September 1980 he announced that the 1975 treaty was null and void, and he demanded recognition by Iran of Iraqi soverignty over the entire Shatt al-Arab. Two other demands were 1) the transfer of certain Arab-populated border areas in Iran to Iraqi control, and 2) the withdrawal of Iranian forces from three small strategic islands in the Strait of Hormuz, which belong to the United Arab Emirates and were seized in 1971 for strategic reasons. Although at this time the two countries were roughly equal in military strength, purges in Iranian army leadership, low morale, and lack of spare parts for weapons due to the US economic boycott convinced Hussain that a limited attack on Iran would almost certainly succeed.[8]

However, the quick and easy victory anticipated by the Iraqis did not materialize. Political expectations proved equally erroneous. Iraq had expected the Arabs of Khuzestan to support the invasion, but they remained loyal to the Khomeini regime. The Iraqi forces failed to capitalize on their early successes and were stopped by determined Iranian resistance. The war quickly turned into a stalemate.

In 1981-1982 the momentum shifted strongly in Iran's favor. The war became a patriotic undertaking as thousands of volunteers, some barely twelve years old, headed for the front. An Iranian operation, appropriately code-named Undeniable Victory, routed three Iraqi divisions. Iran's blockade of Iraqi oil exports put a severe strain on the Iraqi economy. After the defeat, Hussain withdrew all Iraqi forces from Iranian territory and asked for a ceasefire. But Iran refused; Khomeini set the ouster of "the traitor Saddam" as a precondition for peace.

Iraqi forces fared better on their own soil, and threw back a number of large-scale Iranian assaults with huge casualties. Subsequent USSR deliveries of missiles and new aircraft gave Iraq total superiority in the air. In early 1985 the Iraqis launched a campaign of "total war, total peace," combining air raids on Iranian ports and cities with an all-out effort to bring international pressure on Iran to reach a settlement.

The Iran-Iraq War has a high-risk potential for broader regional conflict, and could easily involve other states in the region due to the interconnectedness of the oil industry. But the conflict has probably weathered its most critical period: the 1984 Iraqi effort to interfere with tanker traffic through the Strait of Hormuz by missile attacks. During that period Arab states were divided in their support. Saudi Arabia and other Gulf states provided aid to Iraq but hedged their statements of official support, fearing Iranian pressure on their own Shia populations.[9] Egypt strongly backed Iraq, and with the drop-off in Soviet arms deliveries, Egypt became Iraq's principal supplier. Jordan also supplied arms, and kept the port of Aqaba open for supplies to be trucked across the desert to Iraqi bases, bypassing the Iranian naval blockade. Syria lined up with Iran, underscoring the vicious rivalry between the Syrian and Iraqi Ba'thist regimes, each one claiming itself to be the "true" Arab revolutionary party. But in the final analysis, the commitment of the other Arab states was limited. In this contest between two powerful states for dominance over the Gulf area, their preference was for neither state to win a complete victory.

In March 1985 Iranian forces launched yet another attack aimed toward the Tigris River from their forward bases on the marshy Majoon Islands, captured in 1984. They were beaten back with heavy losses; Iraqi forces were reliably reported to have used chemical weapons in their counterattack. A "battle of the cities" followed, with Iraqi aircraft launching bombing raids on Iranian cities, and Iranian planes occasionally retaliating. But neither the battlefield defeats nor the air raids seemed to have any discernible effect on Iran's determination—at least the determination of its government—to press on with the war until the "cowardly traitor Hussain" had been forced out of office.

The Iran-Iraq War illustrates clearly how little leverage the major powers have in dealing with subregional conflicts. Iraq

These young Iranians, taken prisoner by Iraq, are typical of those fighting in the Iran-Iraq War. The Iranians' patriotic fervor has produced thousands of volunteers, some as young as twelve.

was long considered a Soviet ally, if not a satellite, and Iran an American one. The fall of the shah and the ensuing war upset these relationships. A Soviet embargo on weapons deliveries caused Iraq to turn toward the United States for assistance, while the US lost all leverage with Iran after the Revolution. It has been argued by some observers that both the United States and the Soviet Union need a strong, stable Iran more than a powerful Iraq as a dominant power in the Gulf. Certainly Iran, with its large population and vast resources and territory, has a greater potential than does Iraq to be an effective "policeman of the Gulf." But until both the Iranian and Iraqi governments begin to display the required maturity in their relations toward each other and within the international system, the possibility of peace between them remains remote.

THE ARAB-ISRAELI CONFLICT

The basis of the Arab-Israeli conflict (or, more narrowly, the Palestinian-Israeli conflict) rests on ownership of land. It is not ownership in the proprietary sense, documented by title deeds and mortgages, but in the sense of a *homeland*, a place claimed by a particular people on emotional, symbolic, and physical grounds. The land in question, generally referred to as Palestine (*Falastina*, in Arabic) since Roman times, is the claimed homeland of two peoples, Israelis and Palestinians.

The Israelis are the returned Jews, immigrants to Palestine from many lands plus the small community of Jews who have always lived there. The Palestinians are the dispersed descendants of settlers whose attachment to Palestine dates

back to antiquity. The Jews, as Israelis, have been in possession of their homeland since 1948; yet most of them regard possession as the fulfillment of God's original covenant with Abraham, patriarch of the Hebrew people. The sense of Palestine as a homeland among Palestinians was not based on strong religious feelings; it was more of an automatic attachment based on long residence, something not to be questioned. Nor was it particularly *Arab*, since the Arabs were dispersed over many lands and did not have the overriding sense of a particular place given to them by some divine ordinance. But the exile of the majority of Palestinians after the establishment of the State of Israel in 1948 generated among them an emotional commitment to their Palestinian homeland every bit as strong as that of the Israelis.

In the twentieth century the question of a Palestine homeland was given form and impetus by two national movements, Zionism and Arab nationalism. Zionism, the first to develop political activism in implementation of a national ideal, organized large-scale immigration of dispersed Jews into Palestine. These immigrants, few of them skilled in agriculture or the vocations needed to build a new nation in a strange land, nevertheless succeeded in changing the face of Palestine. In a relatively short time, as an example, a region

ZIONISM

Zionism may be defined as the collective expression of the will of a dispersed people, the Jews, to recover their ancestral homeland. However, the idealized Jewish longing to return to this ancestral homeland was given concrete form by European Jews, in particular Theodor Herzl, a Viennese journalist. Herzl and his associates envisaged a Jewish homeland which would be established by immigration of dispersed Jews from all parts of the world, a secular commonwealth which could become a model for all nations through its revival of the ancient Jewish nation formed by a convenant with God. The Zionist Organization was officially established at a conference in Basle, Switzerland, in 1896. Although consideration was given to a Jewish homeland in other locations, such as Argentina and Uganda, the conference eventually fixed upon Palestine as the logical site for the homeland.

The Zionist program, and the eventual establishment of the State of Israel, brought about sharp disagreement within the global Jewish community. Many Jews, not only Orthodox but also secular (Reform) congregation members, believed that only God could ordain a Jewish state, and that therefore Zionism could only define a homeland for Jews in accordance with the rules and practices of Judaism.

The success of Zionists in creating a Jewish state and reviving Jewish national life has deepened the division between these two views of Zionism. The small "religious" parties in Israel play a role disproportionate to their size in Israeli political life, and debate over such issues as "Who is a Jew?" in the Israeli Knesset (parliament) often takes precedence over important policy matters.

of undeveloped sand dunes near the coast evolved into the city of Tel Aviv, and unproductive marshland was transformed into profitable farms and kibbutz settlements.

Arab nationalism, slower to develop, grew out of the contacts of Arab subject peoples in the Ottoman Empire with Europeans, particularly missionary-educators sent by their various churches to work with the Christian Arab communities. It developed political overtones during World War I, when British agents such as T.E. Lawrence encouraged the Arabs to revolt against the Turks, their "Islamic brothers." In return, the Arabs were given to understand that the United Kingdom would support the establishment of an independent Arab state in the Arab lands of the empire. An Anglo-Arab army entered Jerusalem in triumph in 1917 and Damascus in 1918, where an independent Arab kingdom was proclaimed, headed by the Emir Faisal, leader of the revolt.

The Arab population of Palestine took relatively little part in these events. But European rivalries and conflicting commitments for disposition of the provinces of the defeated Ottoman Empire soon involved them directly in conflict over Palestine. The most important document affecting the conflict was the Balfour "Declaration," a statement of British support for a Jewish homeland in Palestine in the form of a letter from Foreign Secretary Arthur Balfour to Lord Rothschild, a prominent Jewish banker and leader of the Zionist Organization.

Although the Zionists interpreted the statement as permission to proceed with their plans for a Jewish National Home in Palestine, neither they nor the Arabs were fully satisfied with the World War I peace settlement, in terms of the disposition of territories. The results soon justified their pessimism. The Arab kingdom of Syria was dismantled by the French, who then established a mandate over Syria under the League of Nations. The British set up a mandate over Palestine, attempting to balance support for Jewish aspirations with a commitment to develop self-government for the

THE BALFOUR DECLARATION

The text of the Balfour Declaration is as follows:

I have much pleasure in conveying to you on behalf of His Majesty's Government the following declaration of sympathy with Jewish Zionist aspirations which has been submitted to and approved by the Cabinet:

His Majesty's Government view with favor the establishment in Palestine of a National Home for the Jewish people and will use their best endeavors to facilitate the achievement of this project, it being clearly understood that nothing shall be done which may prejudice the civil and religious rights of existing non-Jewish communities in Palestine or the rights and political status enjoyed by Jews in any other country . . .

Arab population, in accordance with the terms of the mandate as approved by the League of Nations. It was an impossible task, and in 1948 the British gave up, handing the "Palestine problem" back to the United Nations as successor to the League of Nations. The UN had approved a partition plan for Palestine in November 1947, and after the termination of the mandate the Zionists proclaimed the establishment of the State of Israel.

Israel was established against the formal opposition of the neighboring Arab states, and since 1948 Israeli resolve has been tested in five wars with them. None of these wars led directly to a peace settlement, and except for Egypt, Israel remains in a state of armistice and nonrecognition with these states.

Most state-to-state disputes are susceptible to arbitration and often outside mediation, particularly when they involve borders or territory. But Palestine is a special case. Its location astride communication links between the eastern and western sections of the Arab world made it essential to the building of a unified Arab nation, the goal of Arab leaders since World War I. Its importance to Muslims as the site of one of their holiest shrines, the Dome of the Rock in Jerusalem, is underscored by Jewish control—a control made possible by the "imperialist enemies of Islam," in the Arab Muslim view. Also, since they lack an outside patron, both the dispersed Palestinians and those remaining in Israel look to the Arab states as the natural champions of their cause.

Yet the Arab states have never been able to develop a coherent, unified policy toward Israel in support of the Palestine cause. There are several reasons for this failure. One is the natural rivalry of Arab leaders, a competitiveness that has evolved from ancient origins, strong individualism, and family pride.

A second reason is the general informality of the Arab political system. The Arab states of today are still struggling to develop separate, viable political systems; and because they still subscribe to the ideal of a single Arab nation, they are torn between efforts to create separate Arab nations or a single Arab nation. In either case, with one exception (Egypt) they have yet to establish a stable, representative, consensual political structure which would enable them to negotiate on a firm basis with Israel. The Arab states are thus probably more of a liability than an asset to the Palestinian cause, as has been amply demonstrated by the experience of the Palestine Liberation Organization (PLO) in Jordan and more recently in Lebanon.

Another reason for Arab disunity over Palestine stems from the relationship of the Arab states with the Palestinians. During the British mandate, the Arab Higher Committee, the nexus of what became the Palestine national movement, aroused the anger of Arab leaders by refusing to accept the leaders' authority over its policies in return for their support. After the 1948 Arab-Israeli War, the dispersal of Palestinians into Arab lands caused further friction; the Palestinians, often better educated than their reluctant hosts and possessed of greater political skills, seemed to threaten the authority of some Arab leaders and to dominate some Arab economies. Finally, the performance of the Arab states in the wars with Israel was a bitter disillusionment to the Palestinians. Constantine Zurayk of the American University of Beirut expressed their shame in his book, *The Meaning of Disaster*:

> Seven Arab states declare war on Zionism, stop impotent before it and turn on their heels . . . Declarations fall like bombs from the mouths of officials at meetings of the Arab League, but when action becomes necessary, the fire is still and quiet . . .[10]

Without the interference of Arab state rhetoric and inept Arab military intervention, it is possible that the Palestinians might have come to terms with their Jewish neighbors long ago. As early as the 1930s, some Jews sought accommodation with Palestinian leaders. Chaim Weizmann, later the first president of Israel, wrote to an American friend: "Palestine is to be shared by two nations . . . Palestine must be built without violating (by) one iota the legitimate rights of the Arabs."[11] Martin Buber, distinguished Jewish philosopher and theologian, argued tirelessly for Jewish-Arab harmony. In 1947, on the eve of the UN partition resolution, he warned: "What is really needed by each of the two peoples . . . in Palestine is self-determination, autonomy . . . but this most certainly does not mean that each is in need of a state in which it will be the sovereign."[12]

More recently, Uri Avnery, a prominent Zionist and Knesset member, writing in the afterglow of Israel's triumph over the Arab states in the Six-Day War, said, "The government (should) offer the Palestine Arabs assistance in setting up a national republic of their own . . . (which) will become the natural bridge between Israel and the Arab world."[13]

Mark Heller, of Tel Aviv University, goes further: "Rather than avoiding a comprehensive peace with the Palestinians, Israel should therefore pursue the Palestine-state settlement as the primary goal of its foreign and national security policy."[14] Peace Now, an organization of Israeli military reservists, students, intellectuals, and young kibbutzim established in 1977, takes dead aim both at the occupation of the West Bank and the building of Jewish settlements there. "We cannot feel free while we rule another people . . . Peace Now stands . . . for the Zionism that bases itself on the ethical right of every people to national self-expression . . . (it) believes that the peace process . . . is necessary for the maintenance of the democratic character of Israeli society."[15]

Unfortunately, there are strong countervailing pressures which work against a Palestinian-Israeli settlement. The Israeli policy of land acquisition from the occupied West Bank, which was accelerated under former Prime Minister Menachem Begin, is clearly an obstacle to reconciliation and respect for Palestinian rights. By 1985 Israel had acquired 51.6 percent of West Bank land through various methods, lead-

The Dome of the Rock in Jerusalem is the site of one of the holiest Muslim shrines. The Israeli control of Jerusalem is one of the reasons the Palestinian Muslims turn to the Arab states for assistance in regaining control of the area.

ing Elias Freij, the mayor of Bethlehem, to observe that without a policy change the situation would very soon be irreversible.[16]

A second countervailing pressure stems from the ambiguities of United States policy toward the conflict. Since US President Harry Truman recognized the State of Israel minutes after Jewish leaders proclaimed its independence, in the wake of the first Arab-Israeli war, seven American presidents have attempted to deal with the issue. It can be argued that only two of them, Dwight D. Eisenhower and Jimmy Carter, were at all successful; Eisenhower for forcing Israel to withdraw from occupied Arab territory (the Sinai) in 1956, and Carter for bringing about the first recognition of Israel by an Arab state, through the Camp David peace treaty. But no American president as yet has been able to close the gap between Palestinian land aspirations and Israeli control of Palestine as the "land of the Covenant." The most positive step yet taken by any US administration toward meeting Palestinian desires was the statement made by former President Jimmy Carter in 1977, when Carter defined for them a homeland as precise as that defined for the Jewish National Home by the Balfour Declaration. But it is a homeland subject to various interpretations and unlikely to be established through serious American efforts.

Domestic political pressures, the broad sympathy of Americans for Israel, and pragmatic support for the country as a dependable key ally in the volatile Middle East, all work against commitments by any US administration to put its weight behind the establishment of a sovereign Palestinian entity. One of the first steps necessary to pursue such an effort would be official recognition by the US of the Palestine Liberation Organization as the legitimate representative of the dispersed Palestinian people, and without statements on the part of the PLO that it is prepared to accept the existence of Israel, recognition remains unlikely.

The evidence of five wars and innumerable small conflicts suggests that the Arab-Israeli conflict will remain localized. Israel's invasion of Lebanon, like its predecessors, remained localized once the US had intervened, and proved only a temporary setback for the PLO, a displacement. Israel and the Arab states continue to be haunted by the Palestinians, an exiled, dispersed people who refuse to be assimilated into other populations or give up their hard-won identity. Mohammed Shadid observes that "Palestine is the conscience of the Arab world and a pulsating vein of the Islamic world . . . perhaps the only issue where Arab nationalism and Islamic revivalism are joined."[17]

The Palestinians are equally present on the Israeli conscience. General Ariel Sharon's Lebanon War, ironically code named "Operation Peace in Galilee," was intended to solve the Palestine problem by rough surgery—decapitation of the PLO head on the assumption that the trunk and arms (the West Bank Palestinians) would have no further reason for resisting incorporation into the Israeli state. The Lebanon War caused the downfall of one Israeli government and the eclipse of Sharon himself, proving for the fifth time in Arab-Israeli

history that military solutions do not work for essentially political problems. And as journalist David Shaham has pointed out, sixty percent of the Israeli electorate is prepared to accept a compromise leading to peace, recognizing the limits to power.

Surrounding the beleaguered Israeli state are the proud new nations of the Arab world, heirs to an ancient tradition of Islamic brotherhood. They are proud of their achievements in a short period of independence, but are frustrated by the presence of an enemy in their midst. These Arab nations have come a long way in a short time, and in some cases have wisely husbanded oil revenues to provide benefits for the children of herders and peasant farmers. Despite some internal problems, these new nations have shown a remarkable degree of political savvy and inter-Arab cooperation on oil policies. The differences over political issues within these states should not obscure the progress toward inter-Arab cooperation and the development of several models for a stable political system. The dilemma is one of transmuting differences among a vital, if friction-oriented, people into solidarity. The key is the Palestinians and the resolution of their conflict with Israel.

THE WESTERN SAHARA: WHOSE DESERT?

It is a fearsome place, swept by sand-laden winds that sting through layers of clothing, scorched by 120° F temperatures, its flat, monotonous landscape broken occasionally by dried-up *wadis* (river beds). The Spanish called it Rio de Oro, "River of Gold," in a bitter jest, for it has neither. Rainfall averages two to eight inches a year in a territory the size of Colorado. The population of about 120,000 is largely nomadic. Before the twentieth century this region, which we know today as the Western Sahara, was outside the control of any central authority. Other than a brief period of importance as the headquarters of the Almoravids, a dynasty that ruled most of North Africa for about a century, the Western Sahara was a backwater.

As a political entity, the Western Sahara resulted from European colonization in Africa in the late nineteenth century. The United Kingdom and France had a head start in establishing colonies. Spain was a latecomer. By the time the Spanish joined the race for colonies, little was left for them in Africa. Since they already controlled the Canary Islands off the West African coast, it was natural for them to claim Rio de Oro, the nearest area on the coast.

In 1884 Spain announced a protectorate over Rio de Oro. The other European powers accepted the Spanish claim under the principle that "occupation of a territory's coast entitled a colonial power to control over the interior."[18] But Spanish rights to the Saharan interior clashed with French claims to Mauritania and the French effort to control the independent Sultanate of Morocco to the north. After the establishment of a joint Franco-Spanish protectorate over Morocco in 1912, the boundaries of the Spanish colony were fixed, with Mauritania on the south and east and Morocco to the north. The nomads of the Western Sahara now found them-

The Western Sahara region is flat, monotonous, and very hot. This inhospitable land currently is contested by groups supported by Morocco and Algeria.

selves living within fixed boundaries defined by outsiders.[19]

The Spanish moved very slowly into the interior. The entire Western Sahara was not "pacified" until 1934. Spain invested heavily in development of the important Western Sahara phosphate deposits, but did little else to develop the colony.

The Spanish population was essentially a garrison community, living apart from the Sahrawis, the indigenous Saharan population in towns or military posts. A few Sahrawis went to Spain or other European countries, where they received a modern education, and upon their return began to organize a Saharan nationalist movement. Other Sahrawis traveled to Cairo, Egypt and returned with ideas of organizing a Saharan Arab independent state. But a real sense of either a Spanish Saharan or an independent Sahrawi identity was slow to emerge.[20]

Serious conflict over the Spanish Sahara developed in the 1960s. By that time both Morocco and Mauritania had become independent. Algeria, the third African territory involved in the conflict, won its independence after a bloody civil war. All three new states were highly nationalistic and were opposed to the continuation of colonial rule over any African people, but particularly Muslim peoples. They encouraged the Sahrawis to fight for liberation from Spain, giving arms and money to guerrilla groups and keeping their borders open.

However, the three states had different motives. Morocco claimed the Western Sahara on the basis of historical ties dating back to the Almoravids, plus the oath of allegiance sworn to Moroccan sultans by Saharan chiefs in the nineteenth and twentieth centuries. Kinship was also a factor; several important Saharan families have branches in Morocco, and the mother and first wife of the founder of Morocco's current ruling dynasty, Mulay Ismail, were from Sahrawi families.

The Mauritanian claim to the Spanish Sahara was based not on historical sovereignty but on kinship. Sahrawis have close ethnic ties with the Moors, the majority of the population of Mauritania, divided into a number of societies. Also, Mauritania feared Moroccan expansion, since its territory had once been included in the Almoravid state. A Saharan buffer state between Mauritania and Morocco would serve as protection for the Mauritanians.

Algeria's interest in Spanish Sahara was largely a matter of support for a national liberation movement against a colonial power. The Algerians made no territorial claim to the colony. But Algerian foreign policy has rested on two pillars since independence: the right to self-determination of subject peoples, and the principle of self-determination through referendum. Algeria consistently maintains that the Saharan people should have these rights.

In the 1960s Spain came under pressure from the United Nations to give up its colonies. After much hesitation, in August 1974 the Spanish announced that a referendum would be held under UN supervision to decide the colony's future.

The Spanish action brought the conflict to a head. King Hassan II declared that 1975 would be the year of testing for Morocco's recovery of the Sahara. A new Sahrawi nationalist organization, Polisario, organized in Mauritania, emerged as the dominant force in the colony. Attacks on Spanish garrisons increased the pressure on Spain to withdraw. Then, in October 1975, Hassan announced that he would lead a massive, peaceful march of civilians, armed only wth Korans, into the Spanish Sahara to recover sacred Moroccan territory. The "Green March" of half a million unarmed Moroccan volunteers into Spanish territory seemed an unusual, even risky, method of validating a territorial claim, but it worked. In 1976 Spain reached agreement with Morocco and Mauritania to partition the territory into two zones, one-third going to Mauritania and two-thirds to Morocco. The Moroccan Zone included the important phosphate deposits.

The Polisario rejected the partition agreement and announced its formation of the Sahrawi Arab Democratic Republic (SADR), "a free, independent, sovereign state ruled by an Arab deomocratic system of progressive unionist orientation and of Islamic religion."[21] The action gave the Polisario a government-in-exile and international maneuvering room. Algeria recognized the SADR in March 1976, setting the stage for the widening of the conflict to involve other states in the region.

Since then Morocco and the SADR (or, more correctly, the Polisario as the military arm of the republic) have been at war. Polisario tactics of swift-striking attacks from hidden bases in the vast desert were highly effective in the early stages. Mauritania was knocked out of the war in 1978 when a military coup overthrew its government. The new Mauritanian rulers signed a peace treaty in Algiers with Polisario representatives, recognizing the new republic. Morocco, not to be outdone, promptly annexed the Mauritanian share of the territory and beefed up its military forces.

Nearly ten years after it began, the Western Sahara conflict is far from being settled. On the Polisario side, a majority of African nations have recognized SADR, but Morocco continues to block the republic's membership in the Organization of African Unity (OAU) or to agree to a referendum on the future of the territory. Algeria, joined for a time by Libya, continues all-out support for the Polisario. The fortified "Sand

Life in the Sahara Desert is often perceived as nomadic, with the people living in tents and riding camels. To some extent this is still true, but there are many towns that offer a more settled way of life, such as this town in the Algerian Sahara.

Wall" from the old Moroccan border down to Mauritania gives the Moroccan army, already superior in weaponry, a strong defensive base from which to launch attacks on its elusive foe. And from behind the wall, Morocco has begun a modest program of economic development in its new Saharan provinces. But the cost to the Moroccan economy is heavy. (King Hassan's recent agreement with Libyan leader Mu'ammar Qadhafi for a union of their two countries is thought to have been dictated by an urgent need for aid, particularly in weapons.) Until some reconciliation of Morocco's historic Islamic claims with the Algerian-Polisario commitment to self-determination for the Sahrawi people is achieved, North Africa will almost certainly continue to be divided and destabilized.

AFGHANISTAN: END OF A BUFFER STATE

Remote, landlocked Afghanistan seems an unlikely setting for conflict between one of the superpowers and a nation of disunited ethnic groups. It is an equally unlikely setting for the installation of a Communist government because of the almost one-hundred-percent Muslim population, strongly traditional in their Islamic values and culture. Yet since 1978 three successive Communist governments have ruled in Kabul, the Afghan capital. The first two were Soviet manipulated; the third and current one was placed in power through a massive Soviet invasion in December 1979.

The current head of state, Babrak Karmal, one of the three founders of the People's Democratic Party of Afghanistan in 1965 and the only survivor, was out of the country when the invasion took place. Hence, Afghanistan is in the unfortunate position of having a government and leader unacceptable to its own people, and being under the control of an occupation army which is anathema to Afghans because it is atheist first and Russian second.[22]

In terms of Middle East conflicts, it is worth noting that no Middle Eastern state has involved itself in more than the most indirect way possible in the Afghan contest with the Soviet Union. Iran provides aid for approximately 500,000 Afghan refugees, but has refrained from public criticism of the Soviet government for its brutal treatment of a fellow Muslim population. Weapons for the Afghan mujahideen (freedom fighters) come from a variety of suppliers (including Egypt and Israel), transferred through a long US-financed arms "pipeline" stretching from Western Europe through the Middle East and on to Pakistan. The US government, caught between the desire to cause difficulties for the Soviet Union at little cost and an honest wish to support the Afghans in their struggle for independence, finds itself in the awkward position of working to undermine, through covert methods, a government which it recognizes, all in the name of a new "Great Game" strategy in Asia.

There remains the question of what effect the Soviet occupation of Afghanistan might have in destabilizing Middle Eastern countries, such as Iran and Turkey, along the Soviet border. The history of Soviet dealings with other Muslim populations, such as the Basmachis of Central Asia, suggests that over time the occupation will result in the transformation of Afghanistan into a Soviet satellite. If and when that happens, the Middle East map will once more be redrawn, with the region clearly separated from the Indian subcontinent and from Soviet Asia as well.

FOOTNOTES

1. Alan R. Taylor, *The Arab Balance of Power* (Syracuse, NY: Syracuse University Press, 1982), Preface, XIII.
2. "Turkistan, Afghanistan, Transcaspia . . . they are the pieces on a chessboard upon which is played out a game for the domination of the World." Lord Curzon, Viceroy of India, quoted in Shabbir Hussain *et al.*, *Afganistan Under Soviet Occupation* (Islamabad, Pakistan: World Affairs Publications, 1980), p. 54.
3. "The Soviet Action in Afghanistan was made necessary by the real threat of seeing the country transformed into an imperialist military platform on the Southern frontier of the USSR." Former Soviet leader Leonid Brezhnev, quoted in Hussain, *op. cit.*, p. 7.
4. Terence O'Donnell, *Garden of the Brave in War* (New York: Ticknor and Fields, 1980), p. 19, states that in visits to remote Iranian villages he was told by informants that the Arabs never washed, went around naked, and ate lizards.
5. Daniel Pipes, "A Border Adrift: Origins of the Conflict," in Shirin Tahir-Kheli and Shaheen Ayubi, eds., *The Iran-Iraq War: New Weapons, Old Conflicts* (New York: Praeger, 1983), pp. 10-13.
6. *Ibid.*, quoted on p. 20.
7. Stephen R. Grummon, *The Iran-Iraq War: Islam Embattled*, The Washington Papers/92, Vol. X (New York: Praeger, 1982), p. 10.
8. William O. Staudenmaier, "A Strategic Analysis," in Tahir-Kheli and Ayubi, *op. cit.*, pp. 29-33.
9. See Nazi N. M. Ayubi, "Arab Relations in the Gulf: The Future and its Prologue," in Tahir-Kheli and Ayubi, *op. cit.*, p. 153.
10. Quoted in Barry Rubin, *The Arab States and the Palestine Conflict* (Syracuse, NY: Syracuse University Press, 1981), p. 7.
11. Letter to James Marshall, January 17, 1930, in Camilo Dresner, ed., *The Letters and Papers of Chaim Weizmann* Vol. 14 (New Brunswick, NJ: Rutgers University Press, 1979), pp. 208-211.
12. Martin Buber, *Land of Two Peoples*, ed. Paul Mendes-Flohr (New York: Oxford University Press, 1983), p. 199.
13. Uri Avnery, *Israel Without Zionists* (New York: Macmillan, 1968), pp. 187, 189.
14. Mark A. Heller, *A Palestinian State: The Implications for Israel* (Cambridge, MA: Harvard University Press, 1983), p. 154.
15. R. D. McLaurin, Don Peretz and Lewis Snider, eds., *Middle East Foreign Policy: Issues and Processes* (New York: Praeger, 1982), p. 154.
16. Arthur Max, *The New York Times*, April 1, 1985.
17. Mohammed Shadid, *The United States and the Palestinians* (New York: St. Martin's Press, 1981), p. 195.
18. John Damis, *Conflict in Northwest Africa: The Western Sahara Dispute* (Stanford, CA: Hoover Institution Press, 1983), p. 10.
19. "The borders zigzagged from Zag in the north to Zug in the south." David Lynne Price, *The Western Sahara*, The Washington Papers/63, Vol. VII (Beverly Hills, CA: Sage Publications, 1979), p. 11.
20. Damis, *op. cit.*, p. 13, notes that a tribal assembly (Jama'a) was formed in 1967 for the Sahrawis, but that its forty-three members were all tribal chiefs or their representatives; it had only advisory powers.
21. Quoted from *Le Monde*, in Damis, *op. cit.*, p. 75.
22. A mass uprising in the city of Herat in March 1979 killed all Soviet military advisers in the city, but spared other Europeans, including Czechs. Anthony Hyman, *Afghanistan Under Soviet Domination 1964-1981* (London: Macmillan, 1982), p. 1010.

Algeria (Democratic and Popular Republic of Algeria)

GEOGRAPHY

Area in Square Kilometers (Miles):
2,460,500 (918,497)
Capital (Population): Algiers (2.5 million)
Climate: mild winters and hot summers on coastal plain; less rain and cold winters on high plateau; considerable temperature variation in desert, February-May

PEOPLE

Population
Total: 21,351,000
Annual Growth Rate: 3.1%
Rural/Urban Population Ratio: 55/45
Ethnic Makeup of Population: 99% Arab-Berber; less than 1% European

Health
Life Expectancy at Birth: 55 years
Infant Death Rate (Ratio): 110/1,000
Average Caloric Intake: 96% (1981) of FAO minimum
Physicians Available (Ratio): 1/2,630 (1980)

Religion(s)
99% Sunni Muslim (state religion); 1% Christian and Hebrew

Education
Adult Literacy Rate: 46%

COMMUNICATION

Telephones: 606,869
Newspapers: 4 dailies; 480,000 circulation

THE CASBAH

The romantic image of the Casbah of Algiers purveyed by Hollywood films is rudely shattered by a walk through the narrow, twisted streets of the old corsair fortress. The tall houses lean inward, producing a claustrophobic gloom. Algiers' Casbah does not have the colorful outdoor markets and artisans of other North African capitals. Today it is an urban slum. Riots broke out there in 1985 protesting its crowded and substandard living conditions. The government responded with force, but agreed to begin demolition of tenements, thus ending two hundred years of colorful existence.

TRANSPORTATION

Highways—Kilometers (Miles): 78,410 (48,724) total; 45,070 (28,006) concrete or bituminous
Railroads—Kilometers (Miles): 3,908 (2,428)
Commercial Airports: 177

GOVERNMENT

Type: republic
Independence Date: July 5, 1962
Head of State: President (Colonel) Chadli Bendjedid
Political Parties: National Liberation Front
Suffrage: universal over 19

MILITARY

Number of Armed Forces: 123,800
Military Expenditures (% of Central Government Expenditures): 7.1%
Current Hostilities: none

ECONOMY

Currency ($ US Equivalent): 5.27 Algerian dinars = $1 (February 1985)
Per Capita Income/GNP: $2,142/$42.9 billion (1982)
Inflation Rate: 15% (1982)
Natural Resources: crude oil; natural gas; iron ore; phosphates; uranium; lead; zinc; mercury
Agriculture: wheat; barley; oats; olives; grapes; dates; citrus fruits; sheep; cattle
Industry: petroleum; light industries; natural gas; petrochemicals; electrical; automotive plants; food processing

FOREIGN TRADE

Exports: $12.9 billion (1982)
Imports: $12.1 billion (1982)

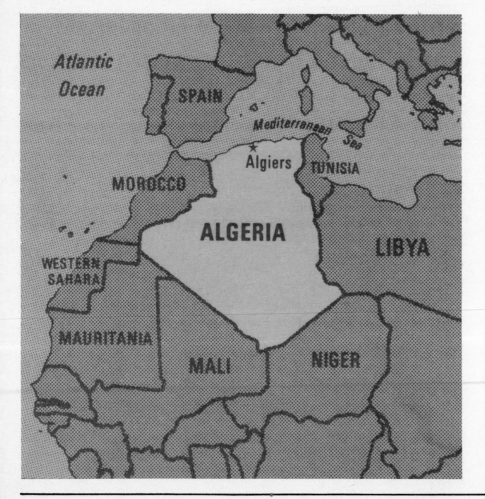

ALGERIA

The modern state of Algeria occupies the central part of North Africa, a geographically distinctive and separate region of Africa which also includes Morocco and Tunisia. The name of the state comes from the Arabic word *al-Jaza'ir,* "the islands," because of the rocky islets along this part of the Mediterranean coast, which were a hazard to ships in the days of sail. The name of the capital, Algiers, is derived from the same origin.

The official name of the country is the Democratic and Popular Republic of Algeria. It is the second largest country in Africa (after Sudan). The overall population density is low considering its size, but Algeria has one of the highest birth rates in the world. The Algerian government is committed to a Socialist system, with wealth from oil and gas exports widely distributed among the population. But rapid population growth and other factors make attainment of this goal difficult.

GEOGRAPHY

Algeria's geography is another obstacle to broad economic and social development. About eighty percent of the land is uncultivable desert, and only twelve percent is arable without irrigation. Most of the population lives in a narrow coastal plain and in a fertile, hilly inland region called the Tell (Arabic for "hillock"). The four Saharan provinces comprise more than half the land area but have only three percent of the population. Yet the mineral resources that have made possible Algeria's transformation in two decades from a land devastated by civil war to one of the Third World's success stories are all located in the Sahara. Also, national prosperity, symbolized by an annual per capita income of $2,142 (in 1982), is misleading, because the large proportion of the population living in the neglected rural areas and the slums of cities do not come close to earning that amount.

Algeria is unique among newly independent Middle Eastern countries in that it gained its independence through a civil war. For more than 130 years (1830-1962) it was occupied by France and became a French department (similar to a US state). With free movement from mainland France to Algeria, and vice versa, the country was settled by large numbers of Europeans who became the politically dominant group in the population, although they were a minority. The modern Algerian nation is the product of the interaction of native Muslim Algerians with the European settlers, who also considered Algeria home.

Algeria's geography is a key to the country's past disunity. In addition to its share of the Sahara desert, Algeria has a number of high and rugged mountain ranges. The Mediterranean coast is backed everywhere by mountains, the most prominent being the Kabylia. The Algerian Atlas range, a continuation of the Moroccan Atlas, is a complex system of deep valleys, high plateaus, and peaks ranging up to six thousand feet. In southeastern Algeria is the most impressive range in the country, the Aurès, a great mountain block with the country's highest peak, Jebel Chélia (7,638 feet). These diverse mountain regions were an obstacle to the development of any form of Algerian social and national unity until recent times. It is significant that the Algerian war for independence from France began in the Aurès.

The original inhabitants of the entire North African region were Berbers, a people of unknown origin grouped into various tribes and speaking different dialects of a now-lost Berber language. (The Tuareg, a nomadic people still living in the Algerian Sahara and neighboring countries, use a written language called Tifinagh. Theirs is the only surviving Berber script, and it is rapidly disappearing as the Tuareg give up their nomadic lifestyle for jobs in the Algerian oil industry.) The Arabs, who brought Islam to North Africa in the seventh century AD, converted the Algerian Berbers after a fierce resistance. The Arabs brought their language as a unifying feature, and religion linked the Algerians with the larger Islamic cultural world. But, in political terms, there was little Berber-Arab mixing to form a homogeneous population. Berber groups in the Aurès and Kabylia accepted Islam, Arabic, and the Arab presence in Algeria, but they remained in isolation in their mountain habitats, a free people and a people apart.

HISTORY: THE CORSAIR REGENCY

The foundations of the modern Algerian state were laid in the sixteenth century with the establishment of the Regency of Algiers, an outlying province of the Ottoman Empire. Algiers in particular, due to its natural harbor, was developed for use by the Ottomans as a naval base for wars against European fleets in the Mediterranean. The Algerian coast was the farthest extent westward of Ottoman power. Consequently, Algiers and Oran, the two major ports, were exposed to constant threats of attack by Spanish and other European fleets. They could not easily be supported, or governed directly, by the Ottomans. The regency, from its beginnings, was a state geared for war.

The regency was established by two Greek-born Muslim sea captains, Aruj and Khayr al-Din (Barbarossa), who had obtained commissions from the Ottoman sultan for expeditions against the Spanish. The two brothers made their principal base at Algiers, then a small port which Khayr al-Din expanded into a powerful fortress and naval base. His government consisted of a garrison of Ottoman soldiers sent by the sultan to keep order and a naval force composed of sea captains called the *corsairs*.

Corsairing or piracy (the choice of term depended upon one's viewpoint) was a common practice in the Mediterranean, but the rise to power of the Algerine corsairs con-

Many colorful traditions remain in evidence in Algeria. This recent marriage ceremony could have taken place hundreds of years ago.

verted it into a more or less respectable profession.[1] The cities of Tunis, Tetuan and Salé in Morocco, and Tripoli, Libya, also had corsair fleets, but the Algerine corsairs were so effective against European shipping that for three hundred years (1500-1800) European rulers called them "the scourge of the Mediterranean." One factor in their success was their ability to attract outstanding sea captains from various European countries. Renegades from Italy, Greece, Holland, France, and England joined the Algerine fleet, converted to Islam, and took Muslim names as a symbol of their new status. Some rose to high rank, such as Hassan (Veneziano), Dragut Reis (an Albanian), and Murat Reis (Moratto Corso).

Government in Algiers passed through several stages and eventually became a system of deys. The deys were elected by the Divan, a council of the captains of the Ottoman garrison. Deys were elected for life, but most of them never fulfilled their tenure due to constant intrigue, military coups, or assassinations. Yet the system provided considerable stability, security for the population, and wealth and prestige for the regency. These factors probably account for its durability; the line of deys governed uninterruptedly from the late 1600s to 1830.

Outside of Algiers and its hinterland, authority was delegated to local chiefs and religious leaders, who were responsible for tax collection and remittances to the dey's treasury. The chiefs were kept in line by generous subsidies. It was a system well adapted to the fragmented society of Algeria, and one which enabled a small military group to rule a large territory at relatively little cost.[2]

The French Conquest

In 1827 the dey of Algiers, enraged at the French government's refusal to pay an old debt incurred during Napoleon's wars, struck the French consul on the shoulder with a fly-whisk in the course of an interview. The king of France, Charles X, demanded an apology for the "insult" to his representative. None was forthcoming, so the French blockaded the port of Algiers in retaliation. But the dey continued to keep silent. In 1830 a French army landed on the coast west of the city, marched overland, and entered it with almost no resistance. The dey surrendered and went into exile.[3]

The French, who had been looking for an excuse to expand their interests in North Africa, now were not sure what they intended to do with Algiers after the conquest. The overthrow of the despotic Charles X in favor of a constitutional monarchy in France confused the situation even further. But the

Algerians considered the French worse than the Turks, who were at least fellow Muslems. In the 1830s they rallied behind their first national leader, the Emir Abd al-Qadir.

Abd al-Qadir was the son of a prominent religious leader, and, more important, was a descendant of the Prophet Muhammad. Abd al-Qadir had unusual qualities of leadership, military skill, and physical courage. For 15 years (1830-1847) he carried on guerrilla warfare against a French army of over 100,000 men with such success that at one point the French signed a formal treaty recognizing him as head of an Algerian nation in the interior. Abd al-Qadir described his strategy in a prophetic letter to the king of France:

> France will march forward, and we shall retire. But France will find it necessary to retire, and we shall return. We shall weary and harry you, and our climate will do the rest.[4]

In order to defeat Abd al-Qadir, the French commander used "total war" tactics, burning villages, destroying crops, killing livestock, and levying fines on peoples who continued to support the emir. These tactics, called "pacification" by France, finally succeeded. In 1847 Abd al-Qadir surrendered to French authorities. He was imprisoned for several years, in violation of a solemn commitment, and was then released by Emperor Napoleon III. He spent the remainder of his life in exile.

Although he did not succeed in his quest, Abd al-Qadir is venerated as the first Algerian leader to unite the peoples in a struggle for independence from foreign control. Abd al-Qadir's green and white flag was raised again by the Algerian nationalists during the second war of independence of 1954-1962, and it is the flag of the republic today.

Algerie Française

After the defeat of Abd al-Qadir, the French gradually brought all of present-day Algerian territory under their control. The last group to submit was the Kabyles, Berbers living in the rugged mountain region east of Algiers. The Kabyles had submitted in 1857, but they rebelled in 1871 after a series of decrees by the French government had made all Algerian Muslims subjects but not citizens, giving them an inferior status to French and other European settlers.

The Kabyle rebellion had terrible results, not only for the Kabyles but for all Algerian Muslims. More than a million acres of Muslim lands were confiscated by French authorities and sold to European settlers. A special code of laws was enacted to treat Algerian Muslims differently from Europeans,

with severe fines and sentences for such minor infractions as insulting a European or wearing shoes in public. (It was assumed that a Muslim caught wearing shoes had stolen them.)

After 1871 Algeria legally became a French department. But in terms of exploitation of natives by settlers, it may as well have remained a colony. One author notes that "the desire to make a settlement colony out of an already populated area led to a policy of driving the indigenous people out of the best arable lands."[5] Land confiscation was only part of the exploitation of Algeria by the colons (French settlers). The colons developed a modern Algerain agriculture integrated into the French economy, providing France with much of its wine, citrus, olives, and vegetables. Colons owned thirty percent of the arable land and ninety percent of the best farmland. Special taxes were imposed on the Algerian Muslims, while the colons were exempted from most taxes.

The political structure of Algeria was even more favorable to the European minority. The colons were well represented in the French National Assembly, and their representatives made sure that any reforms of new laws intended to improve the living conditions or political rights of the Algerian Muslim population would be blocked.

In fairness to the colons, it must be pointed out that many of them had come to Algeria as poor immigrants and worked hard to improve their lot and to develop the country. By 1930, the centenary of the French conquest, many colon families had lived in Algiers for two generations or more. Colons had drained malarial swamps south of Algiers and developed the Mitidja, the country's most fertile region. A fine road and rail system linked all parts of the country, and French public schools served all cities and towns. Algiers even had its university, a branch of the Sorbonne in Paris. It is not surprising that to the colons, Algeria was their country, "Algerie Française." Throughout Algeria they rebaptized Algerian cities with names like Orléansville and Philippeville, with paved French streets, cafes, bakeries, and little squares with flower gardens and benches where old men in berets dozed in the hot sun.

Jules Cambon, governor-general of Algeria in the 1890s, once described the country as having "only a dust of people left her." What he meant was that the ruthless treatment of the Algerians by the French during the "pacification" had deprived them of their natural leaders. A group of leaders developed slowly in Algeria, but it was made up largely of evolués, persons who had received French educations, spoke French better than Arabic, and had accepted French citizenship as the price of status.[6]

Other Algerians, several hundred thousand of them, served in the French Army in two world wars. Many of them became aware of the political rights that they were supposed to have but did not. Still others, religious leaders and teachers, were influenced by the Arab nationalist movement for independence from foreign control in Egypt and other parts of the Middle East.

Until the 1940s the majority of the evolués and other Algerian leaders did not want independence. They wanted full assimilation with France and Muslim equality with the colons. Ferhat Abbas, a French-trained pharmacist who was the spokesman for the evolués, said in 1936 that he did not believe that there was such a thing as an Algerian nation separate from France.

Abbas and his associates changed their minds after World War II. In 1943 they had presented to the French government a manifesto demanding full political and legal equality for Muslims with the colons. It was blocked by colon leaders, who feared they would be drowned in a Muslim sea. On May 8, 1945, the date of the Allied victory over Germany in World War II, a parade of Muslims celebrating the event but also demanding equality led to violence in the city of Sétif. Several colons were killed, and in retaliation army troops and groups of colon vigilantes swept through Muslim neighborhoods, burning houses and slaughtering thousands of Muslims. From then on, Muslim leaders concluded that independence through armed struggle was the only choice left to them.

The War for Independence

November 1 is an important holiday in France. It is called *Toussaint* (All Saints' Day). On that day French people remember and honor all the many saints in the pantheon of French Catholicism. It is a day devoted to reflection and staying at home, a holiday from all work or business.

In the years after the Sétif massacre, there had been scattered outbreaks of violence in Algeria, some of them by a "Secret Organization" (OS) which had developed an extensive network of cells in preparation for armed insurrection. In 1952 French police accidentally uncovered the network and jailed most of its leaders. One of them, a former French Army sergeant named Ahmed Ben Bella, subsequently escaped and went to Cairo, Egypt.

As the date of Toussaint 1954 neared, Algeria seemed calm. But appearances were deceptive. Earlier in the year, nine former members of the OS had laid plans in secret for armed revolution. They divided Algeria into six *wilayas* (departments), each with a military commander. They also planned a series of coordinated attacks for the early-morning hours of November 1, when the French population would be asleep and the police preparing for a holiday. Bombs exploded at French Army barracks, police stations, storage warehouses, telephone offices, and government buildings. The revolutionaries circulated leaflets in the name of the National Liberation Front (FLN), warning the French that they had acted to liberate Algeria from the colonialist yoke and calling on Algerian Muslims to join in the struggle to rebuild Algeria as a free Islamic state.

There were very few casualties as a result of the Toussaint attacks; for some time the French did not realize that they had a revolution on their hands. But as violence continued, regular army troops were sent to Algeria to help the hard-pressed police and the colons. Eventually there were 400,000 French troops in Algeria, as opposed to about 6,000 guerrillas. But the French consistently refused to consider the situation in Algeria as a war. They called it a "police action." Others called it "the war without a name."[7] Despite their great superiority, they were unable to defeat the FLN.

Elsewhere the French tried various tactics. They divided the country into small sectors, with permanent garrisons for each sector. They organized mobile units to track down the guerrillas in caves and hideouts. About two million villagers were moved into barbed-wire "regroupment camps," with a complete dislocation of their way of life, in order to deny the guerrillas the support of the population.

In the end, the war was settled not by military action but by political negotiations. The French government and the people of France, already worn down by the effects of World War II and Indochina (Vietnam), grew sick of the slaughter, the plastic bombs exploding in public places (in France as well as Algeria), and the well-publicized brutality of the army in dealing with guerrilla prisoners. A French newspaper editor expressed the general feeling. He wrote, "Algeria is ruining the spring. This land of sun and earth has never been so near us. It invades our hearts and torments our minds."[8]

The colons and a number of senior French army officers were the last to give up their dream of an Algeria that would be forever French. Together, the colons and the army forced a change in the French government. General Charles de Gaulle, the French wartime resistance hero, returned to power after a dozen years in retirement. But de Gaulle, a realist, had no intention of keeping Algeria forever French. He began secret negotiations with FLN leaders for Algerian independence.

The colons and the army officers made one last effort. In 1961 four generals led an insurrection in Algiers against de Gaulle and demanded his removal from office. But the majority of the army remained loyal. A ceasefire came into effect on March 19, 1962. However, the Secret Army Organization (OAS), a group of army dissenters and colon vigilantes, then launched a new campaign of violence, terror, and indiscriminate murders of Muslims. Bombs exploded in Muslim hospitals and schools; victims were shot at random as they walked the streets. The OAS hoped that the FLN would break the ceasefire to protect its fellow Muslims and thus bring back the French Army. But the FLN held firm.

A REUNITED NATION

Algeria became independent on July 5, 1962. Few nations have started their existence under worse circumstances. Estimates of casualties vary, but by the end of the war hundreds of thousands of men, women, and children, Muslims, colons, and soldiers had been killed or wounded or had simply disappeared. A painful loss to the new nation was the departure of almost the entire European community. The colons panicked and crowded aboard ships to cross the Mediterranean and resettle in various European countries, but especially in France, a land they knew only as visitors. Nearly all of Algeria's managers, landowners, professional class, civil servants, and skilled workers left.

The new Algerian government was also affected by factional rivalries among its leaders. The French writer Alexis de Tocqueville once wrote, "In a rebellion, as in a novel, the most difficult part to invent is the end." The FLN revolutionaries had to invent a new system, one that would bring dignity and hope to people dehumanized by 130 years of French occupation and 8 years of savage war.

The first leader to emerge from intraparty struggle to lead the nation was Ahmed Ben Bella, a former sergeant in the French Army and one of the nine original founders of the FLN. Ben Bella laid the groundwork for an Algerian political system centered on the FLN as a single legal political party, and in September 1963 he was elected president. Ben Bella introduced a system of workers' *autogestion* (self-management), by which tenant farmers took over the management of farms abandoned by their colon owners and restored them to production as cooperatives. Autgestion became the basis for Algerian so-

Establishment of Regency of Algiers **1518-1520**	French conquest, triggered by the "fly-whisk incident" **1827-1830**	Defeat of Abd al-Qadir by French forces **1847**	Algeria becomes overseas department of France **1871**

cialism, the current system of Algerian economic development.

Ben Bella did little else for Algeria, and he alienated most of his former associates by his ambitions for personal power. In June 1965 he was overthrown in a military coup headed by the defense minister, Colonel Houari Boumedienne. Ben Bella was sentenced to prison and became officially a "nonperson." (He was released by President Benjedid in 1980, two years after Boumedienne's death.)

Boumedienne declared that the coup was a "corrective revolution, intended to reestablish authentic socialism and put an end to internal divisions and personal rule."[9] The government was reorganized under a Council of the Revolution, all military men, headed by Boumedienne, who subsequently became president of the republic. After a long period of preparation and gradual assumption of power by the reclusive and taciturn Boumedienne, a National Charter (constitution) was approved by voters in 1976. The Charter defines Algeria as a Socialist state, with Islam as the state religion, basic citizens' rights guaranteed, and leadership by the FLN as the only legal political party. A National Popular Assembly (the first was elected in 1977) is responsible for legislation.

In theory, the Algerian president has no more constitutional powers than the American president. However, in practice, Boumedienne was the ruler of the state, being president, prime minister, and commander of the armed forces rolled into one. In November 1978 he became ill from a rare blood disease; he died in December. For a time it appeared that factional rivalries would again split the FLN, especially as Boumedienne had named neither a vice president nor a prime minister, nor had he suggested a successor.

The Algeria of 1978 was a very different nation from that of 1962. The scars of war had mostly healed. The FLN closed ranks and named Colonel Chadli Bendjedid to succeed Boumedienne as president for a five-year term. (There is no agreement as to his name; some references call him Bendjedid Chadli.) In 1984 he was reelected. Under President Bendjedid, Algeria has continued on the road to socialism and gradual democratization of political life. A prime minister was appointed in 1980. Various political opponents of Boumedienne were freed, including Ben Bella. The structure of the FLN was streamlined, and the number of nonparty members in the 281-member National Assembly was increased in the 1982 elections. Only fifty-five deputies were actually members of the FLN.

FOREIGN POLICY

During the first decade of independence, Algeria's foreign policy was strongly nationalistic and anti-Western. Having won their independence from one colonial power, the Algerians were vocally hostile to the United States and its allies, calling them enemies of popular liberation. Algeria supported revolutionary movements all over the world, providing funds, arms, and training. The Palestine Liberation Organization (PLO), rebels against Portuguese colonial rule in Mozambique, Muslim guerrillas fighting the Christian Ethiopian government in Eritrea—all benefitted from active Algerian support.

Since the mid-1970s Algeria has moderated its anti-Western stance in favor of nonalignment and good relations with both East and West. The government broke diplomatic relations with the US in 1967, due to American support for Israel, and did not restore relations for a decade. Relations improved thereafter to such a point that Algerian mediators were instrumental in resolving the 1979-1980 American-Iranian hostage crisis, since Iran regarded Algeria as a suitable mediator, Islamic yet nonaligned.

The only foreign policy issue on which Algeria remains adamant is the Western Sahara. The Algerians believe strongly in the right of Western Saharan peoples to determine their own future. This commitment has embroiled them in conflict with Morocco, since the Moroccans claim ownership of the Western Sahara as an integral part of their territory. The two countries fought a brief border war in 1963 over ownership of iron mines near the border town of Tindouf. Since 1975 the Algerian policy of allowing sanctuary and bases to the Polisario, the military force of the "Sahrawi Arab Democratic Republic," has led to a number of clashes between Moroccan and Algerian troops. Algeria formally recognized the Sahrawi Republic in 1980 and has led the fight within the Organization of African Unity (OAU) to have it seated as an OAU member.

THE ECONOMY

Algeria's Saharan oil and natural gas resources were developed by the French, and commercial production began in 1958. The French government ruled the Algerian Sahara under a separate military administration. The Sahara was not affected by the war for independence, and exports of crude oil continued, mostly to metropoli-

The rapid growth in the population of Algeria, coupled with urban migration, has created a serious urban-housing shortage, as this apartment building in Algiers testifies.

| Blum-Viollette Plan, for Muslim rights, annulled by colon opposition **1936** | Ferhat Abbas issues Mainfesto of the Algerian People **1943** | Civil war, ending with Algerian independence **1954-1962** | Ben Bella overthrown by Boumedienne **1965** | National Charter commits Algeria to revolutionary Socialist development **1976** | Death of President Boumedienne **1978** |

1980s

| Last street and shop signs in French Algiers replaced by Arabic ones, in Arabization campaign | Trial of Islamic fundamentalists ends with release of majority and short prison terms for leaders | New land redistribution program underway, designed to improve on autogestion system |

tan France, throughout the war. The oilfields were turned over to Algeria after independence, but the French concessionnaires continued to manage them until 1970, when the oil industry was nationalized.

Algeria's petroleum reserves are estimated to be eight billion barrels. The country is a member of the Organization of Petroleum Exporting Countries (OPEC) and follows agreed-upon OPEC guidelines and quotas governing production and pricing. Fortunately for Algeria's ambitious development plans, its low-sulfur crude is in great demand in the industrialized nations, so fluctuations in demand do not seriously affect production. New refineries and pipelines for both oil and natural gas exports have greatly expanded output; revenues from hydrocarbons have averaged $13 billion since 1981.

THE FUTURE

Considering the devastation of an eight-year war, the departure of nearly all skilled professionals and educated leaders in all fields, and vicious infighting among leaders in the period immediately after independence, Algeria has accomplished a great deal in a short time. President Boumedienne brought stability of leadership, intitiated agrarian reform, and defined the direction of development in the 1976 National Charter as a uniquely Algerian form of socialism, Islamic yet suited to the country's special circumstances. His successor, President Bendjedid, has thus far avoided monopoliz-

ing power or developing a personality cult. Wealth from oil and gas exports has enabled the country to diversify its industrial base and maintain a high level of investment and growth; Gross Domestic Product grew by an average of six percent to six-and-one-half percent annually during the 1970s.

Long-term problems revolve around Algeria's agricultural limitations. About 42 percent of the labor force is employed in agriculture, yet the amount of arable land equals less than 2.2 acres per rural resident. Drought and urban migration have adversely affected food production; 70 percent of food needs must be imported at an annual cost of $2.5 billion. Rapid population growth and urban migration have also created a serious urban-housing shortage. Another long-term problem looms with the return of Algerian workers from Europe, due to the economic recession there. Their return would not only add to the unemployment situation but would also eliminate an important source of income from worker remittances.

Algeria's future as a stable, prosperous, progressive nation depends on the resolution of these and other long-term problems. Success depends not only on effective leadership but also on the active participation of a politically apathetic population. In a speech to FLN leaders in February 1985, President Bendjedid warned: "We are on the threshold of the year 2000, when the era when we could count on oil and gas will be finished. Algerians should roll up their

sleeves and stop considering the state as a milking cow."[10]

FOOTNOTES

1. On the corsairs see William Spencer, *Algiers in the Age of the Corsairs* (Norman: University of Oklahoma Press, 1976), Centers of Civilization Series. "The corsair, if brought to justice in maritime courts, identified himself as *corsale* or *Korsan*, never as fugitive or criminal; his occupation was as clearly identifiable as that of tanner, goldsmith, potter or tailor." p. 47.

2. Raphael Danziger, *Abd al-Qadir and the Algerians* (New York: Holmes and Meier, 1977), notes that Turkish intrigue kept the tribes in a state of near constant tribal warfare, preventing them thus from forming dangerous coalitions. p. 24.

3. The usual explanation for the quick collapse of the regency after three hundred years is that its forces were prepared for naval warfare but not for attack by land. *Ibid.*, pp. 36-38.

4. Quoted in Harold D. Nelson, *Algeria, A Country Study* (Washington, DC: American University, Foreign Area Studies, 1979), p. 31.

5. Marnia Lazreg, *The Emergence of Classes in Algeria* (Boulder, CO: Westview Press, 1976), p. 53.

6. For Algerian Muslims to become French citizens meant giving up their religion, for all practical purposes, since Islam recognizes only Islamic law and to be a French citizen means accepting French laws. Fewer than three thousand Algerians became French citizens during the period of French rule. Nelson, *op. cit.*, pp. 34-35.

7. John E. Talbott, *The War Without a Name: France in Algeria, 1954-1962* (New York: Alfred A. Knopf, 1980).

8. Georges Suffert, in *Esprit*, 25 (1957), p. 819.

9. Nelson, *op. cit.*, p. 68.

10. *Africa Research Bulletin*, Political Series, February 1985.

DEVELOPMENT

The new five-year plan shifts emphasis from hydrocarbons and heavy industry to agricultural development. Agriculture employs 42% of the labor force but provides 7% of GDP. A new land-distribution program leases 2- to 8-acre plots to farmers, with ownership vested after 5 years of improved productivity.

FREEDOM

Opposition since independence has been confined to intra-FLN factional conflicts and ended after the Boumedienne takeover. The FLN is the only political party and carefully shepherded Algerians through staged elections. The country has had almost no Islamic fundamentalist violence.

HEALTH/WELFARE

The 1984 Family Code improves significantly the status of Algerian women. The code prohibits polygamy except in rare occasions such as sterility. Women have the right to work but are not obligated to support their families as breadwinners.

ACHIEVEMENTS

During 1980-1984 the government made some progress in dealing with the acute housing shortage and the high unemployment rate. Some 710,000 new jobs were created and 430,000 new housing units built. Production in the non-hydrocarbons sector increased 6%. Inflation has been held in check by price controls and subsidies.

Bahrain (State of Bahrain)

GEOGRAPHY

Area in Square Kilometers (Miles):
678 (260)
Capital (Population): Manama
(100,000)
Climate: hot and humid, April-
October; temperate, November-March

PEOPLE

Population
Total: 409,000
Annual Growth Rate: 3.9%
Rural/Urban Population Ratio: 22/78
(1980)
Ethnic Makeup of Population: 63%
Bahrain; 13% Asian; 10% other
Arab; 8% Iranian; 6% other

Health
Life Expectancy at Birth: 68 years
Infant Death Rate (Ratio): 57/1,000
Average Caloric Intake: n/a
Physicians Available (Ratio): 1/991
(1980)

Religion(s)
66% Shia Muslim; 30% Sunni
Muslim; 4% Christian

Education
Adult Literacy Rate: 74%

COMMUNICATION

Telephones: 72,600
Newspapers: 7 Arabic; 2 English
language (one weekly, one daily)

PEARLING: AN ANCIENT INDUSTRY

Before the discovery of oil, pearl fishing was the main occupation and source of income of Bahrain. As recently as the 1930s there were 900 dhows, with 20,000 divers and crewmen.

Pearl diving dates back 5,000 years; the ancient Epic of Gilgamesh describes a diver tying stones to his feet to descend to the bed of the sea and pluck the magic flowers.

The pearling industry slumped with the introduction of cheaper Japanese cultured pearls, and oil development finished it. But Bahraini pearls are still highly valued, and a few dhows continue to bring them in, using methods unchanged for centuries.

TRANSPORTATION

Highways—Kilometers (Miles): 155
(96) bituminous surfaced
Railroads—Kilometers (Miles): none
Commercial Airports: 3

GOVERNMENT

Type: traditional emirate (cabinet-executive system)
Independence Date: August 15, 1971
Head of State: Isa bin Sulman al-Khalifa, emir
Political Parties: prohibited; several small, clandestine leftist and fundamentalist groups active
Suffrage: none

MILITARY

Number of Armed Forces: Bahrain
Defense Force (army and navy),
2,500
Military Expenditures (% of Central Government Expenditures): 17%
Current Hostilities: none

ECONOMY

Currency ($ US Equivalent): 0.377
Bahrain dinar = $1 (February 1985)
Per Capita Income/GNP: $9,284/$5.5
billion (1983)
Inflation Rate: 4.5% (1982-1984
average)
Natural Resources: oil; associated and nonassociated natural gas; fish
Agriculture: eggs; vegetables; dates; dairy and poultry farming
Industry: petroleum processing and refining; aluminum; ship repair; natural gas; shrimping and fishing

FOREIGN TRADE

Exports: $3.2 billion (1984)
Imports: $3.3 billion (1984)

BAHRAIN

The State of Bahrain is the smallest Arab state. It is also the only Arab island state, consisting of an archipelago of thirty-three islands, five of them inhabited. The largest island, also named Bahrain (from the Arabic *bahr-ayn*, or "two seas"), consists of 216 square miles. This island contains the capital, Manama, and two-thirds of the population. Bahrain's population density is thus one of the highest in the Middle East. The only other inhabited island of importance in the archipelago is Muharraq, formerly a center for pearl fishing and the former residence of the rulers.

Although separated from the Arabian mainland, Bahrain is not far; it is fifteen miles from Qatar and the same distance from Saudi Arabia. A causeway will link Bahrain to Saudi Arabia by late 1985; the causeway will provide advantages to Bahrain's economy, but may also have adverse effects since Saudi society is stricter than the more freewheeling, open society of Bahrain.

Bahrain is unusual among the Gulf states in that it started to develop its economy early. Oil was discovered there in 1932, and exports began in 1934. This head start enabled the government to build up an industrial base over a thirty-year period. Bahrain is also fortunate in having a large skilled labor force of its own people. Bahrain is also different from other Arab oil-producing states in having a native majority of the population.

HISTORY

Archaeologists believe that in ancient times Bahrain was the legendary Dilmun, the land of immortality of the Sumerians of Mesopotamia. On a more practical level, Dilmun was an important trade center between Mesopotamian cities and the cities of the Indus Valley in western India.

During the centuries of Islamic rule in the Middle East, Bahrain (it was renamed by Arab geographers) became wealthy from the pearl-fishing industry. By the fourteenth century it had three hundred villages. Bahraini merchants grew rich from profits on their large, lustrous, high-quality pearls. As recently as 1833 the pearl-fishing fleet numbered fifteen hundred boats. Bahraini sea captains and pearl merchants built lofty palaces and other stately buildings on the islands.

The Portuguese were the first Europeans to land on Bahrain, which they seized in the early sixteenth century as one of a string of fortresses along the coast to protect their monopoly over the spice trade. They ruled by the sword in Bahrain for nearly a century before they were ousted by Iranian invaders. The Iranians, in turn, were defeated by the al-Kalifas, a clan of the powerful

Anaizas. In 1782 the clan leader, Shaykh Ahmad al-Khalifa, established control over Bahrain and founded the dynasty which rules the state today. (The al-Khalifas belong to the same clan as the al-Sabahs, rulers of Kuwait, and are distantly related to the Saudi Arabian royal family.)

A British Protectorate

In the 1800s Bahrain came under British protection in the same way as other Gulf states. The ruler Shaykh Isa, whose reign was one of the world's longest (1869-1932), signed an agreement making the United Kingdom responsible for Bahrain's defense and foreign policy. He also agreed not to give any concessions for oil exploration without British approval. The agreement was important because the British were already developing oil fields in Iran. Control of oil in another area would give them an added source of fuel for the new weaponry of tanks and oil-powered warships of World War I. The early development of Bahrain's oilfields and the guidance of British political advisers helped prepare the country for independence.

INDEPENDENCE

Bahrain became fully independent in 1971. The British encouraged the ruler to join with Qatar and seven small British-protected Gulf states, the Trucial States, in a federation. But Bahrain and Qatar felt they were more advanced economically, politically, and socially than the Trucial States, and therefore did not need to federate.

A mild threat to Bahrain's independence came from Iran. In 1970 Shah Mohammed Reza Pahlavi claimed Bahrain on the basis of Iran's sixteenth-century occupation, plus the fact that a large number of Bahrainis were descended from Iranian emigrants. The United Nations discussed the issue, and recommended that Bahrain be given its independence on the grounds that "the people of Bahrain wish to gain recognition of their identity in a fully independent and sovereign state."[1] The shah accepted the resolution, and Iran made no further claims on Bahrain during his lifetime.

The gradual development of democracy in Bahrain reached a peak after independence. Shaykh Khalifa (now called emir) approved a new Constitution and a law establishing an elected National Assembly of thirty members. The assembly met for the first time in 1973. But two years later it was dissolved by the emir, and it has not been reinstated.

What Had Happened?

Bahrain is an example of a problem common in Middle Eastern countries. It is the conflict between traditional authority and popular democracy. Fuad Khuri describes the problem as one of a "tribally controlled government that rules by historical right,

opposed to a community based urban population seeking to participate in government through elections. The first believes and acts as if government is an earned right, the other seeks to modify government and subject it to a public vote."[2]

Rule in Bahrain is defined in its Constitution as hereditary in the al-Khalifa family, from ruling emir to eldest son. The emir is advised by a Council of Ministers, most of them members of the ruling family. The National Assembly was set up to debate and approve laws prepared by the Council of Ministers. But because political parties are illegal in Bahrain, Assembly members spent their time arguing with one another or criticizing the ruler instead of dealing with issues. When the emir dissolved the Assembly, he said that it was preventing the government from doing what it was supposed to do.

THREATS TO NATIONAL SECURITY

The 1979 Revolution in Iran caused much concern in Bahrain. The new Iranian government revived the old territorial claim to Bahrain, and a Teheran-based Islamic Front for the Liberation of Bahrain called on Shia Muslims in Bahrain to overthrow the Sunni regime of the emir. In December 1981 the government arrested a group of Shia Bahrainis and others and charged them with a plot backed by Iran against the state. The plotters had expected support from the Shia population, but this did not materialize. After seeing the results of the Iranian revolution, few Bahraini Shia Muslims wanted the Iranian form of fundamentalist Islamic government. In May of 1982, seventy-three defendants were given sentences ranging from seven years' imprisonment to life. Bahrain's prime minister told a local newspaper that the plot didn't represent a real danger, "but we are not used to this sort of thing so we had to take strong action."[3]

A STABLE AND DIVERSIFIED ECONOMY

Being one of the first Gulf states to get into the oil business, Bahrain may also be the first to leave it. Its oil reserves are not expect to last beyond 1995. Nor has production ever reached the level of other Arab oil-producing countries. Also, Bahrain exports only refined products, not crude oil. Its refinery, the second largest in the Middle East, depends on purchases of Saudi crude oil for much of its output, and the high price of Saudi crude keeps production down. The world oil glut and other factors caused national income to drop beginning in 1982. Per capita income, $9,284 in 1983, is also well below that of other Arab oil-producing states.

To compensate for lowered production and limited reserves, the government is searching vigorously for other minerals and

Periodic occupation by Iran after Portuguese ouster 1602-1782	al-Khalifa family seizes power over other families and groups 1783	British protectorate 1880	Independence 1971	New Constitution establishes Constituent Assembly, but ruler dissolves it shortly thereafter 1975

■■●■■■■■■■■■■■■■■■■■■■■■■■●■■■■■■■■■■■■■■■■■■■■■■■■■■■■■■■■■■■●■■■■■■■■■■■●■■■■■■■■■■■■■■■■■■●■ 1980s

Iran-backed plot against government thwarted; 60 people, mostly Shia Muslims, arrested

is diversifying the economic base. Natural gas reserves are estimated at nine billion cubic feet. But the most ambitious development project involves aluminum. Using Australian bauxite, the government recently set up a smelter, rolling mill, and extrusion plants for production and export of both raw and finished aluminum products.

CENTER FOR INTERNATIONAL FINANCE

In recent years Bahrain has replaced Beirut, Lebanon as the Middle East's principal international banking and trade center. The Bahraini government established so-called Offshore Banking Units (OBUs). Foreign banks may open OBUs, which cannot provide local banking services but can accept depostis from governments or large financial organizations such as the World Bank and can make loans for development projects. OBUs are "offshore" in the sense that a Bahraini cannot open a checking account or borrow money. But the effectiveness of the system is illustrated by a full-page ad which appeared recently in a US newspaper. The caption read:

Bahrainians would think nothing of doing business with Chase Manhattan. Would you make a deposit in the Bank of Bahrain?[4]

The response is an unqualified *yes*. OBUs bring funds into Bahrain without interfering with local growth or undercutting local banks; Bahrain now ranks among the world's ten largest banking centers. By 1983 there were seventy-seven OBUs in Bahrain, with assets of $62.7 billion. Seventeen per-

cent of the country's income now comes from OBU fees. The offshore banking sector of the economy seems likely to become even stronger, particularly as more and more non-Arab banks are encouraged to join this grwoing financial empire.

THE FUTURE

One key to Bahrain's future may be found in a Koranic verse:

Lo! Allah changeth not the condition of a people until they first change what is in their hearts. (Sura 13:11)

For a brief time after independence, the state experimented with representative government. But the hurly-burly of politics, with its factional rivalries, trade-offs, and compromises found in many Western democratic systems did not suit the Bahraini temperament or experience. Democracy takes time to mature, and Emile Nakhleh reminds us that "any serious attempt to democratize the regime will ultimately set tribal legitimacy and popular sovereignty on a collision course."[5] Also, Bahrain's neighbors are ruled by similar patriarchal governments. It is doubtful that it could move rapidly toward a democratic system unless, or until, these neighbors undertake the same process. To date, the ruling family has succeeded in drawing potential opposition groups into the governing process without giving away too much power. Barring a major upsurge in antigovernment Islamic fundamentalism among the Shia majority, this process should continue in an orderly fashion.

A second action which should help to as-

sure an orderly future for Bahrain was the establishment of the Gulf Cooperation Council (GCC) in 1981, which linked the country in a framework of regional cooperation with Saudi Arabia, Kuwait, Qatar, Oman, and the United Arab Emirates. The GCC was envisaged initially as a mutual defense arrangement, but over the long term its political accomplishments should outweigh the development of a coordinated military system. The members' common goals of gradual democratization, sustained national development, and the building of a successful integrated society are probably most likely to be attained by a tandem movement forward on the part of their patriarchal governments. The power structure in Bahrain, based on the traditional rule of the al-Khalifa family, may appear undemocratic in principle, but in practice it does provide the stable framework within which national life and a new consensus will develop as a matter of course.[6]

FOOTNOTES

1. United Nations Security Council Resolution 287, 1970. Quoted from Emile Nakhleh, *Bahrain* (Lexington, MA: Lexington Books, 1976), p. 9.
2. Fuad I. Khuri, *Tribe and State in Bahrain* (Chicago: University of Chicago Press, 1981), p. 219.
3. *Gulf Daily News*, May 15, 1982.
4. *The Christian Science Monitor*, July 8, 1985.
5. Nakhleh, *op. cit.*, p. 11.
6. See Michael Jenner, *Bahrain: Gulf Heritage in Transition* (London: Longman, 1984), p. 115.

DEVELOPMENT

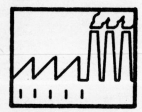

Declining oil revenues in the 1980s slowed down an economic boom that had transformed Bahrain into an industrial and financial center. Capital expenditures for 1984-1985 have been reduced 25% and the 1982-1986 development plan was extended to 1987 to spread out costs.

FREEDOM

The first labor union was approved in 1983, although it is a worker-management committee rather than a trade union. In 1984 the government decreed equal pay for equal work for men and women.

HEALTH/WELFARE

A new University of the Gulf, designed to serve all of the Arab countries and funded by a number of countries including Bahrain, is under construction in Manama. The first phase, a medical school, will open in late 1985. The university will accommodate 5,000 students by the year 2000.

ACHIEVEMENTS

Although Bahrain is a modern state, some aspects of its traditional past survive. One is the art of dhow building. Next door to the huge Arab Shipbuilding and Repair, which handles supertankers, young shipbuilders learn how to build the broad-beamed, seaworthy dhow without plans, measuring tapes, or welding equipment.

Egypt (Arab Republic of Egypt)

GEOGRAPHY

Area in Square Kilometers (Miles):
1,001,258 (386,650)
Capital (Population): Cairo (over
11,000,000 in greater Cairo area)
Climate: dry, hot summers; moderate
winters

PEOPLE

Population
Total: 47,049,000
Annual Growth Rate: 2.7%
Rural/Urban Population Ratio: 55/45
Ethnic Makeup of Population: 90%
Eastern Hamitic (Egyptian, Bedouin,
Arab, Nubian); 10% Greek, Italian,
Syro-Lebanese

Health
Life Expectancy at Birth: 57 years
Infant Death Rate (Ratio): 69/1,000
Average Caloric Intake: 116% of FAO
minimum
Physicians Available (Ratio): 1/970

Religion(s)
94% Muslim (mostly Sunni); 6%
Coptic Christian and other

Education
Adult Literacy Rate: 44%

THE ASWAN DAM

The High Dam at Aswan began as a political decision of the Egyptian government under Gamal Abdel Nasser. Nasser's goal was to increase available cultivable land and generate electricity for industrialization in order to lift Egypt out of poverty. When Western institutions refused to finance the dam, he turned to the Soviet Union. Construction began in 1960 and the dam went into operation in 1971. By 1974 revenues had exceeded construction costs. The dam has made possible electrification of all Egyptian villages, and in Lake Nasser, its reservoir, a fishing industry has been established to replace the sardine industry lost in the Mediterranean due to reduction in Nile flow.

Yet the dam is a mixed blessing for Egypt. Land reclamation through irrigation is proving far more costly than expected. Nile water control has led to increased salinity. And the formerly predictable Nile flow is now dependent on the throwing of a switch by a human technician.

COMMUNICATION

Telephones: 600,000
Newspapers: 11 dailies in Cairo, 6 in
Alexandria

TRANSPORTATION

Highways—Kilometers (Miles): 47,025
(29,221) total; 12,300 (7,643) paved
Railroads—Kilometers (Miles): 4,857
(3,018)
Commercial Airports: 109

GOVERNMENT

Type: republic
Independence Date: 1922
Head of State: President Mohammed
Hosni Mubarak
Political Parties: National
Democratic Party (dominant);
Socialist Liberal Party; Socialist
Labor Party; National Progressive
Unionist Grouping; New Wafd Party;
all must be government approved
Suffrage: universal over 18

MILITARY

Number of Armed Forces: 450,000
*Military Expenditures (% of Central
Government Expenditures):* n/a
Current Hostilities: none

ECONOMY

Currency ($ US Equivalent): 1.83
Egyptian pounds = $1 (March 1985)
Per Capita Income/GNP: $686/$26.8
billion (1983)
Inflation Rate: 11.9% (1970-1982)
Natural Resources: petroleum and
natural gas; iron ore; phosphates;
manganese; limestone; gypsum; talc;
asbestos; lead; zinc
Agriculture: cotton; rice; onions;
beans; citrus fruits; wheat; corn;
barley; sugarcane
Industry: textiles; food processing;
chemicals; petroleum; construction;
cement; light manufacturing

FOREIGN TRADE

Exports: $3.5 billion (1982-1983)
Imports: $8.3 billion (1982-1983)

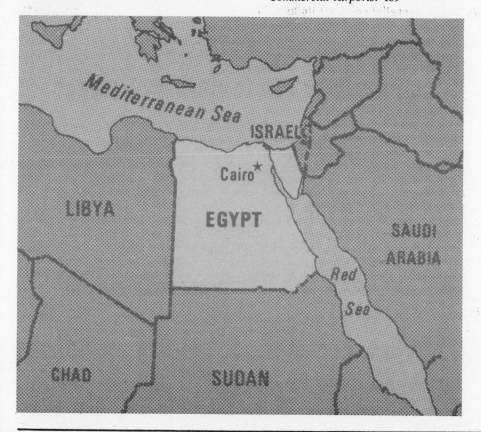

EGYPT

The Arab Republic of Egypt is located at the extreme northeastern corner of Africa, with part of its territory, the Sinai Peninsula, serving as a land bridge to Southwest Asia. The country's total land area is 386,650 square miles. However, ninety-six percent of this area is uninhabitable desert. Except for a few scattered cases, the only settled and cultivable area is a narrow strip along the Nile River. The vast majority of Egypt's population (47,049,000) is concentrated in this strip. Thus, real population density is very high, 5.5 persons per acre. Urban density is also very high. Cairo, the capital and largest city, has about eleven million people in an area designed to hold approximately four million. The growth rate is 2.7 percent per year. The combination of rapid population growth and limited arable land presents serious obstacles to national development.

Modern Egypt identifies itself as an Arab nation and has taken an active part in the development of other Arab states. Not one of the wealthier Arab countries in terms of natural resouces, it has a higher level of education and more skilled professionals than do most other Arab countries. Egyptian teachers, doctors, nurses, engineers, and agricultural specialists have contributed significantly to the development of Arab countries that are wealthier but do not have many skilled workers, such as Libya, Kuwait, and Saudi Arabia.

HISTORY

Although Egypt is a twentieth-century nation in terms of independence from foreign control, it has a distinct national identity and a rich culture that date back thousands of years. The modern Egyptians take great pride in their brilliant past; this sense of the past gives them patience and a certain fatalism which enable them to withstand misfortunes that would crush most peoples. The Egyptian peasants, the *fellahin*, are as stoic and enduring as the water buffaloes they use to do their plowing. Since the time of the Pharaohs, Egypt has been invaded many times, and it was under foreign control for most of its history. When Gamal Abdel Nasser, the first president of the new Egyptian republic, came to power in 1954, he said he was the first native Egyptian to rule the country in nearly three thousand years.

It is often said that Egypt is the gift of the Nile. The mighty river, flowing north to the Mediterranean with an enormous an-

Egypt has a distinct national identity and a history that dates back thousands of years. These pyramids at Giza are some of the most famous mementos of Egypt's brilliant past.

nual spate that deposited rich silt along its banks, attracted nomadic peoples to settle there as early as 6000 BC. Gradually they developed a productive agriculture based on the river's seasonable floods. They lived in plastered mud huts, in small but compact villages. Their villages are not too different from those one sees today in parts of the Nile Delta.

Each village had its "headman," the head of some family more prosperous or industrious (or both) than the others. Gradually the arrival of other nomadic desert peoples brought about the evolution of an organized system of government. Since the Egyptian villagers did not have nearby mountains or wild forests to retreat into, they were easily governable.

The institution of kingship was well established in Egypt by 2000 BC, and in the time of Ramses II (1300-1233 BC) Egyptian monarchs extended their power over a large part of the Middle East. All Egyptian rulers were called *pharoahs*, although there was no hereditary system of descent and many different dynasties ruled during the country's first two thousand years of existence. The pharoahs had their capital at Thebes, but they built other important cities on the banks of the Nile. Pharaonic architecture, based on simple yet accurate instruments and a great deal of human labor, produced extraordinary structures such as the Pyramids, the Sphinx, the Temples at Philae, royal tombs and palaces. These structures, even in ruin, give evidence of the high level of civilization of Pharaonic Egypt.

In the first century BC Egypt became part of the Roman Empire. The city of Alexandria, founded by Alexander the Great, became a center of Greek and Roman learning and culture. Later it became a center of Christianity. The Egyptian Coptic Church was one of the earliest organized churches. The Copts, direct descendants of the early Egyptians, are the principal minority group in Egypt today. When Arab invaders brought Islam to Egypt, they were welcomed by the Copts. In return, Arab Islamic rulers protected the Copts, respecting their Christian faith and not requiring conversion to Islam, although some Copts did convert. The Copts have been useful to Islamic governments in Egypt ever since then because of their high level of education and management skills.

Egypt also had, until very recently, a small but long-established Jewish community which held a similar position under various Muslim rulers. Most of them emigrated to Israel after 1948. Eleven thou-sand were deported in 1956 after the Israeli invasion of the Suez Canal Zone.

Influence of Islam

Islam was the major formative influence in the development of modern Egyptian society. Islamic armies from Arabia invaded Egypt in the seventh century AD, and large numbers of nomadic Arabs followed, settling in the Nile Valley until over time they became the majority in the population. Egypt was under the rule of the caliphs ("successors" of the Prophet Muhammad) until the tenth century, when a Shia group broke away and formed a separate government. The leaders of this group also called themselves caliphs. In order to show their independence, they founded a new capital in the desert south of Alexandria. The name they chose for their new capital was prophetic: al-Qahira, "City of War," the modern city of Cairo.

In the sixteenth century Egypt became a province of the Ottoman Empire. It was then under the rule of the Mamluks, originally slaves or prisoners of war who were converted to Islam. Many Mamluk leaders had been freed and then acquired their own slaves. They formed a military aristocracy, constantly fighting with one another for land and power. The Ottomans found it simpler to leave Egypt under Mamluk control, merely requiring periodic tribute and taxes.

Egypt Enters the Modern World

At the end of the eighteenth century rivalry between the United Kingdom and France for control of trade in the Mediterranean and the sea routes to India involved Egypt. The French General Napoleon Bonaparte led an expedition to Egypt in 1798. However, the British, in cooperation with Ottoman forces, drove the French from Egypt. A confused struggle for power followed. The victor was Muhammad Ali, an Albanian officer in the Ottoman garrison at Cairo, and in 1805 he was appointed governor of Egypt by the Ottoman sultan.

Although he was not an Egyptian, Muhammad Ali had a vision of Egypt as a rich and powerful country under his rule. He began by forming a new army consisting of native Egyptians instead of mercenaries or slave-soldiers. The new army was trained by European advisers and gave a good account of itself in campaigns, performing better than the regular Ottoman armies.[1]

Muhammad Ali set up an organized, efficient tax-collection system. He suppressed the Mamluks and confiscated all the lands they had seized from Egyptian fellahin (peasants) over the years, lifting a heavy tax burden from peasant backs. He took personal charge of all of Egypt's exports. Cotton, a new crop, became the major Egyptian export and became known the world over for its high quality. Dams and irrigation canals were dug to improve cultivation and expand arable land. Although Muhammad Ali grew rich in the process of carrying out these policies, he was concerned for the welfare of the fellahin. He once said, "One must guide this people as one guides children; to leave them to their own devices would be to render them subject to all the disorders from which I have saved them."[2]

Muhammad Ali's successors were called khedives ("viceroys") in that they ruled Egypt in theory on behalf of their superior, the sultan. In practice, they acted as independent rulers.

Under the khedives, Egypt was again drawn into European power politics, with unfortunate results. The Suez Canal was opened in 1869, in the reign of Khedive Ismail. Ismail was the most ambitious of Muhammad Ali's descendants. The Suez Canal was only one of his grandiose public-works projects, by which he intended to make Egypt the equal of any European power. But he used up Egypt's revenues and finally had to sell the Egyptian government's share in the company that had built the Canal to the British government in order to pay his debts.

Ismail's successors were forced to accept British control over Egyptian finances. In 1882 a revolt of army officers threatened to overthrow the khedive. The British intervened and established a *de facto* protectorate, keeping the khedive in office in order to avoid conflict with the Ottomans.

Egyptian Nationalism Emerges

The British protectorate lasted from 1882 to 1956. An Egyptian nationalist movement gradually developed in the early 1900s, inspired by the teachings of religious leaders and Western-educated officials in the khedive's government. They advocated a revival of Islam and its strengthening to enable Egypt and other Islamic lands to resist European control.

During World War I Egypt was a major base for British campaigns against the Ottoman Empire. The British formally declared their protectorate over Egypt in order to "defend" the country, since legally it was still an Ottoman province. The British worked with Arab nationalist leaders against the Turks, and promised to help them form an independent Arab nation after the war. Egyptian nationalists were active in the Arab cause, and although at that time they did not particularly care about being a part of a new Arab nation, they wanted independence from the United Kingdom.

Wafd, an Egyptian delegation, presented demands for independence to the British in 1918. The British refused, whereupon the delegation organized Egypt's first political party under the same name, and began a campaign of agitation against the khedive and the British advisers who really controlled the Egyptian government.

In 1922 the United Kingdom technically abolished the protectorate. Egypt became a constitutional monarchy, although the United Kingdom controlled foreign policy, kept troops there, and advised the new king, Fuad, on all policies. The Wafd and several other political parties took part in national elections, which were allowed under the Constitution. During the 1920s and 1930s the Wafd won the various elections, but neither King Fuad nor his successor, King Farouk, nor his British advisers trusted Wafd leaders to work for the good of the country. So the political system did not work. It became a triangular struggle for power between King Farouk, the Wafd, and the British.

THE EGYPTIAN REVOLUTION

During the years of the monarchy the Egyptian army gradually developed a corps of professional officers, most of them from lower- or middle-class Egyptian backgrounds. There were strongly patriotic and resented what they perceived to be British cultural snobbery, as well as the United Kingdom's continual influence over Egyptian affairs.

The training school for these young officers was the Egyptian Military Academy, founded in 1936. Among them was Gamal Abdel Nasser, the eldest son of a village postal clerk. Nasser and his fellow officers were already active in anti-British demonstrations by the time they entered the academy. During World War II the British, fearing a German takeover of Egypt, reinstated the protectorate. Egypt became the main British military base in the Middle East. This action galvanized the officers into forming a revolutionary movement. Nasser said at the time that it roused in him the seeds of revolt. "It made (us) realize that there is a dignity to be retrieved and defended."[3]

When Jewish leaders in Palestine organized the new state of Israel in May 1948, Egypt, along with other nearby Arab countries, sent troops to destroy the new state. Nasser and several of his fellow officers were sent to the front. The Egyptian army

was defeated; Nasser himself was trapped with his unit, was wounded, and was rescued only by an armistice. Even more shocking to the young officers was the evident corruption and weakness of their own government. The weapons they received were inferior and often defective, battle orders were inaccurate, and their superiors proved to be incompetent in strategy and tactics.

Nasser and his fellow officers attributed their defeat not to their own weaknesses but to their government's failures. When they

returned to Egypt, they were determined to overthrow the monarchy. They formed a secret organization, the Free Officers. It was not the only organization dedicated to the overthrow of the monarchy, but it was the best disciplined and had the general support of the army.

On July 23, 1952 the Free Officers launched their revolution. It came six months after "Black Saturday," the burning of Cairo by mobs protesting the continued presence of British troops in Egypt. The Free Officers persuaded King Farouk

In 1952 the Free Officers organization persuaded Egypt's King Farouk to abdicate. The monarchy was formally abolished in 1954 when Gamal Abdel Nasser became Egypt's president, prime minister, and head of the Revolutionary Command Council (RCC).

to abdicate, and they declared Egypt a republic. A nine-member Revolutionary Command Council (RCC) was established to govern the country.

EGYPT UNDER NASSER

In his self-analytical book, *The Philosophy of the Revolution*, Nasser wrote, ". . . I always imagine that in this region in which we live there is a role wandering aimlessly about in search of an actor to play it."[4] Nasser saw himself as playing that role. Previously he had operated behind the scenes, but always as the leader to whom the other Free Officers looked up. By 1954 Nasser had emerged as Egypt's leader. When the monarchy was formally abolished in 1954, he became president, prime minister, and head of the RCC. Cynics said that Nasser came along when Egypt was ready for another king; the Egyptians could not function without one!

Nasser came to power determined to restore dignity and status to Egypt, eliminate foreign control, and to make his country the leader of a united Arab world. It was an ambitious set of goals, and Nasser was only partly successful in attaining them. But in his struggles to achieve these goals, he brought considerable status to Egypt. The country became a leader of the "Third World" of Africa and Asia, nations newly freed from foreign control.

Nasser was successful in removing the last vestiges of British rule over Egypt. British troops were withdrawn from the Suez Canal Zone, and Nasser nationalized the canal in 1956, taking over the management from the private foreign company that had operated it since 1869. That action made the British very angry, since the British government had a majority interest in the company. The British worked out a secret plan with the French and the Israelis, neither of whom liked Nasser, to invade Egypt and overthrow him. British and French paratroopers seized the canal in October 1956, but the United States and the Soviet Union, in an unusual display of cooperation, forced them to withdraw. It was the first of several occasions when Nasser turned military defeat into political victory. It was also one of the few times when Nasser and the US were on the same side of an issue.

Between 1956 and 1967 Nasser developed a close alliance with the Soviet Union—at least, it seemed that way to the US. Nasser's pet economic project was the building of a high dam at Aswan, on the upper Nile, to regulate the annual flow of river water and thus enable Egypt to reclaim new land

and develop its agriculture. He applied for aid from the US through the World Bank to finance the project, but he was turned down, largely due to his publicly expressed hostility to Israel. Again Nasser turned defeat into a victory of sorts. The Soviet Union agreed to finance the dam, which was completed in 1971, and subsequently to equip and train the Egyptian army. Thousands of Soviet advisers poured into Egypt, and it seemed to American and Israeli leaders that Egypt had become a dependency of the Soviet Union.

The lowest point in Nasser's career came in June 1967. Israel invaded Egypt and defeated his Soviet-trained army along with those of Jordan and Syria, and occupied the Sinai Peninsula in a lightning six-day war. The Israelis were restrained from marching on Cairo only by a United Nations ceasefire. Nasser took personal responsibility for the defeat, calling it *al-Nakba* ("The Catastrophe"). He announced his resignation, but the Egyptian people refused to accept it. The public outcry was so great that he agreed to continue in office. One observer wrote, "The irony was that Nasser had led the country to defeat, but Egypt without Nasser was unthinkable."[5]

Nasser had little success in his efforts to unify the Arab world. One attempt was a union of Egypt and Syria, which lasted barely three years (1958-1961). Egyptian forces were sent to support a new republican government in Yemen after the overthrow of that country's autocratic ruler. But they became bogged down in a civil war there and had to be withdrawn. Other efforts to unify the Arab world also failed. Arab leaders respected Nasser but were unwilling to play second fiddle to him in an organized Arab state. In 1967, after the Arab defeat, Nasser lashed out bitterly at the other Arab leaders. He said, "You issue statements, but we have to fight. If you want to liberate (Palestine) then get in line in front of us."[6]

Inside Egypt, the results of Nasser's eighteen-year rule were also mixed. Although he talked about developing representative government, Nasser distrusted political parties and remembered the destructive rivalries under the monarchy which had kept Egypt divided and weak. The Wafd and all other political parties were declared illegal. Nasser set up his own political organization to replace them, called the Arab Socialist Union (ASU). It was a mass party, but it had no real power. Nasser and a few close associates ran the government and controlled the ASU. The associates took

their orders directly from Nasser; they called him *El-Rais*—"The Boss."

As he grew older, Nasser, plagued by health problems, became more dictatorial, secretive, and suspicious. The Boss tolerated no opposition and ensured tight control over Egypt with a large police force and a secret service that monitored activities in every village and town.

Nasser died in 1970. Ironically, his death came on the heels of a major policy success, the arranging of a truce between the Palestine Liberation Organization and the government of Jordan. Despite his health problems, Nasser had seemed indestructible, and his death came as a shock. Millions of Egyptians followed his funeral cortege through the streets of Cairo, weeping and wailing over the loss of their beloved Rais.

ANWAR AL-SADAT

Nasser was succeeded by Vice President Anwar al-Sadat, in accordance with constitutional procedure. Sadat had been one of the original Free Officers and had worked with Nasser since their early days at the Military Academy. In the Nasser years, Sadat came to be regarded as a lightweight, always ready to do whatever The Boss wanted.

Many Egyptians did not know what Sadat looked like. A popular story was told of an Egyptian peasant in from the country to visit his cousin, a taxi driver. As they drove around Cairo, they passed a large poster of Nasser and Sadat shaking hands. "I know our beloved leader, but who is the man with him?" asked the peasant. "I think he owns that cafe across the street," replied his cousin.

When Sadat became president, it did not take long for the Egyptian people to learn what he looked like. Sadat introduced a "revolution of rectification" which he said was needed to correct the errors of his predecessor.[7] These errors included too much dependence on the Soviet Union, too much government interference in the economy, and failure to develop an effective Arab policy against Israel. He was a master of timing, taking bold action at unexpected times to advance Egypt's international and regional prestige. Thus, in 1972 he abruptly ordered the fifteen thousand Soviet advisers in Egypt to leave the country, despite the fact that they were training his army and supplying all his military equipment. His purpose was to reduce Egypt's dependence on one foreign power, and as he had calculated, the United States now came to his aid.

A year later, in October 1973, Egyptian

Nasser died in 1970 and was succeeded by Vice President Anwar al-Sadat, shown here (left) with UN Secretary-General Kurt Waldheim in 1975. Sadat, virtually unknown by the Egyptian people, took many bold steps in cementing his role as leader of Egypt. Among his actions were ordering fifteen thousand Soviet advisors out of the country in 1972 and signing a peace treaty with Israel in 1979.

armies crossed the Suez Canal in a surprise attack and broke through Israeli defense lines in occupied Sinai. The attack was coordinated with Syrian forces invading Israel from the east, through the Golan Heights. The Israelis were driven back with heavy casualties on both fronts, and although they eventually regrouped and won back most of the lost ground, Sadat felt he had won a moral and psychological victory. After the war, Egyptians believed that they had held their own with the mighty Israelis and had demonstrated Arab ability to handle the sophisticated weaponry of modern warfare.

Anwar al-Sadat's most spectacular action took place in 1977. It seemed to him that the Arab/Israeli conflict was at a stalemate. Neither side would budge from its position, and the Egyptian people were angry at having so little to show for the 1973 success. In November he addressed a hushed meet-

ing of the People's Assembly and said, "Israel will be astonished when it hears me saying . . . that I am ready to go to their own house, to the Knesset itself, to talk to them."[8] And he did so, becoming for a second time the "Hero of the Crossing,"[9] but this time to the very citadel of Egypt's enemy.

Sadat's successes in foreign policy, culminating in the 1979 peace treaty with Israel, gave him great prestige internationally. Receipt of the Nobel Peace Prize, jointly with Israeli Prime Minister Menachem Begin, confirmed his status as a peacemaker. His pipe-smoking affability and sartorial elegance endeared him to US policymakers.

The view that more and more Egyptians held of their world-famous leader was less flattering. Religious leaders and conservative Muslims objected to Sadat's luxurious style of living, his palaces on the Nile and the Mediterranean that reminded them of

King Farouk. The poor resented having to pay more for basic necessities. The educated classes were angry about Sadat's claim that the political system had become more open and democratic, when, in fact, it had not. The Arab Socialist Union was abolished, and several new political parties were allowed to organize. But the ASU's top leaders merely formed their own party, the National Democratic Party, headed by Sadat. For all practical purposes, Egypt under Sadat was even more of a single-party state under an authoritarian leader than it had been in Nasser's time.

Sadat's economic policies also worked to his disadvantage. In 1974 he announced a new program for post-war recovery, *Infitah* ("the Opening"). It would be an open-door policy, bringing an end to Nasser's state-run Socialist system. Foreign investors would be encouraged to invest in Egypt, and foreign experts would bring their technological knowledge to help develop industries. Infitah, properly applied, would bring an economic miracle to Egypt.

Rather than spur economic growth, however, Infitah made fortunes for a few, leaving the great majority of Egyptians no better off than before. Chief among those who profited were the Sadat family. Corruption among the small ruling class, many of its members newly rich contractors, aroused anger on the part of the Egyptian people. In 1977 the economy was in such bad shape that the government increased bread prices. Riots broke out and Sadat was forced to cancel the increase.

On October 6, 1981 President Sadat and government leaders were reviewing an armed-forces parade in Cairo to mark the eighth anniversary of the "The Crossing." Suddenly, a volley of shots rang out from one of the trucks in the parade. Sadat fell, mortally wounded. The assassins, most of them young military men, were immediately arrested. They belonged to Al Takfir Wal Hijra ("Repentance and Flight from Sin"), a secret group that advocates the reestablishment of a pure Islamic society in Egypt—by violence, if necessary. Their leader declared that the killing of Sadat was an essential first step in this process.

Islamic fundamentalism developed rapidly in the Middle East after the Iranian revolution. The success of that revolution was a spur to Egyptian fundamentalists. They accused Sadat of favoring Western capitalism through his Infitah policy, of making peace with the enemy of Islam (Israel), and of not being a good Muslim. At their trial, Sadat's assassins said that they had acted to rid Egypt of an unjust ruler, a proper action under the laws of Islam.

Sadat may have contributed to his early death (he was 63) by a series of actions taken earlier in the year. The remaining Soviet advisers were expelled on charges of encouraging sectarian strife. About sixteen hundred people were arrested in September 1981 in a massive crackdown on religious unrest. They included not only religious leaders but also journalists, lawyers, intellectuals, provincial governors, and leaders of the country's small but growing opposition parties. Many of them were not connected with any fundamentalist Islamic organization. It seemed to most Egyptians that Sadat had overreacted, and at that point he lost the support of the nation. In contrast to Nasser's funeral, few tears were shed at Sadat's. His funeral was attended mostly by foreign dignitaries; one of them said that Sadat had been buried without the people and without the army.

MUBARAK IN POWER

Vice President Hosni Mubarak, former Air Force Commander and designer of Egypt's 1973 success against Israel, succeeded Sadat without incident. Mubarak dealt firmly with Islamic fundamentalism at the beginning of his regime. He was given emergency powers and approved death sentences for five of Sadat's assassins in 1982. But he moved cautiously in other areas of national life, in an effort to disassociate himself from some of Sadat's more unpopular policies. The economic policy of Infitah, which had led to widespread graft and corruption, was abandoned; stiff sentences were handed out to a number of entrepreneurs and capitalists, including Sadat's brother-in-law and several associates of the late president.

Mubarak also began rebuilding bridges with other Arab states which had been damaged after the peace treaty with Israel. Egypt was readmitted to membership in the Islamic Conference, the Islamic Development Bank, the Arab League, and other Arab regional organizations. Egypt backed Iraq strongly with arms and advisors in its war with Iran and in 1984 restored diplomatic relations with Jordan.

The peace treaty with Israel survived, although relations between the two former enemies were badly shaken by a number of Israeli policy actions. After Israel invaded Lebanon in 1982, the Egyptian ambassador to Tel Aviv was withdrawn. Mubarak set three conditions for his return: settlement of ownership of Taba (a small stretch of Sinai beach still controlled by Israel and

Sadat was assassinated in 1981 and was succeeded by Vice President Hosni Mubarak (front row, right). Mubarak has continued his predecessor's moderate stance with regard to the Islamic fundamentalists.

operated by Israeli entrepreneurs as a resort), withdrawal of Israeli forces from Lebanon, and evidence of Israeli willingness to resolve the Palestinian problem. To date only the second of these conditions has been fulfilled.

Escalation of the PLO-Israeli conflict in 1985 created even greater difficulties for Egypt as it sought to keep a balance between loyalty to the Palestinian (and Arab) cause and desire for regional peace. The Israeli air raid on PLO headquarters in Tunis, Tunisia, and the interception by American jets of an Egyptian commercial aircraft carrying the Palestinian hijackers of an Italian cruise ship back to Tunis for presumed disciplining by their PLO peers, were severe blows to Egyptian pride. Mubarak echoed the feelings of his fellow Egyptians when he denounced both incidents as acts of international piracy. In the end, pragmatic concerns were able to smooth ruffled feathers—the peace treaty with Israel that brings Egypt $2 billion a year in aid being the principle advantage.

Although Mubarak's unostentatious

lifestyle and firm leadership encouraged confidence among the Egyptian regime, the system he had inherited from his predecessors remained largely impervious to change. In 1984 elections were held for the presidency and the National Assembly, the first free elections since the Revolution. Several new parties registered in anticipation of presenting candidates for the Assembly. However, a 1983 law required parties to receive at least eight percent of the popular vote to obtain seats. Mubarak was reelected easily for a full six-year term (he was the only candidate). The ruling National Democratic Party won seventy-three percent of seats in the Assembly; the rest went to members of the opposition New Wafd Party, the only one to meet the eight-percent requirement.

The growing success of Islamic fundamentalism in other states, notably Iran, Lebanon, and Tunisia, encouraged Egyptian fundamentalists to make a strong bid toward restoring Islamic law and practice in Egypt in 1985. The fundamentalists took the position that Mubarak's regime, like that of its predecessor, was far too secular and

| Period of the Pharaohs 2500-671 BC | Persian conquest, followed by Macedonians and rule by Ptolemies 671-30 BC | Egypt becomes a Roman province 30 BC | Invading Arabs bring Islam AD 641 | Founding of Cairo 969 | Egypt becomes an Ottoman province 1517-1800 | Napoleon's invasion, followed by rise to power of Muhammad Ali 1798-1831 | The Suez Canal opened to traffic 1869 |

In Egypt there has been a significant migration to urban centers, as illustrated by this scene of the afternoon rush hour in Cairo.

"Westernized" to be truly Islamic. Fundamentalist pressure caused the Constitutional Court to annul a 1979 law giving women rights in divorce cases similar to those held by women in countries such as the United States. When the new National Assembly met in May, there were demonstrations by thousands of fundamentalists demanding that all laws be replaced by Islamic Shari'a law as the law of the land. Some preachers thundered denunciations of the regime from the pulpits of their mosques, calling it secular and un-Islamic. In June 1985 Mubarak cracked down on fundamentalists. The most militant preachers were arrested, jailed, and forbidden to hold services. The government then appointed substitute clerics from the civil service to replace them. The annulment of the 1979 divorce law was reversed by the court in July, under counterpressure not only from women's groups but also from intellectuals, lawyers, and other professionals.

| The United Kingdom establishes a protectorate **1881** | Free Officers overthrow the monarchy, establish Egypt as a republic **1952** | Anglo-French-Israeli invasion of Canal Zone after nationalization of Suez operations **1954, 1956** | Union with Syria into United Arab Republic **1958-1961** | Six-Day War with Israel ends in occupation of Gaza Strip and Sinai Peninsula by Israelis **1967** | Nasser dies; Sadat succeeds as head of Egypt **1970** | Peace treaty signed at Camp David between Egypt and Israel **1979** |

1980s

A STRUGGLING ECONOMY

Egypt's economy rests upon a narrow and unstable base due to rapid demographic growth and limited arable land, and because political factors have adversely influenced national development. The country has a relatively high level of education and as a result is a net exporter of skilled labor to other Arab countries. But the overproduction of university graduates has produced a bloated and inefficient bureaucracy, because the government is required to provide a position for every graduate who cannot find other employment.

Agriculture is the most important sector of the economy, accounting for thirty percent of national income. The major crops are long-staple cotton and sugarcane. Egyptian agriculture since time immemorial has been based on irrigation from the Nile River. In recent years greater control of irrigation water through the High Aswan Dam, expansion of land devoted to cotton production, and higher yields due to improved planting methods have begun to show some results. In 1984-1985 cotton production was up eighteen percent.

The new High Aswan Dam, completed in 1971 upstream from the old one (built in 1906), was expected to increase production and solve population pressure on the land by bringing vast desert areas under cultivation. However, increased costs of reclamation have offset the value of the Dam in providing a regulated flow of Nile water for irrigation. Egypt was self-sufficient in food-stuffs in the early 1970s but now must import approximately one-half of its food requirements. Population growth, migration of farmers to cities with consequent loss of agricultural manpower, and other factors combined to produce this negative food imports balance. Food imports and subsidies for basic commodities are a heavy drain on the budget. Yet the government is afraid to reduce subsidies or increase food prices. Sadat raised the price of bread in 1977 but had to rescind the increase after massive resistance broke out throughout the country.

Egypt has significant oil and natural gas reserves and in recent years has become a major oil-producing country. Proven oil reserves in 1983 were 4.5 billion barrels. Since then, new oil discoveries in the Western Desert and the Gulf of Suez have increased oil production from 420,000 barrels per day in 1977 to 870,000 in 1985. Natural gas showed a similar upward production spiral. In 1985 reserves were estimated at twelve billion cubic feet, sufficient for domestic use plus a large export surplus.

Egypt also derives revenues from Suez Canal tolls and user fees, from tourism, and from remittances from Egyptian workers abroad, mostly working in Saudi Arabia and other oil-producing Gulf states. It was a well-developed manufacturing industry and now produces a variety of military hardware.

But until the Mubarak government can devise a program capable of dramatically

Sadat assassinated; succeeded by Mubarak

Ruling National Democratic Party staggers to predictable victory in People's Assembly elections

Diplomatic relations restored with Jordan

Trial of plotters charged with attempt to overthrow the government ends with convictions and long prison terms

Crackdown on Islamic fundamentalists, with arrests of several religious leaders

reducing food imports, lowering subsidies, expanding the non-oil exports sector, dealing with Egypt's staggering foreign debt, and still providing jobs and prospects for its large population, the economic prospects for Egypt remain dim at best. Attaining even one of these objectives would be difficult enough; attaining all of them would be a Herculean task.

FOOTNOTES

1. An English observer said, "In arms and firing they are nearly as perfect as European troops." Afaf L. Marsot, *Egypt in the Reign of Muhammad Ali* (Cambridge, England: Cambridge University Press, 1984), p. 132.

2. *Ibid.*, p. 161.

3. Quoted in P.J. Vatikiotis, *Nasser and His Generation* (New York: St. Martin's Press, 1978), p. 35.

4. Gamal Abdel Nasser, *The Philosophy of the Revolution* (Cairo, Egypt: Ministry of National Guidance, 1954), p. 52.

5. Derek Hopwood, *Egypt: Politics and Society 1945-1981* (London: George Allen and Unwin, 1982), p. 77.

6. Quoted in Vatikiotis, *op. cit.*, p. 245.

7. Hopwood, *op.cit.*, p. 106.

8. David Hirst and Irene Beeson, *Sadat* (London: Faber and Faber, 1981), p. 255.

9. "Banners slung across the broad throroughfares of central Cairo acclaimed The Hero of the Crossing (of the October 1973 War)." *Ibid.*, pp. 17-18.

DEVELOPMENT

Limits on available arable land and population pressure force Egypt to remain dependent on foreign aid, despite significant progress in some economic sectors. Arab investments in the country have doubled since Sadat's death. One sector showing progress is the Suez Canal.

FREEDOM

Egypt's political system is modelled on that of France under the de Gaulle republic. All decision-making powers are held by the president. The People's Assembly is merely an arena for debate. However, an active journalistic tradition and Cairo's importance as a publishing center encourage considerable press freedom.

HEALTH/WELFARE

Egypt had a long head start over other Arab countries in education and health services. By 1979 14.2% of the population was receiving primary education and 1 million students were enrolled in secondary schools. In 1980 a major campaign to eradicate illiteracy began.

ACHIEVEMENTS

Wealth is unevenly distributed in Egypt. High subsidies on basic commodities keep the poor from starving but contribute to inflation and high budget deficits. Yet the country continues to attract foreign contractors. New ports, steel mills, auto assembly plants, and hotels are under construction.

Iran (Islamic Republic of Iran)

GEOGRAPHY

Area in Square Kilometers (Miles):
1,648,000 (636,294)
Capital (Population): Teheran (6.2 million)
Climate: semiarid; subtropical along Caspian coast

PEOPLE

Population
Total: 43,820,000
Annual Growth Rate: 3.1%
Rural/Urban Population Ratio: 48/52
Ethnic Makeup of Population: 63% Persian; 18% Turkic and Baluchi; 13% other Iranian; 3% Kurdish; 3% Arab and other Semitic

Health
Life Expectancy at Birth: 60 years
Infant Death Rate (Ratio): 46/1,000
Average Caloric Intake: 114% of FAO minimum
Physicians Available (Ratio): 1/6,090

Religion(s)
93% Shia Muslim; 5% Sunni Muslim; 2% Zoroastrian, Jewish, Christian, and Baha'i

---

MODERN IRANIAN LITERATURE

Modern Iranian literature derives from a rich heritage. During the centuries of Islamic greatness, Iranian poets, philosophers, and chroniclers contributed as much to Islamic civilization as did the celebrated Persian miniaturists. The elegant couplets of Hafiz and Sa'di, and the exquisite quatrains of Omar Khayyam's *Rubaiyat,* are examples of this genre.

The literature of twentieth-century Iran descends from this classical Islamic tradition in form but is very different in content. Iranian writers of today grew up in the repressive atmosphere that developed under the regime of Shah Mohammed Reza Pahlavi. Many of them were arrested, tortured, and jailed, while others escaped into exile. Their writings reflect social criticism, protests against authority, and the dark side of national life. A good example is *The Dismemberment,* a banned story by Reza Baraheni, which describes the brutal execution of a condemned man.

Education
Adult Literacy Rate: 48%

COMMUNICATION

Telephones: 1,041,939
Newspapers: 17 dailies (circulation of two largest: 570,000)

TRANSPORTATION

Highways—Kilometers (Miles):
85,000 (52,819) total; 19,000 (11,807) bituminous and bituminous treated
Railroads—Kilometers (Miles): 4,601 (2,859)
Commercial Airports: 161

GOVERNMENT

Type: Islamic republic
Independence Date: February 1, 1979
Head of State: Ayatollah Ruhollah Khomeini, "Guardian Jurisprudent"
Political Parties: Islamic Republic Party; Hojjatiya
Suffrage: universal over 15

MILITARY

Number of Armed Forces: 280,000
Military Expenditures (% of Central Government Expenditures): 22%
Current Hostilities: war with Iraq

ECONOMY

Currency ($ US Equivalent): 97.21 rials = $1 (March 1985)
Per Capita Income/GNP: $1,621/$66.5 billion (1982)
Inflation Rate: n/a
Natural Resources: petroleum; natural gas; some mineral products
Agriculture: rice; barley; wheat; sugar beets; cotton; dates; raisins; tea; tobacco; sheep; goats
Industry: crude-oil production and refining; textiles; cement; food processing; metal fabricating

FOREIGN TRADE

Exports: $19.6 billion (1983)
Imports: $15.5 billion (1983)

IRAN

The Islamic Republic of Iran is the second largest country in the Middle East. Iran is in many respects a subcontinent, ranging in elevation from Mount Demavend (18,386 feet) to the Caspian Sea, which is below sea level. Most of Iran consists of a high plateau ringed by mountains. Much of the plateau is covered with uninhabitable salt flats and deserts, the Dasht-i-Kavir and Dasht-i-Lut, the latter being one of the most desolate and inhospitable regions in the world. The climate is equally forbidding. The so-called "Wind of 120 Days" blows throughout the summer in eastern Iran, bringing dust and extremely high temperatures.

Most of the country receives little or no rainfall. Settlement and population density are directly related to the availability of water. The most densely populated region is along the Caspian coast, which has an annual rainfall of eighty inches. The province of Azerbaijan, in the northwest, the western province of Khuzestan, along the Iraqi border, and the urban areas around Iran's capital, Teheran, are also heavily populated.

Water is so important to the Iranian economy that all water resources were nationalized in 1967.[1] Lack of rainfall caused the development of a sophisticated system of underground conduits called *qanats* to carry water sometimes hundreds of miles across the plateau from a water source, usually at the base of a mountain. Many qanats were built thousands of years ago and are still in operation. They make existence possible for much of Iran's rural population.

Until the twentieth century the population was overwhelmingly rural; but due to rural-urban migration, the urban population has increased steadily. Nearly all of this migration has been to Teheran.[2] Yet the rural population has increased overall. This fact has had important political consequences for Iran under the monarchy as well as under the republic. Attachment to the land, family solidarity, and high birth rates have preserved the strong rural element in Iranian society as a force for conservatism and loyalty to religious leaders, who then are able to influence whatever regime is in power. The rural population has strongly supported the Khomeini regime and contributed much of the volunteer manpower recruited to defend the country after the invasion by Iraqi forces in 1980.

ETHNIC AND RELIGIOUS DIVERSITY

Due to Iran's geographic diversity, the population is divided into a large number of separate and often conflicting ethnic groups. Ethnic Iranians constitute the majority. The Iranians (or Persians, from Parsa, the province where they first settled) are an Indo-European people whose original home was probably in Central Asia. They moved into Iran around 1100 BC and gradually dominated the entire region, establishing the world's first empire (in the sense of rule over various unrelated peoples in a large territory). Although the Persian Empire eventually broke up, the Persian language, system of government, and cultural/historical traditions have given Iran an unbroken national identity to the present day.

The largest ethnic minority group is the Azeri (Azerbaijani) Turks. The Azeris live in northwestern Iran along the Soviet and Turkish borders, while another Azeri group lives across the border in the Soviet Union. They are descended from Turkish peoples who migrated into the region in the eleventh and twelfth centuries AD and were converted to Islam. Their language, Azerbaijani Turkish, and a strong sense of cultural identity separate them from the Iranian majority.

Turkish dynasties originating in Azerbaijan controlled Iran for several centuries and were responsible for much of premodern Islamic Iran's political power and cultural achievements. In the late nineteenth and early twentieth centuries Azeris were in the forefront of the constitutional movement to limit the absolute power of Iranian monarchs. They formed the core of the first Iranian Parliament. The Azeris have consistently fought for regional autonomy from the central Iranian government in the modern period and refer to their province as "Azadistan, Land of Freedom."[3]

The Kurds are the second largest ethnic minority. Iran's Kurdish population is concentrated in the Zagros mountains along the Turkish and Iraqi borders. The Kurds are Sunni Muslims, as distinct from the Shia majority. The Iranian Kurds share a common language, culture, social organization, and ethnic identity with the Kurds in Iraq, Turkey, and Syria. All Kurds are strongly independent mountain people who lack a politically recognized homeland, and who have been unable to unite to form one. The Kurds of Iran formed their own Kurdish Republic, with Soviet backing, after World War II. But the withdrawal of Soviet troops, under international pressure, caused its collapse. Since then, Iranian Kurdish leaders have devoted their efforts toward greater regional autonomy. Kurdish opposition to the central Iranian government was muted during the rule of the Pahlavi Dynasty (1925-1979), but it broke into the open af-

ter the establishment of the republic. The Kurds feared that they would be oppressed under the Shia Muslim government headed by Ayatollah Khomeini, and boycotted the national referendum approving the republic.[4]

Another important minority group is the Arabs (Iran and Turkey are the two Middle Eastern Islamic countries with a non-Arab majority). The Arabs live in Khuzestan province along the Iraqi border. The Baluchi, also Sunni Muslims, are located in southeast Iran and are related to Baluchi tribes in Afghanistan and Pakistan. They are seminomadic and have traditionally opposed any form of central governement control. The Baluchi were the first minority to oppose openly the fundamentalist Shia policies of the Khomeini government.

Lesser non-Muslim minorities include the Armenians, Jews, Assyrians (an ancient Christian sect), and Zoroastrians, adherents of the original fire-worshipping religion of imperial Iran. The Bahais, a splinter movement from Islam, founded by an Iranian mystic named the *Bab* ("Door," i.e., to wisdom) and organized by a teacher named Baha'Ullah in the nineteenth century, are the largest non-Muslim minority group. Although Baha'Ullah taught the principles of universal love, peace, harmony, and brotherhood, his proclamations of equality of the sexes, ethnic unity, the oneness of all religions, and of a universal rather than a Muslim God, aroused the hostilitiy of Shia religious leaders. The Bahais were tolerated and prospered under the Pahlavis, but the republican government, due to its strong insistence on Shia authoritarianism, has undertaken a campaign of violent persecution which some observers have called the "genocide of a noncombatant people."[5]

CULTURAL CONFORMITY

Despite the separatist tendencies in Iranian society caused by the existence of these various ethnic groups and religious divisions, there is considerable cultural conformity. Most Iranians, regardless of background, display distinctly Iranian values, customs, and traditions. Unifying features include the Persian language, Islam as the overall religion, the appeal (since the sixteenth century) of Shia Islam as an Iranian nationalistic force, and a sense of nationhood derived from Iran's long history and cultural continuity.

Iranians at all levels have a strongly developed sense of class structure. It is a three-tier structure, consisting of upper, middle, and lower classes, although some scholars distinguish two lower classes: the urban wage earner, and the landed or land-

Iranian society today has a considerable level of cultural conformity. Shia Islam is the dominant religion of Iran, and observance of this form of Islam permeates society, as this prayer-meeting at Teheran University attests.

less peasants. The basic socioeconomic unit in this class structure is the patriarchal family, which functions in Iranian society as a tree trunk does in relation to its branches. The patriarch of each family is not only disciplinarian and decision maker, but also guardian of the family honor and inheritance.

The patriarchal structure, in terms of the larger society, has defined certain behavioral norms. These include the seclusion of women, ceremonial politeness (ta'aruf), hierarchical authoritarianism with domination by superiors over subordinates, and the importance of face (aberu), maintaining "an appropriate bearing and appearance commensurate with one's social status."[6] Under the republic, these norms are increasingly being Islamized as Khomeini and his fellow religious leaders assert the primacy of Shia Islam in all aspects of Iranian life.

HISTORY

Modern Iran occupies a much smaller territory than that of its pre-Islamic or some of its Islamic predecessors. The Persian

Empire included nearly all of the present Middle East. The Sassanid Kings, contemporaries of Roman emperors (AD 226-641) controlled a territory nearly as large as the Persian Empire. The Sassanid kings made Zoroastrianism the official state religion under a powerful priestly caste. The Sassanid system of administration was taken over by the Arabs when they brought Islam to Iran, because the Sassanids lacked experience in governing.

The establishment of Islam brought significant changes into Iranian life. Arab armies defeated the Sassanid forces at the Battle of Nihavand (AD 641) and gradually occupied all of Iran. But the well-established Iranian cultural and social system provided refinements for Islam which were lacking in its early existence as a purely Arab religion. In a very real sense, the Iranian converts to Islam converted the religion from a particularistic Arab faith to a universal faith. Islamic culture, in the broad sense, embracing literature, art, architecture, music, certain sciences and medicine, owes a great deal to the contributions of Iranian

Muslims such as the poets Hafiz and Sa'di, the poet and astronomer Omar Khayyam, and many others.

Shia Muslims, currently the vast majority of the Iranian population and represented in nearly all ethnic groups, were in the minority in Iran during the formative centuries of Islam. Only one of the Twelve Shia Imams—the eighth, Reza—actually lived in Iran. (His tomb at Meshed is now the holiest shrine in Iran.) Taqiya, or concealment, the Shia practice of hiding their beliefs to escape Sunni persecution, added to the difficulties of the Shia in forming an organized community.

In the sixteenth century the Safavids, who claimed to be descendents of the Prophet Muhammad, established control over Iran with the help of Turkish tribes. The first Safavid ruler, Shah Ismail, proclaimed Shiism as the official religion of his state and invited all Shias to move to Iran, where they would be protected. Shia domination of the country dates from this period. Shia Muslims converged on Iran from other parts of the Islamic world and became a majority in the population.

The safavid rulers were bitter rivals of the Sunni Ottoman sultans and fought a number of wars with them. The conflict was religious as well as territorial. The Ottoman sultan assumed the title of caliph of Islam in the sixteenth century after the conquest of Egypt, where the descendants of the last Abbasid caliph of Baghdad had taken refuge. As caliph, the sultan claimed the right to speak for, and rule, all Muslims. The Safavids rejected this claim and called on Shia Muslims to struggle against him. In recent years the Khomeini government has issued a similar call to Iranians to carry on war against the Sunni rulers of Iraq, indicating that Shia willingness to struggle and incur martyrdom if necessary is still very much alive in Iran.

"King of Kings"

The Qajars, a Turkish people, came to power in the early nineteenth century. The Qajars made Teheran their capital. Most of Iran's current borders were defined in the nineteenth century by treaties with foreign powers—the United Kingdom (on behalf of India), Russia, and the Ottoman Empire. Due to Iran's military weaknesses, the agreements favored the outside powers, and the country lost much of its original territory.

Despite Iran's weakness in relation to foreign powers, the Qajar rulers sought to revive the ancient glories of the monarchy at home. They assumed the old Persian title *Shahinshah,* "King of Kings." At his coronation, each ruler sat on the Peacock Throne, the gilded, jewel-encrusted treasure brought to Iran a century earlier by a Safavid commander from India. They assumed other grandiose titles, such as "Shadow of God on Earth" and "Asylum of the Universe." A shah once told an English visitor, "Your King, then, appears to be no more than a first magistrate. I, on the other hand, can elevate or degrade all the high nobles and officers you see around me!"[7]

Qajar pomp and power, however, masked serious internal weaknesses. The shahs actually ruled by manipulating ethnic and communal rivalries to their own advantage. When they were faced with dangerous opposition, they retreated, and they made concessions only to retract them once the danger was past. Marriages helped to establish a network of power radiating outward from the royal family to leading upper-class families; one shah married 192 times and married off 170 sons and daughters to cement alliances.[8]

Nasr al-Din Shah, Iran's ruler for most of the nineteenth century, was responsible for a large number of concessions to European bankers, promoters, and private companies. His purpose was to demonstrate to European powers that Iran was becoming a modern state and to find new revenues without having to levy new taxes, which would have aroused more dangerous opposition. The various concessions helped to modernize Iran, but they bankrupted the treasury in the process. The shah also wanted to prove to the European powers that Iran had a modern army. A contract was signed with Russia for officers from the Cossacks, a powerful Russian group, to train an elite Iranian military unit, the Cossack Brigade.

Throughout the nineteenth century the religious leaders denounced the government for giving away Iran's assets and resources. But there was little public response until 1892. The shah then gave a fifty-year concession to an Englishman named Talbot for a monopoly over the export and distribution of tobacco. Faced with higher prices for the tobacco they grew themselves, Iranians staged a general strike and boycott, and the shah was forced to cancel the concession. The pattern of local protest leading to mass rebellion, with all population groups uniting against an arbitrary ruler, was to be duplicated in the constitutional revolt of 1905 and again in the 1979 Revolution.

The constitutional movement began as a series of nonviolent protests. The shah initiated several unpopular policies. Public protests in 1906 were met with mass arrests and then gunfire; "a river of blood now divided the court from the country."[9] A general strike was called, and thousands of Iranians took refuge in the British Embassy in Teheran. With the city paralyzed, the shah gave in. He granted a constitution that provided for an elected Majlis (parliament), the first limitation on royal power in Iran in its history. Although four more shahs would occupy the throne, two of them as absolute rulers, the 1906 Constitution and the elected legislature survived as brakes on absolutism until the 1979 Revolution. In this sense, the Islamic Republic is the legitimate heir to the constitutional movement.

The Pahlavi Dynasty

Iran was in chaos at the end of World War I. British and Russian troops partitioned the country, and after the collapse of Russian power due to the Communist Revolution, the British dictated a treaty with the shah which would have made Iran a British protectorate. Azeris and Kurds talked openly of independence, and a Communist group, the Jangalis, organized a

"Soviet Republic" of Gilan along the Caspian coast.

The only organized force in Iran at this time was the Cossack Brigade. Its commander was Reza Khan, a villager from an obscure family who had risen through the ranks on sheer ability. In 1921 he seized power in a bloodless coup, but he did not overthrow the shah. The shah appointed him prime minister and then left the country for a comfortable exile in Europe, never to return.

Iran's neighbor, Turkey, had just become a republic, and many Iranians felt that Iran should follow the same line. But the religious leaders wanted to keep the monarchy. They feared that a republican system would weaken their authority over the illiterate masses. The religious leaders convinced Prime Minister Reza that Iran was not ready for a republic. In 1926 Reza was chosen as the new shah, with an amendment to the Constitution which defined the monarchy as belonging to Reza Shah and his male descendants in succession. Since he had no family background to draw upon, Reza chose a new name for his dynasty: Pahlavi. It was a symbolic name, derived from an ancient province and language of the Persian Empire.

Reza Shah was one of the most powerful and effective monarchs in Iran's long history. He brought all ethnic groups under the control of the central government, and established a well-equipped standing army to enforce his decrees. He did not tamper with the Constitution; instead, he approved all candidates for the Majlis and outlawed political parties, so that the political system was entirely responsible to him.

Reza Shah's New Order

Reza Shah wanted to build a "new order" for Iranian society, and he wanted to build it in a hurry. He was a great admirer of Mustafa Kemal Ataturk, founder of the Turkish republic. Like Ataturk, he believed that the religious leaders were an obstacle to modernization due to their control over the masses. He set out to break their power through a series of reforms. Lands held in religious trust were confiscated, depriving the religious leaders of income. A new secular code of laws took away their control, since the secular code would replace Islamic law. Other decrees prohibited the wearing of veils by women and the fez, the traditional brimless Muslim hat, by men. When religious leaders objected, Reza Shah had them jailed; on one occasion he went into a mosque, dragged the local mullah out in the street, and horsewhipped him for criticizing the ruler in a Friday sermon.

Only one religious leader, a young scholar named Ruhollah al-Musavi al-Khomeini, consistently dared to criticize the shah, and he was dismissed as being an impractical teacher.

Iran declared its neutrality during the early years of World War II. But Reza Shah was sympathetic to Germany; he had many memories of British interference in Iran. He allowed German technicians and advisers to remain in the country, and refused to allow war supplies to be shipped across Iran to the Soviet Union. In 1941 British and Soviet armies simultaneously occupied Iran. Reza Shah abdicated in favor of his son, Crown Prince Shapur Mohammed, and was taken into exile on a British warship.

Mohammed Reza Pahlavi

When the new shah came to the throne, few suspected that he would rule longer than his father and hold even more absolute power. Mohammed Reza Pahlavi was young (22) and inexperienced, and found himself ruling a land occupied by British and Soviet troops and threatened by Soviet-sponsored separatist movements in Azerbaijan and Kurdistan. Although these movements were put down with US help, a major challenge to the shah developed in 1951-1953.

A dispute over oil royalties between the government and the Anglo-Iranian Oil Company aroused intense national feeling in Iran. Mohammed Mossadegh, the prime minister at the time, led a move in the Majlis to nationalize the oil industry. The oil company responded by closing down the industry, and all foreign technicians left the country. The Iranian economy was not affected at first, and Mossadegh's success in standing up to the company, which most Iranians considered an agent of foreign imperialism, won him enormous popularity.[10] Mossadegh became more popular than the shy, diffident young shah, and for all practical purposes he ruled in Iran.

However, by 1953 economic difficulties and Mossadegh's repressive measures had cost him most of his popularity. A contest of wills between the shah and his prime minister followed, ending as the shah left the country. However, the United States, through the CIA (which feared that a Communist plot to take over Iran was behind Mossadegh), helped to mobilize mass demonstrations against Mossadegh, and in August 1953 the shah returned to reclaim his throne. From then on, the shah gradually gathered all authority in his hands and developed the vast internal security network that eliminated parliamentary opposition.[11]

By the 1960s the shah felt that he was ready to lead Iran to greatness. In 1962 he announced the "Shah-People Revolution," also known as the "White Revolution." It had six basic points: land reform, public ownership of industries, nationalization of forests, voting rights for women, workers' profit sharing, and a literacy corps to implement compulsory education in rural areas. The plan drew immediate opposition from landowners and religious leaders. But only one spoke out forcefully against the shah. He was Ayatollah Ruhollah Khomeini, now the most distinguished of Iran's religious scholars. "I have repeatedly pointed out that the government has evil intentions and is opposed to the ordinances of Islam," he said in a public sermon.[12] His message was short and definite—the shah is selling out the country; the shah must go.

Khomeini continued to criticize the shah, and in June 1963 he was arrested. Demonstrations broke out in various cities. The shah sent the army into the streets, and again a river of blood divided ruler from country. Khomeini was released, rearrested, and finally exiled to Iraq. For the next fifteen years he continued attacking the shah in sermons, pamphlets, and broadsides smuggled into Iran through the "bazaar network" of merchants and village religious leaders. Some had more effect than others. In 1971, when the shah planned an elaborate coronation at the ancient Persian capital of Persepolis to celebrate 2,500 years of monarchy, Khomeini declared, "Islam is fundamentally opposed to the whole notion of monarchy. The title of King of Kings . . . is the most hated of all titles in the sight of God. . . . Are the people of Iran to have a festival for those whose behavior has been a scandal throughout history and who are a cause of crime and oppression . . . in the present age?"[13]

Yet, until 1978, the possibility of revolution in Iran seemed to be remote. The shah controlled all the instruments of power. His secret service, SAVAK, had informers everywhere. The mere usage of a word such as "oppressive" to describe the weather was enough to get a person arrested. Whole families disappeared into the shah's jails and were never heard from again.

The public face of the regime, however, seemed to indicate that Iran was on its way to wealth, prosperity, and international importance. The shah announced a four-hundred-percent increase in the price of Iranian oil in 1973, and declared that the country would soon become a "Great Civilization." Money poured into Iran, billions more each year. The army was modernized with the most sophisticated US equipment available. A new class of people, the "petro-bourgeoisie," became rich at the expense of other classes. Instead of the concessions given out to foreign business firms by penniless Qajar shahs, the twentieth-century shah became the dispenser of opportunities to businesspeople and bankers to develop Iran's great civilization with Iranian money—an army of specialists imported from abroad.

In 1976 the shah seemed at the pinnacle of his power. His major adversary, Khomeini, had been expelled from Iraq and was now far away in Paris. US President Jimmy Carter visited Iran in 1977 and declared that, "Under your leadership (the country) is an island of stability in one of the more troubled areas of the world."[14] Yet one month later, thirty thousand demonstrators marched on the city of Qum, protesting an unsigned newspaper article (reputed to have been written by the shah) that had attacked Khomeini as being anti-Iranian. The police fired on the demonstration and a massacre followed.

Gradually, a cycle of violence developed. It reflected the distinctive rhythm of Shia Islam, wherein a death in a family is followed by forty days of mourning and every death is a martyr for the faith. Massacre followed massacre in city after city. In spite of the shah's efforts to bring modernization to his country, it seemed to more and more Iranians that he was trying to undermine the basic values of their society by striking at the religious leaders. Increasingly, marchers in the streets were heard shouting, "Death to the shah!"

Even though the shah held absolute power, he seemed less and less able or willing to use his power to crush the opposition. It was as if he were paralyzed. He wrote in his last book, "A sovereign may not save his throne by shedding his countrymen's blood. . . . A sovereign is not a dictator. He cannot break the alliance that exists between him and his people."[15] The shah vacillated as the opposition intensified. His regime was simply not capable of self-reform, or of accepting the logical consequences of liberalization, of free elections, a return to constitutional monarchy, and the emergence of legitimate dissent.[16]

THE ISLAMIC REPUBLIC

The shah and his family left Iran for good in January 1979. Ayatollah Ruhollah Khomeini returned from exile practically on his heels, welcomed by millions who had fought and bled for his return. The shah's "Great Civilization" lay in ruins. Like a transplant, it had been an attempt to impose a foreign model of life on the Iranian community, a surgical attachment that had been rejected.

In April 1979 Khomeini announced the establishment of the Islamic Republic of Iran. He called it the first true republic in Islam since the original community of believers formed by Muhammad in Mecca. Khomeini said that religious leaders would assume active leadership, serve in the Majlis, even fight Iran's battles as "warrior mullahs." A "Council of Guardians" was set up to interpret laws and ensure that they were in conformity with the sacred law of Islam. Although the republic is governed under a constitution with an elected president and legislature, final authority is held by a "Supreme Legal Guide" who is responsible only to God.

Khomeini, as the first Supreme Guide, embodies the values and objectives of the republic. Because he sees himself in that role, he has consistently sought to remain above factional politics yet to be accessible to all groups and render impartial decisions. But the demands of the war with Iraq, the country's international isolation, conflicts between radical Islamic fundamentalists and advocates of secularization and other divisions have forced the aging Ayatollah into a day-to-day policymaking role. It is a role that he is not well prepared for, given his limited experience beyond the confines of Islamic scholarship. Quite possibly the war with Iraq, for example, could have been settled some time ago if it were not for Khomeini's vision of a pure Shia Iran fighting a just war against the atheistic secular regime of Saddam Hussain.

An unanswered question about the republic is whether it will survive Khomeini. One of the responsibilities of the Council of Guardians is to designate a successor to the Ayatollah when he eventually passes from the scene. In November 1985 the Council named Ayatollah Hossein Ali Montazeri, a close associate of Khomeini's, although he holds no official position, as his eventual successor. Montazeri is even less politically experienced than Khomeini, and the trend toward placing more and more responsibility for national affairs in the hands of secular, technically trained leaders suggests that when Montazeri eventually succeeds Khomeini his role will be that of a new Shia Imam, interpreting and embodying an ancient faith, rather than a dominant decision-making figure.

The Islamic Republic staggered from crisis to crisis in its initial years. Abol Hassan Bani-Sadr, a French-educated intellectual who had been Khomeini's right-hand man in Paris, was elected president in 1980 by

In April 1979 the Ayatollah Ruhollah Khomeini announced the establishment of the Islamic Republic of Iran. Since then his image has become universal in Iran, and to the world Khomeini has become the face of Islamic fundamentalism.

seventy-five percent of the popular vote. But it was one of the few postrevolutionary actions that united a majority of Iranians. Although the US, as the shah's supporter and rescuer in his hour of exile, became Iran's "Great Satan" and thus helped to maintain revolutionary fervor, the prolonged crisis over the holding of American hostages by guards who would take orders from no one but Khomeini embarrassed Iran and damaged its credibility more than any gains made from "tweaking the nose" of a superpower.

Revolutions historically often seem to end by devouring those who carry them out. A great variety of Iranian social groups had united to overthrow the shah. They had different views of the future; an "Islamic republic" meant different things to different groups. The Revolution first devoured all those associated with the shah, in a reign of terror intended to compensate for fifteen years of repression. Islamic tribunals executed thousands of people—political leaders, intellectuals, and military commanders.

The major opposition to Khomeini and his fellow religious leaders came from the radical group Mujahideen-i-Khalq. The Mujahideen favored an Islamic Socialist republic and were opposed to too much government influence by religious leaders. However, the Majlis was dominated by the religious leaders, many of whom had no experience in government and knew little of politics beyond the village level. As the conflict between these groups sharpened,

bombings and assassinations occurred almost daily.

The instability and apparently endless violence during 1980-1981 suggested to the outside world that the Khomeini government was on the point of collapse. Iraqi President Saddam Hussain thought so, and in September 1980 he ordered his army to invade Iran, an action that proved to be a costly mistake. President Bani-Sadr was dismissed by Khomeini after an open split developed between him and religious leaders over the conduct of the war, and he subsequently escaped to France. A series of bombings carried out by the Mujahideen in mid-1981 killed a number of Khomeini's close associates, including the newly elected president of the republic.

The Khomeini regime showed considerable resilience in dealing with its adversaries. The Mujahideen were ruthlessly repressed in 1983. This organization had been in the vanguard of the struggle against the shah, but once the republic had been established the religious leaders came to view its Marxist, and therefore atheist, members as their major internal enemy. The chief Mujahideen leader, Rajavi, escaped to Paris, but most of his associates were hunted down and killed.

The other main focus of opposition was the Tudeh (Masses) Party. Although it is considered a Communist party, its origins go back to the constitutional movement of 1904-1906, and it has always been more nationalistic than Soviet oriented. The shah

| Persian Empire under Cyrus the Great and his successors includes most of ancient Near East and Egypt **5th-3rd centuries BC** | Sassanid Empire establishes Zoroastrianism as state religion **AD 226-641** | Islamic conquest at battle of Qadisiyya **641** | Safavid Shahs develop national unity based on Shia Islam as state religion **1520-1730** | Constitutional movement limits power of shah by Constitution and legislature **1904-1906** |

banned the Tudeh after an assassination attempt on him in 1949, but it revived during the Mossadegh period of 1951-1953. After the shah returned from exile in that year, the Tudeh was again banned and went underground. Many of its leaders fled to the Soviet Union. After the 1979 Revolution the Tudeh again came out into the open and collaborated with the Khomeini regime. It was tolerated by the Shia religious leaders for its nationalism, which made its Marxism acceptable. Being militarily weak at that time, the regime also wished to remain on good terms with its Soviet neighbor. But as the religious leaders became more firmly entrenched, they began to suspect that the Tudeh would unite at the proper time with other anti-Khomeini organizations and move to supplant the Islamic republic by a Marxist one. In 1984 the regime cracked down on the Tudeh in a series of swift surprise moves. Its entire central committee was arrested and sentenced to long prison terms.

PROSPECTS

Seven years after the revolution that overthrew one of the most powerful absolute monarchs on earth by popular consent, the regime of Ayatollah Khomeini remains firmly in power. But the original commitment to Islamic government by religious leaders is slowly being replaced by a more secular configuration. The majority of candidates elected to the 1984 Majlis were technicians or professionals, with far fewer religious leaders than in the previous one. The new Majlis also began to assert a freedom of action not unlike that of Western legislatures. One of its first actions was to reject the appointments of a number of Cabinet ministers on the grounds of nepotism, corruption, or too-close adherence with Hodjatieh, the faction which advocates total adoption of Islamic law and custom in Iran.

The presidential election of August 1985 continued the trend. The ruling Islamic Republican Party nominated President Ali Khamenei for a second term against token opposition. However, Mehdi Bazargan, the last prime minister under the shah and leader of the opposition Freedom Movement,

announced that he would be a candidate. The Council of Constitutional Guardians, which has the final say on all political matters in the republic, eventually vetoed Bazargan's candidacy on the grounds that his opposition to the war with Iraq, although well publicized, would be damaging to national solidarity if he ran for president. Although Khamenei won reelection handily, nearly two million votes were cast for one of the two opposition candidates, a religious leader. The relatively high number of votes for this candidate reflected increasing dissatisfaction with the Khomeini regime's "no-quarter" policy toward Iraq, rather than opposition to the regime itself.

The regime also modified some of the repressive features of the Islamic court system introduced after the 1979 Revolution. In February 1985 the Teheran revolutionary prosecutor, who had come to symbolize the mass jailings, torture, and executions of the early years of the republic, was dismissed. His successor, a religious leader, was also dismissed after complaints by government leaders that he was just as repressive as the first prosecutor. Ayatollah Khomeini then appointed a third prosecutor and scolded both the religious leaders and the government, saying that they should refrain from unnecessary criticism and that unity was all-important.

With active opposition now largely ended, a different form of conflict has emerged, pitting class against class within the framework of adherence to Islamic forms and norms. It is a case of upper and middle classes trying to preserve the freedoms gained under the shah, pitted against lower-class fundamentalists who demand literal obedience to these forms and norms. Thus, in April 1984 violent demonstrations by fundamentalists broke out after the government allowed some relaxation of the strict Islamic dress code, particularly for women. The code was reinstated, but a year later motorcycle-riding militants paralyzed Teheran in a similar demonstration. The demonstration was broken up by police, but was then followed by a counterdemonstration of middle-class youths wearing suits and neckties to demonstrate their rejection of the code. The passage of time, economic de-

velopment and most important, an end of the war with Iraq, may accentuate these differences.

THE ECONOMY

Iran's bright economic prospects during the 1970s were largely dampened by the 1979 Revolution. Petroleum output was sharply reduced, and the war with Iraq crippled industry as well as oil exports. Khomeini warned Iranians to prepare for ten years of grim austerity before economic recovery would be sufficient to meet domestic needs.

Seven years after the Revolution, the country continues to suffer painful economic contractions. The cost of the war with Iraq is estimated at $250 million per month. Unemployment, less than one million in 1976, is now two to three million, inflation is increasing steadily, and the country has difficulty in paying its bills. A further problem stems from factional disagreement in the Majlis over economic-development policies. One faction favors free enterprise; the other favors strict state controls over the economy. As a result, important projects to expand industrial production have been delayed. Iraqi air attacks on Iranian cities and industrial projects caused the foreign technicians working on these projects to be evacuated.

Until 1970 Iran was self-sufficient in food. The White Revolution redistributed a considerable amount of land, most of it from estates which Reza Shah had confiscated from their previous owners. But the new owners, most of them former tenant farmers, lacked the capital, equipment, and technical knowledge needed for a productive agriculture. The revolutionary period caused another upheaval in agriculture, as farmers abandoned their lands to take part in the struggle and fighting between government forces and ethnic groups disrupted production. Production dropped 3.5 percent in 1979-1980, the first full year of the Islamic Republic of Iran, and continued to drop at the same rate through 1982. After 1983 the return of political stabilization motivated farmers to improve production. Wheat imports were reduced to 800,000 tons, a 25-percent improvement.

Bumper crops in 1985, particularly in

| Accession of Reza Shah, establishing Pahlavi dynasty 1925 | Abdication of Reza Shah under Anglo-French pressure; succeeded by Crown Prince Mohammed Reza 1941 | Oil industry nationalized under leadership of Prime Minister Mossadegh 1951-1953 | Shah introduces "White Revolution" 1963 | Revolution overthrows the Shah; Iran becomes an Islamic republic headed by Khomeini 1979-1980 |

1980s

| New Majlis elections reduces number of clerical deputies; 50% of members are new | Major Iranian offensive in Iraqi marshes halted by Iraqi forces, with heavy casualties | New Majlis bill allows peasants who seized lands from landowners after 1979 Revolution to keep them |

wheat and rice, resulted in savings of $500 million in foreign exchange. Although a return to the self-sufficiency of the 1960s was unlikely due to population growth, decline in the rural labor force, and other factors, the country was in better shape agriculturally than during the years of the shah.

Petroleum is Iran's major resource and the key to economic development. Oil was discovered there in 1908, making the Iranian oil industry the oldest in the Middle East. Until 1951 the Anglo-Iranian Oil Company (AIOC) produced, refined, and distributed all Iranian oil. After the 1951-1953 nationalization period when the industry was closed down, a consortium of foreign oil companies—British, French, and American—replaced the AIOC. In 1973 the industry was again nationalized and operated by the state-run National Iranian Oil Company.

After the Revolution, political difficulties affected oil production, as the United States and its allies boycotted Iran due to the hostage crisis, and other customers balked at the high prices ($37.50 per barrel in 1980 as compared to $17.00 per barrel a year earlier). The war with Iraq was a further blow to the industry. Japan, Iran's biggest customer, stopped purchases entirely in 1981-1982. War damage to the important Kharg Island terminal reduced Iran's export capacity by one-third, and the 628,000-barrel-per-day Abadan refinery was put out of action permanently. Special discounts

and incentives to spot purchasers in 1983-1984 enabled Iran to increase its oil sales, but at the expense of long-term development.

Similar problems affect other economic sectors. Disagreements over pricing with the Soviet Union caused the 1981 cancellation of an agreement for natural gas exports, although Iran has proven reserves of 13.7 billion cubic meters. The petrochemicals industry, which the shah had planned to meet all local needs and provide $2 billion annually in export revenues, has been practically closed down. The major project, a $4 billion Japanese-built plant at Bandar Khomeini on the south coast, was closed indefinitely after an Iraqi air raid in February 1984. The most recent budget, for the fiscal year March 1984 - March 1985, anticipates a deficit of $3.6 billion, with over half of revenues to be derived from oil sales. Until such time as there is a solution to the war with Iraq, improved relations with the US, and the resolution of economic policy differences in the Majlis, Iran will probably continue to experience painful economic contractions.

FOOTNOTES

1. Richard F. Nyrop, ed., *Iran, A Country Study* (Washington, DC: American University, Foreign Area Studies, 1978), p. 12.

2. Teheran is a relatively new city for Iran. It was founded in the early nineteenth century and was chosen as the capital due to its central location. In 1900 its population was 200,000. *Ibid.*, p. 77.

3. Byron J. Good, "Azeri," in R.V. Weekes, ed., *Muslim Peoples: A World Ethnographic Survey,* 2nd

edition (Westport, CT: Greenwood Press, 1984), p. 69.

4. Daniel G. Bates, "Kurds," in Weekes, *op. cit.*, p. 425.

5. *cf. The New Yorker,* February 4, 1985, p. 31. The writer notes that "merely being a member of that Bahai community is now, in effect, a crime."

6. Golamreza Fazel, "Persians" in Weekes, *op. cit.*, p. 610. "Face-saving is in fact one of the components of *Ta'aruf,* along with assertive masculinity (*gheyrat*).

7. John Malcolm, *History of Persia,* 2 vols. (London: John Murray, 1829), Vol. II, p. 303.

8. Ervand Abrahamian, *Iran Between Two Revolutions* (Princeton: Princeton University Press, 1982), p. 48.

9. *Ibid.,* p. 83.

10. "Oil is our blood!" The crowds in Teheran chant enthusiastically. Ryszard Kapuscinski, "Reflections—Iran, Part I," *The New Yorker,* March 4, 1985, p. 82.

11. Robert Graham, *Iran: The Illusion of Power* (New York: St. Martin's Press, 1978), pp. 61-62.

12. Imam Khomeini, *Islam and Revolution,* Transl. by Hamid Algar (Berkeley, CA: Mizan Press, 1981), p. 175.

13. *Ibid.,* p. 202.

14. Mohammed Reza Pahlavi, Shah of Iran, *Answer to History* (New York: Stein and Day, 1980), pp. 152-153.

15. *Ibid.,* p. 167.

16. Sepehr Zabih, *Iran's Revolutionary Upheaval: An Interpretive Essay* (San Francisco: Alchemy Books, 1979), pp. 46-49.

DEVELOPMENT

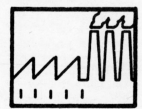

Although most sectors of the economy have been adversely affected by the Revolution and the war with Iraq, progress is marked in certain ones. One is steel. The republican government's goal, like that of its predecessor, is to attain self-sufficiency in steel production as a base for other industries.

FREEDOM

Iran has a long and proud tradition of resistance to tyranny, dating back to the nineteenth century. This should be balanced against some of the worst forms of repression in human history, notably those practiced by the last two shahs. The Khomeini regime initially continued these practices, but conditions have improved.

HEALTH/WELFARE

Since 1980, according to government sources, 4 million Iranians have become literate, increasing the literacy rate by 10%. The infant mortality rate by 1985 had been reduced to 46 per 1,000, and half the country's villages are now supplied with potable water.

ACHIEVEMENTS

Despite total costs of $4.2 billion for the 5-plus years of war with Iraq and difficulties in finding markets for its oil, Iran's economy prospers. Since the 1979 Revolution the country has paid off all foreign indebtedness, including all claims by US banks and companies against the shah's regime.

Iraq (Republic of Iraq)

GEOGRAPHY

Area in Square Kilometers (Miles):
434,924 (167,924)
Capital (Population): Baghdad (3.8
million)
Climate: mostly hot and dry

PEOPLE

Population
Total: 15,000,000
Annual Growth Rate: 3.3%
Rural/Urban Population Ratio: 30/70
Ethnic Makeup of Population: 75%
Arab; 15%-20% Kurdish; 10%
Turkish, Assyrian, and other

Health
Life Expectancy at Birth: 56.1 years
Infant Death Rate (Ratio): 25/1,000
Average Caloric Intake: 127% of FAO
minimum
Physicians Available (Ratio): 1/1,800

Religion(s)
55% Shia Muslim; 40% Sunni
Muslim; 5% Christian and other

BAGHDAD

Baghdad, Iraq's capital, is a "young" city in an ancient land. It was
founded eleven centuries ago at a site centrally located for administering Islam's vast empire. It was planned as a round city of concentric
circles, with the caliph's green-domed palace and mosque at the center.

Baghdad became incredibly wealthy as ships brought luxury goods
from everywhere into its harbor. Scholars, poets and scientists flocked
to the caliph's court. The *Thousand and One Nights Tales* were told here,
devised to save a princess from beheading.

Baghdad was sacked by the Mongols in AD 1258 and fell into ruin.
It revived in the twentieth century with the oil boom. Modern Baghdad
is a city of four million, a fascinating blend of skyscrapers and mosques,
supermarkets and *suqs* where crafts are practiced as they were centuries
ago.

Education
Adult Literacy Rate: 70%

COMMUNICATION

Telephones: 500,000
Newspapers: 4 main dailies in
Baghdad (one in English with
200,000 circulation)

TRANSPORTATION

Highways—Kilometers (Miles): 20,791
(12,920) total; 6,490 (4,033) paved
Railroads—Kilometers (Miles): 1,700
(1,056)
Commercial Airports: 101

GOVERNMENT

Type: nominally republic, under
single party
Independence Date: 1932 as kingdom,
1958 as republic
Head of State: President Saddam
Hussein
Political Parties: Ba'th Party
(dominant); Kurdish Democratic
Party; Kurdish Republican Party
Suffrage: universal for adults

MILITARY

Number of Armed Forces: 648,000
*Military Expenditures (% of Central
Government Expenditures):* n/a
Current Hostilities: war with Iran

ECONOMY

Currency ($ US Equivalent): 0.311
Iraqi dinar = $1 (March 1985)
Per Capita Income/GNP: $2,410/$30
billion (1983)
Inflation Rate: 25% (1984)
Natural Resources: oil; natural gas;
phosphates; sulfur
Agriculture: wheat; barley; rice;
cotton; dates; poultry
Industry: petroleum; petrochemicals;
textiles; cement

FOREIGN TRADE

Exports: $10.3 billion (1982)
Imports: $18.0 billion (1982)

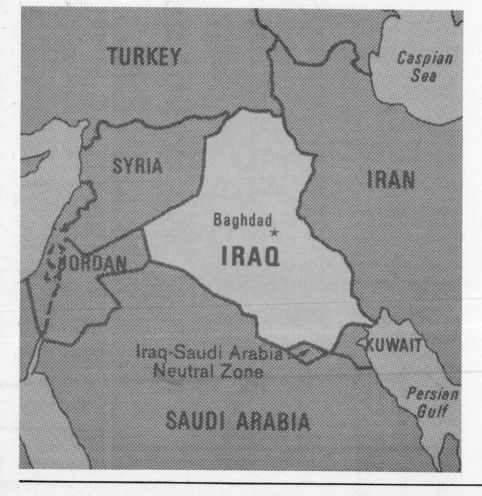

IRAQ

The Republic of Iraq is a young nation in a very old land. In ancient times its central portion was called Mesopotamia, meaning "land between the rivers." The rivers are the Tigris and the Euphrates, rivers that originate in the highlands of Turkey and flow southward for more than a thousand miles to join in an estuary called the Shatt al-Arab, then continuing on to the Persian/Arab Gulf. The presence of these rivers made agriculture possible at a very early date. By 3500 BC a well-established civilization existed in Mesopotamia, with many important cities such as Sumer, Uruk, Eridu, and Ur, the birthplace of Abraham. Some scholars believe that the Garden of Eden was located somewhere in the fertile plain between the two rivers.

Modern Iraq (an Arabic word meaning "cliff," or, less glamorously, "mudbank") occupies a much larger territory than the original Mesopotamia. The current total land area is 167,924 square miles, about the size of California. Iraqi territory also includes a Neutral Zone of 3,522 square miles on the border with Saudi Arabia, which is jointly administered by the two countries. Iraq's other borders are with Turkey, Syria, Jordan, Kuwait, and Iran. These borders were established by the British on behalf of the newly formed Iraqi government, which they controlled after World War I. The only one in dispute is the boundary with Iran down the Shatt al-Arab. This dispute has a long history of bitter conflict behind it, and it was one of the major causes of the war between Iraq and Iran that broke out in 1980.

HISTORY

During its long and rich history, the land between the rivers has seen many empires rise and fall. Assyrians, Babylonians, Chaldeans, Persians, and others contributed layer upon layer to Mesopotamian civilization. These layers are visible in the modern Iraqi town of Erbil (Arbela). Archaeologists digging up Erbil have found relics of cultures that date back even beyond Sumerian times, showing how people lived in terms of their tools, utensils, and homes.

Despite these many varied influences, the most important influence in Iraqi social and cultural life today comes from the conquest of the region by Islamic Arabs. In AD 637 an Arab army defeated the Persians, who were then rulers of Iraq, near the village of Qadisiya, not far from modern Baghdad. (This victory has such symbolic importance for the Iraqis today that during the Iran/Iraq War, the Iraqi government raised money for the war effort by issuing "Qadisiya" war bonds.) Arab peoples settled the region and married with the local population, producing the Iraqi-Arab population of today. Iraq was also the cradle of Shia Islam. The tombs of Ali and Husayn, his grandson, at Najaf and Karbala are places of pilgrimage for Shia Muslims from the entire Islamic world.

In the period of the Abbasid caliphs (AD 750-1258), Iraq was the center of a vast Islamic empire stretching from Morocco on the west to the plains of India. An Abbasid caliph built the walled, round city of Baghdad as his capital. It became a center of science, learning, and the arts as well as a political headquarters at a time when London and Paris were mud-walled villages. In addition to Qadisiya, modern Iraqis treasure the glory days of Baghdad as a symbol of their brilliant past, a symbol which helps to unite them nationalistically.

Baghdad was destroyed by an invasion of Central Asian Mongols in AD 1258. The Mongols overran most of the Middle East. In addition to ravaging cities, they ruined the complex irrigation system which made agriculture possible and productive in the land between the rivers. Modern Iraq has yet to reach the level of agricultural productivity of Abbassid times, even with the use of sophisticated technology.

After the fall of Baghdad, Iraq came under the rule of various local princes and dynasties. In the sixteenth century it was included in the expanding territory of the Safavid Empire of Iran. The Safavid shah championed the cause of Shia Islam, and as a result, the Ottoman sultan, who was Sunni, sent forces to recover the area from his hated Shia foe. Possession of Iraq went back and forth between the two powers, but eventually the Ottomans established control.

Iraq was administered as three separate provinces under appointed Ottoman governors. The governors paid for their appointments and were interested only in recovering their losses. The result was heavy taxation and indifference to social and economic needs. The one exception was the province of Baghdad. It was governed by a man whom today we would call an enlightened administrator. This governor, Midhat Pasha, set up a provincial newspaper, hospitals, schools, munitions factories, and a fleet of barges to carry produce downriver to ports on the Gulf. His administration also ensured public security and an equitable taxation system. Midhat Pasha later became the Grand Vizier (prime minister) of the Ottoman Empire, and was the architect of the 1876 Constitution which limited the powers of the sultan.

The British Mandate

World War I found the United Kingdom and France at war with Germany and the Ottoman Empire. British forces occupied Iraq, which they rechristened Mesopotamia, early in the war. British leaders had worked with Arab leaders in the Ottoman Empire to launch a revolt against the sultan, and in return promised them that they would help the Arabs form an independent Arab state once the Ottomans had been defeated. A number of prominent Iraqi officers who were serving in the Ottoman Army then joined the British and helped them in the Iraqi campaign.

However, the British promise was not kept after the war. The British had made other commitments, notably to their French allies, to divide the Arab provinces of the Ottoman Empire into British and French "zones of influence." An independent Arab state in those provinces was not in the cards.

The most the British (and the French) would do was to organize protectorates, called *mandates*, over the Arab provinces, promising to help the population become self-governing within a specified period of time. The arrangement was formally approved by the new League of Nations in 1920. Iraq became a British mandate, with a government under British advisers, but was headed by its own monarch, King Faisal I.

The British kept their promise with the mandate. They worked out a constitution for Iraq in 1925, which established a constitutional monarchy with an elected legislature and a system of checks and balances. Political parties were allowed, although most of them were groupings around prominent personalities and had no platform other than independence from Britain.[1] In 1932 the mandate formally ended, and Iraq became an independent kingdom under Faisal. The British kept the use of certain air bases, and their large capital investment in the oil industry was protected through a twenty-five-year treaty of alliance. Otherwise, the new Iraqi nation was on its own.

The Iraqi Monarchy, 1932-1954

The new kingdom cast adrift on perilous international waters was far from being a unified nation. It was more of a patchwork of warring and competing groups. The largest minority of the population at that time was Shia Muslims, hostile to the Sunni Muslims for centuries. The next largest minority was the Kurds, fierce non-Arabs noted for their independent spirit and hostil-

Iraq

- International boundary
- ⊛ National capital
- Railroad
- Road
- ✛ International airport

0 — 50 — 100 Kilometers
0 — 50 — 100 Miles

TURKEY · SYRIA · JORDAN · SAUDI ARABIA · IRAN · KUWAIT · PERSIAN GULF

BOUNDARY REPRESENTATION IS
NOT NECESSARILY AUTHORITATIVE

The current area of Iraq is approximately the size of California, and borders Turkey, Syria, Jordan, Saudi Arabia, Kuwait, and Iran. In the south is a Neutral Zone, jointly administered by Iraq and Saudi Arabia. These borders were established after World War I. The only disputed boundary is the Shatt al-Arab area by the Persian Gulf, pictured on this map. The Shatt al-Arab has a long history of bitter conflict and is the main reason for the war that broke out between Iraq and Iran in 1980.

ity to the Arabs. Large Christian and Jewish communities existed; the Christians in particular had been protected by the British and feared reprisals from the Muslim population. The largest gap was between the rural *fellahin* (peasant farmers) and the urban merchants and landowners, a gap which could hardly be narrowed in ten years of British administration.[2]

King Faisal I was the single stabilizing influence in Iraqi politics, and his untimely death in 1933 was critical. His son and successor, Ghazi, was more interested in racing cars than anything else, and was killed at the wheel of one in 1939. Ghazi's infant son succeeded him as King Faisal II, while Ghazi's first cousin became regent until the new ruler came of age.

Lacking strong direction from the top, leadership in the kingdom shifted among a small group of politicians, landlords, wealthy merchants, and local leaders. They controlled the legislature and the Cabinet. One author notes that in the period

1932-1936, there were twenty-two different governments, headed by various prime ministers.[3] No effort was made to broaden the base of participation in the government or to develop responsible political parties. Nuri al-Said, who served many times as prime minister, compared the Iraqi political system to a small pack of cards. You must shuffle them often, he said, because the same faces keep turning up.

THE REVOLUTION OF 1958

By the late 1950s the regime had become out of step with the rest of the Arab world, and out of touch with its people. It was aligned with the West through the 1955 Baghdad Pact, a treaty linking Iraq, Iran, Pakistan, and Turkey with the United Kingdom and sponsored by the United States. Iraq's membership alienated most Iraqi young people, who were Arab nationalists, from their own government. Increasing oil revenues seemed to enrich only the already-

prosperous landlords, merchants, and politicians.

Resentment crystallized in the Iraqi Army. On July 14, 1958 a group of young officers overthrew the monarchy in a swift, predawn coup. The king, regent, and royal family were killed. Iraq's new leaders proclaimed a republic which would be reformed, free, and democratic, united with the rest of the Arab world and opposed to all foreign ideologies, "Communist, American, British or Fascist."[4]

Iraq has been a republic since the 1958 Revolution, and July 14 remains a national holiday. But the republic has passed through many different stages with periodic coups, changes in leadership, and political shifts, most of them violent. Continuing sectarian and ethnic hatreds, maneuvering of political factions, ideological differences, and lack of opportunities for legitimate opposition to express itself without violence have created a constant sense of insecurity among Iraqi leaders. A similar paranoia affects

Iraq's relations with its neighbors. The competition for influence in the Arab world and the Persian/Arab Gulf, and other factors, combine to keep the Iraqi leadership constantly on edge.

This pattern of political instability showed itself in the coups and attempted coups of the 1960s. The republic's first two leaders were overthrown after a few years. Several more violent shifts in the Iraqi government took place before the Ba'th Party seized control in 1968. Since that time, instability has been confined to intraparty struggles; Iraq is for all intents and purposes a one-party dictatorship.

THE BA'TH PARTY IN POWER

The Ba'th Party in Iraq began as a branch of the Syrian Ba'th founded in the 1940s by two Syrian intellectuals, Michel Aflaq, a Christian teacher, and Salah al-Din Bitar, a Sunni Muslim. Like its Syrian parent, the Iraqi Ba'th was dedicated to the goals of Arab unity, freedom, and socialism. However, infighting among Syrian Ba'th leaders in the 1960s led to the expulsion of Aflaq and Bitar. Aflaq went to Iraq, where he was accepted as the party's true leader. This action caused an open break between the Syrian and Iraqi Ba'th Parties, both of which claim to be the legitimate party of Arab unity, freedom, and socialism.

A lack of organized opposition enabled the Ba'th to get on with the job of developing an effective political system. A constitution was issued in 1970 by the Revolutionary Command Council (RCC), the chief decision-making body in the nation. The Constitution defines Iraq as "a sovereign people's democratic republic," with basic rights guaranteed.[5] The Constitution also provides for an elected National Assembly. The first Assembly was elected in 1980 and the second in 1984, Iraq's first national elections since the Revolution. However, seventy-five percent of Assembly members are Ba'thists. Since all laws and policy decisions are made by the RCC, the Assembly's role is limited to ratification of these decisions. The adversary system of political management by specific political parties found in Western nations has never developed in Iraq.

An abortive coup in 1973, which pitted a civilian faction within the Ba'th against the military leadership headed by President Bakr, stirred party leaders to attempt to broaden their base of popular support. They reached agreement with the Iraqi Communist party to set up a National Progressive Front. Later other organizations and groups joined the Front. Although the Iraqi Communist party had cooperated with the Ba'th on several occasions, the agreement marked its first legal recognition as a party. However, mutual distrust between the two organizations deepened as Ba'th leaders struggled to mobilize the masses. The Communists withdrew from the Front in 1979 and refused to participate in parliamentary elections; it was again outlawed in 1980 and went underground.

SADDAM HUSSAIN

Politics in Iraq since the 1958 overthrow of the monarchy have been marked by extreme secrecy. The intrigues and maneuvers of factions within the Ba'th take place off-screen, and there is no tradition of public pressure to bring them to account. In assessing the strengths, capabilities, and prospects for survival of Iraq's Ba'th leaders, a good question beyond "Who are they?" is "Will the Iraqi ruling class please stand up?"[6] A continuous turnover of top leaders, and censorship and suspicion of foreigners, especially journalists, have made Iraq's rulers the least known of any government group in the Middle East. But in the 1980s one leader, Saddam Hussain, emerged to become the new strongman of Iraq.

Hussain, founding member of the Iraqi Ba'th and a revolutionary from early youth, rose through party ranks, surviving coups and countercoups along the way, to become the party's vice-chairman in the late 1970s. When the party chairman retired due to ill health in mid-1979, Hussain succeeded him, to automatically become president of the republic under the Constitution.

But who is Saddam Hussain? He was born in the small town of Tikrit, on the Tigris halfway between Baghdad and Mosul. Tikrit's chief claim to fame, until the twentieth century, was that it was the birthplace of Saladin, hero of the Islamic world in the Middle Ages against the Crusaders. Like Saladin, Saddam Hussain learned early to manipulate people and situations to his personal advantage; and like Saladin, he has surrounded himself with loyal followers from his own clan. Observers often refer to Saddam Hussain's government as the "Tikriti regime" because it includes so many leaders from his hometown.

Saddam Hussain was educated and trained as a lawyer, but it is not known whether or not he ever practiced law. His entire professional life has been spent in politics. He was a founding member of the Iraqi Ba'th Party when still in his twenties, and survived the twists and turns of its fortunes over a quarter of a century to become party secretary-general in the 1970s. For most of that time he worked behind the scenes. But when President Bakr retired due to ill health in 1979, Saddam Hussain succeeded him. He is also chairman of the Revolutionary Command Council, although he has never stood for election, and supreme commander of the armed forces, although he has never served in the military. There are no constitutional provisions for the term of office of any of these positions. Election to the presidency is by two-thirds vote of the RCC; the other two positions follow automatically.

Saddam Hussain's skill in balancing Ba'th factions, his control over the army and security services, and his personal leadership of the war with Iran suggest that he will probably remain in power well beyond the usual term of Iraqi politicians. His war leadership, although yet to be crowned with success, has ironically made him a visible figure not only in Iraq but also in the Western world. His photographs show a portly man with a heavy black moustache, black beetling eyebrows, and the air of a respectable businessman, accentuated by the Paris suits he wears. To present himself as a man of the people and thereby cultivate popular support for the war and his leadership, he has begun to develop a public image. He often wears the checkered *kaffiyeh* (headscarf) of his Tikrit region, visits farms to help with the harvesting, and makes whistle-stop speeches in small towns, where he shakes hands and kisses babies. His personal telephone number is public information, and he accepts calls from anyone with a suggestion or complaint—the equivalent of the daily audience for citizens of rulers in the traditional Islamic world. The most popular item of clothing among Iraqi youth these days is the Saddam T-shirt. It may be that the Iraqi leader sees himself as a Middle Eastern Tito or Castro, seeking a pivotal role for his country appropriate to its resources and important strategic location.[7]

THE KURDS

The Kurds, the largest non-Arab minority in Iraq today, form a relatively compact society in the northern mountains. Kurdish territory was included in the British mandate after World War I, because British troops were already there and the territory was known to have important oil resources. The Kurds agitated for self-rule periodically during the monarchy, and for a few months after World War II formed their own republic in Kurdish areas straddling the Iraq-Iran and Iraq-Turkey borders.

In the 1960s the Kurds rebelled against

| Border province of the Ottoman Empire 1520-1920 | British mandate 1920-1932 | Independent kingdom under Faisal I 1932 | Monarchy overthrown by military officers 1958 | Ba'th Party seizes power 1963 | Algiers agreement between shah of Iran and Hussain ends Kurdish insurrection 1975 | Iraqi forces invade Iran, initiating war 1980s |

War becomes internationalized as Iraqi jets attack tanker traffic in Strait of Hormuz

Diplomatic relations restored with US after 17-year break

Iraq defeats Iranian ground offensive and begins bombing Iranian cities

the Iraqi government, which had refused to meet their three demands (self-government in Kurdistan, use of Kurdish in schools, and a greater share in oil revenues). The government sent an army to the mountains, but was unable to defeat the Kurds, masters of guerrilla warfare. Conflict continued intermittently into the 1970s, with periodic ceasefires. Although the 1970 Constitution named Arabs and Kurds as the two nationalities in the Iraqi nation and established autonomy for Kurdistan, the Iraqi government had no real intention of honoring its pledges to the Kurds.

A major Iraqi offensive in 1974 had considerable success against the Kurdish *Pesh Merga* ("Resistance"), even capturing several mountain strongholds. At that point, the shah of Iran, who had little use for Hussain, began to supply arms to the Pesh Merga. The shah also kept the Iraq-Iran border open as sanctuary for the guerrillas.

In 1975 a number of factors caused the shah to change his mind. He signed an agreement with Hussain, redefining the Iran-Iraq border to give Iran control over half the Shatt al-Arab. In return, the shah agreed to halt support for the Kurds. The northern border was closed, and without Iranian support, Kurdish resistance collapsed. The Iraqi government has yet to implement its promises for Kurdish autonomy. But the collapse of the Pesh Merga and patriotic fervor for the war with Iran, plus the economic advantages to the Kurds of cooperation over resistance to the regime, have kept the Kurdish region relatively peaceful in the last ten years.

THE ECONOMY

Iraq's economy is based on oil production and exports, but it has a well-developed agriculture due to the fertile soil and water resources of the Tigris and Euphrates rivers. It also has a large population and a skilled labor force available for industrial development. The economy is tightly controlled under the Ba'th policy of guided, centralized socialism.

The oil industry was developed by the British during the mandate, but was nationalized in the early 1970s. Nationalization and price increases after 1973 helped to accelerate economic growth during the decade. However, the country is heavily dependent upon pipelines which carry Iraqi oil through neighboring countries to refineries or ports. Disputes with Turkey and Syria over transit fees have forced the suspension of shipments from time to time.

More recently, the war with Iran has seriously affected Iraq's economy. The main Basra refinery was damaged by bombing raids, and Syria (whose Ba'th regime is hostile to the Iraqi Ba'th) closed the pipeline across its territory, leaving Iraq with only the pipeline through Turkey available for its oil exports. For the first time since the oil boom began, the country was unable to meet its import bills and had to default on payments to several contractors. Oil revenues dropped seventy-five percent in 1983.

The war has not only produced high casualties (possibly a million on both sides), but also a heavy drain on Iraqi finances. A peace settlement would relieve the burden on the Iraqi economy, and, if negotiated under terms satisfactory to Iraq, would enable Hussain to capitalize on the broad popular support generated by the war. It seems appropriate to let Iraq's determined leader have the last word: "There should be no halt in the balanced forward movement of our society . . . and our dynamic role in shedding our backward past."[8]

FOOTNOTES

1. The parties had names like "Free," "Awakening," "Nationalists," and "National Independence." Richard F. Nyrop, *Iraq: A Country Study* (Washington, DC: American University, Foreign Area Studies, 1979), p. 38.
2. ". . . sectors were divided within themselves, politicians working against their colleagues, shaykhs perpetuating traditional rivalries . . . fellahin resenting the exploitation of urban landlords and tribal shaykhs alike . . . " Mohammad A. Tarbush, *The Role of the Military in Politics: A Case Study of Iraq to 1941* (London: Kegan Paul, 1982), p. 15.
3. *Ibid.*, p. 50.
4. Nyrop, *op. cit.*, pp. 48-49.
5. *Ibid.*, pp. 184-185.
6. Joe Stork, "State Power and Economic Structure . . ." in Tim Niblock, ed., *Iraq: The Contemporary State* (London: Croom Helm, 1982), p. 44.
7. *Middle East Annual Review* 1981, pp. 177-178.
8. Saddam Hussain, *On Social and Foreign Affairs in Iraq* (London: Croom Helm, 1979), p. 31.

DEVELOPMENT

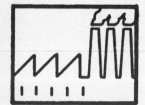

Iraq was hard-hit economically by the war. Government policy of "guns *and* butter" proved unworkable; by 1983 reserves were dangerously low, imports cut 60% and no new projects approved. Massive foreign aid and military success helped stabilize the economy in 1985.

FREEDOM

Basic civil rights are "guaranteed" in the interim Constitution, but in practice the Ba'th Party controls national life. Even owning a typewriter requires a special permit. Opposition to President Hussain within the party has declined since his execution of 21 colleagues in 1979 and his successful war leadership.

HEALTH/WELFARE

Iraqi education took a quantum jump in 1974-1975 when the RCC established free education at all levels. Private education was abolished and private schools (mostly mission schools) merged into the state system. Education is compulsory for the first 6 years. A $42-million US-funded literacy project began in 1979.

ACHIEVEMENTS

Despite delays and shortages of essential materials caused by the war, the Iraqi State Organization for Housing built 400,000 low-cost homes for disadvantaged families in 1979-1980 and anticipates completing 4 million such units by the year 2000.

Israel (State of Israel)

GEOGRAPHY

Area in Square Kilometers (Miles):
20,325 (7,850)
Capital (Population): Jerusalem
(428,700), not recognized by US
and most other governments which
maintain embassies in Tel Aviv (327,300)
Climate: temperate, except in desert
areas

PEOPLE

Population
Total: 3,855,345 (excludes East
Jerusalem and settlements on West
Bank and Gaza Strip)
Annual Growth Rate: 1.5%
Rural/Urban Population Ratio: 10/90
Ethnic Makeup of Population: 85%
Jewish; 15% non-Jewish (mostly
Arab)

Health
Life Expectancy at Birth: 72.1 years
(male); 75.7 years (female)
Infant Death Rate (Ratio): 14.1/1,000
Average Caloric Intake: 115% of FAO
minimum
Physicians Available (Ratio): 1/370

Religion(s)
85% Jewish; 15% Muslim, Druze,
and Christian

Education
Adult Literacy Rate: 88% (Jewish);
48% (Arab)

COMMUNICATION

Telephones: 1,230,000
Newspapers: 36 dailies, 17 in
Hebrew

COOPERATIVE SETTLEMENTS

A unique feature of Israeli society is the cooperative settlements called *moshavim* and *kibbutzim*. They were originally developed to meet the needs of an untrained Jewish immigrant population having to adjust to difficult conditions in a new land. The moshavim are cooperative small landholders' associations. All members work their own land, but their economic and social security are assured by the cooperative in the village where they live. The cooperative handles marketing, farm purchases, and credit. The kibbutzim are collective ownership communities with communal living arrangements, even to sharing of child care. Members pool their labor, income, and expenses. They are not paid for their labor but are provided with all the goods and services they need, sharing duties and rotating work assignments. All kibbutzniks have equal rights; action is voluntary and liability is shared. These settlements contributed significantly to the building of the Israeli state, fostering communality and a united sense of purpose among Jews from many lands.

TRANSPORTATION

Highways—Kilometers (Miles): 4,459
(2,771), majority bituminous
Railroads—Kilometers (Miles): 647
(402)
Commercial Airports: 63

GOVERNMENT

Type: parliamentary multiparty
democracy
Independence Date: May 14, 1948
Head of State: Prime Minister
Shimon Peres (Labor), until Fall
1986; thereafter Yitzhak Shamir
(Likud), until 1988
Political Parties: Likud coalition;
Labor Alignment (also a coalition)
Suffrage: universal over 18

MILITARY

Number of Armed Forces: 140,600
*Military Expenditures (% of Central
Government Expenditures):* 24%
Current Hostilities: state of war with
Arab countries (except Egypt) and
Palestine Liberation Organization
(representing exiled Palestinian Arab
population)

ECONOMY

Currency ($ US Equivalent): 783
Israeli shekels = $1 (March 1985)
Per Capita Income/GNP: $5,612/$23
billion (1983)
Inflation Rate: approached 800% in
1985
Natural Resources: copper;
phosphates; bromide; potash; clay;
sand; sulfur; bitumen; manganese
Agriculture: citrus and other fruits;
vegetables; beef, dairy, and poultry
products
Industry: food processing; diamond
cutting and polishing; textiles and
clothing; chemicals; metal products;
transport and electrical equipment;
potash mining; high-technology
electronics

FOREIGN TRADE

Exports: $4.8 billion (1983)
Imports: $8.3 billion (1983)

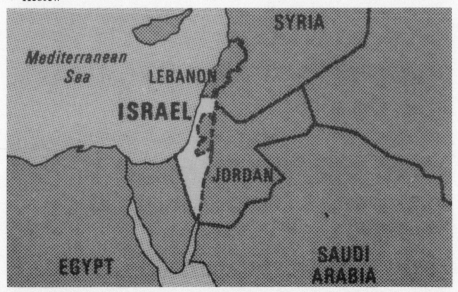

ISRAEL

Despite its small size and population, Israel's territory, boundaries, and its very existence are all in dispute. The country occupies a larger land area than it held at the time of its independence in 1948, due to expansion wars with its neighbors. Its borders with Lebanon, Syria, and Jordan were established by armistice agreements and remain provisional pending a final peace settlement. The border with Egypt, which extends southward from the Mediterranean Sea to the Gulf of Aqaba, along the eastern side of the Sinai Peninsula, was defined by the 1979 Egyptian-Israeli peace treaty and confirmed by the withdrawal of Israeli troops from the Sinai in 1982. Egypt is thus far the only one of its neighbors to have any formal relations with Israel. (A provisional agreement between Israel and Lebanon worked out by United States negotiators for the withdrawal of Israeli troops was subsequently cancelled by the Lebanese government.)

Although it is small, Israel has a complex geography, with a number of distinct regions. The northern region, Galilee, is a continuation of the Lebanese mountains, but at a lower altitude, averaging 4,680 feet in elevation. The Galilee uplands drop steeply on three sides: to the Jordan Valley on the east, a narrow coastal plain on the west, and southward to the Valley of Esdraelon, a broad inland valley from the Mediterranean to the Jordan River. This lowland area is fertile and well watered and has become important to Israeli agriculture.

Another upland plateau, averaging 3,600 feet in elevation, extends south from Esdraelon for about 90 miles. It contains the ancient Jewish heartland—Judaea and Samaria, often referred to as the West Bank—with Nablus, Hebron, and Jerusalem as the main cities. This plateau gradually levels off into semi desert, the barren wilderness of Judaea. The wilderness merges imperceptibly into the Negev, another semidesert region comprising half of the total Israeli land area. Some agricultural projects have been developed in the Negev, using sophisticated irrigation, but its chief value to the country comes from its mineral resources.

CURRENT TERRITORY

Israeli territory currently includes four areas occupied during the 1967 and 1973 wars. They are the Gaza strip on the Mediterranean, the Golan Heights along the Syrian border, the West Bank of the Jordan River, and East Jerusalem. The Gaza Strip was part of Egypt, and the West Bank and

Israelis regard Jerusalem as the political and spiritual capital of Israel. East Jerusalem was annexed from Jordan after the 1967 war, and returning this part of the city to Jordan has never been considered seriously.

East Jerusalem were Jordanian territories. The Golan Heights, which Israel considers strategically important to its defenses, was annexed unilaterally in 1981, although it is legally within Syria, in the United Nations demilitarized zone.

Israeli occupation of the West Bank and East Jerusalem have generated a great deal of controversy within Israel as well as internationally. The West Bank is regarded by some Israelis as an integral part of the original Jewish homeland established in Palestine as the provinces of Judaea and Samaria. Other Israelis, however, feel that the West Bank should either be returned to Jordan or become an autonomous Palestinian state. In recent years a number of Jewish settlements have been established in the West Bank by the first group, to demonstrate their commitment to their goal. The West Bank Data Base Project, funded by The Rockefeller Foundation, reported in April 1985 that the Israeli government owned 51.6 percent of all land in the West Bank, with 7 percent reserved for future Jewish settlements.

In the case of East Jerusalem, there is no disagreement among Israelis. They regard Jerusalem as a single city and as their spiritual and political capital. However, almost all other nations consider Tel Aviv, near the coast, as the Jewish capital and maintain their embassies there. Currently, only El Salvador and Zaire maintain embassies in Jerusalem. A resolution in the US Congress to recognize Jerusalem as the capital has only symbolic significance.

THE POPULATION

The great majority of the Israeli population is Jewish. Judaism is the state religion, and Hebrew, the ancient liturgical language revived and modernized in the twentieth century, is the official language, although English is widely used. Language and religion, along with shared historical traditions, a rich ancient culture, and a commitment to the survival of the Jewish state, have fostered a strong sense of national unity among the Israeli people. They are extremely nationalistic, and these feelings are increased because of hostile neighbors.

Most Israelis believe that their neighbors are determined to destroy their state, and this belief has helped to develop a "siege mentality" among them.

Although Israeli Jews are a unified people, in a state sense, they have come out of widely varying backgrounds and places of origin. Because Jews were dispersed throughout the world for nearly two thousand years, they barely survived as a people. The two main population groups in terms of origin are the Ashkenazi (European) and Sephardic (Oriental) Jews. The Askenazis, the founders of the Jewish state, came from various European countries.[1] The Sephardim, Jews from "Oriental" lands—Turkey, various Arab countries, and North Africa—were later immigrants, except for those indigenous to Palestine. The two groups had little in common except their religion. They had become so isolated from each other over centuries of dispersal that they spoke different languages and could not communicate. Hebrew, until the twentieth century, was the language of a few scholars and was used only in synagogue services; for practical purposes, it was a dead language.

The current differences between Ashkenazi and Sephardic Jews, however, are more economic than linguistic or religious. Sephardic Jews are now in the majority in Israel, but they have not yet gained economic or political equality with the Ashkenazis. In the first three decades of Israeli independence European Jews controlled the government, dominated the Israeli Knesset (parliament), and were more prosperous than the Sephardim.

Another difference among Israelis has to do with religious practice. The Chasidim or Orthodox Jews strictly observe the rules and social practices of Judaism and live in their own separate neighborhoods within cities. Reform Jews, the great majority, are Jewish in their traditions, history, and faith, but modify their religious practices to conform to the demands of modern life and thought.

Differences in their historical experiences have also divided the Ashkenazi. Most of them lived in Eastern Europe, almost completely isolated from other Jews as well as from their Christian neighbors. "They were closed off in a gigantic ghetto called the Pale of Settlement, destitute, deprived of all political rights, living in the twilight of a slowly disintegrating medieval world."[2] However, by the nineteenth century Jews in Western Europe had become politically tolerated, relatively well off, and, due to the "Enlightenment," found most occupations and professions open to them.[3] But the establishment of Israel was largely the work of Eastern European Ashkenazis, despite the fact that the original impetus and organization for settlement came from Western Europeans.

Modern Israel has two important non-Jewish minorities. The first is the Palestine Arabs, descendants of the original Arab population and named for the territory before the establishment of the Israeli state. There are about 640,000 Palestinian Arabs living in Israel. The second minority, the Druze, a community practicing a form of Islam who are also found in Syria and Lebanon, have remained loyal to Israel. They are accepted as a community within Jewish society and serve in the armed forces. The Palestine Arabs, who are distrusted on the assumption that their first loyalty is to their fellow Arabs, are prohibited from military service and tolerated rather than accepted as full citizens.

HISTORY

For most Jews, the establishment of the modern state of Israel is the fulfillment of God's promise of the Land of Canaan to Abraham and his descendants as their home. The original promise still stands to religious Jews, but the people of Israel did not keep their covenant with God according to one interpretation, and at various times in their history were carried off into captivity or dispersed into exile by invaders. Each period of exile is called *Diaspora* ("Dispersion"). The most important one, in terms of modern Israel, took place in the first century AD. At that time, Palestine was part of the Roman Empire. The Jews had rebelled against Rome, and a Roman general (later emperor), Titus, arrived with an army to suppress the revolt. In 70 AD Titus captured Jerusalem. He destroyed most of the city, including the Temple, the focal point of Jewish worship. The majority of Jews either fled into exile or were forcibly deported. (A portion of the Western Wall of the Temple was not destroyed and stands as a place of pilgrimage for devout Jews who come from all over the world to pray beside it. It is called the Wailing Wall.) For two thousand years Jews were dispersed all over the world.

Diaspora Jews were often persecuted in the lands where they lived, and they were

The Wailing Wall, a focal point of Jewish worship, is all that remains of the ancient temple destroyed by the Roman legions led by Titus in AD 70. The Wailing Wall stands as a place of pilgrimage for devout Jews throughout the world. The Jewish tradition shown here requires the separation of men and women during prayer.

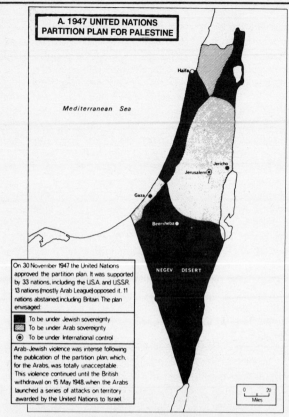

A. 1947 UNITED NATIONS PARTITION PLAN FOR PALESTINE

Mediterranean Sea

Haifa

Jericho

Jerusalem

Gaza

Beersheba

NEGEV DESERT

On 30 November 1947 the United Nations approved the partition plan. It was supported by 33 nations, including the U.S.A. and U.S.S.R. 13 nations (mostly Arab League) opposed it. 11 nations abstained, including Britain. The plan envisaged:

- ■ To be under Jewish sovereignty
- ▨ To be under Arab sovereignty
- ◉ To be under International control

Arab-Jewish violence was intense following the publication of the partition plan, which, for the Arabs, was totally unacceptable. This violence continued until the British withdrawal on 15 May 1948, when the Arabs launched a series of attacks on territory awarded by the United Nations to Israel.

0   20
Miles

JEWISH HISTORY ATLAS, Revised Edn. by Martin Gilbert. Cartography by Arthur Banks and T.A. Bicknell. Used with permission of Macmillan Publishing Co., Inc. Copyright °1969, 1976 by Martin Gilbert.

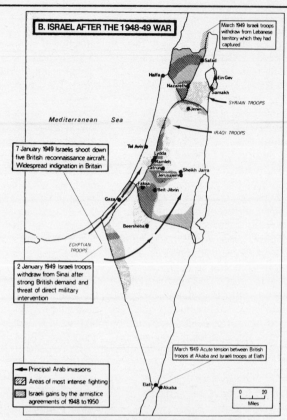

B. ISRAEL AFTER THE 1948-49 WAR

March 1949 Israeli troops withdraw from Lebanese territory which they had captured

Safad

Haifa
Nazareth   Ein Gev
Samakh
SYRIAN TROOPS

Jenin
IRAQI TROOPS

Tel Aviv
Lydda
Ramleh
Latrun   Sheikh Jarra
Jerusalem
Takta
Gaza   Beit Jibrin

7 January 1949 Israelis shoot down five British reconnaissance aircraft. Widespread indignation in Britain

Mediterranean Sea

Beersheba

EGYPTIAN TROOPS

2 January 1949 Israeli troops withdraw from Sinai after strong British demand and threat of direct military intervention

March 1949 Acute tension between British troops at Akaba and Israeli troops at Elath

Elath   Akaba

- → Principal Arab invasions
- ▨ Areas of most intense fighting
- ▨ Israeli gains by the armistice agreements of 1948 to 1950

0   20
Miles

JEWISH HISTORY ATLAS, Revised Edn. by Martin Gilbert. Cartography by Arthur Banks and T.A. Bicknell. Used with permission of Macmillan Publishing Co., Inc. Copyright °1969, 1976 by Martin Gilbert.

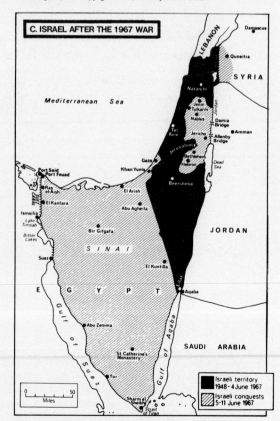

C. ISRAEL AFTER THE 1967 WAR

Damascus

LEBANON

Quneitra

SYRIA

Nazareth

Jenin
Tulkarm
Nablus
Damia Bridge
Tel Aviv
Jericho   Amman
Allenby Bridge
Jerusalem
Gaza   Bethlehem
Khan Yunis   Hebron
Dead Sea
Beersheba

Mediterranean Sea

Port Said
Port Fouad
Ras el-Arish
El Kantara   El Arish
Ismailia   Abu Agheila
Lake Timsah
Bitter Lakes   Bir Gifgafa
Suez
S I N A I
JORDAN
E G Y P T
El Kuntilla
Eilat
Aqaba
Gulf of Suez
Abu Zenima
Gulf of Aqaba
SAUDI ARABIA
St. Catherine's Monastery
Tor
Sharm el Sheikh
Strait of Tiran

0   50
Miles

- ■ Israeli territory 1948-4 June 1967
- ▨ Israeli conquests 5-11 June 1967

JEWISH HISTORY ATLAS, Revised Edn. by Martin Gilbert. Cartography by Arthur Banks and T.A. Bicknell. Used with permission of Macmillan Publishing Co., Inc. Copyright °1969, 1976 by Martin Gilbert.

0 Miles   100

LEBANON
Beirut   SYRIA
Damascus

MEDITERRANEAN SEA
Golan Heights
Haifa
ISRAEL
West Bank   R Jordan
Tel-Aviv   Amman
Jerusalem
Gaza
Dead Sea
Port Said
Suez Canal
JORDAN
Suez
SINAI
EGYPT   Eilat
Aqaba
Gulf of Suez   SAUDI ARABIA
Gulf of Aqaba
RED SEA

- ▨ Israeli-controlled areas

Borders of Israel and Israeli controlled areas as depicted in THE ECONOMIST of July 20, 1985.

almost always distrusted, feared, and restricted to certain occupations. They were better off in some places than in others. In such lands as Islamic (before the Reconquest) Spain and Egypt, Jews served as judges, prime ministers, and financial advisers to local rulers. The Jews in these countries were known as "People of the Book," respected for their knowledge and their sacred books.

But no matter how well or how badly treated Jews were in the lands of the Diaspora, they always felt that they were strangers. Their dream was to return to their homeland.

Zionism

Until the late nineteenth century there was no organized movement among Jews to return to Palestine. A few pious Jews, usually elderly, made the long and dangerous journey to Palestine to live out their days in prayer and perhaps to be buried in the cemetery on the Mount of Olives.[4]

The organized movement for a Jewish return to Palestine to fulfill the Biblical promise is called *Zionism*. It became, however, more of a political movement formed for a particular purpose: to establish by Jewish settlement a homeland where dispersed Jews may gather, escape persecution, and knit together the strands of traditional Jewish faith and culture. As a political movement it differs sharply from spiritual Zionism, the age-old dream of the return. Most Orthodox Jews and traditionalists opposed *any* movement to reclaim Palestine; they believed that it is blasphemy to do so, for only God can perform the miracle of restoring the Promised Land. The establishment of the Israeli state and its development by a secular political system, and policies evolved from modern Jewish nationalism rather than Judaism, have created a dilemma in the Jewish community which has yet to be resolved. [5]

Zionism as a political movement began in the late nineteenth century. Its founder was Theodore Herzl, a Jewish journalist from Vienna, Austria. Herzl had grown up in the Enlightenment period. Like other Western European Jews, he came to believe that a new age of full acceptance of the Jewish community into European life had begun. He was bitterly disillusioned by the wave of Jewish persecution that swept over Eastern Europe after the murder of the liberal Russian czar, Alexander II, in 1881. He was even more disillusioned by the trial of a French army officer, Alfred Dreyfus, for treason. Dreyfus, who was Jewish, was convicted after angry protests that he was

a member of a vast Jewish conspiracy to overthrow the French government.

Herzl concluded from these events that the only hope for the long-suffering Jews, especially those from Eastern Europe, was to live together separate from non-Jews. In his book, *Der Judenstaat* ("*The Jewish State*"), he wrote: :"We have sincerely tried everywhere to merge with the national communities in which we live, seeking only to preserve the faith of our fathers. It is not permitted to us."[6]

In 1897 Herzl organized a conference of Jewish leaders in Basle, Switzerland. This first World Zionist Conference ended with a declaration that "the aim of Zionism is to create for the Jewish people a home in Palestine secured by public law."[7] To reach this goal, the Zionists would promote settlement of Palestine by Jewish farmers, artisans, and tradespeople.

Palestine at that time was part of the Ottoman Empire. The Zionists hoped to be allowed to buy land in Palestine for Jewish settlements. But the Ottoman government would not allow them to do so. Small groups of Eastern European Jews escaping persecution made their way to Palestine and established communal agricultural settlements called *kibbutzim*. Those immigrants believed that hard work was essential to the Jewish return to the homeland. Work was sacred, and the only thing that gave the Jews the right to the soil of Palestine was the "betrothal of toil." This belief held by the kibbutzim movement became a founding principle of the Jewish state.

The Balfour Declaration

Although the Zionist movement attracted many Jewish supporters, it had no influence with European governments, nor with the Ottoman government. It had trouble raising money to finance emigration and land purchases from Jewish bankers.

It appeared in the early 1900s that the Zionists would never reach their goal. But World War I gave them a new opportunity. The Ottoman Empire was defeated, and British troops occupied Palestine. During the war a British Zionist named Chaim Weizmann, a chemist, had developed a new type of explosive that was valuable to the British war effort against Germany. Weizmann and his associates pressed the British government for a commitment to support a home for Jews in Palestine after the war. In 1917 Arthur Balfour, the British foreign secretary, wrote a letter to Lord Rothschild, a wealthy banker and Zionist leader, outlining the British agreement to help

the Zionists establish a Jewish national home in Palestine. Although the letter was general in its terms, the Zionists accepted it as a British commitment to their cause. Since then the letter has been referred to as the Balfour Declaration.[8]

The British Mandate

The peace settlement arranged after World War I by the new League of Nations gave Palestine to the United Kingdom as a mandate. The Zionists understood this to mean that they could now begin to build a Jewish national home in Palestine, through large-scale immigration. They established a Jewish agency under the leadership of Chaim Weizmann to organize the immigration.

However, most of the Zionist leaders had never been to Palestine. They imagined it as an empty land waiting to be developed by industrious Jews, and did not realize that it was already inhabited by a large Arab population. The Palestinian Arabs had been there for centuries; many families still lived in the villages settled by their ancestors. They regarded Palestine as their national home. The basic conflict between the Arabs and Israel arises from the the claim of two different peoples to the same land.

Palestinian Arabs were opposed to the mandate, the Balfour Declaration, and to Jewish immigration. They turned to violence on several occasions, against the British and the growing Jewish population. In 1936 Arab leaders called a general strike to protest Jewish immigration, which led to a full-scale Arab rebellion. The British tried to steer a middle ground between the two communities. But they were unwilling (or unable) either to accept Arab demands for restrictions on Jewish immigration and land purchases or Zionist demands for a Jewish majority in Palestine. British policy reports and White Papers during the mandate wavered back and forth. Thus, in 1937 a report recommended partition, while a 1939 White Paper recommended a self-governing Arab state with an end to Jewish immigration.

One important difference between the Palestinian Arab and Jewish communities was in their organization. The Jews were organized under the Jewish Agency, which operated as a "state within a state" in Palestine. Jews in Europe and the US also contributed substantially to the Agency's finances and made arrangements for immigration. The Palestinian Arabs, in contrast, were led by heads of urban families who often quarreled with one another. The Palestinian Arab cause also did not have outside Arab support; leaders of neighboring Arab states were weak and were still under British or French control.

Adolph Hitler's policy of *genocide* (total extermination) of Jews in Europe, developed during World War II, gave a special urgency to Jewish settlement in Palestine. American Zionist leaders condemned the 1939 British White Paper and called for unrestricted Jewish immigration into Palestine and the establishment of an independent, democratic Jewish state. After the end of World War II the British, still committed to the White Paper, blocked Palestine harbors and turned back the crowded, leaking ships which were bringing desperate Jewish refugees from Europe. World opinion turned against the British. In Palestine itself, Jews formed their own defense organization, Haganah, and underground Jewish terrorist groups such as the Irgun Zvai Leumi and the Stern Gang developed a campaign of murder and sabotage to force the British to end the mandate and establish Palestine as an independent Jewish state.

PARTITION AND INDEPENDENCE

Israel is one of two nations in the world (the other being Libya) that gained its independence through direct action by the United Nations. In 1947 the British decided that the Palestine mandate was unworkable, and asked the United Nations to come up with a solution to the problem of "one land, two peoples." A UN Special Commission on Palestine (UNSCOP) recommended partition of Palestine into two states, one Arab, one Jewish, with an economic union between them. A minority of UNSCOP members recommended a federated Arab/Jewish state, with an elected legislature and minority rights for Jews. The majority report was approved by the UN General Assembly on November 29, 1947 by a 33-13 vote, after intensive lobbying by the Zionists. The partition plan established a Jewish state consisting of fifty-six percent of Palestine, and an Arab state with forty-three percent of the area. The population at that time was sixty percent Arab and forty percent Jewish. Due to its special associations for Jews, Muslims, and Christians, Jerusalem would become an international city administered by the UN.

The Jews accepted the partition plan and made plans to take over their state after the withdrawal of British forces. The Arabs,

now backed by the newly independent Arab states, rejected the plan. Conflict between two communities turned to civil war as the deadline approached for the end of the mandate. On May 14, 1948 the last British soldier left Palestine. Zionist leaders declared the independence of the State of Israel, which was immediately recognized by the United States and the Soviet Union, even as the armies of five Arab states were converging on the new nation to destroy it.

INDEPENDENT ISRAEL

Long before the establishment of Israel, the nation's first prime minister, David Ben-Gurion, had come to Palestine as a youth. After a clash between Arab nomads and Jews from the kibbutz where he lived had injured several people, Ben-Gurion wrote prophetically, "It was then I realized . . . that sooner or later Jews and Arabs would fight over this land, a tragedy since intelligence and good will could have avoided all bloodshed."[9] In the four decades of independence, Ben-Gurion's prophecy has been borne out in five Arab/Israeli wars. In between those wars, conflict between Israel

David Ben-Gurion, pictured here at the head of the table, at an early Israeli Cabinet meeting. Also shown (in front, on the right) is Golda Meir, a future prime minister of Israel.

and the Palestinians has gone on more or less constantly like a running sore.

Approximately a million Palestinians fled Israel during the "War for Independence." After the 1967 Six-Day War, an additional 380,000 Palestinians became refugees in Jordan. Israeli occupation of the West Bank brought a million Palestinians under military control.

The unifying factor among all Palestinians is the same as that which had united the dispersed Jews for twenty centuries: the recovery of the sacred homeland. Abu Iyad, a top Palestine Liberation Organization leader, once said, ". . .our dream . . . (is) the reunification of Palestine in a secular and democratic state shared by Jews, Christians and Muslims rooted in this common land . . . There is no doubting the irrepressible will of the Palestinian people to pursue their struggle . . . and one day, we will have a country."[10]

The land vacated by the Palestinians has been transformed in the four decades of Israeli development. Those Israelis actually born in Palestine—now in their third generation—call themselves Sabras, after the prickly-pear cactus of the Negev. The work of Sabras and of a generation of immigrants has created a highly urbanized society, sophisticated industries, and a productive agriculture in Israel. Much of the success of Israel's development has resulted from large contributions from Jews abroad, from US aid, from reparations from West Germany for Nazi war crimes against Jews, and from bond issues. Yet the efforts of Israelis themselves cannot be underestimated. David Ben-Gurion once wrote, "Pioneering is the lifeblood of our people . . . We had to create a new life consonant with our oldest traditions as a people. This was our struggle."[11]

ISRAELI POLITICS: DEMOCRACY BY COALITION

Israel is unique among Middle Eastern states in having been a multiparty democracy from its beginning. The country has no written constitution, but it has a number of broad laws having constitutional effect. These include the Law of Return (1950), which states that any Jew in the world has the right to emigrate to Israel and be granted full citizenship. Other fundamental laws define and describe rights for women, national election procedures, voting qualifications, national military service, and so on.

The Knesset is the hub of the Israeli political system. Its 120 members are elected for 4-year terms under a system of propor-

The outcome of the 1984 Israeli elections presented a difficult problem. The Labor Party was returned to power but failed to win a majority due to the showing of the Likud Party. A compromise was reached: Prime Minister Shimon Peres, the head of the Labor Party, took power in September 1985, and Yitzhak Shamir (pictured above), the head of the Likud Party, is to become prime minister in October 1986.

tional representation from party lists. The party with the most votes in each election chooses a prime minister and Cabinet to run the government. (The office of president is purely ceremonial.) However, the Israeli Cabinet is responsible to the Knesset for all policies. As is the case with the British political system, the prime minister can be called to account at any time by the Knesset and forced to resign by a vote of no-confidence.

The Labor Party of David Ben-Gurion controlled the government for the first three decades of independence. However, the party seldom had a clear majority in the Knesset. As a result, it was forced to join in coalitions with various small parties. Israeli political parties are numerous. Many of them have merged with other parties over the years or have broken away to form separate parties. The Labor Party itself is a merger of three Socialist labor organizations. The two oldest parties are Agudath Israel World Organization (founded in 1912), which is concerned with issues facing Jews outside of Israel as well as within, and the Israeli Communist Party (Rakah, founded in 1919), one of three with Jewish/Arab membership.

The Labor Party's control of Israeli politics began to weaken seriously after the October 1973 War. Public confidence was shaken by the initial Israeli defeat, heavy casualties, and evidence of Israel's unpreparedness. Austerity measures imposed to deal with inflation increased Labor's unpopularity. In the 1977 elections, the opposition, Likud Bloc, won more seats than Labor but fell short of a majority in the Knesset. The new prime minister, Menachem Begin, was forced to make concessions to smaller parties in order to form a governing coalition.

Begin and his party won reelection in 1981, aided by the national euphoria over the peace treaty with Egypt. But the coalition began to unravel swiftly thereafter. The Israeli invasion of Lebanon put the finishing touches on the unraveling process. It seeemed to many Israelis that for the first time in its existence, the state had violated its own precept that wars should be defensive and waged only to protect Israeli land. As the invasion proceeded and the extent of destruction inflicted on Lebanese civilians became clear, the nation was polarized. Soldiers refused to serve at the front; high-ranking officers resigned their commissions. The cost of the war brought the country closer to economic collapse. In September 1983 Begin, already depressed by the death of his wife and the Lebanese involvement, resigned and retired to private life.[12]

THE 1984 ELECTIONS

Elections were held in July 1984, a year ahead of schedule due to the economic crisis and disagreement over the Lebanese invasion. The Labor Party returned to power, but again failed to win a majority. The two major parties, Labor and Likud, then worked feverishly to form a coalition which would provide a majority in the Knesset. After lengthy negotiations, Labor and Likud reached agreement on the first "government of national unity" in Israel's history. The unusual arrangement provides for alternating two-year terms as prime minister for each party leader. Prime Minister Shimon Peres took office in September 1985, to be succeeded by Yitzhak Shamir, the Likud leader, in October 1986. With a combined majority in the Knesset, it seemed possible for Israel's new political leaders to lead the country out of chaos.

Thus far, however, party unity is more apparent than real. The exposure of a Jewish underground terrorist organization in the West Bank, many of whose members are responsible citizens, underscores the depth of feeling among Israelis regarding continued Israeli rights to this ancestral territory. The coalition government was bitterly criticized after a number of underground members were given life sentences by the court in mid-1985.

Another example of the growth of extremism in Israeli national life was the election to the Knesset of Rabbi Meir Kahane, a Brooklyn, New York-born rabbi who emigrated to Israel some years ago. Kahane, a fiery anti-Arab orator, had founded the Jewish Defense League, a US organization which advocates violent action against Arabs and Arab organizations and has been implicated in a number of bomb attacks on offices of these organizations and on leaders of the American-Arab Anti-Discrimination Committee. In Israel, Kahane organized Kach, a political party which advocates expulsion of all Arabs from the country. After his election to the Knesset—which gave him parliamentary immunity—Kahane began visiting Arab villages, organizing anti-Arab demonstrations, and warning the villagers by loudspeaker to leave Israel or else risk physical harm.

PROSPECTS

The comparison is sometimes made be-

tween the struggling state of Israel in the twentieth century and the Christian Crusader kingdom of medieval Palestine, which lasted for less than a century (AD 1099-1187) before it was overrun by Muslim armies. Palestinian and other Arab leaders who counsel patience rather than violence in dealing with Israel believe at heart that time is on their side, that eventually Allah will lead the faithful to victory and the Israeli state will disappear like its predecessor. Within Israel, the population is divided roughly between those who advocate permanent vigilance, massive retaliation for each incident of violence, and powerful defenses to ensure that the state will survive, and those who are prepared in effect to trade land for peace. Prime Minister Peres has been walking a tightrope between these two opposing viewpoints since he took office, and he can be pardoned for looking over his shoulder at the spectre of time running out as he struggles to unite the Israeli population behind him in serious peace efforts before his hard-line successor takes over.

Peres's leadership has been strengthened by the withdrawal of Israeli forces from Le-

banon, and by divisions within the PLO regarding appropriate responses to peace overtures. An opinion poll taken in October 1985 indicated that sixty-eight percent of the Israeli population supported Peres's policies. This show of support enabled the prime minister to take some steps in 1985 that would have been inconceivable in previous years. More than a thousand Palestinian prisoners, including PLO members, were released from Israeli jails in a swap for three Israelis held by the Arabs. In a speech to the UN, Peres proposed an international conference followed by direct negotiations between Israeli, Jordanian, and Palestinian representatives (including the PLO, which he argued should participate since it was the legitimate representative of the Palestinian people). The proposal was strongly endorsed by the Knesset, which also acted to reduce extremism by passage of a law which bars any political party advocating racism from taking part in national elections. The government also released a suggested plan whereby Israel and Jordan would hold co-dominion over the West Bank for a transitional period to help prepare the population for either federation

Shimon Peres (pictured on the right), head of the Israeli Labor Party, is greeted by UN Secretary-General Javier Perez de Cuellar in 1984.

| Zionist move-
ment organized
by Theodor Herzl
1896 | Balfour
Declaration
1917 | British mandate
over Palestine
1922-1948 | UN partition plan
accepted by Jew-
ish community;
following British
withdrawal, State
of Israel
proclaimed
1947-1948 | Armistices
signed with cer-
tain Arab states
through US
mediation
1949 |

with Jordan or statehood. The initiatives were bold, but time was short. Whether or not Arab disunity could be corrected sufficiently for an effective Arab coalition to emerge capable of responding to them was not clear. But for the moment, those who would trade land for peace seemed to have the upper hand.

THE ECONOMY

In terms of national income and economic and industrial development, Israel is ahead of a number of Middle Eastern states that have greater natural resources. Annual per capita income was $4,041 in 1980 as compared to that of Egypt ($1,177) and Iraq ($2,783) for the same year. Agriculture, although highly developed due to sophisticated technology and the efficient communal organization of the kibbutzim, accounts for only six percent of Gross Domestic Product and employs the same percentage of the labor force. Small industries provide the bulk of the national income. The most important industrial export is diamonds, accounting for twenty-five percent of exports. The aircraft industry is the largest single industrial enterprise, although the electronics, microprocessing, and computer industries are expanding rapidly.

Israel has thirty-four producing oil wells and produces a very small amount of natural gas—73.1 million cubic meters in 1982. This production meets only a fraction of domestic needs. After the 1967 War and the occupation of the Sinai Peninsula, Israel was able to exploit Sinai petroleum resources as well as the Alma oilfields in the Gulf of Suez. Twenty-five percent of domestic oil needs came from the Alma field. In accordance with the Egyptian-Israeli peace treaty, all of these fields were returned to Egypt, with the stipulation that Israel be able to purchase Sinai oil at less than OPEC prices set for Egyptian oil on the world market. Israel has also bought oil from Iran from time to time and from certain African oil-producing countries. But fuel imports are a huge drain on the economy. They reached $2 billion in 1983.

The internal strengths of the Israeli econ-

omy, which include self-sufficiency in food, are more than offset by the weaknesses caused by its international political position. The burden of the more or less permanent state of siege, over a forty-year period, has imposed an artificially high level of military expenditures, usually twenty-four percent of the national budget. Since 1982, military expenditures increased by $1 million a day due to the invasion of Lebanon. Inflation, fed by regular cost-of-living increases under government-labor contracts, was over one hundred percent annually between 1980 and 1984. It reached a plateau of eight hundred percent in 1985. The shekel, which replaced the pound in 1980 as a medium of exchange, was kept artificially high in order to curb inflation, resulting in a drop in export values. Interest on foreign loans, one of the main sources of Israel's prosperity as compared to that of its neighbors, reached $24 billion in 1984. Total foreign indebtedness in 1983 was $22.566 billion, the highest per capita debt ($6,200) in the world.

Israel has survived and prospered economically as a state due to the availability of foreign support. Awareness of this outside resource has kept the nation in an illusion of economic plenty. But just as Israel must one day come to political terms with its Arab neighbors, it must at some point stand on its own feet economically as a Middle Eastern state rather than a dependency of states outside the region. Efforts in this direction would be a healthy sign of a maturing nation.

However, maturity has been slow to develop. Prior to 1977, when the Likud came to power, the economy was managed by the state or by Histadrut, the many-tentacled labor confederation that functions as a union but also as employer and controlling voice in many industries and bargains with the government on equal terms for labor contracts. Likud Prime Minister Begin went all out, abolishing foreign exchange controls, the travel tax, and import licenses, and allowing the currency to float and Israelis to open foreign bank accounts. The result

Agriculture in Israel is highly developed due to sophisticated technology and the efficient communal organization of the kibbutzim.

Six-Day War; Is-
raeli occupation
of East Jerusa-
lem, Gaza Strip,
Sinai Peninsula
1967

Yom Kippur War
1973

Opposition lead-
er Menachem
Begin's Likud
bloc wins
election
1977

Peace treaty with
Egypt
1979

Israeli invasion of
Lebanon

1980s

Knesset elec-
tions result in
deadlock be-
tween Labor and
Likud; resolved
by coalition
government and
two-year alterna-
tion of prime
ministers

Withdrawal of Is-
raeli forces from
Lebanon

Jewish terrorists
sentenced by Is-
raeli court for at-
tacks on West
Bank Arabs

was rampant inflation, balance of payments deficits, and a huge increase in imports of luxury goods paid for in foreign currencies, a major factor in the decline in reserves. But there was no offsetting reduction in the welfare-state structure originally created to absorb immigrants, or in the huge Socialist bureaucracy which had two out of three Israelis working for the government. Government policy of linking wage increases to price rises generated an inflationary spiral that reached 374 percent by 1984. United States aid, because it was disbursed freely without demands that the Israeli government introduce needed structural economic reforms, encouraged Israelis to believe that no matter how profligate they were, Uncle Sam would always bail them out.

The Peres government took office amid warnings from US advisors as well as its own economists that the economy would soon collapse if reforms were not introduced immediately. Warned that even the US Congress might be less willing to consider aid increases without a clear commitment to austerity, the Israeli government introduced a draconian package of reforms in July 1984. It included wage and price freezes and an almost total ban on imports of nonessential goods. An immediate result was a drop of twenty-five percent in personal incomes. Another set of measures, in July 1985, reduced subsidies, raised taxes, devalued the Israeli shekel 18.8 percent,

eliminated cost-of-living increases in labor contracts, and pledged a 3-percent cut in government manpower by abolishing 10,000 jobs. Israelis are still coming to terms with this new world they must live in. The government's latest goal is a $2.2 billion reduction in the budget. As one official observed: "We must think again about certain sacred cows; we have to decide whether we will slaughter them or they will slaughter us."[13]

FOOTNOTES

1. Ashkenazi derived from Ashkenaz (Genesis 10:3) is the name given to Jews who lived in Europe, particularly Germany, and followed particular traditions of Judaism handed down from Biblical days. Sephardim (from Sepharah, Obadiah 1:20) refers to Jews originally from Spain who were expelled and emigrated to the Middle East—North Africa. R.J. Zwi Werblowsky and Geoffrey Wigoder, eds., *The Encyclopedia of the Jewish Religion* (New York: Holt Rinehart & Winston, 1965).

2. Dan V. Segre, *A Crisis of Identity: Israel and Zionism* (Oxford: Oxford University Press, 1980), p. 25.

3. The "Enlightenment" resulted from the French Revolution and its declaration of Liberty, Equality and Fraternity (Brotherhood), meaning that all people are created equal. "Under the new spirit of equality, ghetto walls crumbled." Abraham Shulman, *Coming Home to Zion* (Garden City, NY: Doubleday, 1979), p. 11.

4. Jews believe that those buried there will be the first to be resurrected when the Messiah comes through the "Gate of Compassion" on a white don-

key and proclaims The Day of Judgment. Chaim Bernant, *The Walled Garden* (New York: MacMillan, 1974), p. 249.

5. Segre, *op. cit.*, points out that Israel contains "the first community of Jews officially dissociated from the idea that Jews are a people distinguished from all others by their special relationship with God."

6. Quoted in Shulman, *op. cit.*, p. 14.

7. *The Middle East and North Africa 1984-1985*, 31st edition (London: Europa Publications, 1984), "Documents on Palestine," p. 58.

8. The letter qualifies this commitment by adding that "nothing shall be done which may prejudice the civil and religious rights of existing non-Jewish communities in Palestine . . . " John Kimche, *Palestine or Israel* (London: Secker and Warburg, 1973), Appendix I, p. 343.

9. David Ben-Gurion, *Memoirs* (Cleveland: World Publishing Company, 1970), p. 58.

10. Abu Iyad with Eric Rouleau, *My Home, My Land: A Narrative of the Palestinian Struggle*, transl. by Linda Butler Koseoglu (New York: New York Times Books, 1981), pp. 225-226.

11. Ben-Gurion, *op. cit.*, p. 57.

12. "You start hearing about . . . the war against terrorism, and you wonder: What are they talking about? The Shiites are fighting for their land the only way they know how and according to the norms prevailing there." Editorial in *Ha'aretz* ("The Land"), Israeli newspaper, March 14, 1985.

13. Thomas A. Friedman, *The New York Times*, November 30, 1985.

DEVELOPMENT

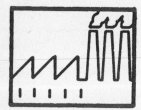

Industry is well developed in Israel. Industrial growth was vigorous in the 1970s, especially in sophisticated industries such as electronics, microchips, and computers. A Law for the Encouragement of Capital Investments provides many investment concessions, particularly for projects financed in foreign currency.

FREEDOM

Israel has no written constitution, but it has a number of organic laws which serve as a constitutional structure. The most important of these is the Law of Return, giving Jews throughout the world the right to emigrate to Israel and be assured of citizenship.

HEALTH/WELFARE

The pattern of Israeli democracy carries over into its court system. Although Israeli law is a blend of Ottoman, British, and pre-independence Palestine Jewish law and precedent, in practice Israeli judges show considerable independence of judgment.

ACHIEVEMENTS

Although it may now be living on borrowed time and has always survived on borrowed funds, the Israeli state itself represents a remarkable achievement, with a vigorous political system, distinctive culture, and productive economy.

Jordan (The Hashimite Kingdom of Jordan)

GEOGRAPHY

Area in Square Kilometers (Miles):
91,000 (35,000)
Capital (Population): Amman
(648,000) (1981)
Climate: predominantly dry

PEOPLE

Population
Total: 2,689,000
Annual Growth Rate: 3.8%
Rural/Urban Population Ratio: 40/60
Ethnic Makeup of Population: 98%
Arab; 1% Circassian; 1% Armenian

Health
Life Expectancy at Birth: 64 years
Infant Death Rate (Ratio): 65/1,000
Average Caloric Intake: 102% of FAO
minimum
Physicians Available (Ratio): 1/1,700

Religion(s)
90%-92% Sunni Muslim; 8%-10%
Christian

Education
Adult Literacy Rate: 71%

"ROSE-RED CITY HALF AS OLD AS TIME"

A sunset view of the rose-red glow of the ancient Jordanian city of Petra, capital of the Nabataeans twenty centuries ago, is a never-to-be-forgotten sight. Built at the crossroads of major caravan routes between Egypt, Arabia, and Mesopotamia, Petra was carved from the red sandstone cliffsides of a narrow valley into a city housing thirty thousand people. The best-preserved building is Pharaoh's Treasury, which was probably a second century AD tomb of a Nabataean king. Petra was the Nabataean capital for four centuries and continued to flourish for another three centuries after conquest by Rome in AD106, until its abandonment due to lack of water.

COMMUNICATION

Telephones: 53,000
Newspapers: 4 dailies (one in
English); 5 weeklies

TRANSPORTATION

Highways—Kilometers (Miles): 6,332
(3,935) total; 4,837 (3,006) paved
Railroads—Kilometers (Miles): 817
(508)
Commercial Airports: 25

GOVERNMENT

Type: constitutional monarchy
Independence Date: May 25, 1946
Head of State: King Hussein I
Political Parties: political-party
activity illegal since 1957
Suffrage: all citizens over 20

MILITARY

Number of Armed Forces: 75,300
*Military Expenditures (% of Central
Government Expenditures):* 25.3%
(1981)
Current Hostilities: none

ECONOMY

Currency ($ US Equivalent): 0.453
Jordanian dinar = $1 (March 1985)
Per Capita Income/GNP: $1,875/$4.9
billion (1982)
Inflation Rate: 9.6% (1970-1982)
Natural Resources: phosphate; potash
Agriculture: vegetables; fruits; olive
oil; wheat
Industry: phosphate mining;
petroleum refining; cement
production; light manufacturing

FOREIGN TRADE

Exports: $751 million (1982)
Imports: $3.2 billion (1982)

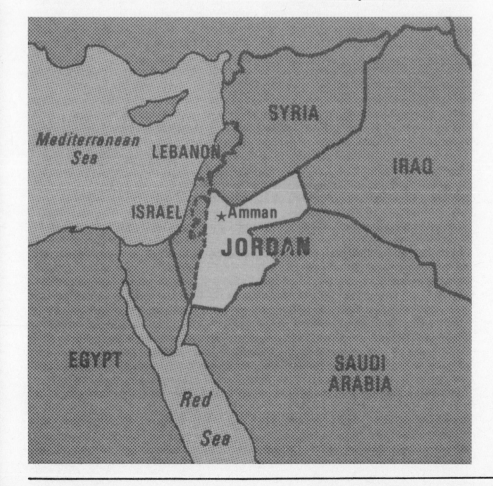

JORDAN

The Hashimite Kingdom of Jordan (formerly called Transjordan; usually abbreviated to Jordan) is one of the smaller Middle Eastern nations. The country consists of two regions, the East Bank (of the Jordan River) and the West Bank. The East Bank is the larger of the two and contains the bulk of the population. The West Bank has been occupied by Israel since 1967, but is technically and legally Jordanian territory. Between 1948 and 1967 Jordanian-occupied territory also included the old city of Jerusalem (East Jerusalem), which was annexed during the 1948 Arab-Israeli War.

Modern Jordan is an artificial nation, the result of historical forces and events that shaped the Middle East in the twentieth century. It had no prior history as a nation and was known simply as the land east of the Jordan River, a region of diverse peoples, some nomadic, others sedentary farmers and herders. Jordan's current neighbors are Iraq, Syria, Saudi Arabia, and Israel. Their joint borders were all established by the British after World War I, when the United Kingdom and France divided the territories of the defeated Ottoman Empire between them.

Jordan's borders with Iraq, Syria, and Saudi Arabia do not follow natural geographical features; the borders were established mainly to keep nomadic peoples from raiding. Over time, these borders have been accepted by the countries concerned. However, a serious border question for Jordan concerns the boundary with Israel. The Israeli occupation of the West Bank and East Jerusalem in June 1967 set up an artificial border between Jordan's two regions. This artificial border not only makes Jordan vulnerable to cross-border conflict, but it also underlines the difficulty the government of King Hussein faces in attempting to develop a successful and integrated Jordanian nation.

HISTORY

Until it became an independent nation in the twentieth century, the territory of modern Jordan was ruled by outside powers. Under the Ottoman Empire, it was part of the province of Syria. The Ottoman authorities in Syria occasionally sent military patrols across the Jordan River to "show the flag" and collect taxes, but otherwise they left the people of the area to manage their own affairs.[1]

This tranquil existence ended with World War I. The Ottomans were defeated, and their provinces were divided into protectorates called *mandates* set up by the League

This is the crowning monument to Rome's occupation of Petra, the Nabataean stronghold in the south Jordan mountains. The city, which had been rock-cut by its Nabataean founders into the tombs and monuments of a death cult, was resculpted by Rome into a Graeco-Roman architectural marvel.

of Nations and assigned to the United Kingdom and/or France to administer and prepare for eventual self-government. The British received a mandate over Palestine, and extended its territory to include Transjordan, the land east of the River Jordan. Due to their commitment to help Jews dispersed throughout the world to establish a national home in Palestine, the British decided to govern Transjordan as a separate mandate.

The terms of the mandate system required the protecting power (in this case, the United Kingdom) to appoint a native ruler. During the war the British had worked with Sharif Husayn, a prominent Arab leader in Mecca who held the honorary position of Protector of the Holy Shrines of Islam, to organize an Arab revolt against the Ottomans. Two of the Sharif's sons, Faisal and

Abdullah, led the revolt, and the British felt they owed them something. When Iraq was set up as a mandate, the British made Faisal its king. Transjordan was a territory of a nomadic population. Abdullah was invited to become its ruler, under British tutelage, but because he considered himself the head of a pastoral society rather than a state (in the modern constitutional sense of the term), he took the title of emir.

EMIR ABDULLAH

Through his father, Abdullah traced his lineage back to the Hashim family of Mecca, the clan to which the Prophet Muhammad belonged. This ancestry gave him a great deal of prestige in the Arab world, and particularly among the nomads of Transjordan, who had much respect for a person's genealogy. Abdullah used the connection assiduously to build a solid base of support among his kinspeople. When the country became fully independent in 1946 and Abdullah took the title of king, he named his new state the Hashimite Kingdom of Jordan.

Abdullah's new country had little to recommend it to outsiders except some fine Roman ruins and a great deal of empty land. It was a peaceful, quiet place, consisting entirely of what is today the East Bank of the Jordan River, with vaguely defined borders across the desert. The population was about 400,000, mostly rural peasants and nomads; the capital, Amman, was little more than a large village spread over some of those Roman ruins.

During the period of the mandate (1921-1946), Abdullah was advised by resident British officials. The British helped him draft a constitution in 1928, and Transjordan became independent in everything except financial policy and foreign relations. But Emir Abdullah and his advisers ran the country like a private club. In traditional Arab desert fashion, Abdullah held a public meeting outside his palace every Friday; anyone who wished could come and present a complaint or petition to the emir.

Abdullah did not trust political parties or institutions such as a parliament, although he agreed to issue a constitution as early as 1928 as a step toward eventual self-government. He also laid the basis for a regular army. A British army officer, John Bagot Glubb, was appointed in 1930 to train the Transjordanian Frontier Force to curb Bedouin raiding across the country's borders. Under Glubb's command, this frontier force eventually became the Arab Legion; during Emir Abdullah's last years, it played a vital role not only in defending the kingdom against the forces of the new state of Israel, but also in enlarging Jordanian territory by the capture of the West Bank and East Jerusalem.[2]

When the United Kingdom gave Jordan its independence in 1946, the country was not vastly different from the tranquil emirate of the 1920s. But events beyond its borders soon overwhelmed it, like the duststorm rolling in from the desert that sweeps everything before it. The conflict between the Arab and Jewish communities in neighboring Palestine had become so intense and unmanageable that the British decided to terminate their mandate. They turned the problem over to the United Nations, and in November 1947 the UN General Assembly voted to partition Palestine into separate Arab and Jewish states, with Jerusalem to be an international city under UN administration.

The partition plan was not accepted by the Palestine Arabs, and as British forces evacuated Palestine in 1947-1948, they prepared to fight the Jews for possession of all Palestine. The State of Israel was proclaimed in 1948. Armies of the neighboring Arab states, including Jordan, immediately invaded Palestine. But they were poorly armed and untrained. Only the Jordanian Arab Legion gave a good account of itself. The Legion's forces seized the West Bank, originally part of the territory allotted to a projected Palestinian Arab state by the UN. The Legion also occupied the old city of Jerusalem (East Jerusalem). Subsequently, Abdullah annexed both territories despite howls of protest from other Arab leaders, who accused him of land grabbing from his "Palestine brothers" and ambitions to rule the entire Arab world.

Jordan now became a vastly different state. Its population tripled with the addition of half a million West Bank Arabs and half a million Arab refugees from Israel. Abdullah still did not trust the democratic process. But he realized that he would have to take firm action to strengthen Jordan and help the dispossessed Palestinians who now found themselves reluctantly included in his kingdom. He approved a new constitution, one that provided for a bicameral legislature (similar to the US Congress), with an appointed Senate and an elected House of Representatives. He appointed prominent Palestinians to his Cabinet. A number of Palestinians were appointed to the Senate, and others were elected to the House of Representatives.

On July 20, 1951 King Abdullah was assassinated as he entered the Al Aqsa Mosque in East Jerusalem for Friday prayers. His grandson, Hussein, was at his side and narrowly escaped death. Abdullah's murderer, who was killed immediately by the royal guards, was a Palestinian. Many Palestinians felt that Abdullah had betrayed them by annexing the West Bank, and because he was thought to have carried on secret peace negotiations with the Israelis. King Abdullah was, more than anything, a reasonable leader, a pragmatist. In his *Memoirs* he wrote, "The paralysis of the

Amman, the capital of Jordan, is a city built on seven hills. Against the slope of one hill is this large Roman amphitheater (center), now restored to its original seating capacity of six thousand spectators.

Arabs lies in their present moral character. They are obsessed with tradition and concerned only with profit and the display of oratorical patriotism."[3]

Abdullah dealt with the Israelis because he despaired of Arab leadership. Ironically, Abdullah's proposal to the United Kingdom in 1938 for a unified Arab-Jewish Palestine linked with Jordan, if it had been accepted, would have avoided five wars and hundreds of thousands of casualties. Yet this same proposal forms the basis for discussion of the Arab-Israeli settlement today.[4]

KING HUSSEIN

Abdullah's son, Crown Prince Talal, succeeded to the throne. He suffered from mental illness (probably schizophrenia) and had spent most of his life in mental hospitals. When his condition worsened, his senior advisers convinced him to abdicate in favor of his eldest son, Hussein, and Hussein became king in 1953.

Hussein has ruled his country for more than thirty years, one of the longest reigns in the world. He has faced and overcome a number of crises during his long reign. The crises stemmed from Jordan's involvement in the larger Arab-Israeli conflict and its pivotal location in that conflict.

Hussein faced a serious threat to his rule shortly after he became king. Elections for the new National Assembly, in 1956, resulted in a majority for parties representing the West Bank.[5] A tug of war between king and Assembly followed. At one point, it was rumored that Hussein had been killed. Hussein, who was very much alive, jumped into a jeep and rode out to the main army base at Zerqa, outside Amman, where he showed himself to his troops to prove he was still in command. The army remained loyal to him, and the alleged coup never materialized. The Zerqa incident illustrates two things about Jordanian politics. One is Hussein's sense of timing, his ability to take bold actions designed to throw his opponents off guard. The second is the importance of army support to the monarchy. The great majority of soldiers in the Arab Legion are still drawn from Bedouins. An observer once said that Jordan is an army with a country attached to it. Through years of attempted assassinations, internal crises, and threats from outside, King Hussein's survival has depended on army loyalty and his own survival skills.

The June 1967 Six-Day War produced another crisis in Jordan, this one not entirely of its own making. Israeli forces occupied ten percent of Jordanian territory, including half of its best agricultural lands.

King Hussein I became the Jordanian head of state in 1953. His rule represents one of the longest reigns in the world.

The Jordanian army suffered six thousand casualties, most of them in a desperate struggle to hold the Old City of Jerusalem against Israeli attack. Nearly 300,000 more Palestinian refugees from the West Bank fled into Jordan. To make matters worse, guerrillas from the Palestine Liberation Organization, formerly based in the West Bank, made Jordan their new headquarters. The PLO considered Jordan as its base for the continued struggle against Israel. Its leaders talked openly of removing the monarchy and making Jordan an armed Palestinian state.

By 1970 Hussein and the PLO were headed toward open confrontation. The guerrillas had the sympathy of the population, and successes in one or two minor clashes with Israeli troops had made them arrogant. They swaggered through the streets of Amman, directed traffic at intersections, stopped pedestrians to examine their identity papers. Army officers complained to King Hussein that the PLO was really running the country. The king became convinced that unless he moved against the guerrillas his throne was in danger. He

declared martial law, and in September 1970 ordered the army to move against them.

The ensuing civil war lasted until July 1971, but in the PLO annals it is usually referred to as "Black September" because of its starting date and because it ended in disaster for the guerrillas. Their bases were dismantled, and most of the guerrillas were driven from Jordan. The majority went on to Lebanon, where they reorganized and in time became as powerful as they had been in Jordan, mainly because the Lebanese government was too weak to control them.

Since 1970 there have been no serious internal threats to Hussein's rule. Jordan shared in the general economic boom in the Arab world that developed as a result of the enormous price increases in oil after the 1973 Arab-Israeli War. Consequently, Hussein was able to turn his attention to the development of a more democratic political system. Like his grandfather, he did not entirely trust political parties or elected legislatures, and he was leery of the Palestinians' intentions toward him.[6] He was also convinced that Jordan should be the natural representative of the Palestinians, rather

Establishment of British mandate of Transjordan 1921	First constitution approved by British-sponsored Legislative Council 1928	Treaty of London; British give Jordan independence and Abdullah assumes title of king 1946	Arab Legion occupies Old City of Jerusalem and West Bank during first Arab-Israeli War 1948	Jordanian forces defeated by Israel in Six-Day War; Israelis occupy West Bank and Old Jerusalem 1967	"Black September"; Civil War between army and PLO guerrillas ends with expulsion of PLO from Jordan 1970-1971	Hussein suspends National Assembly 1974	Hussein reinstates National Assembly

1980s

First elections in 17 years, to fill vacant seats in Assembly; women allowed to vote	Jordan resumes full diplomatic relations with Egypt	Hussein reaches agreement with PLO chairman Arafat to pursue peace with Israel

than the PLO. But he realized that in order to represent them effectively and to build the kind of Jordanian state that he could safely hand over to his successors, he would need to develop popular support in addition to that of the army. Accordingly, Hussein set up a National Consultative Council in 1978, as what he called an interim step toward democracy. The Council had a majority of Palestinians (those living on the East Bank) as members.

The king took another interim step in March 1984 by dissolving the Council and ordering elections immediately for a new House of Representatives. The elections were the first in which women voted. The successful candidates included a number from the West Bank; when the House met for its first session, they were present—the Israelis had allowed them to attend.

It is too soon to tell how well democracy will work in Jordan. King Hussein retains the loyalty of the army, and his descent from the Prophet Muhammad gives him a special position in the eyes of his Muslim subjects. Peter Gubser notes that "the state under Hussein's leadership has created an environment in which people feel they may personally advance and feel personally secure."[7] Considering the obstacles that faced Hussein at the beginning of his rule, this is no small achievement.

THE ECONOMY

Jordan does not have oil, but it is rich in phosphates. Reserves are estimated at two billion tons, and new deposits are constantly being reported. Phosphate rock is the country's main export (6.4 million tons in 1984). Jordan, along with Morocco, Tunisia, and Senegal, is a leading world producer of phosphates.

Although oil has not yet been discovered in commercial quantities, Jordan does have deposits of 800 million tons of shale oil. Shale oil requires vastly greater expenditures and highly sophisticated techniques to produce, and the return per ton is far less in number of barrels than it is from a ton of crude petroleum. Consequently, Jordan is unlikely to become an oil-producing country for years to come.

Next to phosphates and potash (extracted from Jordan's share of the Dead Sea along the Jordanian-Israeli border), the mainstay of the economy is agriculture. The most productive agricultural area is the Jordan Valley. A series of dams and canals from the Jordan and Yarmuk Rivers have increased arable land in the valley by 264,000 acres and have made possible production of high-value vegetable crops for export to nearby countries.

However, politics have continued to interfere with the development of agriculture. The Israeli occupation of the West Bank deprived Jordan of eighty percent of its citrus-growing area and forty-five percent of its vegetable gardens. Israeli bombardments destroyed much of the irrigation system for the Yarmuk and Jordan Rivers in 1967, while Israeli noncooperation has blocked the development of a Tennessee Valley Authority type of project for the Jordan Valley, which would benefit both countries. In view of these political obstacles and

Jordan's own limited resources, the 10.4 percent annual growth rate achieved in recent years is an encouraging example of what can be accomplished by an effective ruler with the cooperation of his people.

FOOTNOTES

1. The Ottomans paid subsidies to nomadic tribes to guard the route of pilgrims headed south for Mecca. Peter Gubser, *Jordan: Crossroads of Middle Eastern Events* (Boulder, CO: Westview Press, 1983).
2. Years later Glubb wrote, "In its twenty-eight years of life it had never been contemplated that the Arab Legion would fight an independent war." Quoted in Harold D. Nelson, ed., *Jordan, A Country Study* (Washington, DC: American University, Foreign Area Studies, 1979), p. 201.
3. King Abdullah of Jordan, *My Memoirs Completed*, translated by Harold W. Glidden (London: Longman, 1951, 1978), Preface, XXVI.
4. The text of the proposal is in Abdullah's *Memoirs*, pp. 89-90.
5. The party with the largest number of seats, the National Socialists, openly opposed most of Hussein's policies. See Naseer Aruri, *Jordan: A Study in Political Development (1925-1965)* (The Hague, Holland: Martinus Nijhoff, 1967), p. 159.
6. The only political movement which is allowed to function in Jordan is the Muslim Brotherhood, a fundamentalist group which advocates a single Islamic Arab state under a new caliph. Hussein permits the Brotherhood to operate in Jordan because it has consistently supported him during his various crises. Gubser, *op. cit.*, p. 111.
7. *Ibid.*, p. 115.

DEVELOPMENT

Jordan's economy has shown remarkable growth, overcoming handicaps of lack of oil, loss of territory and resources in wars with Israel, and civil war with Palestinians. Industry's share of GDP rose from nil in 1950 to the present 20%. Amman has replaced Beirut, Lebanon as a Middle East banking center.

FREEDOM

The reconvening of the National Assembly after a 10-year lapse is an important step toward full constitutional government. But a free political system is still a long way off. In 1985 Minister of Information Leila Sharaf resigned publicly to protest lack of freedom of expression.

HEALTH/WELFARE

Jordan's educational system has shown remarkable results since independence. In addition to public schools there is an important private educational sector which includes Palestinian refuge schools run by the UN Relief and Word Administration (UNRWA), which has cared for the refugees for nearly 40 years.

ACHIEVEMENTS

The large number of educated and technically skilled Jordanians makes them valuable as an expatriate labor force in other Arab countries. Jordan has also been successful in encouraging young people to enter vocational and technical fields, which are shunned in many Arab countries as socially degrading.

Kuwait (State of Kuwait)

GEOGRAPHY

Area in Square Kilometers (Miles):
17,818 (6,880)
Capital (Population): Kuwait
(932,500)
Climate: intensely hot and dry in
summer

PEOPLE

Population
Total: 1,910,000
Annual Growth Rate: 6.2%
Rural/Urban Population Ratio: 9/91
Ethnic Makeup of Population: 39%
Kuwait; 39% other Arab; 9% Indian
or Pakistani; 4% Iranian; 9% other

Health
Life Expectancy at Birth: 70 years
Infant Death Rate (Ratio): 33.9/1,000
Average Caloric Intake: n/a
Physicians Available (Ratio): 1/570

Religion(s)
95% Muslim; 5% Christian, Hindu,
Parsi, and other

Education
Adult Literacy Rate: 71%

COMMUNICATION

Telephones: 214,800
Newspapers: 5 Arabic and 2 English
dailies; 418,000 combined circulation

DRINKING WATER FROM THE SEA

There is almost no fresh water in Kuwait, and less than one percent of the land is arable. Rainfall is rare, less than four inches annually. Aridity was manageable while the population was small, but the demands of growth have put a severe strain on the water supply.

For this reason the government has become a world leader in the desalination of sea water to provide fresh water. It pioneered in the 1950s with a sea-water distillation plant producing eighty thousand gallons of fresh water daily. Other plants followed, and today Kuwait receives all of its fresh water through the desalination process. Production was twenty billion gallons in 1978 and continues to rise. Kuwait's expertise in desalination is now sought by industrialized nations whose own water supplies are threatened by pollution and overuse.

TRANSPORTATION

Highways—Kilometers (Miles): 2,875
(1,787) total; 2,585 (1,606) bituminous
Railroads—Kilometers (Miles): none
Commercial Airports: 11

GOVERNMENT

Type: nominal constitutional
monarchy
Independence Date: June 19, 1961
Head of State: Emir Jabir al-Ahmad
Al Sabah
Political Parties: prohibited
Suffrage: native-born and naturalized
(20-year residency after naturalization
required) males aged 21 and over

MILITARY

Number of Armed Forces: 13,000
*Military Expenditures (% of Central
Government Expenditures):* 8.1%
Current Hostilities: stated as neutral
in Iran-Iraq War but has assisted Iraq
with loans and access through its
territory of Iraqi weapons purchases

ECONOMY

Currency ($ US Equivalent): 0.307
Kuwaiti dinar = $1 (March 1985)
Per Capita Income/GNP: $25,850
(1983)/$27.6 billion (1981)
Inflation Rate: 15.6% (1970-1982)
Natural Resources: petroleum; fish;
shrimp
Agriculture: virtually none
Industry: crude and refined oil;
fertilizer; chemicals; construction
materials

FOREIGN TRADE

Exports: $10.75 billion (1982)
Imports: $7.2 billion (1982)

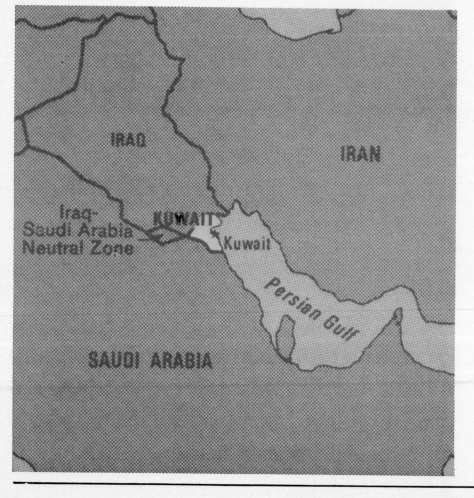

KUWAIT

Kuwait is small, yet it is one of the world's richest nations, with a per capita income of $25,850 (1983). Although revenues have fallen off in recent years due to the global oversupply of oil, reduced prices, and regional tension (particularly in the Iran-Iraq War), the standard of living for Kuwaitis remains one of the highest in the world. Health services, housing, education, and even phone calls are free for all citizens. Kuwait is also unique among Arabian Peninsula nations in having a democratically elected legislature, the National Assembly.

In terms of oil production and twentieth-century world politics, Kuwait has a very important strategic location. It is located at the north end of the Persian/Arabian Gulf, bordering Iraq and Saudi Arabia. Kuwaiti territory includes a Neutral Zone of desert land jointly administered with Saudi Arabia. The two countries share equally in the oil production of the Zone.

HISTORY

Kuwait was inhabited entirely by nomads until the early 1700s. Then a number of clans of the large Anaiza tribal confederation settled along the Gulf in the present area of Kuwait. They built a fort for protection from nomadic raids—*Kuwait* means "little fort" in Arabic—and elected a chief to represent them in dealings with the Ottoman Empire, the major power in the Middle East at that time. The ruling family of modern Kuwait, the al-Sabah, traces its power back to this period.

Kuwait prospered under the al-Sabahs. Its well-protected natural harbor became headquarters for a pearl-fishing fleet of eight hundred dhows (ships). The town (also called Kuwait) became a port of call for British ships bound for India.

In the late 1700s and early 1800s Kuwait was threatened by the Wahhabis, fundamentalist Muslims from central Arabia. Arab piracy also adversely affected Kuwait's prosperity. Kuwait's ruling shaykhs paid tribute to the Ottoman sultan in return for protection against the Wahhabis. However, the shaykhs began to fear that the Turks would occupy Kuwait, so they turned to the British. In 1899 Shaykh Mubarak, who reigned from 1896 to 1915, signed an agreement with the United Kingdom for protection. In return, he agreed to accept British political advisers and not to have dealings with other foreign governments. In this way, Kuwait became an autonomous (self-governing) state under British protection. Shaykh Mubarak's period of reign was important for another reason. During the 1890s Kuwait had given refuge to Ibn Saud, a leader from central Arabia whose family had been defeated by its rivals. Ibn Saud left Kuwait in 1902, traveled in secret to Riyadh, the rival's headquarters, and seized the city in a dawn surprise raid. Kuwait thus indirectly had a hand in the founding of its neighbor state, Saudi Arabia.

INDEPENDENCE

Kuwait continued its peaceful ways under the paternalistic rule of the al-Sabahs until the 1950s. Then oil production increased rapidly. The small pearl-fishing port became a booming modern city. In 1961 the United Kingdom and Kuwait jointly terminated the 1899 agreement, and Kuwait became fully independent under the al-Sabahs.

A threat to the country's independence developed almost immediately, as Iraq refused to recognize Kuwait's new status and claimed the territory on the grounds that it had once been part of the Iraqi Ottoman province of Basra. Iraq was also interested in controlling Kuwaiti oil resources. The ruling shaykh, now called emir, asked the United Kingdom for help, and British troops rushed back to Kuwait. Eventually, the Arab League agreed that several of its members would send troops to defend Kuwait—and, incidentally, to ensure that the country would not revert to its previous protectorate status. The Arab contingents were withdrawn in 1963. A revolution had overthrown the Iraqi government earlier in the year, and the new government recognized Kuwait's independence. Relations have been reasonably good since then, although Iraq still claims an island belonging to Kuwait at the mouth of the Shatt al-Arab estuary. Kuwait has strongly supported Iraq in its war with Iran by providing financial aid and keeping its port facilities open for Iraqi oil exports.

REPRESENTATIVE GOVERNMENT

The Kuwait Constitution provides for a National Assembly of fifty members, elected for four-year terms. Friction between the Assembly and the ruling family developed soon after independence. Assembly members criticized Shaykh Abdullah and his relatives, as well as the Cabinet, for corruption, press censorship, refusal to allow political parties, and insufficient attention to public services. Since all members of the ruling family were on the government payroll, there was some justification for the criticism.

Abdullah died in 1965, but his successor, Shaykh al-Sabah, accepted the criticism as valid. Elections were held in 1971 for a new Assembly, although the voting was hardly representative since only adult male Kuwaiti citizens have the franchise. Since there are no political parties in the country, candidates were elected by profession. The only group approximating a political bloc in the Assembly is the Palestinians, refugees from what is now Israel who fled their homeland after the establishment of the Israeli state in 1948. There are about 300,000 Palestinians in Kuwait, the majority of them better educated and politically more articulate than the Kuwaitis. The Palestinians and/or Palestinian sympathizers in the Assembly are the principal opposition to the ruling family.

Unfortunately for democracy in Kuwait, the new Assembly paid more attention to criticism of the government than to lawmaking. In 1976 it was suspended by Shaykh al-Sabah. He died the following year, but his successor, Shaykh Jabir, reaffirmed the ruling family's commitment to the democratic process. A new Assembly was formed in 1981, with a different membership. The majority were traditional patriarchs loyal to the rulers, along with technical experts in various fields, such as industry, agriculture, and engineering.

VULNERABILITY

Although the general economic progress and distribution of wealth militated against internal unrest in the past, Kuwait's location and its relatively open society make the country vulnerable to external subversion. In the early 1970s the rulers were the target of criticism and threats from other Arab states because they did not publicly support the Palestinian cause. Since then Kuwait has provided large-scale financial aid not only to the PLO, but also to Arab states such as Syria and Jordan which are directly involved in the struggle with Israel because of their common borders. However, in 1985 the Kuwait National Assembly cancelled its aid to Syria.

A new vulnerability surfaced with the Iranian Revolution of 1979 that overthrew the shah. Kuwait has a large Shia Muslim population, while its rulers are Sunni. Kuwait's support for Iraq and the development of closer links with Saudi Arabia (and indirectly the United States) angered Iran's new fundamentalist rulers. Kuwaiti oil installations were bombed by Iranian jets in 1981. In December 1983 truck bombings severely damaged the American and French embassies in Kuwait City. The underground organization Islamic Jihad claimed responsibility for the attacks, and threatened more if Kuwait did not stop its support to Iraq. Kuwaiti police arrested seventeen persons;

Establishment
of al-Sabah
family as rulers
of Kuwait
1756

Agreement with
the United
Kingdom mak-
ing Kuwait a
protectorate
1899

Independence,
followed by Ira-
qi claim and
British/Arab
League
intervention
1961-1963

Elections for
new National
Assembly
1971

Ruler suspends
Assembly on
grounds that it
is a handicap
to effective
government
1976

■■●■■■■■■■■■■■■■■■■■■■■■■■■■■■■■■■■■■■●■■■●■■■■■■■■■■■■■●■ **1980s**

Bombings of
public installa-
tions by Islamic
Jihad; 17 per-
sons arrested

they were later jailed for complicity in the bombings. Since Islamic Jihad claims links to Iran, the Kuwaiti government suspected an Iranian hand behind the violence, and deported six hundred Iranian workers.

These uncertainties led Kuwait to take a major role in forming the Gulf Cooperation Council (GCC) in 1981. The country also began to beef up its armed forces. But its 1984 request to the United States for Stinger antiaircraft missiles for an air-defense system was refused by the US Congress. Subsequently, Kuwait signed an agreement to purchase a Soviet air-defense system, complete with Soviet training advisers, possibly the first to be invited to the Arabian Peninsula. (The exception may be the People's Democratic Republic of Yemen, which is reported to have Soviet military advisers training its armed forces.)

THE PEOPLE:
A MINORITY AMONG MINORITIES

Kuwait has one of the highest birth rates in the world, about six percent annually in recent years. In addition, the rate of immigration is very high, with the result that there are more non-Kuwaitis than Kuwaitis in the population. About twenty-five percent Kuwaitis are Shia Muslims, originally from Iran. Much of the unrest in recent years can be traced to this group or to the Palestinians, most of whom are sympathetic to the Palestine Arab cause. The native Kuwaitis are nearly all descendants of the original Anaiza confederation. Although they are a minority in their own land, they enjoy more privileges than many of the

"new Kuwaitis," such as the right to vote and hold civil-service jobs.

These privileges are a sore point with less fortunate citizens as well as with the masses who migrated to Kuwait in search of work and other opportunities. Yet the continued existence of the National Assembly indicates a positive governmental attitude toward the people. One Kuwaiti official stated that the National Assembly was a good thing for Kuwait "because it acts as a watchdog, and a democracy with one leg is better than none."[1]

Kuwaiti democracy is far from perfect. A 1981 law limits citizenship to Muslims, and a 1982 proposal to give women the right to vote was rejected on the grounds of custom and tradition, although the Constitution affirms the equality of all before the law. To balance these actions, the Assembly rejected, in 1982, a press-censorship law issued as a decree by the ruler which would have established an entirely government-controlled press. In the authoritarian world of the Middle East, the ebb and flow of Kuwaiti democracy is a beacon of light.

THE ECONOMY

Kuwait's only abundant resource is petroleum. Less than 0.1 percent of the land can be cultivated, and there is almost no fresh water. Drinking water comes from sea water converted to fresh by huge desalination plants.

Yet Kuwait's oil production and reserves are such that the country should be able to maintain a high level of material prosperity for years to come. Oil reserves are 67

billion barrels, which should last 200 years at current production rates. The country not only produces but also refines petroleum for export. In the 1980s the Kuwait Petroleum Company, which has a monopoly over Kuwaiti oil production and sale, got into the retail business, purchasing gas-station chains in Italy and other European countries.

Kuwait also has reserves of natural gas, but these are all located in the oilfields. For this reason, cutbacks in oil production also affect the natural gas output. Development of other by-products of the oil industry, such as petrochemicals and fertilizers, has been curtailed in the 1980s because of the drop in oil production.

Kuwait's overall economy is healthy, with consistent foreign-trade surpluses. The government has also invested in a variety of foreign projects. Yet the long-term prospects are for a somewhat reduced standard of living. In 1983, for the first time, Kuwaiti children had to pay for their school meals and uniforms.

FOOTNOTES

1. Colin Legum, *et al.*, eds., *Middle East Contemporary Survey*, Vol. 6, 1981-82 (New York: Holmes & Meier, 1984), p. 500.

DEVELOPMENT

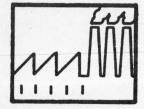

The Kuwaiti government is active in using its wealth for the benefit of less fortunate Third World nations. In 1961 it set up the Kuwait Fund for Arab Economic Development (KFAED), which makes loans to Arab, African, and Asian governments, mainly for power, transporation, and agricultural projects.

FREEDOM

Freedom of speech is guaranteed by the Constitution. There is a relatively free press in both Arabic and English. But freedom is highly restricted for non-Kuwaiti nationals, who may not vote or hold civil-service jobs.

HEALTH/WELFARE

Kuwait has one of the most comprehensive health care and educational systems in the world, all of it free to residents. Education is compulsory to age 14, but most students go on to complete high school and many go on to university. With population growing more than 6% annually, housing is another priority.

ACHIEVEMENTS

The University of Kuwait, with a student body of 17,000, serves the country as well as the larger Arab world with a distinguished faculty and ultramodern facilities, notably in medicine. Kuwait also sends a large number of students abroad for training in technical fields not yet offered at the university.

Lebanon (Republic of Lebanon)

GEOGRAPHY

Area in Square Kilometers (Miles): 10,452 (4,015)
Capital (Population): Beirut (1.1 million)
Climate: Mediterranean (hot, humid summers; cool, damp winters)

PEOPLE

Population
Total: 2,601,000
Annual Growth Rate: 0.1%
Rural/Urban Population Ratio: 23/77
Ethnic Makeup of Population: 93% Arab; 6% Armenian; 1% other

Health
Life Expectancy at Birth: 65 years
Infant Death Rate (Ratio): 39/1,000
Average Caloric Intake: 99% of FAO minimum
Physicians Available (Ratio): 1/540

Religion(s)
55% Christian (Maronite, Greek Orthodox and Catholic, Roman Catholic, and Protestant); 44% Muslim (Sunni and Shia) and Druze; 1% other

Education
Adult Literacy Rate: 75%

AN ANCIENT FORM OF LEADERSHIP

Nationalism in Lebanon is equated with the spirit or ethos of the particular social and/or religious group to which the individual Lebanese gives his or her loyalty. Within the group, loyalty is given to its leader. Leadership tends to be vested in certain families for generations; the leaders of these families, called *zaims* (literally "bosses"), exercise power through their network of contacts and their private militias. This arrangement has lasted up to the present, making Lebanon almost ungovernable in terms of concrete action and consensus politics. But it allows for a fluid system which might work if it were not for continual outside intervention.

COMMUNICATION

Telephones: 150,400
Newspapers: 37 dailies; 30 in Arabic

TRANSPORTATION

Highways—Kilometers (Miles): 7,370 (4,580) total; 6,270 (3,896) paved
Railroads—Kilometers (Miles): 378 (235)
Commercial Airports: 8

GOVERNMENT

Type: parliamentary republic
Independence Date: 1943
Head of State: President Amin Gemayel
Political Parties: numerous political parties exist, most with well-armed militias
Suffrage: compulsory for males over 21; authorized for women over 21 with elementary-school education

MILITARY

Number of Armed Forces: 20,200
Military Expenditures (% of Central Government Expenditures): 26%
Current Hostilities: Civil War between Christians and Muslims and Christian-Muslim factions; continues to be occupied by Syrian troops; Israel makes raids into territory against PLO faction

ECONOMY

Currency ($ US Equivalent): 18.75 Lebanese pounds = $1 (March 1985)
Per Capita Income/GNP: $1,150/$3 billion (1983)
Inflation Rate: 15% (1983)
Natural Resources: limestone
Agriculture: citrus fruit; wheat; corn; barley; potatoes; tobacco; olives; onions
Industry: food processing; cement; oil refining; light industry; textiles; chemicals

FOREIGN TRADE

Exports: $455.4 million (1983)
Imports: $2.8 billion (1983)

LEBANON

The Republic of Lebanon is located at the eastern end of the Mediterranean Sea. The coastal plain, which contains the capital, Beirut, and all other important cities, is narrow, rising just a few miles east of Beirut to a rugged mountain range, Mount Lebanon (ten thousand feet in elevation at its highest point). Beyond Mount Lebanon is the Biqa', a broad fertile villey which is the country's main wheat-growing region. At the eastern edge of the Biqa' the land rises again abruptly to the snow-capped Anti-Lebanon Range, nine thousand feet in elevation. This range separates Lebanon from Syria.

Lebanon's location has always been important strategically as well as commercially. Many invaders passed through it over the centuries on their conquests—Egyptians, Assyrians, Persians, Crusaders, Arabs, and Turks. However, these invaders were seldom able to control Mount Lebanon. For this reason the mountain served as a refuge for ethnic and religious minorities, and it became in time the nucleus of the modern Lebanese state.

Lebanon's commercial importance in history stemmed from the fact that its seaports were a natural outlet for goods from Syria, Jordan, and other inland areas. The port of Beirut, in normal times, is one of the busiest in the world.

Lebanon is not yet a unified nation in the same sense as the American, British, or Japanese nations. Each religious sect, each ethnic group, and sometimes even families within a sect or group distrust and at times mortally hate the others. Abdo Baaklini, a Lebanese political scientist, describes the system as one of a feudal hierarchy with fluctuating political influence, as "powerful families asserted themselves to acquire power and prominence."[1]

HISTORY

In ancient times Lebanon was known as Phoenicia. The Phoenicians were great traders who traveled throughout the Mediterranean and probably out into the Atlantic Ocean as far north as Cornwall in England in search of the tin, copper, and iron ore valued for many uses in the ancient world. Phoenician merchants established trading posts, some of which eventually grew into great cities.

In Phoenicia itself, no central government was ever established. Phoenician towns like Byblos, Tyre, Sidon, and Tripoli were independent states, often in conflict or rivalry over trade with one another. This city-state rivalry has always been a feature of Lebanese life, and is another reason for the lack of a national Lebanese sense of unity.

Lebanon began to develop a definite identity much later, in the seventh century AD, when a Christian group, the Maronites, took refuge in Mount Lebanon after they were threatened with persecution by the government of the East Roman or Byzantine Empire because of theological disagreements over the nature of Christ. The Muslim Arabs brought Islam to coastal Lebanon at about the same time, but they were unable to dislodge or convert the Maronites. Mount Lebanon's sanctuary tradition attracted other minority groups, Muslim as well as Christian. Shia Muslim communities moved there in the ninth and tenth centuries to escape persecution from Sunni Muslims, the Islamic majority. In the eleventh century the Druze, an offshoot of Islam, who followed the teachings of an Egyptian mystic and also faced persecution from Sunni Muslims, established themselves in the southern part of Mount Lebanon. These communities were originally quite separate but in the modern period of Lebanese history have tended to overlap, a fact, as David Gordon says, "that makes both for unity and in troubled times for a dangerous struggle for turf."[2]

Lebanon acquired a distinct political identity in the sixteenth and seventeenth centuries under certain powerful families. The Ottoman Turks conquered it, along with the rest of the Middle East, but were content to leave local government in the hands of these families in return for tribute. The most prominent of these were the Ma'an family, who were Druze. Their greatest leader, Fakhr al-Din (1586-1635), eatablished an independent principality including all of present-day Lebanon, Israel, and part of Syria. It was during al-Din's rule that French religious orders were allowed to establish missions in the country, which facilitated European intervention in Lebanon later on.

The Ma'ans were succeeded by the Shihabs, who were Maronites. Their descendants continue to hold important positions in the country, underscoring the durability of the extended-family system which still dominates Lebanese politics. They also allied the Maronite Church with the Catholic Church in Rome, an action that had great consequences in the twentieth century, when the Maronites came to view Lebanon as "a Christian island in a Muslim sea," preserving its unique Lebanese identity only through Western support.

European countries began to intervene directly in Lebanon in the nineteenth century, due to conflict between the Maronite and Druze communities. In 1860 French troops intervened in the Druze/Maronite conflict, on the side of their fellow Roman Catholics. The European powers forced the Ottoman sultan to establish Mount Lebanon as a self-governing province headed by a Christian governor. The province did not include Beirut. Although many Lebanese emigrated during this period because Mount Lebanon was small, rather poor, and provided few job opportunities, those who stayed (particularly the Maronites) prospered. Self-government under their own leader enabled them to develop a system of small, individually owned farms and to break their former dependence on absentee landowners. A popular saying among Lebanese at the time was, "Happy is he who has a shed for one goat in Mount Lebanon."[3]

The French Mandate

After the defeat of Ottoman Turkey in World War I, Lebanon became a French mandate. The French had originally intended the country to be included in their mandate over Syria, but in 1920, due to pressure from Maronite leaders, they separated the two mandates. "New" Lebanon was much larger than the old Maronite-Druze territory up on Mount Lebanon. The new "Greater Lebanon" included the coast; in short, the area of the current Lebanese state. The Maronites found themselves linked not only with the Druze but also with both Sunni and Shia Muslims. The Maronites already distrusted the Druze, out of bitter experience. Their distrust of Muslims was caused by two factors: fear of a Muslim majority, and fear that Muslims, being mostly Arabs, would work to incorporate Lebanon into Syria after independence.

France gave Lebanon its independence in 1943, but French troops stayed on until 1946, when they were withdrawn due to British and American pressure on France. The French made some contributions to Lebanese development during the mandate, such as the nucleus of a modern army, development of ports, roads and airports, and an excellent educational system dominated by the Université de St. Joseph, training ground for many Lebanese leaders. The French language and culture served until recently as one of the few things unifying the various sects and providing them with a sense of national identity.

THE LEBANESE REPUBLIC

The major shortcoming of the mandate was the French failure to develop a broad-based political system with representatives from the major religious groups. The French very pointedly favored the Maronites. A constitution, originally issued in 1926, established a republican system under an elected president and a legislature. Members would be elected on the basis of six Christians to five Muslims. The president would be elected for a six-year term and could not succeed himself. (The one exception was Bishara Khuri [1943-1952], who served during and after the transition period to independence. The Constitution was amended to allow him to do so.) By private French-Maronite agreement, the custom was established whereby the Lebanese president would always be chosen from the Maronite community.

In the long term, perhaps more important to Lebanese politics than the Constitution is the National Pact. This was an oral agreement made in 1943 between Bishara al-Khuri, as head of the Maronite community, and Riad al-Sulh, his Sunni counterpart. The two leaders agreed that, first, Lebanese Christians would not enter into alliances with foreign (i.e., Christian) nations and Muslims would not attempt to merge Lebanon with the Muslim Arab world; and second, that the six-to-five formula for representation in the Assembly would apply to all public offices. The pact has never been put in writing, but in view of the delicate balance of sects in Lebanon, it has been considered by Lebanese leaders, particularly the Maronites, as the only alternative to anarchy.

Despite periodic political crises and frequent changes of government due to shifting alliances of leaders, Lebanon functioned quite well in its first two decades of independence. The large extended family, although an obstacle to broad nation building, served as an essential support base for its members, providing services that would otherwise have to have been drawn from government sources. These services included education, employment, bank loans, investment capital, and old-age security. Powerful families of different religious groups competed for power and influence, but also coexisted, having had "the long experience with each other and with the rules and practices that make coexistence possible."[4]

The freewheeling Lebanese economy was another important factor in Lebanon's relative stability. Per capita annual income rose from $235 in 1950 to $1,070 in 1974, putting Lebanon on a level with some of the oil-producing Arab states, although the country does not have oil. The private sector was largely responsible for national

After being expelled from Jordan in 1970, the Palestine Liberation Organization (PLO) moved their headquarters to Beirut. In 1982 they were forced out of Lebanon by the Israeli Army, with American assistance. Yasser Arafat, above, is the head and familiar symbol of the PLO.

prosperity. A real-estate boom developed, and many fortunes were made in land speculation and construction. Tourism was another important source of revenues; in 1974 alone, 1.5 million tourists visited Lebanon. Many banks and foreign business firms established their headquarters in Beirut because of its excellent communications with the outside world, its educated, multilingual labor force, and the absence of government restrictions.

THE 1975-1976 CIVIL WAR

The titles of books on Lebanon in recent years often contain adjectives such as "fractured," "fragmented," and "precarious." These adjectives provide a generally accurate description of the country's changed situation as a result of the Civil War of 1975-1976. The main destabilizing element, and the one which precipitated the conflict, was the presence and activities of the Palestinians. A majority of the Palestinians in Lebanon fled there after the 1948 Arab-Israeli War in Palestine and were housed in refugee camps managed by the United Nations Relief and Works Agency (UNRWA). The Lebanese government has never extended citizenship to them, and for all practical purposes they remain stateless refugees. But the Palestinians did not

present a threat to Lebanese internal stability until 1970. After the Palestine Liberation Organization (PLO) was expelled from Jordan, the organization made its headquarters in Beirut. This new militant Palestinian presence in Lebanon created a double set of problems for the Lebanese. Palestinian raids into Israel brought Israeli retaliation that caused more Lebanese than Palestinian casualties. Yet the Lebanese government could not control the Palestinians. To many Lebanese, especially the Maronites, their government seemed to be a prisoner in its own land.

In April 1975, a bus carrying Palestinians returning from a political rally was ambushed near Beirut by the Kata'ib, members of the Maronite Phalange Party. The incident triggered the year-long Lebanese Civil War of 1975-1976. The war officially ended with a peace agreement arranged by the Arab League.[5] But in the broad sense, the bus incident brought to a head conflicts derived from the opposing goals of various Lebanese power groups. The Palestinian goal was to use Lebanon as a springboard for the liberation of Palestine. The Maronites' goal was to drive the Palestinians out of Lebanon and preserve their privileged status. Sunni Muslim leaders sought to reshape the National Pact to allow for equal participation with the Christians in the political system. Shia leaders were determined to get a better break for the Shia community, generally the poorest and least represented in the Lebanese government.[6] The Druze, also interested in greater representation in the system and traditionally hostile to the Maronites, disliked and distrusted all of the other groups.

Like most civil wars, the Lebanese Civil War was fought by its own people. But Lebanon's location, its international importance as a trade, banking, and transit center, and the various factions' need for financial backing ensured outside involvement in the conflict. Syrian troops intervened, at the request of the Arab League, first to enforce the 1976 ceasefire and then to crush the Palestinians. The Israelis helped a Lebanese renegade officer to set up an "independent free Lebanon" adjoining the Israeli border. The complexity of the situation was described in graphic terms by a Christian religious leader:

> The battle is between the Palestinians and the Lebanese. No! It is between the Palestinians and the Christians. No! It is between Christians and Muslims. No! It is between Leftists and Rightists. No! It is between Is-

rael and the Palestinians on Lebanese soil. No! It is between international imperialism and Zionism on the one hand, and Lebanon and neighboring states on the other.[7]

THE ISRAELI INVASION

The immediate result of the Civil War was to divide Lebanon into separate territories, each one controlled by a different faction. The Lebanese government, for all practical purposes, could not control its own territory. Israeli forces, in an effort to protect northern Israeli settlements from constant shelling by the Palestinians, established control over southern Lebanon. The Lebanese-Israeli border, ironically, became a sort of "good fence" open to Lebanese civilians for medical treatment in Israeli hospitals.

In March 1978, PLO guerrillas landed on the Israeli coast near Haifa, hijacked a bus, and drove it toward Tel Aviv. The hijackers were overpowered in a shootout with Israeli troops, but thirty-five passengers were killed along with the guerrillas. Israeli forces invaded southern Lebanon in retaliation and occupied the region for two months, eventually withdrawing after the United Nations, in an effort to separate Palestinians from Israelis, set up a six-thousand-member Interim Force in Lebanon (UNIFIL), made up of units from various countries, in the south. But the Interim Force was not able to do much to control the Palestinians; most Lebanese and Israelis referred sarcastically to the Force as the "United Nothings."

The Lebanese factions themselves continued to tear the nation apart. Political assassinations of rival leaders were frequent. Many Lebanese settlements became ghost towns; they were fought over so much that their residents abandoned them. Some 300,000 Lebanese from the Israeli-occupied south fled to northern cities as refugees. In addition to the thousands of casualties, a psychological trauma settled over Lebanese youth, the "Kalashnikov generation" that knew little more than violence, crime, and the blind hatred of religious feuds. (The Kalashnikov, a Soviet-made submachine gun, became the standard toy of Lebanese children.)[8]

The Israeli invasion of Lebanon in June 1982 was intended as a final solution to the Palestinian problem. It didn't quite work out that way. The Israeli army surrounded Beirut and succeeded with American intervention in forcing the evacuation of PLO guerrillas from Lebanon. Some of the Lebanese factions were happy to see them

Lebanese President Amin Gemayel, addressing the UN General Assembly in 1985.

go, particularly the Maronites and the Shia community in the south. But they soon discovered that they had exchanged one foreign domination for another. The burden of war, as always, fell heaviest on the civilian population. A Beirut newspaper estimated almost fifty thousand civilian casualties in the first two months of the invasion. Also, the Lebanese discovered that they were not entirely free of the Palestinian presence. The largest number of PLO guerrillas either went to Syria and then returned secretly to Lebanon or retreated into the Biqa' valley to take up new positions under Syrian Army protection.

Israeli control over Beirut enabled the Christians to take savage revenge against the remaining Palestinians. In September 1983 Christian Phalange militiamen entered the refugee camps of Sabra and Shatila in West Beirut and massacred hundreds of people, mostly women and children. The massacre led to an official Israeli inquiry and censure of Israeli government and military leaders for indirect responsibility. But the Christian-dominated Lebanese government's own inquiry failed to fix responsibility on the Phalange.

PROSPECTS

Ten years after the supposed "ending" of the Lebanese Civil War, the battles between

sects and factions go on endlessly, with little likelihood that Lebanon can be put together after its great fall. The Israeli invasion brought a change in government, with the Phalange leader, Bashir Gemayel, elected to head a "government of national salvation." Unfortunately for Bashir, his ruthless career had enabled him to compile an impressive list of enemies. He was killed by a bomb explosion at Phalange headquarters before he could take office. Gemayel was succeeded by his older brother, Amin. The new president was persuaded by American negotiators to sign a troop withdrawal agreement with Israel. However, the agreement was not supported by leaders of the other Lebanese communities, and in March 1984 Gemayel unilaterally repudiated it. The Israelis then began working their way out of the "Lebanese quagmire" on their own, and in June 1985 the last Israeli units left Lebanon.

Behind them the Israelis left a country that had become almost ungovernable. Gemayel's effort to restructure the national army along nonsectarian lines came to nothing, since the army was not strong enough to disband the various militias. The growing power of the Shia Muslims, particularly the Shia organization Amal, presented a new challenge to the Christian leadership, while the return of the Palestinians brought bloody battles between Shia and PLO guerrillas. As the battles raged, ceasefire followed ceasefire, conference followed conference, without noticeable success.

Currently the warring factions are no closer to national unity than they were in 1976. The Israeli withdrawal left the Syrians as the major power brokers in Lebanon. In August 1985 the Syrians negotiated a pact with Muslim and Druze leaders and some Christian leaders personally hostile to Gamayel. It would establish a democratic and secular Lebanon, with equitable power-sharing arrangements between the various communities under a new constitution. This was as far as the Syrians could go without all-out intervention. Like the US Marines and Israelis before them, they were reluctant to move deeper into the Lebanese quagmire.

The establishment of Lebanon as a restored and viable nation depends upon both political and economic factors. The most important of these factors is the identification of all Lebanese as nationals first, and members of particular clans, sects, and families second. A second factor is the acceptance and absorption of the Palestinians into the population as full citizens. Two other essential factors are the sharing of political

Establishment of Mount Lebanon as sanctuary for religious communities **9th - 11th centuries AD**	Shihab and Ma'an emirs granted autonomy under overall Ottoman control **1700-1840**	First Civil War, between Maronites and Druze, ending in foreign military intervention **1860-1864**	French mandate **1920-1946**	Internal crisis and first US military intervention **1958**	Civil War, ended (temporarily) by Arab League-sponsored ceasefire and peacekeeping force of Syrian troops **1975-1976**	Israeli invasion and occupation of Beirut **1980s**

Election of Amin Gemayel as president to succeed his murdered brother Bashir; massacre of Palestinians in refugee camps by Christian militiamen	US arranges Lebanese-Israeli agreement for Israeli troop withdrawal; Lebanon unilaterally abrogates Israeli troop-withdrawal agreement	Leaders form government of "National Unity"; withdrawal of Israeli forces from Lebanon completed

power and improvement of the economic and political status of the poorer communities, particularly the traditionally disadvantaged Shia Muslims. The Syrian-sponsored pact of August 1985 offered a mechanism for dealing with these factors. Whether the Christian government of Amin Gemayel, challenged on all sides, could apply the wisdom, accommodation, and maturity needed at this critical juncture to meet its opponents' demands and still salvage something for Christian Lebanon remains to be proven.

THE ECONOMY

Since the Civil War the Lebanese economy has been going steadily downhill. The war and the resulting instability caused most banks and financial institutions to move out of Beirut to more secure locations, notably Jordan, Bahrain, and Kuwait. Aside from the cost in human lives, Israeli raids and the 1982 invasion severely damaged the economy. The cost of the invasion in terms of damages was estimated at $1.9 billion. Remittances from Lebanese emigrants abroad, normally 35 percent of national income, dropped 10 percent in 1984. Customs receipts for 1985 were $13 million, less than 10 percent of the amount budgeted, because militias controlled the Lebanese ports and diverted revenues for their own use. Per capita annual income dropped drastically by 1985. Other Arab states held off on their contributions to the Lebanese budget due to the political uncertainty. The Lebanese pound also plummeted in value.

The long, drawn-out civil conflict has badly affected Lebanese agriculture, the mainstay of the economy. Both the coastal strip and the Biqa' Valley are extremely fertile, and in normal times produce crop surpluses for export. Lebanese fruit, particularly apples (the most important cash crop) and grapes, are in great demand throughout the Arab world. But these crops are no longer exported in quantity. Israeli destruction of crops, the flight of most of the farm labor force, and the blockade by Israeli troops of truck traffic from rural areas into Beirut have had a devastating effect on production.

Lebanon produces no oil of its own, but before the Civil War and the Israeli invasion, the country derived important revenues from transit fees for oil shipments through pipelines across its territory. The periodic closing of these pipelines and damage to the country's two refineries has sharply reduced revenues since 1975. The well-developed manufacturing industry, particularly textiles, has been equally hard hit. The 1982 Israeli invasion resulted in the destruction of twenty-five major industrial establishments. Only half of the twelve hundred textile plants operating before 1975 remain in operation.

In its current condition, the Lebanese economy is vulnerable on several counts. It is vulnerable because Lebanon has not developed as yet a replacement for the financial and trade sectors that departed after the Civil War and are unlikely to return.

Losses of skilled manpower through emigration deprive the economy of its most important asset, effective management. But until the political system is restructured, the economy will continue to slide downhill.

FOOTNOTES

1. Abdo Baaklini, *Legislative and Political Development: Lebanon 1842-1972* (Durham, NC: Duke University Press, 1976), pp. 32-34.
2. David C. Gordon, *The Republic of Lebanon: Nation in Jeopardy* (Boulder, CO: Westview Press, 1983), p.4.
3. *Ibid.*, p. 19.
4. *Ibid.*, p. 25. See also Baaklini, *op. cit.*, pp. 200-202, for a description of the coexistence process as used by Sabri Hamadeh, for many years head of the Assembly.
5. Whether the Civil War ever really ended is open to question. A cartoon in a US newspaper in August 1982 shows a hooded skeleton on a TV screen captioned Lebanon saying, "And now we return to our regularly scheduled civil war." Gordon, *op. cit.*, p. 113.
6. Shia religious leader Imam Musa al-Sadr's political organization was named Harakat al-Mahrumin ("Movement of the Disinherited") when it was founded in 1969-1970. See Marius Deeb, *The Lebanese Civil War* (New York: Praeger, 1980), pp. 69-70.
7. Gordon, *op. cit.*, p. 110.
8. *Ibid.*, p. 125.

DEVELOPMENT

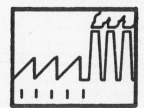

Lebanon's recovery from a decade of civil war and invasion hinges not only on the restoration of political stability but also on external financing. The Council for Development and Reconstruction (CDR), working with the World Bank, issued a 1983-1991 reconstruction plan which will require $17 billion, to come from both external and internal sources.

FREEDOM

Representation in the legislature is set at a ratio of 6 Christians to 5 Muslims. The Shia and Sunni Muslim communities now form a majority, but the Christian Maronites refuse to share power or permit a census. Either of these actions would cause them to lose their privileged status.

HEALTH/WELFARE

Lebanon is unique among Middle Eastern countries in that the majority of secondary schools and colleges and universities are private institutions. Free primary education was established in 1960. Lebanon has a high degree of literacy and most Lebanese are trilingual. Until recently, private institutions were largely exempt from intercommunal violence.

ACHIEVEMENTS

One of the few successful projects in the rebuilding of Lebanon is the UNICEF-sponsored reconstruction program in the south. It began in 1981 with small projects in various villages, such as the provision of a potable water supply, school construction, and health clinics. The funding of just under $2 million comes from other Arab countries.

Libya (Socialist People's Libyan Arab Jamahiriya)

GEOGRAPHY

Area in Square Kilometers (Miles):
1,758,610 (679,536)
Capital (Population): Tripoli
(1,223,000) (1980)
Climate: arid (93% of land is desert
or semidesert)

PEOPLE

Population
Total: 3,684,000
Annual Growth Rate: 5.2%
Rural/Urban Population Ratio: 42/58
Ethnic Makeup of Population: 97%
Berber and Arab; 3% southern
European and southern Asian

Health
Life Expectancy at Birth: 57 years
Infant Death Rate (Ratio): 95/1,000
Average Caloric Intake: 147% of FAO
minimum
Physicians Available (Ratio): 1/730

WATER FROM THE DESERT

Libya's major project in the 1980s is a great "man-made river" from the desert to the sea, a network of pipelines to transport water from vast underground reservoirs in the Sahara northward to densely populated coastal areas. The cost is estimated at $25 billion. The first phase, to be completed in 1985, involves construction of fabrication plants for the pipe and 930 miles of access roads. The project represents Libya's hope for the future, of achieving self-sufficiency in food production. As Qadhafi says, "There is no independence for those who secure their food from abroad."

Religion(s)
97% Sunni Muslim

Education
Adult Literacy Rate: 50%

COMMUNICATION

Telephones: 41,495 (1971)
Newspapers: 1 daily in Tripoli;
circulation of 40,000

TRANSPORTATION

Highways—Kilometers (Miles):
19,300 (11,993) total; 10,500 (6,525)
bituminous
Railroads—Kilometers (Miles): none
Commercial Airports: 116

GOVERNMENT

Type: centralized republic
Independence Date: December 24,
1951
Head of State: Colonel al-Muammar
Qadhafi (no official title; *de facto*
chief of state)*
Political Parties: none
Suffrage: universal adult

MILITARY

Number of Armed Forces: 70,500
*Military Expenditures (% of Central
Government Expenditures):* n/a
Current Hostilities: troops occupy
northern Chad, in opposition to
Chadian government; periodic fric-
tion with Egypt and Tunisia

ECONOMY

Currency ($ US Equivalent): 0.30
Libyan dinar = $1 (March 1985)
Per Capita Income/GNP:
$7,600/$26.5 billion (1983)
Inflation Rate: 16% (1970-1982)
Natural Resources: petroleum;
natural gas
Agriculture: wheat; barley; olives;
dates; citrus fruits; peanuts; livestock
Industry: crude petroleum; food
processing; textiles; handcrafts

FOREIGN TRADE

Exports: $12 billion (1983)
Imports: $9 billion (1983)

*Note: Other commonly used spellings of
Colonel Qadhafi's name include Qaddafi, Gaddafi, and Khadafy.

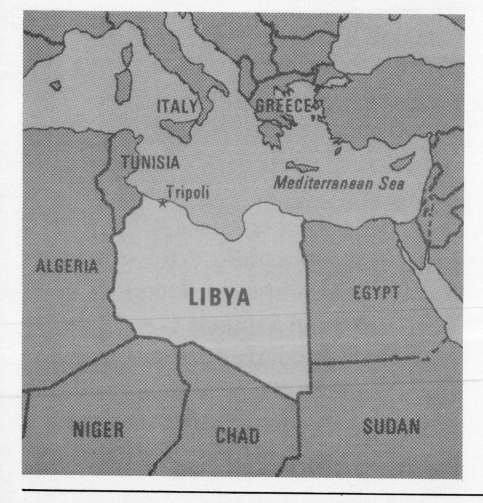

LIBYA

The Socialist People's Libyan Arab Jama-hiriya (Republic), commonly known as Libya, encompasses 679,536 square miles, the fourth largest of the Arab countries. It has a population of 3,684,000. In its fifteen-plus years of existence as a republic, it has played a role in regional and international affairs more appropriate to its size than to its population.

Libya consists of three geographical regions: Tripolitania, Cyrenaica, and the Fezzan. Most of the population lives in Tripolitania, where the capital and major port, Tripoli, is located. Cyrenaica, to the east along the Egyptian border, has a narrow coastline backed by a high plateau (2,400-feet elevation) called the Jabal al-Akhdar (Green Mountain). It contains Libya's other principal city, Benghazi. The two regions are separated by the Sirte, an extension of the Saharan Desert which reaches almost to the Mediterranean Sea. Most of Libya's oilfields are in the Sirte.

The Fezzan occupies the south and south-west part of the country. It is entirely desert except for a string of widely scattered oases. Libya's southern border is with Chad. A 120-mile-wide area called the Aouzou Strip, south of the border, has been occupied by Libyan troops since 1972, the result of Libyan support for one of the factions contesting for power in Chad. The Aouzou is said to have important uranium deposits.

HISTORY

Until modern times Libya did not have a separate identity, either national or territorial. It formed a part of some other territorial unit, and in most cases was controlled by outsiders. However, control was usually limited to the coastal areas. The Berbers of the interior were little affected by the passing of conquerors and the rise and fall of civilizations.

Libya's culture and social structure have been influenced more by the Islamic Arabs than by any other invaders. The Arabs brought Islam to Libya in the early seventh century. Arab groups settled in the region and intermarried with the Berber population to such an extent that the Libyans became one of the most thoroughly Arabized peoples in the Islamic world.

Coastal Libya, around Tripoli, was an outlying province of the Ottoman Empire for several centuries. Like its neighbors, Tunis and Algiers, Tripoli had a fleet of corsairs who made life dangerous for European merchant ships in the Mediterranean. When the United States became a Mediterranean trading nation, the corsairs of Tripoli in-cluded American ships among their targets. The *USS Philadelphia* was sent to Tripoli to "teach the corsairs a lesson" in 1804, but it got stuck on a sandbar and was captured. Navy Lieutenant Stephen Decatur led a commando raid into Tripoli harbor and blew up the ship, inspiring the words to what became the official US Marine hymn: "From the halls of Montezuma to the shores of Tripoli . . . "

The Sanusiya Movement

At various stages in Islam's long history, new groups or movements have appeared, committed to purifying or reforming Islamic society and taking it back to its original form of a simple community of believers led by just rulers. Several of these movements, such as the Wahhabis of Saudi Arabia, were important in the founding of modern Islamic states. The movement called the Sanusiya was formed in the nineteenth century. In later years it became an important factor in the formation of modern Libya.

The founder, called the Grand Sanusi, was a religious teacher from Algeria. He left Algeria after the French conquest and settled in northern Cyrenaica. The Grand Sanusi's teachings attracted many followers. He also attracted the attention of the Ottoman authorities, who distrusted his advocacy of a strong united Islamic world in which Ottomans and Arabs would be partners. To escape from the Ottomans, the Grand Sanusi's son and successor moved Sanusiya headquarters to Kufra, a remote oasis in the Sahara, in 1895.

The Sanusiya began as a peaceful movement interested only in bringing new converts to Islam and founding a network of *zawiyas* ("lodges") for contemplation and monastic life throughout the desert. But when European countries began to seize territories in North and West Africa, the Sanu-si became warrior-monks and fought the invaders.

Italy Conquers Libya

The Italian conquest of Libya began in 1911. The Italians needed colonies, not only for prestige but also for resettlement of poor and landless peasants in Italy's crowded southern provinces. The Italians expected an easy victory against a weak Ottoman garrison. Libya would become the "Fourth Shore" of a new Roman Empire from shore to shore along the Mediterranean.

But the Italians found Libya a tougher land to subdue than they had expected. Italian forces were pinned to Tripoli and a few other points on the coast by the Ottoman garrison and the fierce Sanusi warrior-monks.

The Italians were given a second chance after World War I. The Ottoman Empire had been defeated, and Libya was ripe for plucking. The new Italian government of swaggering dictator Benito Mussolini sent an army to occupy Tripolitania. When the Italians moved on Cyrenaica, the Grand Sanusi crossed the Egyptian boarder into exile under British protection. The Italians found Cyrenaica much more difficult to contol than Tripolitania. It is ideal guerrilla country, from the caves of Jebel Akhdar to the stony plains and dry hidden *wadis* (river beds) of the south. It took nine years (1923-1932) for Italy to overcome all of Libya, despite its vast superiority in troops and weapons. Sanusi guerrilla bands harried the Italians, cutting supply lines, ambushing patrols, and attacking convoys. Their leader, Shaykh Omar Mukhtar, became Libya's first national hero.

The Italians finally overcame the Sanusi by the use of methods which do not surprise us today but which seemed unbelievably brutal at the time. Cyrenaica was made into a huge concentration camp with a barbed-wire fence along the Egyptian border. Nomadic peoples were herded into these camps, guarded by soldiers to prevent them from aiding the Sanusi. Sanusi prisoners were pushed out of airplaines, wells were plugged to deny water to the people, and flocks were slaughtered. In 1931 Omar Mukhtar was captured, court martialled, and hanged in public. The resistance ended with his death.

The Italians did not have long to cultivate their fourth shore. During the 1930s they poured millions of lire into the colony. A paved highway from the Egyptian to the Tunisian border along the coast was complete in 1937; in World War II it became a handy invasion route for the British. A system of state-subsidized farms was set up for immigrant Italian peasants. Each was given free transportation, a house, seed, fertilizers, a mule, and a pair of shoes as inducements to come to Libya. By 1940 the Italian population had reached 110,000, and about 495,000 acres of land had been converted into productive farms, orchards, vineyards, and olive groves.[1]

Independent Libya

Libya was a major battleground during World War II as British, German, and Italian armies rolled back and forth across the desert. The British finally defeated the Germans and occupied northern Libya, while a French army occupied the Fezzan. The United States later built an important air base, Wheelus Field, near Tripoli. Thus the three major Allied powers all had an interest in Libya's future. But they could not agree on what to do with occupied Libya.

Italy wanted Libya back. France wished to keep the Fezzan as a buffer for its African colonies, while the United Kingdom preferred self-government for Cyrenaica, under the Grand Sanusi, who had become staunchly pro-British during his exile in Egypt. The Soviet Union favored a Soviet trusteeship over Libya, which would provide the Soviet Union with a convenient outlet in the Mediterranean. The United States waffled, but finally settled on independence, which would at least keep the Soviet tentacles from enveloping Libya.

Due to lack of agreement, the Libyan "problem" was referred to the United Nations General Assembly. Popular demonstrations of support for independence in Libya impressed a number of the newer UN members, and in 1951 the General Assembly approved a resolution for an independent Libyan state, a kingdom under the Grand Sanusi, Idris.

THE KINGDOM OF LIBYA

Libya has been governed under two political systems since independence: a constitutional monarchy (1951-1969), and a Socialist republic (1969-) that has no constitution because all power "belongs" to the people. Monarchy and republic have had almost equal time in power. But Libya's spectacular economic growth and aggressive foreign policy under the Socialist republic need to be understood in relation to the solid, if unspectacular, accomplishments of the regime that preceded it.

Libya at independence was an artificial union of the three provinces. The Libyan people had little sense of national identity or unity. Loyalty was to one's family, clan, village, and, in a general sense, to the higher authority represented by a tribal confederation. The only other loyalty linking Libyans was the Islamic religion. The tides of war and conquest that had washed over them for centuries had had little effect on their strong, traditional attachment to Islam.[2]

Political differences also divided the three provinces. Tripolitanians talked openly of abolishing the monarchy. Cyrenaica was the home and power base of King Idris; the king's principal supporters were the Sanusiya and certain important traditional families. The distances and poor communications between the provinces contributed to the impression that they should be separate countries. Leaders could not even agree on a choice between Tripoli and Benghazi for the capital. The king distrusted both cities as being corrupt and overly influenced by foreigners. He had his administrative capital at Baida, in the Jebel Akhdar.

The greatest problem facing Libya at independence was economic. Per capita income in 1951 was about $30 per annum; in 1960 it was about $100 per annum. Approximately five percent of the land was marginally usable for agriculture, and one percent could be cultivated on a permanent basis. Most economists considered Libya to be a hopeless case, almost totally dependent upon foreign aid for survival. It is interesting to note that the Italians were seemingly able to force more out of the soil, but one must remember that the Italian government poured a great deal of money into the country to develop the plantations, and credit must be given to the extremely hard-working Italian peasant farmer.

Despite its meager resources and lack of political experience, Libya was valuable to the United States and the United Kingdom in the 1950s and 1960s because of its strategic location. The US negotiated a long-term lease on Wheelus Field in 1954, as a vital link in the chain of US bases built around the southern perimeter of the Soviet Union due to the cold war. In return, US aid of $42 million sweetened the pot, and Wheelus became the single largest employer of Libyan labor. The British had two air bases and maintained a garrison in Tobruk.

After the 1969 Revolution, Libya strove to develop many aspects of the country. These local chiefs are meeting to plan community development.

Political development in the kingdom was minimal. King Idris knew little about parliamentary democracy, and he distrusted political parties. The 1951 Constitution provided for an elected legislature, but a dispute between the king and the Tripolitanian National Congress, one of several Tripolitanian parties, led to the outlawing of all political parties. Elections were held every four years, but only adult, property-owning males could vote (women were allowed the vote in 1963). The same legislators were reelected regularly. In the absence of political activity, the king was the glue that held Libya together.

THE 1969 REVOLUTION

At dawn on September 1, 1969, a group of young army officers abruptly carried out a military coup in Libya. King Idris, who had gone to Turkey for medical treatment, was deposed, and a Libyan Arab Republic proclaimed by the unknown officers. These officers, whose names were not known to the outside world until weeks after the coup, were led by Captain Muammar Muhammad al-Qadhafi. He went on Benghazi radio to announce to a startled Libyan population: "People of Libya . . . your armed forces have undertaken the overthrow of the reactionary and corrupt regime. . . . From now on Libya is a free, sovereign republic, ascending with God's help to exalted heights."[3]

Qadhafi's new regime made a sharp change in policy from that of its predecessor. Wheelus Field and the British bases were evacuated and returned to Libyan control. Libya took an active part in Arab affairs and supported Arab unity, to the extent of working to undermine other Arab leaders whom Qadhafi considered undemocratic or unfriendly to his regime.[4] However, none of his efforts to unite Libya with other Arab states have been successful. The most recent effort, a union with Morocco, signed by Qadhafi and King Hassan II in August 1984, maintains the separate identity and sovereignty of the two states, although the agreement does provide for a federation assembly and joint consultation in foreign policy.

QADHAFI'S SOCIAL REVOLUTION

Qadhafi's desert upbringing and Islamic education gave him a strong, puritanical moral code. In addition to closing foreign bases and expropriating Italian and Jewish properties, he moved forcefully against symbols of foreign influence. The Italian cathedral in Tripoli became a mosque, street signs were converted to Arabic, nightclubs

Muammar al-Qadhafi led a group of army officers in the military coup of 1969 that deposed King Idris. Since then Qadhafi has gained worldwide notoriety for his seeming sanction of terrorism.

were closed, and production and sale of alcohol were prohibited.

But Qadhafi's revoluion went far beyond changing names. In a three-volume work entitled *The Green Book*, he described his vision of the appropriate political system for Libya. Political parties would not be allowed, nor would constitutions, legislatures, even an organized court system. All of these institutions, according to Qadhafi, eventually become corrupt and unrepresentative. Instead, people's committees would run the government, business, industry, and even the universities. Libyan embassies abroad were renamed People's Bureaus and were run by junior officers. (The takeover of the London bureau in 1984 led to counter-demonstration by Libyan students and the killing of a British police officer by gunfire from inside the bureau. The Libyan bureau in Washington, DC was closed by the US Federal Bureau of Investigation (FBI) and the staff deported on charges of espionage and terrorism against Libyans in the US.) As noted earlier, the country was

renamed the Socialist People's Libyan Arab Jamahiriya. Titles of government officials were eliminated. Qadhafi became "Leader of the Revolution," and each government department was headed by the secretary of a particular people's committee.

Qadhafi then developed a so-called Third International Theory, based on the belief that neither capitalism nor communism could solve the world's problems. What was needed, he said, was a middle way which would harness the driving forces of human history—religion and nationalism—to interact with each other to revitalize humankind. Islam would be the source of that middle way, because "it provides for the realisation of justice and equity, it does not allow the rich to exploit the poor."[5]

THE ECONOMY

Modern Libya's economy is based almost entirely on oil exports. Concessions were granted in 1955 to various foreign companies to explore for oil, and the first oil strikes were made in 1957. Ten years later Libya had become the world's fourth largest crude-oil exporter. The industry continued to expand in the 1960s as pipelines were built from the oilfields to new export terminals on the Mediterranean coast. The lightness and low sulfur content of Libyan crude oil has made it highly desirable to the industrialized countries, and, with the exception of the United States, differences in political viewpoint have had little effect on Libyan oil sales abroad. In 1983 Libya was the second largest supplier of crude oil to the European Economic Community, after Saudi Arabia.

After the 1969 Revolution, Libya became a leader in the drive by oil-producing countries to gain control over their petroleum industries. The process began in 1971 when the new Libyan government took over the interests of British Petroleum (BP) in Libya. The Libyan method of nationalization was to proceed against individual companies rather than to take on the "oil giants" all at once. It took more than a decade before the last company, Exxon, capitulated. However, the oil companies continue to provide technical help and to manage a large share of the marketing process. The Libyan National Oil Company is responsible for overall management and holds a majority interest in all concessions, but its actual share of production is about twenty-one percent.

Construction of new refineries and pipelines in recent years along with new oil and gas discoveries have enabled Libya to build a strong industrial sector emphasizing petrochemicals. The industrial complex at Marsa Brega, near Tripoli, is now a major producer of urea and related fertilizer products, with production sufficient for domestic needs and a surplus for export. Libya is also self-sufficient in cement, with five plants in operation. Industrial development success has enabled the government to shift priorities to agriculture, with funds formerly earmarked for industry transferred to agricultural development in the 1985 budget.

Libya is also developing its considerable uranium resources. A 1985 agreement with the Soviet Union provides the components for an 880-MW nuclear power station in the Sirte region. Libya has enough uranium to meet its foreseeable domestic peacetime needs. Whether at some future date Libyan oil revenues could gain access to the plutonium and other fissionable materials and the technical expertise needed to produce nuclear weapons is a matter for political conjecture, although it is economically feasible.

AN UNCERTAIN FUTURE

The revolutionary regime's major success was a redistribution of wealth to bring the benefits of oil revenues to all Libyans. Annual per capita income rose to $2,168 in 1970 and to $9,827 in 1979. (By 1983, however, annual per capita income had dropped to $7,600.) The new wealth brought undreamed-of benefits to Libyans, including permanent homes for the seminomadic Qadadfas of the Sirte, kin of Qadhafi. Free medical care, housing, schools, and other elements of a consumer economy began to change the lives and outlooks of the Libyan people. By 1985 the regime was well on its way to transforming a largely pastoral society into an industrialized one, within less than a generation.

But rule by the people also means rule

Since Qadhafi's rise to power, the resulting redistribution of wealth has meant a very significant change for the better in the lives of all Libyans. These children can look forward to a positive future.

| Establishment of Regency of Tripoli 1711 | Tripoli becomes Ottoman province directly governed, with Sanusiyah controlling interior 1835 | First Italian invasion 1911 | Libya becomes Italian colony, Italy's "Fourth Shore" 1932 | Independent kingdom set up by UN under King Idris 1951 | Revolution overthrows Idris; a Libyan Arab Republic established 1969 | Qadhafi decrees a cultural and social revolution with government by People's Committees 1973-1976 |

1980s

by the strong, as Qadhafi himself stated in *The Green Book*. Over the years most of the leader's old associates became alienated from him, either from disagreements about foreign policy or opposition to the "people's socialism" of *The Green Book*. In the 1980s Qadhafi began to send hit squads abroad to silence the opposition. A number of opposition leaders and dissident students were hunted down and killed in a shadowy war of Libyan against Libyan.

Until recently, opposition to Qadhafi was almost entirely outside Libya. The Libyan leader was popular at home. Libyans were living beyond their wildest dreams, and Qadhafi's foreign policy, if often unsuccessful, attracted international attention. But the gradual drying up of oil revenues has begun to create popular discontent. At the same time, Qadhafi's plan to form "revolutionary committees" to control the armed forces rebounded against him. In May 1984 soldiers sympathetic to the newly formed opposition National Front for the Salvation of Libya, based in Cairo, invaded his Tripoli barracks and attempted to kill him. The attempt failed, as the majority of the army remained loyal. But there is no guarantee that other assassination attempts will not occur as more and more members of the military become disaffected.

Although he eschews any official title other than "Leader of the Revolution," Mu'ammar Muhammad al-Qadhafi, "Brother Colonel" to a generation of Libyans, remains the driving force and iden-

tifying spirit of revolutionary Libya. As the first truly Libyan leader of his land, Qadhafi reflects many of the characteristics of his people—their simplicity, dignity, social egalitarianism, and puritanism born of the stark desert experience. He also embodies the Libyan deep suspicion of the outside world, based on bitter experience. Until very recently the view of Qadhafi held by Libyans was quite different from that of outsiders. The few Libyans who broke with him and went into exile opposed him on grounds of economic mismanagement and refusal to accept intellectual ideas other than his own.

That prevailing view began to change significantly in the mid-1980s, as the economic squeeze affected the good life of Libyans, and as they became aware of Brother Colonel's conflicts with other Arab leaders in the name of Arab unity. The expulsion of Tunisian and Egyptian workers aligned Egypt, Tunisia, and Algeria against Qadhafi, and his "strategic alliance" with non-Arab Iran against Iraq further isolates the colonel on the fluid Arab chessboard. At home, the once-privileged position of the army as Qadhafi's main power base has been seriously eroded through embarrassing military defeats and the activities of pro-Qadhafi revolutionary youth committees who have taken over public security functions. In 1984 and 1985 there were several attempts to overthrow Qadhafi led by army officers. Thus far these efforts have been thwarted by Qadhafi's East German secur-

| Campaign to eliminate Qadhafi's exiled opponents abroad; US imposes economic sanctions in response to suspected Libya-terrorist ties | Commandos attack Qadhafi's military headquarters in Tripoli in unsuccessful coup; mutinies by air force and army units in eastern Libya suppressed | Federation agreement with Morocco; US Congress imposes total ban on trade with Libya |

ity guards, his own vigilance, and the support of loyal army units. But an army is difficult to control when it sees its power and privilege disappear. As this process continues, it is quite possible that another junior officer may emerge from the ranks to seize power in Libya and announce another revolution.

FOOTNOTES

1. " . . . irrigation, colonization and hard work have wrought marvels. Everywhere you see plantations forced out of the sandy, wretched soil . . . " A.H. Broderick, *North Africa* (London: :Oxford University Press, 1943), p.27
2. Religious leaders issued a *fatwa* ("binding Legal decisions") stating that a vote against independence would be a vote against religion. Omar el Fathaly, et al, *Political Development and Bureaucracy in Libya* (Lexington, MA: Lexington Books, 1977).
3. See the *Middle East Journal*, vol. 24, no. 2 (Spring 1970), Documents Section.
4. John Wright, *Libya: A Modern History* (Baltimore: Johns Hopkins University Press, 1982), pp. 124-126. Qadhafi's idol was former Egyptian President Nasser, a leader in the movement for unity and freedom among the Arabs. While he was at school in Sebha, the Fezzan, he listened to Radio Cairo's Voice of the Arabs and was later expelled from school as a militant organizer of demonstrations.
5. *The Times* (London, England), June 6, 1973.

DEVELOPMENT

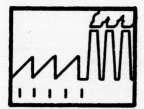

Declining oil revenues and foreign-trade deficits have affected the development program in recent years. In early 1985 some 300 projects deemed "nonessential" were cancelled. A 1983 law requiring replacement of foreign workers by Libyans was implemented in August 1985 by expulsion of 35,000 foreigners.

FREEDOM

Libya has no written constitution, and political parties are outlawed. The main instrument of government is the General People's Congress. The Cabinet is responsible to the Congress. Popular congresses were set up in 1977 to administer regions and municipalities. Popular committees manage all industries and educational institutions.

HEALTH/WELFARE

The republic has vastly expanded education, health, and social services. By 1982 1 million students were enrolled in schools at all levels. There are now 2 universities. Although still dependent on foreign teachers and doctors, Libya in 1984 had more than 2,000 students in medical and teacher training.

ACHIEVEMENTS

The revolutionary regime committed itself from the start to improve living conditions through broad use of oil revenues. By 1985, 745,000 housing units were completed and all towns and villages, even in remote oases, were linked to major cities by paved roads.

Morocco (Kingdom of Morocco)

GEOGRAPHY

Area in Square Kilometers (Miles):
409,200 (171,953)
Capital (Population): Rabat (901,500 in metropolitan area)
Climate: Mediterranean and desert

PEOPLE

Population
Total: 23,565,000
Annual Growth Rate: 2.9%
Rural/Urban Population Ratio: 58/42
Ethnic Makeup of Population: 99.1% Arab-Berber; 0.7% non-Moroccan; 0.2% Jewish

Health
Life Expectancy at Birth: 52 years
Infant Death Rate (Ratio): 125/1,000
Average Caloric Intake: 115% of FAO minimum
Physicians Available (Ratio): 1/10,750

Religion(s)
98.7% Sunni Muslim; 1.1% Christian; 0.2% Jewish

Education
Adult Literacy Rate: 28%

THE URBAN INFLUENCE IN ISLAM

Cities have always held great importance in Islam. The Prophet Muhammad was an urban merchant, and although the design of the Islamic system owes much to the desert influence, its forms and obligations are urban. Moroccan cities were nearly all purely Islamic designs, and due to the French preference for new administrative and residential quarters adjoining the Muslim ones, most of Morocco's Islamic cities have survived. Fez, the first Moroccan capital, survives today as a perfect example of how Muslims lived and worked and traded in medieval times. Old Fez is walled, with streets too narrow for cars. Every street of the *suq* (market) has its specialty, from cloth to spices, to the huge bowls of the coppersmith. Fez has been preserved, through an international effort undertaken by UNESCO, as a monument of the Moroccan past; yet it remains a living city of craftspeople, shopkeepers, and bargainers for carpets, leather, and many other products of the artisan.

COMMUNICATION

Telephones: 227,000
Newspapers: n/a

TRANSPORTATION

Highways—Kilometers (Miles): 55,970 (34,780) total; 24,700 (15,349) bituminous treated
Railroads—Kilometers (Miles): 1,756 (1,091)
Commercial Airports: 79

GOVERNMENT

Type: constitutional monarchy
Independence Date: March 2, 1956
Head of State: King Hassan II
Political Parties: Istiqal Party; Socialist Union of Popular Forces; Popular Movement; National Assembly of Independents; National Democratic Party; Party for Progress and Socialism; the Constitutional Union
Suffrage: universal over 20

MILITARY

Number of Armed Forces: 136,800
Military Expenditures (% of Central Government Expenditures): 22.2%
Current Hostilities: none

ECONOMY

Currency ($ US Equivalent): 9.95 dirhams = $1 (March 1985)
Per Capita Income/GNP: $640/$15.2 billion (1983)
Inflation Rate: 12.5% (1985)
Natural Resources: phosphates; iron; manganese; lead; cobalt; silver; copper; oil shale; fish
Agriculture: wheat; barley; livestock; wine; vegetables; olives; fishing
Industry: phosphate mining; mineral processing; food processing; textiles; construction

FOREIGN TRADE

Exports: $2.1 billion (1983)
Imports: $3.5 billion (1983)

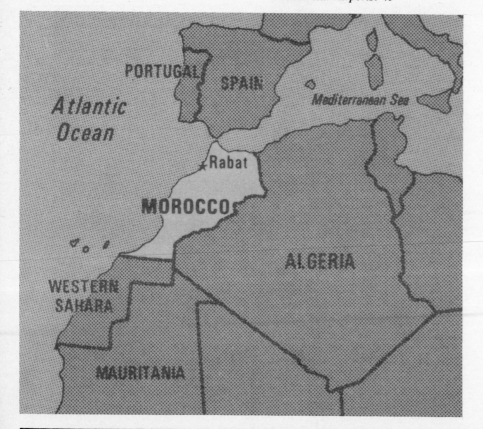

MOROCCO

The Kingdom of Morocco is the westernmost country in North Africa. Morocco has a land area of 171,953 square miles, and its population of 23,565,000 is the second largest (after Egypt) of the Arab states. The current capital is Rabat. Moroccan territory also includes at present the Western Sahara, a former Spanish colony which was annexed in 1976 after the withdrawal of the Spanish administration. The annexation was opposed by a Saharan nationalism movement, the Polisario Front. If Morocco acquires permanent control over the Western Sahara, the country's land area would be increased by 102,000 square miles, a territory the size of Colorado.

Two other territories physically within Morocco remain outside Moroccan control. They are the cities of Ceuta and Melilla, both located on rocky penisulas that jut out into the Mediterranean Sea. They have been held by Spain since the fifteenth century, and are considered parts of mainland Spain. (Spain also owns several small islands off the coast in Moroccan territorial waters.) Morocco periodically claims Ceuta and Melilla, and they were besieged numerous times by Moroccan armies in the past. But thus far the economic advantages to Morocco of the free-port status of the cities and employment of a large Moroccan labor force seem to outweigh the need for political control.

SPLENDID ISOLATION

Morocco is a rugged land, dominated by several massive mountain ranges. The Rif Range, averaging 7,000 feet in elevation, runs parallel to the Mediterranean, isolating the northern region from the rest of the country. The Atlas Mountains dominate the rest of interior Morocco. The Middle Atlas begins south of the Rif, separated by the Taza Gap (the traditional gateway for invaders from the east), and extends from northeast to southwest to join the High Atlas, a snowcapped range containing North Africa's highest peak. A third range, the Anti-Atlas, walls off the desert from the rest of Morocco. These ranges and the general inaccessibility of the country isolated Morocco throughout most of its history, not only from outside invaders but also internally because of the geographical separation of peoples.

Moroccan geography also explains the country's dual population structure. About thirty-five percent of the population are Berbers, descendants of the original North Africans. The Berbers were, until recently, grouped into tribes, often taking the

name of a common ancestor, such as the Ait ("Sons of") 'Atta of southern Morocco.[1] Invading Arabs converted them to Islam in the eighth century, but made few changes in Berber life. Unlike the Berbers, the majority of the Arabs who settled in Morocco were, and are, town-dwellers. To a much greater degree than the Arabs, Berbers were conditioned by traditional family structure and values; "a web of kinship bound the rural individual to his tribal territory, to his immediate family, and to his more distant kin."[2]

The fact that the Arabs were invaders caused the majority of the Berbers to withdraw into mountain areas. They accepted Islam but held stubbornly to their independence. Much of Morocco's past history consists of efforts by various rulers, both Berber and Arab, to control Berber territory. The result was a kind of "balance of power" political system. The rulers had their power base in the cities, while the rural groups operated as independent units. Moroccan rulers made periodic military expeditions called *mahallas* into Berber territory to collect tribute and if possible to secure full obedience from the Berbers. When the ruler was strong, the Berbers paid up and submitted; when he was weak, they ignored him. At times Berber leaders might invade "government territory," capturing cities and replacing one ruler by another more to their liking. When they were not fighting with urban rulers, different Berber groups fought among themselves, so the system did little for Moroccan national unity.

HISTORY

Morocco has a rich and cultural history, with many of its ancient monuments more or less intact. It has had a ruling monarchy for twelve centuries, in some form or other. The ancestors of the present monarch, King Hassan II, came to power in the seventeenth century. One reason for their long rule is the fact that they were descended from the Prophet Muhammad. Thus, Moroccans have a real sense of Islamic traditions and history through their ruler.

The first identifiable Moroccan "state" was established by a descendant of the prophet named Idris, in the late eighth century. Idris had taken refuge in the far west of the Islamic world to escape civil war in the east. Because of his piety, learning, and his descent from Muhammad, he was accepted by a number of Berber groups as their spiritual and political leader. His son and successor, Idris II, founded the first Moroccan capital, Fez. Father and son established the principle whereby descent

from the prophet was an important qualification for political power as well as social status in Morocco.

The Idrisids ruled over only a small portion of the current Moroccan territory, and after the death of Idris II their "nation" lapsed into decentralized family rule. In any case, the Berbers had no real idea of nationhood; each separate Berber group thought of itself as a nation. But in the eleventh and twelfth centuries, two Berber confederations developed that brought imperial grandeur to Morocco. They were the Almoravids and the Almohads. Under their rule, North Africa developed a separate political structure from that of the Eastern Islamic world, and one strongly influenced by Berber values.

The Almoravids began as camel-riding nomads from the Western Sahara who were inspired by a religious teacher to carry out a reform movement to revive the true faith of Islam. (Almoravid comes from the Arabic *al-Murabitun*, "men of the ribat," rather like the crusading religious orders of Christianity in the Middle Ages.) Fired by religious zeal, the Almoravids conquered all of Morocco and parts of western Algeria.

A second "imperial" dynasty, the Almohads, succeeded the Almoravids but improved on their performance. They were the first, and will probably be the last, to unite all of North Africa and Islamic Spain under one government. Almohad monuments, such as the Qutubiya tower, the best-known landmark of Marrakesh, and the Tower of Hassan in Rabat, still stand as reminders of their power and the high level of their architectural achievements.

The same fragmentation, conflicts, and Berber/Arab rivalries that had undermined their predecessors brought down the Almohads in the late thirteenth century. From then on, dynasty succeeded dynasty in power. An interesting point about this cyclical pattern is that despite the lack of political unity, a distinctive Moroccan style and culture developed. Each dynasty contributed something to this culture, in architecture, crafts, literature, and music. The interchange between Morocco and Islamic Spain was constant and fruitful. Poets, musicians, artisans, architects, and others traveled regularly between Spanish and Moroccan cities. One can visit the city of Fez today and be instantly transported back into the Hispano-Moorish way of life of the Middle Ages.

Mulay Ismail

In the late seventeenth century the Alawis, the dynasty currently ruling Moroc-

Morocco has a rich history. The Karaouyine Mosque at Fez was founded in the ninth century AD and is the largest in North Africa. It is also the seat of one of Africa's oldest universities.

co, came to power. The Alawis were originally from Arabia, and were descended from the Prophet Muhammad. They used their prestige from being descended from Muhammad to win the support of both Arabs and Berbers. The real founder of the dynasty was Mulay Ismail (1672-1727), one of the longest reigning and most powerful monarchs in Morocco's history. Mulay Ismail unified the Moroccan nation. The great majority of the Berber groups accepted him as their sovereign. The sultan built watchtowers and posted permanent garrisons in Berber territories to make sure they continued to do so. He brought public security to Morocco also, and it was said that in his time a Jew or an unveiled woman could travel safely anywhere in the land, which was not the case in most parts of North Africa, the Middle East, and Europe.

Mulay Ismail was a contemporary of Louis XIV, and the reports of his envoys to the French court at Versailles convinced him that he should build a capital like it. He chose Meknès, not far from Fez. The work was half finished when he died of old age in his bed. The slaves and prisoners working on this "Moroccan Versailles" threw down their shovels and ran away. The enormous unfinished walls and arched Bab al-Mansur ("Gate of the Victorious") still stand today as reminders of Mulay Ismail's dream.

Mulay Ismail had many wives and left behind five hundred sons, but no instructions as to which one should succeed him. After years of conflict one of his grandsons overcame the other claimants and took the throne as Muhammad II. He is important for giving European merchants a monopoly on trade from Moroccan ports (in wool, wax, hides, carpets, and leather), and for being the first non-European monarch to recognize the United States as an independent nation in 1787.[3]

The French Protectorate

In the nineteenth and early twentieth centuries, Morocco became increasingly vulnerable to outside pressures. The French, who were established in neighboring Algeria and Tunisia, wanted to complete their conquests. The nineteenth-century sultans were less and less able to control the mountain Berbers and were forced to make constant expeditions into the "land of dissidence," at great expense to the treasury. They began borrowing money from European bankers, not only to pay their bills but also to finance arms purchases and the development of ports, railroads, and industries to create a modern economy and prove to the European powers that Morocco could manage its own affairs. Nothing worked; by 1900 Morocco was so far in debt that the French took over the management of its

finances. (One sultan, Abd al-Aziz, had bought one of everything he was told about by European salesmen, including a gold-plated toy train that carried food from the kitchen to the dining room of his palace.) Meanwhile, the European powers plotted the country's downfall.

In 1904 France, the United Kingdom, Spain, and Germany signed secret agreements partitioning the country. The French would be given the largest part of the country, while Spain would receive the northern third as a protectorate, plus some territory in the Western Sahara. In return, the French and Spanish agreed to respect the United Kingdom's claim to Egypt and Germany's claim to East African territory.

The ax fell on Morocco in 1912. French workers building the new port of Casablanca had been killed by Berbers. Mobs attacked foreigners in Fez, and the sultan's troops could not control them. French troops marched to Fez from Algeria to restore order. The sultan, Mulay Hafid, was forced to sign the Treaty of Fez, establishing a French protectorate over southern Morocco. The sultan believed he had betrayed his country, and died shortly thereafter, supposedly of a broken heart. Spain then occupied the northern third of the country, and Tangier, the traditional residence of foreign consuls, became an international city ruled by several European powers.

The French protectorate over Morocco covered barely forty-five years (1912-1956). But in that brief period the French introduced significant changes into Moroccan life. For the first time in its history, southern Morocco was brought entirely under central government control, although the "pacification" of the Berbers was not complete until 1934. French troops also intervened in the Spanish Zone to help put down a rebellion in the Rif led by Abd al-Krim, a *Qadi* ("religious judge") and leader of the powerful Ait Waryaghar tribe.[4]

The organization of the protectorate was largely the work of the first French resident-general, Marshal Louis Lyautey. Lyautey had great respect for Morocco's past and its proud, dignified people. His goal was to develop the country and modernize the sultan's government while preserving Moroccan traditions and culture. He preferred the Berbers to the Arabs, and set up a separate administration under Berber-speaking French officers for Berber areas.[5]

Lyautey's successors were less respectful of Moroccan traditions. The sultan, supposedly an independent ruler, became a figurehead. French colons (settlers) flocked to

Morocco to buy land at rock-bottom prices and develop vineyards, citrus groves, and orchards. Modern cities sprang up around the perimeters of Rabat, Fez, Marrakesh, and other cities. In rural areas, particularly the Atlas, the French worked with powerful local chiefs (*qaids*). Certain unscrupulous qaids used the arrangement to become enormously wealthy. One qaid, al-Glawi, gained huge profits from his position. The Glawi, as he was called, strutted about like a rooster in his territory and often said that he was the real sultan of Morocco.[6]

Morocco's Independence Struggle

The movement for independence in Morocco developed very slowly. The only symbol of national unity was the sultan, Muhammad ibn Yusuf. But he seemed ineffectual to most young Moroccans, particularly those educated in French schools, who began to question the right of France to rule a people against their will.

The hopes of these young Moroccans got a boost during World War II. The Western allies, the United Kingdom and the United States, had gone on record in favor of the right of subject peoples to self-deter-

mination after the war. When President Roosevelt and Prime Minister Winston Churchill came to Casablanca for an important wartime conference, the sultan was convinced to meet them privately and get a commitment for Morocco's independence. The leaders promised their support.

Unfortunately, Roosevelt died before the end of the war, and Churchill was defeated for reelection. The French were not under any pressure after the war to end the protectorate. When a group of Moroccan nationalists formed the Istiqlal ("Independence") Party and demanded the end of French rule, most of them were arrested. A few leaders escaped to the Spanish Zone or to Tangier, where they could operate freely. For several years Istiqlal headquarters was the home of the principal of the American School at Tangier, an ardent supporter of Moroccan nationalism.

With the Istiqlal dispersed, the sultan represented the last hope for national unity and resistance. Up until then he had gone along with the French, but in the early 1950s he began to oppose them openly. The French began to look for a way to remove him from office and replace him with a more cooperative ruler.

In 1953 the Glawi and his fellow qaids decided, along with the French, that the time was right to depose the sultan. The qaids demanded that he abdicate; they said his presence was contributing to Moroccan instability. When he refused to abdicate, he was bundled into a French plane and sent into exile. An elderly uncle was named to replace him.

The sultan's departure had the opposite effect from what was intended. In exile he became a symbol for Moroccan resistance to the protectorate. Violence broke out, French settlers were murdered, and a Moroccan Army of Liberation began battling French troops in rural regions.

Although the French could probably have contained the rebellion in Morocco, they were under great pressure in neighboring Algeria and Tunisia, where resistance movements were also under way. In 1955, somewhat abruptly, the French capitulated. Sultan Muhammad ibn Yusuf returned to his palace in Rabat in triumph, and the elderly uncle retired to potter about in his garden in Tangier. Over the years the Alawi family, which is quite large, acquired palaces and other choice bits of real estate throughout Morocco.

Tangier, Morocco was once a free city and port, and now is Morocco's northern metropolis just across the Strait of Gibraltar.

INDEPENDENCE

Morocco became independent in March 1956. (The Spanish protectorate ended in April and Tangier came under Moroccan control in October, although it kept its free-port status and special banking and currency privileges for several more years.) It began its existence as a sovereign state with a number of assets—a popular ruler, an established government, and a well-developed system of roads, schools, hospitals, and industries inherited from the protectorate. Against these assets were the liabilities of age-old Arab/Berber and inter-Berber conflicts, little experience with political parties or democratic institutions, and an economy dominated by Europeans.

The sultan's goal was to establish a constitutional monarchy. His first action was to give himself a new title, King Muhammad V, symbolizing the end of the old autocratic rule of his predecessors. He also pardoned the Glawi, who crawled into his presence to kiss his feet and crawled out backwards as proof of penitence. (He died soon thereafter.) However, the power of the qaids and pashas ended; "they were compromised by their association with the French, and returned to the land to make way for nationalist cadres, many . . . not from the regions they were assigned to administer."[7]

Muhammad V did not live long enough to reach his goal. He died unexpectedly in 1961, and was succeeded by his eldest son, Crown Prince Hassan. Hassan II has ruled Morocco since then, and while he fulfilled his father's promise immediately with a constitution, in most other ways he has set his own stamp on Morocco.

The Constitution provided for an elected legislature and a multiparty political system. In addition to the Istiqlal, a number of other parties were organized, including one representing the monarchy. But the results of the French failure to develop a satisfactory party system soon became apparent. Berber/Arab friction, urban/rural distrust, city rivalries, and inter-Berber hostility all resurfaced. Elections failed to produce a clear majority for any party, not even the king's own party.

In 1965 riots broke out in Casablanca. The immediate cause was labor unrest. But the real cause lay in the lack of effective leadership by the parties. The king declared a state of emergency, dismissed the legislature, and assumed full powers under the Constitution.

For the next dozen years Hassan II ruled as an absolute monarch. He continued to insist that his goal was a parliamentary system, a "government of national union." But he depended upon a small group of cronies, members of prominent merchant families, the large Alawi family, or powerful Berber leaders as a more reliable group than the fractious political parties. The dominance of "the king's men" led to growing dissatisfaction and a feeling that the king had sold out to special interests. The opposition spread to the army, previously considered Hassan's most loyal supporter. Army officers, most of them Berbers, objected to government corruption and the king's flamboyant lifestyle, his numerous palaces, and free association with foreigners. The king, who has a law degree from a French university, is very much at ease in French and other European cultures as well as in his own Islamic Moroccan culture. The king became identified as the cause of the nation's problems. In 1971, and again in 1972, the military attempted to overthrow him. In both cases the king narrowly escaped with his life, suggesting to most Moroccans that his *baraka* ("charisma") was stronger than that of his opposition. The attempts, however, prompted Hassan II to revive the parliamentary system. A new constitution in 1972 defined Morocco as "a democratic and social constitutional monarchy in which Islam is the established religion."[8] However, the king holds broad constitutional powers. Royal power is based on the leadership of the Alawi family, the king's spiritual role as Commander of the Faithful, and his control of patronage. When Hassan puts on an army uniform, or rides to the mosque on Fridays in the traditional white *jellaba* under an umbrella symbolizing royalty, or meets with his Cabinet dressed in a business suit, he symbolizes these three roles of leadership.

THE WESTERN SAHARA

The Western Sahara, which Morocco annexed after Spain ended its rule over the colony in 1976, is primarily a regional rather than an internal Moroccan problem, although it has adversely affected Morocco's economy due to the heavy cost of occupation. However, the annexation had important results for Moroccan political development. The "Green March," organized by the king, of 350,000 unarmed Moroccans into Spanish territory in November 1975 to dramatize Morocco's claim, was supported by all segments of the population and the opposition parties. In 1977 opposition leaders agreed to serve under the king in a "government of national union." The first elections in twelve years were held for a new legislature, and several new parties, including Socialist and Marxist ones, took part.

Since 1977 the fabric of national unity has remained largely intact. Despite the heavy economic burden of conflict in the Western Sahara between Moroccan forces and guerrillas of the Saharan nationalist movement, the Polisario, which is contesting the annexation, popular support for King Hassan generated by his Saharan policy remains

When Morocco gained its independence from Spain in 1956, King Muhammad V (above right) wanted to establish a constitutional monarchy. He died in 1961 and was succeeded by his son, Crown Prince Hassan (above left), who has ruled successfully ever since.

| Foundations of Moroccan nation established by Idris I and II, with capital at Fez **AD 788-790** | Almoravid and Almohad dynasties, Morocco's "imperial period" **1062-1147** | Current ruling dynasty, the Alawi, establishes its authority under Mulay Ismail **1672** | Morocco occupied and placed under French and Spanish protectorates **1912** | Independence under King Muhammad V **1956** | Accession of King Hassan II **1961** | Unsuccessful attempts by army officers to overthrow Hassan **1971, 1972** | "Green March" into the Western Sahara dramatizes Morocco's claim to the area **1975** |

1980s

| "Bread riots" to protest price increases in basic commodities | Agreement with Libya for a federal union | Completion of fifth and final section of "Sand Wall" protecting the Western Sahara |

high. As a result, the parliamentary system continues to function effectively. Elections for a new national legislature in September 1984 resulted in a strong majority for the promonarchist Constitutional Union Party but with adequate representation for other parties; the opposition Socialist Union of Popular Forces (USFP), the last party to join the government of national union, won ten percent of legislative seats.

The king was also successful in 1984-1985 in gaining support from other African states for his Saharan policy of "annexation without negotiations." Chad and Mauritania signed treaties recognizing the Moroccan claim to the territory. An agreement for a federal union of Morocco and Libya signed in August 1984 gave the Moroccan position an important boost. Libya agreed to end its financial and military aid to the Polisario; perhaps more important, Hassan could now look forward to Libyan aid to ease the burden of defense.

THE ECONOMY

Morocco has too much of certain resources and too little of other critical ones. It has two-thirds of the world's known reserves of phosphate rock and is the number one exporter of phosphates. The major thrust in industrial development is in phosphate-related industries, in large phosphoric acid and fertilizer plants. Development of the huge phosphate deposits at Bou Craa, in the Western Sahara, will increase dramatically Moroccan exports. Production was halted in 1976 when Polisario guerril-

las blew up the conveyor belt carrying phosphate rock from Bou Craa to the Atlantic coast loading terminals some sixty miles away, but was resumed in 1982.

The country has important undeveloped iron-ore deposits and a small but significant production of rare metals such as mercury, antimony, nickel, and lead. But the major obstacle to development is the lack of oil. Years of exploration have produced only empty holes; almost all oil must be imported. Dependence upon oil imports is one of four major economic problems; the others are the cost of the Saharan occupation ($1.5 million per day), low world demand for phosphates, which has depressed prices, and too-rapid population growth. Large amounts of unrepayable foreign aid brought another form of dependence; by 1983 total foreign indebtedness was $13 billion. An economic recovery plan was set up with the help of the World Bank in that year, and by 1985 exports had increased seven percent, the major increases being in citrus, phosphates, and winter vegetables shipped to the European Economic Community countries. In January 1984 the king increased prices and reduced subsidies on basic commodities to comply with World Bank requirements, but violent riots broke out and he was forced to rescind the increases. A year later, with recovery in full swing and bumper crops forecast, a new round of increases drew no public reaction. The recovery has encouraged Morocco's creditors. In March 1985 they agreed to reschedule all debt interest payments and to provide $3 billion in

long-term aid and $750 million in short-term credits over a 3-year period. In the 1980s Morocco seemed more and more likely to be turning into a good credit risk.

FOOTNOTES

1. See David M. Hart, *Dadda 'Atta and His Forty Grandsons* (Cambridge, England: Menas Press, 1981), pp. 8-11. Dadda 'Atta was a historical figure, a minor saint or marabout.

2. Harold D. Nelson, ed., *Morocco, A Country Study* (Washington, DC: American University, Foreign Area Studies, 1978), p. 112.

3. The oldest property owned by the US government abroad is the American Consulate in Tangier; a consul was assigned there in 1791. *Ibid.*, p. 40.

4. See David Woolman, *Rebels in the Rif: Abd el Krim and the Rif Rebellion* (Stanford, CA: Stanford University Press, 1968). On the Ait Waryaghar see David M. Hart, *The Ait Waryaghar of the Moroccan Rif: An Ethnography and a History* (Tucson: University of Arizona Press, 1976). Abd el Krim had annihilated a Spanish army and set up a Republic of the Rif (1921-1926).

5. For a detailed description of protectorate tribal administration see Robin Bidwell, *Morocco Under Colonial Rule* (London: Frank Cass, 1973).

6. He once said: "Morocco is a cow, the Qaids milk her while France holds the horns." Nelson, *op. cit.*, p. 53.

7. Mark Tessler, "Morocco: Institutional Pluralism and Monarchical Dominance," in W. I. Zartman, ed., *Political Elites in North Africa* (New York: Longman, 1982), p. 44.

8. Nelson, *op. cit.*, p. 205.

DEVELOPMENT

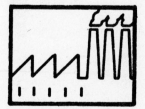

The economic recovery plan initiated in 1983 has brought modest gains, notably a 2.9% GDP growth rate and increased exports. Inflation was held to 12.5% in 1985. Phosphates exports increased 15%. Agricultural production benefitted from favorable weather and rains to increase 4.9% mainly in citrus and winter vegetable exports to Europe.

FREEDOM

The 1972 Constitution defines Morocco as a democratic monarchy with the crown hereditary in the line of Hassan II. The king has broad executive powers, but recently has revived the multiparty system and reinstated the legislature. Although Amnesty International criticizes the government for denial of civil rights of political prisoners, the king has amnestied a large number in recent years.

HEALTH/WELFARE

According to the World Bank, about 50% of Moroccans live in abject poverty. Housing, health services, and educational facilities are all inadequate, a critical situation given the rapid growth rate and extreme youth of the population.

ACHIEVEMENTS

The union with Libya into a "union of states" to be known as the Arab-African Federation promises Morocco considerable economic benefits as well as support for its control of the Western Sahara. Both countries retain full sovereignty over their own affairs, but a joint Libyan-Moroccan Assembly may represent them internationally.

Oman (Sultanate of Oman)

GEOGRAPHY

Area in Square Kilometers (Miles):
299,899 (115,800)
Capital (Population): Muscat (80,000)
Climate: coast, hot and humid;
interior, hot and dry

PEOPLE

Population
Total: 1,009,000
Annual Growth Rate: 3.1%
Rural/Urban Population Ratio: 55/45
Ethnic Makeup of Population: almost
entirely Arab; small Baluchi,
Zanzibari, and Indian groups

Health
Life Expectancy at Birth: 52 years
Infant Death Rate (Ratio): 128/1,000
Average Caloric Intake: n/a
Physicians Available (Ratio): 1/1,900

Religion(s)
75% Ibadhi Muslim; remainder Sunni
Muslim, Shia Muslim, some Hindu

Education
Adult Literacy Rate: 20%

THE SOCIAL USES OF WATER

In inner Oman water has social significance in addition to its household uses. Water is taken from the *falaj* ("irrigation channels"), which
are usually spring fed. In water-scarce Oman, the falaj is not only essential to most household tasks but also serves as community center.
There women wash clothes, scrub pots, clean reed mats, and visit while
children play and bathe nearby.

The collection of a bucket of drinking water from the head of the falaj
is called *gharrafa* (the scooping of enough water to be held in one's hand).
Sunset is a special time for the water ritual, when women gather to pray,
wait their turn for clean water, and talk. But as modern cement houses
are built farther away from the falaj and wells are dug for water, the use
of the falaj as principal water source and gathering place is diminishing.

COMMUNICATION

Telephones: 13,000
Newspapers: 3 dailies

TRANSPORTATION

Highways—Kilometers (Miles):
16,900 (10,502) total; 2,200 (1,367)
bituminous surface
Railroads—Kilometers (Miles): none
Commercial Airports: 140

GOVERNMENT

Type: absolute monarchy
Independence Date: 1951
Head of State: Sultan and Prime
Minister Qabus ibn Said
Political Parties: none; outlawed
Popular Front for the Liberation of
Oman, based in People's Democratic
Republic of Yemen
Suffrage: none

MILITARY

Number of Armed Forces: 24,200
*Military Expenditures (% of Central
Government Expenditures):* 38.4%
Current Hostilities: none

ECONOMY

Currency ($ US Equivalent): 0.346
Omani rial = $1 (March 1985)
Per Capita Income/GNP: $6,828/$6.3
billion (1981)
Inflation Rate: about 10% (1978-1983)
Natural Resources: oil; copper;
asbestos; some marble; limestone;
gypsum
Agriculture: dates; alfalfa; wheat;
bananas; coconuts; limes; vegetables;
fish
Industry: crude petroleum; fisheries;
copper mine and smelter;
construction; cement

FOREIGN TRADE

Exports: $4.4 billion (1982)
Imports: $3.2 billion (1982)

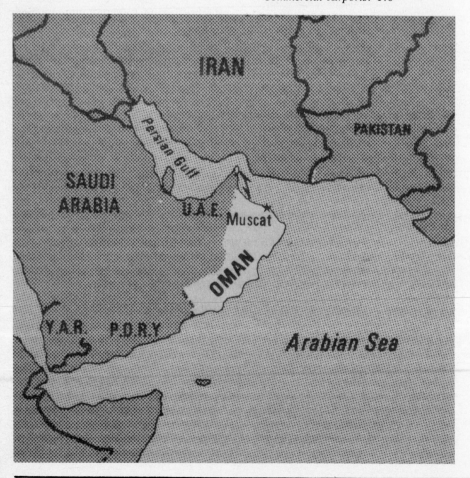

OMAN

The Sultanate of Oman was, at least until 1970, one of the least-known countries in the world. Yet it is a very old country with a long history of contact with the outside world. Merchants from Oman had a near monopoly on the trade in frankincense and myrrh. Oman-built shallow-draught, broad-beamed ships called *dhows* criss-crossed the Indian Ocean, trading with India and the Far East.

In the twentieth century Oman became important to the outside world for two reasons. First, it has been producing oil since the 1960s, and second, it has a strategic location on the Strait of Hormuz, the passageway for supertankers carrying Middle Eastern oil to the industrialized nations. In 1980 an average of seventy-seven ships per day passed down the Persian Arabian Gulf and through the Strait, one every nineteen minutes. Eighty percent of Japan's oil needs passes through Hormuz, and sixty percent of Western Europe's. A Swiss journalist called the Omanis "sentinels of the Gulf" because they watch over this vital traffic.

GEOGRAPHY

Oman is a relatively large country (115,800 square miles) with an estimated population of 1,009,000—certainly not overcrowded. However, the rugged mountain ranges and the desert limit settlement to a few areas. The coastal area around Muscat, the capital, has the largest population. North of Muscat, the Batinah coast supports one-third of the population, due to an ingenious irrigation system of underground canals, some of them more than two thousand years old. The third important area of development is the southwestern coast of Dhofar province, source of the legendary frankincense tree.

Behind Oman's coast is a spine of rugged mountains, the Jabal al-Akhdar ("Green Mountain"), with peaks over ten thousand feet. The mountains form several disconnected chains, interspersed with deep, narrow valleys where village houses hang like eagles' nests from the mountain tops above terraced gardens and palm groves.

Most of Oman's oil wells are located in the interior of the country. The interior is a broad, hilly plain dotted with oasis villages, each one a fortress with thick walls to keep out desert raiders. The stony plain eventually becomes the Rub al-Khali ("Empty Quarter"), the great uninhabited desert of southeastern Arabia.

HISTORY

As was the case elsewhere in Arabia, the social structure of Oman consisted of a number of tribal groups. Many of them were and still are nomadic (Bedouin), while others became settled farmers and herders centuries ago. The groups spent much of their time feuding with one another. Occasionally, several would join in an alliance against others, but none of them recognized any higher authority than their leaders.

In the seventh century AD, the Omanis were converted to Islam. However, they developed their own form of Islam; it was called *Ibadism*, meaning "Community of the Just," and is a branch of Shia Islam. The Ibadi peoples elected their own leader, called an Imam. Imams did not have to be descendants of the Prophet Muhammad, as do the Imams in the main body of Shia Muslims. The Ibadi community believes that anyone, regardless of background, can be elected Imam, as long as the individual is pious, just, and capable. If no one is available who meets those requirements, the office may remain vacant.

Ibadi Imams ruled interior Oman with the support of family shaykhs until the eighteenth century. But well before then, coastal Oman was being opened up to foreign powers. The Portuguese captured Muscat in the 1500s for use as a stopping place for their ships on the trade route to India. (An Omani served as navigator to Portuguese Admiral Vasco da Gama in his voyage across the Indian Ocean to India.) They built two great forts guarding the entrance to Muscat harbor, forts that still stand, giving the town its picturesque appearance. The Portuguese were finally driven out in 1650. Since that time Oman has not been ruled directly by any foreign power.

The current ruling dynasty in Oman is the Al Bu Said Dynasty. It has been in power since 1749, when a chief named Ahmad Ibn Said defeated an Iranian invasion and established his authority over most of Oman. As Middle Eastern rulers go, the Al Bu Saids have been in power for a very long time. But for most of the period, Oman actually had two rulers, a sultan ruling in Muscat and an Imam ruling in the interior at the same time.

The most successful Omani sultan before the twentieth century was Said ibn Sultan (1804-1856). He added Dhofar Province and Zanzibar, on the East African coast, to Omani territory. Sultan Said had good relations with the United Kingdom. He signed a treaty with the British which stated, "the friendship between our two states shall remain unshook to the end of time." The sultan also signed a friendship treaty with the United States in 1833, and in 1836, to the surprise of the New York Port authorities, an Omani ship docked in the New York harbor. Its captain said that the sultan had sent him to get to know the Americans whom he had heard so much about, and to arrange trade contacts. The friendship between the US and Oman is on a very different basis today, as it is the Omanis who allow the US military to use Oman's Masirah Island in the event of a Soviet or Iranian military action in the Gulf. But this friendship had its roots in Sultan Said's mission.

After Sultan Said's death, conflict resumed due to the differences in Omani society. The opening of the Suez canal in 1869 diverted shipping to new Red Sea routes, and ships no longer called at Muscat harbor. Piracy and the slave trade, both of which had provided revenues for the sultan, were prohibited by international law. For the rest of the nineteenth century and most of the twentieth century Oman sank back into isolation, forgotten by the world. Only the United Kingdom paid the Omanis any attention, giving the sultan a small monthly subsidy in the event that Oman might be of some future use to her.

In the early twentieth century the Imams of inner Oman and the sultans ruling in Muscat came to a complete parting of the ways. In 1920 a treaty between the two leaders provided that the sultan would not interfere in the internal affairs of inner Oman. Relations rocked along reasonably smoothly until 1951, when the United Kingdom recognized the independence of the Sultanate of Muscat-Oman, as it was then called, and withdrew its advisers. Subsequently, the Imam declared inner Oman as a separate state from the sultanate. A number of Arab states supported the Imam on the grounds that the sultan was a British puppet. Conflict between the Imam and the sultan dragged on until 1960, when the sultan finally reestablished his authority.

The Ruler Who Stopped the Clock

Oman's ruler throughout this period was Sultan Said ibn Taimur (1932-1970). The most unusual aspect of his reign was the way in which he "stopped the clock" of modernization. Oil was discovered in 1964 in inland Oman, and soon wealth from oil royalties began pouring in. But the sultan was afraid the new wealth would corrupt his people. He refused to spend money for anything, except for the purchase of arms and a few personal luxuries such as an automobile, which he liked to drive on the only paved road in Salalah, his southern capital in Dhofar province. He would not allow the building of schools, houses, roads, or hospitals for his people. Before 1970 there were sixteen schools in all of Oman. The only hospital was the American mission in Muscat, established in the 1800s by Baptist missionaries, and all ten of Oman's qualified doctors were practicing abroad because the sultan did not trust modern medicine. The few roads were rough caravan tracks; many areas of the country, for example the Musandam Peninsula, were completely inaccessible.

The sultan required the city gates of Muscat to be closed and locked three hours after sunset. No one could enter or leave the city. Flashlights were prohibited, since they were a modern invention; so were sunglasses and European shoes. Anyone found on the streets at night without a lighted kerosene lantern was liable to imprisonment. In the entire country there were about one thousand automobiles; to import an automobile, one had to have the sultan's personal permission. On the darker side, slavery was still a common practice. Women were almost never seen in public and were veiled from head to foot if they so much as walked to a neighbor's house to visit. Prisoners could be locked up in the old Portugues fort at Muscat on the slightest pretext and left to rot.

THE COUP d'ETAT OF 1970

As the 1960s came to an end there was more and more unrest in Oman. The opposition centered around Qabus ibn Said, the sultan's son. Qabus had been educated in England, but when he came home his father shut him up in a house in Salalah, a town far from Muscat, and refused to give him any responsibilities. He was afraid of his son's "Western ideas."

On July 23, 1970 supporters of Crown Prince Qabus overthrew the sultan, and Qabus succeeded him. Sultan Qabus brought Oman into the twentieth century in a hurry. The old policy of isolation was reversed. In 1981, worried about a possible spread of the Iran-Iraq war, Oman joined the Gulf Cooperation Council and allowed the United States to use the facilities on Masirah Island in return for $200 million in aid.

At home, Qabus ended the rebellion in Dhofar, a conflict inherited from his father. The rebellion was particularly difficult because the rebels had support from the People's Democratic Republic of Yemen (PDRY) just across the border. The United Kingdom and the late Shah Reza Pahlavi of Iran loaned troops to help Oman. The sultan offered the rebels an amnesty, and earmarked a special fund for Dhofar's development. (One reason for the rebellion was the almost total neglect of Dhofar by the previous government.)

Boys studying the Koran at a village in Oman. When Qabus ibn Said came to power in 1970, replacing his father, he targeted education, health care, and transportation as prime development areas.

| Portuguese seize Muscat and build massive fortresses to guard harbor **1587-1588** | Al Bu Said Dynasty established; extends Omani territory **1749** | British establish de facto protectorate; slave trade supposedly ended **late 1800s** | Independence **1951** | Reactionary Sultan Said ibn Taimur deposed by his son, Prince Qabus **1970** | With Iranian help, Qabus ends Dhofar rebellion **1975** |

▮▮▮ 1980s

Agreement with US allows American military the use of Masirah air base

OMANI SOCIETY

Today, Omanis typically live in two worlds. They may wear both a *kanjar*, the traditional curved dagger, and a digital watch; travel by Land Rover, Datsun, or Mercedes; dress in *dishdasha* and skullcap yet do business by telephone in English; and spend holidays abroad. The pace of modernization is dizzying. Yesterday Muscat had a small dirt airstrip; today a huge industrial park with shops, factories, and high-rise apartments covers the old runway. Broad, paved highways curve along the coast and branch inland to the Imam's old fortress towns and oasis villages, where only camel tracks existed before 1970.

After his accession Sultan Qabus set education, health care, and transportation as his top priorities. The results have been astonishing. By 1983 there were 490 schools, with 7,700 teachers and 150,000 students, one-third of them girls, and plans were well underway for the country's first university. Such is the thirst for education that children often walk many miles to attend the nearest school in their district. In a land where eighty percent of the people are illiterate, one symbol of the new Oman is the schoolchild trudging along a dusty road carrying a bookbag.

The sultan also set out to blanket his country with roads and health clinics. By 1983 all but a few remote Musandam villages were served by graded roads. Medical services used to be provided by the local traditional doctors, but now the health team comes to the villages fully equipped in a Land Rover.

THE ECONOMY

Oman has been exporting oil since 1967, and oil revenues provide ninety-six percent of its income. There are two main oilfields, one near Muscat, the other in Dhofar. Several new Dhofar wells started production in 1985, increasing output to 650,000 barrels per day. Proven oil reserves are estimated at three billion barrels, so at present rates of production Oman should remain an oil-producing state for years to come.

Due to oil wealth, the per capita income of Oman is $6,828, less than that of its neighbors but a dramatic increase over past figures; since 1960 per capita income has gone up 166 percent. Yet income is unevenly distributed. Seventy percent of the population work in agriculture, which provides three percent of the national income. Farming is limited by lack of arable land, undependable rainfall, inefficient methods, and lack of manpower as more and more rural people move to the cities.

The fishing industry employs ten percent of the working population, but obsolete equipment and lack of canning and freezing plants have severely limited the catch in the past. Another problem is the unwillingness of Omani fishermen to move into commercial production; most of them catch just enough fish for their own use. The National Fisheries Company took over the industry in 1979, subsidizing catches, buying motor-powered boats for fishermen, and operating deep-sea trawlers. The company also helped finance storage and processing plants.

PROSPECTS

Oman's long traditions of independence, the national pride which has developed under the rule of Sultan Qabus, and the government's careful use of oil revenues augur well for continued development. A Swiss journalist feels that the Omani character is a great asset. "They have none of the sensitivity of so many new countries; the Omanis look you straight in the eye."[1] An Omani minister put it another way. "We did not choose to be here, at this point on the earth's surface," he said. "God put us here. But once we admit that, we have a responsibility, and one that we intend to fulfill."[2]

FOOTNOTES

1. Liesl Graz, *The Omanis, Sentinels of the Gulf* (London: Longman, 1982), p. 171.
2. *Ibid.*

DEVELOPMENT

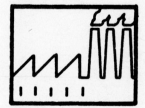

Oman's first oil refinery went into production in 1982, with capacity of 50,000 barrels per day, enough for domestic needs. Development of natural gas reserves, also underway, will allow conversion of domestic fuel systems to gas and will operate the new copper smelter.

FREEDOM

Sultan Qabus set up a Consultative Assembly in 1981 in response to suggestions from advisers that he was unaware of public opinion. The Assembly was enlarged in 1983; 19 of its 55 members are government officials. Members are nominated by the sultan for 2-year terms. The Assembly's function is to make recommendations on development projects.

HEALTH/WELFARE

An institute opened in 1981 is training Omani primary school teachers in order to reduce the country's dependence on expatriate teachers from other Arab countries, mainly Egypt and Jordan. It trains 100 teachers annually.

ACHIEVEMENTS

Oman's membership in the Gulf Cooperation Council (GCO) and its close links with the US provide a measure of political stability which may enable it to resist Islamic fundamentalism from Iran. The US pledged $200 million in 1983 to develop port and airport facilities on Masirah Island.

Qatar (State of Qatar)

GEOGRAPHY

Area in Square Kilometers (Miles):
11,000 (4,427)
Capital (Population): Doha (190,000)
Climate: hot and dry

PEOPLE

Population
Total: 276,000
Annual Growth Rate: 3.3%
Rural/Urban Population Ratio:
13.9/86.1 (1980)
Ethnic Makeup of Population: 40%
Arab; 18% Pakistani; 18% Indian;
10% Iranian; 14% other

Health
Life Expectancy at Birth: 71 years
Infant Death Rate (Ratio): 57/1,000
Average Caloric Intake: n/a
Physicians Available (Ratio): 1/1,333
(1981)

Religion(s)
95% Muslim; 5% other

Education
Adult Literacy Rate: 60%

MAINTAINING RESPECT FOR TRADITIONAL WAYS

Qatar's explosive growth threatens to change forever the traditional Qatari lifestyle, with its customs and links to the past. The National Museum at Doha, completed in 1977, received the Aga Khan award for Architectural Excellence in 1980, not only for its architectural beauty but also because of its function as a storehouse of the Qatari past. The museum surrounds the Amiri Palace, built in the 1800s by the ruling shaykh to underscore his separateness from the Ottomans. A new building, the Marine Museum, has exhibits depicting Qatari life from the Stone Age to the present, emphasizing the duality of desert and sea and the influence of Islam over the people.

COMMUNICATION

Telephones: 53,300
Newspapers: 4 dailies; 4 weeklies

TRANSPORTATION

Highways—Kilometers (Miles): 840
(522) total; 490 (304) bituminous
Railroads—Kilometers (Miles): none
Commercial Airports: 4

GOVERNMENT

Type: traditional emirate
Independence Date: September 3,
1971
Head of State: Khalifa bin Hamad al-Thani, emir and acting prime minister
Political Parties: none
Suffrage: none

MILITARY

Number of Armed Forces: 5,700
Military Expenditures (% of Central Government Expenditures): 25%
Current Hostilities: none

ECONOMY

Currency ($ US Equivalent): 3.64
riyals = $1 (March 1985)
Per Capita Income/GNP: $27,790
(1983)/$7.8 billion (1982)
Inflation Rate: 29.4% (1970-1982)
Natural Resources: petroleum;
natural gas; fish
Agriculture: farming on small scale
Industry: oil production and refining;
natural gas development; fishing;
cement; petro-chemicals; steel;
fertilizer

FOREIGN TRADE

Exports: $4.51 billion (1982)
Imports: $1.95 billion (1982)

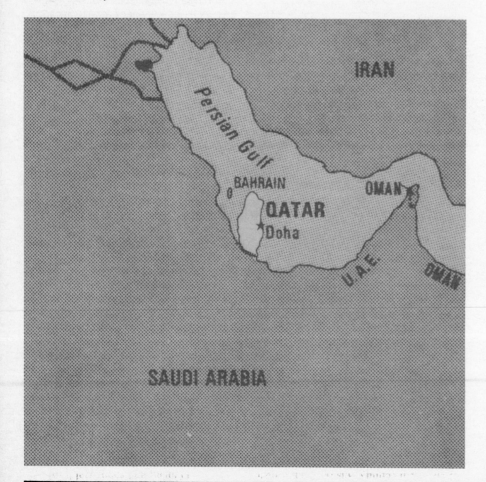

QATAR

Qatar is a shaykhdom on the eastern (Gulf) coast of Arabia, a peninsula 4,427 square miles in area. It is the second smallest Middle Eastern state after Bahrain, but due to oil wealth it has the highest per capita annual income *in the world,* $27,790. Before 1949, when oil exports began, there were about twenty thousand Qataris, all descendants of peoples who had migrated to the coast centuries ago in search of a dependable water supply. Since then, rapid economic growth has attracted expatriate workers and immigrants from other Arab countries and distant Muslim nations such as Pakistan. As a result, native Qataris are outnumbered four to one by immigrants and expatriates, a fact which makes for some tension.

HISTORY

Although the peninsula has been inhabited since 4000 BC, little is known of its history before the nineteenth century. At one time it was ruled by the al-Khalifa family, current rulers of Bahrain. It became part of the Ottoman Empire formally in 1872, but the Turkish garrison was evacuated during World War I. The Ottomans earlier had recognized Shaykh Qassim al-Thani, head of the important al-Thani family, as emir of Qatar, and the British followed suit when they established a protectorate after the war.

The British treaty with the al-Thanis was similar to ones made with other shaykhs in Arabia and the Gulf in order to keep other European powers out of the area and to protect their trade and communications links with India. In 1916 the British recognized Shaykh Abdullah al-Thani, grandfather of the current ruler, as ruler of Qatar, and promised to protect the territory from outside attack either by the Ottomans or overland by hostile Arabian groups. In return, Shaykh al-Thani agreed not to enter into any relationship with any other foreign government and to accept British political advisers.

Qatar remained a tranquil British protectorate until the 1950s, when oil exports began. Since then the country has developed rapidly, but not to the extent of the dizzying change visible in other oil-producing Arab states.

INDEPENDENCE

Qatar became independent in 1971, and the ruler, Shaykh Ahmad al-Thani, took the title of emir. Disagreements within the ruling family led the emir's cousin, Shaykh Khalifa, to seize power in 1972. Shaykh Khalifa made himself prime minister as well

as ruler, and initiated a major program of social and economic development which his cousin had opposed.

Shaykh Khalifa limited the privileges of the ruling family. There were more than two thousand al-Thanis, and most of them had been paid several thousand dollars a month whether or not they worked. Khalifa reduced their allowances, and also appointed some nonmembers of the royal family to the Council of Ministers, the state's chief executive body. He subsequently issued a decree establishing a Consultative Council of thirty elected members to advise the Council of Ministers on legislation and to debate the national budget. Qatar is still a patriarchal state, but the Consultative Council represents an important step toward democracy. The Council may even call ministers to account if their policies seem to violate Qatar's Constitution.

FOREIGN RELATIONS

Because of its small size, great wealth, and proximity to regional conflicts (the Iran-Iraq War in particular), Qatar is vulnerable to outside intervention. The government especially fears that the example of the Iranian Shia Revolution may bring unrest to its own Shia Muslim population. After the discovery of a Shia plot to overthrow the government of neighboring Bahrain in December 1981, Qatari authorities rounded up and deported several hundred Shia Qataris of Iranian origin. But the government has thus far avoided heavy-handed methods, preferring instead to concentrate its efforts on economic and social progress. On the tenth anniversary of independence, the emir said in a speech that "economic strength is the strongest guarantee that safeguards the independence of nations, their sovereignty, rights and dignity."[1]

Vulnerability to possible outside attack led Qatar to sign a bilateral defense agreement with Saudi Arabia in 1982. It had previously joined the Gulf Cooperation Council (GCC) and has been active in developing arrangements to eliminate import tariffs and travel restrictions among GCC members and in setting up a mutual defense system. An earlier British effort to form a federation of Qatar, Bahrain, and the United Arab Emirates in 1968-1969 did not work. Today the threat of subversion draws the three neighbor states ever closer to a federal union.

THE ECONOMY

The Qatari economy is based almost entirely on oil exports. In 1983 these provided eighty-three percent of national revenues.

Oil production is controlled by a government agency, Qatar Petroleum Company. As a member of the Organization of Petroleum Exporting Countries (OPEC), Qatar follows production quotas and prices set by that organization. Its production in 1983 was set by OPEC agreement at 300,000 barrels per day at a price of $29.49 per barrel.

Qatar has huge natural gas reserves, perhaps the world's largest, in the North Dome offshore field (180 billion cubic feet). A $6 billion project for development of this field was started in 1980. However, the collapse of the worldwide liquefied natural gas (LNG) market due to oversupply caused this project to be cancelled.

Development of diversified industries to reduce Qatar's dependence on oil exports has been a top priority for the government since independence. Umm Said, the port of Doha, is the main industrial center. Whereas not long ago it was mud flats, by 1983 Umm Said had a steel mill, fertilizer plants, gas-liquefaction plants for animal feedstock, and a 50,000 barrel-per-day oil refinery.

But water, not oil, is the most critical factor involved in Qatar's progress. There is only one underground water source, and it is being seriously depleted by the daily consumption of ten million gallons. Most of Qatar's fresh water comes from huge desalination plants, which remove the salt content from sea water. Without water for irrigation, agriculture is impossible in this land of little rain, and as recently as 1960 all vegetables, wheat, dairy products, and meat had to be imported. Yet two decades later, Qatar not only grows most of its own food but also exports vegetables to other Gulf states.

SOCIETAL CHANGES

Qatar was originally settled by nomadic peoples, and their influence is still strong. Traditional Bedouin values, such as honesty, hospitality, pride, and courage when faced with adversity, have carried over into modern times. As noted earlier, the al-Thanis and other prominent families are descended from nomads.

Most Qataris belong to the strict puritanical Wahhabi sect of Islam, which is also dominant in Saudi Arabia. They are conservative and cautious. But perhaps because of the large number of immigrants and the presence of a large number of non-Muslim foreign workers, Qataris are less conservative than their Saudi neighbors. For example, movies are shown in Qatar but not in Saudi Arabia.

Unlike other Islamic lands, where wom-

United Kingdom
recognizes
Shaykh Abdul-
lah al-Thani as
emir
1916

Start of oil
production
1949

Abortive
federation with
Bahrain and
the Trucial
States (UAE),
followed by
independence
1971

Ruler deposed
by Crown
Prince Shaykh
Khalifa
1972

1980s

Qatar joins Gulf
Cooperation
Council (GCC)

Qatar takes
part in Opera-
tion Peninsula
Shield, US-
supported joint
military
exercises

en have had to fight every step of the way to gain social and civil rights comparable to those of men, in Qatar the position of women has changed smoothly, almost imperceptibly. The first school for girls opened in 1956, and by 1982-1983 the ratio of boys to girls in primary schools was about the same. However, there were more girls than boys in secondary school and at the University of Qatar. Women are entering many new fields in addition to the traditional ones of nursing and teaching. They work as doctors, journalists, radio or television announcers, and set designers.

The movement of women into the workplace often creates family tensions in other societies, but Qataris seem able to take it in stride. One woman, a designer in her mid-twenties who is married with one child, tells an interviewer, "There are Qataris who allow their wives more freedom than an Englishman would give to his wife. But we hold to our traditions. What I want is for us to change, but wisely. Trouble arises when people try to be modern too fast. Change should take place within the framework of our habits and traditions."[2] A woman doctor says, "I don't want my daughter to wear the *batula* (the black beak-shaped face-mask veil traditionally worn by women in the Gulf). It has no importance now. Times are different. When I was young everybody wore it. Now girls go to school and university and the batula doesn't suit them."[3]

THE FUTURE

What will Qatar be like when the oil stops flowing? Twenty years ago Doha consisted of two rows of mud-brick houses along a ditch; today it is a thriving seaport of 100,000 people, with traffic jams and supermarkets. Qatar, like other oil-producing countries, is affected by global reductions in demand, lower prices, and the inevitable slowdown in development projects. Qatar is more fortunate than most of the oil-producing states, in that its small population can absorb only a limited quantity of imports. The relatively small Qatari oil output is also less affected by price fluctuations. The budget has consistently shown large surpluses, which have been plowed back into housing, hospitals, and other social services.

Qatar's small size and the close links between the ruling family and the people give the country more the appearance of a family-run corporation than of a nation-state. The monarchy is absolute, but it is also wisely paternalistic. Upward mobility and success are common experiences, and for many they occur at a relatively young age; a number of government and industrial leaders are in their thirties. Mohammed, the head of the electricity department of the Ministry of Power and Water, is a typical example. His father was a mechanic, and he knows nothing of his grandfather's people. Yet Mohammed operates comfortably in two worlds, the Western world of high-

powered technology and the world of the traditional close-knit Qatari family. He is the model of the Western technocrat, wearing tailored European suits, his hair short and neatly trimmed. "Yet under this exterior lurks a mind more Arab than Western in its working, never moving on one level only, never accepting anything at face value."[4] These qualities and this distinctive cast of mind seem likely to carry Qatar comfortably into the not-too-distant future when its last oil well runs dry out on the desert.

FOOTNOTES

1. Qatar News Agency, November 2, 1981.
2. Helga Graham, *Arabian Time Machine: Self Portrait of an Oil State* (London: Heinemann, 1978), p. 207.
3. *Ibid.*, p. 183.
4. *Ibid.*, p. 108.

DEVELOPMENT

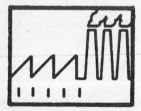

Expansion of agriculture is one of the principal means whereby Qatar hopes to reduce dependence on oil and overuse of newly discovered natural gas reserves. Desalination plants and new irrigation techniques have greatly increased production.

FREEDOM

In theory Qatar is a constitutional monarchy, but in practice absolute power is vested in the ruler. A majority of members of the Council of Ministers (cabinet) are al-Thanis. But, increasingly, high government positions are being filled by technically competent Qataris trained and educated in the West.

HEALTH/WELFARE

Qatar has never drawn up formal development plans. The only goal set by the government is to complete social and economic development programs by the year 2000. By 1983, 6,000 families had been provided with public housing and a noncontributory pension scheme had been set up for all public employees.

ACHIEVEMENTS

The new international airport at Doha went into operation in 1984. Qatar also has one of the world's largest satellite telecommunications station.

Saudi Arabia (Kingdom of Saudi Arabia)

GEOGRAPHY

Area in Square Kilometers (Miles):
2,331,000 (830,000)
Capital (Population): Riyadh
(1,793,000)
Climate: arid, with great extremes of
temperature

PEOPLE

Population
Total: 10,794,000
Annual Growth Rate: 3.3%
Rural/Urban Population Ratio: 31/69
Ethnic Makeup of Population: 90%
Arab; 10% Afro-Asian

Health
Life Expectancy at Birth: 54 years
Infant Death Rate (Ratio): 118/1,000
Average Caloric Intake: 116% of FAO
minimum
Physicians Available (Ratio): 1/1,670

Religion(s)
100% Muslim

Education
Adult Literacy Rate: 52%

COMMUNICATION

Telephones: 760,000
Newspapers: 8 dailies in Arabic; 2
dailies in English

A MOST HOLY PLACE

Mecca, located forty-five miles inland from the Red Sea in western
Arabia, is an unprepossessing place. It lies in the bowl of a dusty valley
encircled by barren waterless hills. Yet this site is the holiest shrine of
Islam. It is not only the birthplace and scene of the ministry of Muhammad but also a place associated with the Judeo-Christian-Muslim legends
of Abraham, Hagar, and Ishmael. These facts explain Mecca's importance. For 800 million Muslims throughout the world, it is the city of
the *hajj* (Great Pilgrimage), the fifth pillar of the House of Islam. Once
each year the Pilgrimage is held under official sponsorship of the Saudi
government.

TRANSPORTATION

Highways—Kilometers (Miles):
50,000 (31,070) total; 22,000 (13,670)
bituminous
Railroads—Kilometers (Miles): 575
(357)
Commercial Airports: 201

GOVERNMENT

Type: hereditary monarchy in al-Saud
family
Independence Date: September 23,
1932 (unification)
Head of State: Fahd bin Abd al-Aziz
al-Saud, king and prime minister
Political Parties: none; prohibited
Suffrage: none

MILITARY

Number of Armed Forces: 44,000
*Military Expenditures (% of Central
Government Expenditures):* 29%
Current Hostilities: none

ECONOMY

Currency ($ US Equivalent): 3.60
Saudi rials = $1 (March 1985)
Per Capita Income/GNP: $14,117/$120
billion (1983)
Inflation Rate: 5.5% (1981-1982)
Natural Resources: hydrocarbons;
iron ore; gold; copper
Agriculture: dates; grain; livestock
Industry: petroleum production;
petrochemicals; cement; fertilizer;
light industry

FOREIGN TRADE

Exports: $40 billion (1983)
Imports: $43 billion (1983)

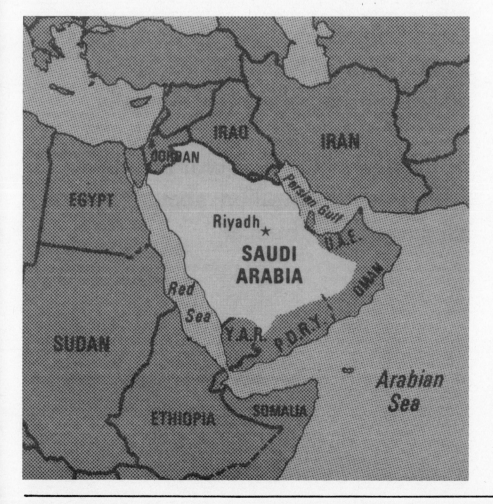

SAUDI ARABIA

The Kingdom of Saudi Arabia is the giant of the Arabian Peninsula, with an area of 830,000 square miles. It is also a giant in the world economy, because of its oil. To many people in the US and elsewhere, the name Saudi Arabia is a synonym for oil wealth. Indeed, its huge oil reserves, large financial surpluses from oil production, and its ability to use oil as a political weapon (as in the 1973 embargo) enable the country to play an important part in regional and in international affairs.

In relation to its size, Saudi Arabia has a small population, estimated at 10,794,000. (The last census was taken in 1974, but the results were never published. The lack of clearly defined borders makes census figures unreliable.) Two-thirds of the people live in urban areas, another unusual feature among Middle Eastern countries. Urban growth is very rapid since only one percent of the land can be used for agriculture and all employment opportunities are in the cities or the oil-producing regions. Due to its small population, the country has had to rely heavily on foreign labor for its programs for rapid development. As a result, immigrant workers greatly outnumber native Saudis.

THE WAHHABI MOVEMENT

In the eighteenth century most of the area included in present-day Saudi Arabia was the home of nomads, as it had been for centuries. These peoples had no central government and owed allegiance to no one except their chiefs. They spent much of their time raiding one another's territories in the struggle for survival. Inland Arabia was a great blank area in the map, a vast, empty desert.

The only part of present-day Saudi Arabia under any government control in the eighteenth century was the Hejaz, a region of barren plains and towering mountains near the Red Sea. The Hejaz, which includes the Islamic Holy Cities of Mecca and Medina, was a province of the Ottoman Turkish Empire, the major power in the Middle East at that time.

Saudi Arabia became a nation, in the modern sense of the word, in 1932. But the origins of the Saudi nation go back to the eighteenth century. One of the tribes that roamed the desert beyond Ottoman control was the tribe of Saud. Its leader, Muhammad ibn Saud, wanted to gain an advantage over his rivals in the constant search for water and good grazing land for animals. He approached a famous religious scholar named Abd al-Wahhab, who lived in an oasis near the present Saudi capital, Riyadh

(then a mud-walled village). Abd al-Wahhab promised Allah's blessing to ibn Saud in his contests with his rivals. In return, the Saudi leader agreed to protect al-Wahhab from threats to his life by opponents of the strict doctrines he taught and preached, and swore an oath of obedience to these doctrines. The partnership between these two men gave rise to a crusading religious movement called Wahhabism.

Wahhabism is basically a strict and puritanical form of Sunni Islam. The Wahhabi code of law, behavior, and conduct is modelled on that of the original Islamic community established in Mecca and Medina by the Prophet Muhammad. Although there has been some relaxation of the code due to the country's modernization, it remains the law of Saudi Arabia today. As a result, Saudi society is not only more conservative and puritanical than many other Islamic societies, it is also governed much more strictly. There is, for example, a ministry of public morals enforcement, and its police squads patrol Saudi streets to ensure that Saudi women are properly dressed and veiled in public, that the ban on eating and drinking during the daytime in the fasting month of Ramadan is observed, and that alcohol and drugs do not get into Saudi hands. So strict is the observance of Islamic law that women (including Western women) are not permitted to drive cars.

Due to the Wahhabi-Saud partnership, religious leaders in the country (many of whom are descendants of Abd al-Wahhab) have a great deal of influence in the government. They may delay or even annul government actions which they believe are contrary to Islamic principles. Thus they have successfully prevented the opening of movie theaters in the kingdom.

HISTORY

The puritanical zeal of the Wahhabis led them to declare a "holy war" against the Ottoman Turks, who were then in control of Mecca and Medina, in order to restore these holy cities to the Arabs. In the early 1800s Wahhabis captured the cities. Soon the Wahhabis threatened to undermine Ottoman authority elsewhere. Wahhabi raiders seized Najaf and Karbala in Iraq, centers of Shia pilgrimage, and desecrated Shia shrines. In Mecca they removed the headstones from the graves of members of the Prophet's family, because in their belief all Muslims are supposed to be buried unmarked.

The Ottoman sultan did not have sufficient forces at hand to deal with the Wahhabi threat, so he called upon his vassal,

Mohammad Ali, the khedive (viceroy) of Egypt. Muhammad Ali had organized an army equipped with European weapons and trained by European advisers. In a series of hard-fought campaigns, the Egyptian army defeated the Wahhabis and drove them back into the desert.

Inland Arabia reverted to its old ways of conflict. The only difference between the Saudis and their rivals was the bond of Wahhabism. It did not help them in their conflicts, and in the 1890s the Saudis' major rivals, the Rashidis, seized Riyadh. The Saudi chief escaped across the desert to Kuwait, a town on the Persian/Arabian Gulf which was under British protection. He took along his eleven-year-old son, Abd al-Aziz ibn Saud.

Ibn Saud

Abd al-Aziz ibn Saud, or Ibn Saud as he is usually known in history, was, like George Washington, the father of his country, in both a political and a literal sense.[1] He grew up in exile in Kuwait, where he brooded and schemed about how to regain the lands of the Saudis. When he reached the age of twenty-one, in 1902, he decided on a bold stroke to reach his goal. Crossing the desert with a small band of followers, he scaled the walls of Riyadh at night and seized the fortress by surprise at daybreak. This daring exploit won him the support of the people of Riyadh, who drove the Rashidis out of the town.

Over the next three decades Ibn Saud steadily expanded his territory. He said his goal was "to recover all the lands of our forefathers."[2] In World War I he became an ally of the British, fighting the Ottoman Turks in Arabia. In return, the British provided arms for his followers and gave him a monthly allowance. The British continued to back Ibn Saud after the war, and in 1924 he entered Mecca in triumph. His major rival, Sharif Husayn, who had been appointed by the Ottman government as the "Protector of the Holy Places," fled into exile. (Sharif Husayn was the great-grandfather of King Hussein I of Jordan.)

Ibn Saud's second goal, after recovering his ancestral lands, was to build a modern nation under a central government. He used as his motto the Koranic verse, "God changes not what is in a people until they change what is in themselves" (*Sura XIII, II*). The first step was to gain recognition of Saudi Arabia as an independent state. The United Kingdom recognized the country in 1927, and other countries soon followed suit. In 1932 the country took its present name of Saudi Arabia, a union of the three provinces of Hejaz, Nejd, and al-Hasa.

SAUDI ARABIA

Ibn Saud's second step in his "grand design" for his new country was to establish order under a central government. To do this, he began to build settlements and to encourage the nomads to settle down, live in permanent homes, and learn how to grow their own food rather than relying on the desert. Those who settled on the land were given seeds and tools, were enrolled in a sort of national guard, and were paid regular allowances. These former Bedouin warriors became in time the core of the Saudi armed forces.

Ibn Saud also established the country's basic political system. The basis for the system was the Wahhabi interpretation of Islamic law. Ibn Saud insisted that "the laws of the state shall always be in accordance with the Book of Allah and the Sunna (Conduct) of His Messenger and the ways of the Companions."[3] He saw no need for a written constitution, and as yet Saudi Arabia has none. (A committee was formed in 1980 to draw up a two-hundred-article "System of Rule," also based on Islamic principles, under pressure from some of the royal princes for political reform. However, it has not yet issued its report.) Ibn Saud decreed that the country would be governed as an absolute monarchy, with rulers always chosen from the Saud family. He was unfamiliar with political parties and distrusted them in principle; political organizations were therefore prohibited in the Kingdom. Yet Ibn Saud was himself democratic, humble in manner, and spartan in his living habits. He remained all his life a man of the people, and held every day a public assembly (majlis) in Riyadh at which any citizen had the right to ask favors or present petitions. (The custom of holding a daily majlis has been observed by Saudi rulers ever since.) More often than not, petitioners would address Ibn Saud not as Your Majesty but simply as Abd al-Aziz (his given name) as a dramatic example of Saudi democracy in action.

Ibn Saud died in 1953. He had witnessed the beginning of rapid social and economic change in his country due to oil revenues. Yet his successors have presided over a transformation beyond the imaginations of the warriors who scaled the walls of Riyadh half a century earlier. Almost the only building left in Riyadh from that period is the Masmak Fort, headquarters of the Rashidi leader, still standing in the midst of tall modern buildings as a reminder to

The Great Mosque at Mecca, in Saudi Arabia, is the holiest of shrines to Muslims. Historically, Mecca was the site at which Islam was founded in the seventh century AD by the Prophet Muhammad. Pilgrims today flock to the Great Mosque to fulfill their Muslim duties as set down by the Five Pillars of Islam.

young Saudis of the epic age in their nation's history.

Ibn Saud was succeeded by his eldest surviving son, Crown Prince Saud. A number of royal princes felt that the second son, Faisal, should have become the new king because of his greater experience in foreign affairs and economic management. Saud's only experience was as governor of the Nejd province of the interior.

The new king was like his father in a number of ways, although he was large and corpulent and lacked Ibn Saud's forceful personality. He was more comfortable in a desert tent than in running a bureaucracy or meeting foreign dignitaries. Also, like his father, he had no idea of the value of money. Ibn Saud would carry a sackful of riyals (the Saudi currency) to the daily majlis and give them away to petitioners. His son, Saud, not only doled out money to petitioners but also

gave millions to other members of the royal family. One of his greatest extravagances was a palace surrounded by a bright pink wall.[4]

By 1958 the country was almost bankrupt. The royal family was understandably nervous about a possible coup supported by other Arab states, such as Egypt and Syria, which were openly critical of Saudi Arabia because of its lack of political institutions. The senior princes issued an ultimatum to Saud: first he would put Faisal in charge of straightening out the kingdom's finances, and when that had been done he would abdicate. The financial overhaul was completed in 1964, and with the kingdom again on a sound footing, Saud abdicated in favor of Faisal.

This incident offers a good example of how the Saudi monarchy operates in crisis situations. Decisions are made collectively, and although the king is an absolute monarch to his subjects, he serves as "head of the family" and in reality must consult with the senior princes on all matters of policy. Decisions are also made in secret in order to give the impression of family unity to the outside world. The reasons for a decision must always be guessed at; the Saudis never explain them. It is a system very different form the open, freewheeling one of Western democracies. Yet it has given Saudi Arabia stability and leadership in at least two occasions when crises threatened the kingdom: the financial crisis under Saud, and the seizure of the Great Mosque in Mecca in 1979.

FAISAL AND HIS SUCCESSORS

The reign of King Faisal (1964-1975) is second in importance only to that of Ibn Saud in terms of state building. One author wrote of King Faisal during his reign, "He is leading the country with gentle insistence from medievalism into the jet age."[5] Faisal's gentle insistence showed itself in many different ways. Encouraged by his wife, Queen Iffat, he introduced education for girls into the kingdom; the first school for girls opened in 1960. Before Faisal, the kingdom had had no systematic development plans. In introducing the first Five-Year Development Plan, the king said that "our religion requires us to progress and to bear the burden of the highest tradition and best manners."[6]

In foreign affairs, Faisal ended the Yemen Civil War on an honorable basis for both sides, took an active part in the Islamic world in keeping with his role as Protector of the Holy Places, and in 1970 he founded the Organization of the Islamic Conference (OIC), which has given the Islamic nations of the world a voice in international affairs. (The Islamic states have succeeded on a number of occasions in passing UN resolutions supporting Palestinian rights to self-determination and condemning Israel for its occupation of the West Bank, Gaza, and the Golan Heights.) Faisal laid down the basic strategy which his successors have followed, namely, avoidance of direct conflict, mediation of disputes behind the scenes, and use of oil wealth as a political weapon when necessary. The king never understood the American commitment to Israel, but he remained adamantly opposed to communism throughout his life. This attitude led him into an alliance with the United States, despite the two countries' divergence of interests.

Faisal was assassinated in March 1975 by a deranged nephew while he was holding

In Saudi Arabia rapid development began in the 1960s. Pictured above is construction work being carried out at a building site in Riyadh.

the daily majlis. The assassination was another test of the system of rule by consensus in the royal family, and the system held firm. Khalid, Faisal's eldest half-brother and junior by six years, succeeded him without incident and ruled until 1982. King Khalid, who was already in poor health, delegated most of his powers to his half-brother Fahd. He died suddenly in 1982, and Crown Prince Fahd, the current ruler, succeeded him.

THE MECCA MOSQUE SIEGE

The most shocking event in Saudi history since the founding of the kingdom was the seizure of the Great Mosque in Mecca, Islam's holiest shrine, by a group of fundamentalist Sunni Muslims in November 1979. The leader of the group declared that one of its members was the *Mahdi* (in Sunni Islam, the "Awaited One") who had come to announce the Day of Judgment. The group occupied the mosque for two weeks. The siege was finally overcome by army and national guard units, but with considerable loss of life on both sides. No one knows yet

exactly what the group's purpose was, nor did it lead to any general expressions of dissatisfaction with the regime. But as David Long suggests, the incident reflects the very real fear of the Saudi rulers of a coup attempted by the ultrareligious right, perhaps a reawakening of the Wahhabi spirit of long ago.

Although the Saudi government remains the most staunchly conservative in the Middle East, it has before it the example of Iran, where a similar Islamic fundamentalist movement overthrew a well-established monarchy. Furthermore, the Shia Muslim population of the country is concentrated in al-Hasa Province, where the oilfields are located. The government's immediate fear after the Great Mosque seizure was of an outside plot inspired by Iran. When this plot did not materialize, the Saudis feared Shia involvement. Outside of increased security measures, the principal result of the incident has been a large increase in funding for the Shia community.

THE ECONOMY

Oil was discovered in Saudi Arabia in 1938, but exports did not begin until after World War II. The oilfields are located in the eastern provinces and in the Neutral Zone. Saudi oil reserves are the world's largest, and, despite high rates of production, more oil has been discovered in recent years than has been taken out of the ground. In 1982 reserves were estimated at 165 billion barrels, along with proven natural gas reserves of 3.2 billion cubic meters. Until 1980 oil production and export was controlled by the Arabian-American Oil Company (Aramco), a consortium of four United States oil companies. The oil industry was nationalized in 1980; it is now managed by Petromin, a Saudi government agency.

King Faisal's reorganization of finances and development plans in the 1960s set the kingdom on an upward course of rapid development. The economy took off after 1973, when the Saudis, along with other Arab oil-producing states, reduced production and imposed an embargo on exports on Western countries as a gesture of support to Egypt in its war with Israel. After 1973 the price per barrel of Saudi oil continued to increase, to a peak of $34.00 per barrel in 1981. (Prior to the embargo it was $3.00 per barrel; in 1979 it was $13.30 per barrel.) The outbreak of the Iran-Iraq War in 1980 caused a drop of about 318 million barrels per day in world production. The Saudis took up the slack, increasing their oil output to 10.3 million barrels per day.

| Wahhabis seize Mecca and Medina **1800** | Ibn Saud captures Riyadh in daring commando raid **1902** | Ibn Saud recognized by British as king of Saudi Arabia **1927** | Oil exports get underway under management of Aramco **1946** | King Saud, eldest son and successor of Ibn Saud, deposed in favor of his brother Faisal **1963** | Faisal assassinated by a deranged nephew; succession passes by agreement to Khalid **1975** | Great Mosque in Mecca seized by fundamentalist Muslim group **1979** |

1980s

Reagan administration sells five AWACS aircraft to kingdom; King Khalid dies; succession passes to Crown Prince Fahd

Saudi jets shoot down Iranian jet for violation of Saudi air space

New budget of $46 billion reflects sharply reduced revenues

The huge revenues from oil have made possible economic development on a scale undreamed of by Ibn Saud and his Bedouin warriors. The old fishing ports of Yanbu, on the Red Sea, and Jubail, on the Gulf, were transformed into new industrial cities, with oil refineries, cement and petrochemical plants, steel mills, and dozens of related industries. By 1983 Jubail had a population of 170,000. Yanbu doubled in size, to 40,000, between 1977 and 1981. Cities were transformed. Riyadh, isolated in the desert, experienced a building boom as Cadillacs bumped into camels on the streets and the shops filled up with imported luxury goods. Every native Saudi, it seemed, profited from the boom with free education and health care, low-interest housing loans, and a guaranteed job.

The boom also attracted a large foreign labor force, drawn by the high wages. Most of this labor force came from poor countries such as the Yemen Arab Republic, Pakistan, South Korea, and the Philippines. The remittances sent home by these workers became a vital source of income to their countries.

The world oil oversupply and falling demand in the 1980s have hit Saudi Arabia hard. The Saudis had become accustomed to a high standard of living, and never expected it to end. But as oil revenues began to drop, the necessary belt tightening did not sit well with them. Many foreign contracts had to be cancelled and projects delayed. The newly rich middle class, many of its members the sons of camel herders, suddenly faced a future of retrenchment, scarce jobs, and a ten-percent profit as opposed to the former one-hundred-percent profit.

THE FUTURE

Saudi Arabia after 1985 is a question mark. The oil wealth is a mixed blessing. As William Quandt says, "Wealth comes from connections, from free wheeling, by good luck—but not primarily because of hard work. There are few incentives for young Saudis to learn a technical skill . . . to use their talents to develop their country."[7] The country is not about to enter into political relations with any Communist country,[8] and in the absence of any means of organized political activity, the Saudis seem unlikely to exchange their well-established family monarchy for a new governing system.

In economic terms, the outlook for Saudi Arabia is for less spending, more husbanding of resources, and diversification of industries to lessen dependence on oil. Thus the 1985-1986 budget sets expenditures at $55 billion, a 6-percent reduction over the previous year. To achieve this reduction, customs duties were raised, wheat subsidies to farmers were reduced, and electricity and water rates were tripled. But the continued high level per capita income and the network of ongoing free social services make such draconian measures acceptable to Saudis as the price they must pay for continued development. This high income level makes the country a good market for foreign business investment even if the enormous profits of previous years are no longer there. And as the head of the Councils of Saudi Chambers of Commerce noted proudly, "We have a beautiful infrastructure now, our schools, airports, ports, roads, power plants and hospitals are 'state-of-the-art.'"[9]

FOOTNOTES

1. He had twenty-four sons by sixteen different women during his life (1880-1953). See William Quandt, *Saudi Arabia in the 1980's* (Washington, DC: Brookings Institution, 1981), Appendix E, for a genealogy.
2. George Rentz, "The Saudi Monarchy," in Willard A. Beling, ed., *King Faisal and the Modernization of Saudi Arabia* (Boulder, CO: Westview Press, 1980), pp. 26-27.
3. *Ibid.*, p. 29.
4. The wall was torn down by his successor, King Faisal. Justin Coe, in *The Christian Science Monitor*, February 13, 1985.
5. Gordon Gaskill, "Saudi Arabia's Modern Monarch," *Reader's Digest*, January 1967, p. 118.
6. Ministry of Information, Kingdom of Saudi Arabia, *Faisal Speaks*, (n.d.), p. 88.
7. Quandt, *op. cit.*, pp. 91-92.
8. John A. Shaw and David E. Long, in *Saudi Arabian Modernization* (New York: Praeger, 1982), point out that the markets in Saudi cities are filled with goods from Communist China. "In Saudi eyes, business is business and politics is politics; to mix them up merely confuses everyone." p. 106.
9. Quoted in *The Christian Science Monitor*, April 18, 1985.

DEVELOPMENT

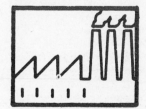

Wealth from oil revenues has enabled Saudi Arabia to move rapidly toward self-sufficiency in food. The main thrust is toward expanding the water supply. Twenty underground aquifers had been located and exploited by 1983. The 1980-1985 Plan allocated almost $28.8 billion in agriculture. Other large sums were invested in desalination plants.

FREEDOM

Saudi Arabia is an absolute monarchy with rule vested in the family of Saud. It has no written constitution and no legislature; political parties are prohibited. However, in 1980 the king formed a committee to draw up a 200-article "system of rule." If this document is completed, it will provide for a Consultative Council to advise the ruler on legislation.

HEALTH/WELFARE

Education holds a high priority in the kingdom. In the 1960s and 1970s thousands of Saudis were sent abroad for technical training, most to the US. A domestic university system was developed rapidly with the help of foreign specialists. Saudi students are not politicized and student unrest is absent.

ACHIEVEMENTS

Saudi Arabia is a major contributor to aid to other Arab states and developing nations. Between 1972 and 1983 $25 billion in Saudi aid went to various states. The bulk of this aid, averaging $1 billion annually, goes to Arab "front-line states" in the struggle with Israel, such as Jordan and Syria.

Sudan (Democratic Republic of the Sudan)

GEOGRAPHY

Area in Square Kilometers (Miles):
2,504,530 (967,500)
Capital (Population): Khartoum (1.25 million) (1981)
Climate: desert in north to tropical in south

PEOPLE

Population
Total: 21,103,000
Annual Growth Rate: 2.7%
Rural/Urban Population Ratio: 77/23
Ethnic Makeup of Population: 52% black; 39% Arab; 6% Beja; 3% other

Health
Life Expectancy at Birth: 47 years
Infant Death Rate (Ratio): 131/1,000
Average Caloric Intake: 99% of FAO minimum
Physicians Available (Ratio): 1/8,930

Religion(s)
70% Sunni Muslim in north; 20% indigenous beliefs; 5% Christian; 5% other

Education
Adult Literacy Rate: 20%

COMMUNICATION

Telephones: 65,030
Newspapers: n/a

SUDAN

Sudan is really two nations, a Muslim Arab north and a Christian and traditional south peopled by various African societies. One of these is the Dinka, incredibly tall, spear-carrying cattleherders. A young Dinka, seven-footer Manute Bol, was the star center on the University of Bridgeport, Connecticut basketball team during the 1984-1985 season, although he had never played the game before coming to the United States.

The southerners fought a seventeen-year war with the north to gain regional autonomy, and President Nimeiri's imposition of Islamic law over them in 1983 led to renewed rebellion. In 1985 the new government abolished Islamic law courts, but it has yet to come to terms with the southerners on regional autonomy.

TRANSPORTATION

Highways—Kilometers (Miles):
20,000 (12,428) total; 1,700 (1,056) bituminous
Railroads—Kilometers (Miles): 5,516 (3,428)
Commercial Airports: 90

GOVERNMENT

Type: republic; currently under military rule; return to civilian government pledged for 1986
Independence Date: January 1, 1956
Head of State: President (General) Abd al-Rahman Swareddahab
Political Parties: currently 38 approved; strongest is Umma Party
Suffrage: universal adult

MILITARY

Number of Armed Forces: 57,500
Military Expenditures (% of Central Government Expenditures): 0.95%
Current Hostilities: none

ECONOMY

Currency ($ US Equivalent): 2.50 Sudanese pounds = $1 (March 1985)
Per Capita Income/GNP: $345/$7.1 billion (1983)
Inflation Rate: 15.2% (1970-1982)
Natural Resources: oil; iron ore; copper; chrome; other industrial metals
Agriculture: cotton; peanuts; sesame; gum arabic; sorghum; wheat
Industry: textiles; cement; cotton ginning; edible oils; distilling; pharmaceuticals

FOREIGN TRADE

Exports: $560 million (1983)
Imports: $1.7 billion (1983)

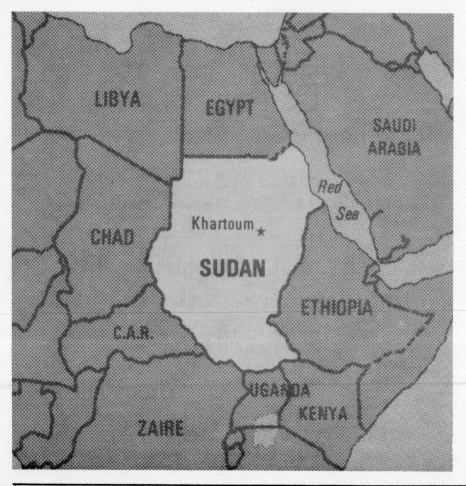

SUDAN

Sudan is the largest nation in Africa, with a land area of 967,500 square miles, four times the size of Texas. It has a population of 21,103,000, with relatively low overall density. The bulk of the population is concentrated in the province of Khartoum (also the name of the capital) and in the central region, which includes the Blue Nile and the White Nile, the country's principal rivers.

The name of the country underscores its distinctive social structure. Centuries ago Arab geographers named it Bilad al-Sudan, "Land of the Blacks." The northern half, including Khartoum, is Arab in language, culture, and traditions, and Islamic in religion. The southern half is sub-Saharan African, made up of a number of black African peoples, the Shilluk, Dinka, Nuer, Azande, and many others. Some of them are Christian due to the efforts of European mission schools established during the British occupation. Others believe in traditional religions. The two halves of Sudan have little or nothing in common. The country's basic political problem is how to achieve unity between these two different societies that were brought together under British rule to form an artificial nation.

HISTORY

The ancient history of Sudan, at least the northern region, was always linked with that of Egypt. Both the pharaohs and later conquerors of Egypt—Persians, Greeks, Romans, and eventually the Arabs, Turks, and British—periodically attempted to extend their power farther south. The connection with Egypt became very close when the Egyptians were converted to Islam by invading armies from Arabia in the seventh century AD. As the invaders spread southward, they converted the northern Sudanese people to Islam, developing in time an Islamic Arab society in the northern Sudan. The southern Sudan remained comparatively untouched because it was separated by geographical barriers, mountain ranges and the great impassable swamps of the Nile.

The two regions were forcibly brought together by conquering Egyptian armies in the nineteenth century. The conquest became possible after the exploration of sub-Saharan Africa by European explorers. After the explorers and armies came slave traders and then European fortune hunters, interested in developing the gold, ivory, diamonds, timber, and other resources of sub-Saharan Africa.

The soldiers and slave traders were the most brutal of all these invaders, particu-larly in the southern Sudan. In fact, many of the slave traders were Muslim Sudanese from the north. The Civil War of 1955-1972 between northern and southern Sudan had its roots in the nineteenth-century experiences of the southerners, as "memories of plunder, slave raiding and suffering" at the hands of slavers and their military allies were passed down from generation to generation.[1]

ORIGINS OF THE SUDANESE STATE

The first effort to establish a nation in Sudan began in the 1880s. The country was ruled by the British as part of their protectorate over Egypt. The British were hated as foreign, non-Muslim rulers. The Egyptians, who made up the bulk of the security forces assigned to Sudan, were hated for their arrogance and mistreatment of the Sudanese.

In 1881 a religious leader in Northern Sudan announced that he was the Mahdi, the "Awaited One" who, according to Sunni Islamic belief, would appear on earth, sent by God to rid the Sudan of its foreign rulers. The Mahdi called for a *jihad* (holy war or struggle) against the British and the Egyptians.

Sudanese by the thousands flocked to join the Mahdi. His warriors, fired by revolutionary zeal, defeated several British-led Egyptian armies. In 1885 they captured Khartoum, and soon thereafter the Mahdi's rule extended over the whole of present-day Sudan. For this reason, the Mahdi is remembered, at least in northern Sudan, as Abu al-Istiqlal, "Father of Independence."[2]

The Mahdi's rule did not last long; he died in 1886. His chief lieutenant and successor, the Khalifa Abdallahi, continued in power until 1898, when a British force armed with guns mowed down his spear-carrying, club-wielding army. Sudan was ruled jointly by the United Kingdom and Egypt from then until 1955. Since the British already ruled Egypt as a protectorate, for all practical purposes joint rule meant British rule.

Under the British, Sudan was divided into a number of provinces, and British university graduates staffed the country's first civil service.[3] But the British followed two policies that have created problems for Sudan since it became independent. One was "indirect rule" in the north. Rather than developing a group of trained Sudanese administrators who could take over when they left, the British governed indirectly through local chiefs and religious leaders. The second policy was to separate southern from northern Sudan through "Closed Door" laws which prohibited northerners from working in, or even visiting, the south.

INDEPENDENCE

Sudan became independent on New Year's Day, 1956, as a republic headed by a civilian government. The country is still officially a republic, but in its three decades of existence it has had five different governments. Only one of them was voted into office. The first civilian government lasted until 1958, when a military group seized power "to save the country from the chaotic regime of the politicians."[4] But the military regime soon became as "chaotic" as its predecessors. In 1964 it handed over power to another civilian group. The second civilian group was no more successful than the first had been, as the politicians continued to feud, and intermittent conflict between government forces and rebels in the southern region turned into all-out civil war.

In May 1969 the Sudanese Army carried out another military coup, headed by Colonel Ja'far (Gaafar) Nimeiri. Successive Sudanese governments since independence, including Nimeiri's, have faced the same basic problems: the unification of north and south, economic development without having any oil resources or a transportation system, and the building of a workable political system. Nimeiri's record in dealing with these difficult problems is one explanation for his longevity in power. A written constitution was approved in 1973. Although political parties were outlawed, an umbrella political organization, the Sudan Socialist Union, provided an alternative to the fractious political jockeying that divided the nation before Nimeiri.[5]

Nimeiri's firm control through the military and his effectiveness in carrying out political reforms were soon reflected at the ballot box. He was elected president in 1971 for a six-year term and was reelected in 1977. Yet broad popular support did not generate political stability. There were a number of attempts to overthrow him, the most serious in 1971 and 1976, when he was actually captured and held for a time by rebels. One reason for his survival may be his resourcefulness. After the 1976 coup attempt, for example, instead of having his opponents executed, he invited them and other opposition leaders to form a government of national unity. One of Nimeiri's major opponents, Sadiq al-Mahdi, great grandson of the Mahdi and himself an important religious leader, accepted the offer and returned from exile. Nimeiri's major achievement was to bring an end to the Civil War between north and south. An agreement was signed in 1972 in Addis Ababa, Ethiopia, mediated by Ethiopian authorities, between his government and the southern Anya Anya resistance movement. The agreement provided for regional autonomy for the south's three provinces, greater representation of southerners in the National People's Assembly, and integration of Anya Anya units into the armed forces without restrictions.

THE COUP OF 1985

Nimeiri was reelected in 1983 for a third presidential term. Most of his political opponents had apparently been reconciled with him, and the army and state security forces were firmly under his control. It seemed that the Sudan's most durable leader would round out another full term in office without too much difficulty. But storm clouds were brewing on the horizon. Nimeiri had survived for sixteen years in power largely through his ability to keep opponents divided and off balance by his unpredictable moves. From 1983 on, however, his policies seemed designed to unite rather than divide them.

The first step in Nimeiri's undoing was the institution of strict Islamic law (Shari'a) throughout the country. This action angered many people, but its impact was particularly heavy on the non-Muslim southern region. Yet Nimeiri followed it up with the reorganization of national and provincial administration into several regions plus the central government region of Khartoum. The idea was to streamline the cumbersome bureaucracy inherited from the British. But the consolidation of the three autonomous provinces of the southern into one province dependent upon the central government was considered by many southerners to be a violation of the commitment made to southern regional autonomy at the end of the Civil War. When Nimeiri pressed ahead with his reforms, a new rebel movement, Anya Anya II, turned again to civil war. The rebels' new strategy was not only to oppose government troops but also to strike at development projects essential to the economy. Foreign workers in the newly developed oilfields in southwestern Sudan were kidnapped or killed, and as a result Chevron Oil Company halted all work on the project.

A crackdown on Islamic fundamentalist groups, particularly the Muslim Brotherhood, added to Nimeiri's growing list of opponents. Members of the Brotherhood had been active in implementing Islamic law as the law of the land, but Nimeiri felt they had gone too far. By late 1984 it appeared that the president had angered or alienated everybody in the country, all for different reasons.

In the end it was the failure of his economic policies rather than anything else which brought about the fall of the leader. The International Monetary Fund (IMF) imposed strict austerity requirements on Sudan in June 1984 as a prerequisite to a $90 million standby loan to enable the country to pay its mounting food and fuel bills. The former were aggravated by famine, the latter by the necessity to import almost all fuel requirements. The IMF insisted on drastic budget cuts, devaluation of currency, and an end to subsidies on basic commodities. If Nimeiri had been able to carry out these reforms he would have stood a chance of restoring the country to solvency and his own rule to respectability. Protests turned to riots, mainly over the end of price subsidies and a consequent thirty-three-percent increase in the prices of such necessities as bread, sugar, and cooking oil. Other protests erupted over the application of Islamic law, especially the ban on alcohol, which brought thousands of Sudanese into the streets shouting "We want beer! We want beer!"

Nimeiri's departure for the United States to seek further economic help triggered a general strike in April 1985. A genuine national movement arose, uniting students, doctors, lawyers, engineers, and other professionals with the urban poor, all demanding that Nimeiri resign. Fearing anarchy or an uprising by young army officers, the senior military leaders moved quickly, took over the government, and ordered Nimeiri deposed. Crowds in Khartoum shouted "Nimeiri the butcher is finished; the country belongs to the people." "He's nothing, let him sell lemons," cried one demonstrator, and others tore Nimeiri's picture from devalued banknotes.[6]

The new military government, headed by General Abd al-Rahman Swareddahab, a highly respected senior officer, promised to hold elections within a year to restore civilian rule and to revive political parties. But the euphoria over the departure of "Nimeiri the butcher" was tempered by the realization that the same set of gigantic problems that had daunted Nimeiri remained to haunt his successors. These included the crushing burden of foreign debt, a weak economy based on inefficient agricultural production, a totally inadequate transportation system, and personal rivalries among political leaders. How long the new unity generated by Nimeiri's policies would last was anybody's guess. An encouraging sign was the formation of a largely civilian cabinet; its only military members were the ministers of defense and interior, and the dreaded internal security service that Nimeiri had formed to implement Islamic law was disbanded.

THE ECONOMY

Although the attainment of political stability remained important to Sudanese development, in the long run it was dependent upon the economy—creating jobs, educating youth, building a future for the country's population that would keep pace with population growth. Unfortunately, the Sudanese economy was, and still is, a weak reed to lean on. The economy is largely dependent upon agriculture. The most important crop is cotton, and cotton exports are affected by world demand and the resulting price fluctuations. Until recently the only other export crop of importance was gum arabic, gathered by hand from the trunks of a small desert tree, the acacia, and used in the manufacture of adhesive, inks, confectionery, and pharmaceutical products.

Because Sudan has a great agricultural potential due to its rivers, alluvial soils, and vast areas of unused arable land, Nimeiri had set out in the 1970s to develop the country into what experts told him could be the "breadbasket" of the Middle East. Enough food could be grown through the expansion of agriculture, he was told, to meet all domestic needs, raise the country's low standard of living, and cover the food needs of all the Arab countries, most of which are not self-sufficient and must import food. To reach this ambitious goal, cotton plantations were converted to production of grain crops. The huge Kenana sugar-refinery complex was started with joint foreign and Sudanese management, the long-established Gezira cotton scheme was expanded, and work began on the Jonglei Canal, intended to drain a vast marshy area called the Sudd (swamp) in the south, in order to bring hundreds of thousands of acres of marshlands under cultivation.

But the breadbasket was never filled. It was almost as if the Sudanese government had had a good idea but had implemented it from the wrong end. Mismanagement and lack of skilled labor delayed some of these projects, while others languished because the roads and communications systems needed to implement them did not exist. The most critical need was for domestic sources of oil. Many foreign oil companies have prospected for years for oil in Sudan, but thus far only one, Chevron, has struck oil in commercial quantities (in 1981). The

| Egyptian province under Muhammad Ali 1820 | Mahdi rebellion against the British and Egyptians 1881 | British recapture Khartoum; establishment of joint Anglo-Egyptian control 1899 | Sudan becomes an independent republic 1956 | Civil War 1956-1971 | Nimeiri seizes power, ends Civil War 1969, 1971 | 1980s |

| Riots and strikes in response to austerity measures | Nimeiri overthrown by army leaders in bloodless coup | Nearly nine million people dying of starvation |

Chevron oilfield is in southwestern Sudan, but the nearest refinery is at Port Sudan on the Red Sea, 840 miles away. Instead of developing a network of roads or building a new refinery near the field, the Nimeiri government decided to build an 840-mile pipeline to Port Sudan. It seemed to the southerners that they would receive none of the benefits from having oil discovered in their part of the country, and the pipeline became one of the main causes of the renewed Civil War.

FAMINE: AN EVER-PRESENT REALITY

Due to its economic difficulties, Sudan ranked near the bottom of the scale defining the "less-developed countries" established by the UN, with a per capita income of $370 per year, in the 1970s. But the individual Sudanese was not so badly off as might appear from this figure, since the economy outside the cities was a barter one in which little money changed hands. Until Nimeiri imposed steep price increases on bread, soap, and cooking oil, the average person was little affected by budget deficits and staggering fuel bills.

But in the early 1980s average Sudanese were increasingly affected by circumstances which were not in their power or their government's power to control. Beginning in 1973 a cycle of drought had spread from the sub-Saharan Sahel region across Africa to affect Sudan and its near neighbors. The drought became critical in 1983, and millions of refugees from Ethiopia and

Chad, the countries most affected, moved into temporary camps in Sudan. Then it was Sudan's turn to suffer; desperate families fled from their villages as wells dried up, cattle died, and crops wilted. By 1985 an estimated nine million persons, half of them native Sudanese, were dying of starvation. Emergency food supplies from many countries poured into Sudan, but due to inadequate transportation, port delays, and diversion of shipments by incompetent or dishonest officials, much of this relief could not be delivered to those who most needed it. Average waiting time for unloading grain at Port Sudan was up to twelve days by July 1985. More than 400,000 bags of grain already unloaded lay on the docks, waiting for trucks that did not come because they were immobilized somewhere else, stuck in the sand or mired in the mud of one of Sudan's few passable roads. Equally distressing things were happening along Sudan's one railroad, from Khartoum to Kosti and on to the heart of the drought-stricken region at Nyala. While refugees starved in Darfur Province, heavy rains to the east washed out track sections, and out of one shipment of six thousand tons, half vanished before arrival at Nyala. "Use your imagination," a UN distribution official told a reporter, indicating corruption or theft, or both.[7] Meanwhile, at the far end of this thin lifeline, children grew weaker daily from malnutrition as their parents waited for the promised rations. Hassan Atiya, Sudanese deputy commissioner for refugees, estimated the death rate for children at two thou-

sand per day in the worst famine of this century.

Muslim Sudanese, like other Muslims, have a profound belief in the power of Allah over all things, and of the consequent inevitability of events that shape their lives. But, understandably, they wonder why starvation is to be their lot, with the limitless possibilities for improvement of their lives promised for years by their national leaders.

FOOTNOTES

1. Dunstan Wai, *The African-Arab Conflict in the Sudan* (New York: Africana Publishing Co., 1981), p. 32.

2. Southerners are not so favorable; in the south the Mahdi's government was as cruel as the Egyptian. *Ibid.*, p. 31.

3. Peter M. Holt, in *The History of the Sudan*, 3rd edition (London: Weidenfeld and Nicolson, 1979), p. 123, quotes the British governor as saying that they were recruited on the basis of "good health, high character and fair abilities."

4. *Ibid.*, p. 171.

5. The SSU is defined as "a grand alliance of workers, farmers, intellectuals, business people and soldiers." Harold D. Nelson, ed., *Sudan, A Country Study* (Washington, DC: American University, Foreign Area Studies, 1982), p. 199.

6. *The Christian Science Monitor*, April 16, 1985.

7. David K. Willis, in *The Christian Science Monitor*, July 11, 1985.

DEVELOPMENT

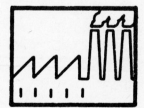

The Kenana Sugar Company, established in 1976, grows under irrigation sugarcane which is refined on site for domestic consumption. The firm employs 12,700 workers. Originally a showcase project, it ran into difficulties due to mismanagement and disagreements among its foreign backers. These difficulties have been resolved and it is now in full production.

FREEDOM

During most of the period of independence before Nimeiri's seizure of power, Sudan had an open political system with numerous parties. The Sudanese Socialist Union became dominant under Nimeiri. But freedom of speech and other rights are widely observed. The country's new leaders have pledged elections for a civilian government in April 1986.

HEALTH/WELFARE

Sudan's population has one of the highest growth rates in the world, and infant mortality is 131 per 1,000. But these rates are likely to change as a result of the current critical famine, affecting both children and adults.

ACHIEVEMENTS

Oil discoveries in 1981 offered hope that Sudan might reduce its fuel bills through domestic production. But the political decision to build a pipeline to the coast rather than a refinery inland near the oilfields triggered renewed civil war, and both pipeline construction and oil production are currently stopped.

Syria (Syrian Arab Republic)

GEOGRAPHY

Area in Square Kilometers (Miles):
185,170 (71,500)
Capital (Population): Damascus
(2,083,000 in metropolitan area)
Climate: predominantly dry

PEOPLE

Population
Total: 10,075,000
Annual Growth Rate: 3.4%
Rural/Urban Population Ratio: 51/49
Ethnic Makeup of Population: 90.3%
Arab; 9.7% Kurd, Armenian,
Circassian, and Turk

Health
Life Expectancy at Birth: 64 years
Infant Death Rate (Ratio): 57/1,000
Average Caloric Intake: 120% of
FAO minimum
Physicians Available (Ratio): 1/2,270

Religion(s)
74% Sunni Muslim; 16% Alawite,
Druze, and other Muslim sects; 10%
Christian

Education
Adult Literacy Rate: 50%

COMMUNICATION

Telephones: 236,000
Newspapers: 3 dailies in Damascus;
others in other major cities

ANCIENT CIVILIZATIONS

In Syria, as in other areas of the Middle East, the visitor is surrounded by the ruined monuments of many long-vanished civilizations. Some
are not only visible but still in use; the Roman waterwheels of Hama
turn creakingly, bringing water up from the Orontes River for thirsty
citizens as they have for centuries. One comes upon others suddenly;
Palmyra (Tadmor), "Bride of the Desert," appears abruptly at the edge
of the ferocious Syrian desert like a mirage of Roman civilization, with
its broken columns and arches. Still others must be dug up laboriously
from mounds. At Tell Mardikh, due north of Hama, archaeologists have
uncovered the ruins of Ebla, a powerful state of four thousand years ago
with a written language and an elaborate royal court. Ebla was a meeting place for ancient civilizations, just as modern Syria is a bridge between
Mediterranean and West Asian cultures.

TRANSPORTATION

Highways—Kilometers (Miles):
16,939 (10,526) total; 12,051 (7,488)
paved
Railroads—Kilometers (Miles): 1,543
(959)
Commercial Airports: 67

GOVERNMENT

Type: republic, under Socialist
regime since March 1963
Independence Date: April 17, 1946
Head of State: President (Lieutenant
General) Hafez al-Assad
Political Parties: Arab Socialist
Resurrectionist Party; Syrian Arab
Socialist Party; Arab Union Socialist
Party; Unionist Socialist Party;
Communist Party of Syria
Suffrage: universal at 18

MILITARY

Number of Armed Forces: 197,500
*Military Expenditures (% of Central
Government Expenditures):* 29%
Current Hostilities: troops in Lebanon as peacekeeping force since 1975,
intervened to halt factional conflicts
in late 1985

ECONOMY

Currency ($ US Equivalent): 3.92
Syrian pounds = $1 (March 1985)
Per Capita Income/GNP: $1,957/$18.4
billion (1981)
Inflation Rate: 13% (1981)
Natural Resources: crude oil;
phosphates; chrome, iron, and
manganese ores; asphalt; rock salt;
marble; gypsum
Agriculture: cotton; wheat; barley;
sugar beets; tobacco; sheep and goat
raising
Industry: petroleum; mining;
manufacturing; textiles; food
processing; construction

FOREIGN TRADE

Exports: $2.0 billion (1982)
Imports: $3.7 billion (1982)

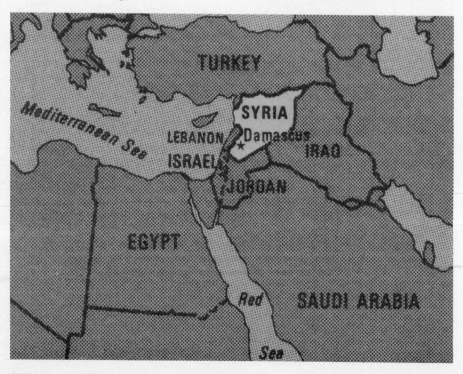

SYRIA

The modern Syrian state is a pale shadow of Syria as it existed centuries ago. Ancient Syria was a powerful kingdom stretching from the Euphrates River to the Mediterranean Sea in the time of Christ. It included the modern countries of Israel, Jordan, Lebanon, Iraq, and southern Turkey. During the first two centuries of Islam, the caliphs ("successors" of Muhammad) ruled a vast empire from their capital at Damascus. Damascus (today the capital of the republic) and Aleppo, Syria's other major city, both claim, with reason, to be the oldest continuously inhabited city in the world. Arab geographers viewed Syria as a large geographical unit, *Bilad ash-Sham* ("the lands of greater Syria").

Modern Syria is a nation of artificial boundaries. Its borders were determined by agreement between France and the United Kingdom after World War I. The country's current boundaries are with Turkey, Iraq, Jordan, Israel, and Lebanon. The only one of these boundaries in dispute is the Golan Heights, which was seized and annexed unilaterally by Israel in the 1970s. The border with Turkey is defined by a single-track railroad, perhaps the only case in the world of a railroad put to that use. Syria's other borders are artificial lines established by outside powers for convenience.

Syria is artificial in another sense: its political system was established by outside powers. Since becoming independent in 1946, the Syrians have struggled to find a political system that works for them. The large number of coups and frequent changes in government are evidence of this struggle. The most stable government in Syria's independent history is the current one, which has been in power since 1970.

Syrian political instability stems from the division of the population into separate ethnic and religious groups. The Syrians are an amalgamation of many different ethnoreligious groups that have settled the region over the centuries. The majority of the population are Sunni Muslim Arabs. The Alawis form the largest minority group. Although the Alawis are nominally Shia Muslims, the Sunni Muslims distrust them not primarily because of religion but because of their secret rituals and because as a minority they are very clannish. A second large minority is the Druze, who are distrusted by both Sunni Muslims and Alawis because their religion, an offshoot of Islam, has Christian and Jewish elements and secret rituals. There are a number of Christian denominations, the most important being the Armenians, and a community of

Jews with ancient origins. Syria also has a number of groups that are distinguished from the rest of the population by language or origin, the largest group being the Kurds (who are Sunni Muslims).

Although Syrian cities are slowly becoming more homogeneous in population, the different communities still constitute a majority in certain areas. Thus, the Alawis make up sixty percent of the population of the northern coast, the Druze (about three percent of the total population) are dominant in the Jabal Druze area in southwestern Syria, and the Kurds live predominantly in the mountains north of Aleppo.

HISTORY

Syria's greatest period was probably that of the Umayyad caliphs (AD 661-750), rulers of a vast Islamic empire. The first Umayyad caliph, Muawiya, is considered one of the political geniuses of Islam. He described his political philosophy to a visitor as follows:

I apply not my lash where my tongue suffices,
nor my sword where my whip is enough.
If there be one hair binding me to my fellow men
I let it not break.
If they pull I loosen;
If they loosen I pull.[1]

During this period of Umayyad rule Damascus became a great center of learning and culture. But later Umayyad caliphs were no more successful than their modern Syrian counterparts in developing effective government. They ruled by fear, repression, and heavy taxation. They also made new non-Arab converts to Islam pay a special tax from which Arab Muslims were exempted. They were finally overthrown by non-Arab Muslim invaders from Iraq. From that time until Syria became an independent republic, its destinies were determined by outsiders.

Syria was ruled by the Ottoman Turks for four centuries as a part of their empire. It was divided into provinces, each province being governed by a pasha whose job it was to collect taxes and keep order (with the help of an Ottoman garrison). In mountain areas such as Lebanon, then part of Syria, the Ottomans delegated authority to the heads of powerful families or leaders of religious communities. The Ottomans recognized each of these communities as a *millet*, a Turkish word meaning "nation." The religious head of each millet represented the

millet in dealings with Ottoman officials. The Ottomans in turn allowed each millet leader to manage the community's internal affairs. The result was that Syrian society became a series of sealed compartments. The millet system has disappeared, but its effects have lingered on to the present day, making national unity difficult.

The French Mandate

In the nineteenth century, as Ottoman rule weakened and conflict developed between Muslim, Christian, and Druze communities in Syria, the French began to intervene directly in Syria to help the Maronite Christians. French Jesuits founded schools for Christian children, and in 1860 French troops landed in Lebanon to protect the Christian Maronites from massacres by the Druze. French forces were withdrawn after the Ottoman government agreed to establish a separate Maronite region in the Lebanese mountains. This arrangement brought about the development of Lebanon as a nation separate from Syria. The Christians in Syria were less fortunate. About six thousand of them were slaughtered in Damascus before Ottoman troops restored order.[2]

In the years immediately preceding World War I, numbers of young Syrian Christians and some Muslims were exposed through the mission schools to ideas of nationalism, self-determinism, and human rights. Gradually, a movement for Arab independence from Turkish rule developed. The movement was centered in Damascus and Beirut. After the start of World War I, the British, with French backing, convinced Arab leaders to revolt against the Ottoman government. The Arab army recruited for the revolt was led by the Emir Faisal, second son of the Sharif Husayn of Mecca, leader of the powerful Arab Hashimite family and the Arab official appointed by the Ottomans as "Protector of the Holy Shrines of Islam." Faisal's forces, along with a British army, drove the Ottomans out of Syria, and in 1918 the emir entered Damascus as a conquering hero. In 1920 he was proclaimed king of Syria.

Faisal's kingdom did not last long. The British had promised the Arabs independence in a state of their own in return for their revolt. However, they had also made secret agreements with France to divide the Arab regions of the defeated Ottoman Empire into French and British protectorates. The French would have Syria and Lebanon; the British would have Palestine and Iraq. The French now moved to collect their pound of flesh. They sent an ultimatum to

Faisal to accept French rule, and when he refused, a French army marched to Damascus, bombarded the city, and forced him into exile. (Faisal was brought back by the British and later installed as king of Iraq under a British protectorate.)

What one author calls the "false dawn" of Arab independence was followed by the establishment of direct French control over Syria.[3] The Syrians reacted angrily to what they considered betrayal by their former allies. Resistance to French rule continued throughout the mandate period (1920-1946), and the legacy of bitterness over their betrayal affects Syrian attitudes toward outside powers, particularly Western powers, to this day.[4]

The French did some positive things for Syria. They built schools, roads, and hospitals, developed a productive cotton industry, established order and peaceful relations among the various communities. But the Syrians remained strongly attached to the goals of Arab unity and Arab independence, first in Syria, then in a future Arab nation.[5]

INDEPENDENT SYRIA

Syria became independent in 1946. The French had promised the Syrians independence during World War II but delayed their departure after the war, hoping to keep their privileged trade position and military bases. Eventually pressure from the United States, the Soviet Union, and the United Kingdom forced the French to leave both Syria and Lebanon.

The new republic began under adverse circumstances. Syrian leaders had little experience in government; the French had not given them much responsibility, and had encouraged personal rivalries in their "divide and rule" policy. The Druze and Alawi communities feared they would be under the thumb of the Sunni majority. In addition to these problems, the establishment of the State of Israel next door in Palestine in 1948 caused great instability in Syria. The failure of Syrian armies to defeat the Israelis was blamed on weak and incompetent leaders.

For two decades after independence Syria had the reputation of being the most unstable country in the Middle East. There were four military coups between 1949 and 1954, and several more between 1961 and 1966. There was also a brief union with Egypt (1958-1961), which ended in an army revolt. One reason for Syria's chronic instability is that political parties, at least until the 1960s, were simply groups formed around leading personalities. At independence, the country had many such parties. Other parties were formed on the basis of ideology,

such as the Syrian Communist Party. In 1963 one particular party, the Ba'th, acquired control of all political activities. Since then, Syria has been a single-party state.

THE BA'TH

The Ba'th Party (the Arabic word *ba'th* means "resurrection") began in the 1940s as a political party dedicated to Arab unity. It was founded by two Damascus school teachers, both French educated: Michel Aflaq, a Greek Orthodox Christian, and Salah Bitar, a Sunni Muslim. In 1953 the Ba'th merged with another political party, the Arab Socialist Party. Since that time, the formal name of the Ba'th has been the Arab Socialist Resurrection Party.

The Ba'th was the first Syrian political party to establish a mass popular base and to draw members from all social classes. Its program called for freedom, Arab unity, and socialism. The movement for Arab unity led to the establishment of branches of the party in other Arab countries, notably Iraq and Lebanon. The party appealed particularly to young officers in the armed forces, and it attracted strong support from the Alawi community because it called for social justice and the equality of all Syrians.

The Ba'th was instrumental in 1958 in arranging a merger between Syria and Egypt in the United Arab Republic (UAR). The Ba'thists had hoped to undercut their chief rivals, the Syrian Communist Party, by the merger. But they soon decided they had made a mistake. The Egyptians did not treat the Syrians as equals but as junior partners in the firm. Syrian officers seized control and expelled the Egyptian advisers. It was the end of the UAR.

For the next nine years power shifted back and forth among military and civilian factions of the Ba'th Party. The process had little effect on the average Syrian, who liked to talk about politics but was wary, with good reason, of any involvement. Gradually, the military faction got the upper hand, and in 1970 Lieutenant General Hafez al-Assad, the defense minister of one of the country's innumerable previous governments, seized power in a bloodless coup.[6]

THE ASSAD REGIME

Hafez al-Assad has been head of Syria longer than any of his predecessors since independence. He was elected president for a seven-year term in 1971, and was reelected in 1978 and again in 1985. Although Assad was slowed down by a heart attack in 1983, he remains the dominant figure in Syrian politics, and his ability to neutral-

ize potential opposition indicates that he will remain in power as long as he wishes.

Under Assad, Syria became a "presidential republic" similar to Tunisia. But Assad's presidency differs from Habib Bourguiba's in Tunisia in important ways. The Syrian head of state has great powers which are confirmed in the permanent Constitution approved in 1973. He decides and executes policies, appoints all government officials, and commands the armed forces. He is also head of the Ba'th Party. Under the Constitution, he has unlimited emergency powers "in case of grave danger threatening national unity or the security . . . of the national territory . . . " (Article 113), which only the president can determine.

Another important difference between Assad and most of his predecessors is that he has made some effort to involve the people in the governing process. In 1973 he organized a National Progressive Front of the Ba'th, and several small leftist or Socialist parties whose programs were acceptable to the majority party were allowed to function. Elections to a new People's Assembly gave the Ba'th sixty percent of the seats, but the fact that forty percent went to former opposition candidates was an encouraging sign of political liberalization. The Syrian Communist Party was allowed to take part in the election as an independent party.

ROLE IN LEBANON

Assad's position was strengthened domestically in the 1970s due to his success (or perceived success) in certain foreign policy actions. The Syrian Army fought well against Israel in the October 1973 War and subsequently received both miltary and financial aid from the Soviet Union as well as its Arab brothers. The invitation by the Arab League for Syria to intervene in Lebanon, beginning with the 1975-1976 Lebanese Civil War, was widely popular among Syrians. They never fully accepted the French action of separating Lebanon from Syria during the mandate period, and continue to maintain a proprietary attitude toward the Lebanese.

Syria's concern over Lebanon deepened after the Palestine Liberation Organization (PLO) established a strong base there following its expulsion from Jordan. The Syrians have been careful not to allow PLO operations against Israel from their territory, and they keep Palestinian forces under a tight reign; the Palestinian al-Saiqa Brigade in Syria is integrated into the Syrian Army.

When the Lebanese Civil War broke out, Assad pledged that he would control the Palestinians in Lebanon, and sent about two

Capital of Umay-
yads removed to
Damascus; Syria
becomes center
of Islamic world
AD 661-750

Ottoman
province
1517-1917

Independent
Arab Kingdom of
Syria proclaimed
under Faisal;
shot down by
French
1920

thousand al-Saiqa guerrillas to Beirut in early 1976. The peacekeeping force approved by the Arab League for Lebanon included thirty thousand regular Syrian troops. For all practical purposes, this force maintained a balance of power among Lebanese factions until the Israeli invasion of June 1982. The Syrian forces then withdrew to the eastern Biqa' Valley, where they remain today. The withdrawal of Israeli forces from all of Lebanon in 1985 has strengthened Syria's position there to the point that President Assad is the principal power broker among the Lebanese factions and the chief prop for the Lebanese government of Amin Gemayel.

INTERNAL OPPOSITION

Since 1979 opposition to the Assad regime has increased steadily. One of the causes is the dominance of the Alawi minority. Although many non-Alawis hold high government positions, the Alawis are the majority in the officer corps, the police, and the intelligence services; the latter two were headed until recently by Assad's brothers. One brother, Rifaat Assad, and his rivals engaged in armed confrontation during the president's illness in a struggle over the succession in 1984. After Assad recovered, he sent Rifaat out of the country for several months. In November Rifaat was reinstated and made one of three vice presidents.

The main opposition to the regime comes from the Muslim Brotherhood, an underground Sunni organization that operates throughout the Arab world. Its goal is a unified, democratic Arab/Islamic state under just leaders. The Brotherhood opposes Assad for what it calls his autocratic leadership, repression of political opposition, and for allowing corruption in government. The Brotherhood was implicated in a wave of assassinations of prominent Alawis which had claimed three hundred victims by 1981. In February 1982 the city of Hama, a Brotherhood stronghold, was almost obliterated by army tanks, artillery, and planes after government forces were ambushed there.[7]

In the long run, the Assad regime must deal effectively with broader forms of discontent than those served up by the Brotherhood. Assad's confidence in the broad

Hafez al-Assad is the dominant figure in Syrian politics, and has been Syria's political head since 1971. While Assad has assumed great powers, he has made some effort to involve the people in the governing process.

support base acquired by the regime due to the Lebanese intervention was shown by his offer of an amnesty to Brotherhood members in February 1985. He said they had gained new convictions and no longer were tools of Syria's enemies. But differences remain. The urban population resents government by people from the provinces. The Alawis are resented by Sunni Muslims because of their high visibility and privileges; it is whispered that they are not true Muslims.[8] Urban rivalries have always been strong in Syria; the rivalry of Damascus and Aleppo goes back centuries. Syria's misfortunes in Lebanon and failure to lead the Arab states to victory over Israel is another

French mandate, followed by independence **1920-1946**	Union with Egypt into United Arab Republic **1958-1961**	Ba'th Party seizes power **1963**	Assad takes control of government; later elected president **1971**	Syrian troops sent to Lebanon as peacekeeping force **1976**	Assad suffers apparent heart attack and is hospitalized for several months
					1980s
Syria cooperates with US in returning body of US citizen killed during hijacking of *Achille Lauro*	Internal power struggle over succession to Assad ends as Assad creates three vice presidents with equal powers under him	Assad is instrumental in obtaining the release of American hostages in Lebanon hijacked by Lebanese Shia gunmen			

source of discontent. But in the last analysis, the regime's survival depends upon its ability to establish a process of succession going beyond Assad, preserving the single-party state in a more representative fashion to provide the just institutions demanded by its opponents.

THE ECONOMY

At independence, Syria was primarily an agricultural country, although it had a large merchant class and a free-enterprise system with considerable small-scale industrial development. When it came to power, the Ba'th Party was committed to state control of the economy. Agriculture was collectivized, land expropriated from large landowners and converted into state-managed farms. Most industries were nationalized in the 1960s. The free-enterprise system all but disappeared.

Cotton was Syria's principal export crop and money-earner up until the mid-1970s. But with the development of oilfields, petroleum became the main export. Petroleum accounted for 74.7 percent of total export earnings in 1983. Syria produced enough oil for its own needs until 1980. However, the changing global oil market, political differences with its Western customers, and the reluctance of foreign oil companies to invest in oil exploration due to the country's strict nationalization policies, have reduced Syria's revenues and hampered economic development. Two encouraging developments in 1985 were the discovery of a new oilfield in the Deir

ez-Zor area and a natural gas find near Homs by Marathon Oil, the last foreign concessionnaire in Syria. If these new discoveries prove to be commercially exploitable as expected, the Syrian hydrocarbons industry will gain a new lease on life.

The main problem with the Syrian economy is not economic. It is political. As an example, disagreements with neighboring Iraq from time to time have shut off Iraqi crude oil shipments through Syrian pipelines to refineries on the Mediterranean. (The pipeline was closed most recently by the Syrians in 1982, after the outbreak of the Iran-Iraq War.) For years Syria earned more from transit fees than it did from its own oil production. In June 1985 Kuwaiti opposition to Syria's policies in Lebanon led the Kuwait National Assembly to cancel $334 million pledged to Syria as a frontline Arab state in the struggle with Israel. The political stability achieved under Assad had just begun to affect the economy when the 1973 Arab/Israeli War caused extensive damage to Syrian factories and refineries. Bad political relations with Jordan and Turkey and the seemingly endless struggle with Israel continue to affect economic stability, and will probably continue to do so in the foreseeable future.

FOOTNOTES

1. The statement is found in many chronicles of the Umayyads. See Richard Nyrop, ed., *Syria, A Country Study* (Washington, DC: American University, Foreign Area Studies, 1978), p. 13.

2. Philip Khoury, *Urban Notables and Arab Nationalism: The Politics of Damascus 1860-1920* (Cambridge, England: Cambridge University Press, 1983), pp. 8-9.

3. Umar F. Abd-Allah, *The Islamic Struggle in Syria* (Berkeley, CA: Mizan Press, 1983), p. 39.

4. A. H. Hourani, *Syria and Lebanon, A Political Essay* (London: Oxford University Press, 1954), p. 54, notes that "His (Faisal's) government had more solid foundations in popular consent than any perhaps since Umayyad times."

5. "Syrians had long seen themselves as Arabs . . . who considered the Arab world as rightly a single entity." John F. Devlin, *Syria: Modern State in an Ancient Land* (Boulder, CO: Westview Press, 1983), p. 44.

6. He was barred from attending a Cabinet meeting, and then surrounded the meeting site with army units, dismissed the government and formed his own. *Ibid.*, p. 56.

7. Devlin notes that the city held out for two weeks. The Assad government has never issued casualty figures. Significantly, no other cities rose in revolt and army units remained loyal, even though Hama religious leaders called for a *jihad* against Assad. *Ibid.*, pp. 73-74.

8. Abd-Allah, *op. cit.*, pp. 42-48, describes them as believing in a Trinity, worshipping natural objects, giving less than absolute obedience to the Koran as the word of God, and following a religious teacher who claimed to be a Prophet and Messenger two hundred years after Muhammad.

DEVELOPMENT

The relationship between politics and economic development in Syria is illustrated by the oil industry. For many years royalties from pipeline transit fees from Iraqi and Saudi oil shipments to Syrian refineries were more profitable than oil exports. But political disagreements have often disrupted this transit trade.

FREEDOM

The 1973 Constitution defines Syria as a Socialist popular democracy with a preplanned Socialist economy. Neither terms are appropriate. In practice Syria is a single-party state with full powers reserved to the president. A People's Council elected by universal adult suffrage holds legislative power, but all legislative decisions are made by Assad and his ministers.

HEALTH/WELFARE

Education and health services in Syria show uneven growth. In 1981-1982 there were more than 2 million students in primary and secondary schools and 113,000 in the country's 5 universities. In contrast, large-scale emigration from rural to urban areas has led to major shortages in housing and health facilities.

ACHIEVEMENTS

Syria's most ambitious development is the Euphrates Dam, begun in 1968 by Soviet technicians and put into operation in 1974. By 1979 it was providing 70% of all electricity needs, and the goal of electric power for every village seemed within reach.

Tunisia (Republic of Tunisia)

GEOGRAPHY

Area in Square Kilometers (Miles):
164,149 (63,378)
Capital (Population): Tunis
(1,000,000)
Climate: hot, dry summers; mild,
rainy winters

PEOPLE

Population
Total: 7,202,000
Annual Growth Rate: 2.6%
Rural/Urban Population Ratio: 46/54
Ethnic Makeup of Population: 98%
Arab; 1% European; less than 2%
Berber and other

Health
Life Expectancy at Birth: 58 years
Infant Death Rate (Ratio): 90/1,000
Average Caloric Intake: 116% of FAO
minimum
Physicians Available (Ratio): 1/3,690

Religion(s)
98% Muslim; 1% Christian; less
than 1% Jewish

Education
Adult Literacy Rate: 62%

PEACE AT LAST

In February 1985, after two thousand years, the mayors of Rome and
Carthage (now a Tunis suburb) signed a treaty symbolically ending the
state of war between their ancestor city-states. The treaty was a reminder
of the great days of Roman Africa with its capital at Carthage. The Bardo
Museum in Tunis houses the world's finest collection of Roman African mosaics in the world. Students came here to work under mosaic
masters from Alexandria (Egypt) in the first century AD. They soon developed their own distinct impressionistic style incorporating native
themes, showing rural hunting and harvesting scenes, fishing expeditions with boat models of the period, and family picnics. One of the
largest mosaics, showing the triumph of Neptune, covers 1,465 square feet.

COMMUNICATION

Telephones: 188,500
Newspapers: 2 Arabic dailies; 3
French dailies

TRANSPORTATION

Highways—Kilometers (Miles): 17,762
(11,037) total; 9,970 (6,195)
bituminous
Railroads—Kilometers (Miles): 2,089
(1,298)
Commercial Airports: 28

GOVERNMENT

Type: republic
Independence Date: March 20, 1956
Head of State: President Habib
Bourguiba
Political Parties: Destourian Socialist
Party (ruling); Communist Party;
Social Democratic Movement;
Popular Unity Movement; last two
legalized in 1983
Suffrage: universal over 21

MILITARY

Number of Armed Forces: 27,600
*Military Expenditures (% of Central
Government Expenditures):* 9%
Current Hostilities: contention with
Libya over oil-rich section of
continental shelf; treaty not yet
concluded

ECONOMY

Currency ($ US Equivalent): 0.93
Tunisian dinar = $1 (March 1985)
Per Capita Income/GNP: $844/$5.83
billion (1983)
Inflation Rate: 9% (1983)
Natural Resources: oil; phosphates;
iron ore; lead; zinc
Agriculture: wheat; barley; olives;
citrus fruits; grapes; vegetables; fish
Industry: mining (phosphates);
petroleum; olive oil; textiles; food
processing; construction

FOREIGN TRADE

Exports: $2.0 billion (1983)
Imports: $3.2 billion (1983)

TUNISIA

Tunisia is the smallest of the four North African countries. With an area of 63,378 square miles, Tunisia is less than one-tenth the size of Libya, its neighbor to the east. However, its population, 7,202,000, is nearly twice the size of Libya's.

Tunisia's long coastline has exposed it over the centuries to a succession of invaders from the sea. The southern third of the country is part of the Sahara Desert, and the central third consists of high, arid plains. Only the northern region has sufficient rainfall for agriculture; this region contains Tunisia's only permanent river, the Medjerda.

The country is predominantly urban. There is almost no nomadic population, and there are no high mountains to provide refuge for independent mountain peoples opposed to central government. The Tunis region and the Sahel, a coastal plain important in olive production, are the most densely populated areas. Tunis, the capital, is not only the dominant city but also the hub of all government, economic, and political activity.

HISTORY

Tunisia has an ancient history which is urban rather than territorial. Phoenician merchants from what is today Lebanon founded a number of trading posts several thousand years ago. The most important one was Carthage, founded by tradition in 814 BC. It grew wealthy through trade and de-

veloped a maritime empire. Its great rival was Rome; after several wars the Romans defeated the Carthaginians and destroyed Carthage. Later the Romans rebuilt the city, and it became great once again, the capital of the Roman province of Africa. Rome's African province was one of the most prosperous in the empire. The wheat and other commodities shipped to Rome from North African farms were vitally needed to feed the Roman population. When the ships from Carthage were late due to storms or lost at sea, or seized by pirates, as sometimes happened, the Romans suffered hardship. Tunisia today has yet to reach the level of prosperity it had under Roman rule.

The collapse of the Roman Empire in the fifth century AD affected Roman Africa as well. Cities were abandoned; the irrigation system that had made the farms prosperous fell into ruin. (A number of these Roman cities, such as Dougga, Utica, and Carthage itself, which is now a suburb of Tunis, have been preserved as historical monuments of this period.)

Arab armies from the east brought Islam to North Africa in the late seventh century. After some resistance, the population accepted the new religion, and from that time on the area was ruled as the Arab-Islamic province of *Ifriqiya*. The Anglicized form of this Arabic word, "Africa," was eventually applied to the entire continent.

The Arab governors did not want to have anything to do with Carthage since they associated it with Christian Roman rule. They

built a new capital on the site of a village in the outskirts of Carthage, named Tunis. The fact that Tunis has been the capital and major city in the country for fourteen centuries has undoubtedly contributed to the sense of unity and nationhood that most Tunisians have.[1]

The original Tunisian population consisted of Berbers, a people of unknown origin. During the centuries of Islamic rule, many Arabs settled in the country. Other waves of immigration brought Muslims from Spain, Greeks, Italians, Maltese, and many other nationalities. Tunisia also had until recently a large community of Jews who were important as traders, jewelers, moneylenders, and craftspeople. Most of the Jews emigrated to the State of Israel when it was founded in 1948. The blending of ethnic groups and nationalities over the years created a relatively homogeneous and tolerant society with few of the conflicts that marked other societies in the Islamic world (such as those in Arabia) where such groups were organized strongly.

The Beylical State

From the late 1500s to the 1880s Tunisia was a self-governing province of the Ottoman Empire. It was called a *regency* because its governors ruled as "regents" on behalf of the Ottoman sultan. Tunis was already a well-established, cosmopolitan city when it became the regency capital. Its rulers, called *beys*, were supported by an Ottoman garrison and a fleet of sea captains

In the 1970s Tunisia experienced a steady and rapid increase in income. Tourism sparked hotel development, such as the one pictured above (left), and exports of phosphates, petroleum, and olive oil fueled substantial economic growth. As demand for these products has decreased, Tunisia's economic future has become uncertain.

called *corsairs*. The corsairs systematically raided the Mediterranean coasts of nearby European countries and preyed on merchant vessels, seizing cargoes and holding crews for ransom.[2]

In the nineteenth century, European powers, particularly France and England, began to interfere directly in the Ottoman Empire and to seize some of its outlying provinces. France and the United Kingdom had a "gentleman's agreement" about Ottoman territories in Africa—the French were given a free hand in North Africa and the British in Egypt. In 1830 the French seized Algiers, capital of the Algiers Regency, and began to intevene in neighboring Tunisia in order to protect their Algerian investment.

The beys of Tunis worked very hard to forestall a French occupation. In order to do this, they had to satisfy the European powers that they were developing modern political institutions and rights for their people. Ahmad Bey (1837-1855) abolished slavery and piracy, organized a modern army (trained by French officers), and established a national system of tax collection. Muhammad al-Sadiq Bey (1859-1882) approved in 1861 the first written constitution in the Islamic world. This Constitution had a declaration of rights and provided for a hereditary (but not an absolute) monarchy under the beys. The Constitution worked better in theory than in practice. Provincial landowners and local chiefs opposed it because it undermined their authority. The peasants, whom it was supposedly designed to protect, opposed it because it brought them heavy new taxes, collected by government troops sent from Tunis. In 1864 a popular rebellion broke out against the bey, and he was forced to suspend the Constitution.

The French Protectorate

In 1881 a French army invaded and occupied all of Tunisia, almost without firing a shot. The French said they had intervened because the bey's government was broke and could not meet its debts to French bankers and capitalists, who had been lending money for years to keep the country afloat. There was concern also about the European population. Europeans from many countries had been pouring into Tunisia, ever since the bey had given foreigners the right to own land and set up businesses.

The bey's government continued under the French protectorate, but it was supplemented by a French administration which held the actual power. The French

collected taxes, imposed French law, and developed roads, railroads, ports, hospitals, and schools. French landowners bought large areas and converted them into vineyards, olive groves, and wheat farms. For the first time in two thousand years Tunisia exported wheat, corn, and olive oil to the lands on the other side of the Mediterranean.

Because Tunisia was small, manageable, and urban, its society, particularly in certain regions, was influenced strongly by French culture. An elite developed whose members preferred the French language to their native Arabic, and who sent their children to French high schools and to colleges or universities in France. The Tunisian Nationalist Movement was developed largely from members of this group, who had matured enough to feel that a friendly association of the two countries as equals would be of mutual benefit. The movement began in the 1920s.[3] The French allowed a certain amount of political freedom, and the nationalists took the name Destour (Arabic *Dustur*), meaning "Constitution."

In the 1930s a new generation of Tunisians began to talk seriously of independence. Most of them had been educated in France. The youths of the new generation became convinced that nationalism, "in order to be effective against the French had to break loose from its traditional power base in the urban elite and mobilize mass support."[4] In 1934 a group of young nationalists quit the Destour and formed a new party, the Neo-Destour. The goal of the Neo-Destour Party was independence from France. From the beginning, its principal leader was Habib Bourguiba.

HABIB BOURGUIBA

Habib Bourguiba (born 1903) once boasted that he had "invented" Tunisia. In a sense, he was right. The Neo-Destour Party, under Bourguiba's leadership, became the country's first mass political party. It drew its membership from shopkeepers, craftspeople, blue-collar workers, and peasants, along with French-educated lawyers and doctors. The party became the vanguard of the nation, mobilizing the population in a campaign of strikes, demonstrations, and violence in order to gain independence. It was a long struggle. Bourguiba spent many years in prison. But eventually the Neo-Destour tactics succeeded. On March 20, 1956 the French ended the Protectorate, and Tunisia became an independent republic led by Habib Bourguiba.

One of the problems facing Tunisia today is that its political organization has changed

very little since independence. A constitution was approved in 1959 which established a "presidential republic," that is, a republic in which the elected president has very great power. Habib Bourguiba was elected president in 1957, and since then he has been reelected four times. He is the republic's first and only head of state, and in 1975 the National Assembly voted him "president-for-life."

The president is also the head of the Neo-Destour Party, the country's only legal political party. The Constitution provides for a national assembly, which is responsible for enacting laws. But to be elected to the Assembly, a candidate must be a member of the Destour Party. Bourguiba's philosophy and programs for national development in his country are often called "Bourguibism." It is tailored to the particular historical experience of the Tunisian people. Since ancient Carthage, Tunisian life has been characterized by the presence of some strong central government able to impose order and bring relative stability to the people. The predominance of cities and villages over nomadism reinforced this sense of order. The experience of Carthage, and even more so that of Rome, set the pattern. "The Beys continued the pattern of strong order while the French developed a strongly bourgeois, trade-oriented society, adding humanitarian and some authoritarian values contained in French political philosophy."[5] Bourguiba has always considered himself the tutor of the Tunisian people, guiding them toward moral, economic, and political maturity as a stern father guides his children.

In 1961 Bourguiba introduced a new program for Tunisian development which he called "Destourian Socialism." It combined Bourguibism with government planning for economic and social development. The name of the Neo-Destour Party was changed to Destour Socialist Party (PSD) to indicate the party's new direction. Destourian Socialism works for the general good, but it is not Marxist; Bourguiba stressed national unanimity rather than class struggle, and opposed communism as the "ideology of a godless state." Bourguiba took the view that Destourian Socialism was directly related to Islam. He said once that the original members of the Islamic community (in Muhammad's time in Mecca) "were socialists . . . and worked for the common good."[6]

For many years after independence Tunisia appeared to be a model among new nations because of its stability, order, and economic progress. Particularly impressive

Wars between Rome and Carthage, ending in destruction of Carthage and rebuilding as a Roman city **264-146 BC**	Establishment of Islam in Ifriqiya, with its new capital at Tunis **AD 800-900**	Hafsid dynasty develops Tunisia as highly-centralized urban state **1200-1400**	Ottoman Turks establish Tunis as corsair state to control Mediterranean sea lanes **1500-1800**	French protectorate **1881-1956**	Tunisia gains independence, led by Habib Bourguiba **1956**	Abortive merger with Libya **1974**	**1980s**

Political liberalization begins as Bourguiba approves multiparty system	"Bread Riots" protesting price increases cause heavy casualties and government shakeup	Strikes, boycott of classes, and clashes between Islamic fundamentalist and Marxist student groups paralyze University of Tunis and branches

were Bourguiba's reforms in social and political life. Islamic law was replaced by a Western legal system with various levels of courts. Women were encouraged to attend school and enter occupations and professions previously closed to them, and were given equal rights with men in matters of divorce and inheritance.

Bourguiba strongly criticized those aspects of Islam that seemed to him to be obstacles to national development. He was against women veiling, polygyny, and ownership of lands by religious leaders, which kept the lands out of production. He even encouraged people not to fast during Ramadan because their hunger made them less effective in their work.

Until the late 1970s there was little opposition either to Bourguiba's autocratic personal rule or to the PSD and its programs. Most Tunisians felt that Destourian Socialism was an effective system for developing a modern Tunisian state. In recent years, however, Bourguiba's periodic ill health, economic problems, and increasing pressure among a new generation of Tunisians for a multiparty political system have raised doubts about Tunisia's future as a one-party state. The succession to the presidency was formally regulated by a constitutional amendment in 1974. The amendment specified that in the event of the death or incapacity of President Bourguiba, the prime minister would succeed him. But as political scientist Elbaki Hermassi observed, "Nobody is big enough to replace Bourguiba. He created a national liberation

movement, fashioned the country and its institutions."[7] The current prime minister, Muhammad Mzali, an education specialist, is the leader among a number of candidates because he is the official successor, but he is not the favorite choice of the party.

THE ECONOMY

Tunisia's development since independence has been fairly impressive. Annual per capita income had a thirteen- to twenty-percent average annual growth rate in the late 1960s and 1970s. However, the growth rate began dropping steadily thereafter, largely due to decreased demand and lowered prices for the country's three main exports, phosphates, petroleum, and olive oil. Tunisia is the world's fourth-ranking producer of phosphates, and the most important industries are those related to production of phosphate fertilizers. Oil exports have increased due to the discovery of several new oilfields in recent years, the majority of them offshore with proven reserves of 1.69 billion barrels.

Yet the economic picture remains uncertain over future leadership, growing unemployment, and the return of large numbers of Tunisian workers from Western Europe due to the economic slowdown there. The country's economic prospects ultimately rest on revitalization of the political system. Tunisia's first antigovernment riots since independence broke out in January 1984, the main cause being a 115-percent increase in the price of bread. Social resentment and economic fustration, however, are, in the

final analysis, protests by a new generation of Tunisians at their inability to find jobs, their exclusion from the decision-making process, unfair distribution of wealth, and the lack of political parties. It is as if there were two Tunisias—the Tunisia of the old politicians and freedom fighters, and the new Tunisia of alienated youths, angry peasants, and frustrated intellectuals—and somehow the two have gotten out of touch with each other.

FOOTNOTES

1. Harold D. Nelson, ed., *Tunisia: A Country Study* (Washington, DC: American University, Foreign Area Studies, 1979), p. 68.
2. Attacks on American shipping by Tunisian corsairs led the US to sign a treaty with the bey in 1799, guaranteeing an annual tribute in return for protection. *Ibid.*, p. 27.
3. The nationalists were nearly all graduates of Sadiki College, a "high school" with a European curriculum that included courses in European politics. They also went on to complete their education in France. *Ibid.*, p. 39.
4. *Ibid.*, p. 42.
5. What Nelson means, in this case, by "authoritarianism" is that the French brought to Tunisia the elaborate bureaucracy of metropolitan France, with levels of administration from the center down to local towns and villages. *Ibid.*, p. 194.
6. *Ibid.*, p. 196.
7. Jim Rupert, in *The Christian Science Monitor*, November 23, 1984.

DEVELOPMENT

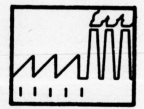

After an impressive growth record over 2 decades of independence, the growth rate since 1980 has dropped sharply, to 3% in 1981, 0.3% in 1982, rebounding to 4.5% in 1983. Falling global phosphate and oil prices, and natural disasters affected performance and led to high unemployment and resultant social unrest.

FREEDOM

In November 1983 Bourguiba approved two opposition parties, Socialist Democrats and People's Unity, as a first step toward a multiparty system. But a 1984 law requiring parties to win 5% of the popular vote to be represented forced the parties off the ballot in local and national elections.

HEALTH/WELFARE

Since independence Tunisia has been a leader among Arab states in social change, especially in women's rights. The 1956 Code of Personal Status outlawed polygyny, set minimum ages for marriage (17 years for females), gave women divorce and inheritance rights equal with men, and guaranteed equal pay for equal work for the sexes.

ACHIEVEMENTS

Economic difficulties and social protests against the rigid leadership are chipping away at Tunisia's image as a success story among new nations. A trend toward revival of Islamic values became noticeable in the 1980s. The impetus was supplied by the Movement for Islamic Tendency (MTI), a fundamentalist organization which is popular among the youth.

Turkey (Republic of Turkey)

GEOGRAPHY

Area in Square Kilometers (Miles):
766,640 (296,000)
Capital (Population): Ankara
(2,800,000)
Climate: coastal areas, moderate;
inland, harsher temperatures

PEOPLE

Population
Total: 50,207,000
Annual Growth Rate: 2.1%
Rural/Urban Population Ratio: 56/44
Ethnic Makeup of Population: 85%
Turkish; 12% Kurdish (Kurds not
recognized as separate ethnic group);
3% other

Health
Life Expectancy at Birth: 63 years
Infant Death Rate (Ratio): 83/1,000
Average Caloric Intake: 122% of
FAO minimum
Physicians Available (Ratio): 1/1,630

Religion(s)
98% Muslim (mostly Sunni); 2%
other (mostly Christian and Jewish)

Education
Adult Literacy Rate: 70%

A TURKISH SHADOW PLAY

One of the most popular forms of entertainment in Turkey is the *Karagoz,* or "shadow play." It dates back to the sixteenth century. There are two main characters: Karagoz, who represents common sense and irony, and his friend Hacivad, who represents formal superficial knowledge.

The most popular legend about the origins of the form is that the two characters were workmen repairing a mosque. Their conversation was so humorous that all work ceased, making the sultan so angry that he had them hanged. He then suffered terrible remorse, and to console him a courtier built a screen and manipulated puppets behind it to represent the two dead men. There are many versions of Karagoz, all requiring great voice skill and knowledge of poetry and music. For a time Karagoz was also used as political satire.

COMMUNICATION

Telephones: 1.9 million
Newspapers: close to 2,000 dailies,
most in Turkish

TRANSPORTATION

Highways—Kilometers (Miles): 60,761
(37,757) total 36,670 (22,787)
bituminous

Railroads—Kilometers (Miles): 8,193
(5,091)
Commercial Airports: 119

GOVERNMENT

Type: republic
Independence Date: 1923
Head of State: General Kenan Evren,
the president, and Prime Minister
Turgut Ozal share executive powers
Political Parties: Motherland Party
(dominant); Democratic Left;
Populist/Social Democrat
Suffrage: universal over 21

MILITARY

Number of Armed Forces: 568,000
*Military Expenditures (% of Central
Government Expenditures):* 17.1%
Current Hostilities: none

ECONOMY

Currency ($ US Equivalent): 493
Turkish lira = $1 (March 1985)
Per Capita Income/GNP:
$1,096/$54.2 billion (1983)
Inflation Rate: 50% (1984)
Natural Resources: coal; chromite;
copper; boron; oil
Agriculture: cotton; tobacco; cereals;
sugar beets; fruits; nuts; livestock
products
Industry: textiles; food processing;
mining; iron and steel; cement;
petroleum; leather goods

FOREIGN TRADE

Exports: $5.7 billion (1983)
Imports: $9.2 billion (1983)

TURKEY

Except for a small area in extreme southeastern Europe called Thrace, the Republic of Turkey consists of the large peninsula of Asia Minor (Anatolia) which forms a land bridge between Europe and Asia. Asiatic Turkey is separated from European Turkey by the Bosphorus, a narrow strait connecting the Black Sea with the Aegean Sea and the Mediterranean Sea via the Sea of Marmara. Throughout history the Bosphorus and the Dardanelles, at the Mediterranean end, have been important strategic waterways, fought over by many nations.

Except for the Syrian border, Asiatic Turkey's borders are defined by natural limits, with seas on three sides and rugged mountains on the fourth. The highest peak is Mt. Ararat (20,143 feet), near the borders with the Soviet Union and Iran. European Turkey's frontiers with Greece and Bulgaria are artificial and fluctuated considerably in the nineteenth and twentieth centuries before the Republic of Turkey was established.

Modern Turkey occupies a much smaller area than its predecessor, the Ottoman Empire. The Ottoman Turks were the dominant power in the Middle East for more than five centuries. After the defeat of the Empire in World War I, Turkey's new leader, Mustafa Kemal Ataturk, turned away from the imperial past, limiting the new republic to territory with a predominantly Turkish population. Since that time Turkey has not attempted to dominate its neighbors and has concentrated mainly on internal development and peaceful relations. The single exception is Cyprus, where Turkish forces have intervened to protect the Turkish minority against the Greek majority of the population.

Asia Minor has an ancient history of settlement. Most of the peninsula is a plateau (average elevation three thousand feet) ringed by mountains. The mountians are close to the coast, and over the centuries, due to volcanic action, the coastline became cracked, with deep indentations and oddly shaped islands just offshore. The inland plateau has an area of arid steppe with dried-up salt lakes at the center, but most of it is rolling land, well suited to agriculture. Consequently, at an early period people settled in small, self-contained villages and began to cultivate the land. Over the centuries nomadic peoples migrated into Asia Minor, but the geographical pattern there did not encourage them to remain nomadic. In terms of national unity, the modern Turkish state has not had the problem of ethnic conflicts which have hampered national unity in many Middle Eastern states.

HISTORY: A PARADE OF PEOPLES

The earliest political unit to develop in the peninsula was the Empire of the Hittites (1600 - 1200 BC), inventors of the two-wheeled chariot and one of the great powers of the ancient Near East. Various peoples succeeded the Hittites; one, the Lydians, invented money as a means of exchange in the time of the Lydian King Croesus. The modern expression "rich as Croesus" comes from this king's habit of panning gold from a nearby river which he pressed into coins to pay for his kingdom's purchases. According to legend, another early Anatolian king, Midas, had the gift of turning anything he touched into gold, hence the expression "the Midas touch."

The Greeks settled Asia Minor still later, followed by the Romans. When Christianity developed as a religion, many cities on the peninsula became important centers of Christian faith, such as Ephesus, Antioch, and Nicaea. A Roman citizen from Tarsus, named Saul, became the greatest missionary of the new Christian Church as the Apostle Paul.

Following the collapse of the Roman Empire in the fifth century AD, Asia Minor became the largest part of the East Roman or Byzantine Empire, named for its capital, Byzantium. The city was later renamed Constantinople, in honor of the Roman Emperor Constantine, after the emperor had become Christian. For a thousand years this empire was a center and fortress of Christianity against hostile neighbors and later the forces of Islam.

The Ottoman Centuries[1]

Various nomadic peoples from Central Asia began migrating into Islamic lands from the ninth century on. Clans from one family group settled mostly in parts of Asia Minor and northwest Iran. The family had no name for itself, but its Chinese neighbors, during its early migrations, called it *Tu-Kueh*, meaning either "helmet," "steep hill," or (perhaps reflecting Chinese feelings about their unwashed neighbors) "dunghill." The Chinese word, translated into the local language, became *Turk*.

The Turks, although divided into families and clans, had from an early stage a real sense of themselves as a nation. There is an ancient legend that describes them as an army of disciplined horsemen, mounted on shaggy steeds, riding slowly toward the sunset, led by a gray wolf. In Asia Minor, the Turkish clans found themselves on the borders of hostile Christian Byzantine and Islamic empires. Islamic activism appealed to them and they joined enthusiastically in the conflict as Ghazis, "warriors for the faith." Asia Minor, having been wrested from the Greeks by the Turks, also gave the Turks a strong sense of identification with that particular place. To them it was Anadolu (Anatolia), "land of the setting sun." These symbols—the gray wolf, the Ghazi tradition, and the "sacred homeland"—continued through their history to give the Turks a strong sense of national identity and unity.

The Ottomans were one of many Turkish clans in Anatolia. They took their name from Osman, a clan leader elected because of certain qualifications considered ideal for a Ghazi chieftain—wisdom, prudence, courage, skill in battle, and justice, along with a strong belief in Islam. [2] Osman's clan members identified with their leader to such an extent that they called themselves Osmanlis, "sons of Osman," rather than Turks, a term they equated with boorish, unwashed peasants.

Although the Ottomans started out with a small territory, they were fortunate in that Osman and his successors were extremely able rulers. Osman's son, Orkhan, captured the important Greek city of Bursa across the Sea of Marmara from Constantinople. It became the first Ottoman capital. The third Osmanli continued the expansion of the state; its rulers were now recognized as sultans. The Ottomans crossed into Europe over a bridge of boats and swept like a tidal wave of conquest across the Balkans. On May 29, 1453, Mehmed II, the seventh Ottoman sultan, captured Constantinople, completing the transformation of a frontier principality of unknown Ghazis into a world empire.

Ottoman power continued to expand after the death of Mehmed II. By the 1600s it included most of Eastern Europe, North Africa, and the Middle East. This large territory was headed by the sultan, who was also the caliph of Islam, ensuring him the spiritual authority over Muslims which supplemented his temporal authority. The Ottomans developed a strong army and fleet that were more than a match for European Christian powers for several centuries. The core of the army was the Janissaries, an elite body of soldiers recruited from Christian villages, forced to convert to Islam, and given special privileges as the sultan's personal guard. Janissary garrisons were assigned to important cities in the empire, and in certain cities, notably the North African provinces, they ran the government, ignoring the sultan's appointed governors.

Another factor that made the Ottoman system work was the religious organization of non-Muslim minority groups as self-governing units called *millets*, a Turkish word meaning "nation." Each millet was headed by its own religious leader, who was responsible to the sultan for the leadership and good behavior of his people. The three principal millets in Turkey were the Armenian and Greek Orthodox Christian communities and the Jews. Although Christians and Jews were not considered equal to freeborn Muslims, they were under the sultan's protection. Usually their lives were not interfered with, and Greek and Jewish merchants in particular rendered important services to the Ottoman government as intermediaries in trade with European countries.

The "Sick Man of Europe"

In the eighteenth and nineteenth centuries the Ottoman Empire gradually weakened, while European Christian powers grew stronger. European countries improved their military equipment and tactics, and began to defeat the Ottomans regularly. The sultans were forced to sign treaties and lost territories, causing great humiliation, since they had never treated Christian rulers as equals before. To make matters worse, the European powers helped the Greeks and other Balkan peoples to win their independence from the Ottomans.

The European powers also took advantage of the millet system to intervene directly in the Ottoman Empire's internal affairs. French troops invaded Lebanon in 1860 to restore order after civil war broke out there between the Christian and the Druze communities. The European powers claimed the right to protect the Christian minorities from mistreatment by the Muslim majority, saying that the sultan's troops could not provide for their safety.

One or two sultans in the nineteenth century tried to make reforms in the Ottoman system. They suppressed the Janissaries, who by then had become an unruly mob, and organized a modern army equipped with European weapons, uniforms, and advisers. One sultan issued a charter stating that all of his subjects would have equal rights "regardless of religion, race or language, in matters such as taxation, education, property rights and encouragement of good citizenship."[3] In 1876 Sultan Abdul-Hamid II, prodded by the British, issued a constitution providing for a Grand National Assembly representing all classes, races,

and creeds within the empire, and limiting the ruler's absolute powers "to the counsel and will of the nation, on the model of the British system of government."[4]

Unfortunately, the forces of reaction, represented by the religious leaders, the sultan's courtiers, and the sultan himself, were stronger than the forces for reform. Abdul-Hamid had no real intention of giving up the absolute powers that Ottoman sultans had always had. The first Grand National Assembly met in 1877, and when the members ventured to criticize the sultan's ministers, he dissolved it.

The European powers became convinced that the Ottomans were incapable of reform. European rulers compared the healthy state of their economies and the growth of representative government in their countries to the grinding poverty and lack of rights for Ottoman subjects, as a healthy person looks at an ill one in a hospital bed. The European rulers referred to the sultan as the "Sick Man of Europe," and plotted his death.[5]

However, the Sick Man's death was easier to talk about than to carry out. The main reason was that the European rulers distrusted one another almost as much as they disliked the sultan. If one European ruler seemed to be getting too much territory, trade privileges, or control over the sultan's policies, the others would band together to block that ruler.

World War I: Exit Empire, Enter Republic

In World War I the Ottoman Empire was allied with Germany against the United Kingdom, France, and Russia. Ottoman armies fought bravely against heavy odds, but were eventually defeated. A peace treaty signed in 1920 divided up the empire into British and French protectorates, except for a small part of Anatolia which was left to the sultan. The most devastating blow of all was the occupation by the Greeks of western Anatolia, under the provisions of a secret agreement that brought Greece into the war. It seemed to the Turks that their former subjects had become their rulers.

At this point in the Turkish nation's fortunes, however, a new "gray wolf" appeared to lead them in a very different direction. His name Mustafa Kemal. During the war, Mustafa Kemal was one of the few successful Ottoman military commanders, organizing brilliant tactical retreats and defeating the British in 1915 when they attempted to capture the Dardanelles.

Mustafa Kemal took advantage of Turkish anger over the occupation of Anatolia by

foreign armies, particularly the Greeks, to launch a movement for independence. It would be a movement not only to recover the sacred Anatolian homeland, but also for independence from the sultan. Mustafa Kemal said that the sultan was no longer the rightful ruler of Turkey; he was a prisoner of foreign interests.

The Turkish independence movement began in the interior, far from Constantinople. Mustafa Kemal and his associates chose Ankara, a dusty village on a plateau, as their new capital. They issued a so-called National Pact stating that the "New Turkey" would be an independent republic. Its territory would be limited to areas where Turks were the majority of the population. The nationalists resolutely turned their backs on Turkey's imperial past.

The Turkish War of Independence lasted until 1922. It was fought mainly against the Greeks. The nationalists were able to convince other occupation forces to withdraw from Anatolia by proving that they controlled the territory and represented the real interests of the Turkish people. The Greeks were defeated in a series of fierce battles, and in 1922 France and the United Kingdom signed a treaty recognizing Turkey as a sovereign state headed by Mustafa Kemal.

THE TURKISH REPUBLIC

The Turkish republic has passed through several stages of political development since it was founded. The first stage, dominated by Mustafa Kemal, established its basic form. "Turkey for the Turks" meant that the republic would be predominantly Turkish in population; this was accomplished by rough surgery with the expulsion of the Armenians and most of the Greeks. Mustafa Kemal also rejected imperialism and interference in the internal affairs of other nations. He once said, "Turkey has a firm policy of ensuring (its) independence within set national boundaries."[6] Peace with Turkey's neighbors and the abandonment of imperialism enabled Mustafa Kemal to concentrate on internal changes. By design, these changes would be far reaching in order to break what he viewed as the dead hand of Islam on Turkish life. Turkey would become a secular democratic state on the European model. A constitution was approved in 1924, the sultanate and the caliphate were both abolished, and the last Ottoman sultan went into exile. Religious courts were also abolished, and new European law codes were introduced to replace Islamic law. An elected Grand National Assembly was given the responsibility for legislation, with executive power held by the president of the republic.

The most striking changes were made in social rather than in political life. Most of these changes bore the personal stamp of Mustafa Kemal. The traditional Turkish costume was outlawed. Polygyny was outlawed. Women were encouraged to work, allowed to vote (in 1930), and given equal rights with men in divorce and inheritance. Turks were required to have surnames; Mustafa Kemal took the name Ataturk, meaning "Father of the Turks."

Mustafa Kemal Ataturk died on November 10, 1938. His hold on his country had been so strong, his influence so pervasive, that a whole nation broke down and wept when the news came. The anniversary of his death is still observed by a moment of silence.

Ismet Inonu, Ataturk's right-hand man, succeeded Ataturk and served as president until 1950. Ataturk had distrusted political parties; his brief experiment with a two-party system was abruptly cancelled when members of the officially sponsored "loyal opposition" criticized the Father of the Turks for his free lifestyle. The only political party he allowed was the Republican People's Party (RPP). It was not a party dedicated to its own survival or to repression, as are political parties in many single-party states. The RPP based its program on six principles, the most important, in terms of politics, being *devrimcilik* ("revolutionism" or "reformism"). It meant that the party was committed to work for a multiparty system and free elections. One author writes, "The Turkish single party system was never based on the doctrine of a single party. It was always embarrassed and almost ashamed of the monopoly (over power). The Turkish single party had a bad conscience."[7]

Agitation for political reforms began in World War II. When Turkey applied for admission to the United Nations, a number of National Assembly deputies pointed out that the UN Charter specified certain rights that the government was not providing. Reacting to popular demands and pressure from Turkey's allies, Ismet Inonu announced that political parties could be established. The first new party in the republic's history was the Democratic Party, organized in 1946. In 1950 the party won 408 seats in the National Assembly to 69 for the Republican People's Party. The Democrats had campaigned vigorously in rural areas, and won massive support from farmers and peasants. Having presided over

Historically, Turkey has been occupied by many different peoples. This recent picture is of rural women washing clothes in a Roman bath in Isikli, western Turkey, that dates back to the fifth century AD.

the transition from a one-party system with a bad conscience to a two-party one, President Inonu stepped down to become head of the opposition.

CIVILIAN POLITICS, MILITARY RULE

Modern Turkey has struggled for more than three decades to develop a workable multiparty political system. An interesting point about this struggle is that the armed forces have seized power three times, and three times they have returned the nation to civilian rule. This fact makes Turkey very different from other Middle Eastern nations, whose army leaders, once they have seized power, are unwilling to give it up. Ataturk deliberately kept the Turkish armed forces out of domestic politics. He believed that the military had only two responsibilities: to defend the nation in case of invasion, and to serve as "the guardian of the reforming ideals of his regime."[8] Since Ataturk's death, military leaders have seized power only when they were convinced that the civilian government had betrayed the ideals of the founder of the republic.

The first military coup took place in the 1960 after ten years of rule by the Democrats. Army leaders charged them with corruption, economic mismanagement, and repression of the opposition. After a public trial, the three top civilian leaders were executed. Thus far they have

been the only high-ranking Turkish politicians to receive the death sentence. (After the 1980 coup a number of civilian leaders were arrested, but the most serious sentence imposed was a ban on political activity for the next ten years for certain party chiefs.)

The military leaders reinstated civilian rule in 1961. The Democratic Party was declared illegal, but other parties were allowed to compete in national elections. The new Justice Party, successor to the Democrats, won the elections but did not win a clear majority. As a result, the Turkish government could not function effectively. More and more Turks, especially university students and trade-union leaders, turned to violence as they became disillusioned with the multiparty system. As the violence increased, the military again intervened, but stopped short of taking complete control.

In 1980 the armed forces intervened for the third time in twenty years. They cited three reasons for their intervention: failure of the government to deal with political violence, the economic crisis, and the revival of Islamic fundamentalism (which they viewed as a total surrender of the secular principles established by Ataturk). (A political party, the National Salvation Party, openly advocated a return to Islamic law and organized huge rallies in several Turkish cities in 1979-1981.) The National

| Founding of Constantinople as Roman Christian capital, on site of ancient Byzantium **AD 330** | Capture of Constantinople by Sultan Mehmed II; city becomes capital of Islamic Ottoman Empire **1453** | Empire expands deep into Europe, with high-water mark with siege of Vienna, Austria **1683** | Defeat of Ottomans and division of territories into foreign protectorates **1918-1920** | Turkey becomes a republic **1925** | Two-party system established, and opposition Democrat Party comes to power **1946-1950** | First military coup overthrows Menderes government **1960** | Military leaders again seize power to halt spiral of leftist-rightist violence |

1980s

| Civilian rule returns with election of new Grand National Assembly under 1981 Constitution | Martial law lifted in all except eastern (Kurdish) provinces | New political party, Democratic Left, organized; two major leftist parties merge into a single opposition party |

Assembly was dissolved, the Constitution was suspended, and martial law was imposed throughout the country. The generals said they would restore parliamentary rule, but not before terrorism had been eliminated.

Thus far Turkey's generals have kept the major part of their promise. A systematic campaign to eliminate political violence has been largely successful. A new constitution was approved in 1982. It moves Turkey closer to a presidential republic, with wide powers reserved for the president. General Kenan Evren, leader of the 1980 coup and head of the ruling National Security Council (NSC) of five generals, was elected president for a seven-year term.

The only real surprise in Turkey's reconstructed political system resulted from the revival of political parties. All former political parties were banned after the 1980 coup. Elections were allowed for a new Assembly in November 1983. Three new parties were allowed to participate, two of them favored by the country's military leaders. The third, the Motherland Party, ran an American-style political campaign, using the media to present its candidates to the country, and won handily. Its leader, Turgut Ozal, became the first prime minister in this newest phase of Turkey's long, slow progress toward effective multiparty democracy.

Whether civilian rule will persevere in its third try is problematical. The new prime minister, an economist by profession, stabilized the economy through a series of drastic cuts and austerity measures when he served as finance minister in 1980-1982. Ozal's government must deal with critical economic problems—fifty-percent inflation, a huge bureaucracy, high taxes, a negative trade balance, and unemployment. Meanwhile, he has five generals looking over his shoulder, not ready to relax martial law, still unsure that Turkey is ready for democracy.

THE ECONOMY

Turkey has a relatively diversified economy, with a productive agriculture based on cotton, wheat, and tobacco, and considerable mineral resources. Cotton is the major export crop, but the country is the world's largest producer of sultana raisins and hazelnuts. Other important crops are sunflower oil seeds, sesame and linseed oil, and cotton oil seeds. Opium was formerly an important crop, but due to illegal exportation, poppy growing was banned by the government in 1972. The ban was lifted in 1974 after poppy farmers were unable to adapt their lands to other crops; production and sale are now government controlled.

Mineral resources include bauxite, chrome, copper, and iron ore, and there are large deposits of lignite. Turkey is one of the world's largest producers of chromite (chromium ore). Another important mineral resource is meerschaum, used for pipes and cigarette holders. Turkey supplies eighty percent of the world market for emery, and there are rich deposits of tungsten, perlite, boron, and cinnabar, all important rare metals.

The major economic weakness is in the lack of petroleum. There is one producing oilfield, with reserves estimated at ten billion barrels. There are four refineries, and the country also receives revenues from fees from the pipeline from Iraqi oilfields. Even so, forty-five percent of energy needs must be imported. The country does have a fairly large skilled labor force, and Turkish contractors have been able to negotiate contracts for development projects in oil-producing countries, such as Libya, with part payment for services in oil shipments at reduced rates.

FOOTNOTES

1. Cf. Lord Kinross, *The Ottoman Centuries: The Rise and Fall of the Turkish Empire* (New York: William Morrow, 1977).

2. *Ibid.*, p.25.

3. *Ibid.*, p. 501.

4. *Ibid.*, p. 511.

5. British Prime Minister William Gladstone said in 1880 that the Ottoman government was "a bottomless pit of fraud and falsehood." *Ibid.*, p.538.

6. V. A. Danilov, "Kemalism and World Peace," in a Kazancigil and E. Ozbudun, eds., *Ataturk, Founder of a Modern State* (Hamden: Archon Books, 1981), p. 110.

7. Maurice Duverger, *Political Parties* (New York: John Wiley, 1959), p. 277.

8. C. H. Dodd, *Democracy and Development in Turkey* (North Humberside, England: Eothen Press, 1979), p. 135.

DEVELOPMENT

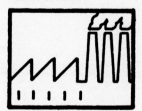

Lack of oil and heavy defense expenditures have made effective economic development difficult. The International Monetary Fund (IMF) and other leading agencies have kept the country afloat since 1977 with loans and rescheduling of debt payments. But in 1984 and 1985 this aid was withheld pending government reforms.

FREEDOM

Turkey has struggled for political democracy and full civil liberties. In the 1970s extremism led to a military coup and curtailment of these liberties. The new Constitution reserves vast powers to the president. Although civilian rule was restored in 1983, a 1985 law gives police broad arrest powers and authority over "public morality."

HEALTH/WELFARE

Education was an early priority in the republic. A new Turkish alphabet replaced the cumbersome Ottoman script in 1928, and adult literacy programs were established throughout the country. Literacy is now 65% in urban areas. By 1981 5.7 million students were enrolled in primary schools.

ACHIEVEMENTS

To compensate for its lack of oil resources Turkey has made a number of profitable barter and trade agreements with oil-producing countries for discounted oil purchases. Turkey's pool of skilled labor is another economic asset. In 1984 remittances from Turkish workers abroad were $1.88 billion, a 23% increase over 1983.

United Arab Emirates

GEOGRAPHY

Area in Square Kilometers (Miles):
82,880 (30,000)
Capital (Population): Abu Dhabi
(225,000) (1981)
Climate: hot and dry

PEOPLE

Population
Total: 1,523,000
Annual Growth Rate: 10.3%
Rural/Urban Population Ratio: 21/79
Ethnic Makeup of Population: 19%
indigenous Arab; 23% other Arab;
50% south Asian; 8% East Asian
and Westerner; fewer than 20% of
population are UAE citizens

Health
Life Expectancy at Birth: 71 years
Infant Death Rate (Ratio): 50/1,000
Average Caloric Intake: n/a
Physicians Available (Ratio): 1/900

FALCONRY

Falconry is a popular sport in the UAE. Once the sport of desert shaykhs, it is now the chief diversion of ordinary citizens. Falcons are a common sight, held on gloved fists, perched on rails outside of banks, on the backs of car and airplane seats, or being trained by a falconer to dive for lures in open spaces. The UAE does not grant tourist visas, but if tourism ever becomes an industry, this ancient sport should become its major travel attraction.

Religion(s)
90% Muslim; 10% Hindu, Christian,
and other

Education
Adult Literacy Rate: 56.3%

COMMUNICATION

Telephones: 208,900
Newspapers: 2 notable dailies; 1
weekly

TRANSPORTATION

Highways—Kilometers (Miles): 1,085
(674) total; 885 (550) bituminous
Railroads—Kilometers (Miles): none
Commercial Airports: 48

GOVERNMENT

Type: federation of emirates
Independence Date: December 2,
1971
Head of State: Shaykh Zayed Al
Nuhayyan, president (chief of state);
Shaykh Rashid Al Maktum, prime
minister and vice president (head of
government)
Political Parties: none
Suffrage: none

MILITARY

Number of Armed Forces: 47,200 plus
air wing (small)
*Military Expenditures (% of Central
Government Expenditures):* 40%
Current Hostilities: none

ECONOMY

Currency ($ US Equivalent): 3.68
dirhams = $1 (March 1985)
Per Capita Income/GNP:
$23,000/$27.5 billion (1983)
Inflation Rate: 16%
Natural Resources: oil; natural gas;
cement aggregate
Agriculture: vegetables; dates; limes;
alfalfa; tobacco
Industry: petroleum; light
manufacturing

FOREIGN TRADE

Exports: $15.4 billion (1983)
Imports: $8.3 billion (1983)

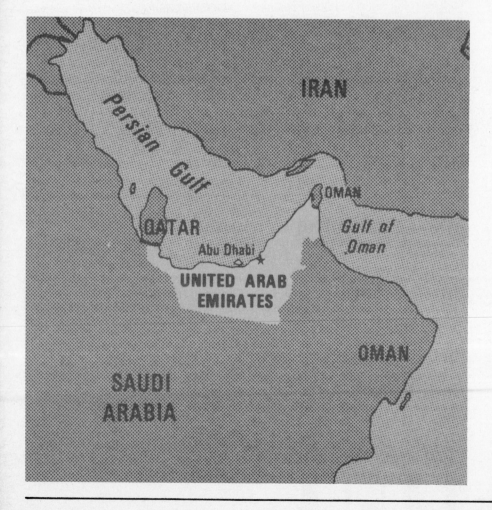

THE UNITED ARAB EMIRATES

The United Arab Emirates (UAE) is a federation of seven independent states with a central governing council located on the northeast coast of the Arabian Peninsula. The seven states—called *emirates*, from the title of their ruler—are Abu Dhabi, Ajman, Dubai, Fujairah, Ras al-Khaimah, Sharjah, and Umm al-Qaiwain. They came under British protection in the 1800s and were given their independence from the United Kingdom by treaty in 1971. At that time they joined in the federal union. From its modest beginnings, the UAE has come to play an important role in Middle East Arab affairs because of its oil wealth.

Abu Dhabi, the largest emirate, contains eighty-seven percent of the UAE in area. Its capital, also called Abu Dhabi, is the largest city in the federation. Dubai, the second largest emirate, has the federation's only natural harbor, which has been enlarged to handle supertankers. Abu Dhabi, Dubai, and Sharjah produce oil, and Sharjah also has important natural gas reserves. The other emirates are less fortunate. Ras al-Khaimah and Umm al-Qaiwain have oil enough for a chain of gas stations. Ajman and Fujairah have plenty of building stone, but little else in terms of natural resources.

HISTORY

The early inhabitants of the area were fishermen and nomads. They were converted to Islam in the seventh century AD, but little is known of their history before the sixteenth century. At that time European nations, notably Portugal, had taken an active interest in trade with India and the Far East. From the time of Prince Henry the Navigator, in the fifteenth century, the Portuguese dominated this trade. Gradually, other European countries, particularly Holland, France, and the United Kingdom, challenged Portuguese supremacy.

As more and more European ships appeared in Arabian coastal waters or fought one another over trade, the coastal Arabs felt threatened with loss of their territory. Meanwhile, the Wahhabis, militant Islamic missionaries, spread over Arabia in the eighteenth century. Wahhabi agents incited the most powerful coastal group, the Qawasim, to interfere with European shipping. European ships were seized along with their cargoes, and their crews were held for ransom. To the European countries this was piracy, but to the Qawasim it was defense of Islamic territory against the infidels. Ras al-Khaimah was their chief port, but very soon the whole coast of the modern UAE became known as the Pirate Coast.

Piracy lasted until 1820, when the British, who now controlled India and thus dominated the eastern trade, convinced the principal chiefs of the coast to sign a treaty that ended pirate activities. A British naval squadron was stationed in Ras al-Khaimah to enforce the treaty. In 1853 the arrangement was changed into a "Perpetual Maritime Truce." Because it specified a *truce* between the British and the chiefs, the region became known as the Trucial Coast and the territory of each chief as a trucial state. A British garrison was provided for each ruler, and a British political agent was assigned to take charge of foreign affairs. The United Kingdom paid the rulers annual subsidies; in most cases, it was all the money they could acquire. There were originally five Trucial States (also called emirates); Sharjah and Ras al-Khaimah were reorganized as separate emirates in 1966.

The arrangement between the United Kingdom and the Trucial States continued to work smoothly for more than a century, through both world wars. Then, in the 1960s, the British decided for economic and political reasons to give up most of their overseas colonies, including those in the Arabian Peninsula, which were technically protectorates rather than colonies. In 1968 they proposed to the Trucial Coast emirs that they join in a federation with Bahrain and Qatar, neighboring oil-producing protectorates. But Bahrain and Qatar, being larger and richer, decided to go it alone. Thus the United Arab Emirates, when it became independent in 1971, included only six emirates. Ras al-Khaimah joined in 1972.

PROBLEMS OF INTEGRATION

Differences in size, wealth, resources, and population have hampered the UAE since it was formed. Another integration problem is poor communications. Until recently, one could travel from emirate to emirate only by boat, and telephone service was nonexistent. These limitations are disappearing rapidly as the UAE develops. One problem that still exists is rivalry among the emirs, and resentment of the rich emirates by the poor ones. The small, poor emirates have been unwilling to give up some of their rights (since they are technically independent) to a federal government. They also resent the domination of Abu Dhabi and Dubai, and feel that wealth is unfairly distributed, that the rich emirates get the lion's share. Also, each emir has been reluctant to give up authority over his British-trained private army to form a unified UAE army.

BUILDING A FEDERAL UNION

Unlike the United States, which has had two centuries to develop its federal system of government, the UAE has had barely a decade and a half. The system was defined in the 1971 Constitution. The government consists of a Supreme Council of the seven emirs, plus a Council of Ministers (cabinet) and a forty-member Federal National Legislature, whose members are appointed from the seven emirates on a proportional basis according to size and population. The federal capital is in Abu Dhabi, and the president of the Supreme Council, Shaykh Zayed, is also ruler of Abu Dhabi. This fact has caused friction, particularly between Abu Dhabi and Dubai. Dubai and Ras al-Khaimah refused for a time to integrate their military units into the UAE armed forces.

The 1979 Revolution in Iran, which seemed to threaten the UAE's security, accelerated the move toward centralization of authority over defense forces, abolition of borders, and merging of revenues. Iran's threat to close the Strait of Hormuz was particularly worrisome, since the UAE economy depends on oil exports. In 1981 the UAE joined with other Gulf states in the Gulf Cooperation Council (GCC) to establish common defense and economic cooperation policies. Abu Dhabi and Dubai also pledged to contribute fifty percent of their revenues toward the federal budget.

The governments of the emirates themselves are best described as patriarchal. Each emir is head of his own large "family" as well as head of the emirate. The ruling emirs gained their power a long time ago from various sources—foreign trade, pearl fishing, or ownership of lands—and in recent years they have profited from oil royalites to confirm their positions as heads of state.

Disagreements within the ruling families have sometimes led to violence or "palace coups." Shaykh Zayed succeeded his uncle when the latter was deposed in 1966, mainly because he was opposed to development.

INTERNAL DIFFERENCES

In general, the new wealth from oil revenues has benefitted most segments of the population and brought vast changes into their lives. But there are some important differences among the emirates. Abu Dhabi and Dubai, the principal oil producers, carry the others on their backs in terms of financing and development funds. They also have the strongest leaders. Shaykh Zayed of Abu Dhabi is credited with bringing the federation into existence, and has been the Federation Council's only

| Peace treaties between the United Kingdom and Arab shaykhs establishing Trucial States **1853, 1866** | Establishment of Trucial Council under British advisers, forerunner of federation **1952** | Independence **1971** | UAE becomes first Arab oil producer to ban exports to US after Yom Kippur War **1973** | Balanced federal assembly and cabinet established **1979** | 1980s |

First free-trade zone established, in Dubai port

Emergency fuel stockpile set up to avoid shortages

president. An observer noted of Shaykh Rashid of Dubai, "The character of Dubai is to some extent the character of Shaykh Rashid, through the grip he exercises by personal decision on almost every major change, on his ability to inspire support, and his capacity as an entrepreneur."[1]

Several of the five smaller emirates have had some success in recent years with their own development programs. Sharjah's one oilfield went into production in 1975, but output was drastically reduced in the early 1980s in order to avoid a too-rapid depletion of reserves. Yet natural gas and gas condensate from the adjoining Sajaa gas field have more than made up for reduced oil revenues.

Ajman and Umm al-Qaiwain are coastal ports with agricultural hinterlands; one author described them as "dormitory towns for the Sharjah-Dubai conurbation, laid out in featureless blocks of flats as depressing as any in the industrial suburbs of the West."[2] Ras al-Khaimah has continually disappointed hopeful oil-seekers; its only natural resource is aggregate, which is used in making cement. Fujairah, the seventh emirate, is physically separated (by Oman) from the rest of the UAE and until recently had few prospects. However, in August 1985 oil was discovered offshore in the Gulf of Oman, and unconfirmed seismic surveys indicated a reservoir of 250 million barrels.

These differences have not only made the development of a unified, balanced economy difficult to achieve, but they have also interfered with progress toward full feder-

ation. The emirs of the smaller states remain reluctant to surrender their power over police protection, tax collection, ministerial appointments, and other reserved powers to federal jurisdiction.

AN OIL-DRIVEN ECONOMY

In the past, the people of the Trucial Coast made a meager living from breeding racing camels, some farming, and pearl fishing. Pearls were the main cash crop; a century ago there were 1,200 boats with 22,000 divers working the shallow waters of the Gulf. But in the twentieth century competition from Japanese cultured pearls ruined the Arabian pearl-fishing industry.

Then, in 1958, oil was discovered in Abu Dhabi. Oil exports began in 1962, and from then on the fortunes of the Gulf Arabs improved dramatically. Production was 14,200 barrels per day in 1962. In 1982 it was 1.1 million barrels per day, indicating how far the country's oil-driven economy has moved in two decades. With reserves of 32.4 billion barrels, plus abundant natural gas, the UAE has a 60-year cushion at current production rates before these fuels run out.

Its wealth has given the UAE the luxury of being able to move away from overdependence on oil. A large industrial zone opened in Jabal Dhanna-Ruwais, Abu Dhabi in 1982 with a 120,000-barrel-per-day refinery, and fertilizer and other plants. Dubai took an early lead in non-oil development, setting up aluminum and petrochemical plants plus the world's largest dry dock.

Economic diversification has had one ad-

verse effect. Due to its small population, the UAE has been forced to recruit foreign labor, mostly from Asia and Africa. By 1982 the majority of the population was non-native. This has caused tensions, because the foreign workers find themselves at the lower end of the economic scale, doing jobs the UAE natives are no longer willing to do, such as garbage collection and janitorial services.

In the long run, the challenge before the UAE is how to adapt a traditional society to the world of high technology. Barely twenty years ago the Gulf Arabs traveled by camels, lived in tents or palm-frond huts, and struggled to survive in a harsh environment. Now they drive Mercedes or Land Rovers, live in air-conditioned homes, vacation in Paris, Rome, or London, and enjoy the latest in electronic gadgets. Sinbad the Sailor, the legendary traveler, would be amazed if he returned to his old harbor, the creek at Dubai. He would hardly know what to think of the sprawling industrial world going up on the old Trucial Coast; many of his fellow Arabs have the same difficulty with their changing would.

FOOTNOTES

1. John Murray, in *Middle East Review 1981* (London: World of Information, 1981), p. 374.
2. *Ibid.*, p. 383.

DEVELOPMENT

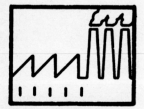

Oil wealth has enabled the UAE to transform a meager agriculture to near self-sufficiency in less than two decades. The total area under cultivation doubled between 1973 and 1979. Large-scale dairy and poultry farms are now in operation.

FREEDOM

The federal system of government leaves local authority to the rulers of the seven emirates. The rulers of Abu Dhabi and Dubai since 1979 have served as president and vice president of the Federation Council respectively. There is a Council of Ministers whose posts are allocated proportionally, and a Consultative Assembly appointed by the rulers.

HEALTH/WELFARE

Education has expanded rapidly since independence. In 1983 there were 100,000 students enrolled at all levels in the five northern emirates alone. Some 600 trained student teachers were graduated from training colleges, helping to reduce UAE dependence on foreign teachers. Health care showed similar increases.

ACHIEVEMENTS

Along with prudently reduced oil production to deal with lessening world demand, the UAE has steadily expanded non-oil sector output. In 1984, the Dubai Aluminum plant produced 155,355 tons, a 27% increase over 1983. Dubai also began exporting raw sulfur, the first shipment, 30,000 tons, going to Japan.

People's Democratic Republic of Yemen (South Yemen)

GEOGRAPHY

Area in Square Kilometers (Miles):
287,849 (110,000)
Capital (Population): Aden (343,000)
Climate: very hot, with minimal rainfall

PEOPLE

Population
Total: 2,147,000
Annual Growth Rate: 2.9%
Rural/Urban Population Ratio: 62/38
Ethnic Makeup of Population: almost all Arab; some Indian Somali, and European

Health
Life Expectancy at Birth: 46 years
Infant Death Rate (Ratio): 140/1,000
Average Caloric Intake: 86% of FAO minimum
Physicians Available (Ratio): 1/7,200

Religion(s)
99% Sunni Muslim; 1% Christian and Hindu

Education
Adult Literacy Rate: 25%

COMMUNICATION

Telephones: 19,000
Newspapers: n/a

DURABLE CULTURE

The overlay of Marxist ideology and heavy doses of scientific socialism have not entirely changed social and cultural life in the republic. In the interior behind Aden, people still live in compact villages and wear traditional clothing. Women are generally unveiled except in Aden, and there mainly due to the presence of non-Muslim foreign communities. The architecture of such towns as Mukalla, on the coast, and Shibam and Saiyun, in the interior, has changed little since Sabaean times. Houses are four- or five-story "skyscrapers" of mud brick, painted in bright colors with elaborate arabesques and calligraphy.

Another custom that has resisted Marxism is the chewing of leaves of *qat*, a mild narcotic grown as a cash crop. The government permits qat chewing in public gatherings on Thursdays and Fridays. On other days it is prohibited.

TRANSPORTATION

Highways—Kilometers (Miles): 5,600 (3,480) total; 1,700 (1,056) bituminous
Railroads—Kilometers (Miles): none
Commercial Airports: 65

GOVERNMENT

Type: Marxist republic, power centered in ruling party
Independence Date: November 30, 1967
Head of State: Ali Nasir Muhammed al-Hasani, chairman, president, and prime minister
Political Parties: Yemeni Socialist Party (only legal party), a coalition of National Front, Ba'th, and Communist parties
Suffrage: all citizens at 18

MILITARY

Number of Armed Forces: 24,500
Military Expenditures (% of Central Government Expenditures): n/a
Current Hostilities: none

ECONOMY

Currency ($ US Equivalent): 0.343 dinar = $1 (March 1985)
Per Capita Income/GNP: $333 (1985)/$810 million (1980)
Inflation Rate: n/a
Natural Resources: fish
Agriculture: cotton; cereals; dates; qat (mild narcotic); livestock
Industry: petroleum; fishing

FOREIGN TRADE

Exports: $580 million (1982)
Imports: $1.2 billion (1982)

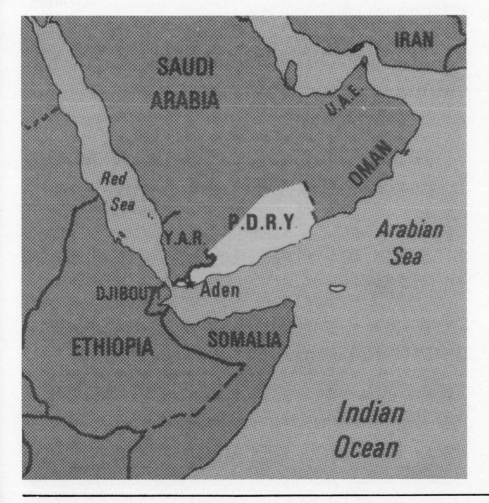

PEOPLE'S DEMOCRATIC REPUBLIC OF YEMEN

The People's Democratic Republic of Yemen (the PDRY) is currently the only Arab state with a Marxist government, although Islam is the state religion and the population is ninety-nine-percent Muslim. It was formed in 1967 from two British territories, the Crown Colony of Aden and the South Arabian Protectorate, a group of twenty emirates or shaykhdoms. The PDRY also includes Perim and Kamaran Islands at the southern end of the Red Sea, and the large island of Socotra off the coast of Oman's Dhofar Province. The PDRY borders Saudi Arabia, Oman, and the Yemen Arab Republic, but none of these boundaries have been formally defined, and in some cases are in dispute. The capital and major city, Aden, was developed by the British as an important naval base and site of the Aden oil refinery, the country's main source of revenue.

The republic occupies an area which is geographically ill favored, with few natural resources, very little rainfall, and a hot, humid climate. The dominant physical feature is the Wadi Hadhramaut, a broad river valley running parallel to the south coast and varying from 100 to 150 miles inland. It is one of the few areas of the country with enough water for irrigation. Except for Aden, the area has little rainfall; in some sections rain may fall only once every ten years. Less than two percent of the land is cultivable.

HISTORY

Despite its bleak and barren appearance today, South Yemen (now the PDRY) in ancient times was home to a flourishing civilization. Two important "inventions" made this civilization possible: the domestication of the camel, and development of an underground irrigation system of channels (falaj). Ships and camel caravans brought the frankincense, myrrh, musk from Socotra, and silks and spices from India and the Far East to northern cities in Egypt, Persia, and Mesopotamia. Aden was an important port for this trade, due to its natural harbor and its location at the south end of the Red Sea. The trade brought large profits to merchants based in Aden. The region's agriculture was well developed due to the falaj and to water provided by the great Marib Dam in northern Yemen. The republic of today has a long way to go to equal the level of productivity and wealth of this ancient civilization.

The people of Yemen were converted to Islam early in the seventh century, in the lifetime of Muhammad according to some scholars. But in terms of political development, southern Yemen remained a backwater, there were no lush farmlands to attract emigrants from other parts of Arabia or the Islamic Middle East. Rivalries between tribes continually disrupted the area, and the collapse of the Marib Dam had adversely affected agriculture.

From the 1500s onward, the south and east Arabian coasts attracted the interest of European powers competing for control of Indian Ocean trade. Aden was a potentially important base, and expeditions by Portuguese and other Europeans tried without success to capture it from the Ottoman Turks who controlled it at the time. In 1839 a British expedition finally succeeded. They found a town of "800 miserable souls, huddled in huts of reed matting, surrounded by guns that would not fire," or so the American traveler Joseph Osgood described the scene.

Under British rule, Aden became an important naval base and refueling port for ships passing through the Suez Canal and down the Red Sea en route to India. For many British families bound for India, Aden was the last land, with the last friendly faces, that they would see before arriving many days later in the strange wonderland of India. The route through the Suez Canal and down the Red Sea past Aden was the lifeline of the British Empire. In order to protect Aden from possible attack by hostile peoples in the interior, the British signed a series of treaties with their chiefs, called shaykhs or sometimes sultans. These treaties laid the basis for the South Arabian Protectorates. British political agents advised the rulers on policy matters and gave them annual subsidies to keep them happy. One particular agent, Harold Ingrams was so successful in eliminating feuds and rivalries that "Ingram's Peace" became a symbol of the right way to deal with proud, independent local leaders.

The March to Independence

After World War II the British began to give independence to their overseas territories. Aden's turn came late; the British wanted to hold on to Aden as long as possible because of its naval base and refinery. It seemed to them that the best way to protect British interests was to set up a union of Aden and the South Arabian Protectorates. This was done in 1963, with independence promised for 1968. However, the British plan proved unworkable. In Aden a strong anti-British nationalist movement developed in the trade unions among the dock workers and refinery employees. This movement organized a political party, the People's Socialist Party, strongly influenced by the Socialist anti-Western, Arab-nationalist programs of President Gamal Abdel Nasser in Egypt.

The Party had two branches, the moderate Front for the Liberation of Occupied South Yemen (FLOSY) and the leftist Marxist National Liberation Front (NLF). About all they had in common was their opposition to the British and the South Arabian sultans, who they called "lackeys of imperialism." FLOSY and the NLF joined forces in 1965-1967 to force the British to leave Aden. British troops were murdered; bombs damaged the refinery. In November 1967 the British had had enough. British forces were evacuated, and the United Kingdom signed a treaty granting independence to South Yemen under a coalition government made up of members of both FLOSY and the NLF.

A MARXIST STATE IN ARABIA

With indpendence, the authority of the South Arabian sultans came to an end, and in 1970 a constitution went into effect. South Yemen was officially renamed the People's Democratic Republic of Yemen.

The PDRY began its existence with serious handicaps. It lost its major sources of income almost immediately. The British payroll stopped, both for its armed forces and the refinery. The closing of the Suez Canal due to the 1967 Arab-Israeli War cut off most port fees and shipping charges, another source of income to the colony while under British rule.

But the main problem was political. A power struggle developed between FLOSY and the NLF. The former favored moderate policies, good relations with other Arab states, and continued ties with the United Kingdom. The NLF were leftist Marxists. By 1970 the Marxists had won. FLOSY leaders were killed or went into exile. The new government set its objectives as state ownership of lands, state management of all business and industry, a single political organization with all other political parties prohibited, and support for anti-government revolutionary movements in other Arab states, particularly Oman and Saudi Arabia. These objectives largely have been achieved, although support for revolutionary movements is not as strong as it used to be.

The PDRY is closely allied with the Soviet Union. It has the same pyramidal structure, with a Presidium at the top, then a Council of Ministers, a Supreme People's Legislative Council, and provincial and district local councils. The only legal party is the Yemen Socialist Party. The party's

Capture of Aden by British naval expedition 1839	South Arabian Protectorates established by British 1882-1914	Protectorates merged with Aden Crown Colony into the Federation of Arab Emirates of the South 1962-1965	British forces withdraw from Aden; National Liberation Front proclaims southern Yemen as independent republic 1967	New Constitution changes country's official name to People's Democratic Republic of Yemen 1970	Agreement on unification with Yemen Arab Republic

1980s

Peace Treaty with Oman ends 15-year conflict over PDRY support for rebels in Dhofar Province (Oman)	Diplomatic relations established with Saudi Arabia; diplomatic relations established with Oman	Rival Marxist faction makes bid to overthrow government

secretary general is also the chairman of the Presidium and the prime minister. Elections to the legislature are strictly controlled by the government. Centralization of power and ruthless repression have practically eliminated internal opposition. However, some liberalization in the system has taken place, following the thaw in relations with neighboring Arab states. In 1985 Ali Nasir Muhammad, prime minister since 1971 and one of the few survivors of the internal conflicts of early independence days, resigned his position to make way for "new blood" and restructuring of the party.

FOREIGN RELATIONS

As might be expected in view of its close alignment with the Soviet Union and its political system, the PDRY has not gotten along well with its neighbors, particularly the patriarchal monarchy in Oman and the moderate republican regime in the Yemen Arab Republic (YAR). It backed a rebellion in Dhofar Province against the sultan of Oman in the 1970s. It was not until 1983, after the complete pacification of Dhofar, that the PDRY dropped its opposition to the sultan and established diplomatic relations.

A more serious rivalry developed with the Yemen Arab Republic. In a broad sense it represents a continuation of the age-old highland-lowland, Sunni Muslim-Shia Muslim conflict in Yemen. The two neighbors fought a brief border war in 1972, again in 1975, and again in 1978 and 1979, this time because of the murder of the YAR president by a bomb in a suitcase carried by an envoy from the PDRY. Both countries have accused each other of subversion and periodic interference in their internal affairs.

Yet the urge for unification of the "two Yemens" is strong, particularly now that both are free from foreign control. In 1979 the border war ended, somewhat surprisingly, in an agreement for their full unification in a "Republic of Yemen." PDRY President Ali Nasir Muhammad (elected in 1980) and YAR President Ali Abdullah Saleh formed a Yemen Presidential Council in 1981, and in 1982 reached agreement on a unitary constitution that would be drafted to govern the unified Yemini nation. What form this state would take, given the differences in ideology and practice, remains to be seen. Meetings of the Presidential Council since 1982 have produced little more than statements of common support for Arab policies toward Israel. But in February 1985 the new PDRY prime minister, Haydar Abu Bakr al-Attas, told his Cabinet that he would press for Yemeni unification within a very short time.

THE ECONOMY

The PDRY has no oil and practically no natural resources; its per capita income of $333 (1985) underscores its contrast with neighboring Oman and Saudi Arabia. The population (2,147,000 in 1984) is growing at an annual rate of 2.9 percent. The country's foreign trade has shown a deficit since independence; the 1983-1984 deficit was $750 million. Government policies of nationalization of the economy and seizure of foreign firms have frightened off foreign investors. About seventy percent of the budget comes from foreign aid, most of it from the Soviet bloc, although as a result of improved relations with other Arab states, aid from them is increasing.

The country's principal resources are its fisheries and the Aden oil refinery. Fisheries exports bring about $56 million in foreign exchange annually. The fishing industry is organized under a national board into cooperatives. Several international lending agencies are supporting fisheries expansion, and in 1985 a $22 million development program financed by the International Development Association, the Kuwait Fund for Arab Economic Development, and the European Economic Community, went into operation to set up a fisheries manpower-training center in Aden and modernize fishing harbors. Oil exploration is almost exclusively run by Soviet and other Eastern bloc companies, and, despite overtures to Western nations, the PDRY remains heavily dependent upon Soviet aid. With the opening up of the neighboring Yemen Arab Republic to Western industry, technology, and tourism because of its newly discovered oil resources, the eventual unification of the two Yemens is likely to bring about considerable modification in the PDRY's rigid Marxism.

DEVELOPMENT

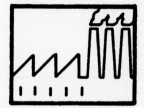

Oil concessions were granted to non-Communist countries such as Italy for the first time in 1979, but thus far results have been negligible. Fishing is the main hope for development of an export industry. A new Soviet-built fishing port at Hedjuff opened in 1985.

FREEDOM

The 1970 Constitution defines the PDRY as a single-party state governed according to "scientific socialism" by the National Liberation Front (NLF). In 1978 the NLF was merged with the Yemeni Socialist Party (YSP), an earlier Marxist organization. The YSP is the sole legal political organization.

HEALTH/WELFARE

The PDRY government has made great efforts in education on the premise that youth is to be prepared for "socially productive work." A campaign for universal literacy began in 1973, and by 1980 6% of GNP was devoted to education. The state is also in the vanguard in women's rights.

ACHIEVEMENTS

In addition to the Hedjuff fishing port, a new 600-line central telephone exchange and the 7,000-line Mukalla rural exchange were completed (by East German technicians) in 1985, for a total of 19,000 lines nationwide. East Germans also built the PDRY's first automatic bakery.

Yemen Arab Republic (North Yemen)

GEOGRAPHY

Area in Square Kilometers (Miles):
195,000 (75,290)
Capital (Population): San'a (275,000)
Climate: interior, temperate; coastal plain, hot and humid

PEOPLE

Population
Total: 5,902,000
Annual Growth Rate: 2.7%
Rural/Urban Population Ratio: 86/14
Ethnic Makeup of Population: 90% Arab; 10% Afro-Arab

Health
Life Expectancy at Birth: 44 years
Infant Death Rate (Ratio): 163/1,000
Average Caloric Intake: 76% of FAO minimum
Physicians Available (Ratio): 1/11,670

Religion(s)
100% Muslim (Sunni and Shia)

A WORLD OF CONTRASTS

The San'a *suq* (market) is a microcosm of modern and medieval Yemen in confusing juxtaposition. Vendors still hawk spices, henna, and *kohl* (antimony paste) from bulging burlap sacks spread on the ground, and men bargain for the *jambiyas* (the curved daggers traditionally worn by male Yemenis) and antique muskets. But alongside these items are the goods of the modern world: cameras, digital watches, calculators, and Sony Walkmans are eagerly snapped up by expatriate workers returning from the Gulf oilfields with thick wads of banknotes. Blacksmiths hammer wrought iron into delicate filigree shapes to the rhythm of Koranic chants, under San'a's medieval skyline of multistory buildings, each topped by a TV aerial. At the day's end, *akhdams,* descendants of African slaves, sweep up the plastic litter with twig brooms.

Education
Adult Literacy Rate: 20%

COMMUNICATION

Telephones: 10,000
Newspapers: n/a

TRANSPORTATION

Highways—Kilometers (Miles): 4,000 (2,486) total; 1,775 (1,103) bituminous
Railroads—Kilometers (Miles): none
Commercial Airports: 23

GOVERNMENT

Type: republic
Independence Date: 1918
Head of State: Colonel Ali Abdullah Saleh, president
Political Parties: none
Suffrage: none

MILITARY

Number of Armed Forces: 22,100
Military Expenditures (% of Central Government Expenditures): 35%
Current Hostilities: none

ECONOMY

Currency ($ US Equivalent): 6.45 riyals = $1 (March 1985)
Per Capita Income/GNP: $460/$3.2 billion (1982)
Inflation Rate: 15.6% (1979-1981)
Natural Resources: rock salt; small deposits of coal and copper; oil (recently discovered)
Agriculture: cotton; fruits and vegetables; cereals; *qat* (mild narcotic); livestock and poultry; coffee
Industry: food processing; building materials; textiles and leather goods; some fishing

FOREIGN TRADE

Exports: $11 million (1981)
Imports: $1.7 billion (1981)

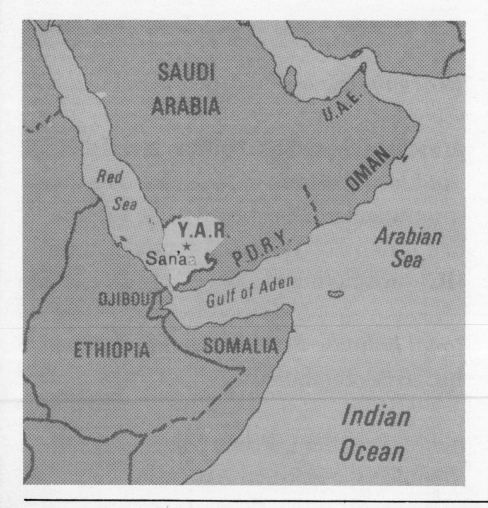

YEMEN ARAB REPUBLIC

The Yemen Arab Republic (YAR) is located in the southwest corner of the Arabian Peninsula. It is composed of two very different geographic regions: a hot, humid coastal strip, the Tihama, along the Red Sea, and an interior region of mountains and high plains that shade off gradually into the bleak, waterless south Arabian desert. The republic forms the largest part of an area that in the past was referred to simply as "Yemen." Today this area contains two separate states, the Yemen Arab Republic and the People's Democratic Republic of Yemen, which extends south and east from the Red Sea along the Arabian Sea to the border with Oman. Due to their locations, the two states are sometimes referred to as North and South Yemen.

The Yemen interior is very different not only from the Tihama but also from other parts of the Arabian Peninsula. It consists of highlands and rugged mountains ranging up to twelve thousand feet. At the higher elevations the mountain ridges are separated by deep, narrow valleys, usually with swift-flowing streams at the bottom. The ample rainfall allows extensive use of terracing for agriculture. The main crops are coffee, cereals, vegetables, and *qat*, a shrub whose leaves are chewed as a mildly intoxicating narcotic.

This part of Yemen has been for centuries the home of warlike but sedentary peoples who have always formed a stable, stratified society living in villages or small cities. These groups have been the principal support for the Shia Zaidi Imams, whose rule was the political nucleus of Yemen from the ninth century AD to the establishment of the republic in 1962. The Yemeni capital, San'a, is located in these northern highlands. It is a fairy-tale capital visually, with its multistory "skyscraper" houses of brick painted in various combinations of beige, pink, blue, and white, with intricate raised designs adorning the brickwork, and latticed balconies from whence the hidden women of San'a can peer down on the streets below.

ANCIENT CIVILIZATIONS

In ancient times the whole of Yemen was known to the Greeks, Romans, and other peoples as Arabia Felix ("Happy Arabia"), a remote land that they believed to be fabulously wealthy. They knew it as the source of frankincense, myrrh, and other spices, as well as other exotic products brought to Mediterranean and Middle Eastern markets by Arab merchants from the East. In Yemen itself, several powerful

kingdoms grew up from profits earned in this Eastern trade. One kingdom in particular, the Sabaeans, also had a productive agriculture based on irrigation. The water for irrigation came from the great Marib Dam, built around 500 BC. Marib was a marvel of engineering, built across a deep river valley (*wadi*). The Sabaean economy supported a population estimated at 300,000 in a region that today supports only a few thousand herders.

The Sabaeans were followed by the Himyarites. Himyarite rulers were converted to Christianity by wandering monks in the second century AD. The Himyarites had contacts with Christian Ethiopia across the Red Sea, and for a time were vassals of Ethiopian kings. An Ethiopian army invaded South Arabia but was defeated by the Himyarites in AD 570, the "Year of the Elephant" in Arab tradition, so called because the Ethiopian invaders were mounted on elephants. (The year was also notable for the birth of Muhammad, founder of Islam.)

Sabaeans and Himyarites ruled long ago, but they are important to Yemenis as symbols of their long and rich historical past. The Imams of Yemen, who ruled until 1962, used a red dye to sign their official documents in token of their relationship to Himyarite kings. (The word *Himyar* comes from the same root as *hamra*, "red.")

THE COMING OF ISLAM

Yemenis were among the first converts to Islam. The separation of the Yemenis into mutually hostile Sunni and Shia Muslims took place relatively early in Islamic history. Those living in the Tihama, which was easily accessible to missionaries and warriors expanding the borders of the new Islamic state, became Sunnis, obedient to the caliphs (the elected "successors" of Muhammad). The Yemeni mountaineers were more difficult to reach, and when they were converted to the new religion it was through the teachings of a follower of the Shi'at Ali, "Party of Ali," those who felt that Muhammad's son-in-law Ali and his descendants should have been chosen as the rightful leaders of the Islamic community. The friction between the lowland Yemenis of the Tihama and the highlanders which exists today has its origins in the ancient dispute.

THE ZAIDI IMAMATE

In the late ninth century AD a feud between certain nominally Muslim groups in inland Yemen led to the invitation to a religious scholar living in Mecca to come and mediate in their dispute. Use of an out-

side mediator was common in Arabia at that time. This scholar brought with him a number of families of Ali's descendants, who sought to escape persecution from the Sunnis. He himself was a disciple of Zaid, Ali's great-grandson. He settled the feud, and in return for his services he was accepted by both sides of the conflict as their religious leader or Imam. His followers received lands and were given a protected status, so that in time they became a sort of theocratic aristocracy. This was the beginning of the Zaidi Imamate, a theocratic state which lasted for a thousand years (until 1962) in Yemen.

Although the first Zaidi Imam had come to Yemen as a mediator, he had some personal qualities which enabled him to control the unruly mountain people and bend them to his will. He was a shrewd judge of Yemeni character, using his knowledge and his prestige as a member of the family of Ali to give personal favors and his power of *baraka* (special powers from God) to one group, or withholding these gifts from another. He also had great physical strength and was reputed to possess magical powers (presumably part of his baraka). It was said of him that he could grind corn with his fingers and pull a camel apart barehanded. He wrote forty-nine books on Islamic jurisprudence and theology, some of which are still being studied by modern Yemeni scholars. He could also bring good (or bad) fortune to a subject merely by a touch or a glance from his piercing black eyes.[1]

The Imams ruled only in the highlands, and they were constantly involved in intergroup conflicts or in wars with Sunni Muslim rulers. In the nineteenth century the Ottoman Turks occupied all of Yemen, placing an Ottoman governor in charge. But this action did not sit well with the mountain peoples. A Yemeni official told a British visitor: "We have fought the Turks, the tribes . . . and we are always fighting each other. We Yemenis submit to no one permanently. We love freedom and we will fight for it."[2]

The Turkish occupation sparked a revolt. Turkish forces were unable to defeat the mountain peoples, and in 1911 they signed a treaty which recognized the Imam Yahya as ruler in the highlands. In return, the Imam recognized Turkish rule in the Tihama. At the end of World War I the Turks left Yemen for good. The British, who now controlled most of the Middle East, signed a treaty with Imam Yahya, recognizing his rule in all of present-day Yemen. (The northern boundary was fixed by treaty with Saudi Arabia in 1934; the eastern boundary with Saudi Arabia and South Yemen has never been defined.)

Imam Yahya ruled Yemen for nearly forty years as an absolute monarch. He took personal charge of the "government," which consisted of little more than a handful of chosen group leaders, religious scholars, his sons and relatives, and himself. John Peterson notes that the Imamate "was completely dependent on the abilities of a single individual who was expected to be a competent combination of religious scholar, administrator, negotiator, and military commander."[3] Yahya was all of these, and his forceful personality and ruthless methods of dealing with potential opposition (with just a touch of magic) ensured his control over the population.

Yahya's method of government was simplicity itself. He held a daily public meeting (*jama'a*) seated under an umbrella outside his palace, receiving petitions from anyone who wished to present them, and signing approval or disapproval in Himyarite red ink. He personally supervised tax collections and kept the national treasury in a box under his bed. The Yemeni unit of currency was the Maria Theresa thaler (or riyal), minted in Trieste, then part of Austria, in large, heavy silver coins. The Imam distrusted the Ottomans, against whom he had fought for Yemeni independence, and refused to accept their coinage. He also rejected British pounds sterling because they represented a potential foreign influence. But the Maria Theresa coins apparently felt good to him; it is doubtful that he knew or cared that the thalers bore a woman's likeness.

Yahya was determined to keep foreign influences out of Yemen and to resist change in any form. Although Yemen was poor by the industrial world's standards, it was self-sufficient, free, and fully recognized as an independent state. Yahya hoped to keep it that way. He even refused foreign aid because he felt it would lead to foreign occupation. But he was unable to stop the clock entirely or to keep all foreign ideas or influences out of Yemen.

Certain actions which seemed to be to his advantage worked against him. One was the organization of a standing army. But in order to equip and train an army that would be stronger than tribal armies Yahya had to purchase arms from abroad, and to hire foreign advisers to train his troops. Promising young officers were also sent for training in Egypt, and on their return they formed the nucleus of opposition to the Imam.

In 1948 Imam Yahya was murdered in an attempted coup. He had alienated not only army officers who resented his repressive rule, but also leaders from outside the ruling family who were angered by the privileges given to the Imam's sons and relatives. But the coup was disorganized, the conspirators unsure of their goals. Crown Prince Ahmad, the Imam's eldest son and heir, was as tough and resourceful as his eighty-year-old father had been.[4] He gathered support from leaders of other clans and nipped the rebellion in the bud.

Imam Ahmad (1948-1962) ruled as despotically as his father had ruled. But the walls of Yemeni isolation inevitably began to crack. Foreign experts came to design and help build the roads, factories, hospitals, and schools the Imam felt were needed. Unlike Yahya, Ahmad was willing to modernize a little. Several hundred young Yemenis were sent abroad for study. Those who had left the country during Imam Yahya's reign returned. Many Yemenis emigrated to Aden to work for the British and formed the nucleus of a "Free Yemen" movement.

In 1955 the Imam foiled an attempted coup. Other attempts, in 1958 and 1961, were also unsuccessful. The old Imam finally died in 1962 in his bed, of emphysema, leaving his son, Crown Prince Muhammad al-Badr, to succeed him.

THE 1962 REVOLUTION

Muhammad al-Badr held office for a week. Then he was overthrown by a military coup. Yemen's new miltary leaders formed a Revolution Command Council and announced that the Imam was dead. Henceforth, they said, Yemen would be a republic. It would give up its self-imposed isolation and would become part of the Arab world. But the revolution proved to be more difficult to carry out than the military officers had expected. The Imam was not dead, as it turned out, but had escaped to the mountains. The mountain peoples rallied to his support, helping him to launch a counterrevolution. About 85,000 Egyptian troops arrived in Yemen to help the republican army. The coup leaders had been trained in Egypt, and the Egyptian government had not only financed the Revolution but also had encouraged it against the "reactionary" Imam.

For the next eight years Yemen was a battleground for civil war. The Egyptians bombed villages and even used poison gas against civilians in trying to defeat the Imam's forces. But they were unable to crush the people hidden in the wild mountains of the interior. Saudi Arabia also backed the Imam with arms and kept the border open.

The Saudi rulers did not particularly like the Imam, but he seemed preferable to an Egyptian-backed republican regime next door.

After Egypt's defeat by Israel in the 1967 Six-Day War, the Egyptian position in Yemen became untenable, and Egyptian troops were withdrawn. It appeared that the royalists would have a clear field. But they were even more disunited than the republicans. A royalist force surrounded San'a in 1968 but failed to capture the city. The Saudis then decided that the Imam had no future. They worked out a reconciliation of royalists and republicans which would reunite the country. The only restriction was that neither the Imam nor any of his relatives would be allowed to return to Yemen.

THE REPUBLIC

The Yemen Arab Republic has had great difficulty in organizing a stable and effective government. Since 1970 it has had four presidents. The first went into exile, and the second and thrid, military officers who seized power, were both murdered. The country's first elected president, Colonel Ali Abdullah Saleh, has remained in office longer than any of his predecessors. He was elected in 1978, and 1983 was reelected for a second five-year term.

The problem faced by any Yemeni leader is one of balancing factions while remaining in overall control of the country. In other Gulf states, oil wealth has been used successfully to develop a broad-based program of social and economic development, which in turn reduces factional conflict. Unity in Yemen is hampered by lack of oil wealth, by friction between lowland Sunnis and highland Shias, and by the mountain people's instinctive distrust of governments.

The Yemen Arab Republic is vulnerable to outside intervention because of its strategic location at the junction of the Red Sea and the Indian Ocean. During the first few years of its existence as a republic the country was aligned with the Soviet Union and China, receiving aid and training advisers for its armed forces. In the 1980s the republic has become more neutral in the East-West struggle, accepting aid from both the United States and the Soviet bloc while committing itself to neither. This nonaligned policy is not only realistic, but also may be an expanded version of the balancing act traditionally practiced by leaders of Yemeni social groups. It might also be a factor allowing eventual union of the two Yemens.

The greatest potential threat to the republic's survival comes from its neighbor

Collapse of Marib Dam, destroying flourishing Himyarite civilization AD 500	Establishment of Zaidi Imamate in highland Yemen 890	Yemen occupied by the Ottoman Turks, eventually becomes an Ottoman province 1517, 1872	Yemen recognized as an independent nation under Imam Yahya 1934	Revolution overthrows Imam al-Badr; military group proclaims a republic 1962	Civil War between supporters of Badr and Egyptian-backed republicans 1962-1969	Intermittent conflict with People's Democratic Republic of Yemen ends with unification agreement

1980s

2,000 guerrillas of Palestine Liberation Organization evacuated from Beirut, Lebanon to YAR	Major oil discovery at al-Jauf, Marib region	Agreement with People's Democratic Republic of Yemen on economic-development projects

to the south. The People's Democratic Republic of Yemen has been at odds with the Yemen Arab Republic for many years, each accusing the other of sabotage, complicity in assassinations of leaders, and subversion. In 1978-1979 the PDRY backed a rebel movement in YAR territory, an action that led to open war. The Arab League arranged a truce, and in 1980, surprisingly, leaders of the two Yemens agreed to unite into a single state. However, progress toward that elusive goal has been slow. A draft constitution was drawn up for ratification in 1982 but has yet to be submitted to referendums in the two states. A joint Yemen Council set up to supervise the unity process in 1981 has met twice, but thus far agreement has been limited to cooperation at the ministerial level. Ideological differences between the YAR and its neighbor continue as obstacles to unity; Prime Minister al-Iryani claimed in 1982 that the Aden regime was supporting an anti-republican movement, the Popular Unity Party of Yemen, with funds and weapons. It is problematical whether the deep-seated suspicion in the North of Marxist-Leninist "subversion" emanating from the progressive South can be overcome easily by the unification of the two Yemeni states.[5]

THE ECONOMY

The Yemen Arab Republic is one of the poorer countries in the Middle East in terms of income and resources available for development. High Yemen was traditionally able to support a comparatively large population (for Arabia), due to dependable

and plentiful rainfall, fertile soil, and the ingenuity of its farmers in making use of all arable land. But with the growth of the oil industry in other parts of the peninsula, the Yemeni economy went out of balance as the oil-less republic struggled to catch up with its neighbors.

Self-sufficiency was replaced by a cash economy as half a million Yemenis emigrated to Saudi Arabia and the Gulf states as temporary labor. The remittances of this expatriate labor force are a vital source of revenue, especially in view of Yemen's chronic trade deficit. But the influx of large amounts of cash, although reduced after 1981 due to cutbacks in Arab oil production, has resulted in inflation, huge increases in imports of consumer goods, and depreciation of the currency.

Agriculture has suffered more than Yemen's fledgling industry with the change in economic patterns. In addition to the reduced available labor force, lack of irrigation and a shortage of credit facilities adversely affect agricultural development. Coffee was formerly the main export crop, but with the shift to a consumer economy, farmers converted much coffee-growing land to production of qat, a mild narcotic, the use of which is addictive in Yemeni society and therefore yields larger profits than coffee. One promising development is the rebuilding, with foreign aid, of the Marib Dam to restore the lands of the Sabeans to their former productivity.

Yemen's major weakness in terms of economic development is its lack of mineral resources. However, the US Hunt Oil Com-

pany made a major oil strike in its concession in the Marib area in October 1984. Indications are that within a few years the YAR will join the ranks of Arab oil-exporting countries, and the common Middle Eastern joke about Yemen, that "it is moving rapidly into the fourteenth century," will no longer be valid.

FOOTNOTES

1. Robin Bidwell, *The Two Yemens* (Boulder, CO: Westview Press, 1983), p. 10.
2. Quoted in Robert Stookey, *Yemen: The Politics of the Yemen Arab Republic* (Boulder, CO: Westview Press, 1978), p. 168.
3. John Peterson, "Nation-building and Political Development in the Two Yemens," in B.R. Pridham, ed., *Contemporary Yemen: Politics and Historical Background* (New York: St. Martin's Press, 1985), p. 86.
4. Yemenis believed that he slept with a rope around his neck to terrify visitors, that he could turn twigs into snakes, and that he once outwrestled the devil. Bidwill, *op. cit.*, p. 121.
5. "You and I are true Arabs from the Yemen, the cradle of all Arabs. Is there any difference between a San'ani, a Rada'i, and Adeni or Hadrami with regard to affiliation with the homeland? All of them are from Yemen, by which I mean 'Natural Yemen' with its fixed and known boundaries. . . ." A leader of the Free Yemeni Movement, quoted in Sultan Nagi, "The Genesis of the Call for Yemeni Unity," in Pridham, *op. cit.*, p. 247.

DEVELOPMENT
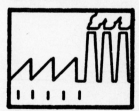
With oil reserves of 200 million barrels and anticipated production of 300,000 b/d when the new refinery is completed late in 1985, the republic is poised for economic takeoff. A Supreme Council was set up in 1985 to supervise minerals development.

FREEDOM

Progress toward a democratic form of government began in 1978 with the formation of a Constituent Assembly. President Ali Abdallah Salih enlarged its membership in 1979 and formed a People's Congress in 1982 to supervise forthcoming presidential elections. In 1983 he resigned, but the Assembly reelected him unanimously for a second 5-year term.

HEALTH/WELFARE

In 1980-1981, 412,573 students at all levels were enrolled in school, 32,000 in secondary schools alone. A new agriculture facility accommodating 600 students opens in early 1986 at the University of San'a, with a Chinese-built medical facility to follow. A recent agreement with Sudan will provide the YAR with 5,000 Sudanese teachers per year.

ACHIEVEMENTS

By 1984 the YAR was self-sufficient in cement production, with plants in operation. A major rural water and power supply project opened, serving the San'a hinterland; since 1979 the government has dug 1,500 wells and provided potable water to 1.5 million villagers through 1,000 water projects.

Articles from the World Press

Annotated Table of Contents for Articles

Middle Eastern Region

1. **Mideast Turning Point,** *World Press Review,* October 1985. This World Press Dialogue reviews the current state of Middle Eastern politics by posing questions designed to highlight the pressure points in the region.   p. 136

2. **The Teflon Palestinian,** *The Economist,* December 21, 1985. The role of the Palestine Liberation Organization (PLO) in Middle Eastern politics has undergone many changes recently, and its leader, Yasser Arafat, seems to have the ability to make setbacks look like successes.   p. 139

3. **Bedouins, Poets and Pirates of the Dunes,** Bruton Bernstein, *Science Digest,* January 1983. The Bedouins are as integral a part of the Sinai as the strategic passes, the flinty plains, and the mauve mountains. They are the living remnants of history, a timeless, proud, and earthy people.   p. 141

4. **Arab Linguists Toil to Keep Language from Being Written Off,** David Lamb, *New Haven Register,* September 1, 1985. To the Arab, the Arabic language is more than a means of communication. It is an object of worship, an almost metaphysical force that draws man closer to God.   p. 142

5. **Cradle of Civilization May Also Be Birthplace of Haute Cuisine,** Erik Eckholm, *Gainesville Sun,* October 12, 1985. A cuisine offering 100 styles of soup, 18 kinds of cheese, 300 types of bread, and the use of innumerable spices, fruits, and vegetables was enjoyed at least 4,000 years ago in the Middle East.   p. 144

6. **Expats' Future in the Gulf,** Zafar Samadani, *Pakistan & Gulf Economist,* June 29 - July 5, 1985. The Gulf states cannot yet do away with the foreign worker, who is needed because of the limited populations of many countries.   p. 145

7. **The Gulf Countries Making Headway,** Zafar Samadani, *Pakistan & Gulf Economist,* August 10-16, 1985. Recently there has been an explosion both in the sports activity of the Arabs and their interest in what is happening on the international scene.   p. 146

Algeria

8. **Crop Production Under Wraps,** David Bradshaw, Special Report—Algeria, *South,* December 1985. The Algerian government is making a bid to boost agricultural production to reduce dependence on imported food by the extensive use of greenhouses.   p. 147

9. **Finding Strength in National Culture,** Kamel Belkacem, Special Report—Algeria, *South,* December 1985. French colonial occupation of Algeria lasted over 130 years, and today the Arab population is striving to regain its cultural identity.   p. 148

Bahrain

10. **Diversification of Economy,** IMF Survey, *Pakistan & Gulf Economist,* August 17-23, 1985. The government of Bahrain has carried out a successful campaign to diversify the economy's base and to reduce the country's dependence on oil through developing its banking, trade, and manufacturing sectors.   p. 149

Egypt

11. **Mubarak Walks a Shaky Tightrope,** Stanley Reed, *The Nation,* December 28, 1985/January 4, 1986. Egyptian President Hosni Mubarak is finding his relations with the United States and Israel strained over his support of recent terrorist hijackings.   p. 151

12. **Egypt's National Film Archive,** Khaled Osman, *The Unesco Courier,* August 1984. Unlike most developing countries, Egypt has a very old film heritage. Films were shown in Cairo and Alexandria as long ago as 1896, and soon afterward films were made in Egypt.   p. 155

13. **Letter from Alexandria,** Geoffrey Bower, *Middle East International,* August 9, 1985. This letter offers a current view of the city of Alexandria.   p. 156

Iran

14. **War and Hardship in a Stern Land,** *Time,* August 26, 1985. The administration of Ayatollah Khomeini has brought with it a level of fanaticism that offers little hope for social change.   p. 157

15. **In Iran, the Stamp of Islam Is Everywhere,** *The Christian Science Monitor,* August 6, 1985. Islam has pervaded all aspects of Iranians' lives; people wear Islamic dress, watch Islamic TV, get an Islamic education, and are policed by Islamic Revolutionary Guards (paramilitary religious police).   p. 158

Iraq

16. **Iraqis Insulated from Economic, but Not Human, Costs in Gulf War,** Mary Curtius, *The Christian Science Monitor,* November 21, 1985. The ruling Ba'thist regime in Iraq has effectively insulated a large part of the population from the economic cost of the Iran-Iraq War by using Iraq's currency reserves, but there is no insulation from the staggering number of casualties.   p. 161

17. **Iraq Grapples with Sandy Solar Collectors,** Richard Wilson, *The Christian Science Monitor,* March 21, 1983. Iraq, like many developing countries, has been fascinated by solar energy. Harnessing this energy source is complicated by the need to keep the ever-present drifting sand off of the collectors.   p. 162

Israel

18. **Israel at a Crossroads,** Xan Smiley, *World Press Review,* September 1985. Israel faces many significant problems: the economy has become very unstable, the government is polarized, and unrest on the West Bank continues to intensify.   p. 163

19. **Israel Is Threatened by an Enemy Within: Its Economy,** Lawrence Meyer, *The Washington Post National Weekly Edition,* January 6, 1986. Israel will remain in serious economic trouble until it figures out how to climb out of its stagnation, create productive jobs, export more than it imports, and pay its bills without huge handouts from abroad.   p. 166

20. **Student Life in Jerusalem,** Hannah Brown, *Congress Monthly,* April 1985. Student life in Israel is examined by an American living and studying in Jerusalem.   p. 168

Jordan

21. **West Bank: Core of Middle East Conflict,** Ned Temko, *The Christian Science Monitor,* October 21, 1985. In the 1967 Arab-Israeli War, the West Bank, the area to the west of the Jordan River, was taken over by Israel. Most Israelis viewed the West Bank as land they would sooner or later swap with Jordan's King Hussein for a peace treaty, but the area has continued to heat up as relations have stalled. — p. 170

22. **Letter from Amman,** Paul Harper, *Middle East International,* December 20, 1985. This letter presents a contemporary view of Amman, Jordan. — p. 173

Kuwait

23. **Kuwait Living on Its Nerves,** K. Celine, *Merip Reports,* February 1985. Kuwaiti shipping has been directly affected by the Iran-Iraq War, and this, coupled with the falling prices for oil, has caused Kuwait's economy to suffer. — p. 174

Libya

24. **Revolution in Recession,** Jon Bearman, *South,* October 1985. Libya's development policy has differed from that of the Gulf oil states. While the Gulf states have used oil revenues in ways that preserve their social structures, Libyan society has been transformed. — p. 176

25. **A Rare Glimpse of Colonel Qaddafi,** Judith Miller, *The New York Times,* January 11, 1986. This article examines some aspects of the Libyan leader's personal life. — p. 178

Lebanon

26. **Life in Lebanon: In the Camps,** *Middle East International,* December 6, 1985. After Israel invaded Lebanon, detention camps were set up for the resident Palestinians. This article notes what life is like in these camps. — p. 180

27. **Who Won Lebanon?** *The Economist,* May 25, 1985. In 1982 Israel invaded Lebanon to rid itself of the danger posed by the presence of the Palestine Liberation Organization; today the Israeli "victory" has actually made for a more dangerous Lebanon. — p. 181

Morocco

28. **Libya and Morocco—Marriage of Necessity,** George Henderson, *Middle East International,* October 11, 1985. The political relationship between Morocco and Libya has survived due to the countries' ability to maintain their own political systems while uniting to combat external threats. — p. 183

Oman

29. **Oman Gives Super Party: It's Come a Long Way,** John Kifner, *The New York Times,* November 19, 1985. Today Oman is a nation starting from scratch to enter the modern world; it is a country creating itself. — p. 185

Saudi Arabia

30. **Cheers for the Saudi Camel Race,** George Joseph Tanber, *The Christian Science Monitor,* March 21, 1983. Each year King Fahd of Saudi Arabia sponsors a camel race that is symbolic of the country's Bedouin heritage. — p. 186

31. **After OPEC,** S. Fred Singer, *The New Republic,* October 21, 1985. The Iran-Iraq War and the worldwide oil glut has forced Saudi Arabia to reevaluate its role in OPEC and face the prospect of lean years ahead. — p. 187

Sudan

32. **Sudan's Hidden Tragedy,** Robert Watkins, *Africa Report,* November-December 1985. The recent drought and famine in Sudan might have been more effectively dealt with if the mammoth logistical problems of delivery had been anticipated and prepared for. — p. 190

Syria

33. **Syria: Key Arab Factor in Mideast Equation,** Mary Curtius, *The Christian Science Monitor,* December 30, 1985. Syria is an important element in Middle Eastern politics, and is consulted when any Middle Eastern event portends peace or unrest. — p. 193

Turkey

34. **In Turkey, a Gain for Rights,** Jeri Laber and Alice H. Henkin, *The New York Times,* December 24, 1985. The human rights climate in Turkey is getting better, but it is a slow process and international pressure should continue. — p. 194

35. **The Magician Who Lost His Touch,** Ergin Yildizoglu, *South,* May 1985. The structural weaknesses of Turkey's industrial sector are threatening the recovery plan launched in 1980 by Prime Minister Turgut Ozal. — p. 196

United Arab Emirates

36. **Rapid Progress in Education,** Fatima Jamal, *Pakistan & Gulf Economist,* July 13-19, 1985. Today the government of the UAE provides free schooling for all ages of students. — p. 198

People's Democratic Republic of Yemen (South Yemen)

37. **Like Clockwork,** *The Economist,* January 18, 1986. The recent attempted coup against President Ali Nasser Mohammed was anticipated because of his divergence from both the Soviet Union and hardline Marxists at home. — p. 200

Yemen Arab Republic (North Yemen)

38. **North Yemen Has Many Reasons for Playing Down Oil Potential,** Ian Steele, *The Christian Science Monitor,* November 12, 1985. As the newest oil producer on the Arabian Peninsula, North Yemen is conspicuous only for a determination to play down its potential. — p. 200

Topic Guide to Articles

TOPIC AREA	TREATED AS AN ISSUE IN:	TOPIC AREA	TREATED AS AN ISSUE IN:
Agriculture	5. Cradle of Civilization May Also Be Birthplace of Haute Cuisine 8. Crop Production Under Wraps 32. Sudan's Hidden Tragedy	**Education**	4. Arab Linguists Toil to Keep Language from Being Written Off 15. In Iran, the Stamp of Islam Is Everywhere 20. Student Life in Jerusalem 36. Rapid Progress in Education
Arts	12. Egypt's National Film Archive	**Emigration**	6. Expats' Future in the Gulf
Commodities	8. Crop Production Under Wraps 23. Kuwait Living on Its Nerves 24. Revolution in Recession 31. After OPEC	**Equal Rights**	14. War and Hardship in a Stern Land 16. Iraqis Insulated from Economic, but Not Human, Costs in Gulf War 34. In Turkey, a Gain for Rights 36. Rapid Progress in Education
Culture	3. Bedouins, Poets and Pirates of the Dunes 4. Arab Linguists Toil to Keep Language from Being Written Off 5. Cradle of Civilization May Also Be Birthplace of Haute Cuisine 9. Finding Strength in National Culture 12. Egypt's National Film Archive 15. In Iran, the Stamp of Islam Is Everywhere 30. Cheers for the Saudi Camel Race	**Family**	3. Bedouins, Poets and Pirates of the Dunes
		Farming	5. Cradle of Civilization May Also Be Birthplace of Haute Cuisine 8. Crop Production Under Wraps
		Food	5. Cradle of Civilization May Also Be Birthplace of Haute Cuisine 8. Crop Production Under Wraps
Current Leaders	1. Mideast Turning Point 2. The Teflon Palestinian 11. Mubarak Walks a Shaky Tightrope 14. War and Hardship in a Stern Land 18. Israel at a Crossroads 24. Revolution in Recession 25. A Rare Glimpse of Colonel Qaddafi 33. Syria: Key Arab Factor in Mideast Equation 35. The Magician Who Lost His Touch 37. Like Clockwork	**Foreign Investment**	19. Israel Is Threatened by an Enemy Within: Its Economy 31. After OPEC 32. Sudan's Hidden Tragedy 35. The Magician Who Lost His Touch
Debt	19. Israel Is Threatened by an Enemy Within: Its Economy 31. After OPEC	**Foreign Relations**	1. Mideast Turning Point 11. Mubarak Walks a Shaky Tightrope 19. Israel Is Threatened by an Enemy Within: Its Economy 21. West Bank: Core of Middle East Conflict 25. A Rare Glimpse of Colonel Qaddafi 28. Libya and Morocco—Marriage of Necessity 37. Like Clockwork
Development	6. Expats' Future in the Gulf 8. Crop Production Under Wraps 9. Finding Strength in National Culture 10. Diversification of Economy 24. Revolution in Recession 29. Oman Gives Super Party: It's Come a Long Way 32. Sudan's Hidden Tragedy 35. The Magician Who Lost His Touch 38. North Yemen Has Many Reasons for Playing Down Oil Potential	**Geography**	3. Bedouins, Poets and Pirates of the Dunes 8. Crop Production Under Wraps 17. Iraq Grapples with Sandy Solar Collectors 32. Sudan's Hidden Tragedy
		Health and Welfare	8. Crop Production Under Wraps 16. Iraqis Insulated from Economic, but Not Human, Costs in Gulf War 26. Life in Lebanon: In the Camps 32. Sudan's Hidden Tragedy
Economy	6. Expats' Future in the Gulf 8. Crop Production Under Wraps 10. Diversification of Economy 19. Israel Is Threatened by an Enemy Within: Its Economy 23. Kuwait Living on Its Nerves 24. Revolution in Recession 29. Oman Gives Super Party: It's Come a Long Way 31. After OPEC 32. Sudan's Hidden Tragedy 35. The Magician Who Lost His Touch 38. North Yemen Has Many Reasons for Playing Down Oil Potential	**History**	3. Bedouins, Poets and Pirates of the Dunes 4. Arab Linguists Toil to Keep Language from Being Written Off 5. Cradle of Civilization May Also Be Birthplace of Haute Cuisine 9. Finding Strength in National Culture 12. Egypt's National Film Archive 29. Oman Gives Super Party: It's Come a Long Way 30. Cheers for the Saudi Camel Race
		Human Rights	9. Finding Strength in National Culture 14. War and Hardship in a Stern Land 15. In Iran, the Stamp of Islam Is Everywhere 26. Life in Lebanon: In the Camps 34. In Turkey, a Gain for Rights

TOPIC AREA	TREATED AS AN ISSUE IN:	TOPIC AREA	TREATED AS AN ISSUE IN:
Import/Export	6. Expats' Future in the Gulf 10. Diversification of Economy 19. Israel Is Threatened by an Enemy Within: Its Economy 31. After OPEC 35. The Magician Who Lost His Touch	**Politics (cont.)**	33. Syria: Key Arab Factor in Mideast Equation 35. The Magician Who Lost His Touch 37. Like Clockwork
		Poverty	32. Sudan's Hidden Tragedy
Industrial Development	6. Expats' Future in the Gulf 10. Diversification of Economy 35. The Magician Who Lost His Touch	**Religion**	3. Bedouins, Poets and Pirates of the Dunes 4. Arab Linguists Toil to Keep Language from Being Written Off 14. War and Hardship in a Stern Land 15. In Iran, the Stamp of Islam Is Everywhere
Labor	6. Expats' Future in the Gulf		
Language	4. Arab Linguists Toil to Keep Language from Being Written Off 9. Finding Strength in National Culture	**Roots**	3. Bedouins, Poets and Pirates of the Dunes 4. Arab Linguists Toil to Keep Language from Being Written Off 5. Cradle of Civilization May Also Be Birthplace of Haute Cuisine 9. Finding Strength in National Culture 12. Egypt's National Film Archive 29. Oman Gives Super Party: It's Come a Long Way 30. Cheers for the Saudi Camel Race
Leadership	1. Mideast Turning Point 2. The Teflon Palestinian 11. Mubarak Walks a Shaky Tightrope 14. War and Hardship in a Stern Land 25. A Rare Glimpse of Colonel Qaddafi 35. The Magician Who Lost His Touch		
Middle Eastern Relations	1. Mideast Turning Point 2. The Teflon Palestinian 11. Mubarak Walks a Shaky Tightrope 18. Israel at a Crossroads 28. Libya and Morocco—Marriage of Necessity 33. Syria: Key Arab Factor in Mideast Equation	**Sex Roles**	15. In Iran, the Stamp of Islam Is Everywhere
		Social Reform	14. War and Hardship in a Stern Land 15. In Iran, the Stamp of Islam Is Everywhere 34. In Turkey, a Gain for Rights 36. Rapid Progress in Education
Migration	3. Bedouins, Poets and Pirates of the Dunes 6. Expats' Future in the Gulf	**Sports**	7. Sports: The Gulf Countries Making Headway 30. Cheers for the Saudi Camel Race
Nationalism	1. Mideast Turning Point 3. Bedouins, Poets and Pirates of the Dunes 4. Arab Linguists Toil to Keep Language from Being Written Off 6. Expats' Future in the Gulf 9. Finding Strength in National Culture 15. In Iran, the Stamp of Islam Is Everywhere 26. Life in Lebanon: In the Camps 28. Libya and Morocco—Marriage of Necessity 30. Cheers for the Saudi Camel Race	**Standard of Living**	10. Diversification of Economy 18. Israel at a Crossroads 19. Israel Is Threatened by an Enemy Within: Its Economy 23. Kuwait Living on Its Nerves 24. Revolution in Recession 31. After OPEC 35. The Magician Who Lost His Touch 36. Rapid Progress in Education 38. North Yemen Has Many Reasons for Playing Down Oil Potential
Natural Resources	8. Crop Production Under Wraps 17. Iraq Grapples with Sandy Solar Collectors 31. After OPEC 38. North Yemen Has Many Reasons for Playing Down Oil Potential	**Trade**	10. Diversification of Economy 24. Revolution in Recession 31. After OPEC
		Urban Life	13. Letter from Alexandria 22. Letter from Amman
OPEC (Organization of Petroleum Exporting Countries)	24. Revolution in Recession 31. After OPEC	**War**	14. War and Hardship in a Stern Land 16. Iraqis Insulated from Economic, but Not Human, Costs in Gulf War 23. Kuwait Living on Its Nerves 27. Who Won Lebanon?
PLO (Palestine Liberation Organization)	2. The Teflon Palestinian 27. Who Won Lebanon?		
Politics	1. Mideast Turning Point 2. The Teflon Palestinian 11. Mubarak Walks a Shaky Tightrope 18. Israel at a Crossroads 21. West Bank: Core of Middle East Conflict 27. Who Won Lebanon?	**Women's Rights**	15. In Iran, the Stamp of Islam Is Everywhere

Article 1

World Press Review, October 1985

Mideast Turning Point

The race to avert a new spiral of violence

ROGER HARDY

IS THE MIDEAST AT ANOTHER TURNING POINT?

Most informed people in the Arab world believe that the peace initiative early this year — when King Hussein of Jordan and PLO chairman Yassir Arafat reached an agreement to work in tandem — especially vis-à-vis Washington — was an important step. We are at a turning point in one basic sense: Either that peace process makes some headway — and that will depend largely on U.S. policy — or it may fail. The prevailing view is that its chances are not good, and that failure might tip the Middle East into a further spiral of violence that would affect the world.

WHAT IS THE NEXT STEP?

There are problems about procedure: Who should be talking to whom about what? We probably have surmounted the hurdle of which Palestinians should be involved. It is possible to circumvent the problem of not talking directly to the PLO. The American priority is to push for talks between the Arabs and the Israelis.

Many people believe that Anwar Sadat was assassinated because he talked with the Israelis and signed the Camp David Accords. That may be simplistic, but it causes concern among Arab leaders. When they talk about multilateral as opposed to bilateral

This World Press Dialogue was conducted by "World Press Review" editorial director Alfred Balk with Roger Hardy, editor of the Arab-oriented monthly "The Middle East" of London.

peace, they are putting their finger on what seems to be the main issue. They do not want to talk on a one-to-one basis with Israel. They want a broad international conference with both superpowers and all the main parties, including the Israelis and the PLO.

The Americans find problems with that. They do not want the Russians in, and they do not want to bring the PLO in directly. We have an impasse.

IS JORDAN'S KING HUSSEIN STRONG ENOUGH TO PLAY A LEADING ROLE?

He certainly has taken a gamble for peace. He also is aware that he must not behave as President Sadat did. He is cautious; Sadat was flamboyant. Though King Hussein's position is secure, it needs to be bolstered by a response from Israel and from the U.S.

The U.S. is the only power that can put pressure on Israel. The Arabs want to see Washington lean on the Israelis to come to negotiations — if possible, on a multilateral basis. The Israelis would not willingly do that, but some compromise could be found.

The Jordanians are saying, "We must have the outward appearance of an international conference, even if it lasts only for a day or less. It would tell the world that here is a broad front for peace. Then the conference could adjourn, and a subgroup would go off and talk peace." It is not beyond the wit of man to devise such a framework.

WOULD THE U.S. AGREE TO SOVIET PARTICIPATION?

The official view has been consistently

no. Secretary of State George Shultz and other key policymakers say that these international conferences are just occasions for rhetoric. They prefer the Henry Kissinger-type step-by-step approach rather than a grand, multilateral event that could be a public failure.

WOULD THE ARABS ACCEPT EXCLUSION OF THE SOVIETS?

The more moderate Arab parties, especially the Jordanians, probably would if they were more certain of success than now. The more radical parties — including some Palestinians and certainly the Syrians, who are the major blocking force in the area — would protest vigorously. That limits King Hussein's freedom of maneuver. He is always looking over his shoulder at Arab opposition.

WHAT ARE THE PRESENT ARAB FACTIONS?

The moderates include Saudi Arabia, Egypt, Jordan, and a new recruit — Iraq. The Iraqis now favor peace, probably because of their war with the Ayatollah. There also is the moderate wing of the PLO under Arafat.

On the radical side, against the peace that is being discussed now, are Syria and Libya. There also is the rather small radical wing of the PLO that broke away from Arafat and is under Syrian control. The key radical party is Syria because it borders Israel, because the Soviet Union has supplied it with sophisticated weaponry — modern missile systems — and because of what has been going on in Lebanon.

The Syrians have a strong interest in keeping the situation unsettled because they seem to be gaining ground — in Lebanon, in arms, and in influence. While not dead set against peace, they want it on the terms they see as being in their interests. And because they probably are the Arab state closest to Moscow, they are ready to dovetail their interests with the Soviets'. Both countries believe that an international conference would strengthen their hand vis-à-vis the U.S., Israel, and the Arab moderates.

The Syrians also have leverage through their alliance with the Iranians. A lot of this has to do with the age-old antagonism between Syria and Iraq as rival Ba'athist states. The fact that Syria and Libya have strong relations with Teheran — which almost certainly include channeling Soviet weapons to the Iranians — also gives them a powerful leverage.

The Syrians are ready to play tough. One can only hope that these are tactics rather than a strategy. King Hussein of Jordan is afraid of the Syrians. He is a brave man in having taken a gamble on peace, but he knows he cannot ignore Syria's power.

WHAT DOES SYRIA WANT?

It wants a slice of the territories occupied by Israel, particularly the Golan Heights. The Israelis say this is a strategic area because from those mountains a hostile force can bomb Israeli settlements. But it is strategic to the Syrians also. They see it as their southern gateway, and claim that under international law it is territory occupied by Israel since 1967.

No Syrian leader could contemplate a peace arrangement with Israel that fell short of the return of the Golan. It is a very difficult demand for the Israelis to meet. One can only hope for a compromise — perhaps a demilitarized Golan Heights that temporarily would belong to nobody.

The Syrians say that if the Hussein-Arafat initiative were to succeed, and if Israel were to withdraw from at least part of the West Bank and a Palestinian entity emerged in confederation with Jordan, "Where would this leave Israel and the U.S., and where would it leave us?" They argue that it would leave Israel strong, it would leave the Arab side weak, and it would strengthen American influence in the region.

Syria is afraid of negotiating as a weak partner with a strong Israel, and in the present balance Israel is very

strong. It has had to withdraw from Lebanon, but it could go back at any time if it felt threatened.

WHAT DO SYRIANS WANT IN LEBANON?

They want, and have largely achieved, a quiet Lebanon. They would like to withdraw as far as they can — because it is costing them a lot of money — and leave behind a Lebanon that poses no threat to Damascus. The Syrians promised to withdraw as soon as the Israelis withdrew, but that never happened. Somehow the world has forgotten about that promise, having been preoccupied with getting the Israelis out with a minimum of damage.

What now remains of the fighting in Beirut and elsewhere could be the last flickers of a fire that has raged in Lebanon for ten years. Lebanon internally has changed to the advantage of the Moslems and to the disadvantage of the Christians, who are a minority that has lost control. Many Christians in Lebanon realize that things can never be as they were.

MIGHT LEBANON BE PARTITIONED?

A formal partition is precisely what the rational parties want to avoid. The irrational forces say, "Our sect, however tiny, comes first, and to hell with the state." The best way to resist them will be to give a lot of autonomy to the communities, and to have a stronger central government authority. President Gemayel scarcely controls the area around his own palace, let alone the capital city.

Lebanon is fragile, and it would become even more fragile were it divided. The Syrian interest is in patching things up. Many other people have tried to be the policeman of Lebanon, and it has never worked. The Syrians are about the only power that could fill that role. You do not have to like the Syrians to see that they are indispensable.

HOW MUCH DOES LEBANON'S STABILITY DEPEND ON OTHER MIDEAST EVENTS?

The Middle East is like a web, with so many parts that pull at other parts that you can never stabilize the whole web. For example, there is the Iran-Iraq war, now five years old. The Iraqis have taken the initiative, and it is a high-risk strategy. They recently bombed Kharg Island, Iran's main oil-export terminal,

and their attacks on tankers in the Persian Gulf continue.

The Iraqis plan to add half a million barrels a day to their output — a 50-per-cent increase. They know there is an oil glut, so this is now an economic war. They are trying to knock some Iranian oil out of the market and replace it with oil of their own.

Still, the Iraqis are desperate for peace. When I visited Baghdad recently I asked the Minister of Information, "What are the terms under which Iraq would consider a ceasefire?" He spelled out four requirements: a comprehensive ceasefire with peace on all fronts; a pullback by both sides to the frontier; an exchange of prisoners-of-war; and — most interesting — a Commission of Inquiry, a longstanding Iranian demand, "to look into who started this war, what caused it."

Unfortunately, there is little likelihood that Iran will come to the negotiating table on that basis. Its people are war-weary, but that does not translate itself into political dissent, for which there is little outlet. Nor would Khomeini's death end the war. His successors, if they felt insecure because they lacked Khomeini's charisma, would stress continuity.

ARE IRAN'S MODERATES PRESSING FOR CHANGE?

There is a paradox in Iran. The decisionmakers — the skilled people in finance and oil, the mullahs, and most members of the Cabinet and the Parliament — now constitute a moderate majority. But that moderate majority is the prisoner of the fundamentalist minority, a small group of mullahs and ayatollahs, most of them close to Khomeini. They are the hardliners on continuing the war.

Now the question is: How long can the apparently acquiescent moderate majority go on acquiescing? They have a direct economic stake in peace. If the war continues at its present level, Iran's war-weariness can only increase. Casualties are high; prices have skyrocketed; the black market is booming; there are shortages of food, weapons, and spare parts for the war machine.

Most observers say that Iraq now has the edge. Both Washington and Moscow would rather see an Iranian than an Iraqi defeat, but not necessarily a victory by either side.

On the American side, an interesting diplomatic development is the resumption of diplomatic relations last year between Baghdad and Washington. The Iraqis are now interested in everything American, from computers to Kentucky fried chicken. After five years of war it matters to them to have Washington's moral support. They hope the U.S. will discourage arms sales to Iran — for example, a reported Chinese arms deal.

HAS RELIGIOUS FERVOR WANED IN IRAN?

Yes. After all, the revolution took place seven years ago and the fervor — some call it fanaticism — could not be sustained for long. The reality for the people who overthrew the Shah is, "How am I going to get meat at today's prices? Am I going to get a deal on the black market? How can I afford a refrigerator or a car, let alone a trip to Europe?" This does not translate into hostility against Khomeini; he is still the great father figure of Iran.

IS THE REGION'S FUNDAMEN-TALIST WAVE WANING?

The West never thought that fundamentalism would reassert itself in the 20th century, so we got it wrong from the beginning. Now the signals seem conflicting. There may be some setbacks for the Iranians and therefore for Khomeini, but there also is a strong assertion by the Shi'ites of Southern Lebanon, who were buoyed by what they saw as a victory against the Israelis. They think that they forced the Israelis out. This was a propaganda victory if nothing else, and it encouraged Shi'ites elsewhere.

We may see setbacks for some of the Sunni, the majority Islamic community, in some Mideast countries. In Egypt President Hosni Mubarak, in the five years that he has been in power, has been very clever in managing this Islamic opposition, but he now seems to be getting into trouble.

We would be wrong to write off Islamic fundamentalism. We have not seen the end of it. It seems to be an expression of protest and alienation over rapid change. It opposes not only the Coca-Cola or Cadillac culture of the West, but also the direct manifestations of Western influence — in the shape of American marines in Beirut or in what the Israelis are doing, because in this context the Israelis are considered a proxy of the West. Any non-Islamic force is regarded as suspect.

COULD THIS BECOME THE BASIS OF A REGIONAL POWER BLOC?

It could. A very modest achievement in the past couple of years has been the Gulf Cooperation Council (GCC). It links together Saudi Arabia and southern Gulf countries. They would like to become a kind of European Economic Community of the Gulf. They hope to remove trade barriers and make it easier for nationals to cross from one territory to another.

If the region can build on that kind of process, then we might see a regional bloc emerging. And if it were like the GCC, it would be a moderate and pro-Western bloc, but use the language of nonalignment.

> "King Hussein's position needs to be bolstered by Israel and the U.S."

WHAT REGIONAL PROJECTS HAS THE GCC LAUNCHED?

The member countries are keen to do things jointly. There is the Arabsat satellite, and a whole range of activity in the communications field. They are likely to move toward common television and radio programs and the opening up of borders — projects at the human level to bring all Arabs together.

A new dimension to the GCC goes far beyond day-to-day economic cooperation. The members realize that they are dependent on Western arms supplies. American, British, and French weaponry are expensive, and they usually have political strings attached — the AWACs aircraft, for example. So there is talk of funding a Gulf arms industry.

The early idea was to establish it in Egypt, to combine Gulf money with Egyptian knowhow and manpower. That coincided with the Camp David Accords, when Egypt was ostracized, so the scheme was abandoned. Now that Egypt is almost back into the Arab club, the plan may be revived. Or, because we live in an age of migrant labor, the base may be in Kuwait, Bahrain, or Saudi Arabia.

HOW GOES SAUDI ARABIA'S RACE TO DIVERSIFY ITS ECONOMY?

Although it has about one quarter of the known oil reserves in the world, the kingdom is trying to build up petrochemicals, electronics, agriculture, and other sectors. But it is experiencing problems of infrastructure and of management. It still is dependent on the U.S., Europe, or Japan for skilled labor and on Pakistan, Bangladesh, or Yemen for unskilled labor. The challenge for the Saudis is to accelerate what they call "Saudi-ization" — training their own people. That is a slow process.

Another problem the Saudis face is competition — especially in petrochemicals. Western producers do not want a market suddenly flooded by cheap products when Saudi industries start producing on a big scale. The Europeans recently imposed tariffs on the Saudis' products, and now Saudis threaten retaliation, saying, "Many Western goods come in either free of tariff or modestly tariffed."

This is a problem for the whole Third World. If the developing countries want to establish industries, they will come into competition with the industrialized world. And industries in the West generally have higher labor costs than in the Third World. This is a classic case where we must have a tradeoff, which ultimately would be in the interests of everybody.

IS LIBYA NOW STABLE UNDER COL. GADDAFI?

He is a remarkable survivor. He was a young military man when he came to power — most Arab leaders are beyond fifty — and he still has a certain charisma among the Libyans, most of whom are from the desert, like Gaddafi. But he has alienated important sectors of the urban middle class. It regards Gaddafi and his regime as unpredictable. It fears that he will suddenly nationalize many businesses. They are alarmed at his adventures in Chad and Morocco, and at his expulsion of Egyptian and Tunisian workers.

After so many years of this unpredictable leader, who has created so many problems within the country and enemies outside, the question is: How long can it go on? He has few friends, but he is fairly close to the Soviet Union — which would like to have a Mediterranean port. Libya also has a reasonable relationship with Syria because the two are fellow radicals. But Gaddafi is so volatile that his friends of today become the enemies of tomorrow, and he has become only a marginal force in the region's affairs.

HOW STRONG IS THE PLO AND WHERE IS ITS HEADQUARTERS?

It has become much less important than anybody had imagined. What happened in 1982 with the Israeli invasion of Lebanon, and subsequently the PLO's eviction from Beirut, and then Arafat's eviction from Tripoli, and the split between the pro-Arafat and the pro-Syrian Palestinians — all caused tremendous damage to the PLO as a movement. The leaders have learned some lessons, and they are regaining ground — enough for Arafat to have some credibility in going ahead with the risky peace initiative along with King Hussein.

It is certainly not popular with all Palestinians, many of whom remember the events of Black September, when the Jordanian forces of the king evicted many Palestinian fighters from Jordan. It is a marriage of convenience, and most Palestinians realize that and are ready to go along. The crunch will come at a point where an offer is on the table, and the Palestinians will be asked by their leadership: Do we go along

with King Hussein and end up with something less than a sovereign independent state?

The Palestinians are dispersed. Some are in Lebanon; some are in Tunisia; some are in Yemen. If the present initiative fails in a way that is clear to everybody, the Palestinian movement may go underground. People have talked in the past of its being a subversive force within the region. If peace fails, it might become one.

Nobody knows where peace can come from the next time around if this attempt fails, because the West Bank probably will have been eaten up by the new Israeli settlements. There will be nothing left on the West Bank front to talk about. And that would produce a dangerous situation in the region.

WHICH WAY IS ISRAEL MOVING?

There has been a polarization within Israeli society ever since the 1982 invasion of Lebanon. Israelis call it "a war of choice," a war they did not have to fight but that their government — the Begin-Sharon leadership at that time — chose to fight. That shocked a tremendous number of Israelis. More than 500 deaths from the Lebanon operation is a high number for a small state like Israel. Israel now has a peace camp, ill-defined but potentially large,

whose adherents come from many political quarters. They believe that the Lebanon war was a terrible mistake.

There also has been an intensification on the right, the emergence of Rabbi Meir Kahane. Most Israelis regard him as an unhealthy phenomenon who is overtly racist. He wants the Arabs evicted from the occupied territory, and wants Israelis and Arabs to have no contact. This is something relatively new, and the fact that he exists, let alone that he got elected to the Knesset, means Israel has a lot to worry about.

The country has a coalition government and a polarized society, and that conveys the scale of its problems. It is difficult for a coalition government to hang together, let alone solve problems. Israel has major economic concerns that require a strong government. If the peace process moves ahead — a big if — and if the U.S. exerts gentle pressure on Shimon Peres, that would be seen in Israel as a symbol for peace.

The Israelis who believe that "we must hold onto the territories that God gave us" appear to be a minority, like the Islamic fundamentalist minority in Iran in a curious sort of way. If that minority is able to hold the majority captive, it will be a terrible thing for Israel.

Article 2

The Economist, December 21, 1985

The Teflon Palestinian

Diplomatic deal-making depends, in the end, on equations of strength. This is why there is reason for hope that a year of grim setbacks for the Palestine Liberation Organisation might be followed by a year of Middle Eastern peace-making. The hope that a battered PLO will reconcile itself to reality must, however, be tempered: in part because of the unpredictable coilings of Middle Eastern politics; but also because the PLO is once again trying to prove its powers of survival and make its setbacks look like successes. Mr Yasser Arafat's failures seem to stick to him no more than Ronald Reagan's gaffes do to him.

One sign of the PLO's resilience is the use it has made of one of the organisation's worst humiliations: the Israeli bombing of its Tunis headquarters in October. This has provided a pretext for it to move many of its offices to Baghdad, which the PLO claims is a much better haven. That is partly wishful thinking. President Saddam Hussein's government will not allow the Palestinians as much freedom of manoeuvre in Iraq as they had

Is there an alternative?

FROM OUR LEVANT CORRESPONDENT

Whatever the PLO's ups and downs, one thing seems immutable: its leader, Mr Yasser Arafat, who has run the Palestinian movement since his own Fatah guerrillas took it over in 1969. From time to time Mr Arafat's diplomatic slipperiness so infuriates not just western governments, which have long questioned his merits, but also Arabs on whose support he depends that there is talk of getting rid of him. The Syrians tried to. Periodically the Saudi Arabians, his main financial backers, quietly suggest an alternative. Relations with Jordan blow hot and cold, and are now on the cool side.

But he is remarkably durable. It will not be easy to replace Mr Arafat, unless he falls to an assassin's bullet or dies in bed. A violent death is always possible; he has many enemies, both Arab and Israeli. Physically, however, he seems in good shape for his 56 years, and rushes to and fro with boundless energy.

A coup against him from within the organisation would be difficult. After 1982, when he was forced out of Lebanon, his forces were scattered across eight Arab countries. But his top soldiers are tried and trusted personal friends, who approve of what is, in PLO terms, Mr Arafat's middle-of-the-road policy. Nor is a constitutional removal very likely. He was elected by the 400-member Palestine National Council, a sort of parliament. The council has been known to criticise him, but it is unlikely to unseat him or to sanction a coup at the top, if only because it shows no sign of thinking who his replacement could be.

If, somehow, he went, one of his close friends from the small group that founded Fatah in 1959 would step forward. (For those who have wondered, Fatah is a back-to-front acronym for "Movement of National Liberation of Palestine".) None of them has Mr Arafat's experience or his aura of being "Mr Palestine". Fatah's official No 2 is Mr Salah Khalaf, better known by his nom-de-guerre of **Abu Iyad**. He is more of an ideologue than Mr Arafat, more left-wing, less inclined to compromise. The conservative Arab governments would be against him.

The official No 3 is Mr Khalil Wazir, better known as **Abu Jihad**. He is the PLO's military leader. In the shadows until Israel's invasion of Lebanon in 1982, he has since travelled all over the

world and may have become Mr Arafat's unofficial deputy. Although he closely follows his leader's policy, he is less temperamental; but he lacks his boss's quickness of mind. He is less dour than Abu Iyad, and would be welcomed as the new leader by most Arab governments if, so to speak, Mr Arafat fell under a camel. With his strong military base, Abu Jihad is the man most likely to succeed.

Sometimes mooted as possible candidates are the **Hassan** brothers, Khalid and Hani, and **Farouk Kaddoumi**. The Hassans have spent most of their careers in Saudi Arabia and Kuwait. The PLO rank-and-file would probably find them too close to those countries and too friendly to America and the West. Mr Kaddoumi, on the other hand, would be thought too close to Syria, where he was once a member of the Syrian Baath Party. He is a left-winger, a "rejectionist", and sometimes appears to confuse fantasy with reality. **Muhammed Milhem**, a former West Bank mayor, has become one of the best known members of the PLO executive, but he officially became a member of the organisation only last year.

Mr Arafat is both head of Fatah, one of eight groups under the PLO umbrella, and chairman of the organisation as a whole. The only other groups besides Fatah that count are Mr George Habash's Popular Front for the Liberation of Palestine and Mr Naif Hawatmeh's Democratic Front. Both groups are Marxist-leaning "rejectionists", now in hock to Syria. Mr Hawatmeh is likelier than Mr Habash to reach an accommodation with Mr Arafat. But unless Syria somehow seized the leadership of the Arab world, neither group would ever produce a leader for the entire PLO.

The whole movement's second-ranking man, and president of the Palestine National Council, is the aged Sheikh Abdul Hamid Sayegh. He would not be a candidate because he is a Muslim cleric; the PLO, which embraces a large minority of Christians as well as Marxist atheists, is secular. The PLO is a very mixed ideological and tactical bag. That is why Mr Arafat, with his all-things-to-all-Palestinians approach, has so successfully clung on to the leadership.

Arafat's leadership, and was, in any event, extremely hostile to Iraq. Besides, Iraq was less than eager to welcome awkward guests at a time when it was doing embarrassingly badly in its war against Iran.

Now Mr Saddam Hussein's government is less hard pressed in the Gulf war. It is more friendly than the Tunisians ever were to the cause of an independent Palestine. The PLO's offices in Baghdad, though much closer to the Palestinian homeland, may be safer from Israeli attack (though the Israeli air force had no trouble reaching a nuclear reactor in the Iraqi capital and putting it out of commission). Syria should not be too huffy about the switch, because President Assad's government has moved a little towards reconciliation with Iraq.

Not that the PLO is moving wholesale to Iraq: it is spreading its bets. The general secretariat is going to Baghdad. The political department, which includes the "foreign ministry", the PLO's executive committee (the organisation's top body), and the Palestinian news agency Wafa will remain in Tunis, at least for a while. The organisation's military headquarters will stay put in North Yemen; and the offices installed in Jordan after King Hussein and Mr Arafat signed their agreement in February will be strengthened by people from Tunis. A few will also go to Algiers and Khartoum.

The PLO's spokesmen argue that it has recaptured political ground among Arabs, especially with its main financiers—Saudi Arabia, Kuwait and the United Arab Emirates—which felt a surge of sympathy after the Tunis raid. They are still hoping that Mr Arafat will co-operate with King Hussein in his drive to open negotiations with Israel. At the same time, the "rejectionist" Arab governments, those most solidly against compromise with Israel, have been mollified by the agreement between hawkish Syria and moderate Jordan.

Egypt, the largest Arab country, continues to take the PLO seriously. President Mubarak, in particular, has been trying assiduously to befriend Mr Arafat's mainstream part of the organisation. Playing the Palestinian card is something that Egypt's government still finds politically useful from time to time. The Palestinian cause remains popular, if not passionately so, among ordinary people throughout the Arab world.

So the PLO, emboldened in its defiance by the sympathy it still arouses, is trying to show that it cannot be pushed around. Mr Arafat says he is having some success in wooing back some members of the small Damascus-based Palestinian groups that had previously rejected his leadership. More important, Mr Arafat has told

first in Lebanon and then in Tunisia. Still, there are some advantages in being under the protection of a strong government, even if elbow-room is not one of them.

Tunis was a strange choice for the PLO's headquarters after the organisation was chased out of Beirut in 1982. Tunisia is a long way from Israel (though not too far for the Israeli air force), and the conservative pro-western government of President Habib Bourguiba has been an uneasy host to a group that still calls itself, even if inaccurately, a "revolution". An additional irony was that the United States was partly responsible for steering the PLO towards Tunisia in the first place.

The Palestinians kept away from Iraq in 1982 because that would have been too provocative to Syria, whose government was (and still is) violently opposed to Mr

King Hussein that he cannot honour the king's request that the PLO make a simple acceptance of Israel's right to exist. He is now insisting that he could do so only if this were part of a package that included United Nations resolutions supporting the Palestinians' right to self-determination.

If the implications of this are what they seem, Mr Arafat is challenging the king to repudiate the agreement that the two men signed last February in Amman. If Mr Arafat succeeded in making King Hussein tear up that document, it would be evidence of a remarkable turnaround in the PLO's fortunes. What it would do to the cause of peace is another matter.

Article 3

Science Digest, January 1983

BEDOUINS
Poets and Pirates of the Dunes

By Burton Bernstein

In the dying light, the Sinai Desert was changing into ever-darker shades of purple. I picked my way around a booth covered with caper plants, then around a disdainful camel, some acacia bushes, and an indistinct mound, which turned out to be a lone Bedouin, prostrating himself for his sundown prayers, facing Mecca. The Bedouins are as integral a part of the Sinai as the strategic passes, the flinty plains, and the mauve mountains. They are the living remnants of history, and the secret of getting along with them is not to be a missionary, not to criticize or patronize behavior that might be alien to Western life; rather, one must accept them for the timeless, proud, earthy people that they are.

As I followed an intermittent stream up the wadi, I recalled what my friend Bailey, a lecturer in Bedouin studies at the University of Tel Aviv, had told me about the Bedouin philosophy of existence in the wilderness. It can be summarized as "I against my brother, my brother and I against our cousin, my brother and I and our cousin against the world." The harshness of life, of course, demands this departmentalization of loyalties.

In the larger world, the Bedouins don't generally take political sides. For all their aggressiveness, the Bedouins have stayed well clear of wars in the region. They have always been good hit-and-run raiders, but with the emphasis on plundering livestock and other valuables, not taking human lives. There is an old Bedouin proverb that translates roughly as: "When the shooting starts, get on the back of camels to the tops of hills."

Burton Bernstein, New Yorker staff writer, visited the Sinai during the Arab-Israeli war of 1969. He returned to the peninsula in 1978, at the time of Israeli occupation.

The Bedouins' fundamental quest in life is for food and shelter on the simplest subsistence level. More than that a Bedouin generally does not covet. Great ambition is alien to him. While some Bedouins have taken up fishing and farming, the majority subsist by herding and menial labor. A favorite Bedouin proverb still is: "When the plow crosses the threshold, manhood departs." As for smuggling (which Bedouins view as merely a profitable occupation), it has brought great wealth to some Bedouins. The contraband includes tape recorders, bolts of cloth, and even burglar alarms, but most of it is hashish.

Bedouins are compulsively hospitable. One day while I was driving with Bailey, a Bedouin man, accompanied by two women (Bedouins are allowed four wives), three children and a flock of goats came into view. We merely wanted directions, but as soon as the man saw us approaching, he went into his mohair tent and brought us a carpet to sit on, not inviting his wife—or

A Bedouin proverb says that when the plow crosses the threshold, manhood departs.

wives—to join us in the ceremonial greeting and tea. He was a handsome man with a dingy turban. Out of respect for his visitors, he often kissed his own right hand, a sign of humility. The directions he eventually gave were in terms of landmarks all but invisible to non-Bedouin eyes—a distant shrub, another tent, a dim white spot of limestone on a far-off hill. "Kadeis is three fingers to the right of the white spot," he said. Desert tracking is a basic Bedouin talent. Having received expert guidance, we roared off across the desert plain under a barrage of *shukrans* (thanks).

In the town, hospitality proved an equally sacred institution. We stayed at the beige one-story house of the Sheikh of Sheikhs Suleiman Ibn Jazi of the Tarabin tribe. In the middle of his sitting room carpet was a round salver, looking like a platter for the world's biggest pizza, on top of which was a mountain of soft white rice and chunks of boiled goat meat. The Sheikh smiled broadly, explaining that just a few hours earlier he had slaughtered his prized goat. At such feasts, the goat's heart, lungs and kidneys are roasted and presented to the guests as appetizers. Following Bailey's example, I broke off a small piece of *pita* and used it as a spoon.

The bilious green walls of the sitting room, I noticed, were peeling and faded, the carpet and mats soiled and dank. How odd that one must remove one's shoes when entering this room—not, obviously, for hygienic reasons, but as a sign of respect. I wondered: If the Sheikh is so powerful and prosperous as befits his station, why does he have such a, well, decrepit house?

But there I go again being a missionary, I thought. Most Arabs who haven't been Westernized are not ostentatious in their house décor; they prefer to put their money in gold, jewelry, livestock, cars, and land. Jazi had made a fortune by smuggling years ago.

The Sheikh's Mercedes-Benz was covered with symbols to ward off the evil eye.

But Bailey added, "He is a simple man who leads a simple Bedouin life, both here and at his tents in the desert." As we left the house, we passed the Sheikh's Mercedes-Benz, with oculiform symbols covering the fenders and hood, placed there to ward off the evil eye.

Long before the Bedouins enthusiastically adopted Islam in the seventh century, they had followed religious patterns of their own design—superstitions, really, based on their star lore, animism, and practical desert laws and customs. Many still believe that the great spirit created man first, and then gave him camels, goats, sheep, and donkeys for his use, along with time and seasons. Some still say that when a man awakens in the morning, the spirit of god is on his right shoulder and the devil is on his left. He must pray and sprinkle himself with water; otherwise the devil will be with him all day. And to this day,

many Bedouins will not attempt a difficult task—a journey, a raid, or sexual intercourse—during unlucky astrological periods.

The legal and philosophical system of the Bedouins is complex, but in the Bedouin culture of subsistence and survival, education comes from the elders, who teach the child by example and imitation. As a rule, only one out of ten Bedouin boys attends school and almost none of the girls. Few Bedouins learn to read or write, which accounts for the emphasis on oral history, law, and entertainment.

Though some have called the Bedouin "wild, untamable animals," the noted contemporary biblical scholar William Albright has said that Bedouins "are the heirs of over thirty centuries of camel-nomadism and of some thirteen centuries of Islam." The fact that they, direct descendants of the original Arabs of the desert, were among the earliest promulgators of Islam has given them a sense of superiority over all other Moslems to this day. Despite the centuries of wrangling over the peninsula, in truth, the Bedouins and the citizens of the towns own the Sinai.

This article was excerpted from *Sinai: The Great and Terrible Wilderness* by Burton Bernstein, copyright © 1979, reprinted by permission of Candida Donadio & Associates.

THE BEDOUIN IN BRIEF

Religion: Islam **Language:** Arabic **Numbers:** About 1,200,000 (45,000 in Sinai).
Habitat: The desert from the western border of Egypt to western Iran.
Tribes: About 18 tribes or tribal federations called the *asilin*.
Social Structure: Extended family. Patriarchal (father heads each family) and patrilocal (couples reside near or with the bridegroom's father).
Marriage: Polygyny; arranged by the family on a strictly commercial basis.
Occupation: Nomadic herders of camels, goats, horses and sheep; some farming.
Housing: Chiefly mohair tents; some stone huts, each with an opening facing west.
Diet: Milk products, dried fruits, dates, some grains; meat is a luxury.
Government: The "ideal human condition" is *mafish hakuma*, which means "no government."

Article 4

New Haven Register, September 1, 1985

Arab linguists toil to keep language from being written off

By David Lamb
Los Angeles Times Service

CAIRO — Few people attach more importance to language than does the Arab.

To the Arab, his language is more than a way of communicating. It is an object of worship, an almost metaphysical force that draws man closer to God.

For the Koran is written in Ara-

bic, and the Koran is regarded as the word of God. Moslems believe that every thought, every word man needs is written in the Koran, expressed 13 centuries ago in Allah's revelations to the illiterate merchant Mohammed.

Master Arabic, and the wisdom of the Koran is unlocked. Protect the purity of Arabic and God's word remains unsullied forever.

Yet there is concern, from Saudi Arabia to Morocco, that the pressures of the modern world are challenging Arabic to keep up with the times.

If it cannot, some scholars suggest, classical Arabic may join Latin in the category of admired, studied — but dead — languages.

"Hardly a day passes without some prominent person complaining that Arabic is being corrupted by the influence of foreign words," observed Said Bedaui, a noted Egyptian scholar on the Arabic language. "People will tell you the Arabs are losing mastery over their language.

"They believe that if they allow the language to develop, to become more contemporary, they will fail to understand the Koran. The language academy is concerned; the Ministry of Education is concerned; everyone is concerned."

How, for instance, should the language accommodate the word "sandwich," which is used to described a thing that was not eaten in Mohammed's time?

How about "television," "automobile" and the thousands of scientific, medical and mathematical terms that have crept into other languages?

In colloquial Arabic — which purists dismiss as a low-grade spoken language without fixed rules — in the news media and in casual conversation, foreign words have simply been adopted.

"Sandwich" is "sandawitshat;" "television" is "tilivizyoon;" "bus" is "autubiis;" "radio" is "radio."

The 54 scholars at the Egyptian Language Academy, established in 1934, have tried to counter this practice, without success, by finding appropriate words from the Koran.

For sandwich, they came up with a term that translated as "a divider and a divided thing together with something fresh inside." For automobile, their alternative was "that which goes by itself."

Predictably, no one says that he is getting into his "that which goes by itself" to find a cheese "divider and a divided thing together with something fresh inside." He gets into his sayra and goes off to buy a cheese sandawitshat.

The academy's offerings, which at first were ridiculed, are now simply ignored.

The Egyptian academy — along with similar institutes in Syria, Iraq, Jordan and Morocco, all of which are making conflicting decisions — also is trying to cope with the scientific and medical demands of the 20th century.

Its members have made slow progress, but only now are they looking for words to describe what the West produced or discovered about 1970.

Their pace seems to indicate that classical Arabic will increasingly be rooted in the past, useful primarily as a medium for religious and intellectual discussion.

Virtually no one outside religious circles speaks classical Arabic in informal conversation. Colloquial dialects have taken its place, but they vary so much from region to region that a Tunisian, say, cannot understand a Bahraini without major semantic changes.

For example, to say "I want," a Moroccan would use the word "brit;" a Saudi might use "uriid" or "uhib."

Even within Egypt — and the Egyptian dialect is widely understood because Egyptian movies and TV soap operas are seen throughout the Arab world — Bedaui has found five distinct linguistic levels, each with its own syntax and speech sounds.

A sheik will speak on one level in the mosque and on another in addressing the vegetable vendor, much as educated Egyptians casually shift from Arabic to French to English in the same conversation.

"So if you're a Westerner and you want to learn Arabic, you've got a problem," Amin Hosni, a professor of Arabic at the American University of Cairo, said.

"Do you want to learn classical and spend five years in a library? Or do you want to read newspapers and talk to people? And in

what country do you want to talk to them? What you've actually got to learn is two languages in one."

More than 600 English words, among them "algebra," "alcohol," "assassin," "cotton," "magazine," "traffic" and "tariff," have Arabic derivations, and a handful of Moslem scholars argue that Western thought has been greatly influenced by Arabic.

The phrase "amir al bhr," for example, means "prince of the sea," and the argument goes that the French and English had trouble pronouncing it so they gradually altered it until it became the word "admiral."

Westerners have trouble with Arabic, a Semitic language and thus related to Hebrew, that is spoken by 167 million people.

In Arabic, there is an almost complete absence of cognates, or words derived from recognizable roots. It sounds different and it looks different; it has a different alphabet (there are 28 letters); the vowel system is different, and the tenses are imprecise.

Also, there is no unanimity on how to transliterate Arabic words into the Roman letters used in the West.

Will classical Arabic eventually die? No, Arab scholars say.

As the language of the Koran, it is deeply ingrained in Islam. It is part of the spirit of Arab nationalism. Indeed, in the ancient debate over who is an Arab, the one thing everyone agrees on is that an Arab is someone who speaks Arabic.

In an effort to adapt classical Arabic to modern demands, the Arab League set up a language academy in Morocco, and in the mid-1970s, its representatives met in Algiers to consider a list of words that included "gram."

They debated, often heatedly, for days.

The Egyptians insisted it should be "gram," as in English. The Lebanese were just as insistent on "jram."

Finally, the league compromised on "gjram," which may be unpronounceable in any language.

Article 5   *Gainesville Sun*, October 12, 1985

Cradle of civilization may also be birthplace of haute cuisine

By ERIK ECKHOLM
New York Times News Service

NEW YORK — Imagine a cuisine offering a hundred styles of soup and 18 kinds of cheese. A place where 300 types of bread are made with different flours, spices or fruit fillings and can be ordered in special shapes ranging from a heart to a woman's breast. A place where truflelike fungi are harvested for the table and pickled grasshoppers are served for snacks.

It may sound like latter-day California, or perhaps the Left Bank in Paris. But new findings reveal that these varied delights and more were enjoyed at least 4,000 years ago in the Middle East. The princes and priests of ancient Mesopotamia, it turns out, were gastronomes of the first order; their chefs, masters.

Mesopotamia, the strip of land between the rivers Tigris and Euphrates that is now part of Iraq, has long been called the cradle of civilization. Now it may also become known as the birthplace of haute cuisine.

Deciphering cuneiform symbols on stone tablets housed at Yale University, the French scholar Jean Bottero has discovered what are by far the oldest extant recipe books. Written in Akkadian, an ancient Babylonian language, the recipes were apparently carved onto stone around 1700 B.C. Previously the tablets had been thought to contain pharmaceutical formulas.

Bottero, an eminent Assyriologist and a good cook himself, wrote in a recent issue of Biblical Archaeology magazine that the tablets reveal "a cuisine of striking richness, refinement, sophistication and artistry, which is surprising from such an early period. Previously we would not have dared to think a cuisine 4,000 years old was so advanced."

The best-preserved of the tablets features 25 recipes, with a heavy emphasis on aromatic meat stews. Stag, gazelle, kid, lamb, mutton and pigeon and other birds are to be prepared in, among other concoctions, a red stew, a clear stew, a tart stew and a stew with bread crumbs sprinkled on top. Garlic, onions and leeks are favored flavorings, but mint, juniper berries, and what appear to be mustard, coriander and cumin are also called for along with some unfamiliar herbs and spices.

These recipes are not for the culinary amateur. Often just a few lines long, they list essential ingredients laconically, leaving quantities and cooking times to the discretion of the cook. In this they resemble modern cookbooks written for the use of professional chefs such as Auguste Escoffier's "Guide Culinaire."

Up to now, the earliest preserved cookbook worthy of the name had been that of Apicius, a Roman gourmet whose "On Culinary Art" was probably compiled in the fourth century A.D. Some Greeks are known to have collected recipes, but only tantalizingly brief references, by one Athenaeus of Naucratis in his second-century work "The Learned Banquet," have survived.

To the unending frustration of culinary historians, cooking technique is ignored in the Bible. Archeologists can surmise what basic foods the Egyptians ate, but nary a hieroglyphic recipe has been found to tell them how they prepared them.

In addition to the newly deciphered tablets, other written records, artistic depictions and archeological remains indicate the wide range of foods enjoyed by the Babylonians and their predecessors in Mesopotamia, the Sumerians. One text, a sort of Sumerian-Akkadian, Akkadian-Sumerian dictionary on 24 stone tablets, provides terms in the two languages for 800 different foods and beverages. Other artifacts suggest that a complete menu of available consumables would be twice that long.

The choices, at least for the elite, included meats both domestic and wild, fish, turtles and shellfish and a host of grains, vegetables, tubers, fruits, mushrooms and herbs. One text even describes meat-stuffed intestinal casings, the world's first sausages. A bas-relief portrays a servant carrying a snack plate of pomegranates and pickled grasshoppers.

In another pattern that may sound familiar, the Mesopotamian master chefs were all men, whereas in ordinary households the women invariably did the cooking. The masters prepared feasts for the upper classes in spacious, well-equipped kitchens and with unique access to costly ingredients.

Would-be experimenters with the ancient recipes should beware, Bottero warned.

Re-creating the Mesopotamian dishes would be practically impossible, and not just because of the difficulty of matching ingredients precisely. Every cuisine, he observed, "is made up primarily of tricks of the trade." Without a chance to watch a Babylonian Julia Child demonstrate proper technique, one cannot hope to reproduce the gustatory magic encapsulated in the cuneiform symbols.

Just how tasty today's epicures would find the dishes is uncertain in any case. "It appears that their concept of good food and ours are worlds apart," said Bottero. "For instance, they adored their foods soaked in fats and oils, they seem obsessed with every member of the onion family, and, in contrast to our tastes, salt played a rather minor role in their diet."

Article 6   *Pakistan & Gulf Economist*, June 29 - July 5, 1985

Expats' future in the Gulf

The Gulf states cannot yet do away with the foreign worker who is also needed because of the limited populations of many countries.

By ZAFAR SAMADANI

The Gulf region is currently undergoing two experiences, both relevant to expatriate workers and the countries they represent. Oil revenues are declining and the Gulf countries are economising. A reduction in the size of the foreign work-force appears to be the target. For the locals, part of the effort is development of indigenous labour, an end impeded by the presence of foreign workers though because of many other reasons also.

While these countries are promoting their individual and collective interests, for those who have tuned their economies to earnings of expatriates, and Pakistan is one of them, the news should be less than heartening. But the development is not sudden nor unexpected. The picture and the changes in it have been available for some time. Statistics have been telling the story and issuing plain and unambiguous warnings. If no one has heeded then, the fault lies with the countries who provide the force, because reduction in foreign workers of the region has been progressively increasing since 1981.

According to a study conducted in the region, the changes are striking. The expatriate labour force, says the study, peaked in 1981 when its total was 7.5 million. By the end of the last year it had receded to 5.8 million, of which four million were in Saudi Arabia alone while the rest were shared by other States in the Gulf. During 1984, approximately 700,000 expatriate workers were sent back from the region. Projections pursue the same course, prophesying that in the next five years, Saudi Arabia plans to axe 600,000 workers and that other countries have similar plans with less daunting figures because of the smaller work-force.

Retrenchement is to be seen in many sectors, most notably in construction. The boom which had become an identification factor for these states is long over. It has vacated the position of the fastest growing sector to become a somewhat static scene, one marked by reduced jobs. Two developments have caused this transformation, for the expatriate, from the rosy to the gloomy: the process of creation of the basic infrastructure is nearing completion in most cases; slashed budgets have led to shelving of many other projects or to a readjustment in their sizes to suit the changed and changing revenue and resource situations. The aim is to make the maximum effort to live within the resources and, at the same time, groom the local work-force to replace expatriates. Both are laudable ends. But are they achieveable too? From the looks of things, not fully and not instantly, at least.

The region seems to have developed the white collar syndrome. An AFP report quoting an important official of the Ministry of Labour and Social Welfare of the UAE says: "Fathers tend to steer their children away from what they consider menial work and young people refuse to enter technical jobs because the society looks down on those attending technical institutes instead of universities." This indicates that the dependence on foreign workers is not to be given up entirely nor too soon, certainly not in the near future.

The example of Kuwait itself provides the argument contradictng the policy. According to the report of the last census carried out in the country, foreigners, who make up sixty per cent of the 1.7 million population of the country, fulfill seventy-seven per cent of the manpower requirements of Kuwait, ninety-eight percent of workers in the construction sector, 92 per cent of those in transport and communication and storage sectors and 93 percent in the commercial, restaurant and hotel sectors. Most of them, according to a survey, are Asian. Like other countries of the Gulf, Kuwait also has embarked on a policy of cutting down the number of foreign workers. It is however to be doubted that it can be effectively done unless the Kuwaitis cast off their disdain for manual work, a change in attitude for which there is little evidence. The commitment to university education as being superior to technical education has to be negotiated and the importance of the latter must be recognised before something meaningful can happen on this front. The two need not be at the cost of each other, but there has to room for both.

Still, considering that Kuwait and Saudi Arabia are two of the richest nations of the region with high per capita incomes (around 19,830 US dollars (1980) for Kuwait and $11,260 for Saudi Arabia (1980) the attitude is at least not exactly surprising that the same psychological resistance to manual work persists all over the region. In Bahrain, for instance, with a population of 351,000 and certainly not as affluent as other states, the foreign workers total 58 percent of the local employment scene.

Evidently the Gulf states cannot yet do away with the foreign worker who is also needed because of the limited population of many countries.

Still, the picture has completely altered over the years and for understandable reasons. A curve of change has been carved and recent policy decisions are thickening it as well as maintaining an upward movement in its growth in the favour of the locals. New contracts for the expatriates are at lower salaries and many benefits such as overtime allowances and accomodation facilities are in the process of being brought down (partially by preferring bachelors to married people), replacing expensive western experts with comparatively lower paid Asians and reviewing costs in general with a view to economising and providing more opportunities to locals. This was inevitable.

Unfortunately the countries benefiting from expatriates' earnings have failed to consolidate to their advantage and invest it into a better and secure future. Pakistan has certainly not done that with the result that increasing unemployment over the next few years can be forecast. Nevertheless, it is still far from being all over. To be exact, a period of about five years is available till the roof caves in. This period can be utilised for ensuring that a period of prosperity is not followed by one marked by disaster. Those presiding over the scene should start worrying and planning.

Article 7   *Pakistan & Gulf Economist*, August 10-16, 1985

THE GULF COUNTRIES MAKING HEADWAY

By ZAFAR SAMADANI

Although the Arabs hae been keen sportsmen all through history, their pursuits have been restricted mainly to traditional sports of the region. In recent years, they have broken into modern times in this field too, as in many others. There has in fact been an explosion both in the sports activity of the Arabs and their interest in what is happening on the international scene.

One example of their involvement is the premium they place on sports coverage over local television networks. There is never an important event which the networks miss taking directly on satellite. On course their romance does not extend to all sports, but the ones which have conquered their hearts are always there.

Football for instance: Arabs are crazy about the game. They play it all over, all the time; they watch it whenever a match worth watching takes place anywhere, at home or abroad, physically presenting themselves in an arena or making an irrevocable appointment with television. Within the countries of the region, practically each city has a well equipped and finely constructed stadium equipped with the latest facilities usually exceeding local requirements. Only on a rare evening is a football ground deserted. A match is invariably in progress, just as predictably, spectators are around. Not simply that either. On a scorchingly hot afternoon, a while after midday to be exact, I have seen barefooted Omani boys play football right under the sun with a fervour not affected by the heat. They would be barefooted not for lack of resources, but because this suits their unfettered spirit. Invariably a sports-loving crowd would be present to encourage and criticise the youngsters.

In the United Arab Kingdom, I have been surprised more than once by the time local television devotes to sports, particularly international events, not that local fixtures get ignored. Here too, football is prime programme. I was told that all through the region the World Cup is taken directly and not only be the contests between the last sixteen teams. Preliminary matches are also enthusiastically watched when they are taken on satellite.

This is not to say that traditional sports have started leaving the Arabs cold; falconry is just as popular and camel racing is a festival event attended, in the case of important contests, by VVIP's. But these aren't sports for all. That honour goes to football.

Camel racing has, however, to compete with car racing. Car rallies sponsored by major international automobile companies are a regular feature of the Gulf life. The champion drivers are regarded as heroes as much as they are in Europe; nor are all of them foreigners. Many Arabs out-race their Western counterparts with more famous and prestigious reputations. These rallies are not confined to any one country or state. The interest is the same all over.

While all countries of the region have numerous football tournaments of various levels, the top events are the Arab Cup and the championships in the Pan Arab Games. In the Pan Arab Games which took place early this month in Morocco, the event which had almost one hundred per cent participation was football. Twenty of the twenty-one member countries participated in the football championship which started on August 5. The matches were played at four centres, Rabat, Casablanca, Mohammadia and Settat. The country that stayed away was Sudan, which cited financial reasons for the absence. Needless to report the matches were televised live in most Arab countries and in all the countries of the Gulf without exception. All local championships in Gulf countries invariably have foreign teams participating in them.

While football occupies the prime place, cricket has also hit the front pages in the last few years. That has indeed been a remarkable feat as, while football is widely played in the region, cricket has a restricted following. Very few Arabs are actively engaged in playing it. The credit for bringing this spectator sport which has been traditionally limited to the English speaking world goes wholly to two individuals, Sharjah businessman Abdur Rahman Bukhatir and Pakistan's former test captain, Asif Iqbal. With Bukhatir financing the promotion of the game and Asif Iqbal using his training from Australia's World Cup Cricket of Packer, they have managed to place the region in general, and UAE and Sharjah in particular, on the cricket map.

Cricket has brought a large number of visitors to the region, also. Last year, when the Rothmans Cup took place in Sharjah with teams from England, Australia, India and Pakistan participating, the region was flooded with tourists. The Cup matches, like the Asia Cup of the year before, drew tremendous crowds and presented cricket of the highest and most exciting quality. Locally, the impact of these contests has generated enough excitement to ensure that cricket matches between teams composed mainly of expatriates have some locals on them. An Arab playing cricket is no longer a novel sight. The game has certainly come to the region. Though other countries of the area have comparatively a lesser interest in the game, Oman has exhibited more than a passing patronage. The game is restricted to expatriates, generally, but Omanis are also to be frequently seen turning their arm for a bowl or walking up to the wicket all padded in locally played matches.

It is however not just cricket or football or other sporting activities; there is a noteworthy awareness of sport and an extremely keen interest that at times exceeds that of the countries boasting of longer traditions in the field.

One aspect of the increased attention on sports is intense media focus comprising live telecasts and detailed coverage of local events. Another is a boost to construction activities otherwise marked by decline, through the building of stadiums. Although many construction plans of the region have been slashed in recent times, those related to sports are unaffected. If anything, greater attention is being paid to them.

And this keenness is not limited to a few countries; the whole of the Arab world has been caught up by a wave of enthusiasm for sports, with the result that the entire Middle East presents a constant scene, one vast arena of joy for sportsmen and spectators. In Egypt, for instance, the country's Higher Sports and Youth Council had 23 sports projects in hand last year, including a stadium at Medina Nasr with a capacity for 12,000 seats in an indoor arena. In view of the limited capacity of some of the existing stadiums used by local football clubs of Cairo, new stadiums are being planned for them to accommodate the large crowds thronging football grounds irrespective of the importance of a match.

Qatar, already possessing considerable facilities for its sports lovers, is now further improving the quality of state support for sports. Its main stadium has the tallest floodlights in the world. The 63.5 metre high floodlights costing 2 million dollars are however only one of the attractions at the Bousher stadium which has cost 90 million dollars.

Saudi Arabia too, has no dearth of stadiums. It has nevertheless embarked on a policy of creating more and more modern facilities. It is to have a new stadium in Riyadh with a capacity for

70,000 spectators. The stadium, costing 340 million dollars is to comprise, besides other facilities, a royal box offering seats for 1,000 VIPs and parking space for 7,500 cars. The West German firm which is constructing the Riyadh sports arena has already completed three stadiums in the past, the last one at Shaqura at a cost of 35 million dollars. The Riyadh stadium is expected to be completed this year. The Presidency of Youth and Sports overseas has made developments in the sports sector in Saudi Arabia. It is following a continuous programme to create new facilities and improve existing facilities on a nationwide basis, a policy which is benefiting clubs all over the country. Saudi Arabia still has the main focus on football and most programmes are geared towards its promotion, though athletics and some other sports such as basketball are also receiving due attention.

For most countries of the region, sports and youth affairs go together. Last year, when Oman celebrated the Youth Year, the activities were of a diverse nature but emphasis on sports was clear. The year's celebration concluded with a tournament between youth teams of the region. The programme for the year was chalked out and supervised by the Ministry of Youth Affairs. Nine years back Oman completed the construction of a major sports complex in Muscat. Now it is reported to have plans for five sports centres in different parts of the Sultanate.

Like many other countries of the Gulf, Kuwait, too, has football on top of the list of sports priorities. Over the last two decades, the local scene has been transformed in an amazing manner. According to a report, Kuwait Football Association was founded in 1962. At that time, the country's football team used to play its international contests on a school ground which could not be called a stan-

dard pitch by any stretch of imagination. It is a different story today. The country now has four major stadiums with a capacity for 25,000 spectators and a number of smaller sized arenas offering the latest facilities to players. The country has also succeeded in substantially improving its standards. In the World Cup Football, 1982, the performance of the Kuwaiti team won a lot of praise from sports experts.

In UAE, sports are more diversified than in many other countries of the region. It has an interest in golf and rugby besides football and cricket, though admittedly locals are scarcely involved in golf or other such sport. They mainly have an expatriate following. The country is also focusing equally clearly on traditional sports and providing attention, backing, and facilities to such sports as camel racing. Camel race tracks have been developed alongside facilities for modern sport.

Morocco, which held the ninth Mediterranean Games in September 1983, has considerable modern facilities which were improved upon at that time and have recently been further updated for the Pan Arab Games. As in other fields, the region has also entered contemporary times in the arena of sports, too, and can compete, in terms of facilities, with many countries regarded as far more developed. So far, the sportsmen of the region have not been able to take the maximum benfit from the increased attention on sports but the standards have generally improved and more and more games are being played. If the emphasis remains, and judging from current policies, it is not only likely to sustain but also further increase, the impact should soon be perceptible in the performance of the region's sportsmen.

Algeria:

Article 8   *South,* December 1985

Crop production under wraps

The Algerian government is making a bid to boost agricultural production to reduce dependence on imported food. Two thirds of all food consumed in Algeria is imported, and food imports cost US$2-billion annually—one sixth of foreign exchange earnings. One way of increasing production of fresh fruit and vegetables without extending the cultivated area is to grow them in extensive greenhouses under transparent plastic film—plasticulture as it is called in Algeria. This method is heavily promoted by the ministry of agriculture.

As the end of the summer approached, the bare skeletal frameworks of greenhouses were covered with plastic film. Inside the structures, farmers have begun to prepare the soil for fruit and vegetables which will be grown and harvested throughout the winter months. Farming under plastic means that the crops can be spaced out as required and made available throughout the year. The crops—tomatoes, peppers, pimentoes, cucumbers, beans, lettuces and melons—are also usually superior to those grown outside and they need less water.

Even more important, when grown under plastic in an ideal micro-climate free from wind and rain, crops can be made to increase their yields in an almost magical fashion. Tomatoes have yielded 30-50 tonnes per hectare under plastic, while grown in the open field they would have rendered 10 tonnes at most. Such impressive returns have encouraged the government to commit itself to increase the area of land under the regime, and plasticulture is one of the priority sectors of agriculture under the new five year plan. The aim is to triple the area under plastic to 8,000 hectares by promoting the technique in both the private and the public farming sectors.

Plasticulture also covers a wide range of applications of plastic film in agriculture—from greenhouses and tunnel cultivation of melons, carrots and peppers to mulching, the lining of irrigation canals, drainage ditches and small reservoirs, to hay protection and animal storage. The film produced by the local plastics industry has a big role to play in the modernisation of Algerian agriculture.

Still the greenhouses are the most famous example of plasticulture. The technique is not new to Algeria and was first introduced under a programme run by the FAO in the late 1960s. At that time its crops of tomatoes, peppers and cucumbers were intended to go for export as primers to Europe. But it is to meet

the needs of the rapidly growing Algerian population that the newly planned plasticulture regions are intended, although in future, surplus production could again find its way to Europe.

Until recently, plasticulture was restricted to the coastal plain, especially near the capital, and in the important Mitidja plain to the south. But it is now spreading fast in the deep south too, in the Saharan zones where the technique has also been found to boost yields dramatically. Technical back-up is provided by the Institute for the Development of Market Gardening at Staoueli, west of Algiers, which has carried out basic experimental work.

Plasticulture is not without problems. Farmers must familiarise themselves with the strains of crops best suited to greenhouse cultivation. There are new

technical demands, new diseases to combat such as mildew, and farmers must learn how to use thermometers and hydrometers to monitor the temperature and humidity of soil and air to get the best out of the technology.

Another drawback of the technique is its expense. The wooden or tubular frameworks, which last up to 10 years, cost up to US$40,000 per hectare and the plastic film adds another US$5,000. The Algerian film only lasts one season, compared with foreign makes lasting three to four seasons. The government has, however, offered credit of up to US$40,000 per hectare to encourage plasticulture, and with returns of 30 tonnes per hectare, the investment can quickly pay for itself.

David Bradshaw

Article 9
Finding strength in national culture

SOUTH DECEMBER 1985

The computer and *rai*, the popular musical form from western Algeria, have penetrated deeply into Algerian society, becoming as popular as the national football team, World Cup finalists for the second consecutive time. These are not extraordinary, but for a population with 70 per cent under 30 years of age, these are the first indications that herald a change at the socio-cultural level, after the bloody history of eight years of the war of liberation from the French army and a colonial occupation lasting over 130 years.

Newly independent Algeria began to construct at full speed an autonomous national economy, not being content with the neo-colonial status that the manipulators of post-colonial France tried to impose by their favourite means, economic, cultural and political destabilisation. If the intentions of certain circles within the French state in 1985 remain unchanged, the methods have undergone some revisions. Various actions along the lines of the "Greenpeace affair" have been tried without success, and from the Algerian point of view, there is no reason to make distinctions as to their nature (secret agents or political manoeuvres involving third states), when their target is Algerian sovereignty and peace within the region. In these circles, which persist in thinking that the Algerian war is not yet over (the example of Le Pen is pertinent in this respect), it is felt that Algeria's Achilles heel lies in its cultural fragility.

A direct, brutal colonisation of more than a century tried to erase all traces of national identity, reducing the Arab language to a ghetto existence, falsifying history and restricting schooling to the primary level. (At independence there were only 450 Algerian university students, including those expatriated in France.) This process mocked religion, and included special laws of exclusion comparable to those applied to the Indians in North America. After all this, the country's reconstruction entailed precise objectives, including a bid gradually to restore the Algerians' national language without rejecting the French tongue.

Today the renaissance takes on a variety of aspects and expresses itself among the country's student circles, comprising 5-million young Algerians (men and women), and nearly 120,000 university students. Strongly receptive to universal values, Algerian education retains the handicap of a double culture, Arab and French, but has as its vector its own cultural identity, much of whose heritage was concealed or distorted by colonialism. This explains why the Algerian, after having overcome the problems entailed by the choice between his own language and a foreign one, devotes all his attention and thought to the conception of a language which has infiltrated into every

education and university mechanism and which is destined to create and stimulate the development and progress of scientific research and social transformation. At the first *Salon de l'Université* exhibition visited several weeks ago by President Chadli Bendjedid, the research sections gave demonstrations of the advances achieved in information technology, electronics, earth sciences and other fields which represent the modern era of an Algeria which is breaking away from its dependence on oil income and is counting on its own resources from now on. Recently the weekly *Algérie Actualité* ran a front-page headline, "Oil out, Ideas in".

Algeria was attacking this very system of thought, inherited from the long colonial night followed by a conservative, neo-colonialist cultural environment both internally and externally, by pursuing a young, innovative type of society in conformity with the socialist goals which the country set for itself after its liberation.

National identity cannot be separated from its main component, the history of Algeria, which has mobilised researchers, academics, historians and ordinary citizens who bear witness in the written press and on television to their contributions in a key period, the Algerian war. Others go back further into the past to the first settlements of the Berber people, from before the Roman invasion until the advent of the civilising force of Islam in this part of Africa. All Algerians today are aware that Tariq Ibn Ziad, who conquered Spain and the southwest of France many centuries ago, commanded mainly Maghrebian troops.

Algerians have known for a long time that their ancestors were not the Gauls of France, and that, at the time when Arab civilisation was at its peak, Haroun el Rachid made a gift to Charlemagne of the first clock in the history of France. Beyond these anecdotal aspects, Algerians who lived through the colonial era, along with the younger generation, cannot forget colonial horrors and follow with a keen interest all of the seminars and television productions devoted to history, where they can listen to the first-hand accounts of the heroes of the war of liberation, who have come out of their silence to reveal that Algerian independence was wrenched from the French at that cost of great sufferings and that General de Gaulle, who made peace with the political and military leadership of the FLN, only did so after having subjected the whole country, from north to south and from east to west, to a monstrous bloodbath.

Young Algerians, born after independence and less affected than their elders who underwent the war, approach the end of the 20th century with ambitions of a kind which already have one foot planted in the year 2000. It is significant that a new evening newspaper set up in recent months and catering to the concerns of young people is titled *Horizon 2000*. It is an untroubled younger generation which has learned to assert itself, taking more and more key posts within the state, in business firms, in the university and in medicine; a development which on the economic level is extremely perturbing to Algeria's trading partners when they present themselves in the guise and with the ulterior motives of the former coloniser. Graduates of prestigious universities in the United States, England, France, the socialist countries and the Arab world, notably from Algeria itself, the ranks of young Algerian managers, made up to a large extent of women, have today earned the respect of their partners and are no longer content with dreaming of a transfer of technology.

The airlines receive them in ever greater numbers, crisscrossing the globe, a young generation thirsting for discoveries and new faraway horizons like their illustrious geographer ancestor, Ibn Batouta.

In Algeria the authorities have perceived in this generation signs of maturity, of adaptability, and natural tendencies to live in harmony within a revolutionary context, which does not require them to abstain from enjoying themselves through music and dance, or to take up more serious occupations such as in the scientific workshops, sports and the other leisure activities for which the state provides considerable material and financial resources.

Between their frank sympathy for the people's struggle in Palestine, in South Africa and the Western Sahara, and their fascination with the progress of western societies, including even Hollywood films, a large portion of the younger generation has taken up the most noble aspects of the Islamic heritage. In the face of a conservative Islamic upsurge, it opposes rigour and practises an open-mindedness, aware that Islam was one of the bulwarks preventing French attempts at depersonalisation in Algeria, and that the country needs no lessons on the part of these missionaries inspired from abroad (Libya, Saudi Arabia, etc). In actual fact, this severely limited phenomenon is not comparable to what is happening in Tunisia, Egypt or Morocco, where the social tensions resulting from the poverty of the underprivileged have provided favourable ground for extremist activities. □

Kamel Belkacem

Bahrain:

Article 10

Pakistan & Gulf Economist, August 17-23, 1985

DIVERSIFICATION OF ECONOMY

The Government of Bahrain has carried out a successful campaign to diversify the economy's base and to reduce the country's dependence on oil. Spearheading the diversification has been the expansion of the services sector, including banking and trade, along with manufacturing. Expansion of these sectors has more than offset substantial declines in petroleum output in recent years, with the result that growth of the real gross domestic product (GDP) in Bahrain has averaged around 7 per cent annually. At the same time, the domestic rate of inflation has slowed down, in line with declining world inflation; prices in Bahrain rose by about 3 per cent annually in both 1983 and 1984.

Notwithstanding the growing importance of the non-oil sector in the Bahraini economy, petroleum remains the principal earner of foreign exchange and the major contributor to budgetary receipts. As a result, the softness of world oil prices in recent years has weakened Bahrain's fiscal and external accounts. The Government has responded to the deterioration in its fiscal position primarily by restraining current expenditures and by delaying capital spending. By helping to contain the growth of overall demand, these measures are expected to contribute to an improvement in the current account position over the medium term.

The opening of a causeway linking Bahrain and Saudi Arabia in late 1985 is expected to enhance Bahrain's future economic performance by providing new growth opportunities for Bahrain's services sector, especially in the areas of transportation, tourism, and real estate.

Petroleum-related activities

Bahrain is a member of the Organization of Arab Petroleum Exporting Countries (OAPEC). Although it is not a member of the Organization of Petroleum Exporting Countries (OPEC), its oil pricing policies are generally in accord with OPEC decisions.

Crude oil production accounted for about 14 per cent of Bahain's GDP in 1983, compared with 23 per cent just five years earlier. Partly responsible for this contraction was a decline in output of the Jebel al-Dukhan onshore field, which accounts for just under half of Bahrain's oil production. Output of this field has been falling steadily since 1970, when it reached its peak of 76,000 barrels per day(b/d). After stabilizing in 1983 and 1984 at about 41,800 b/d, output from the Jebel al-Dukhan field is expected to resume its downward trend in 1985. About 54 per cent of Bahrain's oil output comes from the Abu Saafa offshore field, whose production is shared equally by Bahrain and Saudi Arabia. Output from this field varies in response to policy decisions by Saudi Arabia. Production increased significantly in 1983, more than offsetting the decrease in onshore oil output. As a result, Bahrain's total crude oil production that year rose by more than 3 per cent. Output of the Abu Saafa field is estimated to have risen by about 9 per cent in the first nine months of 1984, relative to the corresponding period of 1983.

All of the country's oil output is refined domestically at the Bahrain Petroleum Company (Bapco) refinery, which processes crude oil into (principally) gas oils, fuel oil, naphtha, jet fuel, gasoline, and kerosene. The refinery also processes crude oil imports from Saudi Arabia and, in recent years, from India. In the face of declining demand for its products, the Bapco refinery's output fell sharply in 1982, and in 1983 contracted further to a record low of 175,000 b/d. While the production level recovered in 1984 to an average of 209,000 b/d, output was still below the refinery's rated capacity of 260,000 b/d.

Bahrain has substantial natural gas resources, which are expected to last another 50 years at the 1983 extraction rate of 504 million cubic feet per day (mmcfd). Production rose to an average of 537 mmcfd in the first nine months of 1984, with a further increase to 670 mmcfd expected by 1986 as a result of a four-year plan to intensify extraction of natural gas from the Khuff Zone. This field currently accounts for 75 per cent of Bahrain's gas output, with natural gas associated with petroleum production accounting for the remainder.

Gas processing is an important activity in Bahrain's economy. Much of Bahrain's gas output is processed at the gas liquefaction plant operated by the Bahrain National Gas Company (Banagas). In 1983 this plant produced about 3.1 million U.S. barrels of natural gas liquids—propane, butane, and naphtha—primarily for export. By far the largest development project in the gas sector, however, is an export-oriented ammonia and methanol plant scheduled to begin operations in late 1985. Owned jointly by Bahrain, Kuwait, and Saudi Arabia, the plant will have a rated capacity of 1,000 metric tons daily for each of the two products.

The non-petroleum sector

One of the first countries in the Gulf to begin oil exploration and production, Bahrain was also among the first to experience output decline and to embark on a diversification effort. While the initial aim of the authorities was to establish oil-based industries, the focus during the past decade has been on the services sector. At the same time, the Government has fostered the expansion of industries, with particular emphasis on aluminum, iron, and steel products.

The country's industrial policy has focused on the development of both large-scale facilities for the manufacture of export-oriented goods and small-scale projects specializing in items intended for domestic consumption. The growth of non-oil manufacturing has been led, to a large extent, by the aluminum sector. Output of the country's aluminum smelter, Aluminium Bahrain (Alba), has expanded rapidly since it began operations in 1971. Alba's output accelerated after 1981, when the productive capacity of the facility was expanded by over 40 per cent. In 1983, Alba's operations accounted for more than half of the real value added in the non-oil manufacturing sector.

The aluminum industry in Bahrain also includes a number of "downstream" operations, including an aluminum powder plant, a company producing overhead transmission cables, and a firm that makes aluminum products for construction and general engineering purposes. The industry will be expanded further in late 1985, when the Gulf Aluminium Rolling Mill Company begins operations.

Bahrain's manufacturing diversification efforts have also included new projects in the iron and steel sector. The Arab Shipbuilding and Repair Yard, (ASRY) owned jointly by the seven OAPEC members, started operations in 1977. Faced with weak demand for its services as a result of unfavourable market conditions, competition from abroad, and the strength of the U.S. dollar (in which prices are quoted), the yard has recently begun to use its spare capacity for steel fabrication. Another project in the iron and steel sector is the iron ore pelletizing plant of the Arab Iron and Steel Company, which began operations in 1984. All of its output (expected to reach the full capacity level of 4 million tons by 1986) is to be exported.

The services sector also has played an important role in the Government's diversification efforts during the past decade. As a result, the contribution of the services sector to real GDP has grown from 39 per cent in 1978 to 48 per cent in 1983. A leading force in this growth has been offshore banking, whose real value added more than doubled between 1978 and 1983. The growth of offshore banking units slowed significantly in 1983, however, signalling the beginning of a consolidation phase. The services sector also encompasses trade, tourism, and transport activities. These subsectors have grown steadily over most of the past decade and they are expected to expand further once the causeway between Bahrain and Saudi Arabia is opened to the public.

Another activity that has contributed to the rapid growth of the non-oil sector has been construction. With strong demand by the private sector for housing and office facilities, and with public sector construction projects expanding at relatively high rates, real value added by this sector grew substantially in the 1970s. Following setbacks from 1979 through 1981, construction has experienced a recovery, which was especially pronounced in 1983.

The construction boom of the 1970s had an adverse effect on agriculture, however. Rising land values lead many small farmers to sell their fields to developers, with the result that the amount of land under cultivation has fallen sharply in recent years. This reduction in usable farm land, along with growing pressures on scarce water resources, has depressed agricultural output levels. In response, the Government has introduced a number of farming subsidies and imposed new water fees to promote more efficient water use.

Fiscal policy

Revenues from the petroleum and gas sector have accounted for around 70 per cent of total fiscal revenues and grants in recent years. In spite of declining crude oil output, however, Bahrain's fiscal position was relatively strong through 1981 as a result of higher world oil prices. The budget surplus for 1981 reached a record of 159 million Bahrain dinars, while the overall surplus (including extra-budgetary operations) peaked at BD 197 million in the same year. The country's fiscal position weakened in 1982, however, because of higher current and capital outlays and a deficit in extra-budgetary operations. The budget surplus was thus almost halved to BD 83 billion, while the overall fiscal balance shifted into a deficit of BD 89 million.

Faced with the prospect that revenues would not resume former growth rates because of weaker oil demand and prices, the Government introduced a programme in early 1983 to contain the expansion of fiscal outlays. The most important provision of the programme was the extension of the time frame for completing the economic and social investment programme to 1982-87 and the reduction of outlays under the plan by about 6 per cent to BD 1 billion. This programme is Bahrain's first attempt at medium-term planning for public sector investment expenditures.

Despite the introduction of these measures, the rate of growth of capital outlays increased in 1983, since work on many of the projects scheduled for that year was too far along in the planning process to be shelved. This increase was more than offset, however, by a significant reduction in the growth rate of current outlays. As a result, the expansion in total expenditures slowed to 13 per cent in 1983 from 24 per cent in the previous year.

These expenditure-restraining measures were accompanied by actions to increase non-oil revenues, which in 1983 accounted for about 23 per cent of total fiscal resources. The growth of non-oil fiscal resources nevertheless slowed—rising by only 12 per cent in 1983, compared with 17 per cent in 1982. The deceleration in the growth of non-oil receipts, combined with an 18 per cent decline in oil and gas revenues, resulted in a 13 per cent decrease in total government income in 1983, compared with a 3 per cent increase a year earlier.

The decline in total resources and the growth in outlays led to a further weakening in the Government's budgetary position in 1983, with the budget surplus of 1982 turning into a deficit of BD 50 million and the overall deficit widening to BD 103 million.

Bahrain's domestic banking sector includes the Bahrain Monetary Agency (BMA) (whose functions are similar to those of a central bank), 18 commercial banks (3 of which are locally incorporated with Bahraini ownership), an Islamic Bank, and a Housing Bank.

Credit to the private sector has expanded at annual rates of 11 to 16 per cent since 1979. Most of the increase since 1981 have been accounted for by trade, construction, and personal credit expansion. There was net government borrowing in 1982, but the Government rebuilt its net deposit position in 1983.

Apart from the domestic banking system, Bahrain is a major world offshore financial centre that has grown rapidly since 1975. By the end of 1983, the total assets of offshore banking units had reached $63 billion, compared with $28 billion at the end of 1979; over the same period, their number expanded from 51 to 75. For the most part, the market handles assets and liabilities with maturities of three months or less. The offshore banking units have recently expanded the scope of their activities in response to a slowdown in their asset growth rates.

Balance of payments

Bahrain's external accounts have been weakened by the softening of oil markets. Export earnings of the petroleum sector have fallen sharply since 1981, when they peaked at BD 1.5 billion; in 1983, these earnings amounted to only BD 972 million. At the same time, the continued high level of economic activity in Bahrain has led to an expansion in non-oil imports. As a result of these develpments, Bahrain's trade balance shifted into deficit in 1983; the shortfall continued in 1984. In 1983, the deterioration in the trade balance was partially offset by an improvement in the services and private transfers balance, though weaker, remained positive. In the first half of 1984, however, Bahrain's current account posted a deficit of about BD 94 million, compared with one of BD 5 million in the corresponding period of 1983.

The deterioration of the current account in 1983 was partly offset by an improvement in the net balance of capital flows and official grant receipts. As a result, the overall balance of payments posted a surplus of BD 46 million in 1983.

Bahrain's gross official reserves at the end of June 1984 amounted to BD 548 million, which was equivalent to about five months of total imports or nine months of non-oil imports. The country's external public debt amounted to BD 91 million at the end of 1983, or about 5 per cent of GDP. Most of the debt reflects loans from neighbouring countries extended on concessional terms; debt-service payments represented less than 1 per cent of export earnings in 1983.

Courtesy—IMF Survey.

Egypt:

Article 11

The Nation, December 28, 1985/January 4, 1986

■ EGYPT AFTER MALTA

Mubarak Walks a Shaky Tightrope

STANLEY REED

In the storm of recriminations in Egypt that followed the Achille Lauro fiasco, the provocative leftist weekly *Al Ahaly* asked a pertinent question: "Will the crime of hijacking the Egyptian plane be the calamity that puts us back on the right track, which we have forsaken for the last 15 years?" By that the paper meant, Will Egypt at last acknowledge the folly of maintaining close ties with the United States and take a more independent approach to resolving the Arab-Israeli dispute and reviving the economy? A break with the United States by the most powerful Arab

Stanley Reed is a writer who specializes on the Middle East.

state—the only one to have signed a peace treaty with Israel—would have almost as profound an impact on the region as the Iranian revolution had.

Officially the Egyptians say no change is in the offing. President Hosni Mubarak is trying to undo whatever damage his hot words about "piracy" might have caused him in Washington following the U.S. interception of the Egyptian airliner carrying the Achille Lauro hijackers. By granting U.S. "antiterrorist" specialists the privilege of playing an advisory role in the ill-fated storming of the hijacked Egyptair jet in Malta, he gratified his American patrons. (Maltese officials prevented the United States from direct participation.) Now he is allowing the joint U.S.-Egyptian military exercises planned for this month to go ahead, although the Arab press had reported that he intended to cancel them. He is also resuming talks with the Israelis on border disputes, which he had suspended to protest the October 1 bombing of Palestine Liberation Organization headquarters near Tunis.

No one should be fooled by Mubarak's attempts to pretend that all is well between Cairo and Washington and that even Egyptian-Israeli relations are not so bad. The displays of anti-American and anti-Israeli feeling in Egypt in the past two months have been more than isolated outbursts of emotion. The "normal" and "neighborly" relations with Israel prescribed in the 1979 peace treaty negotiated at Camp David have not materialized. As the Egyptian economy deteriorates and the peace process remains stalled, it is becoming increasingly difficult for Mubarak to justify the close relationship with the United States that was supposed to produce wondrous improvement on both fronts. To give just one example, in last year's parliamentary election the three main opposition parties took positions highly critical of the Camp David accords, and Mubarak's own National Democratic Party thought it the better part of valor to minimize the nation's ties with the United States and Israel. Its 8,000-word platform mentioned neither Camp David nor Anwar el-Sadat, the party's founder.

Many close observers of U.S.-Egyptian relations say that a confrontation like the one that occurred over how to dispose of the Achille Lauro hijackers was inevitable. Mohammed Hakki, a Washington-based consultant who served as press counselor at the Egyptian Embassy from 1975 to 1981 and as head of the State Information Service from 1981 to 1982, was in Cairo shortly after the incident and was able to compare the reactions of officials and journalists in both capitals. "It was like being on two completely different planets," he said. "There is a complete lack of proper communication between the two countries."

Poor communication was certainly a factor in the debacle. Political counselor Osama al-Baz, who is normally the best channel to Mubarak, was in Tunis at the time, so Cairo relied on Foreign Minister Esmat Abdel Megid, who proved an unsatisfactory conduit. The embassy does not have the easy access to this Egyptian president that it had to Sadat. That estrangement may be attributable in part to the abrasive personality of Ambassador Nicholas A. Veliotes, whose call for Egypt to "prosecute those sons of bitches" (overheard in a ship-to-shore telephone conversation with an aide) made him a hero in America but touched off demands for his recall in Cairo. Mubarak and his aides had recognized that Egypt was a low-priority concern in Washington after Jimmy Carter's defeat in 1980, but they had not anticipated that the Reagan Administration would consider the offended dignity of a friendly Arab country a small price to pay for the opportunity to bring terrorists to justice. In an interview with a local magazine, al-Baz termed the interception of the Egyptian plane by U.S. Navy jets "unimaginable on the part of any country, let alone one that we consider a friendly state with a principal role in the peace process." He should have known better.

Al-Baz, a graduate of Harvard Law School, has been Mubarak's political mentor since the late 1970s, and is the architect of a strategy that is likely to lead to further tension with Washington unless the Administration shows more flexibility than it did during the Achille Lauro incident. Acting on the assumption that Sadat was destroyed partly because he was too pro-American, al-Baz, with Mubarak's endorsement, is trying to restore at least the appearance of in-

dependence. "Egypt is not a part of NATO, not a part of the United States and not a part of the strategy of the West," he told me a year ago. "Egypt's purpose is to forge a strategy for the Arab world. That is why we cannot accept any military bases here in Egypt." He complained: "Some people in Washington [that is, Congress] want something tangible to show in return for U.S. aid. The fact that Egypt is a friend is not enough."

When Egypt's privileged position as the second-largest recipient of American aid, after Israel, is in question, however, the leadership plays a different tune. A few weeks after my conversation with al-Baz the State Department received a confidential document from Cairo describing Egypt as a major "strategic asset" of the United States. The communiqué, which was drawn up to support a request for a $995 million increase in U.S. economic and military assistance in 1986, cited the numerous times that Cairo had allowed U.S. forces to use Egyptian facilities to support operations elsewhere in the region, including Lebanon, the Sudan and Oman. While making the obligatory bows to nonalignment, "regional priorities" and full control over military bases, the document emphasized that "none of these problems will prevent steadily closer cooperation between Egypt and the U.S."

The Achille Lauro incident was only the most recent indication of the difficulties Egyptians face in staying in the good graces of the Reagan Administration and at the same time trying to regain acceptance in the Arab world. The American demand that Mubarak hand over the hijackers for trial forced the Egyptian leader to choose between placating the United States and breaking an agreement with the Palestinians. Predictably, he received little help from either side. Washington was unsympathetic, and Yasir Arafat, who Mubarak said had agreed to take custody of the gunmen in Tunis, suddenly became unavailable.

The decision to involve Arafat seems to have been an ill-conceived attempt to force him to act like a responsible international figure. Handing the hijackers over to the P.L.O. for trial and punishment, Mubarak explained, "would have proved to the whole world Arafat's commitment to his statements condemning terrorism." In late 1984 al-Baz apparently convinced Mubarak, who had previously avoided staking his prestige on diplomatic gambits, that Egypt could reconcile its American and Arab objectives only by leading an "Arab initiative" to lure the United States back into an active role in Middle East diplomacy. Egyptian efforts contributed greatly to an apparent breakthrough: the agreement in February between Arafat and King Hussein that the P.L.O. and Jordan would "move together toward . . . a peaceful and just settlement of the Middle East crisis . . . on the basis of . . . United Nations and Security Council resolutions." From the Egyptian point of view that statement came close enough to the long-sought recognition of Israel's right to exist to warrant Herculean American efforts to drag the Israelis to the bargaining table. Instead, the U.S. negotiators allowed themselves to be drawn into a bizarre wrangle over which Palestinians the Israelis would let them speak to in preliminary talks.

In the fall events took a turn that the Egyptians viewed with great alarm. President Reagan's endorsement—later changed to mild disapproval—of the Israeli raid on P.L.O. headquarters near Tunis indicated that the Israelis were winning the Administration over to their view that the P.L.O. is purely a terrorist organization and as such deserves no place in future peace negotiations. The harsh U.S. stance on the Achille Lauro incident was further evidence of this trend. "All the maneuvers of the United States indicate that it has agreed to this plan to exclude the P.L.O. from any coming settlement," said al-Baz in an interview published in Egypt on November 1, "and we consider this a dangerous mistake." The Egyptians believe there is no alternative to working with Arafat. Like others in the Arab world, they are exasperated with him and have doubts about whether he still has enough clout to sell an agreement to his people, but they see no credible challenger to his leadership.

The most revealing aspect of Egypt's reaction to the Achille Lauro affair received little attention in the United States. Although the P.L.O. chief's close associate Mohammed Abbas had planned the takeover of the Italian ship, the Egyptians invited Arafat to Cairo and gave him a hero's welcome in November. On previous occasions the government had tightly restricted Arafat's movements, but this time Mubarak permitted him to make a grand political tour, visiting the headquarters of the political parties, private homes, the Islamic University al-Azhar and even Pope Shenuda III, the Patriarch of the Coptic Christian Church. The government-controlled papers ran long interviews with Arafat. An *Al Ahram* headline, "Egypt's stand is necessary to resist the Israeli and American plot against the Palestinian people," sounded the main theme of the visit. Behind the scenes, however, Mubarak and al-Baz browbeat Arafat into pledging that future guerrilla operations would be confined to the "occupied territories."

In a telephone interview, Mohamed Sid-Ahmed, an Egyptian political analyst, drew two conclusions from the Egyptian regime's royal treatment of Arafat. First, he said, "Mubarak cannot afford to lose Arafat because he is his only window into the Arab world." Second, hosting Arafat was "a way to stand up to the Americans after the humiliation suffered at their hands." Mubarak was trying to tell the Americans, "You cannot hit me as you have and assure stability in Egypt. I cannot be ill treated in this way; I cannot afford to be identified only with the U.S. and Israel as Sadat was."

Sid-Ahmed does not think that Egypt is on the verge of a precipitous break with the United States and Israel analogous to Sadat's surprise expulsion of Soviet advisers in 1972. Al-Baz's presence makes such an impulsive action unlikely. "He is very good at keeping things from getting out of control," he said. Still, Sid-Ahmed considers the U.S.-sponsored peace treaty with Israel to be in growing peril. He rightly pinpoints the continued resistance to the development of normal and neighborly relations with Israel as

the chief cause of concern. The Egyptians are delighted to sell Israel about $400 million worth of oil each year, and they are keeping their embassy open in Tel Aviv. But they are discouraging nearly all other exchanges between the two countries. Israeli tourists visiting Egypt outnumber Egyptians going in the other direction by at least ten to one. There has been no Egyptian ambassador in Tel Aviv since 1982, when Mubarak withdrew his emissary to protest the Israeli invasion of Lebanon. Although the Israelis have sent their best and brightest Arabists to Cairo in hopes of establishing valuable contacts, the vast majority of the Cairo elite refused to mix with them.

An unpleasant expression of anti-Israeli sentiment occurred on October 5, just after the raid on Tunis, when a 24-year-old Egyptian border guard opened fire on a party of bathing suit–clad Israeli tourists who approached his position near a beach in Sinai. Seven were killed, including two women and four children. Mubarak sought to minimize the killings as "a small accident" that was the work of a man "who lost his mind," and *Al Ahaly* published an apparently scurrilous report that the tourists had provoked the young man by taunting him and spitting on an Egyptian flag. Another opposition paper, *Al Shaab*, reported that at his trial by military tribunal, from which the press was barred, the soldier told the court, "I don't care if you execute me to please America and Israel." To their credit the Israelis limited their response to this ugly incident to bitter complaints about the conduct of the local authorities, who, according to Israeli Health Minister Mordechai Gur, "did not take the minimum steps to treat casualties" and prevented Israeli medical personnel on hand from administering first aid. The Israelis also were careful not to hold Egypt responsible for the August attack in Cairo in which an employee of their embassy was killed and two others wounded by an unidentified gunman, who sprayed machine-gun fire through their car window. Sooner or later a similar incident could touch off a serious confrontation between the two countries.

The stunted growth of Egyptian-Israeli relations is worrisome because little binds the two countries together beyond the special relationship both have with the United States and the ever-present threat that Israel will reoccupy the Sinai. Egypt's ties to America are much more substantial than those to Israel, mostly because of the massive economic and military assistance programs that U.S. administrations have mounted in Egypt since the 1973 war. Egypt is scheduled to receive $1.3 billion in military aid and $1.29 billion in economic aid in 1986. Certainly the Egyptian leadership would be reluctant to provoke an aid cutoff, particularly at a time when its main sources of foreign exchange are drying up, but those programs no longer guarantee America enormous leverage over Egyptian policy. Egyptian attitudes toward the aid programs have changed radically since the death of Sadat, in 1981. They are no longer seen as a cornucopia of blessings but rather as small potatoes compared with what Israel receives and a sinister means of imposing American tutelage on Egypt.

Some of the strongest supporters of the American connection are senior military officers, who do not wish to see their main source of arms jeopardized. Defense Minister Abdel-Halim Abu Ghazala, a former military attaché in Washington, quickly came to the defense of the United States after the Achille Lauro incident and was sharply criticized in *Al Ahaly* for putting his ties to America ahead of the national interest. The leftist paper also reported that Abu Ghazala pushed Mubarak into the disastrous decision to storm the Egyptair jet in Malta, over the objections of al-Baz.

Egypt's loan repayments to the United States have become a special source of friction between the two countries. With foreign exchange earnings in decline, Egypt is hard pressed to service its $31.5 billion debt. Although all U.S. aid to Egypt is now in the form of grants, military procurement loans prior to 1984 carried interest rates as high as 15 percent. Principal and interest payments on these obligations in 1986 will be $557.3 million. Mubarak's repeated requests for relief have been spurned by Washington. The turndowns rankle for two reasons. First, the terms on Israel's debt are continually being eased; the latest rescheduling proposal could cost the U.S. treasury $531.7 million in 1986. Second, the opposition uses the debt issue to support its contention that Egypt is following a pro-Western foreign policy because of economic blackmail. On September 18, as Mubarak prepared to make his second pilgrimage of 1985 to Washington, *Al Ahaly* commented, "The West is exploiting Egypt's rising debts to step up the pressure so that Egypt does not withdraw from its assigned role in the Western strategic framework." To demonstrate his irritation with the United States, the Egyptian President has let the arrears on Egypt's military debt to the United States build up to more than $400 million.

The opposition would have less to complain about if the economy was still expanding at the 8 percent clip of the late 1970s, but even that high growth turns out to have been illusory. It was fueled almost entirely by revenues from oil exports, Suez Canal tolls, Egyptians working abroad, tourism and foreign aid, all of which were vulnerable to forces beyond Egypt's control, and which have either leveled off or gone into decline. Egypt benefited more from the Arab oil boom than most people realize, and it is feeling the effects of the bust more than some of the exporters in the Persian Gulf because it lacks their ample financial reserves. Lower oil prices have eroded petroleum export earnings from a peak of $2.8 billion in 1981 to $2.3 billion in 1984. The money sent home by the approximately 3 million Egyptians working abroad has also been affected, since Saudi Arabia, Libya, Kuwait and other employers of expatriate labor have slashed their spending and forced as many as 500,000 Egyptian workers home.

Mubarak must discover a way of closing an overall payments deficit that the I.M.F. projects at $1.3 billion for 1985. That will not be an easy task. Word of Egypt's problems is already beginning to affect its ability to borrow. For example, the British government's export finance agency has dropped Egypt's credit rating to the poorest-risk category.

In managing the domestic economy, the Egyptians play a game similar to the one they play in foreign affairs. Recent Egyptian governments have talked about self-sufficiency and independence, but in practice they have taken on as much debt and foreign aid as possible in order to avoid hard decisions. Sadat allowed imports to increase 20 percent annually during the fat years of the late 1970s, and in the four months prior to last year's parliamentary elections Mubarak permitted a 30 percent jump in food imports to put his constituents in a good mood. Egypt spends about $5 billion per year on subsidies that stimulate consumption and benefit the rich as well as the poor because the government has never bothered to limit distribution of subsidized items, such as 2 cent loaves of bread, to the neediest.

Now that the lean years are here Mubarak must deal with the consequences of past inaction. He has brought in his third Prime Minister in four years, Ali Lotfi, an economics professor, who is reputedly an austerity-minded budget cutter. The government is holding its first serious negotiations since 1978 with the International Monetary Fund, whose pressures for austerity are widely blamed for the riots that followed the increase in food prices in 1977. In hopes of securing a $1.5 billion loan, Lotfi is promising to cut the subsidies and provide more incentives for foreign investment. There is no reason to think that pain will be any easier to sell in 1985 than it was in 1977. Mubarak's standing is no better now than Sadat's was then, and in 1977 there were no opposition newspapers to tell the masses that they were being asked to make sacrifices for the benefit of the rich and Egypt's American creditors. On the popular black market, the Egyptian pound, always a good barometer of the nation's mood, has already given Mubarak a vote of no confidence by plunging to its all-time low against the dollar.

Mubarak enters what promises to be the most trying period of his presidency in poor shape. Although few doubt either his honesty or his good intentions, his handling of both the Achille Lauro and the Egyptair hijacking have revived the old questions about his leadership. More troubling, he has yet to carve out a constituency for himself. Those who thrived under Sadat mistrust him, while the Nasserites and other leftists will never accept him until he completely repudiates Sadat's policies. Even the military officers, who should be his most reliable supporters, are smarting from their bungling of the Malta raid and unproved charges that they leaked Mubarak's plans for the Achille Lauro gunmen to the Americans.

Barring economic and diplomatic miracles, Mubarak faces stepped-up pressure from the leftists, the liberals and the Islamic fundamentalists, who, although incapable of toppling him, are already making his job difficult. It is not hard to foresee a chaotic political atmosphere developing that might provoke an impulsive move by Mubarak or someone else. ☐

Article 12   *The Unesco Courier,* August 1984

Egypt's national film archive

by Khaled Osman

UNLIKE most developing countries, Egypt has a very old film heritage. The Lumière brothers organized film shows in cafés in Cairo and Alexandria as long ago as 1896, and shortly afterwards films began to be made in Egypt, at first by foreigners (mainly French, Italian and German film-makers) and then, from 1927 on, by Egyptians.

This heritage, almost a century old, is a mine of information for the film historian to whom it reveals traces of a conception of cinema which has to a large extent been inherited by modern Egyptian film-makers, and also for the general historian seeking to reconstitute a historical period.

In Egypt the problem of preserving films was for many years neglected by the authorities who did not appreciate the interest films could hold for future generations.

If many old films have been preserved or rediscovered in spite of the absence of provisions for mandatory deposit in the past, it is due to private initiatives which were praiseworthy but imperfect and necessarily incomplete.

A special role in the field of preservation was played by Misr Studios, which were founded in 1935 by the great Egyptian economic and industrial pioneer Talaat Harb. When the Studios were created, storage facilities were built for the preservation of both newsreel films (which began to be made on a regular basis in 1925) and feature films.

But such concern was extremely rare at that time, when films were considered

KHALED OSMAN, *of Egypt, is a graduate of the Ecole des Hautes Etudes Commerciales in Paris, and holds a law degree from the university of Paris. He is engaged on research into the Egyptian cinema.*

primarily as products for short-term use, as revealed in this anecdote. When the great actress Fatma Roshdi was about to release "Under the Sky of Egypt", her previous film "Catastrophe over the Pyramids" appeared, was panned by the critics and booed by the public. So as to maintain her status as a star by preventing the second film (which was in the same vein as the first) from being shown to the public, Fatma Roshdi, who was also the film's producer, simply decided to destroy *all* existing copies of it. Such losses are irreparable, and the only information we have about these vanished films is to be found in the many fascinating art magazines published at that time.

The initiative taken by Misr Studios was extremely laudable, and it was a heavy blow for Egypt when a fire caused by the negligence of a janitor ravaged part of the Studios in July 1950, notably affecting the archive premises.

A growing awareness of the problem of film preservation in the mid-1950s led to the creation of the Egyptian Film Archive by the Office of Arts. In the same year Egypt participated for the first time (as an observer) in the work of the International Federation of Film Archives (FIAF).

But the odds seemed to be stacked against the Egyptian Archive, for in August 1958 another fire, in this case caused by the spontaneous combustion of nitrate film, destroyed part of the collection which had been patiently assembled from gifts of Egyptian and foreign films and from films seized by the Customs.

After the fire the Archive continued to be supplied in this way, with the addition of a more important source in 1968 when the Ministry of Culture was persuaded to establish a mandatory deposit obligation.

The tide now began to turn, although some restrictive practices continued to exist. The 1968 decree was not backed up by sufficiently dissuasive sanctions; the authorities banked on the hope, which proved vain, that private producers would co-operate with them, following the example of the Egyptian General Cinema Organization, a public body. In 1971 the Organization ceased its production activities because of an enormous chronic deficit. However, a step forward had been taken the year before when Egypt joined FIAF.

But piecemeal measures were no longer tolerable; legislation was needed. Such legislation now exists in the shape of Law no. 35 of 1975, which requires producers and distributors jointly to deposit at the Film Archive (now known as the National Archives) a 35 mm copy made at their own expense of any film produced for public showing in Egypt or elsewhere.

Initial application problems have been overcome, and today the law has given the Archives a new lease of life; the practice of mandatory deposit is satisfactorily carried out since copies are subject to quality control.

Nevertheless, the situation is still fragile; certain producers and distributors would like, on grounds of lack of film, to replace the mandatory deposit requirement by payment of a guarantee.

But this is not of central importance. Today the path to be followed has been signposted, and the importance of the preservation of films is fully recognized. Directly or indirectly, Egypt's film heritage bears witness to the country's tormented history in this century, with its joy and pain, its defeats and victories, its fears and hopes. Fortunately, the major part of it has been saved. ∎

Middle East International, August 9, 1985

Letter from Alexandria

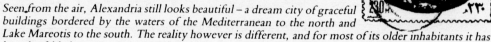

Seen from the air, Alexandria still looks beautiful – a dream city of graceful buildings bordered by the waters of the Mediterranean to the north and Lake Mareotis to the south. The reality however is different, and for most of its older inhabitants it has lost the fabled aura it once possessed. Only in memory does the old city live on as one of the great cosmopolitan centres of the region.

The poems of Cavafy, the observations of Forster and the novels of Durrell also speak of an Alexandria that no longer exists, and a glance at the visitors' book in the Cecil Hotel tells one of the comings and goings of those who contributed to its former distinction. Memory and nostalgia are very much part of the atmosphere of the modern city. Alexandria only yields up its secrets grudgingly, and echoes of the recent and historic past seldom intrude on the present. A few scattered ruins and some faded names on crumbling buildings are all that a casual observer might notice.

Younger Alexandrians shrug off such romantic references to a vanished age, an age in which aristocratic and foreign influences predominated, and in which they and their forbears played only an insignificant role. Alexandria now belongs to its own people who live in the frenetic present. On the narrow strip of land between lake and sea the city threads its way from west to east. Into this thin ribbon of congestion are crowded nearly three million people. From five in the morning till midnight its main arteries roar with the din of never ceasing traffic conveying a populace which seems forever on the move from one end of the city to the other. From the modern port in the west which handles 90 per cent of Egypt's trade, through to the city centre and commercial district, and eastwards to the resorts of Montazah and Mamoura, all is movement.

The outlines and layout of the old streets, squares and gardens still exist. The facades of many buildings are unchanged. But the beauty has faded, the sense of quiet order gone. Roads and pavements which were once washed daily are now neglected. Suburbs like Roushdi which once housed elegant villas surrounded by trees and open spaces have now been invaded by rows of tower blocks. For the rest, Alexandria has become infected by all the ills of the late 20th century – pollution, overcrowding and overstretched municipal services. Yet some of the old magic lingers. Public gardens with their bougainvileas, oleanders and flame trees still offer a measure of tranquillity. Pavement cafes like Pastroudis, patisseries like the Trianon and open air news-stands selling international newspapers and periodicals give the city a cosmopolitan feel.

For the inquisitive traveller Alexandria has much of interest. The Museum of Antiquities tells of the city's early history. The catacombs of Kom al-Shugafa are unique in their fusing of Greco-Roman and Egyptian decorative styles. The colourful old quarter of Anfushi and the mosque of Abu'l Abbas al-Mursi breathe of traditional Islam. A short drive away in the western desert lie the ruins of an ancient Christian city and a temple dedicated to Osiris. Nelson's island, which marks the site of the battle of the Nile in 1798, can be reached by boat from Aboukir, a fishing village east of Alexandria. A few miles further on is the little town of Rashid (Rosetta), where in 1799, Napoleon's soldiers found the famous trilingual inscription which led to the decipherment of the language of ancient Egypt. For visitors who are patient and persistent there is much to see and learn.

The summer holiday season is now at its height. This climax to the Alexandrian year sees nearly two million Cairenes and others pour into the city to escape the deadening heat of the capital and the south. Already strained facilities are stretched to breaking point. The visitors congregate mostly in the cafes and restaurants along the Corniche and on the miles of beaches, bright with umbrellas, below it. The Corniche, a six-lane highway, begins alongside the magnificent bay of the eastern harbour, a haven for yachts and fishing boats. Once dominated by the ancient Pharos, it is today overlooked by the 15th century fort of Qait Bey. From here the road follows the coastline eastwards in a series of majestic bends to the former palace and estate of ex-King Farouk at Montazah, now an attractive public park. It provides the main thoroughfare for Alexandria's holiday traffic.

Alexandrians and their visitors delight in life out of doors after dark, and the city's cafes, restaurants, shops, night clubs and markets stay open long after midnight. The seafront, public gardens, squares and bazaars are ablaze with light. People of all ages, in groups large or small, in traditional or modern dress, stroll in the cooling sea breezes. Some take rides in horse-drawn cabs. Some browse in shops or stalls. Others while away long hours in cafes gossiping and playing backgammon or chess. The noise and bustle continue into the early hours after which there is a brief respite. But before long the first trams and buses, crammed with workers, begin clanking and wheezing along the streets. Life goes on and people go about their daily work. Alexandria today might have lost some of its former glory but it is nevertheless a vibrant and lively city with a vital role to play in the life of Egypt and its people.

Geoffrey Bowder

Iran:

Article 14

TIME, AUGUST 26, 1985

War and Hardship in a Stern Land

A rigid theocracy harbors fanaticism and little hope for change

Banner headlines in Iraqi newspapers last Friday proclaimed WE DESTROYED KHARG ISLAND. The papers reported a "massive blitz" by Iraqi planes against the terminal, one of the world's largest, through which flow 90% of Iran's crude-oil exports of 1.6 million bbl. a day. If indeed Iraq had destroyed the terminal, it would have been a turning point in the five-year-old gulf war. By late last week, however, oil-industry experts concluded that although Iraqi jets had managed to penetrate the heavily defended southeastern, landward side of the complex known as "T terminal," the strike would not seriously disrupt the oil exports on which Iran's economy relies. Correspondent John Borrell recently spent nine days in Iran and came away with, among other impressions, the belief that Iran, under the rule of its Shi'ite Muslim theocracy, has not weakened in its resolve to carry on the war. His report on life in Iran today:

The Gohari family reunions take place in the Behesht-e Zahra Cemetery at the edge of the dusty Veramin plain on the outskirts of Tehran. Hussein Gohari, 14, squats next to the graves where his father Essa and his brothers Hassan and Ali lie, all killed in the conflict with Iraq. His mother, like many of the other widows at the cemetery, carefully washes her husband's gravestone, then sits with one hand on it in prayer. "We come every Friday," says Hussein. Soon his mother may be left alone to tend the graves. Hussein is ready, eager even, to join the war. "My mother doesn't want to lose me," he says, gazing steadyeyed at the sobbing woman. "But yes, I will go because I hate [Iraqi President] Saddam Hussein and I want to avenge the deaths of my brothers and father."

This gathering of the living and the dead and the vows of vengeance have become a weekly ritual for Iranian families since the conflict with neighboring Iraq began to reap its harvest of victims, estimated at between 100,000 and 200,000. The graves at Behesht-e Zahra are tightly packed, sometimes no more than 6 in. apart, and they are advancing rapidly in tree-lined squares toward the perimeter of the 1.5-sq.-mi. cemetery. Aluminum-and-glass display cases contain photographs of the dead, many of them teenagers, along with family heirlooms. Most also bear a picture of the Ayatullah Ruhollah Khomeini, the octogenarian who guides Iran's side of the bloody campaign, as he does every other facet of life in Iran.

When Iraq launched its first air raids on Tehran three months ago, thousands of people fled to the surrounding countryside every night. But despite the continuing threat of high-level bombing runs, there is little about the city to suggest that it is the capital of a country at war. Streetlights are turned off at night but restaurants are crowded, and even when air-raid warnings whine from radios, it seems that no one bothers to seek cover.

The war is only one hardship that presses in on Iranians. It is an irony of the Ayatullah's revolution that six years after the Shah's ouster, the average Iranian is no better off materially. And it would appear that the country has swapped one set of constraints on personal freedom for another. There is still abundant evidence of overcrowding and wretchedness. Two pounds of meat that cost just over a dollar in 1978 now costs $12 on the open market. Medical services have deteriorated, foreign travel is difficult.

But perhaps the greatest irony of all is that despite these harsh realities, Khomeini remains a revered, inspirational figure for Iran's masses. There are rumblings of discontent, but there seems no serious challenge to his conservative Shi'ite theocracy. There is little question either that the Islamic Republic will survive, if not flourish, after his death. The explanation lies in the application of a skillful mix of repression, which is being eased somewhat as the regime gains confidence, and the presenting of Islam as a unifying and controlling element in what remains a loose and still evolving political structure. "People may well be poorer than they were under the Shah," says a Western ambassador in Tehran. "But they feel they have won self-respect. That is very important psychologically. As long as the oil flows, the regime is secure."

The Imam, as Khomeini is now called, towers over Iran with all the power and prestige of Darius, one of the most famous of the pre-Islamic Persian kings. Khomeini's image is everywhere, painted in oils and hung in heavy frames in hotel lobbies and government buildings and vacant lots, and festooned in glossy photographs over thousands of martyrs' graves. Even his sayings are etched in brass and copper and hung in frames or daubed in paint on the sides of buildings. WHOEVER FIGHTS AGAINST THE TRUTH SHALL BE DEFEATED is one such framed homily, hanging in the baggage hall at Tehran's airport. A short distance away, a blunter sign, painted on the side of a hangar, reads DEATH TO AMERICA.

Although he is 85, Khomeini still regularly receives visitors at his modest but heavily guarded villa in the capital's northern suburbs. Even dignitaries must follow the procedure of removing shoes and sitting cross-legged in his presence. And while the twelve-man guardian council is constitutionally the state's supreme decision-making body, the Imam is without question the ultimate authority on everything from religious doctrine to the conduct of the war against Iraq. "He is more powerful than the Shah ever was," says an East bloc diplomat. "He sits very close to God in the eyes of most people."

But not, perhaps, in those of middle class Iranians, who have not been cowed or shorn of their natural bellicosity and are thus still suspect to many of the regime's leaders. They voice their criticism of the regime relatively freely, if privately. They crack jokes about the clergy, often at the expense of Ayatullah Hussein Ali Montazeri, Khomeini's heir apparent, who is regarded as pious but simple. "The clerics are making a mess of the economy," says a businessman who complains bitterly about the shortage of foreign exchange. "They should stick to preaching and let us run the economy."

There is a shortage of consumer goods as a result of strict import quotas, made necessary by declining oil revenues. Many factories are running at 40% or less of capacity because of a shortage of imported raw materials. Oil revenues are likely to be as low as $12 billion this year, down from $21 billion in 1983. But there is a flourishing black market that enables boutiques on Tehran's fashionable Vali-Asr Avenue to sell designer jeans for $120 a pair. Whisky can be found for $100 a bottle, despite the regime's strict ban on the use of alcohol.

In private homes, middle-class families watch American movies on smuggled videocassettes: *Rambo—First Blood Part*

II is currently doing the rounds of Tehran's northern suburbs. Affluent Iranians eat at American-style fast-food restaurants, and despite the difficulties of getting an exit visa, even for an official fee of $500, many still vacation abroad. Says one Western diplomat in Tehran who has served in two East European capitals: "Things are a lot more open here than Eastern Europe."

Yet while the middle class is able to sidestep some of the regime's strictures in the privacy of their homes, the 150,000-strong Revolutionary Guard still enforces a strict public acceptance of dress regulations, particularly for women. All women, Iranians and foreigners alike, have to dress in Islamic fashion, which means either a dark, tentlike chador, or at least a long smock over a modest dress or trousers, with the head covered by a scarf. Even at holiday resorts on the Caspian Sea, where women once swam in bikinis, the rules are rigidly applied, and women are required to cover themselves from head to toe while swimming.

The activities of the Revolutionary Guards and neighborhood Islamic committees as sentinels of the new morality have been curtailed somewhat, and Khomeini has personally forbidden arbitrary searches of private homes. Even so, these watchdogs have considerable power. On one recent evening on the promenade at Bandar Anzali, a popular weekend getaway for Tehranis, five guards, three of them veiled women, drove in a Nissan van through the strolling crowds. A woman was stopped and told to roll down her three-quarter-length sleeves. Another was admonished for allowing a lock of hair to escape from under her scarf. Sometimes female guards carry cotton and cleansing cream and insist on helping transgressors remove their makeup.

The regime likes to blame much of what it regards as decadent behavior on Western influence, particularly that of the U.S. And there is no more powerful symbol of Iran's rigid stance before the outside world than the 25-acre American embassy compound at Ayatullah Talagani Street. Today it is in the hands of the Revolutionary Guards, its walls still daubed with the students' anti-American slogans.

Recent disclosures of Iranian efforts to make clandestine purchases of American weaponry and spare parts demonstrate that Iran's condemnation of the U.S. does not prevent it from coveting American technology. These covert attempts to secure what Iran's bellicose anti-Western policies prevent it from obtaining openly suggest one of the Islamic Republic's long-term weaknesses. Unlike the Shah, who tried to open up Iran to the West and turn it into an industrial power, Khomeini has turned the country back on itself. Science and technology are neither condemned nor encouraged. Admissions to the University of Tehran are down—partly the result of political vetting, which weeds out many of the best students—while admissions to theological colleges are up.

"Iran can buy its way out of the trouble its policies create for as long as the oil lasts," says one Western diplomat. "So perhaps Iran could survive religious medievalism for another 40 years." After that, and perhaps even long before, there seems little doubt that Iran will be forced to come to terms with the West, probably even with America itself. ∎

Article 15

The Christian Science Monitor, August 6, 1985

In Iran, the Stamp of Islam

Special to The Christian Science Monitor

Tehran, Iran

Islam is the operative word in today's Iran.

Since the Islamic revolution in 1979, even the national Iranian dish, *chelo kebab* (rice with meat) is now advertised by restaurants as *chelo kebab Islami.*

The country is now known as the Islamic Republic of Iran. The old imperial crest has been converted to a symbol that reads in Arabic as both "Allah" and "There is no God but Allah," the Muslim confession of faith.

Islam has pervaded all aspects of Iranians' lives.

People wear Islamic dress, watch Islamic TV shows, get an Islamic education at school, are policed by Islamic Revolutionary Guards (paramilitary religious police), give their children Islamic names instead of traditional Persian ones, and even drink "Islamic beer," which has no alcohol.

Mosques are being built in neighborhoods where previously there were none. In city centers where statues of the Shah once stood, new monuments are being built to look like Al Aqsa mosque in Jerusalem, the third-holiest Muslim shrine after Mecca and Medina. Muslims originally faced Al Aqsa rather than Mecca when they prayed. The need to recapture this mosque—as well as Jerusalem, or Qods, as it is referred to by the Islamic Republic and other Arabs—is a major theme of the government.

Iranians are constantly reminded by posters and in the news media that after Karbala (a major Shiite pilgrimage town in Iraq) is regained by victory in the war against Iraq, the Iranian Army can then sweep on to liberate Qods. The government has declared an annual holiday called "Qods Day" to increase awareness of the issue.

Much of the structure of today's Iranian government is based on Ayatollah Ruhollah Khomeini's book "Islamic Government," written in 1971 while he was in exile. In it he says the first principle of Islamic government is that no one but God has the right to govern anyone.

However, he interprets the Koranic quotation, "Obey God, His prophet, and those who are in authority among you" to mean that Islamic jurisprudents, called mujtahids, should rule in God's place.

Iran is ruled by high-ranking religious scholars. The Constitution gives supreme authority to a religious leader and Ayatollah Khomeini is entitled to hold this position for the rest of his life.

Hojatolislam Ali Khamenei is President, Hojatolislam Hashemi Rafsanjani is the speaker of parliament, and Ayatollah Mussavi Ardebili is the chief justice.

("Hojatolislam" and "ayatollah" are the two main ranks of mujtahid.)

The ulema, or Islamic scholars, fill many other important positions in the Iranian government. At the local level, the imam jomehs, leaders of Friday prayers in towns and cities, have the most power. They have generally been appointed as Khomeini's personal representatives.

The ulema have become somewhat of a privileged class in Iran. "Before the Revolution, there used to be so many clerics walking in the streets—but now they drive around in cars," one housewife remarks. Most clerics in high

positions are accompanied by large escorts of armed Revolutionary Guards.

Islamic law is the law of the land. A prominent sign in a hotel tea room reads, "Women without their *hijab* [head covering] arranged properly will be sentenced to 74 beatings with a stick."

How strictly these laws are enforced is difficult to estimate. Around the corner from where I was staying in Tehran, one woman was reportedly given 100 lashes for adultery. But my host, a European who had lived in Iran since the revolution, said it was the first time he had heard of such a happening. He felt many of the horror stories circulating in the West about harsh punishments for infringements of Islamic law are exaggerated.

The educational system has also been infused with Islam. Many academics and professors fled Iran at the time of the revolution, and clerics have taken their places. Religious scholars now constitute the majority of university admissions committees, and one-sixth of the questions on the entrance examination are now on Islam, a freshman at Tehran University said.

The student said the questions cover subjects ranging from Islamic philosophy ("Describe how God has justice in the world") to details of prayer procedure ("If you realize part way through that you forgot a step, should you continue or start again?"). Once enrolled at university, students must take several courses in Islamic studies, he said.

Iranians react differently to the pervasive influence of Islam in their lives.

"We are a people with a deep spiritual sense. The revolution started because we felt we had lost our spiritual core to Western consumerism," one Shiite, a teacher of English, explained. "Now it has been restored. Look at the hundreds of thousands of people that have thronged to Friday prayers every week since the revolution."

But a young Kurdish woman disagreed.

"I am sick of Islam. All we hear is Islamic this, Islamic that. I'm about ready to convert to Zoroastrianism," she said. "All they [Zoroastrians] ask is that you have good thoughts, good words, and good deeds—who can argue with that?"

Iran's Islamic system has a strong attraction for some foreign Shiites.

"I've been to most of the Muslim countries, and I just came back from Mecca, but Iran is the most Islamic place in the world," says a Lebanese woman visiting the shrine of Imam Reza in Mashhad. "It's like a dream, it's so spiritual here. Look at how these people give everything for the war against Iraq: themselves, their money, their jewelry."

Her daughter adds: "People have been so kind to us. The shopkeeper did not want to let me pay for my *chador* when he heard I was from Lebanon. He said I was his Muslim sister."

The Islamization of Iranian society does not appear to have resulted in the persecution of the country's religious minorities, with the exception of the Bahais, who are regarded as heretics for recognizing another prophet after Muhammad.

But Christians, Zoroastrians, and Jews, all considered "People of the Book" (monotheists with a revealed scripture) have largely been left alone. Since many of them are businessmen, professionals, or involved in other independent occupations, they have generally not been adversely affected by the priority given to Shiites for government jobs. The biggest problem voiced was the closing of the Armenian schools for two years. The government allowed them to reopen last fall.

"We all celebrated when we heard the good news," said one Armenian man. "It was quite a worry for us, since there was no way for our children to study the Armenian language. The only other major change is the *chador*. It's not that much of a problem for our women; after all, the Virgin Mary wore a veil, so they figure they can, too."

The freedom of worship of the protected minority religions is relatively unhampered.

Explains an Anglican priest: "I still conduct services every Sunday in my church, and the government allows me to operate my Christian bookshop. After all, Islam honors Christ as a great prophet. Nonetheless, we try to keep somewhat of a low profile."

The sacred fire has not stopped burning for 2,000 years at the main fire temple in Kerman, with the exception of a few days during the Arab invasion which converted Iran from Zoroastrianism to Islam in the 7th century. Here, and at Yazd, the two remaining Zoroastrian centers in Iran, the ancient practices are followed without restriction despite the resurgence of Islamic fervor since the 1979 revolution.

Some do's and don'ts in the Islamic Republic

Since Iran's revolution in 1979, the regime has instituted sweeping changes to make Iranian society more Islamic. Some areas that are regulated in accordance with Ayatollah Khomeini's teachings:

• **Sports.** Participatory sports are discouraged and there are few spectator sports. According to the head of the Physical Education Department, sports are not needed in the Islamic Republic, especially for women who get enough exercise running a household. Swimming, recommended by Ayatollah Khomeini, is allowed as long as men and women are separated and the women wear a special "swimming *chador*." A rare weightlifting competition on TV opened with a prayer by a turbaned cleric and was performed under a large picture of Ayatollah Khomeini.

• **Alcohol.** Consumption is forbidden by the Koran.

• **Friday, the Islamic holy day.** All businesses are shut, in marked contrast to the Shah's time, when even on Fridays bazaars and cinemas were open.

• **Undergraduate study abroad.** High school graduates may no longer to to foreign countries for college. It is considered that the Western cultural influence they bring back harms the country. Graduate students may still go overseas, but Iran is planning to expand the capacity of universities so that this will not be necessary, said a regime official.

• **Travel abroad.** A previous ban on taking more than one overseas trip per year was lifted this year, but Iranians are still allowed to take only $500 out of the country. They are also not allowed to take Persian carpets out of Iran.

• **Western publications.** Those showing unveiled women are forbidden. No fashion magazines are allowed

into the country, and magazines like Time and Newsweek are usually for sale only on the black market or in censored versions. The Economist, a British newsmagazine, is found in some bookstores.

• **Music.** Western music is frowned upon, though classical music is sometimes heard. Most acceptable are Koranic recitations or lively revolutionary songs urging patriots to go to the warfront as their religious duty.

• **Cosmetics.** Makeup is prohibited, including perfume. Long fingernails are frowned upon; they are considered unsanitary for eating with the hands. At least one young woman was given an unwelcome manicure by a vigilant Revolutionary Guard.

• **Clothing.** Women must wear either a *chador* (the head-to-toe veil), usually in black or a small paisley print, or a manteau (a loose smock worn over pants, from the French word for coat) with a scarf on the head. Usually the manteau outfit is blue or some other dark color. Some women try to add a little spice with gold-threaded or designer scarves and high heels. An occasional nonconformist might appear in orange or yellow. Women must wear socks and cover their arms above the wrist.

Men cannot wear short sleeves or T-shirts and should button the tops of their shirts. Ties, regarded as a Western accouterment, are strongly discouraged in government offices. Government officials set the style with suit jackets over shirts buttoned at the collar.

So popular as to be a virtual uniform for young men are green Army jackets, giving a revolutionary mystique, particularly when worn with a beard. The Revolutionary Guards wear these jackets in a brighter green color.

Iraq:

Article 16   *The Christian Science Monitor*, November 21, 1985

Iraqis insulated from economic, but not human, costs in Gulf war

By Mary Curtius
Special to The Christian Science Monitor

Baghdad, Iraq

The most chilling reminders of Iraq's five-year-old war with Iran are the somber black flags dotting the rooftops of homes in almost every neighborhood of this capital. Each flag commemorates a father, son, or brother, who has died in battle.

Western analysts estimate that as many as 300,000 Iraqis may have died in this war. There is no confirmation of that figure from the Iraqis, who consider even weather reports top secret information. What officials do not deny, however, is that in this nation of 14 million, the war has left few families untouched.

The ruling Baathist regime has effectively insulated a large part of the population from the economic cost of the war — by using up Iraq's prewar foreign currency reserves to finance large-scale development projects during the first three years of fighting.

But there is no insulation from the staggering number of casualties.

Iraqi officials agree that their nation, with a population one-third that of Iran, can't afford a continued war of attrition. They say that Iraq's 40 air strikes since mid-August against Iran's Kharg Island oil terminals, renewed strikes on oil tankers in the Gulf, and bombing raids on Iranian industrial plants, are all evidence of Iraq's determination to increase military pressure on Iran.

"He [Iran's Ayatollah Ruhollah Khomeini] wants to dominate the world," says Naim Haddad, a member of the Revolutionary Command Council. The council func-

Iraqi soldiers at front are now fighting 'defensive war'

tions as executive and legislative authority in Iraq.

Iraq, Mr. Haddad says, had held back in its military effort to see if Iran would respond to numerous third-party efforts to start negotiations. Now, however, "we will continue hitting them and to destroy their economy and their military machine until their minds will be awakened," Haddad says. "Khomeini is a political man, not a religious man. When he finds he cannot achieve his aim, when he finds the bullets return to him, he will change his mind. Increasingly, the destruction will change his mind."

But Western analysts say that Iraq has threatened before that it was going to step up its attacks, then has failed to follow through.

"No military analyst can understand Iraq's strategy," says one Western diplomat. "Either the military is incompetent, or the decisions are being made for political reasons."

Western analysts worry, the diplomat says, about the tenacity of the Iranians in their pursuit of the war on the ground. "There's too much complacency about this war. The Iranians haven't quit. Every time, after another Iranian assault, when the dust has settled you find them [the Iranians] controlling a little more territory [in Iraq]," said the diplomat.

The Iranians now control an estimated 2,500 square miles of Iraqi territory in the southern marshes and northern mountains. This week, Iraqi military sources accused Iran of preparing another massive ground assault because the Iranians have resumed shelling Iraqi cities.

The Iraqi response is to fight what Western military

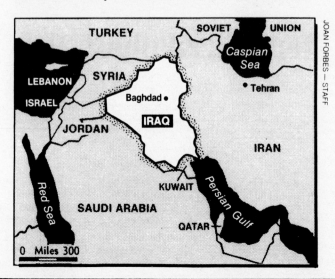

analysts describe as a "very conservative, defensive war" and to continue appealing to the Arabs, the West, and the Soviet Union to push Iran toward a negotiating table.

"All the Iraqis can hope for [now] is to defend their territory, their regime, and their system," one diplomat says. "It is no longer a question of winning, it's a question of not losing."

For the ruling Baath Party and Iraqi President Saddam Hussein, the Iranian threat is twofold: it challenges the territorial sovereignty of Iraq and the very existence of the Baath, which as a radical, pan-Arabist secular regime is antithetical to Khomeini's brand of Muslim fundamentalism.

Khomeini's demands as preconditions for peace have remained constant — that Iraq must admit it started the war, that it must pay billions in reparations and that President Hussein must be overthrown.

The Iraqis insist that by focusing on Hussein, Khomeini actually has strengthened the President and helped the party to foster a sense of nationhood in a country that traditionally has been torn by ethnic and religious divisions.

"The effects of the war have been positive and negative," said Sad'un Hammadi, another member of the Revolutionary Command Council and former Iraqi Foreign Minister. "We have lost human life and resources. But the country also has been vitalized, the people have been united. Our patriotic and nationalist feelings have been intensified."

The regime continues to create symbols of nationalism — ranging from the building of several war monuments and museums to the constant public statements by Iraqi officials that Iraq, an Arab nation, has for centuries suffered from the non-Arab, Persian "aggresion" of its eastern neighbor.

About 12 miles south of Baghdad lies a three-story modernistic brick building that houses a gigantic mural depicting the first Qadisiyah battle. It is a regular stopping place for busloads of Iraqi schoolchildren and officials guiding visiting diplomats.

The first Qadisiyah battle took place in Iraq during the seventh century. It marked the Arab defeat of the Persian Sassanid empire and the establishment of Baghdad as the seat of Islam for the next 500 years. The war with Iran now is frequently referred to by Iraqis as the"second Qadisiyah," or "Saddam"s Qadisiyah."

The symbols and the appeal to Iraqi nationalism have been bolstered by the government's pragmatic payments to the families of slain soldiers. Each family receives cash, a new car, and an apartment.

Despite the rhetoric of the regime that the war has its positive points, Iraqi officials interviewed last week universally insisted that they will not tolerate the stalemate much longer. "We will not let the war drag on," insisted Dr. Hammadi."On the ground, there is stalemate, yes. But in the air and on the sea it is active."

Article 17   *The Christian Science Monitor*, March 21, 1983

Modern-day Babylonians still looking to the sun and stars for progress

Iraq grapples with sandy solar collectors

By Richard Wilson
Special to The Christian Science Monitor

Baghdad, Iraq

Astronomy, the oldest branch of science, originated with the Babylonians in Mesopotamia, between the Tigris and Euphrates rivers, where Iraq now lies.

Today, like modern-day Babylonians, the Iraqis are looking to the sun (for energy) and the stars (through giant telescopes).

Iraq, like many developing countries, has been fascinated by solar energy. One experimental solar house here is heated and cooled by the sun's rays of energy. It is a guest house for distinguished visitors (and serves excellent food) but there is a problem with the solar collectors,one that is not present in most Western countries.

The ever-present sand in Iraq covers the collectors. For solar heating this is unimportant because the system will still operate. But for solar cooling it reduces the crucial temperature difference between the high temperature of the collector and the low temperature of an evaporative cooling tower —reducing the efficiency drastically.

Removing the sand in a cheap and simple way is a major research topic for the Iraqis, but it will be of importance to all countries in desert regions.

A day's drive from Baghdad is the National Astronomical Observatory, where two large optical telescopes and one radio telescope are being constructed. As

Iraq's new eye on the universe, they are located on 6,400-foot-high Mt. Konek near Arbil, in the Kurdish region of Iraq. Dr. May Kaftan-Kassim, who worked at Harvard University in the 1950s, is project manager. He is sure that the Kurdish rebels will not disturb the operation of the observatory.

In the last 10 years, the new wealth that has accompanied the increased price of oil has stimulated the Iraqis to think about encouraging science.

The observatory is one way of capturing an ancient tradition. The Babylonians were the first to name the 12 constellations in the zodiac, and the spiral minaret at Samarra was built as an astronomical observatory. The Abbasid Caliph Haroun ar-Rashid (AD 787-809) brought to his court at Baghdad scientists and medical men from all over the civilized world. And the astronomer Abbattani, in 929, determined the length of the year to be 365 days, 5 hours, 46 minutes, and 24 seconds with the remarkably small error of 2½ minutes.

In the intervening thousand years, the scientific tradition lapsed and the pursuit of science passed to the West. Under the Ottoman Empire Iraq was neglected. The fruits of technology were imported and science ignored. For example, the Iraqi national railway, with its main line linking Turkey to Baghdad and Basra, was built by Germans.

There were false starts. At the time of the revolution of July 14, 1958, when Col. Abdul-Karim Qasim overthrew and killed King Faisal II and his advisers, there was an important Jesuit college in Baghdad. This had trained many of the country's leaders—both Muslims and Christians. The college was nationalized and incorporated into the University of Baghdad. Standards immediately fell, and many Iraqis regret its passing.

A major effort is being made to increase the quantity and quality of higher education. There are eight universities.

Before 1968, when Ahmad al-Bakr and Saddam Hussein took power in the name of the Ba'ath party, there was some communication with the USSR. This has been largely broken, and Iraq plans to send its best students to the West to do graduate work.

It is also unclear what effects the repressive government has on the activities of scientists. The scientists I talked with would like cooperaton with other countries, but they complain there is not enough freedom of movement—even to other Arab states.

Research is concentrated in the Scientific Research Council. One of the largest sections of the council's laboratories in Baghdad concentrates on work connected with the oil industry.

Dr. Wilson is chairman of the physics department at Harvard University. He has been an adviser to the Iraqi government on its nuclear power program.

Israel:

Article 18

World Press Review, September 1985

Israel at a Crossroads
Polarization, economic crisis, and a restive West Bank

XAN SMILEY

Those who doubt Israel's ability to survive have been finding supporting evidence recently. The 1982 invasion of Lebanon has damaged Israel's diplomatic standing. More recently its army has looked vulnerable at the hands of Shiite Moslem guerrillas in south Lebanon. An exhausting polarization threatens the country.

The economy has become so unstable that many hardnosed businessmen doubt that it ever will recover. One day, many Israelis fear, the Americans may tire of picking up the bills, sending guns, and incurring the displeasure of the oil-rich Arabs.

Inflation last September reached an annual rate exceeding 1,000 per cent; the country's per-capita foreign debt is the highest in the world — about $6,200 per person; over the past three years annual economic growth has

This report is excerpted from the newsmagazine "The Economist" of London.

Jerusalem—"trying to redefine Zionism."

William Karel/Sygma

slumped to as low as 1.1 per cent; unemployment is expected to reach 10 per cent by year end; immigration has slowed almost to a halt; and some reports suggest that 30,000 Israelis —

nearly 1 per cent of the Jewish population — may leave this year.

The possibility of a Moslem fundamentalist regime in Cairo, a Syrian-blessed one in Amman, or even an Iranian victory in the Persian Gulf war sends shivers down the sturdiest Israeli spine. Militarily Israel remains the most powerful country in the Middle East. Yet, with today's coalition cabinet sharply divided between hawks and doves, it cannot decide whether it is worth trying to convince neighbors — and itself — that peace is possible between Arab and Jew.

Against this backdrop Israelis are

> "Israel now gets 17 per cent of all American overseas aid."

trying to redefine Zionism. In 1948 when the state was born, most settlers were the heirs of Theodor Herzl and Chaim Weizmann, the founders of modern Zionism. Their party was the Labor Party. For eighteen years David Ben-Gurion, Weizmann's chief lieutenant, ran it — and Israel.

A more militant brand of Zionism came into its own when Menachem Begin, head of a bloc of right-wing parties known as the Likud, was elected to power in 1977 and again in 1981. In 1983 Prime Minister Begin suddenly resigned, leaving Yitzhak Shamir briefly as prime minister.

Last year the old caught up with the new — but failed to overthrow it. After a drawn election, Labor's Shimon Peres managed to grasp the premiership, but only on condition that his party would rule in coalition with Shamir's.

The mainstream Zionists, led by Weizmann, believed in a secular, Socialist, egalitarian state. The manner of its acquisition would be based mainly on compromise with the British, who had taken Palestine from the Ottoman Turks at the end of World War I. There was no doubt in the minds of most early Zionists that Jewish interests would have to prevail over local Arab ones.

Another strand of Zionist thought is the religious one. Though it has been getting stronger, it remains a minority strand — and a tangled one, because many religious Jews are anti-Zionist. That has not prevented some of them, with semantic acrobatics, from sitting in the Knesset, Israel's Parliament, or accepting ministerial portfolios.

Israel's political center has proven increasingly barren. In last year's election, Likud's support shrank 5 per cent while Labor's dipped nearly 2 per cent. The left half of the electorate hardly gained at all. Much of Likud's loss was a gain to parties even farther to the right, including that of the virulent Rabbi Meir Kahane, whose avowed aim is to expel all Arabs from territories under Israel's control.

It is doubtful whether Prime Minister Peres can bring many voters back into the Labor fold, because Labor has the stamp of the past on it. Peres admits that his party is now "social-democratic" rather than Socialist. That may not offend the bulk of Israel's educated voters, who are moving away from the pioneering egalitarian ideals.

Israelis still take for granted the welfare state system on which the post-Hitler state of Israel was founded. Basic food is heavily subsidized, along with public transport and public housing. The Utopian idealism of the kibbutz — the communal rural settlement that once was the sparkling symbol of Zionism — has faded. Only 3 per cent of Israelis now live in the country's 277 kibbutzim, where farming and other enterprises are conducted communally, and a larger number in the moshavim, where organization is communal but land is owned individually.

Because the kibbutzniks were touted for so long as Israel's heroic elite, the average underprivileged Sephardic Israeli tends to view them as Ashkenazic snobs. Except for the Palestinian question, the most contentious problem in Israel is the socioeconomic gap between Israeli Jews of European origin — the Ashkenazim — and those from Afro-Asia — the Sephardim (literally "Spanish," because many North African Jews had been expelled from Spain in the Middle Ages, but now taken to mean all non-European Jews).

In the 1984 election some 80 per cent of Likud's support came from the Sephardim. The history of Labor's decline is underlined by the Ashkenazic-Sephardic culture clash. When the huge waves of immigration from Morocco and Iraq occurred in the 1950s and 1960s, the newcomers formed an underlayer of Israeli society, and until 1967 — when cheap Arab labor became available — they performed nearly all the dirty jobs.

Sephardic political attitudes differ sharply from those of the early pioneers

from Europe. The newcomers were not influenced by Zionism's 19th-century liberalism. Many of them see no merit in a democratic system that allows a voice for opponents — especially Arabs. They want a strong messianic leader — a Begin or an Ariel Sharon — even though those two happen to be Ashkenazim.

The Ashkenazic-Sephardic conflict can distort and embitter politics, but in time it will be resolved. A confident new Sephardic bourgeoisie continues to come into its own. Ben-Gurion said that a homogeneous Israel would have proved itself once there was a Sephardic chief of general staff. Today's, Gen. Moshe Levy, is of Iraqi origin.

It is hardly surprising that tension has been sharp among Israel's Jewish communities. The achievement is that with such bare tools — a 3,000-year-old religion, a shared feeling of isolation and vulnerability, and a Hebrew language reconstituted from holy books understood a century ago by only a few — the Jews of Israel have gathered together 3 million people from different backgrounds and have hewn so vital and viable a society.

Israeli politics are by far the most open in the Middle East — with the proviso that Arabs in the territories oc-

> "Not certain that turning Jordan into Palestine would be a solution."

cupied in 1967 are allowed little voice. The electoral system needs overhauling, but turnout at elections is more than 80 per cent. Violence has never marred a poll. The steadily increasing Arab vote now accounts for 12 per cent of the Knesset seats — enough to hold the balance of power.

The country's press is vigorous and varied; many Israeli journalists are fearless, inquisitive, and hardhitting. Foreigners have easy access to information, and though Israel's propaganda machine is among the best oiled in the world, there is no difficulty in seeking out the ugly features of life or voices of dissent both Arab and Jewish. Despite censorship of "security matters," the war in Lebanon was scrutinized in the press by an often savagely critical eye.

It is notable, too, that, after the massacre of Sabra and Shatila in 1982, when some 800 Palestinians were slaughtered in Beirut, the only spontaneous demonstration of public anguish in the Middle East, outside Lebanon, was by 100,000 Israelis in Tel Aviv. And though certain Israeli leaders were gravely responsible through negligence or worse, it was — after all — an Arab massacre of Arabs. Nor did the subsequent Israeli inquiry dodge Israel's responsibility.

Now that Prime Minister Peres and, to give him his due, Mr. Shamir, have calmed the political atmosphere, Israel's first priority is the economy. Its three main culprits have been the greedy war machine, a flabby welfare state maladministered by a Socialist bureaucracy, and weak governments. Many Israeli leaders have assumed that American generosity is inexhaustible.

The U.S. is crucial to Israel's economy (Israel now gets 17 per cent of all American overseas aid), but aid on excessively generous terms probably has done more harm than good. Between 1948 and 1971, average annual American aid was only $60 million. From the 1973 watershed until 1981, the U.S. spent $18 billion on Israel. Three quarters of that was military aid.

Shimon Peres, unlike Menachem Begin, is interested in economics. He has a plan whose first element is to cut, cut, cut. Target Number One for the hatchet will be defense, which now consumes about a third of the operational budget.

He also plans to cut $2 billion out of the $12-billion budget; to reduce inflation to 200 per cent (the September, 1984, rate — projected on an annual basis — was more than 1,000 per cent); to reduce the trade deficit by $1.5-2-billion; to increase exports by 15 per cent; and to keep unemployment down while improving on the current near-zero-level growth rate.

Its massive military spending can be drastically reduced, however, only if Israel — reborn in bloodshed ar ' preoccupied with five wars since it became a nation — can find peace in an Arab world. The crux of its problem remains the question: Can Palestinian Arab and Jewish Israeli minds meet?

The heart of Palestine these days is the West Bank of the Jordan River. The 760,000 Palestinian Arabs on the West Bank and the 500,000 in Gaza have virtually no legal political representation. The region has undergone a relentless process of being woven into the fabric of the rest of Israel.

There are 42,500 Jewish settlers dotted about the land, and advocates of Jewish settlement are convinced that there will be more than a million by the end of the century — but that is unlikely. Israeli policy is to exert total control and to inhibit the growth of Palestinian economic or political independence. The aim is to prevent an uprising and to snuff the Palestinian spirit.

The number of West Bank settlers should, strictly speaking, include annexed East Jerusalem's new Jewish population of 88,000, which is expected to rise to 120,000 by next year, while the Palestinians have dwindled to 110,000. There can be no doubt of the intention of all Israeli governments since 1967: Jerusalem must stay undivided and predominantly Jewish.

The West Bank plight should not, however, be exaggerated. Under the Hashemite kings of Jordan inhabitants had few political rights, frequent detentions, large disparities in wealth, and a far less free press than today. Arabs now can buy newspapers with such headlines as ISRAEL COUNTERS LEBANESE RESISTANCE WITH TERROR.

Many West Bank residents have become richer, although quite a few have become poorer. Many have improved living standards. Some 80,000 Palestinian laborers commute daily to Israel proper, and though they earn far less than the Israelis for the same jobs, they have more to spend than before.

West Bank law is a tangle of knots. Israel has turned confusion to its advantage, using Ottoman law here, British and Jordanian rules there — whichever suits best. The main body of law is Jordanian, to which the Israelis have added some 1,300 "military orders" affecting everything from what vegetables may be planted to water rights, censorship, and detention provisions. Jewish settlers are subject to different laws — those of Israel.

Nowhere is the application of law more onesided than in questions of use and ownership of land. Meron Benvenisti, former deputy mayor of Jerusalem, reports, "The Israeli authorities, in their quest to take possession of the land [in the West Bank and Gaza], have been using every legal and quasi-legal means in the book and are inventing new ones to attain their objectives." The authorities have control of 52 per cent of the land of the West Bank.

On the Palestinian question differences along the political spectrum are slight. The vast body of Labor opinion — from David Ben-Gurion and Golda Meir to Abba Eban, one of today's more thoughtful and allegedly dovish Labor leaders — shares Likud's Zionist belief: There is no such thing as a Palestinian nation. "Jordan is Palestine" is the cry of many Zionists, both Labor and Likud. Let King Hussein fall, as surely one day he will, argue most Israelis, and the Palestinians will have their own country.

But it is not certain that turning Jordan into Palestine, which probably would mean deposing King Hussein, would be a solution. Such a state would probably be just as committed to recovering some of the rest of Palestine to the west. That is why King Hussein remains the key to a lasting peace. It is he who may be able to infuse a sense of reality into the many Palestinians still imprisoned in the myth of recovering all of their former territory.

The Palestinians themselves have the ability to make a breakthrough, and there is little doubt that Yassir Arafat is still their most popular leader. It is for Arafat to convince the Israelis that his aims have changed. An overwhelming majority of West Bank inhabitants favors an outright recognition of Israel — provided that Israel makes reciprocal recognition of Palestinians' right to some kind of nationhood. No Israeli government could agree to an independent Palestinian state. It would be electorally unthinkable.

But there are peaceminded Palestinians and Israelis who might eventually accept a formula by which a Palestinian political entity had a broad measure of territorial control, while Amman ran foreign policy and security — independence within Jordanian limits.

The trouble is that the two sides have been far apart for so long that any set of proposals for peace requires contemplation of the apparently ridiculous. Does Mr. Arafat have the courage to risk an initiative? Would Israel have the courage to respond? Everything that has happened suggests that the attempt is unlikely to be made, and that if it were made it would fail. But that is no reason for not trying. (July 20) □

Article 19   *The Washington Post National Weekly Edition*, January 6, 1986

Israel Is Threatened by an Enemy Within: Its Economy

The state has to restructure a system kept afloat by foreign handouts, imports and public-works projects

By Lawrence Meyer

JERUSALEM—With its military enemies and the plague of quadruple-digit inflation at least temporarily at bay, the Israeli government is approaching a decision of watershed dimensions that it has avoided for all the country's 37 years:

Will it continue to build the Jewish state by using the nation's economy as a kind of massive public-works project—with all the featherbedding that the term implies?

Or will it risk driving Jews from Israel by tolerating unemployment in order to steer Israel toward economic efficiency, encouraging enterprises that are productive and allowing those that are not to die? The goal would be to build an economy that can support the western lifestyle Israel's citizens so clearly want.

The simple fact is that Israel's economy suffers from serious structural problems. It has a low-wage, labor-intensive Third World economy. But it has managed—by massive borrowing—to satisfy First World tastes for such commodities as video cassette recorders, luxury automobiles and vacations abroad.

The inflation rate, once as high as 1200 percent annually, has been reduced to between 40 and 50 percent. But slowing inflation—the problem that has preoccupied Israeli economists and Reagan administration policy-makers—will not resolve the fundamental dilemma.

Even leaving out military expenditures, Israel will remain in serious economic trouble until it figures out how to climb out of its stagnation, create productive jobs, export more than it imports, and pay its bills without huge handouts from abroad.

What life-support systems are to dying patients, American foreign aid has become to Israeli life. Without the continuing flow of that aid—roughly 19 percent of the government's budget in 1985—Israel would not be able to defend itself while maintaining a society that boasts five universities, sees one-seventh of its citizens travel abroad annually, has 50 percent of its work force employed in government, finance and service jobs (ranking behind only the United States and Canada—countries far more developed than Israel), and has 29 percent of its civilian work force on the government—which is to say the public—payroll.

Israel has a lower percentage of workers employed in industrial jobs than any of the seven leading industrial countries (the United States, Germany, Japan, Canada, the United Kingdom, Italy and Sweden) except Canada.

In its 1978 report, the Bank of Israel analyzed structural problems in the country's economy. It found that in "recent years there has been a marked structural change in employment, with the public-services sector absorbing most of the additional manpower. Since the government's ability to siphon off more money through taxes is limited . . . and since a diminished dependence on external sources of finance (foreign aid) has become a prime national target, there is no escaping the need to reduce the share of public services in total resource use.

"In other words, the freezing, and perhaps even absolute decrease, of public sector employment is necessary for relieving pressure in the labor market and making more resources available to the business sector."

This warning was not heeded by the government of former prime minister Menachem Begin. If anything, rather than reducing Israel's dependence on American foreign aid, the Likud government increased that dependence.

Civilian consumption was not brought under control, even when the Israel invasion of Lebanon in 1982 resulted in an absolute decline in productivity. Consumption in that year increased. An analysis of the distribution of employment in the Israeli economy among the various sectors finds no significant difference today from what the Bank of Israel described in 1978.

Of course there are reasons for the fix that Israel is in, reasons that make it all the more difficult to solve the problem.

One of the unique features of Israel as the Jewish State has been the role of the economy—even before the state was created—as an instrument of nation-building. In political Zionism—the ideology that saw the creation of a Jewish State as the only realistic solution to the "problem" of European Jewry—the state was the end point.

A corollary of Zionist ideology in the pre-state days held that Jews should do the work, among other reasons in order to provide jobs for the Jews who were coming to Palestine in answer to Zionism's call. In the history of the United States, immigrants came to fill jobs; in Israel's history, jobs were created to hold immigrants.

After the state was founded, full employment became a governmental goal—not simply because it was better to have able-bodied persons working, and not simply because the country was desperately in need of development, but also because Jews who did not have jobs would leave Israel. In the last 10 years in Israel, unemployment has run from a low of 2.9 percent in 1979 to the current rate somewhere between 7 and 8 percent, although the possibility of a rate as high as 11 percent has been mentioned.

Americans have grown accustomed to unemployment rates that Israelis find high precisely because the U.S. government has backed away from massive spending programs as a way to stimulate employment. To a large extent, then, Israel's economy from its early days can be viewed as a kind of continuing public-works project.

This strategy has had its benefits. In its first 30 years, Israel increased its exports by 3,600 percent, to use just one index of success. An infrastructure, including roads, bridges and a complex water-supply system, was built. But there is no way to measure how much more successful the Israeli economy would have been if higher unemployment rates—in the short term at least—had been tolerable.

They were not. Where other nations might use standards of efficiency to measure the benefit of investments, Israel was willing for years to subsidize businesses that otherwise could not survive because they provided jobs. By the same token, government payrolls were padded with unnecessary workers doing nonessential jobs because economic efficiency was not a primary consideration.

Not all the jobs in Israel were make-work, to be sure. Thousands of jobs were created by privately-owned (and some government-owned) companies where economic efficiency was extremely important. Israel's sophisticated high-tech industries have to compete in world markets against other companies that receive no government subsidies or help. Some of these workers, better educated and often of European descent, prospered in their private-enterprise jobs. A wealthy class developed alongside the middle class and the poor.

This situation made it especially difficult for a popularly-elected government to change policies and to begin using economic efficiency as a standard for measuring policy. As consumption among wealthier Israelis increased, the poorer class of Israelis—often "Oriental" or Sephardic Jews—began to demand their share of the pie. A succession of Israeli governments responded by continuing the official make-work policy, supplemented by a combination of subsidies and welfare programs.

This policy would have been expensive enough without the enormous defense costs that Israel has had to bear, especially in the last 18 years.

But whatever the reasons for Israel's economic predicament, the question is, what happens next? If inflation is really under control—and despite the optimism of many Israelis on the subject, it's still a big if—where does the Israeli economy go from here? The central fact of the Israeli economy is that it is not growing. Indeed, after years of growing, the Israeli economy has been contracting.

According to figures released by the government's finance ministry, Israel's national income for 1985 will be about

$400 million less than it was in 1981. Israel has three clear economic choices: continued education, stagnation or growth. The first two are obviously undesirable, but how can growth be resumed? Since the founding of the Jewish state, a substantial amount of economic growth has been achieved by borrowing—from other countries, especially the United States, from world Jewry and from banks. In the current Israeli government budget, debt service accounts for slightly more than half of the total. As a result, in the near term at least, Israel probably will have to forgo large-scale borrowing as a way to resume growth.

The other classic way to achieve economic growth is to increase productivity, and this gets to the core of the problem: Increasing productivity in Israel would require substantial structural changes, changes that run against the Israeli ideological and political grain.

Israel never has had a year in which its exports exceeded its imports. The reason for achieving higher productivity would be to reverse this situation, turning a deficit into a surplus. If we think of productive labor as being that which brings capital into Israel—whether the job is in the industrial or service sector—then part of what Israel needs to become self-sufficient is clear. Thousands of workers now on government payrolls, or working in factories producing items under Israeli government contract, or working as social workers, are not doing productive labor under this definition. They are not helping Israel pay its bills abroad, a vital necessity for a country that must import virtually all of its raw materials.

If it were within a government's power to wave a wand and move workers from one sector of the economy to another painlessly—that is, without unemployment—the problem still would not be solved. Israel is one of the most heavily unionized countries in the world. More than 75 percent of the Israeli work force belongs to a union. Even white-collar workers and professionals have their unions.

Virtually all the unions in Israel are components of the Histadrut, the unique labor union that is also a worker-owned industrial conglomerate and the largest nongovernmental employer in Israel. Because of its size and power, and because the Histadrut predated the state, it has been characterized as a state within a state.

As a labor union, the Histadrut watches out for the interest of its members, who vote for the leadership in periodic, partisan elections. And, as a labor union, the Histadrut enforces the work rules and principles it has negotiated with management to safeguard the union's idea of what is best for the workers. It will come as no surprise to anyone familiar with labor unions that the idea of a worker producing more without necessarily being paid more, or producing more without fully sharing in the benefit of his or her increased production, does not sit well with unions.

Nor does the idea of laying people off on the basis of merit rather than seniority sit well with labor unions. Keeping a junior worker who happens to be more capable while laying off a more senior worker is anathema to the labor-union ethic.

But that, in stark terms, is what increasing productivity is all about. What is needed in Israel is a sea change in public policy. If the Israeli economy is ever to be self-sustaining, the Israeli government may have to tolerate a period of relatively high unemployment—perhaps 10 percent or more—and resist the temptation to create jobs to put people back to work. The whole idea of this exercise would be to let ingenuity—which Israelis have in abundance—guided by market demand, determine where Israeli workers earned their pay.

The joker in the deck is that no Israeli government—for practical as well as ideological reasons—can tolerate substantial emigration of Jews. Israel's most capable technicians, scientists and engineers are on a par with quality professionals anywhere in the western world. If they can't find work in Israel, they can find it abroad. And it is no different for less highly-trained workers, who take the responsibility of providing for their families just as seriously.

The other major restraint against a basic restructuring of Israel's economy is political. Israel is a democracy, albeit one at present with a government of national unity. Under the best of circumstances, it is hard for democracies to undertake programs that require long-term sacrifice by the population. Even if the government's policy is well-conceived, the temptation by the opposition party to engage in demagoguery may prove irresistible.

Given the pre-existing splits in Israeli society—between the religious and nonreligious, between European and Oriental Jews, between those who would give up the West Bank for peace and those who would not—it is hard to imagine (not inconceivable, but hard to imagine) that a government could sustain a long-term policy of austerity in order to restructure the economy without unrest creating pressure to change the government.

These are the choices facing the Israeli government. It is understandable that Israelis, and those in the United States who wish them well, may fasten on the apparent success that Israel has enjoyed in curbing inflation. But that apparent success ought not to obscure the deeper, more complex and potentially far more momentous economic problem Israel has yet to confront.

Article 20   *Congress Monthly*
                                                                      April 1985

Student Life in Jerusalem

Hannah Brown

WINTER IN Jerusalem. . . . When it isn't raining, the sunlight is still golden, but indoors, the stone floors seem to have turned to ice. Most buildings have no central heating, and although it is rarely colder than 40° F., you have to work at keeping warm. The "layered look" is a matter of necessity and not of fashion. People survive by using space heaters, usually run on gas or *neft* (kerosene) rather than electricity, which increased in price over 60 percent in one month before the price freeze began. It has been a mild winter so far, I'm told, and the streets are often warmer than the apartments, which were designed to keep out the heat of the sun.

On a recent visit to the Givat Ram campus of the Hebrew University of Jerusalem in the early evening, I smelled a strong odor as I approached the dormitories. Was it a gas leak — or a bomb? Stepping inside, I saw a half-dozen students lighting kerosene heaters in the hall. Kerosene gives off an especially bad smell when it is first lit, so people usually light their heaters in a hall or stairwell. I stood watching them, and noticed that the walls and door were completely bare except for a schedule of *shmira* (guard duty — students are required to take turns guarding their dormitory), and that the hall was

silent. It was after seven, and the library was already closed. Some students were cooking dinner in the kitchen at the end of the hall (there is a cafeteria, but few students can afford to eat in it every day), but most were in their rooms, studying. I was suddenly struck by the contrast between this dormitory and the college dormitory I lived in until last spring. The noise level in American dormitories is infamous, and the halls are usually decorated with posters and signs advertising meetings, parties, and sports events. After spending several months in Jerusalem and taking courses at the Hebrew University, I have come to realize that the stark halls and subdued atmosphere on the campus here reflect more than a different style of university life. They reflect problems and circumstances unique to Israel that find expression on the university campus as well as in every other area of Israeli society.

The strongest influence on Israeli students is the experience of army service. Israeli men — except for most Arabs and anti-Zionist religious Jews — serve three years in the Israel Defense Forces (four years if they become officers), from the age of eighteen to twenty-one, and women serve from eighteen to twenty. Many Israelis take a year or two after the army to work or travel. In general, Israelis enter the university at an age when most Americans are completing their studies.

This age difference, along with the maturity that comes from the boredom, discipline, and danger of spending years in the IDF, explains the studiousness and reserve of the students.

HANNAH BROWN, *a recent graduate of Swarthmore College, is currently living and studying in Jerusalem.*

They don't come to the university to get out of their parents' house, or to learn how to drink, or to play basketball — they have just spent years patrolling in Lebanon or the West Bank, doing tank maneuvers on the Golan Heights or Air Force drills in the Negev, sleeping in tents or barracks, awakening at five in the morning. So it is not surprising that the demands of university life — eight o'clock classes, sharing rooms, unannounced quizzes — do not seem especially difficult to them.

Israeli army service does not end after the initial three-year period, however. Men are required to do *miluim* (reserve duty) until the age of fifty-four, and women until age twenty-four. Since the beginning of the war in Lebanon, *miluim* can be as much as fifty days a year, and most women serve only two weeks or less. *Miluim* duty is no less dangerous than the original period of service, and soldiers on reserve duty are stationed in Lebanon and along the borders. Students (and professors) are routinely called to serve in the middle of the semester. As a result of these disruptions, deadlines have to be flexible, and final exams are offered twice or three times to give those who missed classtime a better chance.

Soldiers who would rather be students complain bitterly of the cycle of *miluim*, falling behind in their studies, and trying frantically to catch up. Imagine the difficulties that face a student forced to miss the second and third weeks of an organic chemistry course, for example. Another problem is the tension that comes from switching back and forth between such different routines and responsibilities so quickly. A twenty-five-year-old student calculates that he has served over six months of *miluim* since "getting out of the army." "Sometimes I wake up in the morning and don't know whether to go to class or to pick up a gun," he says. Students stationed in Lebanon tend to be the most resentful, both because of the danger and because many (if not most) feel that the IDF should withdraw from Lebanon as soon as possible. "I'm counting the minutes," a student on leave from his *miluim* in Lebanon told me. He had ten more days to serve and missed the beginning of the semester. I sometimes wonder if the Shi'ites, the Druse, or the Syrians resent the Israeli presence in Lebanon as much as the Israelis who serve there do.

Another drain on the students' energy is the failing economy. Most students work at one or two part-time jobs in order to pay their tuition and living expenses. Between work and the army, it isn't surprising that most students don't find time for extracurricular activities. There are intramural sports teams, but they are not popular. A newspaper is published every two or three weeks, but the editors have trouble filling it up. There are almost no plays, except occasional presentations by students in the theater department, and few concerts or dance performances of any kind. Loud parties are held only by the American students, and the more studious Israelis try to live on halls without Americans. Israeli parties are casual by American standards: guests talk and sing, and often drink nothing stronger than coffee and tea. A great many Israelis go home for *Shabbat*, leaving the campus almost deserted.

More surprising is the lack of political activity on campus. There are some political groups, but they are not especially active. All last fall I cannot remember a single on-campus demonstration. This is especially noteworthy, given the fact that between 10 and 20 percent of the students at the Hebrew University are Arab. This figure is only an estimate — no university official I spoke to would give me an exact figure, but all the students I asked estimated that Arab students comprise about 15 percent of the university population. Whether or not their guesses are accurate, it is clear that there is a sizable group of Arab students, enough to form a political group.

At Bir Zeit University on the West Bank, there is a great deal of political protest, so much so that the government has closed it down on several occasions. At the Hebrew University, however, political activity is generally limited to protests against speakers. A representative of the Christian Lebanese Forces in Israel, Pierre Yazbek, who was invited to speak at the university in February, was shouted down by Arab students for over two hours. He was finally able to speak after one hundred Arab students were removed by the campus security forces and border police.

The following week, Member of Knesset Meir Kahane planned to demonstrate against the Arab students' protest against Yazbek. When Kahane addressed the crowd with his usual, "Shalom, Jews and dogs," and continued in the same vein, telling Arab students that there was no place for them at the university or in the country, people began throwing stones at him. In the melée that followed, fourteen students, both Arab and Jewish, were arrested. Kahane has since been banned from speaking on Israeli campuses, because he inevitably incites such riots.

Although day-to-day relations between Jewish and Arab students are generally cordial, there is very little social contact between them. As a rule, Jewish and Arab students do not share dormitory rooms. At Tel Aviv University, where there are more students who want on-campus housing than the university can provide for, Arab students have requested priority in dormitory space, because they cannot find landlords in Tel Aviv who will rent to them. Predictably, some Jewish students resent the fact that Arabs have access to the relatively cheap dormitory rooms while they live at home or in more expensive apartments. All the tensions in the country as a whole — ethnic, economic, and political — exacerbate the usual campus problems.

A final contrast between American and Israeli university life is the graduation ceremony. In America, students dress in black robes and listen to speeches about the challenges that await them in the "real world." Israeli graduations are less formal. Students finish their studies at different times (because of *miluim*) and many skip the ceremony altogether. The ceremonies in which soldiers affirm their loyalty to the IDF, usually held at the Western Wall or Masada, are much more emotional. Unlike American students, Israelis never have a chance to forget the realities of the world outside their classroom. For them, the university is a place to earn a degree — and perhaps to get a little rest.

Jordan:

Article 21

The Christian Science Monitor, October 21, 1985

West Bank: core of Middle East conflict

Violence threatens to undermine moves toward settlement

By Ned Temko
Staff writer of The Christian Science Monitor

Jerusalem

The West Bank issue, once seen as a potential bridge for Mideast peace, threatens to undermine current moves toward an Arab-Israeli settlement.

The leaders of Israel and Jordan, in separate visits to Washington within the last month, have signaled fresh interest in exploring Mideast peace.

Yet the West Bank — Item 1 on any serious Arab-Israeli negotiating agenda — is increasingly gripped by the inertia of conflict.

The recent violence there is a reminder that at the core of the Arab-Israeli conflict lies the question of the Palestinians. These are Arabs who

for generations have lived on the land that, in 1948, became the modern state of Israel — expanded since by the Israeli occupation of the West Bank and the Gaza Strip near Sinai after the 1967 Arab-Israeli war. The Palestinians have never had a state, and their leadership is divided. But all evidence is that they still can exert at least veto power in any negotiating move by Israel and Jordan.

Also complicating any fresh initiative is the heightened tension between Israel and Egypt — signatories, in 1979, of history's only formal Arab-Israeli peace treaty.

In Washington, President Reagan remains less actively engaged in Mid-

east diplomacy than was President Jimmy Carter. Especially since the failure of its Lebanon policy, the Reagan administration has signaled that the parties directly involved in the Mideast dispute must make real progress in narrowing differences before the United States will plunge into any new initiative.

Their recent dovish statements aside, observers here say, Israeli Prime Minister Shimon Peres and Jordan's King Hussein must do two things to give peace a chance.

The first is to agree to negotiate with each other—a hitch which has defied resolution by Hussein and a succession

Israeli soldiers stroll through marketplace in Nablus, occupied West Bank

FILE PHOTO — WILLIAM KABEL/SYGMA

of Israeli leaders for more than a decade.

The second is to find at least sufficient common ground to have something to talk about—notably on the West Bank issue.

In addition to rising tension in the territory, the past year has seen signs of grating differences among rival Israeli and Arab visions of how to achieve eventual peace there.

Both of the West Bank's most recent tenants—Israel and Jordan—are also beset by internal political problems that make it hard for their leaders to take the kinds of risks peacemaking must entail.

King Hussein rules a country, the majority of whose citizens are native Palestinians. He cannot ignore the rise of Palestinian nationalism since the 1967 war and the emergence of Palestinian leader Yasser Arafat's Al-Fatah guerrilla group on its heels.

Prime Minister Peres heads a misleadingly entitled "national unity" government with the rival, right-wing Likud bloc of retired former Premier Menachem Begin. By a "rotation" agreement, Likud chief and Foreign Minister, Yitzhak Shamir is to get Peres's job about a year from now.

Against this background, the recent statements from King Hussein and Peres have impressed even hardboiled skeptics among Mideast analysts by their extent and consistency.

The Jordanian monarch said publicly in Washington that he was "prepared to join all parties in pursuing a negotiated [Arab-Israeli] settlement, in an environment free of belligerent and hostile acts."

Foreign diplomats attach equal importance to the King's relatively restrained approach on a number of recent Arab or international moves to condemn Israel—notably since its bombing of the Palestine Liberation Organization's headquarters in Tunisia on Oct. 1.

Hussein also sided publicly with Britain in its dispute with a PLO official whom the British said had reneged on a pledge to formally recognize Israel's right to exist. The pledge was to precede a milestone meeting between the British Foreign Secretary and a joint Jordanian-Palestinian delegation which

was scheduled for last Monday but abruptly cancelled.

Peres issued remarks, en route his current US visit, praising Hussein's recent approach as a change from past Jordanian policy. The statement coincided with a front-page story last Wednesday in Israel's respectable daily, Haaretz, implying that Peres may have met secretly with the Jordanian monarch about a week earlier. Predictably, the Likud sniped at Peres back home, charging he was fixing to make concessions his "national unity" partners could not permit.

The Israeli prime minister has said he feels Jordan is truly serious about making peace and should come forward for direct talks.

Particularly amid signs that Peres's economic austerity program is finally reducing the inflation rate, the prime minister's inner circle has been hinting he might opt to call early elections in search of a widened leadership mandate instead of making good on "rotation" with Likud's Mr. Shamir.

In the opinion polls, although these have proved notoriously misleading in recent Israeli political history, Peres's standing far outstrips Shamir or anyone else as preferred prime minister. And so close was last year's election, that even if Peres's Labor Party gains only a few seats in parliament in fresh elections, it might still put together a coalition without Likud.

But election or no election, in Israel serious snags in any Israel-Jordon peace process are already evident.

Peres has linked his comments for Hussein to an insistence that the King

exclude Palestinians who are members of the PLO from such talks.

One reason for the Israeli leader's upbeat mood in Washington has been his sense that the recent hijacking of an Italian liner and alleged Palestinian breach of assurances in London have so battered the PLO's image that the rest of the world—Hussein included—will gladly cut the organization out of any Mideast negotiating process.

The King, despite his implicit slap at the PLO over the recent London mix-up, has so far seemed either unwilling or unable to do so. Western diplomats here say he will not do so now either. The PLO, while weakened by the war in Lebanon and its recent crises, can still credibly claim recognition among most Palestinians as symbol and spokesman for their national aspirations.

Unless Hussein can be confident of getting so good a deal from Israel on the West Bank as to preemptively silence all Arab critics, Western diplomats feel, he remains unlikely to break with the PLO altogether. "He needs," says one diplomat, "Palestinian cover."

The message of recent West Bank tension is that so difficult and divisive are the issues there that no one, neither Hussein nor Peres, is likely to get the deal he wants.

One issue is central: Whose land is it?

By Israeli standards, Peres is a moderate on this question. He has never presented control of the West Bank as an historical, or Biblical, imperative that some settlers base their claims on.

One negotiating option would be the traditional Labor Party approach of "territorial compromise" on the West Bank.

But what territory would be compromised?

Israeli political analysts of all party stripes agree that the city of Jerusalem—as formally annexed after the 1967 war—would not be put on the "territorial compromise" table.

But Hussein's longtime position has been that real peace would require Israel's returning virtually the entire West Bank and the predominantly-Arab eastern portion of Jerusalem, holy to Muslims as well as Jews and Christians. Hussein ruled old Jerusalem and the West Bank until 1967.

"It's hard to see what would be in

it for Hussein" to make a territorial compromise, says political consultant Zeev Chafets. Jordanian officials have always held that such a compromise, among other things, would amount to their recognizing Israel's spoils of the 1967 war.

The other alternative would be to revive the Begin-era approach of "functional" rather than territorial compromise. That is, the West Bank would remain a single entity. Peace would entail a negotiated division of authority among Israel, the local Palestinians, and Jordan.

But so far at least, Hussein seems to feel that this would also amount to tacit recognition of Israel's capture of the territory on the battlefield.

As one Western economic expert, who has frequent dealings in Jordan, puts it, any such functional compromise retaining a major say for Israel risks being seen by Hussein as "merely taking down a fence on the Jordan River; a nonstarter."

There have been specifically discouraging signs from the West Bank already.

In the past year, the Peres government has taken initial steps on a pledge to encourage peace prospects by improving the West Bank Palestinians' "quality of life." Several officials in the Israeli administration there have been replaced by figures who, local Palestinians say, seem generally more pleasant to deal with. Various foreign-funded economic development projects—including cooperatives, long politically taboo—have received the requisite Israeli OK after long pre-Peres delays.

But the effects of the process on

prospects for overall peace have been minimal so far. Peres told reporters recently that the upsurge of Arab violence had limited the scope of this quality-of-life campaign.

In local Palestinians' view, that is not the issue.

Typifying the response is lawyer Raja Shehadeh. He and other Palestinians are bitter over the scope of the Israeli crackdown in response to the upsurge in violence—including revival for the first time in several years of the weapon of "administrative detention" without formal court hearing or trial, of suspected Arab troublemakers.

But, Mr. Shehadeh says, what most grates on Palestinians transcends both the recent cycle of violence and Peres's concept of quality of life. What matters is whether the Israelis plan to cede political control of the majority-Arab territory captured in 1967.

Shehadeh and other Palestinians see no evidence of this so far. Thus Peres's generally softer verbal line and his quality-of-life moves are seen, in Shehadeh's words, as a means by which Israel can secure both the West Bank and good relations with the rest of the world.

On Hussein's side of the West Bank equation, there have been equal difficulties.

Jordan's recent worry has been a gradual exodus of West Bank Palestinians who, as the economies of oil-rich Gulf nations lagged, increasingly sought employment across in Jordan.

Hussein's kingdom has economic challenges of its own, and the arrival of large numbers of West Bankers could only complicate them. The outflow, involving mostly young Palestin-

ians recently out of school, also seemed likely to ease Israeli control of the West Bank in the long run.

So by the end of 1982 Jordan applied new, tougher regulations on Palestinians leaving the West Bank. But under Palestinian pressure from a West Bank that is bubbling with record youth unemployment—up to 12,000 men out of work, according to the estimate of one Arab economic expert—Jordan again eased entry formalities.

Jordan, say the Palestinians, had no choice.

This, indeed, is increasingly the refrain heard on all sides of the West Bank dispute.

Those who do speculate about peace agree that so complex and ossified is the conflict that only a psychological breakthrough along the lines of the 1977-79 process between Egypt and Israel can jolt things forward.

Two rival demonstrations—one favoring concessions for West Bank peace, the other against them—saw Peres off to the US a few days ago.

More striking than the rallies, however, was their size—or lack of size. At most, 6,000 people took part in either event.

At least two of the various foreign embassies contacted in preparation of this Monitor series seemed to place the issue of conflict and conciliation on the West Bank in similar perspective.

No, officials from each mission explained apologetically, they weren't exactly up to date on various recent West Bank developments:

It had been summer. Staff was short. The West Bank was one issue left slack—something unthinkable a few years back.

Article 22   *Middle East International,* December 20, 1985

Letter from Amman

It's early Friday night in Amman's "al-Balad" district, what Americans would call downtown. Crowds push their way along pavements crammed with merchandise overflowing from shop fronts and from displays of clothes, toys and all sorts of trinkets and gadgets laid out by street traders. At least half the human congestion is stationary, clustered round pungent falafel stalls or cafes, or just lounging at street corners to gossip and inhale the assault on the senses of food cooking, garish neon signs or fairy lights flashing, cars honking and electronic music blaring. For although it's the Muslim day of rest, the streets could hardly be more alive: even the lottery ticket sellers are shouting out over the din for punters.

The carnival-like atmosphere is completed by the endless rows of banners strung across the road at the level of first storey balconies (on which more people are grouped surveying the scene) in honour of the recent 50th birthday of the Jordanian monarch. The neatly calligraphed banners proclaim virtually identical messages, differing only in the name of the sender: "The al-Fulan Electrical Appliances Company salutes His Majesty King Hussein on this happy anniversary", etc. etc.

And then everyday chaos suddenly turns into bedlam. A group of youths with green bands tied around their heads and each holding aloft a corner of a huge green flag dances wildly out into the heavy traffic, cheering and laughing. A grey-clad policeman, his cape and spiked helmet giving him the bizarre appearance of a cross between a Parisian gendarme and a remnant of the Kaiser's army, lashes out angrily in an attempt to restore order. But on his own he's helpless: the youths surround and taunt him, making him desperate and ridiculous. All the while the tooting of horns and squealing of brakes is building up to an insane crescendo, as the cars swerve to avoid the scuffles in the road. Traffic grinds to a complete halt.

For what must be one of the most well-ordered and controlled of Arab cities, it's all very strange. Who are these green-clad marauders in a country where public dissent is seemingly unknown? If you have ever passed through London's East End on a Saturday afternoon, you have probably already guessed. Green is the colour of one of Jordan's two main football teams, and these unruly young men are celebrating today's cup final victory over their sporting heroes' arch-rivals. To know this, however, is to glimpse only the surface of something that presses hard on the absolute core of Jordan's national existence.

The team of the greens is al-Wahdat and takes its name from one of Jordan's many Palestinian refugee camps. The rival team is al-Faisali, which takes its title from the Hashemite monarch of the same name. The intense competition between the two, or rather between their many hundreds of thousands of supporters, is the only obvious sign of the dichotomy between the country's original inhabitants, now about 20 per cent of the population, and the Palestinian majority. The latter, of course, support al-Wahdat, with all the pride and fervour that elsewhere (the Israeli-occupied West Bank for instance) would be manifested through the usual channels of Palestinian nationalist expression. But no Palestinian flags or pictures of Arafat will you see in Jordan, nor will you hear the sentimental Palestinian ballads and revolutionary songs. The fracas on the streets of "al-Balad" between the police, who like the army's executive echelons are virtually Jordanian to a man, and the al-Wahdat fans is about the only example the casual visitor is likely to see of a departure from the concept of what the local media refer to as "the one Jordanian-Palestinian family". The man in the street, if not the refugee camp, certainly thinks twice before confessing his nationality to a stranger as anything other than Jordanian, though the chances are that he or his immediate forbears came from the other rather than this side of the River Jordan. And it would be a brave man who did not prominently display at least one Jordanian flag or royal portrait in his workplace throughout the weeks-long celebration of King Hussein's personal golden anniversary.

Jordan is the only Arab country to have offered the Palestinians the security and settled prosperity acquired through the exercise of full citizenship rights. Jordanians and Palestinians, 15 years after a war between them which equalled in bitterness and hatred any between Arab and Israeli, now co-exist in genuine peace, tolerance and mutual liking. Is the price the restriction of any expression of a separate Palestinian identity to a mild outbreak of soccer hooliganism? The ultimate price may be much higher. The outwardly successful campaign to get Jordan's Palestinians to identify themselves with the state, and above all with the monarchy, as exemplified by the mind-numbing outpourings of the royal birthday media extravaganza, carries sinister echoes of a favourite theme of Israel's right-wing: that Jordan is "the Palestinian state", and hence the convenient solution to the Palestinian problem. How this malicious propaganda, with its ominous implications for the Palestinians of the Israeli-occupied territories, can be rebutted in practice, without destabilising Jordan, is part of the dangerous balancing act King Hussein must continue to pull off to ensure his survival.

Paul Harper

Kuwait:

Article 23   Merip Reports ● February 1985

Kuwait Living on its Nerves

K. Celine

The traveller landing at Kuwait doesn't have to wait long for signs that the small city-state is in some kind of crisis. While citizens of the six countries belonging to the Gulf Cooperation Council (GCC) procede swiftly through immigration, the rest of us stand in long, slow-moving lines before submitting to the detailed check of visas, work permits and residences introduced to maintain a tight control over new arrivals. In the city itself, the low walls of concrete blocks around the American Embassy—just like the ones surrounding the White House in Washington—are an ugly reminder of the truck bomb attack by partisans of Iraq's outlawed Dawa' Party in December 1983. It takes only a little longer to notice that the big hotels are starkly empty and that many of the stores in the smart new air-conditioned shopping centers—some of which commanded $2 or $3 million in key money only a few years ago—have closed down.

Kuwaitis, of course, are used to living on their nerves. And never more so since the start of the Iran-Iraq war, which brought fighting close to Basra, only two hours' drive to the north. In many ways, 1984 seems to have been the most difficult yet. Kuwaiti shipping was directly affected by the intensification of the Gulf tanker war not many miles offshore. Security has been stepped up drastically; regular police sweeps of political undesirables and illegal immigrants produce at least 200 deportations a month. Perhaps most dangerous of all, Iran appears convinced, in spite of official Kuwaiti denials, that Kuwait has leased two uninhabited northern islands, Bubiyan and Warba, to Iraq for military purposes. This has exposed the country to the threat of direct Iranian armed intervention. The uncharacteristically outspoken attacks on Tehran for allegedly aiding and abetting the hijackers of the Kuwaiti plane just before Christmas illustrated just how frayed some nerves have become.

Nineteen eighty-four had important implications for Kuwait's traditional policy of neutrality and independence in the face of increasing pressure from its three most powerful neighbors, Iran, Iraq and Saudi Arabia. Determined to find better ways of defending its airspace after three Iranian raids, it turned to Moscow for supplies of SAM (surface-to-air) missiles and to Paris for Mirage interceptor planes after Washington had vetoed its request for Stinger anti-aircraft missiles. Perhaps to hammer the point home, Kuwait also refused to accept the credentials of the new American ambassador-designate, on the grounds that he had previously served in Israel.

At the same time, Kuwait continued to come under ever-

increasing pressure to coordinate its defenses with the other GCC countries under the American AWACS umbrella. A meeting of the Gulf rulers in Kuwait, held in great splendor yet amid signs of an almost paranoid obsession with security in late November, decided to set up the GCC's own small rapid deployment force of perhaps two batallions, probably to be stationed in Saudi Arabia. By making concessions on relatively unimportant points, the Kuwaiti ruling family evidently hopes to postpone acceptance of the larger Saudi demands for an integrated Gulf Defense Command until the war is over and the international situation looks a bit better.

Kuwait's present economic situation constitutes just as much of a minefield. The recession triggered off in 1982 by falling oil prices, the disruptive effect of the Iran-Iraq war and the traumatic crash of the unofficial stock exchange, the Suq al-Manakh, continues. Of these, the war seems to have had the most serious immediate consequences. It has cut Kuwait's lucrative transit trade with both Iran and Iraq severely. It has also forced the government to pay so much attention to local security that many would-be visitors are having the greatest difficulty in obtaining visas. Indeed, many here believe that one reason the government agreed to house the Gulf rulers' conference in some of the bigger hotels was to meet their owners' criticism that the new regulations had turned nearly all their trade away.

The Stock Market Crash

In the long run, the Suq al-Manakh crash may prove to have been the more dangerous event. For one thing, it has ruined the country's hard-won reputation for careful fiscal management. It has also planted a future time-bomb by leaving almost every important financial institution in possession of many heavily over-valued assets such as real estate and the post-dated checks used by brokers to meet their debts in the Suq al-Manakh. It seems that if they employed proper accounting methods in their annual balance sheets, many of them would prove to be technically bankrupt.

The Suq crash had its origins in the acute shortage of local investment opportunities for the huge private fortunes made during the oil boom of the late 1970s. This led to the emergence of an unofficial market in the shares of companies located in other Gulf states, which could not be legally traded in Kuwait, as well as in paper companies, many of which were created simply for the purpose of having some marketable stocks to play with. Soon the amounts involved in buying and selling such shares exceeded even the astronomical sums available to the oil millionaires. Traders and speculators took recourse to payments by post-dated check: this form of credit is perfectly legal in Kuwait, where banks are required to clear any check presented to them regardless of its date. The system worked so long as those holding such checks kept to a kind of gentleman's agreement not to try to cash them. But as soon as some of the very big ones came up for presentation, credit and confidence evaporated and the bubble simply burst. During the boom itself, the universal desire to make money out of what seemed like a special Kuwaiti version of Monopoly drew in a large proportion of the local population, both Kuwaiti and non-Kuwaiti. The crash, when it came, left few households unscathed.

Why the government—the al-Sabah ruling family—let the whole business get so out of hand in spite of repeated warnings from some of its own ministers, such as the well-respected Abd al-Latif al-Hamad, is still a matter of debate. At least one member of the royal family was himself heavily involved; it turns out that he owes his small creditors alone at least a billion dollars. Also involved were any number of rulers and their relations in surrounding Arab countries. Darker rumor has it that the whole thing was deliberately allowed to balloon by other members of al-Sabah on the grounds that this would destroy much of the economic (and thus political) power of the merchant class, which had grown so rich from the oil boom that it could no longer be controlled by the traditional reins of state patronage.

The immediate result of these triple blows—the war, falling oil prices and the Suq al-Manakh crash—came in 1982, when the gross national product actually fell. This was followed by a longer period of economic stagnation marked by a drop in civilian imports, an increase in the number of unoccupied buildings, a huge reduction in private lending and, until it was checked a few months ago, a significant flight of Kuwaiti capital abroad. The general loss in business confidence has led to louder and louder calls for government intervention. But the government itself has moved at only a snail's pace to sort out the tangled web of credit and obligations left by the Suq al-Manakh crash, prosecuting just a few of the major brokers, paying off some of the smaller investors who had lost money and, for the rest, trying to get some of the larger debtors—like Shaikh Khalifa al-Sabah—to make individual repayment arrangements. It has resisted all calls to pump large sums of money into the economy, preferring to refer the matter to a high-level commission under the minister of oil, which has been asked to produce its own plan for economic revival by February 1985.

The government has also signally failed to press on with its policy of using a temporary budgetary deficit on current account as a justification for charging money for services which are now free, such as health. Plans to introduce such charges were hastily withdrawn in September 1984. One reason may have been the vocal criticism in the National Assembly and the feeling that the issue could easily be used as an effective rallying cry by opposition forces during the forthcoming general election. In particular, the new charges might provoke further militancy from members of Kuwait's 40,000-strong trade union movement; some had already organized a series of work stoppages in the oil industry to protest plans to withdraw privileges granted in the days of foreign control. But almost certainly the most telling argument must

have been the one which asked how the government could possibly expect the people to bear new burdens at a time when Suq al-Manakh brokers were still making free with billions of dollars of investors' money, and when the government itself was earning so much from its overseas investments that it could easily meet any temporary shortfall in its ordinary revenues over and over again.

Approaching Elections

Some of these issues have been aired in the campaign for the general election scheduled for this February 20th. The electorate is confined to those 57,747 male Kuwaitis over 21—3.5 percent of the population of 1.7 million—who are first-category citizens (those who can prove that their family lived in Kuwait in 1920). The 25 two-member constituencies have been gerrymandered in such a way as to give a built-in majority to the bedouin supporters of the royal family. Still, it will be taken as an important test both of public opinion and of government intentions. Speech is relatively free. Public meetings of over 20 persons require a special permit; much of the electioneering goes on either in special tents put up so that a candidate can entertain his electorate (never more than 2-3,000) or in informal meetings in private houses (*diwaniyas*) where family members and their friends meet to hear the candidate speak or to ask him questions.

Political parties are banned by ministerial order, but certain recognized trends exist among some of the candidates. These include the associates of the veteran Arab nationalist politician and social reformer, Ahmad al-Khatib, and two religious organizations, the Ikhwan (Muslim Brothers) and the more conservative Salafiyya. Most of the other candidates are identified simply in terms of their community of origin, like the Shi'as, or particular bedouin tribes. For al-Khatib, the main issues of the campaign are the state of the economy, the government's failure to punish people who acted illegally during the Suq al-Manakh frenzy, and the government's short-lived attempt to amend the constitution — attempts withdrawn after provoking widespread opposition in May 1983. This last issue, generally taken as an example of the ruling family's desire to obtain greater powers for themselves against the National Assembly, probably at the insistence of the Saudis, can be used to generate discussion about some of the larger questions relating to Kuwait's difficult political future. While no one believes that more than a handful of the government's critics can possibly get elected, it may well suit the royal family to be able to point out that the National Assembly is not simply a rubber stamp, particularly when it comes to trying to protect Kuwaiti independence against Saudi pressure.

Beyond the short-term interest in the election and its outcome, there is a great deal of both fatalism and fear. Conversations with Kuwaitis of all classes have a way of coming to a sharp halt when they bump suddenly up against the brute facts which underlie their economic and political position. There also seems to be a general feeling that, whatever opportunities there may have been a few years ago to transform Kuwait into a different type of society, this time is now past; there is now nothing left to do but to play out the role of being a tiny rentier state, heavily reliant on foreign labor and foreign expertise and threatened by powerful and greedy neighbors.

Politically, the ruling family once tried to establish a neutral position in the Gulf, friendly to all (it was the only GCC country to recognize the People's Democratic Republic of Yemen) and always ready to use its wealth for constructive development through respected institutions like the Kuwait Fund. Today they find themselves forced to take sides in the Iran-Iraq war and simultaneously regarded as a threat by their own ally, Saudi Arabia, as they hold out against Saudi plans to place Gulf defense on a new footing. Economically, the ruling family tried to diversify activity while spreading the wealth—albeit unequally—to most Kuwaitis, giving them jobs and allowing them to derive great benefit from their extremely privileged position vis-a-vis the foreigners who now make up over three-quarters of the labor force. But diversification has gone no further than a successful move downstream to refine and export a larger share of its own oil, leaving the government with little alternative but to invest more and more of its revenues abroad in other people's industry rather than its own.

Meanwhile, with few honorable exceptions, including some senior members of the Kuwaiti trade union movement, the Kuwaiti population has gotten so used to its privileges that it is ready to support ever more extreme measures to deny them to anyone else, even to the extent of contemplating rules which would make it difficult for Kuwaiti citizens to marry non-Kuwaitis without giving up their children's right of citizenship. If there was a moment when the trading city of Kuwait might have seemed on its way to becoming the Venice of the Gulf, it now seems more and more like a Middle Eastern version of Miami—

palm trees, air-conditioning, migrant labor, manipulation from outside political centers and all.

— January 1985

Postscript: Kuwaitis went to the polls on February 20th. Out of 50 seats in the National Assembly, 28 new members were elected. The results were important for three reasons. One was the return to the Assembly, after a four year absence, of Dr. Khatib, together with three others associated with his group, including Sami al-Manis, the editor of the group's weekly journal, *Al-Tali'a*. The second was the defeat of two of the leading Muslim fundamentalists, leaving only two others in the Assembly to represent this trend. The third was the high turnover of members and the defeat of a number of prominent men close to the ruling family. Although the Assembly will maintain its large majority of conservatives loyal to the al-Sabah family, many have interpreted the results as a significant vote of protest against the government's failure to restimulate the stagnant economy. Other significant features were the election of only one prominent Shi'i and the victory of 'Abd Allah al-Nafisi, a man close to the Muslim Brothers but a bitter critic both of the government and of Saudi interference in Kuwaiti affairs. The new Assembly can be expected to be both active in its debates and more watchful of what members take to be the interests of native-born Kuwaitis as against migrants or outside economic interests. ∎

Libya:

Article 24

SOUTH OCTOBER 1985

Revolution in recession

Libya The country's unique development programme is in jeopardy. Oil exports – on which progress towards self-sufficiency depends – have fallen to just 890,000 barrels a day from the 1970 peak of 3,312,900 b/d. Oil revenues this year are expected to be lower than 1984's US$10-billion and, according to a survey in Wharton's *Middle East Economic Outlook*, Libya will be running a 0.9 per cent current account deficit by the end of 1986.

Libya's development policy has differed radically from that of the conservative Gulf oil states. While the Gulf states have used oil revenues in a way that preserves their social structures, Libyan society has been transformed.

By 1980 Libyans' average annual income had risen to US$19,000; more significantly, since Colonel Muammar al Qadhafi's takeover in 1969, major social reforms and an attack on inequality have been implemented. Homelessness was a serious problem. Qadhafi gave housing high priority, eliminating homelessness by 1976.

Clearing the development path: Qadhafi bulldozes last shanty in Libya, June 1976

Revenues were systematically allocated to build a comprehensive health service. Between 1968 and 1978 the number of hospitals increased by 50 per cent, the number of beds rising from 5,646 to 13,347. For the remoter areas a flying doctor service was started. Malaria was effectively eradicated and trachoma and tuberculosis sharply curbed. Day nurseries were started, enabling women to work outside the home. One of Qadhafi's first actions, in 1970, was to decree equality of the sexes and pay parity.

Spending on education increased tenfold. Between 1969 and 1979 the number of schools and colleges increased two-and-a-half times; primary school attendance became compulsory and higher education free. A literacy campaign meant that by 1976 half the adult population could read and write, instead of only 10 per cent under the monarchy that preceded Qadhafi.

Yet the change was most striking in economic development. The monarchy had accepted virtual subordination to the oil companies, which irked Qadhafi. In 1973 the authorities gained majority control of oil company operations in Libya, and began using revenues to diversify the economy away from oil, which on known reserves and rates of depletion was not expected to last much beyond 2020.

The Libyan leadership is now responding to the slide in oil prices by trying to increase agricultural and industrial self-sufficiency. The fall in financial reserves from US$8.7-billion in January 1982 to US$3.7-billion in June this year has not induced them to cancel key diversification projects.

When the downward drift of oil prices began in 1981, Libya decided to concentrate resources on strategic projects, including the "industrial fortresses" – heavy industrial plants aimed at cutting reliance on crude exports.

These "fortresses" fall into two categories: diversification in hydrocarbons, such as at the Abu Khamash petrochemical complex, the Mersa Brega methanol and ammonia plant, and the Ras Lanuf ethylene steam cracker; and development of mineral resources through such ventures as the iron and steel plant at Misrata and the aluminium complex at Zuwara.

More recently, the emphasis has been placed on agriculture. In the 1985 development budget the allocation to industry was down 20 per cent, with resources being mobilised for the Great Manmade River project, which at US$9-billion overwhelms other schemes in scale and expense.

The "river" is a pipeline designed to transform Libyan agriculture by carrying water 1,900km from artesian wells at Sarir and Tazerbo in the desert south to Ajedabiya on the coast. Completion is scheduled for 1989, after which a second stage is to link wells in the Fezzan in the southeast

Libya's lean years

	1980	1981	1982	1983	1984	1985
Oil production ('000 b/d)	1,790	1,215	1,115	1,105	990	910[a]
Revenues from oil production (Estimates in US$'000)	22,000	15,000	14,000	11,500	10,000	10,000[b]
Estimated financial reserves (US$millions)	10,400	8,700	6,700	4,500	4,100	3,700

Sources: BP Statistic Review of World Oil Industry; Opec; Wood Mackenzie and Company, Edinburgh; Middle East Economic Digest; Middle East Economic Survey; OECD

a: Mid-year projected average based on released export figures and domestic consumption.
b: Mid-year forecast.

with Tripoli, and a third stage will extend the network from Ajedabiya to Tripoli and Tobruk.

Self-reliance in agriculture has been a recurring theme throughout Qadhafi's leadership. In September 1969, within days of deposing King Idris, Qadhafi launched a green revolution, but the first results were disappointing. The exodus from the country to the towns accelerated. In 1973 the authorities responded with a 10-year integrated plan for agriculture.

But many of the government projects were unable to absorb investment allocations because of shortages of manpower, especially skilled labour, and water. The state had to hire foreign workers.

In 1976 the leadership, facing a temporary balance of payments deficit, was forced to revise the diversification strategy. The result was a marked shift from agriculture to industry.

To diversify away from the oil sector and generate self-sustained industrial growth, Qadhafi decided to bring the resources in the private sector under state control. In 1976 a state monopoly of foreign trade was established as a prerequisite for import substitution.

Having consolidated his domestic position by cracking down on the merchants and their allies, the urban clergy, in 1979 Qadhafi expropriated all privately-owned industry. Industrialists were obliged to surrender their factories and assets to the control of workplace committees, called vocational congresses. This was the base for proposals for the country's industrialis-

US Trade with Libya

	Exports	Imports
	(US$-million)	
1974	139.4	1.4
1975	231.5	1,044.6
1976	276.6	2,406.2
1977	313.7	3,796.1
1978	425.0	3,779.3
1979	468.1	5,256.0
1980	508.8	8,594.7
1981 (January-September)	610.1	4,916.9
1982 (January-September)	224.8	493.5
1984	200.2	9.7

Source: US Department of Commerce

ation, culminating in the 1981-85 transformation plan.

The plan's emphasis on heavy industry was encouraged by the 1979 rise in oil prices. The subsequent deterioration in the oil market soon led to doubts about the viability of industrialisation, particularly in view of a lack of world demand for Libyan oil products and for Libyan steel and aluminium.

But the authorities have persisted with heavy industry because they believe that the market in refined products and chemical by-products is more secure than the market in crude oil and that heavy industry is vital for self-sustained growth outside the oil sector. The investment required by the 1981-85 plan has forced more drastic changes. In 1981 bank deposits were seized virtually without warning and it was announced that the private retail sector would be abolished with state supermarkets replacing retail outlets.

The leadership's attempt to redistribute resources, including manpower, from non-productive to productive sectors sparked a serious backlash, yet failed to achieve the desired transfer of manpower. Economic sabotage took place and the exile opposition movement grew up.

Qadhafi's action to suppress externally-based opposition presented the US, Libya's biggest oil customer, with a pretext for an oil embargo. This came into effect in March 1982, precipitating a slump in Libyan oil production from 1.2-million b/d to 660,000 b/d, a two-month ban on consumer goods imports and other measures.

The leadership countered the loss of the US market with remarkable success. Envoys were dispatched worldwide to diversify oil sales. Qadhafi visited Eastern Europe three times in six months, tying up barter deals, which now account for 300,000-400,000 b/d, half of Libya's oil exports. By the end of 1982 Libya had recovered from much of the harm inflicted by Reagan's boycott (which included US technology to Libya) but still faced falling oil prices and lower Opec production ceilings.

Further expenditure controls followed in 1984. The congress agreed in principle to remove all subsidies from the service industries, such as electricity, water and television, which were reorganised along financially autonomous lines. It also passed a resolution instructing the central bank to balance monthly revenue and spending.

Acute cash flow problems resulted. Foreign contractors are still experiencing long delays in payment. Estimated trade debts have risen from US$2-billion to US$3-billion in October 1982 to more than US$5-billion now. Libya has tried to meet these debts by bartering oil, but key creditors, notably Turkey and Spain, are refus-

Breaking the blockade

The speed with which Libya established friendly relations with Sudan, since President Gaafar Nimeiri of Sudan was deposed in April, has unsettled its opponents Egypt and the US. It is the most important breakthrough yet in Colonel Muammar al Qadhafi's campaign to reduce Libya's isolation in the Arab world and has punched a hole in the US trade blockade of Libya.

Nimeiri was Libya's most extreme opponent in the region and his fall was greeted with open rejoicing in Tripoli. Libya was the first country to recognise the new government of General Abdel Rahman Sawar el Dahab.

The Libyan opposition was expelled from Sudan, diplomatic links restored, and Libyan aid offered for the reconstruction of Sudan.

In May Qadhafi visited Khartoum for talks with Sawar el Dahab. A military cooperation agreement was made. Senior members of the revolutionary committee movement were appointed to Libya's New Brotherhood Bureau in Khartoum.

Less spectacular improvements in Libya's foreign relations have been made with several other previously hostile states. The most significant was the reconciliation with Morocco culminating in the Oujda Treaty of Union, signed by King Hassan and Qadhafi in August 1984. Relations have been normalised with Saudi Arabia, following bitter exchanges in 1979-82 over Saudi oil policy and the stationing of US Awacs surveillance aircraft in the Arabian peninsula.

Libyan security had become increasingly vulnerable before these initiatives were launched towards the end of 1982. Qadhafi had clashed with a number of pro-US Arab and African states, especially Egypt, Sudan and Morocco. Then came the confrontation with the US.

The Reagan administration barely concealed its intention to topple a leadership which actively contested the US presence in the region. In August 1981 the US sixth fleet held exercises in the Gulf of Sirte, which Libya claimed as territorial waters, and two Libyan planes surveying the manoeuvres were brought down. The previous month French intelligence sources had revealed that a team from the Israeli general staff had been seconded to Egypt's President Anwar Sadat to formulate a strategy for the invasion of Libya. When the Sirte clash occurred, 200,000 Egyptian troops were deployed along the Libyan frontier.

Qadhafi's immediate response was a programme of mass militarisation. The aim was the creation of Qadhafi's long-proposed society of "the armed people".

But while mobilisation could to some extent deter aggression, it was useless against the other US weapons of diplomatic isolation and trade sanctions.

Qadhafi made urgent efforts to improve relations with Western European countries, especially France and Italy. He visited Austria as the guest of Chancellor Bruno Kreisky. The day he arrived, Washington declared a unilateral boycott.

The Libyan leadership hit back with a successful campaign to diversify oil marketing, linked with diplomatic initiatives to reduce Libya's political isolation. Qadhafi flew to Beijing, where he called for Third World solidarity, and arranged a series of trade protocols. The rupture of relations with Britain in April 1984, following the shooting in St James's Square, London, was no more than a setback.

Qadhafi has displayed a remarkable degree of pragmatism. To improve relations with Morocco he ended military support for the Polisario Front; to develop this year's reconciliation with Sudan he withheld supplies to the Sudanese People's Liberation Army. Even before the fall of Nimeiri he had approached Sudan for negotiations, and he has recently made overtures to Iraq and Niger. □

J B

---

ing these terms, and construction schedules have suffered.

The one project exempt from the rigid fiscal policy is the Great Manmade River. This is funded by a purchase tax on consumer goods and, reputedly, an oil counter-trade agreement with South Korea, the home of the main contractor, Dong Ah Construction.

The "river" is an immense gamble. There is no guarantee that it will bring self-reliance in agriculture. Its over-dependence on foreign technology and labour encapsulates a dilemma of the whole development programme. The technology is US, British, Swedish and Swiss; the labour is Thai and South Korean.

The same features are evident in all the major development projects. The workforce is 36 per cent non-Libyan. Even in agriculture Egyptians and Pakistanis form a high percentage of manpower.

The advance towards self-sufficiency in technology would doubtless enable Libya to achieve a certain degree of self-sufficiency in production. It is already self-sufficient in eggs, poultry, vegetables and fruit, and, according to Qadhafi, 66 per cent in wheat and barley and 60 per cent in meat. But without the inputs, self-reliance would be impossible. □

Jon Bearman

Article 25

THE NEW YORK TIMES, SATURDAY, JANUARY 11, 1986

A Rare Glimpse of Colonel Qaddafi

By JUDITH MILLER
Special to The New York Times

TRIPOLI, Libya, Jan. 10 — Col. Muammar el-Qaddafi, the Reagan Administration's symbol of international terrorism, says he was born in the Islamic month of Muharram, the month of peace.

"In this month, we must not fight," the Libyan leader said. "And if we are fighting, we must stop during this period."

The colonel said he was not sure what month in the Gregorian calendar that Muharram is, since it varies from year to year in the Islamic calendar, which is lunar. But he says he thinks he was born in March.

Muharram is also the first month of the Islamic year, in effect a new beginning. That, Colonel Qaddafi said, is essentially what he has tried to achieve in Libya since coming to power in a coup that overthrew the monarchy 16 years ago.

His political dream, he said in an interview with five Western reporters Thursday, has always been to set up an Islamic utopia in this tribal country, a progressive democracy without race, class or sex distinctions, a society in which arms and the means of production would be in the hands of the masses. He was 29 years old at the time this vision came to him.

Young Ruler, Long Tenure

Now he is 44, still among the Arab world's youngest rulers. But he is among those who have been in power the longest.

Most Western officials and students of Libya say Colonel Qaddafi has created not a people's paradise, but a ruthless police state. The United States has accused him of having backed the Vienna and Rome airport attacks on Dec. 27 in which 19 people died, 5 of them Americans, and more than 100 were wounded.

Colonel Qaddafi has denied involvement in those attacks. His aides say he is not troubled by the portrait of him as an archterrorist that is drawn by the United States and other foes.

In the interview, however, Colonel Qaddafi tried to dispel that image by discussing his political goals and aspirations, his personal likes and dislikes, the crisis between Libya and the United States, and his personal and family life.

The interview, conducted in English, revealed a side of the leader that few journalists see — a man determined, at least in this encounter, to be likable, nonaggressive, almost jovial.

Curiosity and Naïveté

At the same time, he came across as a man ignorant of many political facts of life in the West, an isolated leader who often displayed an almost childlike curiosity and naïveté.

He expressed astonishment, for example, when told by one reporter that President Reagan was loved by many Americans.

"They love him?" Colonel Qaddafi said incredulously. "But he has created so many crises in the world," he said, shaking his head in disbelief.

Colonel Qaddafi was born in the town of Sirte, the son of an illiterate Bedouin. He went to school for only a few years and is basically a self-taught man. He learned English, which he speaks fairly well, in Tripoli and in Wilton, England, where he was a junior officer in a staff course in signals communication in 1966.

He disliked Britain, friends say, adding that he felt lost there and found the English cold and condescending.

He has traveled outside the Middle East relatively infrequently, and he has been unwelcome in many European countries for several years. He has never been to the United States, but said he admired what ordinary Americans had built. "It's hard to develop a country," Colonel Qaddafi said.

Reagan Is Called Weak

President Reagan, he asserted, was a weak man who was "under the domination of the Zionists." President Carter was also weak, he said. "But he was a good man," the colonel added.

Throughout the session, Colonel Qaddafi delighted in posing his own questions to the reporters. He asked, for example, whether Americans did not feel that their country was being destroyed and their relationship with the Arabs damaged by the country's close ties to Israel.

"Don't you realize that you are being pushed to the brink of war?" he said. "Of course," he continued, "none of you is Jewish."

One reporter objected. Her father is Jewish, she said.

"I see," the colonel replied. "But your mother?"

She was Roman Catholic, the reporter replied.

"To which one do you belong?" Colonel Qaddafi pressed.

"To both of them," the reporter responded. "And to my country."

"But your father, he is not a Zionist?" the colonel asked hopefully.

"Oh, yes," the reporter said. "He is an ardent Zionist, Colonel Qaddafi, as are many Americans."

"But how can they not understand the suffering of the Palestinian people?" the colonel said. "People whose land has been taken away?"

A Conciliatory Message

Colonel Qaddafi used the interview to deliver a conciliatory message similar to the one he gave Western European ambassadors who were summoned to meet with him Wednesday night. He vowed that he would try to persuade what he called his Palestinian brothers to limit their struggle to "military Israeli objectives."

Just before the interview, he had refused at a news conference to condemn the airport attacks.

Throughout the interview, Colonel Qaddafi demonstrated his ability to direct messages to appropriate audiences. When he speaks for Libyan or Arab consumption, he is savage. The official Libyan press agency, for example, has continued all week to praise the airport attacks as "heroic acts." Meeting with the ambassadors, however, the colonel said he did not approve of these "tragic events."

His mood at the news conference differed sharply from his mood at the interview with the five reporters, all of whom were women. He was far more relaxed during the interview, and joked with the reporters about finding Libyan husbands for them.

The Status of Women

The interview was conducted in a spartan inner office at the Bab el-Azzazir military barracks, a heavily fortified complex on the outskirts of Tripoli, where the news conference was also held. During the interview, he wore a camel-colored, gold-embroidered Arabic cloak.

The colonel did not say why he had decided to give the interview to women only. But he noticed immediately when one woman who was among the journalists at the news conference was not among those ushered into his inner sanctum.

He inquired about her and, in Arabic, asked an assistant, "How could you have forgotten her?" The reporter was quickly summoned back to the barracks.

One Wife and 7 Children

The colonel also emphasized his determination to improve the status of women. He said Libya was considering a law designed to end polygamy and to give women as well as men the right to demand a divorce.

He has one wife and seven children, only one of whom was a girl, "unfortunately," the colonel said. He said he would have liked more girls.

Colonel Qaddafi said encouraging his people to adopt more progressive ideas was among the biggest challenges he faced. "Petroleum societies are lazy everywhere," he said. "People are used to having more money and want everything available. The revolution wants to change this life and to promote production and work, to produce everything by our hands. But the people are lazy."

Utopia in Green Books

Colonel Qaddafi listed several political leaders he admired: Washington, Lincoln, Garibaldi, Sun Yat-sen, Gamal Abdel Nasser and Mahatma Ghandi. "Not Indira," he said.

The Green Books, the three slim volumes in which he outlines his eclectic view of the socialist Islamic utopia, were his own invention, he said. They were the product of his study of "history, human experience, life of ordinary people, what people need and how we make them happy, why one man is happy and another is sad," the colonel said.

There would be no more Green Books, he said, just interpretations of them.

As pastimes, Mr. Qaddafi listed music—classical music, especially Beethoven, he said—as well as horseback riding and reading.

Among his favorite books, he said, were Arabic translations of Alex Haley's "Roots," "Uncle Tom's Cabin" by Harriet Beecher Stowe and a book by the British author Colin Wilson, titled "The Outsider."

Lebanon:

Article 26   *Middle East International*, December 6, 1985

Life in Lebanon
In the camps

This article is by a correspondent who has recently returned from living and working in Lebanon

"I am a Palestinian. A citizen of the camp. I love the camp more than Palestine because I was born there. I have always lived there."

One of the most profound effects of the Israeli invasion and occupation of Lebanon has been to turn the camp into both a refuge and a death trap for Palestinians; an environment where they feel most secure, yet where their enemies come to hunt them down. Nowhere in the world is Palestinian existence more precarious, yet nowhere is it more important to preserve the camps as communities, thereby guaranteeing the Palestinians' continued presence in Lebanon.

Though they are more like villages, the camps are still something of ghettos for the Palestinians. They are over-crowded and economically depressed, with unemployment estimated at around 60 per cent of the active work-force. With the UNRWA budget shrinking in real terms every year, basic health care and sanitation are rudimentary. Even the main roads through a camp like Ain al-Hilweh have yet to be paved, and major sewers are left uncovered.

But in a country where there is virtually no government and no state provision of welfare or education services, the Palestinians are relatively well-off, particularly in comparison with many poor Shi'ites. The degree of independence and autonomy enjoyed by the Palestinians within their camps can be measured by the efforts of their enemies to break them up: immediately after invading Lebanon the Israelis tried for months to prevent the reconstruction of the largely decimated Ain al-Hilweh, grudgingly allowing tents but no permanent structures. In the same way, negotiations between UNRWA and the Lebanese government reached deadlock over whether Mieh Mieh, destroyed in the fighting in Sidon in March and April, should be rebuilt, a deadlock which was only broken by the residents themselves taking the matter into their own hands and setting to work. Again, reconstruction in Sabra/Chatila in West Beirut was stalled for a month after the "War of the Camps" this summer, partly by force, partly by threat, while rumours flew that there were to be tenement blocks built for the people, with wide roads criss-crossing the camp. Had such roads been built in Ain al-Hilweh before the invasion, the Palestinians would not have been able to resist Israeli tanks with such ferocity.

As a direct result of the invasion and occupation the

> *Palestinians cling to their existence within the camps because it is the closest thing they have to Palestine...*

Palestinians are now the most vulnerable community in Lebanon – the issue of whether they will be able to remain in the country has still not been resolved. Borj al-Barajneh and Sabra/Chatila are even now surrounded by the men and tanks of the Amal militia, creating great fear and despondency among the Palestinian community in Beirut. Many thousands have fled the capital, east to Baalbek or south to the one remaining "independent" camp in Sidon, and are still uncertain whether they will be able to return.

Meanwhile, Palestinians cling to their existence within the camps because it is the closest thing they have to Palestine, despite the fact that the camps are closely-packed, surroundable targets. Outside the camps there are too many hostile "no-go" areas, too many checkpoints, once manned by the Phalange, then by the Israelis, now by Amal – just south of Beirut at Khaldeh is now known as "Barbara", after the notorious checkpoint in East Beirut manned by the Lebanese Forces.

The tenacity of Palestinians determined to stay within the confines of the camps despite bombardments is remarkable – one old man stayed in Ain al-Hilweh throughout the five week assault on the camp from the hills controlled by the Lebanese Forces because he wanted to tend his beautiful garden. "I made the mistake

> *"It's not sardines we want, it's security."*

of leaving Palestine," he said, "and I'm not going to make the same mistake twice." Such an attitude is not difficult to understand when one considers the alternative: during the "War of the Camps" many Palestinians took refuge in empty basements and mosques in the areas just to the north of Sabra/Chatila, huddling in overcrowded conditions for days in fear in an area predominantly controlled by Amal. Separated from friends and family, the displaced made do as best they could on the tins of fish and bags of sugar handed out by relief workers. "It's not sardines we want", one woman shouted at me, "it's security." Nor is fleeing the camp necessarily safer than staying within its confines: scores of Palestinians were picked up off the streets of West Beirut during the summer. Some were shot, others have not been heard of since. During the war in Sidon in the spring, some of the displaced Palestinians who had taken shelter in the industrial city found themselves targetted once more and died amongst the lathes.

Two significant social changes have taken place within the Palestinian communities following this increased vulnerability within Lebanon. The first is the central role that women now play in running the camps. There are not large numbers of women serving on the camps' "Popular Committees" but in the areas of education, social welfare and community activity, most of the work is done by women. There are historical and cultural reasons for this: on the one hand Palestinian women have been used to coping while a significant proportion of their menfolk found work in the Gulf. In addition, after the Israeli invasion, the majority of men between the ages of 15 and 60 spent at least a year in Ansar or one of the other detention centres. And now, given the nature of the arbitrary and brutal nature of the fighting that has followed the Israelis' withdrawal, it is often only the women who have adequate mobility inside and outside the camps to maintain the necessary links between communities. In general, women are not regarded as militarily threatening and are allowed to come and go as they please by most militiamen. This is not true in all cases, and at least one woman I met had been detained overnight by Amal and had been interrogated and manhandled. Yet it seems that cognisance is finally being given to the important role women played during the siege of Borj al-Barajneh in June and July. One particular press photograph showed a middle-aged Palestinian woman demonstrating the wooden catapult she had constructed, which she used to shoot tin cans packed with explosives. And it was the women who first returned to Sabra/Chatila after this summer's fighting and began the long process of reconstructing the camp. Palestinian women are the social cement of their community at a time when all the pressures are for greater fragmentation.

The second social change is the increased radicalisation and Islamicisation of young people. This is due partly to the upsurge of fundamentalism in Lebanon as a whole, partly to the increased rapprochement between the Islamic groups and Fatah, and partly to the diminishing range of options and opportunities open to young Palestinians. These latter range from the danger of setting foot outside the camp, to the widespread disillusionment among young people with the current Palestinian leadership. In addition, the Middle East's largest vocational training school, Sibline, has now closed, drastically curtailing the chance of most young Palestinians to gain access to further education. Evidence of increased Islamicisation can be found among young girl Fatah scouts, who are encouraged to wear headscarves and Islamic dress, and among young fighters who tend more and more to go off to battle with green head-bands with "There is no god but God" inscribed in white. A number of educated young Palestinians I know in Ain al-Hilweh read the *Tawheed* newspaper, the publication of the Sunni fundamentalist from Tripoli, Said Shaaban, and talk of the need for Palestinians to find a religious leader of the quality of Khomeini to restore power to the *Umma*, the community of believers. Although Palestinian communities are nowhere near as fundamentalist in tenor as the Shi'ite communities in the south, for example, the change is significant enough for Palestinians themselves to be commenting on it, and to be unclear, as yet, whether it will last or not.

Because of the prevailing insecurity for everyone living in Lebanon there can be no certainties, no guarantees that what is true today will be true tomorrow. In the meantime, the Palestinians are desperate defenders of the little autonomy they have left, and continue to pick themselves up, brush themselves off and get on with the business of maintaining their lives.

Article 27

THE ECONOMIST MAY 25, 1985

Who won Lebanon?

Three years ago next month Israel catapulted its army over its northern border to change the political map of Lebanon. With one important exception, the plan failed. The map has changed (see next page), but mostly not in the way intended by Mr Menahem Begin, then Israel's prime minister, and his defence minister, Mr Ariel Sharon. From the Israeli viewpoint, many of the changes on the map mean an uglier, more dangerous, Lebanon than before.

But not all. One of Israel's aims in invading Lebanon was to rid itself of the danger posed by the presence of the Palestine Liberation Organisation's guerrillas on neigbouring soil. The guns of the PLO now control neither west Beirut nor the southern section of Lebanon—including the frontier with Israel—which used to come under their sway. There are still pockets of Mr Yasser Arafat's men in Sidon and in Beirut, but even in the capital's southern slums, over the past week, the last armed Arafat units have been under attack by the Amal militia of the Shia Moslems, apparently with Syrian

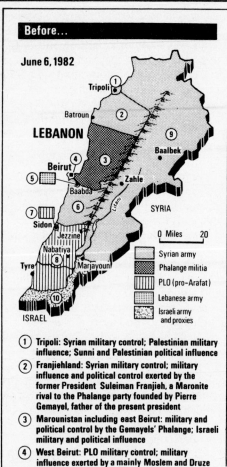

Before...

June 6, 1982

Syrian army
Phalange militia
PLO (pro-Arafat)
Lebanese army
Israeli army and proxies

① Tripoli: Syrian military control; Palestinian military influence; Sunni and Palestinian political influence

② Franjiehland: Syrian military control; military influence and political control exerted by the former President Suleiman Franjieh, a Maronite rival to the Phalange party founded by Pierre Gemayel, father of the present president

③ Marounistan including east Beirut: military and political control by the Gemayels' Phalange; Israeli military and political influence

④ West Beirut: PLO military control; military influence exerted by a mainly Moslem and Druze

coalition; Sunni political control

⑤ Presidential enclave at Baabda, including headquarters of Lebanon's national army

⑥ Druzistan: Syrian military control; military influence and political control exerted by the Jumblatt family, led by Walid Jumblatt; patches of Maronite political influence, exerted mainly by the family of the former president, Camille Chamoun

⑦ Sidon: PLO military control; military influence and

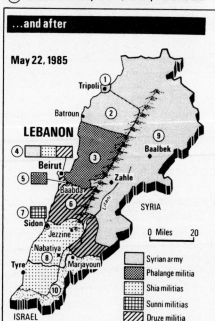

...and after

May 22, 1985

Syrian army
Phalange militia
Shia militias
Sunni militias
Druze militia
Israeli army and proxies

political control exerted by Sunnis

⑧ The south: PLO military control; military and political influence exerted by Shias, Communists and the Popular Syrian party (PPS)

⑨ The Bekaa valley: Syrian military and political control; Shia, Sunni and PPS political influence

⑩ Haddadland: Israeli military and political control largely via Major Saad Haddad, a Lebanese Christian proxy; Maronite military and political influence

① Tripoli: Syrian military and political control except in city centre dominated by pro-Arafat Sunni fundamentalists

② Franjiehland: same as 1982

③ Marounistan including east Beirut: military control exerted since March, 1985, mainly by pro-Israeli rebel faction of Maronites' Phalange; political contest for control of the Phalange between rebel faction and President Amin Gemayel's Syrian-blessed faction

④ West Beirut: Syrian, Shia and Druze military control; Syrian, Shia and Sunni political influence

⑤ Presidential enclave at Baabda, including headquarters of Lebanon's national army plus Phalange militias loyal to President Gemayel; Syrian political influence

⑥ Druzistan: Druze and Syrian military and political control

⑦ Sidon: Sunni and pro-Syrian PLO military control; Shia military influence; Sunni political control

⑧ The south: Shia military and political control, exerted mainly by secular Amal party; Communist, PPS and Hezbollah (fundamentalist Shia) military influence

⑨ The Bekaa valley: same as 1982, but some pro-Syrian PLO military influence

⑩ Lahadland: Israeli military and political control via General Antoine Lahad and his Christian-led South Lebanese Army; Maronite military and political influence

approval. Since Israel's withdrawal from the south speeded up, a number of Palestinian guerrillas have been trickling towards the border, but they belong to factions tightly controlled by Syria. Mr Arafat's military power in Lebanon seems on the verge of collapse.

But if Mr Arafat has lost, Israel has not gained in proportion to his loss. Mr Sharon's aim had been a pro-Israeli Lebanese government run by Maronite Christians. The result, today, is an exceedingly feeble pro-Syrian government with a Christian president who is little more than a figurehead.

The irony is that, although Syria was trounced by Israel at the start of the Lebanese war, Syria has none the less emerged as the chief beneficiary of the Israeli invasion. Syria's President Assad has not yet succeeded in imposing a full *pax Syriana* on all the Lebanese factions. All the same, he has seen Syria's influence percolate throughout the country, except along a thin strip of the southern border and perhaps in the area around Sidon. If anyone is almost in control of Lebanon, it is Mr Assad.

If there are any Lebanese map-win-

ners, they are the Shias and the Druzes. The losers are the Sunni Moslems and—above all—Israel's chief allies, the Maronites. The Sunnis, whose rather conservative political leaders once spoke with some authority for Lebanon's Moslems, have been pushed into the shade, and their militias brushed aside. Practically nowhere in Lebanon lies under Sunni military control, except corners of Tripoli and Sidon.

The Maronites' reverse has been even more drastic. All their territorial pockets south of Beirut have been overrun, except for the vulnerable little enclave of Jezzine and the frontier strip held, courtesy of Israel, by the dwindling band of unhappy militiamen under General Antoine Lahad. The Maronites still hold the coast and hinterland north of Beirut and south of Tripoli. But they are divided. Lebanon's President Amin Gemayel, head of the family which founded the Phalange party and has been helped by Israel for nearly three decades, has been forced to bend the knee to Mr Assad. This has provoked a revolt by the Phalange's hardliners, who probably command the party's sympathy. But, with the Syri-

ans standing balefully in support of Mr Gemayel, the presidential faction may yet prevail. If it does, Israel will have lost its Maronite connection and any hope of political sway over Lebanon.

The greatest territorial gain has been made by the Druzes. They have cleared their Chouf hills of almost all the remaining Christian influence, and extended their fief down to the Mediterranean in the west and across to the Syrian border in the east. In terms of pure muscle, however, the Shias, Lebanon's largest single community, have emerged as the brawniest new power, with the balance of guns and—if there is ever another Lebanese election—votes in their favour. Most important, they have displaced the PLO both in west Beirut and in southern Lebanon, and have claimed that it is they who are chiefly responsible for harrying the Israelis home.

Now, after the loss of 654 Israeli and at least 12,000 Lebanese lives, the Israelis are almost back to the border. Their remaining, modest, aim is to achieve a truce with the new Shia masters of southern Lebanon. There are signs that a tentative one may already have been arranged. While much of the rest of Lebanon is at war as usual, a strange calm has descended on the southernmost strip. Since May 1st Shia guerrillas have virtually stopped attacking Israeli soldiers.

Will the new semi-peace last? There are a host of imponderables. First, Israel wants Mr Nabih Berri and his more secular-minded Shias to assert themselves over the wilder, more fundamentalist ones who look for inspiration to Iran. Mr Berri is winning the intra-Shia competition in southern Lebanon, but is having a harder time of it in Beirut.

With Syrian approval, Mr Berri's militiamen were this week clobbering the Palestinians in Beirut. They seem determined to sweep Beirut clean of the PLO. By May 22nd at least 100 Palestinians had been killed by Mr Berri's men in Beirut in fighting that started on May 19th and, by May 23rd, the Shias claimed they had wrested control of the Sabra and Chatila refugee camps from the PLO.

The message Mr Berri is delivering is music to Israeli ears. If he can be so ruthless in Beirut, maybe he can enforce his party's paramountcy in southern Lebanon, and keep the border peaceful. But it is not clear that Mr Berri is yet willing to be as vigorous in confronting the Shia militants in Beirut and the Bekaa valley—who may be just as anxious as Mr Arafat's Palestinians to raid Israel over the frontier.

The trickiest part of any Israeli-Shia deal would be the buffer zone. The Israelis hope that the Shias will drop their threat to fight on until General Lahad's Israeli-armed militia disintegrates. They want the general's men to control the border strip. If that proves impossible,

the Israelis are asking themselves—and perhaps Mr Berri—whether it would be feasible for Israel to entrust the border to small groups of Shia and Christian militiamen responsible for keeping armed strangers out of their own villages.

If Mr Berri proves unable to call off the guerrillas or seal the border, Israel says Syria must do the job—or else. Some Israelis claim to believe that the entire guerrilla war in the south has been orchestrated by the Syrians. Ergo, if Israel is to come to terms with the southern Lebanese, Syria has to be argued or threatened into tacit co-operation. How? Another war does not seem to be on the cards at the moment. The Israelis continue to hint that it is always a possibility. It is not a possibility that Mr Assad relishes. But neither do most Israelis.

Morocco:

Article 28

Middle East International, October 11, 1985

Libya and Morocco—marriage of necessity

by George Henderson

The extraordinary political marriage between Morocco and Libya has, despite all the gloomy prognostications, survived its first year. The treaty, which was based on a plan put to Colonel Qadhafi by King Hassan during a meeting in August 1983, formally came into being on 1 September 1984. It caused an immediate outcry of protest in other North African capitals, particularly in Algiers, where the treaty was seen as a deliberate riposte to Algerian attempts to create Maghrebi unity through its March 1983 treaty with Tunisia, to which Mauritania adhered in December 1983.

Morocco and Libya had both been unable to adhere to the Algerian treaty, because neither of them could fulfil the conditions laid down by Algeria – a resolution of outstanding disputes in the region, particularly with respect to the Western Sahara, and the delimitation of regional borders. Libya was excluded because of a long-standing dispute over its common border with Algeria, and even though Tunisia suggested ways to permit Libyan adherence, Algeria remained opposed – not least because Libya had reduced its support for the Polisario Front, the Sahrawi national liberation movement, in its struggle with Morocco for control of the Western Sahara. This support had noticeably declined since mid-1983 largely because of

Qadhafi's rapprochement with Morocco and his decision to rebuild his bridges with moderate states in the Middle East, particularly Saudi Arabia. Indeed, his rapprochement with Morocco had originally been largely conditioned by Algeria's continued spurning of Libyan overtures for closer relations.

Although outstanding border disputes between Morocco and Algeria had been theoretically resolved in a

> *The slow abandoning of the SADR and the [Polisario] Front was not too difficult a step for Colonel Qadhafi to take.*

1972 treaty (which still awaits ratification), the Western Sahara conflict made any close link between the two quite unthinkable. The surprise meeting between King Hassan and the Algerian president, Chadli Ben Jedid, in February 1983 marked an end to the frigid atmosphere that had characterised the Boumedienne era, but did not really signify a change of heart by either state.

In this context, the sudden decision of Morocco and Libya to form their own union seems much less surprising, despite the profound differences in their political structures and international aspirations. Libya was, after all, the world's first *jamahiriyah* (state of the masses) – the embodiment of direct popular democracy even if Colonel Qadhafi maintained a firm, even repressive control. Morocco, on the other hand, was a traditional Islamic sultanate in which the ruler had the added quality of *caliph* or religious leader of his people and mediator for them with Allah. The system was modified by an element of guided democracy in which a large number of political parties ebulliently disputed the restricted political terrain proffered to them by the royal palace. The treaty arrangements mirrored these profound differences by enabling each state to maintain its own political system, while binding each to support the other against external threats. The provision for other states to join the "Arab-African Union", as the treaty was called, emphasised the continued individuality of member states – unlike the Algerian alternative, which required compromise.

The most immediate benefit of the treaty for both countries was that each could consider that it had successfully broken out from the isolation imposed upon it by regional events – Libya from the constrictions of Algeria's border demands and Tunisian anxiety over mutual relations, and Morocco from the growing diplomatic crisis over the Western Sahara. Indeed, the initial benefits for Morocco were by far the most compelling, since the Moroccan government's continued refusal to honour a June 1981 pledge to hold a referendum over the Western Sahara issue was clearly going to lead to a major crisis inside the Organisation for African Unity (OAU). In the light of this refusal, it became clear that the OAU would have to seat a delegation from the Saharan Arab Democratic Republic (SADR), the political wing of the Polisario Front, at its next meeting in November 1984. Algeria, in the wake of the Libyan-Moroccan treaty, had decided that it no longer believed in Moroccan protestations of willingness to comply with international resolutions – in both the OAU and the UN – over self-determination for the Sahrawi, and stepped up its military support for the Front.

The Libyan-Moroccan treaty, then, offered Morocco an effective means of breaking the growing diplomatic opposition to its occupation of the Western Sahara – ironically enough at a time when its military status was being steadily improved by the strategy of defensive walls which since 1980 had steadily pushed Moroccan control from the Layyoune-Smara-Bou Craa triangle towards the Algerian border and southwards towards the Atlantic coastal town of Dakhla, which in August 1985 was finally brought into the Moroccan defensive system. Libya, for its part, while it did not originally approve of Morocco's occupation and offered the Polisario Front increasing military and humanitarian support, decried the "Balkanisation", as Colonel Qadhafi saw it, implied by the creation of yet another state in North Africa. As a result, the slow abandoning of the SADR and the Front was not too difficult a step for Colonel Qadhafi to take.

The consequences of this move were first seen in Libya's abstention over issues involving the Western Sahara issue at the OAU and the UN in November 1984

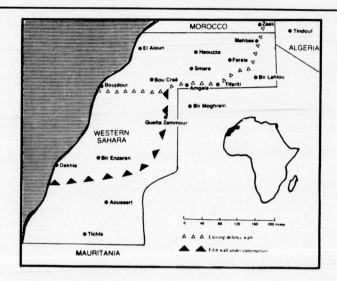

and in its refusal to host a joint meeting of the Arab League and the OAU in Tripoli in April 1985. In addition, King Hassan has been able to rest content that the Front is now totally dependent on Algeria for military supplies and that the 120,000-150,000 Saharan refugees in camps around Tindouf depend on continued Algerian support for their survival (see page 20). Strangely enough, despite the collapse of Libyan material and diplomatic support for the Saharan cause, Libya has not withdrawn its recognition of the SADR and still figures among the 63 states worldwide that have recognised it.

Apart from the Western Sahara issue – clearly the most important aspect as far as Morocco is concerned – and the wider issue for Libya of generalised support for an avowedly moderate, pro-American state such as Morocco, in the face of continuing and virulent hostility from the Reagan administration and the US Congress, the treaty has had other, albeit minor, benefits. Morocco has been able to anticipate economic benefits – opportunities for Moroccan workers seeking an alternative to chronic unemployment; access to Libyan oil supplies, a vital consideration for a country that spends the equivalent of half its export earnings on oil imports; and the opportunity for Moroccan business to penetrate a potentially useful market.

Not surprisingly the reality has not lived up to the ideal. Libya faces a major economic crisis with its oil revenues cut by more than half from the 1980 level of $22 billion to a likely level of only $7.5 billion this year – and its foreign reserves falling by more than sixfold from their 1983 level of $6 billion. It has been forced to expel foreign workers in large numbers, which makes it unlikely that more Moroccan workers can find employment there, although up to 35,000 Moroccan workers already in Libya have not been affected by the recent expulsions. At the same time, Morocco has also been offered $100m by Libya to help with wheat purchases – about half the total cost of Moroccan wheat imports this year. Several joint companies have also been formed and Libya is to help in Morocco's current drive to discover oil. Moroccan companies have been bitterly disappointed, however, by the complexities of

On the economic front, the results have been far from dramatic.

operating in the Libyan market and by the consequences of the fall in oil revenues.

On the economic front, therefore, the results have been mixed and far from dramatic. Politically, however, relations have, on occasion, been explosive. King Hassan was reportedly furious that Libya should have decided in June to strengthen its relations with Iran, given Morocco's moderate alignment with Jordan, Egypt and Iraq in the Middle East. Libya found King Hassan's recent conference in August over the Palestinian issue and the current Jordanian-inspired peace moves for peace with Israel unpalatable in the extreme and sent only a low level delegation to the preliminary meetings for the Casablanca summit and stayed away from the meeting proper. There have been other, more concealed, conflicts over Middle Eastern affairs, but Libya has, at least, been instrumental in healing a long-standing rift between Morocco and Syria

earlier this year, while Morocco has continued to act as honest broker in discussions between the authorities in N'Jamena and Libya over the future of Chad.

Moroccan displeasure with Libya is underlined by the fact that King Hassan has still not made his long promised visit to Tripoli and sent a low-level delegation to the 16th anniversary celebrations of Libya's revolution. Nonetheless, despite these surface disagreements, Morocco and Libya need each other. Libya is about to face another onslaught from the Reagan administration, while Morocco still has to cope with the continuing Algerian diplomatic campaign in support of the SADR. Currently, moves are under way to have Morocco condemned by Third World opinion at the non-aligned summit meeting in Luanda and here continued Libyan support will be vital. Nonetheless, the issue does underline the critical role played by the Arab African Union for both countries – for Libya as a bulwark against the USA and for Morocco as a guarantee against diplomatic isolation in the Third World over the Sahara. In short, the imperatives are exactly as they were one year ago, with the one exception that the divisions in North Africa – ironically caused by moves towards regional unity – are now more profound than ever.

Oman:

Article 29

THE NEW YORK TIMES, TUESDAY, NOVEMBER 19, 1985

Oman Gives Super Party: It's Come a Long Way

By JOHN KIFNER
Special to The New York Times

MUSCAT, Oman, Nov. 18 — The Bedouins are in from the desert for the celebration, camped at the far edge of the city: dark, whippet-lean men with hawklike faces, few teeth and daggers in their belts, hobbling their camels out by the silvery disk antennas of the television satellite station.

Fifteen years ago, this far edge of the Arabian Peninsula was a medieval place, kept isolated by its absolute ruler, the reclusive and curmudgeonly Sultan Said bin Taimur, who forbade smoking, listening to the radio, playing drums or the stringed oud, and the wearing of eyeglasses or European shoes.

There were only six miles of paved road then — from the royal palace to the airport — but there was little demand for more because the Sultan decided who could have a car and allowed few of them. Similarly, he decided who could get married, be educated or legally leave the country. For himself, he avoided the use of gasoline, preferring to have his automobile pushed along by slaves.

Oman today is a nation yanked into the modern world. Starting from scratch, propelled by 500,000 barrels a day worth of oil money, it is a country creating itself. Construction is going on at such a rate that people who leave the capital for a few months often cannot find their way around when they return, because of all the new highway overpasses and skyscrapers.

Coup Is Turning Point

The turning point came on July 23, 1970, when Sultan Qabus bin Said, then a shy 29-year-old graduate of Sandhurst, the British military academy, who had been kept under virtual house arrest for four years, overthrew his father with the aid of discontented tribal sheiks and a certain amount of counseling by a British Army captain on assignment here, Timothy Landon.

Slaves who were supposedly on guard waved a small raiding party into the palace, the windows of which had been painted blue so no one could see in. Trying to pull a pistol, the old Sultan shot himself in the foot to become the only casualty of the day. He left on a

British Royal Air Force plane and died in his suite at the Dorchester Hotel in London two years later.

Today, Sultan Qabus and Oman began a celebration of 15 years of his rule in a flourish of visits by representatives from some 60 countries, including half a dozen heads of state. The occasion is National Day, which does not mark any particular historic event but coincides with the Sultan's birthday.

The events began early this morning when the Sultan, in a gold-encrusted blue and red uniform, reviewed a full-dress parade of his British-trained troops. There will be camel races by the Bedouins and a multimillion-dollar Hollywood-produced fireworks display.

"Its a coming out day," said a Western diplomat, who added that the country had been on "a sustained high since 1979," when the oil revenues really began rolling in.

"The Sultan seems to be saying now is as good a time as any to say to the world, 'We are a mature country,'" the diplomat said.

Amid the preparations for National Day, it is beginning to look a lot like Christmas here, with red, green and white lightbulbs outlining everything from the turrets of the old Portuguese forts on the rocky heights above the picture-book harbor to the new ministries and high-rise buildings to the construction cranes themselves.

The highways are decorated with flashing lights, and the street light stanchions are bedecked with illuminated representations of butterflies, castles and potted flowers. There are 1,797 Omani flags along the way to the brand-new $232 million Al Bustan Palace Hotel.

Fifteen years ago, Omanis love to tell their visitors, there were only three schools in the country, all of them elementary schools, with 900 students, all boys. Now there are 591 schools with 225,000 students, 43 percent of them women or girls, and a concentration on spreading education to the vast rural areas and on practical studies such as agriculture and nursing.

Under government scholarships, about 200 students graduate from foreign universities each year now, but a new Sultan Qabus University is under construction. Other statistics show the quantum leap: 2,100 miles of paved roads, 2,600 new hospital beds, a 40-fold rise in per capita income to about $8,000 a year.

A Wasteland Transformed

Vast stretches of houses and stores rise on what was wasteland a decade ago. There are ubiquitous Japanese four-wheel-drive pickup trucks for the Bedouins now, and aluminum or fiberglass motorboats are replacing the

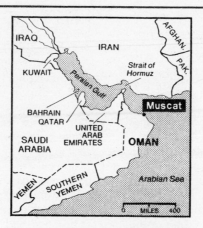

The New York Times/Nov. 19, 1985

Skyscrapers have rapidly changed the face of the capital, Muscat.

high-prowed wooden fishermen's rowboats.

"In 1970 there was nothing," Minister of Education Yahya al-Mantheri said in an interview. "We are running, not walking, to get the infrastructure to work."

So far, diplomats here say, Oman seems to have avoided much of the garish excess that has accompanied new oil wealth in the Middle East. "They've learned a lot from their gulf neighbors; there's a lot fewer white elephants around here," a Western diplomat said.

The Sultan, another expert noted, has also shown a concern for historical scholarship and for the environment. A campaign is under way, for example, against beach litterers who have been disturbing the nesting areas of the loggerhead turtle.

Much of the policy here has been shaped by a coterie of advisers to the

Sultan, most of them British and some reputed to have backgrounds in intelligence.

The British influence is still strong here, particularly in the military. Britain sent crack Special Air Service troops to help the Sultan put down a rebellion of mountain tribesmen backed by Communist Southern Yemen at the beginning of his rule. Some 200 British officers are on loan to the Sultan's army, while about 1,000 Britons are under hire as contract, or mercenary, officers.

The Chief of the Defense Staff, the highest-ranking military officer, is a British lieutenant general, the Air Force commander a British air vice marshal and the naval commander a British rear admiral.

Slow 'Omanization'

There is an official policy of "Omanization," or replacing expatriates with Omanis not only in the military but throughout the economy. The process is proceeding slowly, one diplomat said, because the Sultan "doesn't want Omanization at the cost of efficiency, and in any case you won't ever Omanize the menial jobs."

More than two-thirds of the work force here is made up of foreigners, many from the Indian subcontinent. Oman is dependent on foreigners for almost everything, including the armies of street cleaners who make this a uniquely neat country in the Arab world.

At the new hospital in the southern city of Salala, where some tribesmen refuse to check the old Lee-Enfield rifles that are a standard male accessory, none of the 52 doctors or 200 nurses is an Omani. The mail room has special slots marked to send letters to India Sri Lanka and Pakistan.

Saudi Arabia:

Article 30

The Christian Science Monitor, March 21, 1983

Cheers for the Saudi camel race

King tries to keep an old Bedouin tradition

By George Joseph Tanber
Special to The Christian Science Monitor

Riyadh, Saudi Arabia

On the last turn it was Al Harab out front and all alone.

As the crowd rose to cheer, the young jockey continued to flail his stick against his mount's backside, driving him toward the end. Then, after crossing into glory, 11-year-old Solaiman Obeid jumped down from his camel, bounded up the stairs of the royal pavilion, and came face to face with the King of Saudi Arabia.

King Fahd presented the seemingly unawed young boy with $10,000, a gold dagger, and the keys to a 20,000-gallon water

tanker. Al Harab had to settle for 1,000 bags of fodder for his 35-minute, 12-mile run.

And so it went during the King's Camel Races, held earlier this month at the Janadriyeh Race Track just outside Saudi Arabia's capital city.

The races became an annual event nine years ago under the late King Faisal, who wanted to bring the monarchy and the people together for an occasion symbolic of the country's heritage, according to Abdullah al-Bassam, manager of the Equestrian Club, a co-sponsor with the National Guard.

"For centuries the Bedouin have been racing their camels and horses at informal events, but with the rapid modernization of Saudi Arabia King Faisal foresaw a time when perhaps it would end," said Mr. Bassam. "This race guarantees that it (the tradition) will continue."

The race is primarily a Bedouin affair. Craggy-faced nomads—National Guard reserves—in well-worn robes and Arab headdresses lined both sides of the mile-long entrance road, clutching their single-shot, bolt-action rifles. The Guard traditionally lines the route the King takes on special occasions.

Meanwhile, boy jockeys, sons of Bedouins, and their trainers were busy prepping their camels, which are scruffy and ornery-looking even on the best of days. Red numbers were painted on their necks for the race.

As the entrants filed out onto the track, fans scrambled for seats in the small public viewing stand. Next-door the royal family began filtering into the royal pavilion with its Persian carpets and plush chairs. Joining King Fahd were his brothers Prince Abdullah and Prince Sultan, second and third in line for the throne. United Arab Emirates President Sheikh Zayed was a special guest of the King.

Once the King and senior princes arrived, security tightened considerably. Throngs of policemen in green-denim uniforms blanketed the spectator and track areas.

There were 586 camels (most between four and six years old) entered in the opening race. Of Sudanese breeding, they are larger and faster than the Arabian camels raced in the afternoon. The race is broadcast live across the kingdom and is also replayed in the evening. The royal pavilion is fitted with a live television monitor.

The pack started out on the far side of the looped track, a distance requiring binoculars to identify the racers. Some of the boys rode bareback while others used leather saddles or blankets; some sat directly atop the hump while others chose to ride more toward the animal's backside. All the jockeys used stick-whips and shouts and whoops to motivate their mounts.

On the second lap a number of camels began to tire or lose interest and dropped out. One, No. 246, plopped down in front of the pavilion, snorting and foaming at the mouth. The jockey lashed and cursed at the animal, but it refused to budge. Three race stewards pushed from behind in an attempt to get it going, but to no avail.

Between races the spectators and guardsmen retreated to tents for Saudi-style tailgate parties—lamb, rice, and fruit followed by naps and afternoon tea. In one such setting Khaled al-Tmammy, the public relations assistant for the Guard, was asked if there was any gambling during the event.

"Absolutely forbidden!" he replied.

The second race, also a 12-mile run, was more hotly contested. These were the plodders trained for long-distance riding, and the 700-plus camels in this event stayed closely bunched throughout. King Fahd and his entourage chose a new vantage point for watching the race—a customized bus that followed the leaders around the track.

Ahmed Rahman, 12, brought Dabiaan home first in the afternoon race just ahead of Al-Husan and Rabba to claim the same kind of prizes Solaiman Obeid had won earlier.

An inquiry into who kept what of the bounty was answered when the announcer said the winning owner was Prince Muhammad ibn Saud. Prince Mohammad, it turned out, also owned the first three finishers in the morning race. "Most of the top camels belong to men of means, so the boys (jockeys) normally get to keep everything," said a spectator.

After the race, King Fahd led his group in the early evening prayer. Down on the track spectators once again mixed with the jockeys and their mounts. Enterprising photographers with instant cameras did a brisk business posing rider and camel at $3 a shot. And to the cheers of his admirers, Ahmad Rahman and his father drove their new water tanker off into the sunset.

Article 31

THE NEW REPUBLIC
OCTOBER 21, 1985

The party's over for Saudi Arabia.

AFTER OPEC

THE KINGDOM of Saudi Arabia is in a fix, financially and politically. For the past 12 years it has been the linchpin of the oil cartel, the 25-year-old Organization of Petroleum Exporting Countries. In order to survive, it may now be forced to cast off OPEC and go its own way.

The reason for the crisis is the precipitous decline in Saudi oil income, from $110 billion in 1980 to $25 billion in 1985 (even less if the depreciation of the dollar is taken into account). The cause of the decline is the 1979-80 tripling of prices from $12 to $36 a barrel. The bonanza proved to be short-lived, but it has created a long-term problem for Saudi Arabia and other Arab countries that have large oil reserves. The price jump spawned a massive effort of conservation and fuel switching that has cut world oil consumption, created a glut, and led Riyadh to reduce its oil production from over ten million barrels per day to 2.5 mbd. Even this huge cut, and smaller cuts by other OPEC members, have not been able to stem the slide in oil prices, now down to about $26 a barrel, and still falling.

AS OIL INCOME rose from $36 billion in 1977-78, the Saudi budget climbed as well. The annual deficit is now about $20 billion. With financial reserves reputed to be about $100 billion—and not all of them liquid—the outlook is not bright. Cutting government expenditures to fit income is painful and can even be hazardous. Raising oil production to increase income could also turn out to be risky. If Riyadh doubles production to five mbd, it would lower the price to below $20 and cause serious problems for all other oil producers—including Iran, Iraq, and Egypt, all of them powerful neighbors.

This dilemma has been evident ever since the 1980 price rise, but the Saudis have been lucky. Their major threat in the gulf has been Iran; in the Arab world their rival has been Iraq. For five years, however, these two nations have been locked in an exhausting conflict brought on by the ill-advised decision of Saddam Hussein, Iraq's dictator, to invade Iran's oil region. The conflict has been prolonged by the stubbornness of the Ayatollah Khomeini, who is literally demanding Hussein's head as his price for peace.

Yet from the point of view of Saudi Arabia and the other Arab gulf states (Kuwait, Qatar, Bahrein, and the United Arab Emirates), the war has produced a double bonus: it has removed an imminent military threat (Iraq has long claimed part of Kuwait or even all of it); and it has drastically cut oil exports from Iran and Iraq, allowing other OPEC members to sell more oil. Unfortunately, Saudi Arabia and Kuwait have been forced into multibillion-dollar subsidies of Iraq to enable it to withstand Iran's counterassault.

The establishment of the state of Israel has worked to Riyadh's advantage. Arab radicals and others who might have attacked Saudi Arabia in an effort to take over the oil wealth of the Arab peninsula have focused their aggression instead on Israel. There is no reason to doubt Riyadh's opposition to Zionism, often coupled with crude anti-Semitism, but it has been said that if Israel did not exist, Saudi Arabia would have had to invent it.

In the mid-1960s Gamal Abdel Nasser, supported by Soviet Russia, had his troops in Yemen in the southern tip of the Arabian peninsula. There is firm evidence that he was using poison gas in an effort to subdue the tribes. Riyadh, in the meantime, was supporting the royalists in North Yemen with indifferent success. Nasser disappeared as a threat to Saudi Arabia after Israel defeated his armed forces in the Six-Day War of 1967.

By 1973, when Egypt had recovered its strength and Syria had become a major military power (thanks to Soviet arms and Saudi financial support), Israel repeated its 1967 performance—although at much greater cost. In the interim and after, Israel dealt with the PLO and assorted radical groups, mostly financed by Saudi Arabia. It is clear from the PLO's war matériel captured in the Lebanon operation in 1982 that it had received generous funds from the Saudis, which it had used to buy Soviet arms.

The existence of Israel thus has enabled Riyadh to deflect intra-Arab threats by playing the role of a "moderate" in Western eyes while supporting the radical states opposed to Egypt and Jordan's making peace with Israel. More important, by using a relatively small part of its oil income, Riyadh has removed from the agenda the question of who owns Arabian oil resources: ruling families, nations set up mostly by Western governments, or the whole Arab entity. If there is really an Arab nation, some Arabs believe, then the oil should be looked at as an Arab or even Islamic patrimony. In this respect, Libya's Muammar al-Qaddafi has been quite forthright, using his oil wealth for what he declares to be Arab and Islamic objectives, including terrorism against the West.

But Riyadh's luck is running out. Iraq is exporting more oil, an extra one mbd by 1986, and will want to maintain its quota in spite of the falling need for OPEC oil. Khomeini is exporting both oil and subversion. He is helped by the fact that the Arab population of the gulf oil region is mostly Shiite. The recent assassination attempt on Kuwait's ruler by Shiite terrorists may be a preview of things to come.

Syria looms as a possible threat—politically and as an oil exporter. Hafez al-Assad is not likely to attack Saudi Arabia; Iraq is a much more tempting target. But Syria, as the region's strongest military power and the training base for Shiite terrorists, may extract what it wants by blackmail and threats. A recent oil discovery at Deir ez Zor means that Syria will soon join the ranks of oil exporters.

STILL, the foreign threats pale beside the domestic one: the deficit. Saudi Arabia's fourth Five-Year Plan (1985-90), issued in March 1985, may already be out of date. It evidently envisions an annual oil income of about $50 billion, based on a production of five mbd and a price of about $30. But with current production of 2.5 mbd and falling prices, the average annual oil income over the next five years may be more like $20 billion to $25 billion.

Some of Riyadh's ambitious development projects in areas such as education, agriculture and industry, health, and housing, are likely to be stretched out. Many capital projects are likely to be canceled, once revenues are factored in. The current budget (March 1985-86) is thought to be $75 billion (including military expenditures of $17 billion). It probably does not include "foreign aid," the so-called loans to Iraq and other Arab groups. With investment income at perhaps ten billion dollars and only minor tax income, oil income is by far the largest planned source of revenues—and it may be off by 50 percent. Clearly expenditures will have to be cut and revenues enhanced.

Of course, budget cuts can be hazardous to the regime in power. We have witnessed demonstrations elsewhere, in Egypt and even in Israel, when the government tried to reduce subsidies or tampered in some way with the standard of living. In the Saudi case, expectations have been built up for a wider distribution of the oil wealth, and there will be great disappointment for the merchant class, technocrats, and military who haven't yet gotten their share. The distribution of oil wealth in Saudi Arabia has been based on the original trickle-down mechanism: subsidies, and commissions paid whenever the government spends money. This may be a reason for keeping arms purchases high. It will be important for the government to demonstrate that the burden is spread equitably. Will it try taxation on a large scale to pay for social programs?

The key to avoiding a crisis may lie in attracting private capital to invest in Saudi development projects. That is the main theme of the Fourth Development Plan, which devotes much attention to providing incentives to investors. There is no doubt about the huge oil wealth held by private Saudis, not only by members of the royal family. But it is not certain that these Saudis can be persuaded to invest and demonstrate their faith in the viability of the kingdom.

I N THE PAST, Riyadh has been able to obtain outside investments, mainly from foreign oil companies, by promising them access to oil. But as these companies have belatedly discovered, oil can always be obtained, without making any special concessions, by paying the market price. Mobil and Shell have invested in Saudi oil refineries designed to export oil products, only to find that they are uneconomical because of high maintenance and operation costs, and high transport costs of products to European markets. Many other development projects may turn out to be white elephants—hardly a way to attract new investors.

Any realistic appraisal of Saudi Arabia's financial prospects for the next several years would give only moderate weight to budget cutting without causing social unrest, and little weight to harnessing private Saudi wealth to the kingdom's development. The planned elimination of foreign workers would save up to five billion dollars per year, but with serious repercussions in Yemen and Egypt, which depend heavily on remittances from citizens working in Saudi Arabia. Taxation, whether on income, wealth, foreign travel, or imports, has its limits. At best, these measures would only prolong the period before financial reserves are exhausted.

It is not possible to state categorically that financial reserves will disappear by a certain date. There are too many uncertainties about the actual rate of expenditures in the next five years. As regards the liquidity of the Saudi reserves, one suspects that a large percentage of the remaining $100 billion is tied up in investments or in loans that cannot be readily turned into cash. But it is not necessary

to be precise. A continuing deficit that spells an exhaustion of reserves could have damaging political consequences to the Saudi regime if it is perceived to be weakening or losing its hold.

A drastic change in policy is required. Saudi Arabia has been willing over the last five years to act as the swing producer for OPEC. Riyadh has unilaterally reduced its oil production from over ten mbd to 2.5 mbd in order to defend the oil price jump of 1979-80. It should have been immediately apparent that this price of over $30 was too high and would lead to large-scale substitutions by cheaper fuels. The drop in oil use has been the major cause of the glut and the weakening in price. Saudi Arabia's production cuts have only delayed the inevitable price drop, and made money for other oil producers, including those in the United States.

Now the Saudis must follow a new course: increase production, letting the price fall if necessary below $20 a barrel in order to maximize their own long-term profit stream. This may mean a break with most of OPEC. It will certainly displease other producers—among them Iran, Iraq, Egypt, and Syria. The gulf sheikhdoms, now allied with Saudi Arabia in the Gulf Cooperation Council, may join since they have similar long-term interests—or they may abandon Riyadh.

The choices facing the Saudi rulers are either unpleasant or dangerous. But they have shown themselves to be survivors in the past and may yet find a way out of their difficulties. There is probably little the West can do or should do. And even if there is a change in regime, the new rulers in all likelihood will continue to sell oil to the world market.

S. FRED SINGER

S. Fred Singer is Visiting Eminent Scholar at George Mason University. He served as deputy assistant secretary of interior and as a consultant to the Department of Energy and the U.S. Treasury. His latest book is *Free Market Energy* (Universe Books).

Sudan:

Article 32

AFRICA REPORT • November–December 1985

Sudan's Hidden Tragedy

The devastation from the drought and famine in Sudan might have been minimized had donors and the former government foreseen the mammoth logistical problems the relief effort would encounter. Now that the drought appears to have subsided, international and domestic efforts must focus on addressing the country's basic infrastructural and developmental needs to prevent a repeat of the disaster.

BY ROBERT WATKINS

International relief agencies operating in Sudan are breathing a guarded sigh of relief now that it appears, at least by most accounts, that the "unparalleled disaster" that was predicted only a few months ago for Sudan's drought-ravaged western regions has been averted. Those who have been involved in the relief effort since its belated inception realize that for the most part, the disaster was averted mainly because of the dramatic reversal in climatic conditions which had prevailed in the northern part of the country for the last five years, and almost in spite of international relief efforts.

Abundant rainfall in the western regions of Darfur and Kordofan and in the east in the large grain-producing areas around Gedaref has enabled farmers to sow a crop that should reach harvest by mid-October to mid-November. Lands that only a few months ago were parched, devoid of vegetation, and subject to scorching mid-winter temperatures as high as 120 degrees fahrenheit are now grown over with a dense, verdant cover. In some areas of Darfur

Robert Watkins is a freelance journalist.

where rain has been particularly plentiful, 'dura' (sorghum) crops have already reached a height of five to six feet, covering the dessicated remains of camels and donkeys that once littered the landscape. Many agriculturalists are even predicting a second crop in some areas before the coming of the dry winter weather in early December.

Despite the more optimistic outlook for Sudan, questions remain about the speed with which the former Nimeiry government recognized and admitted to the world that it was confronting a situation beyond its control, and the efficacy of the international community in responding to Sudan's appeal. For although large quantities of food aid—relative to the requirements of the population—have been allocated for Sudan since November 1984 (1.475 million metric tons had been pledged as of August 1985 according to UN sources), only a small portion has actually made its way to those in the most affected areas. In human terms, this has meant that the entire population of Darfur (2.8 million) and Kordofan (2.9 million) has been receiving only 20-35 percent of the targeted food aid.

People living in the remote areas of

these two western regions have unquestionably suffered the most during the drought. The amount of grain and medical supplies that reached them—most notably in the isolated regions of northern Darfur—was so small as to be insignificant in many cases. Perhaps most disturbing is that the magnitude of the disaster in these areas will never be fully known. Although estimates that put the death toll in Darfur alone at 100,000 may be exaggerated, there is no doubt that the loss of life has been substantial. As during past periods of drought and deprivation, those villagers living far from large settlements have quietly died in the desert far from the view of relief workers and television cameras.

Responsibility for this 'hidden' tragedy could easily be attributed to the former government of Sudan for its reluctance to sound the alarm that would have helped draw world attention away from Ethiopia to its own plight; or to the international relief organizations which failed to respond quickly enough to the crisis; or to the international donor community at large which would not listen attentively enough to the organizations which were already predicting disaster

"The virtual breakdown of the western railway link meant that the truck or 'souk lorry' was the only viable surface connection"

in Sudan more than a year ago. Finger pointing at this stage, however, would serve no useful purpose. But the transport and logistical problems must be examined if similar mistakes are to be avoided in the future.

During the early stages of the emergency, when the primary concern of relief agencies was to focus world attention on Sudan in order to procure food aid supplies, those involved in food distribution assumed that the country's transport facilities were adequate to meet the large requirements of the population in the west.

The U.S. Agency for International Development and the European Economic Community (EEC), the two main donors responsible for the supply and distribution of food aid to the west, relied on the Sudan Railways Corporation (SRC) and private trucking firms to transport supplies from Port Sudan to the region. From the offloading process at the port to the distribution centers in the west, the Sudanese transportation system has been subject to numerous unforeseen bottlenecks. Yet people with only limited experience in the country predicted these problems, especially the inability of the railways to cope with the needs during the May to August rainy season.

By all accounts, expecting the Sudanese railway system to deliver the 1,200 metric tons of cereals required in Darfur alone was totally unrealistic—even if the railway rehabilitation schemes planned by the major donors had been implemented. The torrential rains of the summer months have habitually hampered the operation of the railways. Although the rains had been insubstantial for the last few years throughout the country, any scenario involving transport should have considered the devastation that the rains can wreak on the rail lines. Some realistic contingency planning should have been undertaken in the event that the rains did arrive.

By July, it was obvious that the railway system was completely incapable of coping with the transport of food to the west if only because of weather conditions. Not only were tracks washed out in almost a dozen places along the line, but a major bridge collapsed between Kosti and Nyala, 700 miles outside Khartoum, halting the already insufficient number of train shipments to the west. Two locomotives and seven railway wagons valued at $1 million each were lost in the accident.

The rains thus immobilized the railway transport system for some time, as the equipment needed to replace the washed out bridge and repair the line was hundreds of miles away in Atbara. It is unlikely that the railway will contribute much to transportation of food relief deliveries this year. The EEC, among others, is helping to rehabilitate and upgrade the tracks, rolling stock, and communication system of the SRC, but these efforts cannot be expected to revitalize the system for a few years yet.

Despite the unpredictable weather conditions, a number of factors could have been assessed, but were ignored by those organizing the rail shipments. While the political turmoil would have been difficult to predict, the former government's commitment to expediting food aid through the SRC was overestimated. Improving the management capability of the SRC was not seriously considered until it was far too late, and even then the organization demonstrated little interest in self-examination and improvement.

It was clear that if any important managerial changes were to be made, they would have to be at the direct and firm behest of the new Transitional Military Council led by General Rahman Sawar-Dahab. In an effort to improve the railways, senior government officials and the SRC itself have recently indicated their willingness to implement the necessary managerial reforms, restructure the trade unions, and accept foreign technical assistance.

The virtual breakdown of the western railway link meant that the truck or 'souk lorry' was the only viable surface connection. Yet, once again because of the rains, food deliveries by truck—normally taking anywhere from six to ten days during optimal, dry season conditions—took up to six weeks in some cases. During the critical summer months, a time when the last harvest runs out and the current one is not yet in, very little food aid reached Darfur. It is estimated that of the 1,200 metric tons per day needed, only 250 metric tons arrived during this period.

Many people have claimed that Sudan's trucking facilities are adequate to transport the necessary volume of food supplies. Regardless, with the breakdown of the railway system, truck transport prices escalated, rapidly depleting the resources many donors had set aside to cover transport. Truck transport prices to the west traditionally increase during the rainy season. Not only is the journey more arduous and time-consuming, but truck owners risk damaging or even losing their vehicles. It is clear, nevertheless, that the trebling of truck transport prices between March and July was the result of the increased dependence on their services after the railway broke down.

To make matters worse, some aid agencies—eager to move their food and medical supplies at the expense of other agencies—offered large sums of money to Sudanese trucking firms, thereby increasing the market rate. Greed on the part of some trucking firms undoubtedly played a role in the rate increase, as the market forces of supply and demand came into play. At the same time, many truckers were bitter about the huge profits made by the Sudanese-American cargo transport company, Arkel-Talab. Earlier in the year, USAID granted the firm a concession on the transport of American grain to the west. The transaction was questioned by many. While a lavish sum was paid to the company, the rates actually received by the truckers, especially on the long haul trips to Darfur, were considered very low.

In any case, much of the private trucking sector, and to some extent the military, has been involved in the relief effort. It became clear, however, that even their efforts were not enough to move the required volume of food to the west. Concerned by the complete failure of the local transportation infrastructure to cope with the amount of food aid entering the country, some bilateral donors and international agencies requested outside assistance. The Italian government, for example, donated 103 Fiat trucks with a seven-ton carrying capacity. Only 53 had arrived by the end of August.

Many of the other trucks which were pledged for Sudan were not expected to arrive and become fully operational until the end of October at the earliest. By the time the trucking fleet is assembled to transport badly needed food supplies to the west, those who needed the food will have perished. Those lucky enough to have planted and who received enough food to last until October-November will be harvesting their crops— that is, providing the rains continue at their present level.

It would be wrong to assume, however, that the international fleet of trucks moving full steam to the west will be unable to reach those still in need. Many lives can still be saved if the food is distributed from centers in Nyala and El Fasher in Darfur province. Although it is abundantly clear that the relief effort was started too late and has been out of step with the needs, a certain momentum has been established. World attention must continue to focus on Sudan's plight.

"Those villagers living far from large settlements have quietly died in the desert far from the view of relief workers and television cameras."

Proper health care, water and sanitation facilities, reforestation projects, and other rehabilitation and development efforts must now replace emergency work. This can only be done if the world follows developments in Sudan. Moreover, it cannot be assumed that because there was rain this year, there will be rain next year. Buffer food stocks must be built up and adequate storage facilities constructed if a similar tragedy is to be avoided.

At the same time, as food aid stocks are replenished in key distribution centers in the west, close attention must be paid to the impact of food aid on local market prices. Agricultural economists have pointed out that many farmers found themselves without seeds, not only because they were forced to eat the stock which they normally reserve from each harvest, but also because local merchants had artificially raised prices through hoarding. The interplay between food aid and local market prices is complex and needs to be seriously addressed in the Sudanese context.

There will also be a problem when it comes time to dismantle the trucking operation. It is expected that once the rains subside and the trucks that have been pledged arrive, trucking costs will decrease. The international fleet will undoubtedly compete to some extent with private local operators. The impact on the economy needs to be examined. Clearly, the fleet should be disbanded as quickly as possible so that transportation work can be handled uniquely by local expertise.

The new Sudanese government has moved to create its own Relief and Rehabilitation Commission modeled after a similar organization in Ethiopia. Although it is suffering from an acute lack of funds and has yet to clearly define its mandate, the commission could go a long way in preparing the country for another major relief operation should the drought continue or recur in a few years time.

The relief aspect of the emergency may be nearly over, but given the nature of the drought that has afflicted the entire Sudano-Sahelian region for the last decade, much work remains to be done. This is especially true if the country is to develop the ability to face the prospect of recurring drought without relying on the vicissitudes of international assistance. □

Syria:

Article 33

The Christian Science Monitor, December 30, 1985

Syria: key Arab factor in Mideast equation

By Mary Curtius
Special to The Christian Science Monitor

When Israel debates a response to terrorist attacks against its airline in Europe, it takes account of Syria. When Lebanese factions sign a peace pact, they hail its broker — Syria. When Jordan floats a peace plan, it seeks Syria's view. All highlight Syrian President Assad's key regional role.

The first summit in 10 years between Jordan's King Hussein and Syrian President Hafez Assad could have a dramatic impact on the chances for an Arab-Israeli peace conference taking place next year.

The shaky Mideast peace process could collapse if King Hussein either cannot persuade President Assad to join in a conference or cannot secure his acquiescence to such a conference taking place, diplomatic sources here say. The prospects look bleak for Hussein winning Assad over to his point of view in pursuing a settlement, Jordanian sources acknowledge.

Hussein is scheduled to arrive in Damascus today, at a time when:

• Assad has just reinforced his image as the chief power-broker in Lebanon, presiding over a pact designed to end the Lebanese civil war.

• Syria is the focal point of increasing tension with Israel over Syrian deployment of antiaircraft missiles within and along the Lebanese border.

• Assad continues to oppose efforts by King Hussein and Palestine Liberation Organization chief Yasser Arafat to jointly negotiate peace with Israel.

In addition, last Friday's Palestinian terrorist attacks on airports in Rome and Vienna, in which 18 people were killed and 121 people were injured, could provoke conflict if Israel retaliates by attacking Palestinian strongholds in Lebanon.

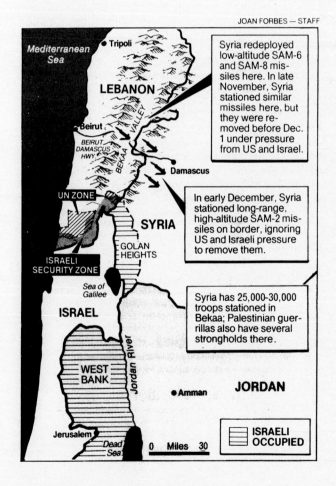

JOAN FORBES — STAFF

Syria redeployed low-altitude SAM-6 and SAM-8 missiles here. In late November, Syria stationed similar missiles here, but they were removed before Dec. 1 under pressure from US and Israel.

In early December, Syria stationed long-range, high-altitude SAM-2 missiles on border, ignoring US and Israeli pressure to remove them.

Syria has 25,000-30,000 troops stationed in Bekaa; Palestinian guerrillas also have several strongholds there.

ISRAELI OCCUPIED

The Syrians have recently redeployed mobile missile batteries in Lebanon's eastern Bekaa Valley. The Israelis say the missiles threaten their ability to fly reconnaissance flights over Lebanon. The weapons, clearly, are a Syrian challenge to that claimed right.

Syria first deployed the missiles in the Bekaa after Israel shot down two Soviet-supplied Syrian jets over Syrian territory Nov. 19. Largely through United States diplomatic efforts, the missiles were removed. But Israeli Prime Minister Shimon Peres announced last week that the Syrians had again deployed the missiles.

The situation has been made more volatile by the terrorist attacks Friday on Israeli airline counters in airports in Vienna and Rome. The Israelis have vowed revenge for the attacks. The attackers were identified as Palestinians, and one likely target for Israeli retaliation could be the Syrian-controlled Bekaa Valley, where several Palestinian guerrilla groups have bases. Should Israel attack the Bekaa, the Syrians could decide to use their missiles, in turn provoking further Israeli retaliation.

Lebanese accord enhances Syria's prestige

Syria has demonstrated its influence in Lebanon by engineering a pact which was signed in Damascus Saturday by the leaders of Lebanon's three most powerful militias. Details of the agreement were not released, but a new government is to be formed, and it is believed that the power of the traditionally dominant Christian minority will be reduced, and more power will go to the Muslim community. If the accord — which is backed by the presence of an estimated 25,000 Syrian troops — succeeds, it will greatly enhance Syria's prestige.

It is doubtful that Assad will want to invest his newly-earned political capital on convening a peace conference this year, Western observers say. The US, Israel, Jordan, Egypt, and the PLO have all been manuevering toward such a conference since last February, when Hussein and PLO chief Arafat signed an accord to jointly pursue negotiations based on trading land for peace.

Syria has remained adamantly opposed both to the accord and to Mr. Arafat. In fact, Hussein and Assad only a few months ago were seemingly implacable foes. In addition, Hussein backs Iraq in the Persian Gulf war, while Syria supports Iran, and has sought to depose Arafat as leader of the PLO. The Jordanians have said they are willing to negotiate directly with Israel in the context of an international conference, but the Syrians say "no" to direct negotiations.

Jordanian officials insist it is too early to tell if the dif-

ferences between Syria and Jordan will prove too fundamental to reconcile. That will be determined, sources say, by the meeting between Hussein and Assad.

Hussein has grown more interested in drawing close to Syria in the face of a series of disappointments, Jordanian sources say. Hussein reportedly feels let down by the Americans, who have failed to provide him with arms and have refused to meet with the PLO. The King also feels betrayed by the PLO, which has equivocated on publicly accepting United Nations Security Council resolutions 242 and 338 which enshrine the concept of an Israeli withdrawal from Arab territory occupied in 1967 — in return for the right to live in peace. These resolutions have been accepted by Israel, Jordan, and the US as the basis for negotiations.

Privately, the Jordanians say they will continue to explore the possibility of convening an international conference until March. That is when the US Congress is scheduled to consider the arms package to Jordan. It is also the red line, many analysts believe, for Israel's Mr. Peres to extricate himself from the coalition government that keeps him bound to the hardline Likud bloc. The Likud opposes negotiations with Jordan that would return any Israeli-occupied territory.

The Americans fear that Assad may exert such pressure that Hussein may not be willing to wait even until March before he pulls out of the process altogether.

Although the question of who should represent the Palestinians in an international conference remains unresolved, US, Israeli, and Jordanian officials all say that progress has been made recently on agreeing to a framework for an international conference.

Assad's view of an international conference differs fundamentally from Hussein's conception, and would never be accepted by the Israelis or the Americans, Western sources say.

The Syrian President believes the conference should be chaired by the Soviet Union and the US who would sit "sort of as judges in an international tribunal," one diplomatic source explained.

If the King were to agree to that concept, there would be little chance that a conference could be convened, sources here say.

Turkey:

Article 34   THE NEW YORK TIMES, TUESDAY, DECEMBER 24, 1985

In Turkey, a Gain for Rights

By Jeri Laber
and Alice H. Henkin

Jeri Laber is executive director of Helsinki Watch, a human rights organization. Alice H. Henkin is a lawyer with the Aspen Institute for Humanistic Studies.

The human rights climate in Turkey seems to be getting better, slowly. America and the rest of Europe should of course welcome this progress, tentative as it is, but we should also keep up the scrutiny and pressure that spurred it in the first place.

On Dec. 10, five nations — France, Norway, Denmark, the Netherlands and Sweden — announced that they had reached a friendly settlement with

Turkey and were dropping the complaints they had lodged against it in 1982 in the European Commission of Human Rights. Turkey hailed the announcement as a reaffirmation of its place in the European community. The United States welcomed it as an acknowledgment of Turkey's efforts to restore democracy. It was also wel-

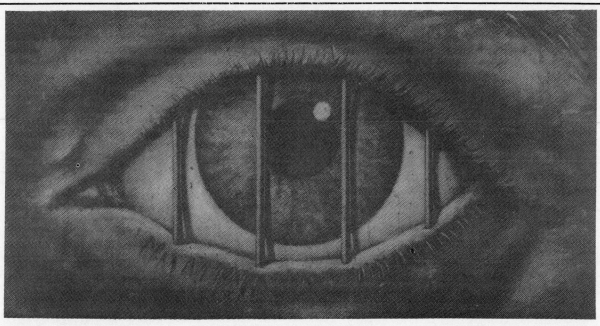
Rafal Olbinski

comed, though somewhat more cautiously, by Turkish victims of human rights abuse. They hope that the agreement — and the expectations that come with it — will bring them further relief.

We were in Turkey when the settlement was announced. During this visit, in dramatic contrast to a previous mission in 1983, we were given unlimited opportunities to meet with whomever we wished, including Prime Minister Turgut Ozal, members of the Government and the new Parliament, party leaders and private citizens from all walks of life. We explored a confusing landscape — a combination of encouraging changes and severe human rights violations.

A new openness in Turkish society — it all began with the legislative elections in November 1983 — is most apparent in its exuberant, outspoken press. Private citizens who are critical of the system also seem less fearful than they were two years ago, more inclined to speak out, both publicly and privately. Parliamentarians and other political leaders are engaged in lively, often acrimonious debate on subjects that would have been unmentionable a short time ago, including prison conditions, torture and human rights violations.

Yet abuses continue. There is torture in police detention centers where suspects are denied the right to see their families or lawyers. Interroga-

tion techniques routinely include electric shocks, suspension by the arms and merciless beating of the soles of the feet. Prison conditions are abominable, and the many thousands of young people who were swept up on terrorism charges in 1980, following

But scrutiny and pressure should continue

the military takeover, are still awaiting the outcome of prolonged group trials. Members of the Turkish Peace Association — prominent people such as the former head of the Turkish Medical Association, a well-known theater director and the wife of the former mayor of Istanbul — have spent three years in military prisons, for views expressed before 1980.

At the same time, human rights have become a major domestic issue: A recent poll indicated that if elections were held now, the majority of votes would go to a left opposition

party that has made human rights its focus. Some Turks claim that the opposition is "using" human rights as a convenient issue with which to attack the Government. Others question the sincerity of the Government's response — its claims to be correcting these abuses. But no one denies that Turkish politicians have become extremely sensitive to international pressure for human rights.

Contradictions abound. Martial law has been lifted in all but nine of 67 provinces. It has, however, been replaced in most places by an emergency-measures law that is almost as severe. There is a new "police law" that reduces the permissible period of police detention, but it is still possible, and usual, to hold a suspect incommunicado for as long as 15 days. The Government, which has taken some steps to punish torturers, claims difficulty in bringing the police under control. Yet it was easy for us to find major torture centers in both Istanbul and Ankara.

Nevertheless, we are hopeful. We met many courageous people fighting for freedom despite a restrictive constitution and other repressive legislation. Human rights issues are being discussed everywhere, and there is strong momentum for change. What's needed now is continued attention from abroad to encourage the moral leadership and political will of Turkey's highest authorities.   □

The magician who lost his touch

The structural weaknesses of Turkey's industrial sector are threatening the monetarist recovery plan launched by Turgut Özal in 1980

The heady mix of monetarist and neo-liberal policies which provided Turkey with its vaunted economic miracle is fading, five years after it was pushed through by the junta.

Prime Minister Turgut Özal, who devised the strategy in 1980 to take the economy out of a state of near collapse was *Euromoney* magazine's Man of the Year in 1981. Now he seems to have run out of ideas.

As elsewhere, the policy mix has given few signs of effecting the permanent changes in the underlying structure of the economy that are necessary to sustain the short-term gains from austerity.

Like many Latin American countries, Turkey's industries are domestically oriented. Vital industries like the car industry, machinery, chemicals, pharmaceuticals, rubber and plastics are almost fully controlled by multinationals.

The economy as a whole is also heavily dependent on imports, which provide between 35 and 75 per cent of the content of goods produced in many industries.

Neither exports nor tourism has been able to provide adequate foreign currency to meet industry's import needs. Turkey started exporting workers to Europe in the early 1960s and initially their remittances helped. But the economy has an insatiable

The making of a monetarist

Turgut Özal, the architect of Turkey's economic recovery package, became Prime Minister in December 1983. He had been associated with a Suleyman Demirel government, as a top state planner, at the beginning of the 1970s. When Demirel had to resign following the military coup in 1971, Özal also quit and went to work in the World Bank for two years, where he probably cultivated his monetarist views. When he returned to Turkey, he entered the private sector, becoming a member of the executive committee of MESS (the Confederation of Metal Industry Employers), and later its chairman.

Özal retained close contacts with Demirel, whom he had always addressed as *agabey* (elder brother). When Demirel became Prime Minister in 1979, Özal presented him with two reports,

analysing the causes of the crisis. He identified Turkey's "enemies" as inflation, communism, statism and foreign currency shortages; and proposed a shift towards "economic liberalism".

But when he later attempted to implement his ideas, he ran into strong opposition from a broad political spectrum. Bulent Ecevit, leader of the opposition Republican Peoples Party, a social-democratic group, warned that these "policies would inevitably lead us into a Latin American type of military regime".

In 1980, a military junta took over, paving the way for the unhindered implementation of the policies. While Demirel and Ecevit were banned from politics and their parties disbanded, Özal became the new regime's economy minister.

appetite for foreign exchange; the more it grew, the more it needed – foreign credits were essential to sustain economic growth. Between 1964 and 1980, Turkey's foreign debt rose from about US$1-billion to US$12-billion. The import substitution model of economic development was thus based on foreign credits and direct multinational investment.

The impressive 9 per cent growth rate of the 1950s, when industrial capacity was being built up, was only possible because

of high tariff barriers. But it is an approach which also depended on state credits, support prices, subsidies and extremely low real interest rates – minus 2.9 per cent in 1970; minus 14.4 per cent in 1974 and minus 67 per cent in 1980 – and creeping inflation.

The real cause of the 1979 economic crisis, in fact, was not excess money supply as 'monetarist' economists claimed but the industrial structure which made such policies imperative. While excess money

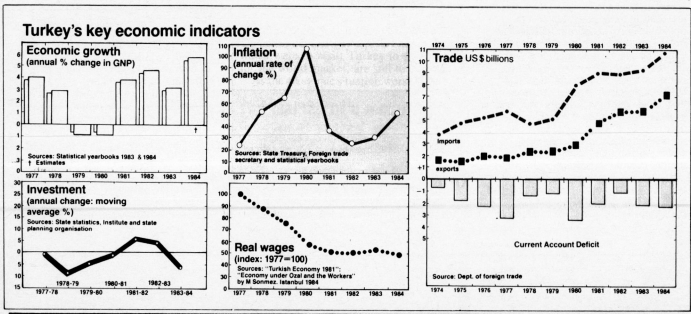

Turkey's key economic indicators

Economic growth (annual % change in GNP)

Sources: Statistical yearbooks 1983 & 1984
† Estimates

1977 1978 1979 1980 1981 1982 1983 1984

Investment (annual change: moving average %)

Sources: State statistics, Institute and state planning organisation

1977-78 1978-79 1979-80 1980-81 1981-82 1982-83 1983-84

Inflation (annual rate of change %)

Sources: State Treasury, Foreign trade secretary and statistical yearbooks

1977 1978 1979 1980 1981 1982 1983 1984

Real wages (index: 1977=100)

Sources: "Turkish Economy 1981": "Economy under Ozal and the Workers" by M Sonmez. Istanbul 1984

1977 1978 1979 1980 1981 1982 1983 1984

1974 1975 1976 1977 1978 1979 1980 1981 1982 1983 1984

Trade US $ billions

Imports

exports

Current Account Deficit

Source: Dept. of foreign trade

1974 1975 1976 1977 1978 1979 1980 1981 1982 1983 1984

can be mopped up quite quickly, the necessary radical economic reconstruction is a much bigger and tougher task.

The economic distress signals have been evident since the 1960s. The country's first deep recession in 1968-73 came at a time of military rule. The second, more acute slump came in 1977 after the oil price shock and the increase in world prices for capital goods.

By November, 1979, when Suleyman Demirel, leader of the conservative Justice Party, was asked to form a government, the economy was on the verge of collapse. "We inherited a wreck", he said when he took over. The figures were eloquent: with only US$30-million in the state coffers, imports of oil and many essential raw materials were drying up, and use of industrial capacity slumped to about 40-45 per cent. The black market became a way of life. Turkey was neither able to service its debts nor find anybody willing to make it the new loans necessary to run its industries. With inflation hovering around 100 per cent, a new round of negotiations with the unions was about to begin.

The much-needed rescue operation came with the 1980 Özal austerity package, launched with strong western backing. Its main aim was to open the economy to market forces. Measures included tight controls over money supply growth and the removal of state subsidies, to reduce domestic demand and force industrialists to seek new markets abroad, and the opening up of the economy to international competition through the removal of import barriers. This was intended to eliminate uneconomic and uncompetitive enterprises, clearing the way for the development of export-orientated industries. The lira was then devalued by 50 per cent. This was followed by price increases – 300 to 400 per cent in some cases – of key goods produced by state enterprises. The subsidies removed included those on several key commodities, among them important wage goods such as cereals, tea, sugar and meat, as well as those on industrial and agricultural inputs, like oil and fertiliser.

Interest rates were also decontrolled, and stamp duty on imports fell from 25 to one per cent. At the same time, export promotion policies were adopted; low interest credits were provided for exporters, who also got easy access to foreign currency and tax rebates of five to 20 per cent.

Outside Turkey, strategic considerations induced the West to help one of Nato's key members. Debts were rescheduled, big new credits were mobilised – almost US$4-billion was pledged between 1979 and 1982 under the OECD's special assistance programme for Turkey – and the IMF gave the biggest loan that it could.

Özal's policies seemed to be working successfully up to 1983. Economic growth

recovered and inflation fell to 25 per cent in 1982. The ratio of exports to imports increased from 36 per cent to 56 per cent between 1980-82, while the current account deficit decreased from US$3.9-billion to US$1.2-billion and the foreign trade deficit declined from US$4.9-billion to US$3.9-billion. Use of industrial capacity increased. Corporate profits, too, began to recover and fixed capital investments started to improve.

But this recovery was bound to be short-lived because it did not involve the reconstruction of industry. There was real need for a big rise in productivity and a broadening of the industrial base, to produce a wider variety of goods. Instead, recovery was based on three rather shaky foundation stones. First, trade unions were suspended, industrial action banned and real wages depressed to below their 1963 levels. This formed the basis for the increase in capacity utilisation – more people for the same wage bill – and the rise in production and profits. The second was the increase in revenue from exports and overseas construction contracts, which removed foreign exchange constraints. The export increase did not, however, result from a strengthening of industry, but from new export regulations, which provided millions to exporters in the form of credits, subsidies and tax rebates – while consumer and producer subsidies were simultaneously reduced. This made it possible for them to sell on world markets below production prices. The Iranian revolution and the ensuing war with Iraq also helped boost exports; Turkey happily sold to both sides.

The third was the deregulation of interest rates, which immediately shot up from 10-15 per cent, and at one point 150 per cent, attracting all the small investors. But the consequent high cost of industrial borrowing, coupled with successive mini-devaluations, increased production costs. When some finance companies and banks began to run into difficulties, a chain reaction was triggered that ended in a crash. Small investors lost billions, often their life savings.

This was one of many signs that the Özal programme was creating economic and political tensions. Over the last two years the cracks have steadily widened.

Exports increasingly became monopolised by a handful of holding companies, 25 of which accounted for 70 per cent of total exports in 1983. According to Ibrahim Bodur, chairman of the Istanbul Chamber of Industry, this had a negative effect on exports as it limited their further diversification and expansion.

Worsening market conditions in the Middle East and North African markets, due to declining oil prices, also hit exports. In 1983, economic indicators slumped. Although growth in 1984 was an impressive 5.7 per cent, capital investment has been

declining since 1983. At the same time, it is increasingly clear that the recovery in many industries has proved to be weaker than during the previous period of recovery.

But the biggest setback for Özal came on the inflation front: after falling to 26 per cent in 1982, it suddenly soared to 55 per cent in 1984, a year when the boldest monetarist policies were being implemented.

Devaluations, the elimination of subsidies and attempts by large producers to raise profits in a deregulated economy all added to upward pressure on prices. Despite claims that the Özal package was producing an economic reconstruction, the basic structure of industry is now little different from what it was five years ago. The pattern of imports continues to show the characteristics of an import-substituting industrial structure.

In 1979, investment goods together with raw materials, accounted for 98 per cent of all imports. In 1984, the figure was still around 95 per cent. Imports continued to be financed by rapidly rising debts which climbed from US$16-billion to US$20-billion. Although Turkey's credit-worthiness may have increased, and a series of free trade zones have been set up, the forecast foreign capital investments which were to assist Turkey in producing for the world market, are still to come.

As the economic situation worsened, the major policy tools of monetarism began to be counter-productive. High interest rates and the progressive decline in the lira's value increased the burdens on small and medium-sized businesses. Even larger companies without direct links to the banks have started to complain.

While policies aimed at reducing inflation through tight money policies may have had initial success, the chairman of the Federation of Chambers of Commerce and Industry, Mehmet Yazar, argues: "These policies are, today, nursing another source of inflation by increasing costs and prices." He calls for "a shift towards policies which would increase demand."

But despite all the criticism and apparent failures, the Prime Minister still says there are no alternatives to his policies, which he says will work in the long run. Özal is not alone in this deep faith; his policies still enjoy the support of the large holding companies which have most readily adapted to the new economic regime. Ali Kocman, former chairman of Tusiad, the organisation grouping the biggest holding companies, says the need to pursue policies that boost exports is Turkey's fate. There can be no shift away from these policies, whatever changes may occur.

Workers and others suffering most under the Özal economic programme have no channels through which to express their feeling: the new Constitution has made any serious opposition to the government impossible and, having seen their independent trade unions banned by the junta and their right to organise curtailed under new labour laws, workers are bitter but powerless – at least for now.

The chairman of Turk Is – a pro-regime trade union which was not banned by the military – has bluntly told the government that the workers have nothing left to give. He also warned of the danger that worker militancy could take root in the soil of economic discontent.

As Özal progressively runs out of steam, divisions widen inside the business community which until recently gave him full support, splits paralleled by growing discontent elsewhere in society. □

Ergin Yildizoglu

United Arab Emirates (UAE):

Article 36
Pakistan & Gulf Economist, July 13-19, 1985

Rapid progress in education

By FATIMA JAMAL

Before the existence of the federation, there was no educational system in the UAE except four schools in Sharjah and Dubai. Now the government provides free schooling at all levels.

In 1971, the year of independence, the law of compulsory education was formulated. In a demographically tiny but wealthy and developing state like the UAE, it was imperative that education policies formulated be geared towards moulding each and every citizen, young and old, for a role in nation-building. The educational system has undergone overall development and expansion in the last eleven years. The number of schools and students has increased dramatically. In addition to that, campaigns to eradicate illiteracy among the grown-ups and old-aged have been going full steam.

The UAE embarked itself on a policy of annually investing as much as 24 percent in 1979 of the Federal Budget on education. The amount in absolute terms increased from Dh 247 million in 1973 to over Dh 1 billion in the mid-70s and Dh 1,721 billion in 1983.

Abu Dhabi gave its education department Dh 360 million in 1983 alone to build more schools, increase the number of classrooms in existing schools and to maintain some schools. Nearly half of the funds were invested on infrastructure, such as school buildings and ancillary facilities, including equipment. Now the number of schools has jumped from a mere 66 in the 1970-71 academic year to the current 360 spread throughout the country, serving children in the urban as well as farflung rural areas.

Despite reduced oil earnings in recent years, the country has continued with literacy work. The 1983-84 academic year was attended by 160,000 boys and girls of all ages, which represents a 12 per cent increase over the 1982 student population. Some 24 new schools were to be built in 1983. They were financed from the Ministry of Education's 1983 budget of Dh 1.721 billion, with 14 secondary schools planned. Five were to be built in Abu Dhabi at a cost of Dh 45 million while four were to be erected in Al Ain at a cost of Dh 33 million. Three girls' schools were to be built in Dubai at a cost of Dh 26 million, with a boys' school in Sharjah costing Dh 9 million and a girls' school in Ras al Khaimah costing Dh 10 million.

Long before the formation of the UAE, Sharjah pioneered the growth of education in the Trucial states. Nineteen years before the Federal government made primary education compulsory for all nationals over six years of age, Sharjah set up its first school in the region.

Established in 1953, the school, which enrolled 450 boys above the age of six, was set up with assistance from Kuwait and Britain.

Sharjah's historic role in the growth of education on the Trucial coast was acknowledged by other Emirates right at the start of the Federation a decade ago.

Over the years Sharjah has maintained its lead in the field of education. According to a statistical report, the number of school buildings in the Northern Emirate as a whole had increased by 7.5 per cent. The number of schools in Sharjah totals 40, offering a range and choice of the best educational facilities anywhere in the Emirate.

The increased construction by the federation has made rapid progress in the field of education in recent years. Sharjah's achievement in this sphere has been steady and evenly distributed. Although geographically separated by as much as 150 km, the educational needs of enclaves like Khor Fakkan and Kalba have been well taken care of.

University education

At the tertiary level, educational opportunities for the UAE youths are greater than ever. The UAE University is now offering a large number of seats. At the same time, offers of scholarships for education in foreign educational facilities have also increased substantially. The UAE university took 5000 students in its various departments or faculties in the 1983-84 semester. The number of students was reported to have increased sevenfold in the six years since the university opened. Not only has the university student population increased, but their educational standards, too, have been upgraded.

The Emirates' university, established as the region's most ambitious project of higher education in 1977, is today poised to expand into a "city of learning." In fact, the university has been expanding rapidly from the very first day with the number of its students now standing at 3,000. The number of teaching departments has also gone up considerably, with the nuclear physics department being the latest one planned to be added shortly.

It was decided to have a university in Al Ain because the town has several advantages. The first is that Al Ain is significantly poised for the development of the Emirates. It was one of the earlier centres of settlement and civilization. The university opened with four main colleges. They covered humanities and social sciences, natural science education, public administration and political science. Students were given teachers' training in the education college and an Islamic law section was added in 1978.

The university is still new, but the total number of students has been steadily rising. During the first year, around 500 were admitted, about 650 in the second year, 800 in the third and 950 in 1983. About 80 per cent of them are citizens of the Emirates; with others coming from other Gulf countries. There are also other Arabs who are presently living in this country including Palestinians, Egyptians, and Sudanese. There are about 15 different nationalities on the campus. The university has become a popular place for women to study. It is a significant fact that about 43 per cent of the students are girls.

The girls that come here have very serious attitude towards

The number of schools jumped from a mere 66 in the 1970-71 academic year to the current 360 spread throughout the country, serving children in the urban as well as farflung rural areas.

work and are doing very well. There could be several reasons why the number is so high.

The educational system of the country has developed into a balanced way with good opportunities for both boys and girls. It may be because boys have more opportunities to study abroad or take up jobs straight away after leaving school. Much effort is being put into keeping academic standards as high as possible. There are now some 200 lecturers, including 92 who took up their posts during the current academic year. Along with its teaching role, the university has important work to do in research and community services. These functions have been developed from the start and they have evolved further.

Research projects have been carried out already in different departments and a new research center is being started in social studies, natural science and development projects.

Technical education

Those school graduates who decide not to go to universities are also provided with opportunities. These are offered in the technical and vocational institutions. The Ministry of Education has three technical schools, one each in Dubai, Sharjah and Ras al Khaimah, and one commercial college in each of the same cities.

Students are accepted for technical school at the earliest upon completing their six years of primary education at the age of 12 or 13—but they can enter at any time during the following years once they have completed their compulsory years of education. The full technical courses last six years and are divided into three stages.

In the technical schools, three options are offered for specialisation: mechanical engineering, electrical engineering and woodwork.

The commercial schools are attached to the technical schools at Dubai. They offer a three-year course after the students have completed nine years of education. Here the normal subjects are taught along with secondary skills; on completing this course of study, students are ready for work in the large national companies or banks.

The three-year agriculture course is conducted by the Ministry of Education in Ras al Khaimah. Students must have nine years of prior education. Here, basic agricultural economy is taught with methods of irrigation having a high priority. Animal husbandry, social science and botany are studied.

There are about 700 students in the three technical schools. Of these 15 per cent to 20 per cent take on jobs after the completion of the course.

Not long ago expatriates working in the UAE would think twice before having their families join them. The primary reason was paucity of proper educational facilities for their children.

Though education provided by the Federal Government has always been free, for the expatriates the concern was to give their children a course of study that would have continuity with the one they had back home. Even in the case of small children who had to do preparatory work prior to joining a school, the question was of choosing a school with a suitable system of education. The problem was daunting, as in most cases the expatriates were never quite sure of the length of their stay there.

Over the years, however, the problem was solved with the mushrooming of private schools set up by small communities of various nationalities, each providing a course of education on the pattern of its respective country. This became possible only with the cooperation of the Education Ministry and generous donations of land and resources by the Rulers.

Today there are about 90 private schools in the UAE, representing almost every major expatriate nationality, with a combined student strength running into thousands in Dubai, which had the country's first private school. St. Mary's has the largest number of them, mostly managed by boards of investors and in some cases by individuals.

Adult education

Facilities of adult education have also been vastly improved. When the programme was launched in 1972, there were 13 centres. Today there are 573 literary classes conducted at 137 centres and attended by 14,065 adult students all over the country. In 1983, 71 adult education centres were opened, with over 12,000 men and 7,894 women enrolled in that year.

People's Democratic Republic of Yemen (South Yemen):

Article 37

The Economist, January 1986

South Yemen

Like clockwork

The attempted coup against President Ali Nasser Mohammed of South Yemen should have come as no surprise to him. Three previous left-wing presidents of this Marxist country have been victims of coups from even farther to their left. Like them, President Nasser Mohammed had strayed from the path of ideological correctness, to the irritation of both hardline Marxists at home and the Soviet Union. Fighting both in the capital and in the countryside seemed to be continuing on the 16th, when it was reported that the government was talking to the rebels.

The organisers of the attempt, which began on January 12th, seem to have included the previous president, Mr Abdul Fatah Ismail, whom Mr Nasser Mohammed had deposed in 1980 but who had the continued backing of the Russians. Tribal leaders, including the former defence minister, Mr Ali Ahmed Nasser Antar, supported the coup. On January 16th, anti-government tribesmen from the countryside were said to be marching on the capital.

South Yemen, one of the world's poorest countries, has a population of only 2m or so (nobody has properly counted); it is economically uninteresting but strategically important for the Soviet Union. It is Russia's only friend in the Arabian peninsula, and provides a useful base for Soviet ships and nuclear submarines. The airport runway at the capital, Aden, is being extended. This would let the Russians use it for long-range surveillance aircraft, and thus give them coverage of the American base at Diego Garcia, 2,200 miles away in the Indian Ocean.

No president of South Yemen has ever got very far in installing communism. Half of GNP and most of agriculture was still accounted for by the private sector in

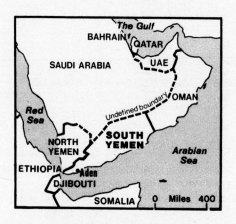

1982, proportions little different from ten years before. Between 1969 and 1978 there were three successful coups by hardline Marxists, each criticising his predecessor's failure to transform South Yemen into a model communist state. The third, in 1978, brought in Mr Fatah Ismail, as faithful a disciple as Moscow could wish for. He was unpopular at home, however, having made a serious effort to nationalise more land and property. President Nasser Mohammed got rid of him in 1980, and he fled to Moscow.

President Nasser Mohammed continued to co-operate with the Russians, but also tried to make better friends with the generally Russophobe Arab countries of the Gulf. He stopped supporting guerrillas fighting the governments of North Yemen and Oman, and restored diplomatic relations with Oman and Saudi Arabia. The rapprochement has been profitable. Since 1980 South Yemen has been getting money from OPEC and the Arab Monetary Fund, as well as some aid from individual Gulf countries.

But for the past two years hardliners have been making life difficult for President Nasser Mohammed. He had to let Mr Fatah Ismail back into the country last year.

And the Russians have been in a position to make their influence felt. Despite Mr Nasser Mohammed's diversification efforts, South Yemen still depends heavily on the Russians for money—they are the country's biggest creditor—and for trained manpower. There are about 1,000 Russians in South Yemen in military and another 1,000 in administrative jobs; Cubans and East Germans also have big roles. The Russians seem to be promoting a settlement; talks were being held in the Soviet Embassy.

Yemen Arab Republic (North Yemen):

Article 38

North Yemen has many reasons for playing down oil potential

By Ian Steele
Special to The Christian Science Monitor

Sana, North Yemen

As the newest oil producer on the Arabian Peninsula, North Yemen is conspicuous only for a determination to play down its potential.

The first and last official hurrah was in July 1984, when President Ali Abdullah Saleh announced a flow of 7,800 barrels of

THE CHRISTIAN SCIENCE MONITOR

INTERNATIONAL
TUESDAY, NOVEMBER 12, 1985

oil and 50 million cubic feet of gas a day from the nation's first test well.

Since then, the government and the successful prospector, Hunt Oil Company of the United States, have been silent.

Hunt is said by observers here to have explored four fields with a capacity of producing from 200,000 to 400,000 barrels a day within four years. But North Yemen's longer-term oil future has been left to the speculation of foreign businessmen, diplomats, and the overseas aid community.

President Saleh has several reasons for keeping the lid on information about the nation's reserves:

● Even if the resources are extraordinary, it could take four years or longer to develop them for export if the world glut continues. A more immediate concern is how to husband this otherwise poor country through the interim.

● At least half of Yemen's 2 million workers are in neighboring Saudi Arabia, and the last thing the president wants is a stampede for home. Yemenis in Saudi Arabia sent their families almost $1 billion last year — a figure equal to almost one-third of the gross national product.

While most of the money bypassed the treasury, it helped Yemenis to start small businesses and buy land, equipment, and other benefits beyond the capacity of the domestic economy. The government can ill afford to have these workers at home, unemployed and disgruntled.

● Saleh is also keen to preserve Yemen's favored-nation treatment as a so-called least developed country. Donors have been willing to overlook foreign remittances boosting the annual average per capita income from a qualifying low of $420 to about $1,500. But the oil find is forcing some to rethink their position.

"We have just begun a new four-year planning cycle for Yemen and aid will be maintained at current levels through that period," says Jan Roos, the Dutch chargé d'affaires. "But beyond that we might have a new set of circumstances."

Among those considerations, according to British and American officials, could be a swing from cash grants and loans to less flexible arrangements for technical assistance, coupled with smaller loans or a steep rise in interest rates from today's concessional 2½ percent.

Dragoslav Zdravkovic, who heads the United Nations Development Program in the capital city of Sana, agrees that oil money could put a crimp in Yemen's aid budget. But, he adds, a stronger economy would probably mean more rather than less activity in social development. "The needs here are enormous and they won't disappear overnight," he says. "Seventy-

JOAN FORBES — STAFF

five percent of the population is illiterate. The infant mortality rate is one of the highest in the world. The development agencies will stay, but they might ask the Yemenis to pay more of their share."

According to Scott Robinson, a former British civil servant in Yemen now working with the Shell Oil Company, the opening of an oil refinery next year could save the country about $120 million a year from its current $400 million balance of payments deficit.

"I have a gut feeling that they have at least as much oil as Oman, and perhaps considerably more," Mr. Robinson says.

"The interesting thing to me is that when Oman found oil it had very little else. Yemen already has roads, schools, hospitals. So that oil — while it might not be all that significant in terms of world prices in the near future, as it has been for countries like Saudi Arabia and Kuwait in the recent past — will have very considerable influence on Yemen's capacity for development."

Oil will also give a psychological lift to President Saleh, whose interest in better relations with his counterpart, Ali Nasser Muhammad in South Yemen, makes his northern Saudi Arabian neighbors very nervous. South Yemen is a Marxist state with close ties to the Soviet Union.

The fear of a unified Yemen with left-wing leanings and a population of 13 million is a constant in Saudi politics. Saudi Arabia feeds millions of dollars a year into North Yemen's budget and gives considerable indirect aid to foster better ties. Given the Saudi desire to maintain ties with noncommunist North Yemen, it is apparent that financial independence is not something the Saudis wish for their neighbor.

British and American observers appear less concerned by talk of unity and say that the present North- South Yemen ties are preferable to the conflict of the late 1970s when South Yemen sponsored raids on the north.

"The Soviet Union provides a lot of military aid and the Americans, although they provide less military aid, are the major donors of civilian aid," says one British expert. "I don't think they particularly love the Americans, but I don't think the relationship with the Soviets is a natural one at all. As long as both sides are prepared to continue giving, then the Yemenis will tug their forelock to both."

Credits

MIDDLE EASTERN REGION

Page 136 Article 1. Copyright © 1986 *World Press Review*, 230 Park Ave., New York, NY 10169.
Page 139 Article 2. © 1985 The Economist, reprinted by permission.
Page 141 Article 3. Originally from *Science Digest*, January 1983. Reprinted by permission.
Page 142 Article 4. From *New Haven Register*, September 1, 1985. Reprinted by permission of David Lamb, Los Angeles Times Service.
Page 144 Article 5. Copyright © 1985 by the *Gainesville Sun*, October 12, 1985. Reprinted by permission.
Page 145 Article 6. From *Pakistan & Gulf Economist*, June 29-July 5, 1985.
Page 146 Article 7. From *Pakistan & Gulf Economist*, August 10-16, 1985.

ALGERIA

Page 147 Article 8. Reprinted from *South*, December 1985, p. 96 by permission.
Page 148 Article 9. Reprinted from *South*, December 1985, p. 107 by permission.

BAHRAIN

Page 149 Article 10. From *Pakistan & Gulf Economists*, August 17-23, 1985, pp. 44-46.

EGYPT

Page 151 Article 11. Reprinted by permission of *The Nation*, December 28, 1985, pp. 705-708.
Page 155 Article 12. Reproduced by permission from *The Unesco Courier*.
Page 156 Article 13. Reprinted by permission of *Middle East International*, August 9, 1985.

IRAN

Page 157 Article 14. Copyright 1985 Time Inc. All rights reserved. Reprinted by permission from TIME.
Page 158 Article 15. Reprinted by permission from *The Christian Science Monitor*. © 1985 The Christian Science Publishing Society. All rights reserved.

IRAQ

Page 161 Article 16. Reprinted by permission from *The Christian Science Monitor*. © 1985 The Christian Science Publishing Society. All rights reserved.
Page 162 Article 17. Reprinted by permission from *The Christian Science Monitor*. © 1983 The Christian Science Publishing Society. All rights reserved.

ISRAEL

Page 163 Article 18. © 1985 *World Press Review*, reprinted by permission.
Page 166 Article 19. From *The Washington Post National Weekly Edition*, January 6, 1986. Reprinted by permission of the author.
Page 168 Article 20. Reprinted by permission from *Congress Monthly*, April 1985, pp. 13-14.

JORDON

Page 170 Article 21. Reprinted by permission from *The Christian Science Monitor*. © 1985 The Christian Science Publishing Society. All rights reserved.
Page 173 Article 22. Reprinted by permission of *Middle East International*, December 20, 1985.

KUWAIT

Page 174 Article 23. "Kuwait Living on its Nerves," K. Celine, *MERIP Report*, February 1985, pp. 10-12. Reprinted by permission from *MERIP Report*, 475 Riverside Dr., Rm #518, New York, NY 10115.

LIBYA

Page 176 Article 24. Reprinted from *South*, October 1985, pp. 27-28 by permission.
Page 178 Article 25. Copyright © 1986 by The New York Times Company. Reprinted by permission.

LEBANON

Page 180 Article 26. Reprinted by permission of *Middle East International*, December 6, 1985.
Page 181 Article 27. © 1985 *The Economist*, reprinted by permission.

MOROCCO

Page 183 Article 28. Reprinted by permission of *Middle East International*, October 11, 1985.

OMAN

Page 185 Article 29. Copyright © 1985 by The New York Times Company. Reprinted by permission.

SAUDI ARABIA

Page 186 Article 30. Reprinted by permission from *The Christian Science Monitor*. © 1985 The Christian Science Publishing Society. All rights reserved.
Page 187 Article 31. Reprinted by permission of *The New Republic*, © 1985, The New Republic, Inc.

SUDAN

Page 190 Article 32. Reprinted by permission of *Africa Report*. Copyright © 1985 by the African-American Institute.

SYRIA

Page 193 Article 33. Reprinted by permission from *The Christian Science Monitor*. © 1985 The Christian Science Publishing Society. All rights reserved.

TURKEY

Page 194 Article 34. Copyright © 1985 by The New York Times Company. Reprinted by permission.
Page 196 Article 35. Reprinted from *South*, May 1985, by permission.

UNITED ARAB EMIRATES

Page 198 Article 36. From *Pakistan & Gulf Economist*, July 13-19, 1985.

PEOPLE'S DEMOCRATIC REPUBLIC OF YEMEN (SOUTH YEMEN)

Page 200 Article 37. © 1986 *The Economist*, reprinted by permission.

YEMEN ARAB REPUBLIC (NORTH YEMEN)

Page 200 Article 38. Reprinted by permission from *The Christian Science Monitor*. © 1985 The Christian Science Publishing Society. All rights reserved.

Glossary of Terms and Abbreviations

Abd   Slave, servant of God (as in Gamal Abdel Nasser: Abd al-Nasir).

AFESD (Arab Fund for Economic and Social Development)   Established in 1972 to make low-interest loans for projects in the Arab states. Membership: all of the Arab states.

Alawi (Nusayri)   A Shia Muslim minority group in Syria, currently in power under President Assad.

Arab League (League of Arab States)   Established in 1945 as a regional organization for newly independent Arab countries. Membership: all of the Arab states (Egypt's membership was suspended after the 1979 peace treaty with Israel) plus the Palestine Liberation Organization.

Asabiyya   Tribal or group solidarity, a concept developed by the fourteenth-century Islamic philosopher Ibn Khaldun to explain Muslim, particularly North African, social behavior.

Autogestion   Self-management, a French term describing the workers' takeover and management of former French-owned estates in Algeria after the owners' departure.

Ayatollah   "Sign of God," the title of highest rank among the Shia religious leaders in Iran.

BADEA (Arab Bank for Economic Development in Africa)   Established in 1975 to make low-interest loans of up to forty percent of the cost of development projects in Africa. Membership: All of the Arab states except the Yemen Arab Republic and the People's Democratic Republic of Yemen. Headquarters: Khartoum, Sudan.

Ba'th (Arab Socialist Resurrection Party)   A Socialist political party which has two main branches, ruling in Syria and Iraq respectively, plus members in other Arab countries.

Caliph (in Arabic, Khalifa)   Agent, representative, or deputy; in Sunni Islam, the line of successors to Muhammad.

Colon   Settler, colonist (French), a term used for the French population in North Africa during the colonial period (1830-1962).

Dar al-Islam   "House of Islam," territory ruled under Islam. Conversely, Dar al-Harb, "House of War," denotes territory not under Islamic rule.

Dhow   The traditional broad-beamed, gaff-rigged fishing boat of the Arabian coasts.

Druse (Druze)   An offshoot of Islam that has developed its own rituals and practices and a close-knit community structure; Druse populations are found today in Lebanon, Jordan, Syria, and Israel.

Emir (Amir)   A title of rank, denoting either a patriarchal ruler, provincial governor, or military commander. Today used exclusively for rulers of certain Arabian Peninsula states.

Evolués   A French term used to describe those North African Muslims who adopted the French language, culture, and values during the protectorate period.

Faqih   One knowledgeable in Islamic law; also a Koranic teacher. The root word is *fiqh*, "jurisprudence."

Fatwa   A legal opinion or interpretation delivered by a Muslim religious scholar-jurist.

FLN (National Liberation Front)   The resistance movement against the French in Algeria which succeeded in establishing Algerian independence and is Algeria's only legal political party.

GCC (Gulf Cooperation Council)   Established in 1981 as a mutual defense organization by the Arab Gulf states. Membership: Bahrain, Kuwait, Oman, Qatar, Saudi Arabia, and the United Arab Emirates. Headquarters: Riyadh, Saudi Arabia.

Hadith   "Traditions" of the Prophet Muhammad, the compilation of sayings and decisions attributed to him which serve as a model and guide to conduct for Muslims.

Hajj   Pilgrimage to Mecca, one of the Five Pillars of Islam; also used as a title for one who has made the pilgrimage.

Hijrah (Hegira)   The Prophet Muhammad's emigration from Mecca to Medina in AD 622 to escape persecution; start of the Islamic calendar.

Histadrut   An Israeli labor confederation.

Ibadi   A militant early Islamic group that split with the majority (Sunni) over the question of the succession to Muhammad. Their descendants form the majority of the population in Oman and the Yemen Arab Republic.

IBRD (International Bank for Reconstruction and Development)   Established on December 27, 1945 to make loans at conventional interest rates to countries for development projects. Headquarters: Washington, DC. Affiliated organizations are the International Development Assistance Organization (IDA), the International Finance Corporation (IFC), and the International Monetary Fund (IMF).

IDB (Islamic Development Bank)   Established in 1973 to provide interest-free loans to member states. Membership: Islamic countries (43). Headquarters: Jiddah, Saudi Arabia.

Ihram   The seamless white robe worn by all Muslims making the hajj.

Ijma   Consensus, the agreement of the majority of members of a particular Islamic community for collective action on important matters, such as a peace treaty.

Ijtihad   Independent reasoning and interpretation of matters of Islamic law. When made authoritatively, as by an ayatollah, such interpretations have the force of law.

Ikhwan   Brothers, as in a religious confraternity. When capitalized (*i.e.*, Ikhwan al-Muslimin), refers to the Muslim Brotherhood, a secret but widespread Sunni organization opposed to Muslim secular governments.

Imam Religious leader, prayer-leader of a congregation. When capitalized, refers to the descendants of Ali who are regarded by Shia Muslims as the rightful sucessors to Muhammad.

Islam Submission, *i.e.*, to the Will of God, as revealed in the Koran.

Ismailis Members of a branch of Shia Islam who accept a line of only five Imams descended from Muhammad through Ali. Their spiritual leader is the Aga Khan.

Ithna 'ashariyyah "Twelvers," the main body of members of Shia Islam who accept a line of twelve Imams ending with the Hidden Imam or Mahdi.

Jahiliyya The "time of ignorance" of the Arabs before Islam. Sometimes used by Islamic fundamentalists today to describe secular Muslim societies, which they regard as sinful.

Jama'a The Friday communal prayer, held in a mosque (*jami'*). By extension, the public assembly held by Muslim rulers for their subjects in traditional Islamic states such as Saudi Arabia.

Jamahiriyya Popular democracy (as in Libya).

Jihad The struggle of Muslims collectively or individually to do right and defend the community; commonly, "holy war."

Jizya A poll-tax or tithe imposed on non-Muslim peoples living in the territories of Islam.

Khan A title of rank in eastern Islam (Turkey, Iran, etc.) for military or clan leaders.

Kharijites An early Muslim group who opposed the sucession in Muhammad's family but also opposed the election of the first four caliphs as undemocratic. They assassinated Ali after he had negotiated a truce with his opponents upon becoming caliph; in their view, he had bartered away his right to the office.

Khedive Viceroy, the title of rulers of Egypt in the nineteenth and twentieth centuries who ruled as regents of the Ottoman sultan.

Kibbutz A collective settlement in Israel.

Koran (in Arabic, Qur'an) "Recitation," the book of God's revelations to Muhammad via the Angel Gabriel, which form the basis for Islam.

Maghrib "West," the hour of the sunset prayer; in Arabic, a geographical term for North Africa.

Mahdi "The Awaited One" in both Sunni and Shia Islam, the Messiah, who will appear on earth to reunite the divided Islamic community and announce the Day of Judgement. In Shia Islam he is the Twelfth and Last Imam (al-Mahdi al-Muntazir) who disappeared twelve centuries ago but is belived to be in a state of occultation (suspended between heaven and earth).

Majlis Assembly, parliament, legislature.

Mandate An arrangement whereby an occupying power assumed the responsibility on behalf of the League of Nations to train the population of the occupied territory for eventual self-government.

Marabout Particularly in North Africa, a local saint or holy man respected for his intercessory powers with God on behalf of a community.

Millet "Nation," a non-Muslim population group in the Ottoman Empire recognized as a legitimate religious community and allowed self-government in internal affairs under its own religious leaders, who were responsible to the sultan for its behavior.

Muezzin A prayer-caller, the person who announces the five daily obligatory prayers from the minaret of a mosque.

Mufti A legal scholar empowered to issue fatwas. Usually one mufti is designated as the Grand Mufti of a particular Islamic state or territory.

Mujahid (plural, Mujahiddin) "Fighter for the faith," one who undertakes a jihad against the enemies of Islam.

Mujtahid An independent legal interpreter whose judicial opinions reflect one of the four schools of Islamic law.

Muslim One who submits (to the Will of God). *cf. Islam*.

OAPEC (Organization of Arab Petroleum Exporting Countries) Established in 1968 to coordinate oil policies—but not setting prices—and to develop oil-related inter-Arab projects, such as an Arab tanker fleet and dry-dock facilities. Membership: all Arab oil-producing states. Headquarters: Kuwait.

OIC (Organization of the Islamic Conference) Established in 1971 to promote solidarity among Islamic countries, provide humanitarian aid to Muslim communities throughout the world, and provide funds for Islamic education through construction of mosques, theological institutions of Islamic learning, etc. Membership: all states with an Islamic majority or significant minority. Headquarters: Jiddah, Saudi Arabia.

OPEC (Organization of Petroleum Exporting Countries) Established in 1960 to set prices and coordinate global oil policies of members. Middle East members: Algeria, Iran, Iraq, Kuwait, Libya, Qatar, Saudi Arabia, and the United Arab Emirates. Headquarters: Vienna, Austria.

PLO (Palestine Liberation Organization) Established in 1964 to represent the Palestinian Arabs in exile and to develop political and military strategies for the liberation of Palestine from Israeli control and the establishment of an independent Palestinian state. The PLO is split into a number of factions although in theory it operates under a centralizing authority, the Palestine National Congress (PNC). Current headquarters: Tunis, Tunisia.

Polisario A national resistance movement in the Western Sahara which opposes annexation by Morocco and is fighting to establish an independent Saharan Arab state, the Sahrawi Arab Democratic Republic (SADR).

PSD (Parti Socialiste Destourien) The dominant political party in Tunisia since independence, and until recently the only legal party.

Qadi (Cadi, Kadi) An Islamic judge.

Qaid (Caid, Kaid) Particularly in North Africa, a native Muslim official appointed to administer a region or territory by the French during the protectorate period.

Qasba (Casbah, Kasba) A fortified section of an Islamic city; citadel.

Qibla The section of wall in an Islamic mosque which faces in the direction of Mecca, marked by a recess or niche (*mihrab*).

Qizilbash ("Red heads" in Turkish, from their red battle-caps.) An eastern Islamic group who helped found the sixteenth-century Safavid monarchy in Iran.

Quraysh The group of clans who made up Muhammad's community in Mecca.

Sahrawi A member of the population of the Western Sahara, currently annexed by Morocco.

Salat The five obligatory daily Islamic prayers, the second of the Five Pillars of Islam.

Shahada The confession of faith by Muslims, the first of the Five Pillars of Islam.

Shari'a "The Way," the corpus of the sacred laws of Islam as revealed to Muhammad in the Koran.

Sharif "Holy," a term applied to members of Muhammad's immediate family and descendants through his daughter Fatima and son-in-law Ali.

Shaykh (Sheikh, Sheik) Patriarchal leader of an Islamic community, usually elected for life; also used for certain religious leaders and community elders as a title of honor.

Shia (Shiite) Originally meant "Party," *i.e.*, of Ali, those Muslims who supported him as Muhammad's rightful and designated successor. Today, broadly, a member of the principal Islamic minority.

Sufi An Islamic mystic.

Sunna Custom or procedure, the code of acceptable behavior for Muslims based on the Koran and hadith. Not to be confused with Sunni, the name for the majority group in Islam.

Suq (Souk) A public weekly market in Islamic rural areas, always held in the same village on the same day of the week, so that the village may have the word incorporated into its name. Also refers to a section of an Islamic city devoted to the wares and work of potters, cloth merchants, wood workers, spice sellers, etc.

Taqiyya Dissimulation, concealment of one's religious identity or beliefs (as by Shia under Sunni control) in the face of overwhelming power or repression.

Tariqas The religious brotherhoods or orders of Sunni Islam.

UAR (United Arab Republic) The name given to the abortive union of Egypt and Syria (1958-1961) and subsequently assumed by Egypt as its official name.

Ulema The corporate body of Islamic religious leaders, scholars, and jurists.

Umma The world-wide community of Muslims.

UN Observer Missions Various peacekeeping forces established to monitor truces between Israel and the Arab states. They are: UNDOF (UN Disengagement Observer Force), established in 1974 to maintain the border truce between Israel and Syria; UNIFIL (UN Interim Force in Lebanon), established in 1978 to patrol the Israeli-Lebanese border; and the UN Multinational Observer Force in the Sinai, set up to monitor the staged withdrawal of Israelis from Egyptian territory in the Sinai.

UNRWA (United Nations Relief and Works Agency for Palestine Refugees) Established in 1950 to provide food, housing, and health and education services for Palestinian refugees who fled their homes after the establishment of the State of Israel in Palestine. Headquarters: Vienna, Austria. Refugee camps are located in Lebanon, Jordan, the Gaza Strip, and the West Bank.

UN (United Nations) Established on June 26, 1945 through official approval of the charter by delegates of fifty nations as a global international organization. All of the Middle Eastern countries are members; the PLO holds observer status. Headquarters: New York City. Two sub-agencies of the UN operate directly in the Middle East.

Wilayat al-Faqih Supreme guardianship of the Law, the formal position held by Ayatollah Khomeini in the Islamic Republic of Iran according to Iran's 1980 Constitution.

Zakat Compulsory almsgiving, or today the tax or tithe required of Muslims for the support of the community, the Fourth Pillar of Islam.

Sources for Statistical Summaries

US State Department, *Background Notes*

The World Factbook (1984)

World Statistics in Brief (1983)

Information Please Almanac (1985)

The Stateman's Yearbook (1985-1986)

Statistical Yearbook (1985)

World Bank, World Development Report (1984)

Whitaker's Almanack (1985)

Bibliography

GENERAL WORKS

James A. Bill and Carl Leiden, *Politics in the Middle East* (Boston, MA: Little, Brown & Co., 1979).
> An excellent study focused on leadership, ideology, and oil politics.

A.S. Cusdi and Ali Dessouki, eds., *Islam and Power* (Baltimore, MD: Johns Hopkins University Press, 1981).
> Informative essays by various scholars, including one on Khomeini's concept of Islamic government.

R. Hrair Dekejian, *Islam in Revolution* (Syracuse, NY: Syracuse University Press, 1985).
> Thorough analysis of Islamic fundamentalism, with case studies of fundamentalist politics in several Middle Eastern countries.

John J. Donohue and John L. Esposito, eds., *Islam in Transition: Muslim Perspectives* (New York: Oxford University Press, 1982).
> Translations of the writings of important Muslim intellectuals.

Dale F. Eickelman, *The Middle East: An Anthropological Approach* (Englewood Cliffs, NJ: Prentice-Hall, 1981).

Sydney Fisher, *The Middle East: A History,* third ed. (New York: Alfred A. Knopf, 1979).
> The best standard history of the region, although it excludes North Africa.

Michael Hudson, *Arab Politics: The Search for Legitimacy* (New Haven, CT: Yale University Press, 1977).
> A thorough discussion of the problem of identity and consequent legitimacy that affects Arab governments.

Fazlur Rahman, *Islam* (Chicago, IL: University of Chicago Press, 1979).
> A historical study of the development of Islam from its beginnings to the present.

William Spencer, *The Islamic States in Conflict* (New York: Franklin Watts, 1983).
> An introduction to conflict in the Middle East, between (and among) Arab and non-Arab Islamic states.

John O. Voll, *Islam: Continuity and Change in the Modern World* (Boulder, CO: Westview Press, 1982).
> A useful history.

NATIONAL HISTORIES

Algeria

Alistair Horne, *A Savage War of Peace: Algeria 1954-1962* (London, England: Macmillan, 1977).

Henry F. Jackson, *The FLN in Algeria: Party Development in a Revolutionary Society* (Westport, CT: Greenwood Press, 1977).

William Spencer, *Algiers in the Age of the Corsairs* (Norman: University of Oklahoma Press, 1976).

John Talbott, *The War Without a Name: France in Algeria, 1954-1962* (New York: Alfred A. Knopf, 1980).

Bahrain

Michael Jenner, *Bahrain: Gulf Heritage in Transition* (London, England: Longman, 1984).

Fuad I. Khuri, *Tribe and State in Bahrain* (Chicago, IL: University of Chicago Press, 1981).

Egypt

Raymond W. Baker, *Egypt's Uncertain Revolution Under Nasser and Sadat* (Cambridge, MA: Harvard University Press, 1979).

Mark N. Cooper, *The Transformation of Egypt* (London, England: Croom Helm, 1982).

Derek Hopwood, *Egypt: Politics and Society 1945-1981* (London, England: George Allen & Unwin, 1982).

Afif L. Marsot, *Egypt in the Reign of Muhammad Ali* (Cambridge, England: Cambridge University Press, 1984).

Iran

Ervand Abrahamian, *Iran Between Two Revolutions* (Princeton, NJ: Princeton University Press, 1982).

Michael M. Fischer, *Iran from Religious Dispute to Revolution* (Cambridge, MA: Harvard University Press, 1983).

John D. Stempel, *Inside the Iranian Revolution* (Bloomington: Indiana University Press, 1981).

Iraq

Phoebe Marr, *A History of Modern Iraq* (London, England: Longman, 1983).

Tim Niblock, ed., *Iraq: The Contemporary State* (London, England: Croom Helm, 1982).

Edith Penrose and E.F. Penrose, *Iraq: International Relations and National Development* (Boulder, CO: Westview Press, 1978).

Israel

Michael J. Cohen, *Palestine: Retreat from the Mandate* (New York: Holmes and Meier, 1978).

Grace Halsell, *Journey to Jerusalem* (New York: Macmillan, 1981).

Don Peretz, *The Government and Politics of Israel* (Boulder, CO: Westview Press, 1979).

Dan V. Segre, *A Crisis of Identity: Israel and Zionism* (Oxford, England: Oxford University Press, 1980).

Jordan

Peter Gubser, *Jordan: Crossroads of Middle Eastern Events* (Boulder, CO: Westview Press, 1983)

Richard D. Nyrop, ed., *Jordan: A Country Study* (Washington, DC: American University, Foreign Area Studies, 1979).

Patrick Seale, ed., *The Making of an Arab Statesman: Sharif Abd al-Hamid Sharaf and the Modern Arab World* (London, England: Quartet Books, 1983).

Kuwait

Stephen Gardiner and Ian Cook, *Kuwait: Making of a City* (London, England: Longman, 1983).

Jacqueline Ismail, *Kuwait: Problems of Modernization* (Syracuse, NY: Syracuse University Press, 1981).

Lebanon

David C. Gordon, *Lebanon: Nation in Jeopardy* (Boulder, CO: Westview Press, 1983).

Walid Khalidi, *Conflict and Violence in Lebanon: Confrontation in the Middle East* (Cambridge, MA: Harvard University Press, 1979).

Jonathan Randal, *The Tragedy of Lebanon* (London, England: Chatto and Windus, 1983).

Libya

J.A. Allen, *Libya: The Experience of Oil* (London, England: Croom Helm, 1981).

Marius K. Deeb and Mary Jane Deeb, *Libya Since the Revolution* (New York: Praeger, 1982).

John Wright, *Libya, A Modern History* (Baltimore, MD: Johns Hopkins Press, 1982).

Morocco

Harold D. Nelson, ed., *Morocco: A Country Study* (Washington, DC: American University, Foreign Area Studies, 1978).

William Spencer, *Historical Dictionary of Morocco* (New Brunswick, NJ: Scarecrow Press, 1980).

I. William Zartman, ed., *Political Elites in Arab North Africa* (New York: Longman, 1982).

Oman

Christine Eickelman, *Women and Community in Oman* (New York: New York University Press, 1984).

Liesl Graz, *The Omanis: Sentinels of the Gulf* (London, England: Longman, 1982).

J.E. Peterson, *Oman in the 20th Century* (London, England: Croom Helm, 1978).

Qatar

Helga Graham, *Arabian Time Machine: Self Portrait of an Oil State* (London, England: Heinemann, 1978).

Saudi Arabia

David Holden and Richard Johns, *The House of Saud* (New York: Holt, Rinehart and Winston, 1981).

Yusuf A. Sayigh, *Arab Oil Policies in the 1970's* (London, England: Croom Helm, 1983).

John A. Shaw and David E. Long, *Saudi Arabian Modernization: The Impact of Change on Stability* (The Washington Papers/89, Vol. X. New York: Praeger, 1982).

Sudan

Peter M. Holt and M.W. Daly, *The History of the Sudan,* third ed. (London, England: Weidenfeld and Nicolson, 1979).

Harold D. Nelson, ed., *Sudan: A Country Study,* third ed. (Washington, DC: American University, Foreign Area Studies, 1982).

Dunstan Wai, *The African-Arab Conflict in the Sudan* (New York: Africana Publishing Company, 1981).

Syria

Umar F. Abd-Allah, *The Islamic Struggle in Syria* (Berkeley, CA: Mizan Press, 1983). (Should be read with extreme caution due to its anti-Assad bias, but contains useful material on the Muslim Brotherhood.)

John F. Devlin, *Syria: Modern State in an Ancient Land* (Boulder, CO: Westview Press, 1983).

Philip S. Khoury, *Urban Notables and Arab Nationalism* (Cambridge, England: Cambridge University Press, 1983).

Turkey

Antony Bridge, *Suleiman the Magnificent* (New York: Franklin Watts, 1983).

William Hale, *The Political and Economic Development of Modern Turkey* (London, England: Croom Helm, 1981).

Lord Kinross, *The Ottoman Centuries: The Rise and Fall of the Turkish Empire* (New York: William Morrow, 1977).

William Spencer, *The Land and People of Turkey,* second ed. (New York: J.B. Lippincott, 1972).

Tunisia

Wilfred Knapp, *Northwest Africa: A Political and Economic Survey,* third ed. (Oxford, England: Oxford University Press, 1977).

Richard Lawless and Allan Findlay, eds., *North Africa: Contemporary Politics and Economic Development* (London: Croom Helm, 1984).

Harold D. Nelson, ed., *Tunisia: A Country Study* (Washington, DC: American University, Foreign Area Studies, 1978).

United Arab Emirates (UAE)

Frauke Heard-Bey, *From Trucial States to United Arab Emirates* (London, England: Longman, 1982).

Ali M. Khalifa, *The United Arab Emirates: Unity in Fragmentation* (London, England: Croom Helm, 1980).

Rosemarie S. Zahlan, *The Origins of the United Arab Emirates* (London, England: Macmillan, 1978).

People's Democratic Republic of Yemen (South Yemen)

B.R. Pridham, ed., *Contemporary Yemen: Politics and Historical Background* (New York: St. Martin's Press, 1985).

Robert Stookey, *South Yemen: A Marxist State in Arabia* (London, England: Croom Helm, 1982).

Yemen Arab Republic (North Yemen)

Robin Bidwell, *The Two Yemens* (Boulder, CO: Westview Press, 1983).

J.E. Peterson, *Yemen, the Search for a Modern State* (London, England: Croom Helm, 1981).

B.R. Pridham, ed., *Contemporary Yemen: Politics and Historical Background* (New York: St. Martin's Press, 1985).

Robert Stookey, *Yemen: The Politics of the Yemen Arab Republic* (Boulder, CO: Westview Press, 1978).

LITERATURE IN TRANSLATION

Roger Allen, ed., *In the Eye of the Beholder: Tales of Egyptian Life from the Writings of Yusuf Idris* (Minneapolis, MN: Bibliotheca Islamica, 1978).
Short stories by one of Egypt's greatest writers.

Sami Bindari, *The House of Power* (Boston: MA: Houghton Mifflin, 1980).
Dramatic novel about life in an Egyptian village.

Leo Hamalian and John D. Yohannan, eds., *New Writing from the Middle East* (New York: Mentor Books/New American Library, 1978).
Short stories, poems, and dramas from Arabic, Armenian, Persian, Israeli, and Turkish literature.

Aziz Nesin, *Istanbul Boy: The Autobiography of Aziz Nesin*, in two parts (Austin: University of Texas Press, 1977).
The autobiography of a distinguished satirist and writer, with his observations on everyday Turkish life.

Amos Oz, *The Hill of Evil Counsel* (New York: Harcourt Brace Jovanovich, 1976).
Three short stories set in Palestine in the years just before Israeli independence.

Nicolas Saudray, *The House of the Prophets* (New York: Doubleday, 1985).
A novel by a French writer set in a fictional land which is a composite of Egypt, Lebanon, Syria, and Iraq.

CURRENT EVENTS

To keep up to date on rapidly changing events in the contemporary Middle East and North Africa, the following are especially useful:

Current History, A World Affairs Journal
One issue per year is usually devoted to the Middle Eastern region.

Africa Research Bulletin (Exeter, England)
Monthly summaries of political, economic, and social developments in all of Africa, with coverage of North-Northeast Africa.

Africa Report
Bimonthly, with an "African Update" chronology for all regions.

MEED (Middle East Economic Digest) (London, England)
Weekly summary of economic and some political developments in the Middle East-North African region generally and in individual countries. Provides special issues from time to time on such topics as "Japan in the Middle East," "The Transportation Industry," and "Kuwait: A Profile."

PERIODICALS

The Christian Science Monitor
One Norway Street, Boston, MA 02115

The Economist
25 St. James's Street, London, England

The Middle East Journal
1761 N Street, NW, Washington, DC 20036
This quarterly periodical, established in 1947, is the oldest one specializing in Middle East affairs, with authoritative articles, book reviews, documents, and a quarterly chronology.

Middle Eastern Studies
Gainsborough House, Gainesborough Road, London, England
Quarterly historical magazine.

The Middle East and North Africa
Europa Publications, 18 Bedford Square, London, England
A reference work, published annually and updated, with country surveys, regional articles, and documents.

Le Monde (Weekly edition, in English)
7 Rue des Italiens, Paris, France
A summary of the previous week's news, with separate sections on various geographical regions. The Middle East and North Africa are treated separately.

New Outlook
9 Gordon Street, Tel Aviv, Israel
Bimonthly news magazine, with articles, chronology and documents. Reflects generally Israeli leftist peace-with-the-Arabs views of the movement Peace Now, with which it is affiliated.

Index

Abbasid dynasty, 47, 53
Abdullah, Emir (Jordan), 68-69, 70
Abdur Rahman Bukhatir, 146
Abraham, 53, 59, 99, and Jewish homeland, 19;
    Muslim view of, 6
Abu Dhabi, 123
Abu Saafa oilfield, 149
Achille Lauro incident, 151, 152, 153, 154
Afghanistan, Soviet Union in, 16, 24-25
ariculture, in Algeria, 147-148; in ancient South
    Yemen, 126; in Bahrain, 150; in Israel, 65;
    in Jordan, 71; in Lebanon, 79; in Libya, 82;
    in Morocco, illus. 91; in Oman, 95; in
    Qatar, 97; in Sudan, 106; in Turkey, 121; in
    United Arab Emirates, illus. 124; in Yemen
    Arab Republic, 129, 131
Agudath Israel World Organization (Israeli
    political party), 63
Ain al-Hilweh refugee camp (Beirut, Lebanon),
    180, 181
Alawis, 87-88, 89, 90; in Syria, 109, 110
Alawite (Shia) community, and terrorism, 5
Al Bu Said Dynasty, of Oman, 93
al-Dawa, and concept of Jihad, 5; and Mid-East
    terrorism, 4
Alexander the Great, 37
Al-Fatah, 140
Algeria, Democratic and Popular Republic of,
    26-31; agriculture in, 147-148; France in, 115;
    and Spanish Sahara, 24; sports in, 148
Algerian Atlas mountain range, 27
Algerian treaty (1984), 183
al-Kalifas, and Bahrain, 33, 34; and Qatar, 97
Almoravids, in Morocco, 87; and Western
    Sahara, 22, 23
al-Nakba, and 6-day War, 39
al-Saiga guerrillas, in Beirut, 111
Al Takfir Wal Hijra (Egyptian secret group), 40
aluminum industry, in Bahrain, 150
Amal (Shia organization in Lebanon), 4, 78,
    180, 181
American-Arab Anti-Discrimination Committee,
    64
Amman, Jordan, illus. 69, 173; Israel in, 70
Anaizas peoples, 33
Anglo-Iranian Oil Company, 51
Anya Anya resistance movement (Sudan), 106
Anya Anya II (Sudanese resistance), 106
Aouzou Strip (Lybia-occupied), 81
Arab-African Federation, illus. 91
Arab Higher Committee, 20
Arabic language, 16, 142 fol., 148
Arab-Israeli conflict, 19 fol., see also, Arab-
    Israeli War; Six-Day War
Arab-Israeli War (1948), 20, 68, 77; (1967), 126
Arab League, 41, 77; language academy of, 143;
    and OAU, 184; and Syria, 110; and two
    Yemens, 130
Arab Legion, 69
Arab nationalism, and Palestine homeland,
    19-20, 22; during World War I, 37-38; see
    also, Palestinian Liberation Organization
Arabs, in Algeria, 27; Druze, 59; in Iran, 45;
    and Iranians compared, 17; development of
    Islam, 6; Palestinian, 59; see also, Arab
    nationalism; Islam
Arab Socialist Union (ASU), 39, 40
Arafat, Yassir, illus. 77, 140; eviction of, from
    Tripoli, 139; and Israel, 165; and King
    Hussein, 136, 137, 141, 171, 194; in Lebanon,
    181-182; and Mubarak, 152
architecture, Islamic, 11-12
armed services, in Israel, 169

Armenians, in Iran, 45; and Syria, 109
arms supplies in Mideast, 138, 158, 174
Assad, Pres. Hafez al-, 110, illus. 111; 112
Assyrians, in Iran, 45
Atlas Mountains, 87
Aurès mountains (Algeria), 27
autogestion, in Algeria, 29-30
Azeri (Azerbaijani) Turks, 45, 47

Baaklini, Abdo, 76
Baghdad Pact (1955), 54
Baha'Ullah (religious leader), 45
Bahrain, State of Bahrain, 32-34, 97; economy
    of, 149-151; and United Arab Emirates, 123;
    see also, Bahrain Monetary Agency; Bahrain
    Petroleum Company refinery
Bahrain Monetary Agency (BMA), 151
Bahrain Petroleum Company (Bapco) refinery,
    149
Bakr, President Ahmad al- (Iraq), 55, 163
Balfour, Arthur, 20
Balfour declaration, and Jewish homeland in
    Palestine, 20, 61
Bani-Sadr, Abol Hassan, 49
Bardo Museum (Tunis), 113
Basmachis, Soviet dealings with, 25
Ba'th party, 110, 112, 137; in Iraq, 55, 161, 162,
    163
batula (traditional garment), 98
Bedouins, 141 fol., and King's Camel Races,
    186; in Oman, 93, in Qatar, 97
Begin, Menachem, 21, 40, 63, 64, 65, 164, 165,
    166, 171, 181
Beirut, Lebanon, 76, 137; PLO in, 77, 78; Sabra
    and Shatila massacre in, 165; U.S. Marines
    in, 4, 138
Bendjedid, President Chadli (Algeria), 30, 31,
    148
Ben-Gurion, David, illus. 62; 63, 164
Berbers, 27, 148; and Libya, 81; in Morocco, 87,
    88, 90; in Tunisia, 114
beverages, Middle Eastern, 13, 14; see also,
    food
"Black Saturday," 38
Black September, 139
Black Stone, and Islam, 11
Blue Nile river (Sudan), 105
Bol, Manute, 104
Bosporous strait, 118
Boumedienne, President Houari (Algeria), 18,
    30, 31, 183
Bourguiba, President Habib (Tunisia), 115-116;
    and PLO, 140; and President Assad,
    compared, 110
Britain, see United Kingdom
Buber, Martin, 21
Byzantine Empire, 118
Byzantium, 118

Cairo, Egypt, 36, 37; illus. 42
Caliph, Muslim, 7; illus. 8
Camp David peace treaty, 22, 136, 138, 152
Carter, Jimmy, 22, 48, 170, 179
Carthage, Tunis, 114, 115
Casbah of Algiers, 26
celebrations, Muslim and Jewish, 13; see also,
    Ramadan
Chad, drought in, 107; and Libya, 81; and
    Morocco, 91, 185
China, and Yemen Arab Republic, 131
Christianity, relationship of, to Islam, 6; see
    also, Christians
Christian Phalange (Lebanon), 78

Christians, in Egypt, 37; in Iran, 159; in Iraq,
    54; in Lebanon, 77, 78, 79, 182, 194; and
    Muslims, 9; in Syria, 109; in Turkey, 118,
    119
Churchill, Winston, 89
colons, French settlers in Algeria, 28
communism, and South Yemen, 200
Constantine, 118
Coptic Church, 37, 153
Corsair Regency of Algiers, and Mediterranean
    piracy, 27-28, 81, 115
Cossack Brigade (Iranian military unit), 47
Council of Guardians (Iran), 49
Croesus, King, 118
Crusades, 6, 9
Cuellar, Javier Perez de, illus. 64
Cyrus the Great, 17

da Gama, Vasco, 93
Damascus, Syria, 109; and Aleppo, 111; role of,
    in Islam, 8
Dar al-Harb ("House of Dissidence"), and
    jihad, 5
Dar al-Islam ("House of Islam"), and jihad, 5
Dawa' Party (Iraq), 174
de Gaulle, Charles, 148
desalination, in Kuwait, 72
desert, effect of, on Middle Eastern social
    organization, 15-16; see also, Sahara
Destour (Tunisian nationalists), 115; see also,
    Destour Socialist Party
Destour Socialist Party (PSD), 115, 116
Dhofar rebellion (Oman), 94
Diaspora Jews, 59, 61
Diego Garcia (American base), 200
Dilmun (legendary land), 33
Dismemberment, The, 44
Dome of the Rock (Jerusalem Muslim shrine),
    20; illus. 21
domino theory, and Middle East, 16-17
drought, in Sudan, 107
Druze, in Lebanon, 76, 182; in Syria, 109, 110

East Jerusalem, 58, 68; Jordanian capture of, 69
Eban, Abba, 165
education, secular: in Algeria, 148; in Egypt,
    43; at Hebrew University of Jerusalem,
    168-169; Muslim, 14; in Oman, 94, 95; in
    PDRY, 127; in Saudi Arabia, illus. 103; in
    Turkey, 121; in United Arab Emirates, illus.
    124; in YAR, illus. 131
Egypt, 35-43; economy of, 151, 154; and Iran-
    Iraq War, 18; and Israel, 20, 38, 153; and
    Jordan, 41; national film archive of, 155;
    and Ottoman Turks, 9; and peace process,
    58, 136; social tensions in, 149; Soviet
    Union in, 17, 39; sports in, 147; and the
    Sudan, 105; and U.S., 151-154; and Yemen,
    130; see also, Arab-Israeli War
Egyptian-Israeli peace treaty (1979), 58
Egyptian Military Academy, 38
Eisenhower, Dwight D., 22
Ethiopia, drought in, 107; and Sudan, 190, 192
Euphrates Dam (Syria), illus. 112
Euphrates river, 53, 144
European Commission of Human Rights, 194
European Economic Community (EEC), and
    famine relief, 191
Europeans: influence of, in Middle East, 15, 16,
    17, 20, 191; and Mediterranean pirates, 28;
    and Morocco, 88; and Tunisia, 115; and
    United Arab Emirates, 123; see also,
    individual European countries

Fahd, King, 102, 186, 187
Faisal I, 53, 54, 68, 101, 102
Faisal II, 54, 163, 186
Faisal, Emir, 20, 109
family, Muslim, 13, 14
Farouk, King, 38, 156
fellahin (Egyptian peasants), 37
Fez, Treaty of (1912), 88
Fezzan, the (Libya), 81
fishing industry: in Oman, 95; in PDRY, 127;
    see also, pearl fishing
Fitr, Id al- (Moslem celebration), 13
Five Pillars of Islam, 6
FLN, see National Liberation Front
food, Middle Eastern, 13-14, 144
France, 16, 20; and Algiers, 27, 28; and Egypt,
    37, illus. 43; and Iraq, 53; and Jordan, 68;
    and Lebanon, 76, 77, 119; and Libya, 81;
    and Morocco, 88-89; and Syria, 109, 110;
    and Tunisia, 115
Free Officers (Egyptian secret organization), 38
Fuad, King, 38

Gaddafi, see Qadhafi, Muammar al-
Galilee, 58
Gaza strip, 58, 165
Gemayel, Amin, 78, 79, 182
Gemayel, Bashir, 78, 111, 137
Germany, and Morocco, 88
Ghazi, King (Iraq), 54
Gilgamesh epic, 32
Golan Heights, 58, 137
Grand Sanusi, 81, 82
Great Mosque (Mecca), seizure of (1979), 102
Green Books: of Qadhafi, 83, 85, 179
"Green March" into Spanish territory, 24, 90
Green Mountains, see Jabal al-Akhdar
Gulf Cooperation Council (GCC), 34, 74; and
    Kuwait, 174; Oman in, 94, 95; as regional
    power bloc, 138; and Saudi Arabia, 189; and
    United Arab Emirates, 123

Habash, George, 140
Hafiz (Iranian poet), 44, 46
hajj (Great Pilgrimage), 99
Hamid II, 119
Hasan (son of Ali), 7
Hashishin (secret society), 5
Hassan (Veneziano) and Algerian pirates, 28
Hassan II, King (Morocco), 13, 24, 83, 90, 91,
    178, 183, 185
Hebrew language, 143, 164
Hejaz region (Saudi Arabia), 100
Herzl, Theodore, 19, 164
Himyarites, 129
Histadrut (Israeli labor union), 167
Hittites, 118
Hizbullah (Muslim faction), 4, 10
Hodjatieh (Iranian faction), 50
Hormuz, Strait of, 16, 18, 93, 123
Hosni, Amin, 143
housing, in Algeria, illus. 30; in Iraq, illus. 56;
    in Libya, illus. 85; in Morocco, illus. 91;
    Muslim, 12-13
Husayn, Sharif (son of Ali), 7-8, 53, 68, 100
Hussain, President Saddam (Iraq), 55
Hussein I, King (Jordan), 13, 17, 18, 49, 68, 69;
    illus. 70; 163, 165, 170, 171, 172, 173; and
    Arafat, 136, 137, 139, 141, 171, 194; and
    Assad, 193; and Iran, 188; and Israel, 193;
    and Khomeini, 162; and PLO, 140, 141, 152;
    and Syria, 137

Istiqlal, Abu al- (the Mahdi), 105
Ibadism, 93
Ibn Said, Ahmad, 93
Ibn Saud, King, 14, 101
ibn Saud, Prince Muhammad, 100, 187
ibn Sultan, Said, 93
ibn Taimur, Sultan Said, 93, 94
Idris, King (Grand Sanusi of Libya), 82, 83, 177
Idris II (Morocco), 87
Ikhwan, see Muslim Brotherhood
Iman (Islamic leader), 8, 93
Infitah (Egyptian economic program), 40
Interim Force in Lebanon (UNIFIL), 78
International Federation of Film Archives
    (FIAF), 155
International Monetary Fund (IMF), 154; and
    Sudan, 106; and Turkey, 121
Iran, Islamic Republic of, 44-51; and
    Afghanistan-Soviet conflict, 25; and Algeria,
    30; and Bahrain, 33; and concept of jihad,
    5; government of, 137; and Iraq, 54; and
    Kuwait, 174; and Libya, compared, 10-11;
    Qajar dynasty of, 15; and Oman, 94;
    Revolution in, 18, 19; Sassanid Empire of,
    17; and Saudi Arabia, 188; Shia Muslims in,
    8, 47; and Turkey, 118; and UAR, 123; and
    U.S., 16, 19, 158; women in, 14; see also,
    Iran-Iraq War; Islamic fundamentalism;
    Khomeini; Persian Empire
Iranian hostage crisis, 4, 49
Iranian people, 45-46; and Arabs, compared, 17
Iran-Iraq War: 16, 17-19, 49, 50, 53, map 54;
    157; effect of, on Iran, 161-162; and Kuwait,
    73, 174, 176; and Lebanon, 137; and oil
    prices, 102; and PLO, 140
Iraq, 52-56; and Kuwait, 174, 188; and PLO,
    140; solar energy in, 162-163; Sunni
    Muslims in, 47; and Syria, 109, 137; and
    Turkey, 121; and U.S., 16, 138; see also,
    Hussein I; Iran-Iraq War
Irgun Zvai Leumi (Jewish terrorist group), 62
Islam, 4; achievements of, 9; architecture of,
    11-12; Baghdad as seat of, 162; celebrations
    of, 13; and concept of jihad, 5-6;
    development of, 6; divisions of, 7-8; in
    Egypt, 37; and Europe, 9; food, 13-14; in
    Iran, 45, 46, 48, 157, 158-160; in Oman, 93;
    under Pahlavi dynasty, 47-48; reform
    movements in, 10-11; sacred places of, 99,
    100, 102, 158; and sports, 160; in Sudan,
    106; in Tunisia, 116; in Turkey, 8, 119; in
    Yemen, 126, 129
Islamic Conference, 41
Islamic Development Bank, 41
Islamic Front for the Liberation of Bahrain, 33
Islamic fundamentalism: in Algeria, illus. 31; in
    Bahrain, 34; in Egypt, 41-42, 163; in Iran,
    10, 137, 138, 157; in Lebanon, 181; in Saudi
    Arabia, 102; see also, Khomeini, Ayatollah
Islamic Jihad: "holy war" definition of, 5; and
    Kuwait, 74; and terrorism, 4, 5
Islamic unity: and Middle East social
    organization, 16; and terrorism, 5
Israel, 57-66; and Arab states, 20; economy of,
    163, 165, 166-168; and Egypt, 38, 153; and
    Golan Heights, 137; and Lebanon, 78, 79,
    139, 163, 181, 182-183; and Palestinians, 173;
    and peace process, 152, 153; role of, in
    peace negotiations, 136; and Syria, 110, 194;
    territory occupied by, map 193; and U.S.,
    165; and Zionism, 19

Israel Defense Forces (IDF), 168-169
Istiqlal party (Morocco), 89, 90

Jabal al-Akhdar, 93
Jamaat al-Jihad ("Society of the Struggle"), and
    Great Mosque in Mecca, 5
Jangalis (Iranian political group), 47
Japan, and Iran, 51
Jerusalem, 58; after 1967 war, 171
Jesus, Muslim view of, 6
Jewish Defense League, 64
Jews, 13; Ashkenazi, 59, 164; Diaspora, 59, 61;
    in Egypt, 37; in Iran, 45, 159; in Iraq, 54;
    in Israel, 58 fol.; and Palestinian homeland,
    19-20; Reform, 59; Sephardic, 59, 164; in
    Syria, 109; in Tunisia, 114
Jordan, Hashemite Kingdom of, 67-72; and
    Egypt, 41; and Nasser, 39; and peace
    process, 136, 185; and Syria, 193; see also,
    Hussein I; Iran-Iraq War
Jordan River, East and West Banks, 68
Jordan Valley, 58
Judaea, 58; see also, West Bank

Ka'ba, and Islam, 11
Kabyles peoples, 28
Kach (Israeli political party), 64
Kahane, Rabbi Meir, 64, 139, 164
"Kalashnikov generation" of Lebanese youth, 78
Karagoz ("Shadow play"), 117
Karaouyine Mosque (Fez, Morocco) illus. 88
Karbala (Iraq), shrine at, 8, 53, 100, 158
Kenana sugar refinery (Sudan), 106
Kerman temple (Iran), 160
Khalid, King, 102
Khan, Reza, 47
Kharg Island oil terminal (Iran), Iraqi bombing
    of, 51, 137, 157, 161
Khartoum, province and capital of Sudan, 105,
    106
Khedive (Egyptian viceroy), 37, 100
Khomeini, Ayatollah Ruhollah al-Musavi al-, 8,
    10, 11, 48, illus. 49, 157, 158, 159, 162;
    cultural effects of, 14; and Hussein, 188;
    and Iraq, 17, 18, 45, 137, 161; and Mideast
    peace process, 136; setbacks for, 138;
    support of, 45, 50
kibbutzim (Israeli cooperative settlement), 20,
    57, 65, 164
kinship, Moslem, 12
Kissinger, Henry, 136
Knesset (Israel) parliament, 59, 63, 164
Kom al-Shugafa catacombs (Egypt), 156
Koran, 5, 6, 14; and Arabic language, 142-143
Kordofan, Sudan, 190
Kurds: and Iran, 18, 45, 47, 159; in Iraq, 53-54,
    55-56; in Syria, 109
Kuwait Fund for Arab Economic Development
    (KFAED), illus. 74; 176
Kuwait, 72-74; economy of, 174-176; labor force
    of, 145; and Iraq, 188; rulers of, 33; sports
    in, 147; and Syria, 112; and U.S., 174

labor: in Egypt, 154; expatriate, 145, 154, 200,
    201; in Libya, 177; in Third World, 138; see
    also, labor unions
Labor Party (Israel), 63, 64
labor unions: in Bahrain, 34; in Israel, 167; in
    Kuwait, 175, 176; in Turkey, 198
Law of Return (1950) (Israel), 63
League of Nations, and Syria, 20

Lebanon, Republic of, 75-79; before and after Lebanese War, map 182; Israeli invasion of, 63-64, 181; and Mideast peace process, 136, 137; Palestinian refugee camps in, 180-181; and Syria, 109, 110, 112; U.S. in, 17; violence in, 16, 165; women in, 14; see also, Lebanon War

Lebanon War, 22, map 182

Levy, Moshe, 164

Libya (Socialist People's Libyan Arab Jamahiriya [Republic]), 80-85; economy of, 176-178; and Iran, compared, 10-11; and Islamic fundamentalism, 10; and Mediterranean piracy, 28; and Mideast peace process, 136; and Morocco, 183-185; illus. 91; and Sudan, 178; in Turkey, 121; and U.S., 177

Likud (Israeli party), 64, 65, 164, 165, 171

Ma'an family (Lebanon), 76

Mahdism, 102; and Islamic fundamentalism, 10; in Sudan, 102, 105

Majlis (Iranian parliament), 47, 49, 50

mandates: British over Israel, 61-62; France in Lebanon, 76; U.K. and France over Jordan, 68, 69; during World War II, 53; see also, United Nations

Maronites, in Syria, 109; in Lebanon, 76, 77, 182

Marxism: in Iran, 49, 50; in Yemen, 125, 126

Mauritania, 183; and France, 22; and Morocco, 91; and Western Sahara, 23, 24

Meaning of Disaster, The, 21

Mecca, Saudi Arabia, 100; role of, in Islam, 6, 8, 11, 99, 158

Medina, Saudi Arabia, 100

meerschaum, 121

Meir, Golda, 165; illus. 62

Midas, King, 118

Middle East: American perception of, 4; foreign powers in, 16, 17; geography of, 15, 16; housing in, 12

millet, Turkish geopolitical unit, 119

Mohammed, Ali Nasser, 200, 201

Mohammed Reza Pahlevi (1919-1980), 8, 33, 44, 48, 94

Montazeri, Ayatollah Hossein Ali, 49

Morocco, Kingdom of, 15, 86-91; and France, 22; history of piracy in, 28; and Libya, 24, 83, 178, 183-185; social tensions in, 149; sports in, 146, 147; and Western Sahara, 23, 24

Moses, Muslim view of, 6

Moshavim (Israeli cooperative settlement), 57

mosque, Islamic, 11

Motherland Party (Turkey), 121

Movement for Islamic Tendency (MTI), in Tunisia, 116

Mubarak, Hosni, 41, 42, 43, 73, 154; and Islamic fundamentalism, 138; and PLO, 140, 151-153

Muhammad V, illus. 90

Muhammad the Prophet, 6, 86, 87, 99, 100, 129; and divisions of Islam, 7; and Egyptian leaders, 37

Muhammad Ali, 37

Muhammad the Messenger, and fundamentalist Islam, 5

Muhammad II (Morocco), 88

Mujahideen-i-Khalq (Iranian radical group), 49

Muslim Brotherhood, 5, 111, 175, 176

Muslims: American perception of, 4; and Christians, 9; cultural differences among, 11; divisions of, 7-8; duties of, 6; family life, 13; in French Algeria, 28; in PDRY, 127; in Sudan, 107; in Yemen Arab Republic, 131; see also, Islam; Islamic fundamentalism

Mussolini, Benito, 81

Nablus, Israel, 58

Najaf, Iraq, holy shrine in, 8, 53, 100

Napoleon Bonaparte, in Egypt, 37

Nasser, Gamel Abdul, 35, 36, 38, 39; influence of, in Aden, 126; and Saudi Arabia, 188; in Yemen, 188

National Astronomical Observatory (Baghdad, Iraq), 162

National Democratic Party (Egypt), 40

nationalism, in Iraq, 162; see also, Arab nationalism

National Liberation Front (FLN), in Algeria, 29, 30, 148

nationalization, in Libya, 84

National Pact (Lebanon), 77

National Progressive Front (Iraq), 55

National Salvation Party (Turkey), 120

NATO, and Turkey, 197

natural gas resources, in Bahrain, 150

New Wafd Party, 41

Nihavand, Battle of (641 AD), 46

Nile River, Egypt, 35, 36-37

Nimeiri, President Ja'far (Sudan), 104, 105-106, 107, 178

North Yemen, see Yemen Arab Republic

Offshore Banking Units (OBUs), 34

oil industry: in Algeria, 30-31; in Bahrain, 33, 34, 149, 150, 151; in Egypt, 43; in Iran, 48, 50, 51; in Iraq, 56; in Israel, 65; in Jordan, 71; in Kuwait, 73; in Lebanon, 79; in Libya, 81, 83-84; illus. 85; in Oman, 93, 95; in Qatar, 97, 98; in Saudi Arabia, 100, 102, 138, 187-189; in Sudan, 106-107; in Syria, 112; Tuareg workers in, 27; in Tunisia, 116; in United Arab Emirates, 122, 124; in Yemen, 126, 201

Oman, Sultanate of, 92-95; modernization of, 185-186; and PDRY, 127, 200; sports in, 146

"Operation Peace in Galilee," 22

Organization for African Unity (OAU) and Western Sahara, 24, 30, 184

Organization of Arab Petroleum Exporting Countries (OAPEC), 149, 150

Organization of Petroleum Exporting Countries (OPEC), members of, 31, 97, 149; and Saudi Arabia, 187, 188, 189; and South Yemen, 200

Organization of the Islamic Conference (OIC), 102

Osmanlis, 118

Ottoman Turks, 15; and Christianity, 9; and Egypt, 37; and Europeans, 13-14, 20; geographical sphere of, 17; and Iran, 47; in Iraq, 53, 163; in Israel, 164; in Jordan, 68; in Lebanon, 76; in Libya, 81; and modern Turkey, 118-119; and Qatar, 97; and Saudi Arabia, 100; and Shatt al-Arab, 18; in Syria, 109; in Tunisia, 114-115; and Yemen, 126, 129

Oujda Treaty of Union (1984), 178

Pahlavi dynasty, 45, 47; see also, Mohammed Reza Pahlevi; Reza Shah Pahlevi

Pakistan: and Iraq, 54; labor force of, 145

Palestine: and Arab-Israeli conflict, 19; British mandate in, 68, 69; partition of, 62; see also, Palestinian homeland; Palestine Liberation Organization; Palestinian Arabs; Palestinian Refugee Camps

Palestine Liberation Organization (PLO), 20, 22, 63, 64; illus. 77; and Algeria, 30; dispersement of, 139; expulsion of, from Beirut, 139; in Jordan, 70; and Kuwait, 73; in Lebanon, 77, 78, 181, 183; and Mideast peace process, 136, 193; and Nasser, 39; and Saudi Arabia, 188; and Syria, 110, 193; in Tunisia, 171

Palestinian Arabs, 19, 61; and Lebanon, 77-78; see also, Palestinian Liberation Organization

Palestinian refugee camps: in Jordan, 173; in Lebanon, 180-181

Pan Arab games, 146

Passover seder, 13

Peacock Throne (Iran), 47

pearl fishing, in Bahrain, 32, 33

"People of the Book," 159

People's Socialist Party (Aden), branches of, 126

Peres, Shimon, illus. 63, 64; 139, 164, 165, 170, 194

Perpetual Maritime Truce (1853), 123

Persian Empire, 45, 46; and Iraq, 53; and Ottomans, 18

Persians, see Iranians

Pesh Merga (Kurdish resistance movement), 56

Phalange party (Lebanon), 76, 77, 182

Philosophy of the Revolution, The, 39

Phoenicia, 76; see also, Lebanon

Phosphate mining: in Jordan, 71; in Morocco, 91; in Tunisia, 116

piracy: in Corsair Regency of Algiers, 27-28; and Oman, 93; in Tunisia, 114; and United Arab Emirates, 123

Polisario (Popular Front for the Liberation of Saquia al-Hamra and Rio de Oro), 16, 24, 87, 90, 91, 183

Port Sudan, pipeline to, 107

Portugal: and Bahrain, 33; and Oman, 93; and UAR, 123

pyramids, illus. 36, 37

Qadadfas of the Sirte (Libya), 84

Qadhafi, Muammar al-, 10, 11, 80, 83, 84, 85, 138-139; and Morocco, 24, 83, 183, 184; and Polisario, 183; social and economic reforms of, 176, 177; and terrorism, 188

Qatar, State of, 33, 96-98; sports in, 147; and UAR, 123

Rajavi (Mujahideen leader), 49

Rakah (Israel Communist party), 63

Ramadan (Muslim celebration), 13, 100, 116

Ramses II, 37

Rashidi peoples, 100

Reagan, Ronald, 16, 17, 139, 152, 153, 170; and Qaddafi, 178, 179, 185

Republican People's Party (RPP), 120

Revolutionary Command Council (RCC), in Iraq, 55

Revolutionary Command Council (RCC), in Egypt, 38, 39

Revolutionary Guards of Iran, 160

revolutions: Iranian, 48, 50; Iraqi, 54-55

Reza Shah Pahlevi (1877-1944), 18, 47-48, 50

Riyadh, Saudi Arabia, 100, 101, 103, illus. 102; 103

Roosevelt, Franklin D., 89

Rubaiyat, 44

Russia, and Iran, 47; see also, Soviet Union

Sabaean kingdom, 129

Sabah family (Kuwait), 33, 73, 175, 176

Sabra/Chatila refugee camp (Beirut, Lebanon), 180, 181

Sadat, Anwar al-, 5, 17, 39-41, 152, 154; and Camp David accords, 136

Safavid dynasty (Iran), 46-47, 53

Sahara: mineral resources of, 27; in Tunisia, 114

Saharan Arab Democratic Republic (SADR), 184

Sahel region, drought in, 107

Sahrawi Arab Democratic Republic (SADR), 24

Sahrawi peoples, 23, 24; nationalism among, 184

Salafiyya (Kuwait religious organization), 175

Samaria, 58; see also, West Bank

San'a, Yemen, 129

Sanusiya movement, and Islamic fundamentalism, 10, 81

Sassanid Empire of Iran, 17, 46, 162

Saudi Arabia, Kingdom of, 99-107; and Bahrain, 33-103, 149; economy of, 187-189; and Iran, 188; and Iran-Iraq War, 18

and Islamic fundamentalism, 10; and Kuwait, 73, 174; labor force in, 145; and Libya, 81; and peace process, 136; radio in, 14; sports in, 147, 186, 187; and Yassir Arafat, 140; and Yemen, 130, 200

Saul, 118

SAVAK (Iranian secret service), 48

Secret Army Organization (OAS), in Algeria, 29

Sétif massacre (May 8, 1945), 29

Shahinshah (Persian "King of Kings"), 47

Shah-People's Revolution in Iran, 48, 50

Shatt al-Arab waterway (Iraq), 53, map 54; dispute of, 18; and Kuwait, 73

Shia Muslims, 7; in Bahrain, 33; in gulf oil region, 188; and Ibddism, 93; in Iran, 45, 46, 48; in Iraq, 17, 53; in Kuwait, 73, 74; in Lebanon, 76, 78, illus. 79, map 182; persecution of, 8; in Qatar, 97; and terrorism, 4

Shia Zaidi Imams, in YAR, 129

Shultz, George, 136

Sinai Peninsula, 36, 58

Six-Day War, 21, 39, 63, 66; and Jordan, 70; effect of, on Yemen, 130

slavery, in Oman, 94; see also, slave trade

slave trade: and Oman, 93; and Sudan, 102

Socialism: in Israel, 164; in Tunisia, 115, 116; see also, Marxism

Socialist Union of Popular Forces (USFP), 91

solar energy, in Iraq, 162-163

South Arabian Protectorate, 126

South Yemen, see People's Democratic Republic of Yemen

Soviet Union: in Afghanistan, 24-25; and Egypt, 35, 39, 41; and Iran, 45, 48, 51; and Kuwait, 74; and Lebanon, 78, 188; and Libya, 82, 84, 138; and Mideast peace process, 136, 137, 162; in Middle East, 16, 19; and PDRY, 126, 127, 200; and PLO, 188; and Syria, 110; illus. 112; and Yemen Arab Republic, 131, 201; see also, Russia

Spain: and Morocco, 88; in Western Sahara, 22, 23, 24

Sphinx, the (Egypt), 37

sports, in Mideast, 146-147

Stern Gang (Jewish terrorist group), 62

Succoth (Jewish celebration), 13

Sudan, Democratic Republic of the, 104-107; drought and famine in, 190-192; and Libya, 178

Sudan Railways Corporation (SRC), and famine relief, 191

Suez Canal, 37; and Egyptian economy, 43; and Oman, 93

Suez Canal Zone: British withdrawal from, 39; Israeli invasion of, 37

Sumerians, 144

Sunni Muslims, 7; Iranian support of, 18; in Iraq, 17; in Kuwait, 73; in Lebanon, 76; illus. 79; 182; and Shia Muslims, illus. 8; in Syria, 109; see also, Wahhabis

Sunni-Shia split, illus. 8

Suq al-Manakh (Kuwait stock market), 174-175

Syria (Syrian Arab Republic), 108-112; and Iran-Iraq War, 18; effect of Israeli invasion of Lebanon on, 182; and Jordan, 193; and League of Nation's mandate, 20; and Mideast peace process, 136, 137

Taba (Sinai beach), 41

Talal, King (Jordan), 70

tea ceremony, Middle Eastern, 14

Teheran, Iran, 45; Qajars in, 47

Tel Aviv, Israel, 20

terrorism: Achille Lauro, 151; Athens, 4; Beirut, 4; Egypt's attitude toward, 151 fol.; Iran, 4; and Qadhafi, illus. 83; 178; see also, Islamic Jihad

Third International Theory, 83

Thousand and One Nights Tales, 52

Tigris river, 53, 144

Transjordan, see Jordan, Hashimite Kingdom of

Trucial States, 33, 123, 198

Truman, Harry, 22

Tuareg nomads, 16; language of, 27

Tudeh (Masses) Party (Iran), 49-50

Tunis, Tunisia, 114; Israeli raid on, 153

Tunisia, Republic of, 113-116; housing in, 12; and the PLO, 139, 140, 171; social tensions in, 149

Tunisian Nationalist Movement, 115

Turkey, and Afghanistan-Soviet conflict, 25; economy of, 196-198; human rights in, 194-195; and Iraq, 54; war of independence, 119

UAE University, 198

ulema (Islamic scholars), 159

Umayyad empire, in Syria, 109

Umma community (Lebanon), 181

United Arab Emirates, 122-124; education in, 198-199; sports in, 146

United Kingdom: and Arab nationalism, 20; and Bahrain, 33; and Egypt, 37-38; and Iran, 47, 48; and Iraq, 53; and Israel, 61, 164; and Jordan, 68; and Kuwait, 73; and Libya, 82; role of, in Middle East, 16, 18; and Morocco, 88, 89; and Oman, 93, 94, 186; and Ottoman Empire, 119; and PLO, 171; and Saudi Arabia, 100; and Sudan, 105; and Syria, 110; and United Arab Emirates, 123; and Western Sahara, 22; and Yemen, 126, 129; see also, United Nations

United Nations, 107; and Bahrain, 33; famine relief, 107; and Golan Heights, 58; and Israel, 62; and Jordan, 68, 69, illus. 71; and Lebanon, 78, illus. 79; and Morocco, 86; and North Yemen, 201; and Palestine homeland, 20, map 60; 102, 141; and

Spanish colonies, 24; and Turkey, 120; see also, United Kingdom

United Nations Relief and Works Agency (UNRWA), in Lebanon, 77

UN Special Commission on Palestine (UNSCOP), 62

United States, and Afghanistan-Soviet conflict, 25; and Arab-Israeli conflict, 22; and Egypt, 39, 151-154; and Iran, 48, 49, 137-138, 158; and Iraq, 54, 138; and Israel, 63, 66, 152-153, 165; and Kuwait, 74, 174; and Libya, 81, 82, 83, 177; Middle East policy of, 16, 19, 58, 136, 170, 194; and Morocco, 89; and Oman, 93, 94; and PLO, 140; and Saudi Arabia, 102; and Syria, 110

University of the Gulf, illus. 34

U.S. Agency for International Development (USAID), and famine relief, 191, 192

Wafa (Palestinian news agency), 140

Wafd (Egyptian delegation and political party), 38

Wahhabis, 10, 73, 81, 97, 123; in Saudi Arabia, 100, 101

Wailing Wall (Israel), illus. 59

"War of the Camps," in Lebanon, 180

Weir, Benjamin, 4

Weizmann, Chaim, 21, 61, 164

West Bank, 58, 63, 64, 69, 165; peace process in, 170-172

West Bank Data Base Project, 58

Western Sahara, 90-91; political history of, 22-24

White Papers, and British mandate over Israel, 61, 62

"White Revolution," see Shah-People's Revolution

women: in Bahrain, 34; in Iran, 46, 158, 159, 160; in Israel, 63; in Libya, 83, 179; in Muslim societies, 14; in Oman, 94; in Qatar, 98; in Saudi Arabia, 100; in Tunisia, 116; in Turkey, 120; in Yemen, 125

World War I: and Arab nationalism, 20; Egypt's role in, 37; effect of, on Iran, 47; effect of, on Iraq, 53; effect of, on Jordan, 68; and Libya, 81; and Ottoman Empire, 119

World War II: effect of, on Algerians, 29; Iran in, 48; and Israel, 61, 62; and Libya, 81; effect of, on Middle East geography, 15; and Turkey, 120

Yahya, Imam, 129-130

Year of the Elephant (570 AD), 129

Yemen, People's Democratic Republic of, 125-127, 200; and King Faisal of Saudi Arabia, 102; and Kuwait, 176; and Oman, 94; and Soviet Union, 74

Yemen Arab Republic, 128-131; housing in, 12; oil industry in, 200-201; and PDRY, 127

Zaidi Imamate, in Yemen, 129

Zaire, and Jerusalem, 58

Zam Zam (sacred well of Islam), 11

Zerga incident (Jordan), 70

Zionism, 19-20, 61, 166; Israeli redefinition of, 164

Zionist Organization, 19

Zoroastrianism: in Iran, 45, 159, 160; in Sassanid empire, 46

Zurayk, Constantine, 21